Scene of the Cybercrime
Second Edition

Michael Cross

KEY	SERIAL NUMBER
001	HJIRTCV764
002	PO9873D5FG
003	829KM8NJH2
004	BAL923457U
005	CVPLQ6WQ23
006	VBP965T5T5
007	HJJJ863WD3E
008	2987GVTWMK
009	629MP5SDJT
010	IMWQ295T6T

PUBLISHED BY
Syngress Publishing, Inc.
Elsevier, Inc.
30 Corporate Drive
Burlington, MA 01803

Scene of the Cybercrime, Second Edition

Printed in the United States of America
1 2 3 4 5 6 7 8 9 0

ISBN 13: 978-1-59749-276-8

Page Layout and Art: SPi Publishing Services
Copy Editor: Audrey Doyle
Project Manager: Andre Cuello

For information on rights, translations, and bulk sales, contact Matt Pedersen, Commercial Sales Director and Rights, at Syngress Publishing; email m.pedersen@elsevier.com.

Author

Michael Cross (MCSE, MCP+I, CNA, Network+) is an internet specialist/programmer with the Niagara Regional Police Service. In addition to designing and maintaining the Niagara Regional Police's Web site (www.nrps.com) and intranet, he has also provided support and worked in the areas of programming, hardware, database administration, graphic design, and network administration. In 2007, he was awarded a Police Commendation for work he did in developing a system to track high-risk offenders and sexual offenders in the Niagara Region. As part of an information technology team that provides support to a user base of over 1,000 civilian and uniformed users, his theory is that when the users carry guns, you tend to be more motivated in solving their problems.

Michael was the first computer forensic analyst in the Niagara Regional Police Service's history, and for five years he performed computer forensic examinations on computers involved in criminal investigations. The computers he examined for evidence were involved in a wide range of crimes, inclusive to homicides, fraud, and possession of child pornography. In addition to this, he successfully tracked numerous individuals electronically, as in cases involving threatening e-mail. He has consulted and assisted in numerous cases dealing with computer-related/Internet crimes and served as an expert witness on computers for criminal trials.

Michael has previously taught as an instructor for IT training courses on the Internet, Web development, programming, networking, and hardware repair. He is also seasoned in providing and assisting in presentations on Internet safety and other topics related to computers and the Internet. Despite this experience as a speaker, he still finds his wife won't listen to him.

Michael also owns KnightWare, which provides computer-related services like Web page design, and Bookworms, which provides online sales of merchandise. He has been a freelance writer for over a decade and has been published over three dozen times in numerous books and anthologies. When he isn't writing or otherwise attached to a computer, he spends as much time as possible with the joys of his life: his lovely wife, Jennifer; darling daughter Sara; adorable daughter Emily; and charming son Jason.

Author of First Edition

Debra Littlejohn Shinder, MCSE, MVP is a technology consultant, trainer and writer who has authored a number of books on computer operating systems, networking, and security. These include *Scene of the Cybercrime: Computer Forensics Handbook,* published by Syngress, and *Computer Networking Essentials,* published by Cisco Press. She is co-author, with her husband, Dr. Thomas Shinder, of *Troubleshooting Windows 2000 TCP/IP,* the best-selling *Configuring ISA Server 2000, ISA Server and Beyond,* and *Configuring ISA Server 2004.* She also co-authored *Windows XP: Ask the Experts* with Jim Boyce.

Deb is a tech editor, developmental editor and contributor to over 20 additional books on subjects such as the Windows 2000 and Windows 2003 MCSE exams, CompTIA Security+ exam and TruSecure's ICSA certification. She formerly edited the Brainbuzz A+ Hardware News and currently edits Sunbelt Software's WinXP News and VistaNews, with over a million subscribers, and writes a weekly column on Voice over IP technologies for TechRepublic/CNET. Her articles on various technology issues are regularly published on the CNET Web sites and Windowsecurity.com, and have appeared in print magazines such as Windows IT Pro (formerly Windows & .NET) Magazine and Law & Order Magazine.

She has authored training material, corporate whitepapers, marketing material, and product documentation for Microsoft Corporation, Hewlett-Packard, GFI Software, Sunbelt Software, Sony and other technology companies and written courseware for Powered, Inc and DigitalThink.

Deb currently specializes in security issues and Microsoft products; she has been awarded Microsoft's Most Valuable Professional (MVP) status in Windows Server Security for the last four years. A former police officer and police academy instructor, she lives and works with her husband, Tom, on a beautiful lake just outside Dallas, Texas and teaches computer networking and security and occasional criminal justice courses at Eastfield College (Mesquite, TX). You can read her tech blog at http://deb-tech.spaces.live.com.

Contents

Chapter 1

Facing the Cybercrime Problem Head-On

Topics we'll investigate in this chapter:

- Defining Cybercrime
- Categorizing Cybercrime
- Reasons for Cybercrimes
- Fighting Cybercrime

☑ Summary

☑ Frequently Asked Questions

Introduction

Today we live and work in a world of global connectivity. We can exchange casual conversation or conduct multimillion-dollar monetary transactions with people on the other side of the planet quickly and inexpensively. The proliferation of personal computers, easy access to the Internet, and a booming market for related new communications devices have changed the way we spend our leisure time and the way we do business.

The ways in which criminals commit crimes are also changing. Universal digital accessibility opens new opportunities for the unscrupulous. Millions of dollars are lost by both businesses and consumers to computer-savvy criminals. Worse, computers and networks can be used to harass victims or set them up for violent attacks—even to coordinate and carry out terrorist activities that threaten us all. Unfortunately, in many cases law enforcement agencies have lagged behind these criminals, lacking the technology and the trained personnel to address this new and growing threat, which aptly has been termed *cybercrime.*

Even though interest and awareness of the cybercrime phenomenon have grown in recent years, many information technology (IT) professionals and law enforcement officers have lacked the tools and expertise needed to tackle the problem. To make matters worse, old laws didn't quite fit the crimes being committed, new laws hadn't quite caught up to the reality of what was happening, and there were few court precedents to look to for guidance. Furthermore, debates over privacy issues hampered the ability of enforcement agents to gather the evidence needed to prosecute these new cases. Finally, there was a certain amount of antipathy—or at the least, distrust—between the two most important players in any effective fight against cybercrime: law enforcement agents and computer professionals. Yet, close cooperation between the two is crucial if we are to control the cybercrime problem and make the Internet a safe "place" for its users.

Law enforcement personnel understand the criminal mindset and know the basics of gathering evidence and bringing offenders to justice. IT personnel understand computers and networks, how they work, and how to track down information on them. Each has half of the key to defeating the cybercriminal. This book's goal is to bring the two elements together, to show how they can and must work together to defend against, detect, and prosecute people who use modern technology to harm individuals, organizations, businesses, and society.

Defining Cybercrime

Cybercrime is a broad and generic term that refers to crimes committed using computers and the Internet, and can generally be defined as a subcategory of computer crime. If this sounds strange, consider that whether someone commits Internet fraud or mail fraud, both forms of deception fall under a larger category of fraud. The difference between the two is the mechanism that was used to victimize people. Cybercrime refers to criminal offenses committed using the Internet or another computer network as a component of the crime. Computers and networks can be involved in crimes in several different ways:

- The computer or network can be the tool of the crime (used to commit the crime).
- The computer or network can be the target of the crime (the "victim").
- The computer or network can be used for incidental purposes related to the crime (for example, to keep records of illegal drug sales).

Although it is useful to provide a general definition to be used in discussion, criminal offenses consist of specific acts or omissions, together with a specified culpable mental state. To be enforceable, laws must also be specific. In many instances, pieces of legislation contain definitions of terms. This is necessary to avoid confusion, argument, and litigation over the applicability of a law or regulation. These definitions should be as narrow as possible, but legislators don't always do a good job of defining terms (and sometimes don't define them at all, leaving it up to law enforcement agencies to guess, until the courts ultimately make a decision).

To illustrate this, we can look at the Council of Europe's Convention on Cybercrime treaty, which you can view at http://conventions.coe.int/Treaty/EN/Treaties/Html/185.htm. The treaty attempts to standardize European laws concerning crime on the Internet, but one of the biggest criticisms of the treaty is its use of overly broad definitions. For example, the definition of the term *service provider* is so vague that it could be applied to someone who sets up a two-computer home network, and the definition of *computer data*, because it refers to any representation of facts, information, or concepts in any form suitable for processing in a computer system, would comprise almost every possible form of communication, including handwritten documents and the spoken word (which can be processed by handwriting and speech recognition software). Likewise, the U.S. Department of Justice (DOJ) has been criticized for a definition of *computer crime* that specifies "any violation of criminal law that involved the knowledge of computer technology for its perpetration, investigation, or prosecution" (reported in the August 2002 *FBI Law Enforcement Bulletin*). Under such a definition, virtually any crime could be classified as a computer crime, simply because a detective might have searched a computer database as part of conducting an investigation.

Understanding the Importance of Jurisdictional Issues

Another factor that makes a hard-and-fast definition of cybercrime difficult is the jurisdictional dilemma. Laws in different jurisdictions define terms differently, and it is important for law enforcement officers who investigate cybercrime, as well as network administrators who want to become involved in prosecuting cybercrimes that are committed against their networks, to become familiar with the applicable laws. In the case of most crimes in the United States, that means getting acquainted with local ordinances and state statutes that pertain to the offense. Generally, criminal behavior is subject to the jurisdiction in which it occurs. For example, if someone assaults you, you would file charges with the local police in the city or town where the assault actually took place.

Because cybercrimes often occur in the virtual "place" we call cyberspace, it becomes more difficult to know what laws apply. In many cases, offender and victim are hundreds or thousands of miles apart and might never set foot in the same state or even the same country. Because laws can differ drastically in different geographic jurisdictions, an act that is outlawed in one location could be legal in another.

What can you do if someone in California, which has liberal obscenity laws, makes pornographic pictures available over the Internet to someone in Tennessee, where prevailing community standards—on which the state's laws are based—are much more conservative? Which state has jurisdiction? Can you successfully prosecute someone under state law for commission of a crime in a state where that person has never been? As a matter of fact, that was the subject of a landmark case, *U.S. v. Thomas and Thomas* (see the "CyberLaw Review" sidebar in this section).

CyberLaw Review

U.S. v. Thomas and Thomas

Robert and Carleen Thomas, residents of California, were charged with violation of the obscenity laws in Tennessee when a Memphis law enforcement officer downloaded sexually explicit materials from their California bulletin board system (BBS) to a computer in Tennessee. This was the first time prosecutors had brought charges in an obscenity case in the location where the material was *downloaded* rather than where it *originated*. The accused were convicted, and they appealed; the appeals court upheld the conviction and sentences; the U.S. Supreme Court rejected their appeal.

Even if the act that was committed is illegal across jurisdictions, however, you might find that no one wants to prosecute because of the geographic nightmare involved in doing so (see the "On the Scene" sidebar in this section for an example of one officer's experience).

On the Scene

Real-Life Experiences

From Wes Edens, criminal investigator and computer forensics examiner
Here's how *the* typical multijurisdictional case complicates the life of a working police detective. Put yourself in this detective's shoes: Bob Smith, who lives in your jurisdiction in Oklahoma, reports that he has had some fraudulent purchases on his credit card. In addition, he has been informed that two accounts have been opened using his information via the Internet at two banks: Netbank, based in Georgia, and Wingspan, which was recently bought by Bank One.

The suspect(s) applied for a loan to buy a car in Dallas. As a result, the suspects changed Bob's address on his credit profile to 123 Somewhere Street, Dallas. This is a nonexistent address.

In the course of your investigation, you contact Netbank (Georgia) and they inform you that they do not keep Internet Protocol (IP) addresses of people opening accounts online. You obtain a copy of the online credit application. It contains all of

Continued

Bob Smith's credit information, but the address is now 321 Elsewhere Street, Dallas. This is also a nonexistent address.

You contact all the companies at which purchases have been made with Bob's bogus credit cards. Half won't speak *to* you unless you have paperwork, and half of *those* say that the paperwork has to be from a court in the state where they are located, not where you are. Now you have to find police departments in five different states that are willing to help you generate court papers to get records. Because you have filed no charges and the victim (and presumably the suspect) does not live in their jurisdiction, most of these organizations are reluctant to get involved.

You get the paperwork from half of the companies. Of 10, only one actually has an IP address. It is an America Online (AOL) account, which means it could have been accessed from anywhere in the world—further complicating the jurisdictional nightmare, but you press on. You get a subpoena for AOL, requesting the subscriber information for that IP address at that date and time. Three weeks later, AOL informs you that they keep logs for only 21 days, so you're out of luck because the target IP date and time occurred two months ago.

You run down the 15 phone numbers used on the various suspect accounts and applications. All 15 are different. Three are in Dallas, two are in Fort Worth, and the remainder is either disconnected numbers or in a random spattering of towns across South Texas. There is no apparent connection between any of the numbers. You get the addresses used to ship the purchased items. Every address is different; three are in Dallas and two are in Fort Worth. Several are either pay-by-the-week rentals or "flop houses" where people come and go, as in a bus station. A couple of them are mail drops. You subpoena those records, only to find that all the information they contain is bogus.

You decide to visit with your boss and explain to him that you need to travel to another state for a few days to solve *this* $1,500 caper. He listens intently until you start to mention going to Georgia, Maryland, and Texas. You then tell him you also have three other such cases that involve nine other states, and you'll probably have to go to all those locations, too. You can hear him laughing as he walks out the door.

You decide to visit with the DA just for the heck of it. You explain the case thus far, and she asks What crime was committed here? (Your answer: Well, none that I know of for sure.) Does the suspect live here? (Probably not.) Can we show that any exchange of money or physical contact between suspect and victim took place here? (No, not really.) Do you have any idea where the suspect is? (Probably in Texas.) Were any of the purchases made in Oklahoma? (No.) Why are you conducting this investigation? (Because the victim is standing in my office.)

The DA tells you that the victim needs to report this crime to the Texas authorities. You give the victim a list of seven different agencies in Texas, one in Georgia, and one in Maryland. You tell him that he needs to contact them. He calls you back three days later and says that they want him to go to each place to fill out a crime report and he can't afford to take off two weeks and travel 2,000 miles to report that he is a victim. You suggest he call the FBI, even though deep down you know that they are not going to touch a $1,500 fraud case.

Continued

> You give up on that case and pick up the other three identity-theft cases that landed on your desk while you were spinning your wheels on this one. You note that all three were done entirely through the Internet, and like the first one, they all involve a multitude of states.

Although we'll discuss jurisdictional issues in greater depth in Chapter 16, it is important that we also notice the other edge of this double-edged sword. Legislation in different states or countries may be in direct conflict or diverge from the intent of different laws or constitutional rights. For example, in 2001, a number of nonmember States of the Council of Europe signed the Convention on Cybercrime treaty that we discussed earlier. These included Canada, Japan, and the United States. The treaty was ratified by the U.S. Senate in 2006 and put it into force January 1, 2007, improving international cooperation in cybercrime investigations. However, this has created some controversy, as the treaty doesn't require dual criminality, whereby an act must be criminal under the laws of both countries. This would enable one country to spy on the Internet activities of citizens of another country, where no laws have been broken. Under the terms of the treaty, a service provider would need to cooperate with search and seizures (without reimbursement), and may be prevented from deleting logs or other data related to a person who is law abiding in that country.

Quantifying Cybercrime

Although the potential infringement on a person's rights may seem like something out of George Orwell's *1984*, we would do well to remember that sacrificing privacy and certain freedoms has become a norm in the twenty-first century. For better or worse, the Internet has largely grown beyond the anonymous free-for-all that was seen in its early years. Fears of terrorism, identity theft, predators on the Internet, and other criminal activity have brought about new laws, and it will take years to iron out the inconsistencies in courts, political debates, and public forums such as the Internet. Although cybercrime once sounded like the stuff of futuristic science fiction novels, law enforcement, computer professionals, and the general public have grown to recognize it as a contemporary problem.

- The Internet Crime Complaint Center (IC3) is a partnership between the Federal Bureau of Investigation (FBI) and the National White Collar Crime Center (NW3C), and provides a way to report Internet crimes online. The IC3 began as the Internet Fraud Complaint Center (IFCC), and during its first year of operation (May 2000 and May 2001) its Web site received 30,503 complaints of Internet fraud. Changing its name to reflect the broadened scope of Internet crimes, in June 2007 the IC3 received its 1 millionth complaint, with 461,096 of the cases reported to it being referred to federal, state, and local law enforcement. Of this, these cases reflected an estimated loss of $647.1 million, or a median loss of $270 per complainant. You can find annual reports reporting these figures on the IC3 Web site (www.ic3.gov/media/annualreports.aspx).

- In its 2007 Annual Report, the IC3 reported that the majority of cybercrime complaints (44.9 percent) involved cases of Internet auction fraud, where people would bid online for various items. Of these complaints, 19 percent involved situations in which people had paid for items but never received the merchandise, or in which the merchandise had been sent to a bidder and payment was never received (www.fbi.gov/majcases/fraud/internetschemes.htm).

- According to the Computer Security Institute's *Computer Crime and Security Survey* for 2007, 494 computer security professionals in U.S. corporations, government agencies, universities, and financial and medical institutions reported that fraud was the greatest source of financial losses, with losses resulting from virus attacks falling into second place for the first time in seven years. In addition to this, 29 percent of the organizations suffered a computer intrusion that they reported to law enforcement (www.gocsi.com).

- According to the Cybersnitch Voluntary Online Crime Reporting System, the most-reported Internet-related crime is child pornography, with other crimes ranging from desktop forgery to such potentially violent crimes as electronic stalking and terrorist threats. (A full list of reported cybercrimes is available at www.cybersnitch.net/csinfo/csdatabase.asp.)

CyberStats

Charting the Online Population

Although it is difficult to have an accurate total for the number of people using the Internet, the Web site www.internetworldstats.com estimates that by the end of 2007, there were 1,319,872,109 people online. The Central Intelligence Agency (CIA) World Factbook (https://www.cia.gov/library/publications/the-world-factbook/fields/2153.html) reveals the increase in Internet users, showing that two years previous only 1,018,057,389 people were online. The CIA also provides a breakdown of users by country, showing that the European Union, United States, and China have the largest number of Internet users in the world. As the global population becomes increasingly "connected," the opportunities for criminals to use the Net to violate the law will expand, and cybercrime will touch more and more lives.

Although almost anyone has the potential to be affected by cybercrime, two groups of people must deal with this phenomenon on an ongoing basis:

- IT professionals, who are most often responsible for providing the first line of defense and for discovering cybercrime when it does occur

- Law enforcement professionals, who are responsible for sorting through a bewildering array of legal, jurisdictional, and practical issues in their attempts to bring cybercriminals to justice

Although it is imperative to the success of any war against cybercrime that these two groups work together, often they are at odds, as neither has a real understanding of what the other does or of the scope of their own roles in the cybercrime-fighting process. Police may have misgivings about civilians being involved in an investigation, whereas private sector businesses may want to avoid bad publicity or the headache of being ensnared in legal processes. These and other issues hinder the efforts to catch and prosecute cybercriminals, and they create an atmosphere where cybercrime can thrive.

Differentiating Crimes That *Use* the Net from Crimes That *Depend on* the Net

In many cases, crimes that we would call cybercrimes under our general definition are really just the "same old stuff," except that a computer network is somehow involved. That is, a person could use the Internet to run a pyramid scheme or chain letters, set up clients for prostitution services, take bets for illegal gambling, or acquire pornographic pictures of minors. All of these acts are already criminal in certain jurisdictions and could be committed without the use of the computer network. The "cyber" aspect is not a necessary element of the offense; it merely provides the means to commit the crime. The computer network gives criminals a new way to commit the same old crimes. Existing statutes that prohibit these acts can be applied to people who use a computer to commit them as well as to those who commit them without the use of a computer or network.

In other cases, the crime is unique and came into existence with the advent of the Internet. Unauthorized access is an example; although it might be likened to breaking and entering a home or business building, the elements that comprise unauthorized computer access and physical breaking and entering are different. By statutory definition, breaking and entering generally requires physical entry onto the premises, an element that is not present in the cyberspace version of the crime. Thus, new statutes had to be written prohibiting this specific behavior.

CyberLaw Review

Theft of Intangible Property

Theft of intangible property, such as computer data, poses a problem under the traditional theft statutes of many U.S. jurisdictions. A common statutory definition of theft is "unlawful appropriation of the property of another without the effective consent of the owner, with the intent to deprive the owner of the property." (This definition comes from the Texas Penal Code, Section 31.03.)

This definition works well with tangible property; if I steal your diamond necklace or your new Dell laptop, my intent to deprive you of the use of the property is clear. However, I can "steal" your company's financial records or the first four chapters of the great American novel you're writing *without* depriving you of the property or its use at all. If I were prosecuted under the theft statute, my defense attorney could argue that the last element of the offense wasn't met. This is the reason new statutes had to be written to cover theft of intangible or intellectual properties, which are not objects that can be in the possession of only one person at a time.

"Traditional" intellectual property laws (copyright, trademark, and the like) are civil laws, not prosecuted in criminal court other than under special newer laws

Continued

pertaining to only narrowly defined types of intellectual property such as software and music. Some federal laws prohibit theft of data, but the FBI and federal agencies have jurisdiction in only certain circumstances, such as when the data is stolen from federal government computers or when it constitutes a trade secret. In most cases, it's up to the state to prosecute. States can't bring charges under federal law, only under their state statutes. Until recently, many states didn't have statutes that covered data theft because it didn't fit under traditional theft statutes and they didn't have "theft of intellectual property" statutes.

Working toward a Standard Definition of Cybercrime

Why is it so important for us to develop a standard definition of cybercrime? Unless we all use the same—or at least substantially similar—definitions, it is impossible for IT personnel, users and victims, police officers, detectives, prosecutors, and judges to discuss the offense intelligently. As we saw when discussing the European Convention on Cybercrime treaty, poor or omitted definitions of technology can create issues that can impact the rights and business practices of law-abiding citizens. In addition to this, as we'll discuss later in this chapter, it is impossible to collect meaningful statistics that can be used to analyze crime patterns and trends. If we can't agree on what something is, we can't compile statistics on it.

Crime analysis allows agencies to allocate resources more effectively and to plan their own strategies for responding to problems. It is difficult for agency heads to justify the need for additional budget items (specialized personnel, training, equipment, and the like) to appropriations committees and governing bodies without hard data to back up the requests. Standard definitions and meaningful statistical data are also needed to educate the public about the threat of cybercrime and involve communities in combating it. Crime analysis is the foundation of crime prevention; understanding the types of crime that are occurring, where and when they are happening, and who is involved is necessary to develop proactive prevention plans.

Even though we have no standard definitions to invoke, let's look at how cybercrime is defined by some of the most prominent authorities.

U.S. Federal and State Statutes

We have already mentioned the somewhat broad definition of computer crime adopted by the U.S. DOJ. Individual federal agencies (and task forces within those agencies) have their own definitions. For example, the FBI investigates violations of the federal Computer Fraud and Abuse Act, which lists specific categories of computer and network-related crimes:

- Public switched telephone network (PSTN) intrusions
- Major computer network intrusions
- Network integrity violations
- Privacy violations

- Industrial/corporate espionage

- Software piracy

- Other crimes in which computers play a major role in committing the offense

USA PATRIOT Act and Protect America Act

Many aspects of the Computer Fraud and Abuse Act were amended by the USA PATRIOT Act, which increased penalties and allowed the prosecution of individuals who *intended* to cause damage, as opposed to those actually causing damage. The USA PATRIOT Act is an acronym for *Uniting and Strengthening America by Providing Appropriate Tools Required to Intercept and Obstruct Terrorism*. As its clumsy and cumbersome title indicates, it was created after the September 11, 2001 terrorist attacks on the United States, and was pushed through the U.S. Senate to give law enforcement enhanced authority over monitoring private communications and accessing personal information.

Another act that was signed into law by President Bush in August 2007 is the *Protect America Act* (nicknamed by many as PATRIOT II). It also provides greater authority to law enforcement, and allows the government to perform such actions as:

- Access the credit reports of a citizen without a subpoena

- Conduct domestic wiretaps without a court order for 15 days after an attack on the United States or congressional authorization of use of force

- Criminalize the use of encryption software used in the commission or planning of a felony

- Extend authorization periods used for wiretaps or Internet surveillance

The focus of the Protect America Act was to update the Foreign Surveillance Act and deal with shortcomings in the law that don't address modern technology. However, these acts were controversial enough to require the U.S. DOJ to create www.lifeandliberty.gov, a Web site designed to provide information and disclaim arguments against these two acts.

State Laws

Title 18 of the U.S. Code, in Chapter 47, Section 1030, defines a number of fraudulent and related activities that can be prosecuted under federal law in connection with computers. Most pertain to crimes involving data that is protected under federal law (such as national security information), involving government agencies, involving the banking/financial system, or involving intrastate or international commerce or "protected" computers. Defining and prosecuting crimes that don't fall into these categories usually is the province of each state.

Most U.S. states have laws pertaining to computer crime. These statutes are generally enforced by state and local police and might contain their own definitions of terms. For example, the Texas Penal Code's Computer Crimes section (which is available to view at http://tlo2.tlc.state.tx.us/statutes/pe.toc.htm) defines only two offenses:

- Online Solicitation of a Minor (Texas Penal Code Section 33.021).

- Breach of Computer Security (Texas Penal Code Section 33.02), which is defined as "knowingly accessing a computer, computer network, or computer system without the effective consent of the owner." The classification and penalty grade of the offense are increased according to the dollar amount of loss to the system owner or benefit to the offender.

Section 502 of the California Penal Code (Section 502), on the other hand, defines a list of eight acts that constitute computer crime, including altering, damaging, deleting, or otherwise using computer data to execute a scheme to defraud; deceiving, extorting, or wrongfully controlling or obtaining money, property, or data; using computer services without permission; disrupting computer services; assisting another in unlawfully accessing a computer; or introducing contaminants (such as viruses) into a system or network. Additional sections of the penal code also address other computer and Internet-related crimes, such as those dealing with child pornography and other crimes that may incorporate the use of a computer. However, as stated earlier, these are not necessarily dependent on the use of computers or other technologies.

Depending on the state, the definition of computer crime under state law differs. Once again, the jurisdictional question rears its ugly head. If the multijurisdictional nature of cybercrime prevents us from even defining it, how can we expect to effectively prosecute it?

International Law: The United Nations' Definition of Cybercrime

Cybercrime spans not only state but also national boundaries, so perhaps we should look to international organizations to provide a standard definition of the crime. At the Tenth United Nations Congress on the Prevention of Crime and Treatment of Offenders, in a workshop devoted to the issue of crimes related to computer networks, cybercrime was broken into two categories and defined thus:

a. **Cybercrime in a narrow sense (computer crime): Any illegal behavior directed by means of electronic operations that targets the security of computer systems and the data processed by them.**

b. **Cybercrime in a broader sense (computer-related crime): Any illegal behavior committed by means of, or in relation to, a computer system or network, including such crimes as illegal possession [and] offering or distributing information by means of a computer system or network.**

Of course, these definitions are complicated by the fact that an act may be illegal in one nation but not in another. The paper goes on to give more concrete examples, including:

- Unauthorized access
- Damage to computer data or programs
- Computer sabotage
- Unauthorized interception of communications
- Computer espionage

These definitions, although not completely definitive, do give us a good starting point—one that has some international recognition and agreement—for determining just what we mean by the term *cybercrime*.

IT professionals need good definitions of cybercrime to know when (and what) to report to police, but law enforcement agencies *must* have statutory definitions of specific crimes to charge a criminal with an offense. The first step in specifically defining individual cybercrimes is to sort all the acts that can be considered cybercrimes into organized categories.

Categorizing Cybercrime

Cybercrime is such a broad and all-encompassing term that it is all but useless in any but the most general discussion. Certainly if you called the police to report that your home was burglarized, you wouldn't start by saying that you'd been the victim of a "property crime." For police to have a chance of identifying the criminal or to bring charges against that person once identified, they must know the specific act that was committed.

Categorizing crimes as property crimes, crimes against persons, weapons offenses, official miscon-duct, and so on is useful in that it helps us organize related, specific acts into groups. That way, general statistics can be collected and law enforcement agencies can form special units to deal with related types of crime. Furthermore, officers can specialize and thus become more expert in particular categories of crime.

Similarly, it's useful to define categories of cybercrime and then place specific acts (offenses) into those categories. First, we must realize that cybercrimes, depending on their nature, can be placed into existing categories already used to identify different types of crime. For example, many cybercrimes (such as embezzling funds using computer technology) could be categorized as *white-collar crimes*, generally defined as nonviolent crimes committed in the course of business activities, usually (although not always) motivated by monetary profit and often involving theft, cheating, or fraud. On the other hand, Internet child pornographers are usually classified as sex offenders (pedophiles) and regarded as violent or potentially violent criminals.

This crossover into other categories and the widely diverse acts that constitute cybercrime make it difficult to break cybercrime into its own narrower categories. However, most agencies that deal with cybercrime want to do so if only because it also helps them identify the type of suspect they're looking for. (The profile for a person who operates a child pornography site on the Internet is different from that of a person who hacks into others' computer systems, which in turn is different from that of a person who uses e-mail to run a chain letter scheme.)

NOTE

We discuss the types of cybercriminals and their common characteristics in detail in Chapter 3, "Understanding the People on the Scene."

Collecting Statistical Data on Cybercrime

At the beginning of this chapter, we provided some statistical information gathered by agencies formed to deal with cybercrime issues. However, reporting crimes to these agencies is voluntary. This means that the figures are almost certainly much lower than the actual occurrence of network-related crimes. This is because not only do an unknown number of cybercrimes go unreported (as with all crimes), but many or most of those that *are* reported to police are not reported to the agencies that collect these statistics.

In fact, currently it is practically impossible to even get an accurate count of the number of cybercrimes reported to police. To understand why that's true, let's look at how crime data is reported and collected in the United States.

Understanding the Crime Reporting System

Local law enforcement agencies—municipal police departments and county sheriffs' offices—are individually responsible for keeping records of criminal complaints filed with their agencies, the offenses they investigate, and the arrests they make. There is no mandated, standardized recordkeeping system; each agency can set up its own database, use one of many proprietary recordkeeping software packages marketed to law enforcement, or even keep the records manually as police agencies did for years prior to the computerization of local government operations.

In an effort to provide national crime statistics, the FBI operates the Uniform Crime Reporting (UCR) program. Local law enforcement agencies complete a monthly report that is sent to the FBI. This information is consolidated and issued as reports documenting the "official" national crime statistics. The program has been in place since the 1960s; more than 18,000 agencies provide data, either directly or through their state reporting systems. These statistics are made available to the media and through the FBI's Web site at www.fbi.gov/ucr/ucr.htm.

In the 1980s, the UCR program was expanded and redesigned to become an incident-based reporting system in which crimes are placed into predefined categories. The National Incident-Based Reporting System (NIBRS) specifies data to be reported directly to the FBI through data-processing systems that meet the NIBRS specifications. (Agencies that don't have the requisite equipment and resources still file the standard UCR reports.)

Categorizing Crimes for the National Reporting System

NIBRS collects more details on more categories of crime than the UCR, which provides only summaries of various crime categories. Even so, the 22 Group A offense categories and the 11 Group B offense categories for which NIBRS collects data include no category that identifies an offense as a cybercrime. (See the "CyberStats" sidebar in this section for a list of the NIBRS categories.)

CyberStats

NIBRS Crime Categories

According to the *NIBRS Data Collection Guidelines* and *UCR Handbook* (both available from the FBI Web site at www.fbi.gov/ucr/ucr.htm), offenses are categorized into the

Continued

following groups. Extensive data is collected for Group A offenses, whereas only arrest data is collected for Group B offenses.

Group A offense categories:

Arson

Assault (aggravated, simple, and assault by intimidation)

Bribery

Burglary/Breaking and Entering

Counterfeiting/Forgery

Destruction/Damage/Vandalism of Property

Drug/Narcotic Offenses (including drug equipment violations)

Embezzlement

Extortion/Blackmail

Fraud Offenses

Gambling Offenses

Homicide Offenses

Kidnapping/Abduction

Larceny/Theft (excluding motor vehicle theft)

Motor Vehicle Theft

Pornography/Obscenity

Prostitution Related

Robbery

Sex Offenses (forcible)

Sex Offenses (nonforcible)

Stolen Property Offenses (excluding theft)

Weapons Law Violations

Group B offense categories:

Bad Checks

Curfew/Loitering/Vagrancy

Disorderly Conduct

Driving Under the Influence

Drunkenness

Family Offenses (nonviolent)

Liquor Law Violations

Voyeurism ("Peeping Tom")

Continued

Runaway

Trespass

All Other Offenses

As you can see from the list of NIBRS offense categories shown in the sidebar, a local agency reporting a cybercrime must either find a standard category into which it fits (for example, an online con game that asked people to send money to a "charity" under false pretenses would be classified under "Fraud Offenses," whereas entering a computer's files from across the Internet and stealing trade secrets would be classified as "Theft") or place it into the catchall "All Other Offenses" category. Either way, no information in the national crime reports generated from this data indicates that these offenses are cybercrimes.

Agencies that deal with cybercrime must formulate their own cybercrime-specific categories for internal recordkeeping, to accurately determine the types of cybercrimes occurring in their jurisdictions. Agencies that have technically savvy officers or in-house IT specialists will be able to do this without outside help. In many cases, however, local law enforcement personnel don't have the technical expertise to understand the differences between different network-related crimes. Police officers might understand the concept of "hacking," for example, but they might not be able to differentiate between a hacker who gains unauthorized access to a network and one who disrupts the network's operations by launching a denial-of-service (DoS) attack against it.

This is where IT professionals can work with law enforcement to help define more clearly and specifically the elements of an offense so that it can be investigated and prosecuted properly. Agencies might need to hire outside IT security specialists as consultants and/or officers might need to receive specialized training to understand the technical elements involved in various cybercrimes. In many cases when these officers are trained, it allows the creation of a formal technology crime unit, which specializes in investigating or assisting in the investigation of cybercrimes.

We discuss the law enforcement–IT professional relationship in detail, along with more specifics about how the two can work together, in Chapter 15.

Developing Categories of Cybercrimes

We can categorize the various cybercrimes in several ways. We can start by dividing them into two very broad categories: those crimes committed by violent or potentially violent criminals, and nonviolent crimes.

Violent or Potentially Violent Cybercrime Categories

Violent or potentially violent crimes that use computer networks are of highest priority for obvious reasons: These offenses pose a physical danger to some person or persons. Types of violent or potentially violent cybercrime include:

- Cyberterrorism
- Assault by threat
- Cyberstalking
- Child pornography

The U.S. Department of State defines terrorism as "premeditated politically motivated violence perpetrated against noncombatant targets by subnational groups or clandestine agents." *Cyberterrorism* refers to terrorism that is committed, planned, or coordinated in cyberspace—that is, via computer networks.

This category includes using e-mail for communications between coconspirators to impart information to be used in violent activities as well as recruiting terrorist group members via Web sites. More ambitiously, it could include sabotaging air traffic control computer systems to cause planes to collide or crash; infiltrating water treatment plant computer systems to cause contamination of water supplies; hacking into hospital databases and changing or deleting information that could result in incorrect, dangerous treatment of a patient or patients; or disrupting the electrical power grid, which could cause loss of air conditioning in summer and heat in winter or result in the death of persons dependent on respirators in private residences if they don't have generator backup.

Assault by threat can be committed via e-mail. This cybercrime involves placing people in fear for their lives or threatening the lives of their loved ones (an offense that is sometimes called *terrorist threat*). It could also include e-mailed bomb threats sent to businesses or government agencies.

Cyberstalking is a form of electronic harassment, often involving express or implied physical threats that create fear in the victim and that could escalate to real-life stalking and violent behavior.

Child pornography involves a number of aspects: people who create pornographic materials using minor children, those who distribute these materials, and those who access them. When computers and networks are used for any of these activities, child pornography becomes a cybercrime.

CyberLaw Review

National Child Pornography Laws

In the United States, it is a federal crime (18 USC 2251 and 2252) to advertise or knowingly receive child pornography. The Child Pornography Prevention Act of 1996 (CPPA) expanded the definition of *child pornography* to any visual depiction of sexually explicit conduct in which the production involved the use of a minor engaging in sexually explicit behavior, even if the visual depiction only *appears to be* of a minor engaging in such conduct or is advertised or presented to convey the impression that it is of a minor engaging in such conduct. The Free Speech Coalition sued to have the law struck down as unconstitutional, and a federal appellate court did strike down the statute. In October 2001, the Supreme Court heard arguments in the case *Ashcroft v. The Free Speech Coalition* on the constitutionality of the CPPA. In April 2002, the Supreme Court ruled that the provisions of USC 2256 that prohibit "virtual child pornography" (computer-generated images of children engaging in sexual conduct) are overly broad and unconstitutional.

In the United Kingdom, under the Protection of Children Act (1978) and Section 160 of the Criminal Justice Act of 1988, it is a criminal offense for a person to possess

Continued

either a photograph or a "pseudo-photograph" of a child that is considered indecent. The term *pseudo-photograph* is defined as an image made by computer graphics or that otherwise appears to be a photograph. Typically this is a photograph that is created using a graphics manipulation software program such as Adobe Photoshop to superimpose a child's head on a different body (the same type of "virtual child pornography" addressed by the U.S. Supreme Court in its April 2002 decision).

Most countries have laws addressing child pornography. For a synopsis of national laws compiled by Interpol (the International Criminal Police Organisation), see the Interpol SexualOffenses Against Children Web site at www.interpol.int/Public/Children/SexualAbuse/NationalLaws.

Child pornography is generally considered a violent crime, even if some of the persons involved have had no physical contact with children. This is the case because sexual abuse of children is required to produce pornographic materials, and because people who are interested in viewing these types of materials often do not confine their interest to pictures and fantasies but are instead are practicing pedophiles, or aspire to be, in real life.

On the Scene

Real-Life Experiences

From Detective Glen Klinkhart, Anchorage Police Department Computer Crimes Unit
Not too long ago, a friend of mine with the FBI called me with a request. He told me that he had received a transcript from an Internet Relay Chat (IRC) session, and he wanted to tell me about it. During the IRC correspondence, one of the participants had written a detailed plan about preparing the kidnap and rape of a young boy from a shopping mall. The chat indicated that the mall might be somewhere in our city. The FBI agent asked if I would be interested in reading the chat session logs and giving him my opinion of the situation.

When the agent arrived I took a look at the transcript and was horrified by what I read. The IRC session showed what appeared to be two people chatting online. One, called "PITH," apparently sent the FBI the computer chat logs, and the other was the suspect, known only as "Kimmo." PITH saved the chat log file and then contacted law enforcement about the incident. The chat was a chilling and frightening view into a demented mind.

The eight pages of chat noted extremely graphic, sexually explicit details, which included the very specific ways that the suspect said he would enjoy "raping" and "torturing" his victim. During the rest of the chat, the suspect, Kimmo, gave details about the specific shopping mall that he had scoped out and the general location of

Continued

his cabin, north of the city. Kimmo was very specific about the sexual acts that he was going to perpetrate against his victim. It was apparent that Kimmo had been thinking and fantasizing about this attack for some time.

The FBI and our department immediately began working on the case. At one point, we had 14 agents and police detectives working on this single investigation. We continued to track the location of our suspect by going undercover into Internet chat rooms looking for Kimmo, tracing his IP address, and using tools such as search warrants and subpoenas to gather a trail of information leading to our suspect.

The trail led to a divorced father living on the outskirts of the city. Agents began watching him and his house. Others checked into his background and learned more about how he operated. He appeared to have no criminal history; however, he was very adept at using computers. He also matched many of the details that had been communicated to PITH during the disturbing chat session.

We obtained search warrants for the suspect's house and prepared to search his office as well. On a clear, cold morning, we hit the office and the house of our suspect. Another group of officers attempted to interview the suspect.

When confronted, the suspect played it as though he didn't know what we were talking about. He denied any knowledge of the chat session between PITH and Kimmo. When presented with irrefutable evidence, including an electronic trail that led directly to his home computer, he finally admitted that he was Kimmo. He stated that he participated in the chat because he was heavily intoxicated at the time. He told investigators that he had never harmed a child and that he would never hurt anyone.

His computer systems at home and at work told another tale. On his home computer and on various computer media, we found hundreds of images of child pornography, including images of children being forced into bondage and raped. Kimmo had also developed a fondness for collecting hundreds of computer drawings depicting children having their bodies sliced, mutilated, and displayed in disturbing and gory fashion.

The suspect was arrested. He later pleaded guilty to possession and distribution of child pornography. He is currently serving his time in federal prison.

Was the suspect merely drunk when he was chatting with PITH? Would he really "never harm a child," as he told us? Would he have grabbed a kid from the mall and taken him to a cabin to be raped and tortured? We might never know for certain. I do know that for at least the next few years, this guy will not have a chance to make good on his plans, thanks to the hard work of the FBI, the U.S. Attorney's office, and our team of dedicated investigators.

Nonviolent Cybercrime Categories

Most cybercrimes are nonviolent offenses, due to the fact that a defining characteristic of the online world is the ability to interact without any physical contact. The perceived anonymity and "unreality" of virtual experiences are the elements that make cyberspace such an attractive "place" to commit crimes.

Nonviolent cybercrimes can be further divided into several subcategories:

- Cybertrespass
- Cybertheft

- Cyberfraud
- Destructive cybercrimes
- Other cybercrimes

A number of more specific criminal acts can fit into each of these categories.

Cybertrespass

In *cybertrespass* offenses, the criminal accesses a computer's or network's resources without authorization but does not misuse or damage the data there. A common example is the teenage hacker who breaks into networks just "because he (or she) can"—to hone hacking skills, to prove him- or herself to peers, or because it's a personal challenge.

Cybertrespassers enjoy "snooping," reading your personal e-mail and documents and noting what programs you have on your system, what Web sites you've visited, and so forth, but they don't do anything with the information they find. Nonetheless, cybertrespass is a crime in most jurisdictions, usually going under the name of "unauthorized access," "breach of network security," or something similar.

Law enforcement professionals need to be aware of the laws in their jurisdictions and avoid automatically dismissing a complaint of network intrusion simply because the victim can't show loss or damage. Network administrators need to be aware of this crime, because under criminal statutes, a company can prosecute intruders simply for accessing the network or its computers without permission. In this regard, it might be easier to build a criminal case than a civil lawsuit, because the latter often requires proof of damages in order to recover.

Cybertheft

There are many different types of *cybertheft*, or ways of using a computer and network to steal information, money, or other valuables. Because profit is an almost universal motivator and because the ability to steal from a distance reduces the thief's risk of detection or capture, theft is one of the most popular cybercrimes. Cybertheft offenses include:

- *Embezzlement*, which involves misappropriating money or property for your own use that has been entrusted to you by someone else (for example, an employee who uses his or her legitimate access to the company's computerized payroll system to change the data so that he is paid extra, or who moves funds out of company bank accounts into his own personal account)

- *Unlawful appropriation*, which differs from embezzlement in that the criminal was never entrusted with the valuables, but gains access from outside the organization and transfers funds, modifies documents giving him title to property he doesn't own, or the like

- *Corporate/industrial espionage*, in which persons inside or outside a company use the network to steal trade secrets (such as the recipe for a competitor's soft drink), financial data, confidential client lists, marketing strategies, or other information that can be used to sabotage the business or gain a competitive advantage

- *Plagiarism*, which is the theft of someone else's original writing with the intent of passing it off as one's own

- *Piracy*, which is the unauthorized copying of copyrighted software, music, movies, art, books, and so on, resulting in loss of revenue to the legitimate owner of the copyright

- *Identity theft*, in which the Internet is used to obtain a victim's personal information, such as Social Security and driver's license numbers, to assume that person's identity to commit criminal acts or to obtain money or property or use credit cards or bank accounts belonging to the victim

- *DNS cache poisoning*, a form of unauthorized interception in which intruders manipulate the contents of a computer's domain name system (DNS) cache to redirect network transmissions to their own servers

On the Scene

Counterfeit Software on eBay

When most people think of software piracy, they think of a person with a bootleg copy of Windows or the latest computer game or application. This was not the case when copies of Rockwell Automation computer software began to appear for sale on eBay. Rockwell Automation produces (among other products) specialized management software that's used for factory production lines and machinery. As reported through press releases on the U.S. DOJ Web site (www.usdoj.gov), in 2007, nine individuals were convicted of felonies involving the sale of counterfeit Rockwell Automation computer software on eBay, which sold for a fraction of a combined retail value of approximately $30 million.

- Courtney Smith of Anderson, Indiana, admitted to holding 32 or more separate eBay auctions in which more than $700,000 in software was sold for a personal profit of $4,149.97.

- Robert Koster of Jonesboro, Arkansas, admitted to holding 105 or more separate online auctions on eBay, in which copies of the software were sold to make him a personal profit exceeding $23,000. The actual retail value was more than $5 million.

- Yutaka Yamamoto of Pico Rivera, California, admitted to holding 92 or more separate auctions on eBay, in which he made more than $6,000 in profit, selling counterfeit copies of the software that had a retail value of approximately $543,000.

- Eric Neil Barber of Manila, Arkansas, admitted to holding 217 or more separate auctions on eBay, in which he made approximately $32,500 selling software that had a retail value of $1.4 million.

Continued

- Phillip Buchanan of Hampton, Georgia, admitted to holding 67 or more separate auctions on eBay, in which he made approximately $13,100 selling software that had a retail value of $2 million.

- Wendell Jay Davis of Las Vegas admitted to holding 53 or more separate eBay auctions, in which he made approximately $17,000 selling software that had a retail value of almost $8 million.

- Craig J. Svetska, of West Chicago, Illinois, admitted to holding 376 separate eBay auctions, in which he made a profit of approximately $59,700 selling software that had a retail value of more than $7.6 million.

Network administrators should be aware that in many cases, network intrusion is much more than simply an annoyance; cybertheft costs companies millions of dollars every year. Law enforcement officers need to understand that theft does not always necessarily involve money; a company's data can also be stolen, and in most jurisdictions, there are laws (including, in some cases, federal laws) that can be used to prosecute those who "only" steal information.

Cybertheft is closely related to cyberfraud, and in some cases the two overlap. This overlap becomes apparent when you encounter cases of cyberfraud that involve misappropriation of money or other property.

Cyberfraud

Generally, *cyberfraud* involves promoting falsehoods to obtain something of value or benefit. Although it can be said to be a form of theft, fraud differs from theft in that in many cases, the victim knowingly and *voluntarily* gives the money or property to the criminal—but would not have done so if the criminal hadn't made a misrepresentation of some kind.

Cyberfraud includes the same types of con games and schemes that were around long before computers and networks. For example, the con artist sends an e-mail asking you to send money to help a poor child whose parents were killed in an auto accident, or promising that if you "invest" a small amount of money (by sending it to the con artist) and forward the same message to 10 friends, you'll be sent thousands of times your "investment" within 30 days. Other frauds involve misrepresenting credentials to obtain business (and often not providing the service or product promised). The Internet simply makes it easier and quicker for these con artists to operate and gives them a greatly expanded number of potential victims to target.

Fraudulent schemes, cyber-based or not, often play on victims' greed or good will. Law enforcement professionals find that these crimes can often be prosecuted under laws that have nothing to do with computer crime, such as general fraud statutes in the penal code or business code. Fraud is often aimed at individuals, but network administrators should be aware that con artists also sometimes target companies, sending their pleas for charity and "get rich quick" schemes to people in the workplace, where they can find a large audience. Such spam should be reported to the corporate IT department, where steps can be taken to report the abuse to the authorities and/or block mail from the con artist's address if it is a continuing problem.

Cyberfraud can take other forms; any modification of network data to obtain a benefit can constitute fraud (although some states have more specific computer crime statutes that apply). For example, a student who hacks into a school system's computer network to change grades or a person who accesses a police database to remove his arrest record or delete speeding tickets from his driving record is committing a form of fraud.

Destructive Cybercrimes

Destructive cybercrimes include those in which network services are disrupted or data is damaged or destroyed, rather than stolen or misused. These crimes include:

- Hacking into a network and deleting data or program files

- Hacking into a Web server and defacing (electronically vandalizing) Web pages

- Introducing viruses, worms, and other malicious code into a network or computer

- Mounting a DoS attack that brings down the server or prevents legitimate users from accessing network resources

Each of these in some way deprives the owners and authorized users of the data and/or network of their use.

Cybervandalism can be a random act done "just for fun" by bored hackers with a malicious streak, or it might be a form of computer sabotage for profit (erasing all the files of a business competitor, for example). In some cases, cybervandalism might be performed to make a personal or political statement (as in *cybergraffiti*).

CNN.com reported on January 8, 2002 that the number of "defaced" Web sites increased more than fivefold between 2000 and 2001. Immediately following the crash landing of a U.S. spy plane in China in 2001, numerous incidents of Chinese and U.S. hackers defacing each other's Web sites were reported in a so-called "cyberwar." More often, and for less political reasons, there have been a significant number of other cybervandalism. An increase was also seen 2003, but this was due to a contest held by cybervandals to deface Web sites.

A common theme of cybergraffiti involves *tagging* the Web site, in which a hacker will have his or her alias splashed across a Web page (similar to normal graffiti that is spray-painted on a wall). Alternatively, a hacker may add an additional Web page to the site, indicating that he or she was there. Cybervandalism is so common that you can visit www.zone-h.com to view Web sites that have recently been defaced, or view archived snapshots of sites that have been defaced in the past.

The increase in cybervandalism points up the necessity of not only setting up general intrusion detection systems (IDSes), but also ensuring that known vulnerabilities in Web servers are addressed by staying up-to-date on the latest attack types and faithfully applying the updates and "fixes" released by vendors to patch such security holes. IT professionals need to be aware that older operating systems and applications were not designed with high security in mind, simply because the risk was not as great and security was not as well understood at the time they were released. On the other hand, new operating systems and applications could have security vulnerabilities that haven't yet been discovered. Most software vendors are quick to address security problems once they become known, but that often doesn't happen until a hacker discovers and exploits the problem.

Law enforcement officials, in many cases, need legislation that specifically addresses network intrusion to prosecute cybervandals, because it might be difficult to fit these activities into the elements of existing vandalism laws.

Viruses and other malicious code comprise a huge problem to all Internet-connected computers. A computer *virus* is a program that causes an unwanted—and often destructive—result when it is run. A *worm* is a virus that replicates itself. A *Trojan* (or *Trojan horse*) is an apparently harmless or legitimate program inside which malicious code is hidden; it is a way to get a virus or worm into the network or computer.

Malicious code does millions of dollars' worth of damage to computer systems, and virus writers are very active, continually turning out new viruses and worms and modifying old ones so that they won't be detected by antivirus (AV) software. The advent of modern e-mail programs that support Hypertext Markup Language (HTML) mail and attachments has made spreading viruses easier than ever. It's no longer necessary to break into the network to introduce malicious code—now you can simply e-mail it to one technically unsophisticated user and it will quickly spread throughout the local area network (LAN) and beyond.

AV software such as that marketed by Symantec (Norton Antivirus or Symantec AntiVirus, shown in Figure 1.1) and McAfee is an essential part of every network's security plan. Whichever AV package is used, it is essential that its *virus definition files*, used to identify and red-flag known malicious code, be updated frequently.

Figure 1.1 Symantec AntiVirus, One of Several AV Products Designed to Protect Network Security

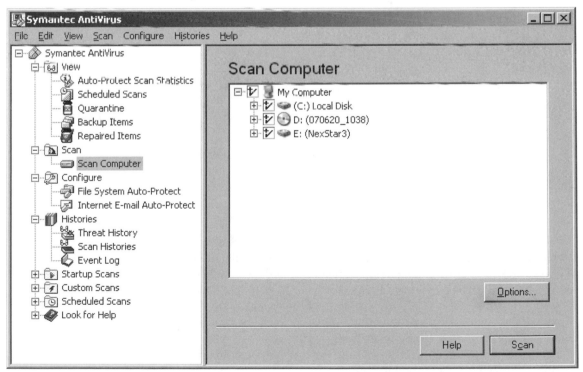

We will discuss viruses, worms, and Trojans in much more detail in Chapter 10.

Other Nonviolent Cybercrimes

There are many more nonviolent varieties of cybercrime. Again, many of these only incidentally use the Internet to accomplish criminal acts that have been around forever (including the world's oldest profession). Some examples include:

- Advertising/soliciting prostitution services over the Internet

- Internet gambling

- Internet drug sales (both illegal drugs and prescription drugs)

- *Cyberlaundering*, or using electronic transfers of funds to launder illegally obtained money

- *Cybercontraband*, or transferring illegal items, such as encryption technology that is banned in some jurisdictions, over the Internet

Prostitution is illegal in all U.S. states except Nevada and in many countries. The statutes in most states are written in such a way so that soliciting sexual services using the Internet falls under the law. Additionally, according to Mike Godwin of the Electronic Frontier Foundation, in an interview titled "Prostitution and the Internet" (published at www.bayswan.org/EFF.html), it is a federal offense to use interstate commerce to solicit "unlawful activity"; 18 USC 1952 defines "prostitution in violation of state laws" as an unlawful activity. 18 USC 1952 itself is available to view at the Cornell University Law School Web site at www4.law.cornell.edu/uscode/18/1952.html.

Nonetheless, one merely needs to use a search engine to find that high-tech hookers are advertising their services extensively on the Internet. Often, these are under the thin guise of "massage" or "escort services," although their sites provide little doubt as to what's actually for sale. Many of the sites give rates by the hour and night, and some will even provide information on where women are willing to fly on a plane to meet with you (needless to say, not something normally associated with therapeutic massage). Online prostitution is also often closely affiliated with online pornography services, which (unless children are involved) are generally protected as speech in the United States under the First Amendment to the Constitution.

An interesting law enforcement issue is that of *cyberprostitution*, which involves trading *virtual* sex for money. In such an activity, a person pays another person to engage in sex acts over the Internet. The customer can watch the prostitute pose or perform sex acts through live streaming video, while dictating the e-hooker's actions. In some cases, the prostitute may also be paid to engage in *cybersex* or *sex chat*, in which the two exchange sexually explicit textual messages or teleconference online. Because no physical contact actually takes place, these activities don't fall under most states' prostitution statutes. In 1996, the U.S. Congress passed the Communications Decency Act, which prohibited "indecent" or "patently offensive" communications on the Internet. Then, in 1997, in *Reno v. ACLU*, the Supreme Court struck down the law as unconstitutional (a violation of First Amendment free speech). It is important for law enforcement professionals to realize that the laws governing online sexual conduct and content are constantly evolving; this is an area in which it is vital to stay up-to-date because what's legal today could be illegal tomorrow, and vice versa.

Network professionals have other issues to consider regarding sexual content. Even if not a crime, posting or allowing sexually offensive material on a company network can result in civil lawsuits alleging sexual harassment. Employers who create a "hostile workplace" environment can be sued under Title VII of the Civil Rights Act of 1964.

Internet gambling has flourished, with online customers able to place bets in virtual casinos using credit cards. In July 2000, the U.S. House of Representatives voted on and rejected a proposed Internet Gambling Prohibition Act. However, the federal government has used the 1961 Interstate Wireline Act (18 USC 1084) to prosecute online gambling operations. This act prohibits offering or taking bets from gamblers over phone lines or through other "wired devices" (which include Internet-connected computers) unless authorized by a particular state to do so. As with many other Internet crimes, jurisdiction is a problem in prosecuting Internet gambling proprietors.

In 2006, a new version of the Internet Gambling Prohibition Act was attached to the SAFE Port Act (Security and Accountability For Every Port Act), which addresses port security. Title VIII of this act, which is also cited as the Unlawful Internet Gambling Enforcement Act, prohibits the transfer of funds to Internet gambling sites or the banks representing these sites, with some exceptions such as fantasy sport teams. A copy of this act is available to view at www.rules.house.gov/109_2nd/text/hr4954cr/hr49543_portscr.pdf.

CyberLaw Review

Offline and Online Gambling

In the United States, offline gaming is legal in some states and not in others. Some countries, such as Antigua and other Caribbean states, permit and license Internet gaming operations. Some states have enacted statutes prohibiting Internet gambling. In 2000, South Dakota passed such a law, the Act to Prohibit the Use of the Internet for Certain Gambling Activities, which makes Internet gambling a felony in that state. (The state lottery and casinos licensed in South Dakota are exempt from prosecution, however.)

Internet gambling is another area in which laws can change quickly and vary tremendously from one jurisdiction to another. Indeed, some states themselves engage in online gambling, offering lottery sales on the Internet.

Internet drug sales comprise another big business. Both the trafficking of illegal drugs and the sale of prescription drugs by online pharmacies are growing problems. The Internet's impact on the international trafficking of illegal drugs such as opium has been studied by the United Nations and individual governments. In March 2000, the UN passed a resolution with the objective of "deterring the use of the World Wide Web for the proliferation of drug trafficking and abuse," encouraging its members to adopt a set of measures to prevent or reduce sales of illicit drugs through the Internet.

Internet-based pharmacies that sell controlled substances might be legal, legitimate businesses that work much the same as traditional mail-order pharmacies, abiding by state licensing laws and processing prescriptions issued by patients' doctors. Other online pharmacies provide prescription drugs based merely on a form filled out by the "patient," which is purportedly evaluated by a physician who has never seen the "patient" and without requiring any verification of identification. Spammers bombard the mailboxes of e-mail users with unsolicited advertisements for drugs such as Viagra, diet pills, Prozac, birth control pills, and other popular prescription medicines.

In the United States, the Internet Pharmacy Consumer Protection Act was introduced by a House Committee but failed to make it to the House floor. Nonetheless, a number of existing laws were applicable to the Internet, allowing law enforcement to arrest individuals involved in the cyber drug trade. The Controlled Substances Act and the Food, Drug, and Cosmetic Act can be used to prosecute offenders under federal law, and each state has laws regarding licensing of pharmacies and requirements for prescribing and dispensing drugs. Even though the Internet Pharmacy Consumer Protection Act failed to become law, others have taken up the torch. Senator Dianne Feinstein introduced the Online Pharmacy Consumer Protection Act of 2007, which is designed to amend the Controlled Substances Act and impose restrictions and regulations on Internet pharmacies.

The DOJ, the Food and Drug Administration (FDA), and the Federal Trade Commission (FTC) have all cracked down on companies selling controlled substances over the Net without valid prescriptions. In addition, several state attorneys general have sued such online pharmacies to prevent them from doing business in those states. In March 2001, federal and local authorities cooperated to close down an Oklahoma-based pharmacy that allegedly sold prescription drugs illegally online. Law enforcement officials should become familiar with the many state and federal laws that regulate the sales of prescription drugs as well as those that address sales and possession of illicit drugs.

On the Scene

Operation Cyber Chase

In 2005, a year-long investigation of Internet pharmaceutical traffickers resulted in 20 arrests in eight U.S cities and four foreign countries. The Drug Enforcement Agency (DEA) investigation was conducted in cooperation with the FBI, U.S. Postal Service, Royal Canadian Mounted Police (RCMP), and other agencies and law enforcement. It culminated in arrests over a 48-hour period, taking down more than 200 Web sites that sold controlled substances over the Internet. The operation focused on traffickers who shipped Schedule II-V pharmaceutical controlled drugs to customers, regardless of their age or whether they had a medical examination as required by U.S. law.

Cyberlaundering involves using the Internet to hide the origins of money which was obtained through illegal means. Money laundering is a very old crime, but the relative anonymity of the Internet has made it easier for criminals to turn "dirty money" into apparently legitimate assets or investments.

The Internet gambling operations discussed earlier provide one way to launder money: A criminal uses the illegally obtained cash in gambling transactions. Online banking also offers opportunities for criminals, who can open accounts without meeting banking officials face to face. Money can be deposited in a secret offshore bank account or transferred electronically from one bank to another until its trail is difficult or impossible to follow. Although criminals still face the challenge of initially getting large amounts of cash deposited into the system without raising suspicions, once they do they can move these funds around and manipulate them much more easily and quickly with the convenience of today's electronic transfers.

Cybercontraband refers to data that is illegal to possess or transfer. For example, in the United States, the International Traffic in Arms Regulations (ITAR) prohibits the export of strong cryptographic software and invokes prison and/or fines of up to $1 million for sending such software to anyone outside the United States. In 1997, a U.S. district judge ruled that the regulations were unconstitutional and violated First Amendment rights to freedom of speech. In 2000, the Clinton administration adopted new, more relaxed encryption export regulations. The U.S. Department of Commerce's Bureau of Industry and Security (www.bis.doc.gov) is responsible for controlling cryptography exports from the United States. It is seeking to tighten export regulations and impose harsher penalties through fines and imprisonment under the Export Enforcement Act of 2007.

Under the Digital Millennium Copyright Act (DMCA), software that circumvents protection of copyrighted materials is illegal to make available to the public. A Russian cryptographer named Dmitri Sklyarov was arrested in Las Vegas in 2001 for "trafficking in" a software program that breaks the encryption codes created by Adobe to protect its eBook product. This, the first criminal case brought under this section of the DMCA, generated a great deal of controversy, especially because the software in question is legal under the laws of Sklyarov's own country, Russia. It resulted in much disagreement over interpretations of various sections of the DMCA; an interesting aspect is that the act does not appear to prohibit possession (or even use) of the software by end users, only the "provision" of such software to others. It also resulted in a great deal of public support for Sklyarov and his employer, ElcomSoft Inc., with a large number of Web sites appearing with names such as www.freesklyarov.org and calls to boycott Adobe products. In the end, Adobe formally withdrew its support to pursue the criminal case against Sklyarov, prosecutors agreed to set aside charges in exchange for his testimony, and ElcomSoft was found not guilty.

In the United States, most data is currently protected under the First Amendment, although there are obvious exceptions, such as child pornography (discussed earlier in this chapter). The concept of cybercontraband is a relatively new—and controversial—one. Law enforcement professionals are still feeling their way in this area, along with legislators who attempt to balance the freedoms and rights of Internet users with the desire to protect society from "harmful" information.

Prioritizing Cybercrime Enforcement

As cybercrime proliferates, it will obviously be impossible for law enforcement agencies to devote the time and effort required to investigate and prosecute every instance of Internet-related criminal activity. Establishing crime categories helps agencies prioritize enforcement duties.

Factors to consider when deciding which types of cybercrime will get top enforcement priority include:

- **Extent of harm** Crimes that involve violence or potential violence against people (especially crimes against children) are normally of high priority; property crimes that result in the largest amount of monetary loss generally take precedence over crimes for which the amount of loss is less.

- **Frequency of occurrence** Cybercrimes that occur with more frequency usually result in more concerted efforts than those that seldom occur.

- **Availability of personnel** Cybercrimes that can be investigated easily by one detective might get more agency attention simply because there are not sufficient personnel resources to set up sophisticated investigations that require many investigators.

- **Training of personnel** Which cybercrimes are investigated and which aren't sometimes depends on which ones investigators have the training to handle.

- **Jurisdiction** Agencies generally prefer to focus their resources on crimes that affect local citizens. Even if the agency has legal jurisdiction, it might choose not to spend resources on cybercrimes that cross jurisdictional boundaries.

- **Difficulty of investigation** Closely related to the two preceding factors, the difficulty of the investigation and the likelihood of a successful outcome could affect which crimes get top priority.

- **Political factors** The prevailing political climate often influences an agency's priorities. If the politicians who govern the agency have a special concern about specific crimes, enforcement of those crimes is likely to take precedence.

In dealing with law enforcement officials on cybercrime cases, it is important for IT professionals to understand how these factors might cause some cybercrimes to be investigated more enthusiastically and prosecuted more vigorously than others.

Reasons for Cybercrimes

Although we discuss the people involved in cybercrimes in Chapter 3, it is important to realize that criminals have begun to incorporate computers and the Internet in their crimes for specific reasons. For the pedophile seeking pornography, the Internet makes it easier to acquire what he or she wants, and is perceived as more anonymous. For a person committing fraud, using e-mail or a Web site to procure victims offers the potential to reach more people. Even when the attack is direct, as in the case of a former employee hacking a network or disseminating viruses, there is no physical evidence to show who committed the crime. The computer and the Internet become a useful tool, suiting the criminal's needs and making the crime possible to achieve or easier to commit.

Most of us equate the ills of the Internet with what we see on TV, in movies, or on the news: hackers gaining access to sensitive government information, pornographic images of attractive adults, and so on. In reality, computer crimes more often than not include copyright piracy (software, movie, sound recording), child pornography, planting of viruses and worms, password trafficking, e-mail bombing, and spam. As with most things seen in the media and movies, the reality is different from the romanticized version.

The reasons someone commits a cybercrime can be as varied as the people committing the crimes. Cybercrimes can be committed for such reasons as:

- Financial, as in cases involving fraud, embezzlement, and so on

- Emotional, as in cases of threats sent via e-mail, hackers seeking a thrill from defacing a Web site, or disgruntled programmers using logic bombs to disseminate viruses or to bring down a network out of revenge against an employer

- Intellectual, such as when certain hackers attempt to gain access to a secure site or crackers attempt to break passwords

- Accessibility, as when a person downloads pirated software, music, or other material because it's extremely easy to do so

- Curiosity, as when people visit sites or download files that they know contain illegal content, but do so anyway

- Deviant behavior, as when a person accesses child porn or other illegal images, video, or other materials

From this, you can see that a computer crime is intentional, not accidental. Regardless of the type of crime, the person is often organized and has given some thought to committing it. It is not like the teenager who has a sudden urge to shoplift, or the hungry homeless person who decides to steal a loaf of bread. At the most basic level of committing the cybercrime, the person must boot the computer, log on, and perform specific actions to commit the crime. Because of this, in most situations a sudden impulse to commit a crime isn't even possible.

Fighting Cybercrime

To successfully fight cybercrime, as with any other type of crime, we must first understand it. *Know thine enemy* is good advice, regardless of the type of war we plan to wage. The first step in developing a plan to fight cybercrime is to define it, both generally and specifically. This chapter has given you some definitions to serve as a starting point in identifying just what cybercrime is—and what it isn't.

Another important element in determining our strategy against cybercrime is to collect statistical data so that we can perform an analysis to detect patterns and trends. Without reliable statistics, it is difficult to establish effective prevention and enforcement policies.

Statistics are the basis for the next step: writing clear, enforceable laws when needed to address cybercrimes that aren't covered by existing laws.

Finally, an effective crime-fighting effort must educate all those who deal with or are touched by cybercrime: those in the criminal system community, those in the IT community, and those in the community at large.

Determining Who Will Fight Cybercrime

By necessity, the fight against cybercrime must involve more than just the police. Legislators must make appropriate laws. The IT community and the community at large must be on the lookout for signs of cybercrime and report it to the authorities—as well as taking measures to prevent themselves from becoming victims of these crimes. The law enforcement community must investigate, collect evidence, and build winnable cases against cybercriminals. Jurors must weigh the evidence and make fair and reasonable determinations of guilt or innocence. Courts must assign fair and effective penalties. The corrections system must attempt to provide rehabilitation for criminals who might not fit the standard "criminal profile."

A major problem in writing, enforcing, prosecuting, and interpreting cybercrime laws is the lack of technical knowledge on the part of people charged with these duties. Legislators, in most cases, don't have a real understanding of the technical issues and what is or is not desirable—or even possible—to legislate. Police investigators are becoming more technically savvy, but in many small jurisdictions, no one in the department knows how to recover critical digital evidence. The budget might not allow for bringing in high-paid consultants or, for instance, sending a disk to a high-priced data recovery service (not to mention the fact that both of these options can create chain-of-custody issues that might ultimately prevent the recovered data from being admissible as evidence). Because larger police departments are often overwhelmed with their own cases, they are unable or unwilling to take on the tasks of performing computer forensics for those who don't have the skills and equipment to do it themselves.

Prosecutors have the advantage of being able to bring in expert witnesses to explain the intricacies, but prosecutors must have a minimal grasp of the technical issues involved to know what to ask those witnesses on the stand. Juries, too, are often in over their heads when evaluating the merits of a cybercrime case. If jury members don't have enough technical understanding to determine for themselves whether the elements of an offense have been proven, they must rely on conflicting opinions presented by the attorneys and the experts without really understanding the basis of those opinions. For this reason, we thoroughly discuss the topic of providing expert testimony in Chapter 17.

On the Scene

Real-Life Experiences

Here's an illustration of how technically complex cybercrime cases can present a challenge to jurors beyond that of, for example, a murder case:

In determining whether a defendant is guilty of murder, the jury will hear testimony, such as eyewitness accounts that the defendant picked up a gun, aimed it at the victim, and fired, or testimony of forensics experts who testify that the defendant's fingerprints were on the gun. The veracity of the witnesses' statements might be in question, and the defense attorney could argue that the defendant had handled the

Continued

gun previously but didn't use it to kill the victim, but the basic issues are not difficult to understand. Everyone on the jury knows what a gun is, and it is pretty well established that fingerprints are unique and can be positively identified as belonging to a specific person.

In a case involving hacking into a computer network, on the other hand, jurors might hear testimony about open ports and Transmission Control Protocol/Internet Protocol (TCP/IP) exploits and how IP spoofing can be used to disguise the origin of a network transmission. These terms probably mean little to jurors whose only exposure to computers is as end users, and the finer points of network communications and security are not topics that can be easily explained in the limited amount of time that's usually available during trial testimony. If the jurors don't understand *how* the crime occurred, it will be difficult for them to decide whether a particular defendant committed it.

Judges, too, often have a lack of technical expertise that makes it difficult for them to do what courts do: interpret the laws. The fact that many computer crime laws use vague language exacerbates the problem.

Lack of technical understanding also comes into play when judges hand down sentences. In an attempt to "make the punishment fit the crime," in many jurisdictions, judges exercise creativity in dealing with computer-related crimes. Rather than assigning the penalties normally associated with criminal conduct—fines and/or imprisonment—judges are imposing sentences such as probation with "no use of computers or networks" for a specific period of time. In today's world, where computers are quickly becoming ubiquitous, a strict interpretation of some sentences would prohibit a person from even using the telephone network and would make it practically impossible for that person to function—and certainly impossible for him or her to gain productive employment.

Corrections officials don't need technology expertise to deal with cybercriminal inmates, but they are challenged by a growing population of prisoners unlike the formerly typical lower-class, undereducated criminal they are used to handling. White-collar criminals could be at special risk within a general prison population, yet providing separate facilities for them might bring complaints from politicians and pundits that they are being housed in "country clubs" and given preferential treatment. This situation could escalate to debates charging racial discrimination, because a majority of convicted cybercriminals are white—the opposite of the prison population in general.

The answer to all these dilemmas is the same: education and awareness programs. These programs must be aimed at everyone involved in the fight against cybercrime, including:

- Legislators and other politicians
- Criminal justice professionals
- IT professionals
- The community at large and the cyberspace community in particular

Educating Cybercrime Fighters

An effective cybercrime-fighting strategy requires that we educate and train everyone who will be involved in preventing, detecting, reporting, or prosecuting cybercrime. Even potential cybercriminals, with the right kind of education, could be diverted from criminal behavior.

Educating Legislators and Criminal Justice Professionals

Those who make, enforce, and carry out the law already understand the basics of legislation, investigation, and prosecution. They need training in the basics of IT: how computers work, how networks work, what can and cannot be accomplished with computer technology, and most important, how crimes can be committed using computers and networks.

This training, to be most useful, should be targeted at the criminal justice audience, rather than be a repackaging of the same material that is used in the same way to train IT professionals. Although much of the information might be the same, the focus and scope should be different. A cybercrime investigator doesn't need to know the details of how to install and configure an operating system. He or she *does* need to know how a hacker can exploit the default configuration settings to gain unauthorized access to the system.

The training necessary for legislators to understand the laws they propose and vote on is different from the training needed for detectives to ferret out digital evidence. The latter should receive not only theoretical but also hands-on training in working with data discovery and recovery, encryption and decryption, and reading and interpreting audit files and event logs. Prosecuting attorneys need training to understand the meanings of various types of digital evidence and how to best present them at trial.

Police academies should include a block on computer crime investigation in their basic criminal investigation courses; agencies should provide more advanced computer crime training to in-service officers as a matter of course. Many good computer forensics training programs are available, but in many areas these tend to be either high-priced, short-duration seminars put on by companies in business to make a profit, or in-house programs limited to larger and more urban police agencies. Enrollees primarily tend to be detectives. Few states have standard mandated curricula for computer crime training in their basic academy programs or as a required part of officers' continuing education.

In rural areas and small-town jurisdictions, few if any officers have training in computer crime investigation, although this situation is slowly changing. Again, officers who do have training are usually detectives or higher-ranking officers—yet it is the patrol officer who generally is the first responder to a crime scene. He or she is in a position to recognize and preserve (or inadvertently destroy or allow to be destroyed) valuable digital evidence.

Ideally, all members of the criminal justice system would receive some basic training in computer and network technology and forensics. However, that is an unrealistic goal in the short term. The next best solution is to establish and train units or teams that specialize in computer-related crime. If every legislative body had a committee of members who are trained in and focus on technology issues; if every police department had a computer crime investigation unit with special training and expertise; and if every district attorney's office had one or more prosecutors who are computer crime specialists, we would be a long way toward building an effective and coordinated cybercrime-fighting mechanism.

For years, law enforcement lagged behind in the adoption of computer technology within departments. Over the past decade, the law enforcement community has begun to catch up, and as younger individuals with existing computer skills are recruiting, the gap between technology and experience is closing. Federal agencies such as the FBI have excellent computer forensics capabilities. Large police organizations such as the International Association of Chiefs of Police (IACP) and the Society of Police Futurists International (PFI) have embraced modern technology issues and provide excellent resources to agencies. Metropolitan police departments and state police agencies have recognized the importance of understanding computer technology and have established special units and training programs to address computer crime issues. But law enforcement in the United States and other countries still has a long way to go before all law enforcement agencies have the technical savvy to understand and fight cybercrime.

Those agencies that are still lacking in such expertise can benefit greatly by working together with other, more technically sophisticated agencies and partnering with carefully selected members of the IT community to get the training they need and develop a cybercrime-fighting plan for their jurisdictions. The Internet reaches into the most remote areas of the country and the world. Cybercrime cannot remain only the province of law enforcement in big cities; cybercriminals and their victims can be found in any jurisdiction.

Educating IT Professionals

IT professionals already understand computer security and how it can be breached. The IT community needs to be educated in other areas:

- **Computer crime awareness** This area requires an understanding of what is and isn't against the law, the difference between criminal and civil law, and penalty and enforcement issues.

- **How laws are made** This area includes how IT professionals can get involved at the legislative level by testifying before committees, sharing their expertise, and making their opinions known to members of their governing bodies.

- **How crimes are investigated** This area includes how IT professionals can get involved at the investigative level by assisting police, both as victims and interested parties and as consultants to law enforcement agencies.

- **How crimes are prosecuted** This area includes how IT professionals can get involved at the prosecution level as expert witnesses.

- **The basic theory and purpose behind criminal law and the justice system** This area includes why IT professionals should support laws against computer crime.

Perhaps a more controversial issue surrounds the attitude of many IT professionals toward those in law and law enforcement. Although by no means universal, an antipathy toward the government and authority figures is common in some parts of the IT community.

There are undoubtedly a number of reasons for this attitude. Technological prowess is highly valued, so skilled hackers garner a certain amount of admiration, even among many corporate IT pros. The IT industry is young, compared with other professions, and has been largely unregulated. IT professionals fear the inefficiency and increased difficulty that overregulation will impose on them in the course of doing their jobs, as they have seen in some other professions. Many tech people are not familiar with legal procedure, and distrust of the unknown is a common human reaction. When they do cooperate with authorities, they are often faced with a lack of respect, unlike other professionals that police may deal with. For example, an officer may have some experience setting up a home network of two computers, and may act as though he or she is equal to or superior in technological expertise to the IT professional. When treated with a lack of respect, the IT professional returns it in kind. Finally, many technical people buy into the hacker mantra that "information wants to be free" and disagree with at least some of the cybercrime laws (particularly those restricting encryption technologies and making software and music or movie copyright violations criminal offenses).

To actively engage the IT world in the fight against cybercrime, we face the challenge of educating IT personnel in how cybercrime laws actually work to their benefit. We won't be able to do this unless we can show IT professionals that the laws themselves are fair, that they are fairly enforced, and that they can be effectively enforced. Network administrators and other IT professionals are generally busy people. Even if they believe that cybercriminals should be brought to justice, they won't take the time to report suspected security breaches or work with law enforcement in investigations if they have no confidence in the competence or integrity of the criminal justice system.

One way IT personnel can become more familiar with and more comfortable with the legal process is through more exposure to it. Law enforcement personnel should actively solicit their help and involve them as much as possible in the fight against cybercrime, giving IT professionals a personal stake in the outcome.

Educating and Engaging the Community

Finally, we must educate the community at large, especially that subset which consists of the end users of computer and network systems. These are the people who are frequently direct victims of cybercrime and ultimately indirect victims in terms of the extra costs they pay when companies they patronize are victimized and the extra taxpayer dollars they spend every year in response to computer-related crimes.

Just as neighborhood watch groups and similar programs have given citizens a way to become proactive about crime prevention in their physical localities, educational programs can be developed to teach citizens of the virtual community how to protect themselves online. These programs would teach network users about common types of cybercrime, how to recognize when they are in danger of becoming cybercrime victims, and what to do if they do encounter a cybercriminal. In some areas, such as online scams and fraud, this type of education alone would greatly reduce the success of con artists' schemes. Organizations such as CyberAngels (www.cyberangels.org) have been created for this purpose.

Crimestoppers

Cybercrime Fighting Organizations

The National Cyber Security Alliance is a cooperative effort between industry and government to foster awareness of cybersecurity through educational outreach and public awareness. More information is available at www.staysafeonline.info.

The United States Computer Emergency Readiness Team (US-CERT) was established in 2003 to protect the Internet infrastructure of the United States. It is a partnership between the Department of Homeland Security and the public and private sectors, and provides information online at www.us-cert.gov.

Continued

The International Association of Computer Investigative Specialists (IACIS) is an international volunteer nonprofit organization from local, state, and federal law enforcement agencies. IACIS provides training and education in the field of forensic computer science. More information is available at www.cops.org.

Law enforcement and IT professionals need to work more closely with the community (including businesses, parents, students, teachers, librarians, and others) to build a cybercrime-fighting team that has the skills, the means, and the authority necessary to greatly reduce the instances of crime on the Internet.

Getting Creative in the Fight against Cybercrime

The fight against cybercrime has the best chance for success if we approach it from many different angles. The legal process is just one way to fight crime. The best methods are *proactive* rather than *reactive*—that is, it's best to prevent the crime before it happens. Failing that, this section discusses some creative ways that businesses and individuals can shield themselves from some of the consequences of being victims if a cybercrime does occur.

Using Peer Pressure to Fight Cybercrime

One way to reduce the incidence of Internet crime is to encourage groups to apply peer pressure to their members. If cybercriminals are shamed rather than admired, some will be less likely to engage in the criminal conduct. This method is especially effective when it comes to young people. Many teenage hackers commit network break-ins to impress their friends. If more technology-oriented young people were taught a code of computer ethics early —emphasizing that respect for others' property and territory in the virtual world is just as important as it is in the physical world—hackers might be no more admired by the majority of upstanding students than are the "bad kids" who steal cars or break into houses.

On the Scene

Real-Life Experiences

Jorge Gonzalez, the owner of one Internet file-sharing portal, Zeropaid.com, took an innovative approach to combating the swapping of child pornography through his site. He has posted a number of bogus files on the site, which uses the popular Gnutella file-sharing program. These bogus files are identified as child porn images, although they are not. When users try to access those files, they are "busted." The user's IP address (which can be used to trace his or her identity) is recorded and posted on the site's Wall of Shame. (The Wall of Shame site was actually created by a Gnutella

Continued

user who identifies himself as Lexx Nexus.) This tactic is similar to the tactics of some newspapers that print the names of people arrested for crimes such as drunk driving or prostitution. The premise is that the fear of publicity will deter some people from committing these crimes.

Certainly it's been shown that peer pressure and changes in peer group attitudes can affect behavior. To a large degree, the increasing social stigma associated with smoking has been linked with a decline in the percentage of smokers in the United States.

Of course, some people will commit crimes regardless of peer pressure, but this pressure is a valuable tool against many of those cybercriminals who are otherwise upstanding members of the community and whose criminal behavior online erroneously reflects the belief that "everyone does it."

Using Technology to Fight Cybercrime

In the spirit of "fighting fire with fire," one of our best weapons against technology crimes is—you guessed it—technology. The computer and network security industry is hard at work, developing hardware and software to aid in preventing and detecting network intrusions. Operating system and other software vendors are building more and more security features into software.

In addition to this, third-party security products, from biometric authentication devices to firewall software, are available in abundance to prevent cybercriminals from invading your network or system. Monitoring and auditing packages allow IT professionals to collect detailed information to assist in detecting suspicious activities. Many of these packages include notification features that can alert network administrators immediately when a breach occurs.

Data recovery products assist law enforcement personnel in gathering evidence despite criminals' efforts to destroy it, and police can—with a search warrant—get into criminals' protected systems using the same tools that hackers use to illegitimately break into systems. We discuss all of these technologies and more throughout numerous chapters of this book.

Finding New Ways to Protect against Cybercrime

To combat cybercrime, we need to remember that as technology progresses, new venues and methods of committing crime also present themselves. E-mail and programs used to be limited to computers, but personal digital assistants (PDAs) and cell phones have allowed crimes to be committed from mobile devices, which must also be understood if the evidence is to be retrieved from them. In the same way, while files and information could almost exclusively be shared in chat rooms, newsgroups, and Web sites, forums such as Facebook and MySpace provide new avenues for cybercriminals to find victims and exchange data. As each new technology or feature of the Internet arises, a new twist to combating cybercrime presents itself.

Gaining an advantage over cybercriminals can be attained through a collaboration of law enforcement and IT professionals. An example of this is the Child Exploitation Tracking System (CETS), which was developed by Microsoft Canada, the Royal Canadian Mounted Police (RCMP), and the Toronto Police Service. CETS was designed to track child predators on the Internet, and allows police around the world to share information on those who were exploiting children. Although vendors and other IT professionals have a firm understanding of what technology can do, and how systems can work to achieve a goal, the police understand what is needed to capture criminals. Collaborating between them, they can not only keep up with cybercriminals, but also gain an advantage over them.

Because cybercriminals often get involved with technology at an early age, it is important that a clear message is sent to those of young ages. *Cyberbullying* involves a child or teenager intimidating, threatening, or otherwise tormenting his or her peers using Internet technology. In some cases, cyberbullies have even gone so far as to modify pictures of the victim, as we discussed earlier when talking about virtual child pornography. Some bullies have posed as their victim online, setting up blogs or sending instant messages (IMs) to the victim's classmates or friends, claiming he or she performs sexual acts or otherwise defaming or ostracizing the victim. By not taking cyberbullying seriously, school officials and law enforcement send a clear message that the cyberbully can get away with this. The bully, victim, and everyone else who has contact with the situation may then presume (somewhat correctly) that the police and school system are incapable of helping the victim or catching the culprit. Because they've gotten away with it in the past, the bully or others familiar with the case may decide to pursue other illegal activities online.

It is not possible to prevent all cybercrime or to always avoid becoming a cybercrime victim. However, organizations and individuals can take steps in advance to minimize the impact that cybercrime will have on them or their organizations. In addition to using backups of data to restore data, spare servers, or other methods we'll discuss in Chapter 12, cybercrime insurance can be used to recoup losses. *Cyberinsurance* originated in the late 1990s to protect companies from losses resulting from Y2K, but continued to provide coverage against various cybercrimes. Admittedly, the cost of such insurance is affordable to only mid-size and large companies, but it serves as an example of one of the new ways that potential victims can protect themselves from financial loss.

Summary

Cybercrime is already a big problem all over the world, and it's growing fast. The law enforcement world is scrambling to catch up; legislators are passing new laws to address this new way of committing crime, and police agencies are forming special computer crime units and pushing their officers to become more technically savvy.

However, the cybercrime problem is too big and too widespread to leave to politicians and police to solve. The former often don't have the technical expertise to pass effective laws, and the latter lack sufficient training, manpower, and time—not to mention an understanding of the confusing issue of jurisdiction—to tackle any but the most egregious of Internet crimes.

Cybercrime, like crime in general, is a social problem as well as a legal one. To successfully fight it, we must engage people in the IT community (many of whom might be reluctant to participate) and those in the general population who are affected, directly or indirectly, by the criminal activity that has found a friendly haven in the virtual world.

We can use a number of tactics and techniques, including the legal system, peer pressure, and existing and emerging technologies, to prevent cybercrime. Failing that, we can develop formal and informal responses that will detect cybercrime more immediately, minimizing the harm done and giving us more information about the incident, maximizing the chances of identifying and successfully prosecuting the cybercriminal.

We're all in this boat together. The only way to stop cybercrime is to work together and share our knowledge and expertise in different areas to build a Class A cybercrime-fighting team.

Frequently Asked Questions

Q: Is the law enforcement community opposed to the use of encryption?

A: Most law enforcement professionals who specialize in cybercrime do not oppose use of encryption for legitimate communications. The Department of Justice states its official position on the www.cybercrime.gov Web site: "We do not oppose the use of encryption—just the opposite, because strong encryption can be an extraordinary tool to prevent crime. We believe that the use of strong cryptography is critical to the development of the 'Global Information Infrastructure,' or the GII. We agree that communications and data must be protected—both in transit and in storage—if the GII is to be used for personal communications, financial transactions, medical care, the development of new intellectual property, and other applications. The widespread use of unrecoverable encryption by criminals, however, poses a serious risk to public safety."

Q: Is software piracy really a big problem?

A: According to some estimates, the average purse snatcher gets only $20 or $30 per stolen purse, and the average strong-arm robbery (mugging) yields $50 or less. In contrast, pirated software programs often cost from several hundred to several thousand dollars. Thus, economically, one act of software piracy is several times more "serious" than victimization by a petty thief or robber.

Q: Why, then, do many people feel that software piracy is not a serious crime?

A: There are a number of reasons. Software piracy doesn't carry the emotional, face-to-face impact that purse snatching and robbery do. Software is "intangible"; it is made up of bits and bytes of electronic data, unlike a piece of physical property. Software piracy is not "theft" in the traditional meaning of the word because it is taken by copying, not by depriving the owner of its use. Many people feel that software vendors' licensing terms are unfair, and thus piracy is somewhat justified retaliation. There is also a general feeling that because copying of software is so widespread and appears to do no harm, it's not a "real crime" (similar to the way many people, who would never think of running a red light, feel about speeding).

Q: With all the computer and network security products currently on the market, why aren't all systems completely secured?

A: Despite all the excellent products available, the only completely secure computer is one that is turned off. In law enforcement firearms training, officers learn about "security holsters" that are designed to prevent a criminal from taking away an officer's weapon and using it against him or her. The first thing an officer who tries a security holster learns is that it is more difficult to use than a traditional, nonsecure holster and that the officer must practice diligently or he won't be able to draw his weapon quickly when it's needed. The simple truth is that the only totally secure holster is one into which the gun is permanently glued. Then it's not accessible to the bad guy, but it's not accessible to the officer, either. Computer and network security includes this same balancing act of security and accessibility, and the two factors will always be at odds. The more secure your systems are, the less accessible they are, and vice versa. Because the very purpose of a computer network is accessibility, no network can ever be 100 percent secure.

Chapter 2

The Evolution of Cybercrime

Topics we'll investigate in this chapter:

- Exploring Criminality in the Days of Stand-Alone Computers

- Understanding Early Phreakers, Hackers, and Crackers

- How Online Services Made Cybercrime Easy

- Introducing the ARPANET: The Wild West of Networking

- Watching Crime Rise with the Commercialization of the Internet

- Bringing the Cybercrime Story Up-to-Date

- Looking to the Future

☑ Summary

☑ Frequently Asked Questions

Introduction

How old is the phenomenon of cybercrime? It's safe to say that soon after the first computer networks were built, some people were looking for ways to exploit them for their own illegal purposes. The idea of theft is as old as the concept of privately owned property, and an element of almost all societies is dedicated to taking as much as possible of what isn't theirs—by whatever means they can.

As soon as it was widely recognized that computers store something of value (information), criminals saw an opportunity. But just as it's more difficult to target a robbery victim who stays locked up in his own home every day, the data on closed, stand-alone systems has been difficult to steal. However, that data began to move from one computer to another over networks, and like the robbery victim who travels from place to place, this data became more vulnerable. Networks provided another advantage: an entry point. Even if the information that was of value was never sent across the wire, the comings and goings of other bits of data opened up a way for intruders to sneak inside the computer, like a robber taking advantage of the victim's housemates who leave the doors unlocked on their way out.

However, cybercrime didn't spring up as a full-blown problem overnight. In the early days of computing and networking, the average criminal didn't possess either the necessary hardware or the technical expertise to seize the digital opportunity of the day. Computers were million-dollar main-frame monstrosities, and only a few of them were in existence. An aspiring cybercriminal could hardly go out and buy (or steal) a computer, and even if he did, it's unlikely that he would have known what to do with it. There were no "user-friendly" applications; working with early systems required the ability to "speak" *machine language*—that is, to communicate in the 1s and 0s of binary calculation that computers understood.

The cybercrime problem emerged and grew as computing became easier and less expensive. Today almost everyone in industrialized countries has access to computer technology; children learn to use PCs in elementary school, and people who can't afford computers of their own can use PCs in public libraries or on college campuses for free, or they can rent computer time at business centers or Internet cafés. Applications are "point and click" or even voice-activated; it no longer requires a computer science degree to perform once-complex tasks such as sending e-mail or downloading files from another machine across the Internet. Some of today's cybercriminals are talented programmers (the hacker elite), but most are not. Advanced technical abilities make it easier for cybercriminals to "do their thing" and cover their tracks, but these abilities are by no means a job requirement.

In this chapter, we take a look at these issues:

- The challenges of computer crime in the days of stand-alone computers

- How early network-connected criminals operated

- How members of ARPANET (the predecessor to the Internet) increased the opportunities for criminal activity

- How the phenomenal growth of the commercial Internet led to the equally phenomenal rise in cybercrime

- How the advent of easy-to-use online services such as CompuServe and America Online (AOL) made online criminality even easier

- Where we are today and how the "latest and greatest" technologies have created new security vulnerabilities

First, let's go back to the 1940s, when Dr. J. Presper Eckert and Dr. John W. Mauchly devised one of the first digital computers, the Electronic Numerical Integrator and Computer (ENIAC).

Exploring Criminality in the Days of Stand-Alone Computers

ENIAC was a behemoth, requiring more than 1,500 square feet of floor space—more than many of today's "starter homes." This gigantic machine used more than 17,000 vacuum tubes and could do about 1,000 calculations per second, compared with the millions of calculations per second attained by compact, inexpensive modern PCs.

ENIAC was quite an accomplishment, but the good doctors involved in its development didn't rest on their laurels. In 1949, they introduced the Binary Automatic Computer (BINAC), which stored data on a magnetic tape. Shortly thereafter, they invented the Universal Automatic Computer (UNIVAC), the first commercially marketed computer, under a grant from the U.S. government.

When the first UNIVAC was delivered to the U.S. Census Bureau in 1951, it was the size of a room and cost $1 million. The manufacturer eventually built 46 UNIVACs for government and business customers. The UNIVAC used magnetic tape, which was faster than the IBM punch card system that was its direct competitor.

NOTE

Going even further into the past, the first punch card tabulation machines were invented in the late 1800s by an engineer named Herman Hollerith. Like the UNIVAC, punch card technology was originally developed for the U.S. Census Bureau to use in sorting and analyzing its data. Hollerith's Tabulating Machine Company, founded in 1896, was acquired by IBM in 1924.

These early computers had some inherent security advantages: They were huge and expensive, they were stand-alone systems, and most of the world didn't really know what a computer was, much less how to use it.

Sharing More Than Time

It wasn't long before scientific-minded people were enamored with computers. The Programmed Data Processor (PDP-1), developed and marketed by Digital Equipment Corporation (DEC) in the 1960s, was the first computer used for commercial time sharing (that is, the owners of the computer rented computer time to other businesses, schools, laboratories, and programmers who couldn't afford to buy computers of their own).

Because numerous people and businesses were using the same computer, the data and programs stored on it were vulnerable. Thus, the first doors to hacking were opened—and despite the efforts of system administrators, security product vendors, and law enforcement, those doors have not been closed since.

    The first hackers' group came about, not surprisingly, at the Massachusetts Institute of Technology (MIT) in 1961 shortly after MIT got its first PDP-1. The group, called the Tech Model Railroad Club, was made up of members who programmed for the sheer joy of it—the essence of hacking in its original sense.

The Evolution of a Word

In the 1960s, the term *hacker* was used to refer to someone who was considered a "real programmer," who had mastered the computer systems of the day and was able to manipulate programs to do more than they were originally intended to do. According to the Internet Users' Glossary, which is the Internet Engineering Task Force's Request for Comments (RFC) 1392 (www.ietf.org/rfc/rfc1392.txt), a hacker is a "person who delights in having an intimate understanding of the internal workings of a system, computers and computer networks in particular."

    In the late 1960s and early 1970s, hacking became associated with the radical underground ("yippie") movement and took on an antiestablishment flavor. Law enforcement agencies began to arrest *phreakers* for tampering with the phone system, as we discuss in more detail in the following section. In the 1980s, the FBI made some of the first high-profile arrests of computer hackers (including that of Kevin Mitnick, who arguably became something of a "martyr to the cause" in the hacking community). Movies such as John Badham's *WarGames* (1983), Phil Alden Robinson's *Sneakers* (1992), and Iain Softley's *Hackers* (1995) brought into the mainstream the concept of the hacker as a brilliant and somewhat romantic figure who breaks the law (but usually for noble purposes).

    Even though in the community of computer enthusiasts, the term *hacker* continued to be used in its original context whereas *crackers* (which we'll discuss in the next section) were people who would maliciously crack the security of systems, public perception of the two became intermingled. Despite this, or perhaps more because of it, those who broke into systems were viewed with some reverence. After all, it could be argued that they weren't creating the vulnerabilities that existed in poor programming or meager security; they were simply taking advantage of it. The hackers were using their talents to do things that were beyond the abilities of the common computer user or person on the street, who may have never even seen a computer at this point in time. To many, including those in the criminal justice system, the concepts were beyond their grasp.

Understanding Early Phreakers, Hackers, and Crackers

Hacking in the modern sense of the word—as applied to someone who breaks into systems, usually remotely—couldn't have come into its own without the network. However, we mustn't forget that networks existed long before there were computers. In the 1940s, when the first real computers were being developed, today's huge global telephone network, the construction of which began in the late 1800s, had already been steadily growing for 60 years.

    The first electronic hackers broke into the phone system to make long distance calls without having to pay for them. These telephone network hackers became known as *phreakers*. Yet another term that originated during the early years of electronic communication is *cracker*, used to describe someone who "cracks" a system's security; this term now often refers to someone who specializes in cracking passwords. The various designations help to define what security system is being attacked or broken.

Hacking Ma Bell's Phone Network

The person who has been attributed as being the father of phreaking is Joe Engressia, who as a blind child in the 1950s discovered that by whistling in a certain pitch, he could reset the telephone company's automated system that played disconnected phone messages. The tone he discovered was the same frequency used by the 2600 Hz tone system, and although he didn't immediately realize it, it allowed him to reset the trunk system and thereby make free long distance telephone calls.

Another of the earliest phreaks was Stewart Nelson. As a student at MIT in 1964, Nelson became part of the first generation of hackers by figuring out how to use MIT's computer to generate the tones to access the phone company's long distance service. In doing so, he too was able to exploit the phone system's vulnerability.

Although some especially talented phreakers such as Engressia were able to reproduce these tones merely by whistling, most phreakers used a device called the *blue box*, a tone generator set to reproduce the 2600 Hz frequency. Today's phone systems don't use the 2600 Hz tone for long distance access, but there is still an active contingent of phone phreakers who take advantage of the complexities of modern systems to find new ways to exploit the telephone system technology to their benefit.

Phamous Phreakers

John Draper, a U.S. Air Force veteran and engineering technician for National Semiconductor, who went by the alias of Captain Crunch, is generally credited with designing the original blue box after discovering that the toy whistle included in boxes of Cap'n Crunch cereal could produce the 2600 Hz signal that granted access to AT&T's long distance service. Draper was arrested and served time in a California minimum security prison for this infraction. According to legend, he held seminars while in prison, teaching other inmates how to hack the phone system. He was later arrested again in New York, but went on to create the word processing application *EasyWriter* for the Apple II and IBM PC.

Prior to founding Apple Computer, in the early 1970s Steve Jobs and Steve Wozniak made and sold blue boxes. According to John Draper's Web site (www.webcrunchers.com), Steve Wozniak contacted Draper after he tried and failed to make a functioning blue box. Draper agreed to meet the pair at the University of California at Berkeley, where they learned how to use the box, and Wozniak attempted to use the device to call the Pope in Rome. Jobs and Wozniak began to sell the boxes for $150 apiece, complete with instructions and inscribed with the words "He has the whole world in his hands." On Steve Wozniak's Web site at www.woz.org, you can see a photo of the pair in 1975 holding a blue box.

NOTE

2600 Magazine and its Web site (www.2600.com) are popular resources for the hacker underground; the magazine got its name from the 2600 Hz phone phreaking frequency.

Phreaking on the Other Side of the Atlantic

The British phone system had its own phreakers, dating back to the time when the "Toll A" hack was discovered and exploited to make free long distance calls. Later, British phreakers constructed "bleeper boxes" that served the same purpose as the blue box in the United States but used different sets of frequencies.

A Box for Every Color Scheme

In addition to the original blue box, phreakers constructed a number of other devices to outwit the phone system. The *red box* replicates the tones that are produced when coins are deposited in a pay phone, and a *black box* allows calls placed *to* the phone to which it is attached to be made free of charge.

Not all phone phreaking was done for the purpose of circumventing long distance charges. Manipulation of the phone system was also popular with people engaged in other criminal activities, to cover their tracks when conducting illegal business over the phone. The *cheese box* was devised to connect two lines at a location in such a way as to allow bookies or drug dealers to receive calls from another remote location and go through the cheese box to disguise the number at which they were actually located.

From Phreaker to Hacker

While early phreakers were experimenting and finding how systems worked, phreaking progressed to a subculture of people stealing services or circumventing the authorities. Even as the public became aware of this, it was difficult for people to have sympathy for the victim (the telephone company) as they paid inflated fees for long distance services. Few realized that the losses suffered from crimes are added to everyone else's bill.

A huge wealth of information about phreaking is available on the Web, including detailed instructions for "wannabe" phreakers. The phreaker "attitude" (disdain for large corporations such as the telephone company and a belief in the "right" of those who are clever enough to rip off these corporations) formed the basis of the later hacker subculture. Many of the first computer hackers began their criminal careers as phone phreakers.

Living on the LAN: Early Computer Network Hackers

In the 1970s, the first affordable personal computer, the Altair 8800, became available. The machine was sold as a kit that the buyer had to put together, and it didn't do much once it was built because the owner also had to write his or her own programs for it. Nevertheless, the Altair gave birth to hacking as we know it today; this device made it possible for individuals to own their own computers and learn to program.

Other relatively low-cost computers followed; the Commodore 64 was a popular "toy" that introduced many youngsters, mostly teenage boys, to the joys of programming and, later, full-fledged hacking. Radio Shack's TRS-80 (affectionately known as the Trash 80) and the original IBM PC brought more powerful computing to people who were eager to find new ways to exploit the systems' capabilities. But it was the PC network that really opened the floodgates for all hacking that followed.

The first computer "networks" were not actually made up of networked computers. Rather, they consisted of one computer—a mainframe—and many terminals that connected to the mainframe, ran programs on it, and accessed its files. Although these terminals were networked in one sense of the word, they were "dumb" terminals that possessed no processing power of their own. This mainframe timesharing linked multiple users and allowed them to share files and printers. It also allowed early hackers to access the files of other mainframe users.

Disadvantages of mainframe computing included the high cost of the computer and the single point of failure that it represented. If the system went down, no one on the network could do any computing, because the terminals they operated were dumb. *Minicomputers* (such as the DEC PDP and VAX, and the IBM AS/400) were created as lower-cost, more compact alternatives to the full-fledged mainframe, but these machines still relied on dumb terminals and worked in essentially the same way as the older devices. Eventually, the search for a better way led to the development of smaller, less expensive computers (then called *microcomputers* and later called *personal computers,* or *PCs*) that could sit on a desktop. With each worker having a full-fledged computer on the desktop, there was much more fault tolerance than with the mainframe; if one computer went down, everyone else could keep computing.

However, workers missed some of the advantages of the mainframe environment, such as the ability to easily share files with others. "Sneakernet"—copying files to a floppy disk and physically transporting the disk to another computer—was the workaround, but that system didn't work so well when the users who wanted to share files were in different parts of the building or the files were too large to fit on a floppy. The solution was to connect the stand-alone desktop computers in a network, providing the resource-sharing benefits of mainframe computing with the fault tolerance of decentralized computing. Networked PCs give us, in many ways, the best of both worlds. They also give the hackers among us a way to access our information, whether we want to share it or not.

In the 1970s, researchers at Xerox's Palo Alto Research Center (PARC) developed Ethernet, which still forms the basis of most local area networks (LANs) today. DEC, Intel, and Xerox got together in 1979 to create Ethernet standards (originally called DIX after the company names) to make it easy for vendors to create compatible products. In 1983, the Institute of Electrical and Electronics Engineers, Inc. (IEEE) released the 802.3 specifications based on thick coaxial cable and called 10Base5.

Ethernet gave companies a way to link their computers easily and relatively inexpensively, especially after the IEEE developed and standardized a second version based on thin coax (10Base2) in 1985. Networked PCs began to emerge as a popular alternative to mainframe computing (or in some cases, an addition to it) in the 1980s.

How BBSes Fostered Criminal Behavior

In addition to networking PCs together at one location to create a LAN, PCs could be used to link to one another from remote locations using a modem and a telephone line. This led to the advent of the *bulletin board system (BBS)*, a computer system equipped with one or more modems so that users can dial in and use its services. BBSes were a predecessor of the Internet, providing many of the services people are familiar with today. Although BBSes were generally text-based, users were able to download files, exchange private e-mail, post messages to a "board" to carry on public virtual discussions, play online games, and use many other features. And though message networks were used to discuss topics with others throughout the world, BBS users would generally dial into systems that were local to them.

Ward Christensen and Randy Suess developed the software for the Computerized Bulletin Board System (CBBS) in the 1970s in Chicago. They described it in an article published in *Byte Magazine* in 1978. The system was a huge success, and BBSes sprang up all over the country. To see how popular they were, you can see a historical list of BBSes at http://bbslist.textfiles.com.

Early hackers and phreakers seized on the BBS idea as a way to communicate with one another and share their tricks and techniques. Most boards included both the public forum and e-mail service between members of the BBS. Although many BBSes were legitimate "places" where computer hobbyists could gather and share the software they'd written themselves or discuss issues of the day, the BBS had a natural appeal to the criminal element. The BBSes spawned the first large-scale method of distributing *warez* (hacker jargon for pirated software), often computer games. Other BBSes specialized in the sharing of pornographic pictures and/or stories.

Early BBSes were slow (2400-baud modems were top of the line at the time) and expensive unless you were lucky enough to live in the same locality as your cohorts or you were a phreaker who didn't pay for long distance calls. It was often difficult to get connected because most BBSes were operated out of someone's home on a limited budget, so the average systems operator, or sysop (the person who ran the BBS), didn't have a large number of modems and phone lines. Although some sysops ran these systems for love, many (especially those who dealt in pornography) charged members a monthly or annual fee to connect.

The popularity of these forums began to decline in the late 1990s, when Internet access became commercially available at an affordable price and the graphical nature of the World Wide Web made the BBS systems with their ASCII drawings seem hopelessly outdated.

On the Scene

Bulletin Board Systems

What was allowed on a particular BBS was dependent on the system operator (sysop) who owned the computer. Whereas most boards were community-based forums for computer enthusiasts, others existed that provided hacking tools and information, pirated software, copies of virus files, or distributed child pornography.

Because sysops in a particular area were generally in contact with one another, they (and the other BBS users) often knew which boards allowed illegal material and which users were troublemakers. Unfortunately, because computer-related crime wasn't generally understood and few laws existed, it wasn't unheard of for local police to brush off those who called to complain. In addition to this, there was a fear of police seizing the complainant's computer as evidence, as the officer might not understand how remote computers were being accessed. Keep in mind that at the time, it cost a few thousand dollars to buy a PC, so they weren't as common as today, and most people didn't really understand them. To put this period into further perspective, the controversy about sharing music involved taping it on cassettes.

Continued

Most sysops monitored what was happening on their systems, and acted accordingly. In most cases, users who uploaded illegal material or harassed other users would simply be banned from the board. Word might then spread to other sysops, who would likewise ban them. As BBSes policed themselves, sysops acted as the sheriffs of their online communities.

How Online Services Made Cybercrime Easy

In the early days of the commercial Internet, getting online was not necessarily an easy proposition. Unlike today's operating systems, the operating systems in use then (mostly Windows 3.*x*) didn't come with the Transmission Control Protocol/Internet Protocol (TCP/IP) stack built in; also not included was the software required to make a dial-up connection to the Internet and use its applications (Winsock). The correct software had to be downloaded, complex text configuration files had to be edited, and it took a certain amount of technical savvy (not to mention patience) to put it all together and successfully log on to the Internet. In addition, users had to log on through the first commercial Internet service providers (ISPs), which were often brand-new ventures launched by a couple of nerds on a shoestring budget, working out of an apartment. These entrepreneurs generally didn't provide user-friendly setup CDs to configure the settings for you, as most ISPs do today.

There was, however, an easier way to get online: the online service. Companies such as CompuServe, Prodigy, and AOL offered access to their network "communities." Once logged on to the service, users could download software, post messages to bulletin boards, find information on a wide variety of topics, and waste amazing amounts of time in chat rooms or holding private conversations through instant messaging (IM).

The big lure of these services was ease of use. They provided a disk that usually installed the proper software automatically and configured users' computer settings, so users didn't have to know anything about much of anything to get "connected." In their early days, the services were excruciatingly expensive by modern standards; in the 1980s it cost $25 an *hour* to connect to CompuServe. Prices dropped in the early 1990s to around $3 an hour, and eventually the services went to unlimited usage plans that cost less than $20 a month.

The online services were *not*, in their early days, ISPs. Rather, they were private wide area networks (WANs) in which members interacted with each other but not with the "outside world" of the Internet—they were like BBSes on steroids. Later the services provided e-mail gateways so that their members could exchange e-mail with others outside the private network. They also added access to the World Wide Web. Today, online services are synonymous with ISPs, and the ease of going online has attracted criminals (along with legitimate users) who are not particularly technically proficient.

Another attraction of online services for criminals is the anonymity they offer. Generally, if you set up an account with a regular ISP, you're assigned a user account name and an e-mail address based on that name. It's possible to get the ISP to change your account name, but it's a lot of trouble and can't be done too frequently. Services such as AOL allow users to create secondary "screen names" that they can change whenever they want, making it easier for a criminal to change identities and cover his or her tracks.

Introducing the ARPANET: The Wild West of Networking

In the beginning (or what was the beginning of today's vast global internetwork), there was the ARPANET. The ARPANET eventually begat the Internet.

Sputnik Inspires ARPA

Back in 1957, no one could have foreseen the communications system that today connects friends, relatives, business partners, and strangers all over the world. In 1957, President Dwight Eisenhower authorized the creation of the Advanced Research Projects Agency (ARPA) in response to the launch of the Soviet Union's first artificial Earth-orbiting satellite, Sputnik.

ARPA's first project was to develop a satellite of its own for the United States; it was not until years later that the agency began to work on computer and networking technology. In the 1960s, as the Cold War with the Soviet Union continued, the government considered the possibility of nuclear war and how to maintain communications if the unthinkable occurred. This is where ARPA's involvement with computing began.

ARPA Turns Its Talents to Computer Technology

Dr. J.C.R. Licklider was appointed to run ARPA's computer technology project in 1962. He was largely responsible for building the beginnings of a WAN connecting government/military and university sites, using redundant links so that if one node was taken out, messages could still get through by taking a different path. This network, based on packet-switching technology developed in the 1960s, was called the *ARPANET*.

The first node of the network was installed at the University of California at Los Angeles (UCLA) in 1969. Additional nodes were installed at Stanford, U.C. at Santa Barbara (UCSB), and the University of Utah, located in Salt Lake City.

Network Applications Come into Their Own

In the early 1970s, e-mail—still the Internet's "killer application" in terms of popularity—was invented. Gateways were devised to connect networks using different architectures, and specifications were developed for what would become File Transfer Protocol (FTP).

By the end of the 1970s, Usenet newsgroups had been established, and the first interactive multiple-user sites, called *multiuser dungeons*, or *MUDs*, had appeared. By that time, the ARPANET had been up and running for more than 10 years, although it was still limited mostly to university and government sites.

The Internetwork Continues to Expand

In the early 1980s, the TCP/IP suite was defined as the standard for communications on the ARPANET. Soon after, name servers were created to handle the translation of "friendly" computer names and paths to the Internet Protocol (IP) addresses computers use to route messages to one another.

William Gibson's sci-fi novel *Neuromancer*, published in 1984, coined the term *cyberspace* as a description of the online world. At that time, no one had any idea just how crowded cyberspace would soon become.

The ARPANET of the 1980s

The worldwide network was steadily growing, but in 1986 there were still only about 5,000 hosts (computers) on the Net. About this time, the National Science Foundation (NSF), which maintained the Internet backbone, established five supercomputer centers, which resulted in a dramatic increase in available connections. The next year, 1987, the number of hosts had risen to either 10,000 or 28,000 (depending on the source you consult), and a year after that, the NFSNET backbone was upgrade to 1.544 Mbps (a T1 line). By 1989, all sources agree that there were more than 100,000 hosts on the network.

The Internet of the 1990s

In 1990, the ARPANET ceased to exist, and the Internet was born. Actually, ARPA had already been split into two parts in the 1980s: MILNET (for military use, which was integrated into the Defense Data Network) and the NSFNET, which handled civilian communications. NSF upgraded the backbone again, to T3 speed (44.736 Mbps). The NSFNET grew into today's commercial Internet, and by 1992, there were more than 1 million Internet hosts. In 1995, NSFNET gave the backbone services to interconnected commercial Network Access Providers (NAPs) and became a research network again, establishing the very high-speed Backbone Network Service (vBNS) that connected the five supercomputer centers. The commercialization of the Internet had begun.

The Worm Turns—and Security Becomes a Concern

During the early ARPANET days, security was both a major concern to the military contingent and almost a nonissue to research scientists, who were more interested in what the technology could do than in securing it)—hence the break-up of the network. The small number of nodes on the network limited the scope of the threat posted by security breaches. However, in 1988, a *worm* (a self-replicating program) was released on the Internet and attacked computers running Berkeley UNIX, spreading all across the United States, infecting thousands of computers and shutting down a large portion of the Internet. This was the wakeup call; Internet users suddenly realized that some in their midst harbored malicious intent. Many more virus attacks and hacks were to follow.

Watching Crime Rise with the Commercialization of the Internet

By 1991, e-mail users had begun to consider the possibility that their Internet communications would be intercepted. Philip Zimmermann released an encryption program called Pretty Good Privacy (PGP) that could be used to protect sensitive messages. PGP was also used by criminals to hide evidence of their crimes from police.

The first cyberbank, called First Virtual, came online in 1994, opening up vast new opportunities for hackers. Also that year, researchers began work on the "next generation" of the Internet Protocol, called IPv6. The primary purpose of the new version was to address the anticipated shortage of IP addresses using the current IPv4's 32-bit address space, but another concern addressed by the new protocol version was to be IP security.

In 1995, the U.S. Secret Service and the Drug Enforcement Agency (DEA) obtained an Internet wiretap to help build a case against suspects who were accused of producing and selling illegal cell phone cloning equipment.

In 1996, Congress became concerned about the amount of pornography that was being exchanged over the Internet and passed the Communications Decency Act (CDA), which was later declared unconstitutional. Meanwhile, a cracker was able to shut down the Public Access Networks Corporation in New York using a hack attack that was described in *2600 Magazine*. A "cancelbot" launched on Usenet destroyed more than 25,000 newsgroup messages, and in the same year, the U.S. Department of Justice (DOJ), Central Intelligence Agency (CIA), and Air Force computers (among others) were hacked.

In the next three years, many more government agencies and prominent companies had their systems hacked, including the U.S. Department of Commerce, UNICEF, and *The New York Times*. eBay, Microsoft, and the U.S. Senate Web sites also fell victim to hackers. The Melissa virus caused company e-mail servers to shut down. A fraudulent Web page that was designed to appear to be a Bloomberg financial news story resulted in the shares of a small tech company increasing 31 percent in response to the false "news."

As we entered the 2000s, a huge, distributed denial-of-service (DoS) attack shut down major Web sites such as Yahoo! and Amazon. Apache, RSA Security, and Western Union were hacked, the Code Red worm attacked thousands of Web servers, and the Sircam virus hit e-mail accounts all over the world.

However, malicious code and hack attacks comprised only a small portion of the overall criminal activity that in some way used or depended on the Internet. From the infamous "Nigerian letter" scam to the use of the Net to plot the September 11, 2001 terrorist attacks, crime was running rampant on the network—and still is today.

Bringing the Cybercrime Story Up-to-Date

The new millennium brought with it the growing popularity of new and exciting technologies, such as wireless networking and low-cost, high-speed "always-on" connectivity options through Digital Subscriber Line (xDSL) and cable modem. These technologies have become available in increasing numbers of places. Unfortunately, these technologies also provide new opportunities for cybercriminals, for a number of reasons, which we explore here.

Understanding How New Technologies Create New Vulnerabilities

Most of us are much more security-conscious today than we were a decade ago, in regard to both our computers and our lives in general. Certainly, more security products are on the market today than a few years ago. Lawmakers all over the world have "cracked down" on behaviors such as unauthorized access, which recently weren't covered by criminal statutes.

We seem to have all of the most important elements for reducing the incidence of cybercrime: We have the laws ("with teeth"); we have the tools; we even have the widespread awareness that is sometimes the most difficult component of a crime prevention effort. Why, then, is cybercrime not only *not* going away, but steadily increasing?

An important reason for the increase in cybercrime is the whirlwind pace at which new technologies are being developed to make our computing experience more productive, easier, faster, and more fun. However, convenience and performance often come with a price, and that price is security.

Cybercriminals love new technologies, including:

- Broadband

- Wireless

- Mobile computing and remote access

- Sophisticated Web technologies such as Java, ActiveX, and so on

- Fancy e-mail programs that support Hypertext Markup Language (HTML) and scripting

- E-commerce and online banking

- IM

- New operating systems

Cybercriminals also love standardization. If everyone uses the same operating system, or the same Web browser, or the same e-mail client, or if all vendors adhere to the same specifications, the potential attacker has much less to learn and a much larger playing field. For example, a reason why Macintosh computers are less prone to viruses is because it doesn't make sense for a programmer to write viruses that attack a system that is used by a minority of people. It makes more sense to write viruses that attack Microsoft operating systems and software, which most people have.

Let's discuss the reasons these new technologies and the standardization of computer and networking technologies are so dear to the heart of the cybercriminal.

Why Cybercriminals Love Broadband

Broadband technologies such as DSL, cable modem, and satellite Internet services have made Internet users' lives easier, but they have also made it easier for hackers to invade those users' computers and networks. Because individual computers attached to broadband networks such as cable modem or DSL behave more like computers attached to a network than like individual computers that use telephone lines to dial into the Internet, it is easier to exploit the technology to gain unauthorized access. As a consequence, broadband users need to be much more security conscious than dial-up Internet users.

CyberStats

Internet Connectivity

According to the Pew Internet & American Life Project's report "Broadband Adoption in 2007" (www.pewinternet.org/pdfs/PIP_Broadband%202007.pdf), more people are using broadband to connect to the Internet than ever before. Of those who use the Internet from home, 70 percent have a high-speed connection and 23 percent use dial-up.

Of the residential high-speed lines that were used as of December 31, 2006, the Federal Communications Commission (www.fcc.gov/wcb/iatd/comp.html) reported that the following high-speed services were used:

- Cable modem, 53 percent
- Asymmetric Digital Subscriber Line (ADSL), 39.1 percent
- Symmetric Digital Subscriber Line (SDSL) and traditional wireline, 0.2 percent
- Fiber, 1.3 percent
- All other, 5.8 percent

The Problem with 24/7 Connectivity

A network is vulnerable to an attack from outside only when it is connected to an outside network. When most users and companies were connecting to the Internet with analog modems or dial-up Integrated Services Digital Network (ISDN) connections, their vulnerability to attack was limited because the system was available to outsiders only during a session. When you finished doing what you wanted to do on the Net, you disconnected and your system "disappeared" from the Internet.

Additionally, most ISPs use Dynamic Host Configuration Protocol (DHCP) to assign IP addresses to dial-up users. This means your Internet-connected computer gets a new IP address each time you hang up and reconnect.

DSL and cable are referred to as "always-on" technologies. You don't have to dial up a connection each time you want to get onto the Internet; instead, you stay connected 24 hours a day, seven days a week. This makes it quicker and easier for you to access Internet resources. It also makes it easier for you to run a server, allowing other authorized users to remotely access shared files on your system. Because your IP address generally stays the same, since you don't disconnect, these authorized clients can find your server more easily from one communication session to the next. Of course, turning off your DSL modem or powering down the computer will break the connection, and "shuts the door" to potential hackers. However, computers can run continuously, and many users never turn their systems off.

The problem with 24/7 technologies is that they make it easier for *unauthorized* folks to access your system, too. Your exposure is much greater because you're "always open for business," giving a hacker more time to mount a brute force attack to guess your password or figure out which Transmission Control Protocol/User Datagram Protocol (TCP/UDP) ports might be open and vulnerable. Furthermore, because your IP address stays the same, it's easier for these hackers to return to your system the next time they want to do a little virtual breaking and entering.

The Problem with High-Speed Connectivity

Another advantage of broadband is the increased connectivity speed. Unlike an analog modem that's limited to 56 Kbps (and practically speaking, less than that due to federal regulations and line considerations), DSL and cable companies offer high-speed downloads and often higher upload speeds as well. This means improved performance on your end—but if your service offers a high upload speed, it also means an intruder will be able to snatch your files more quickly.

Luckily, in terms of security if not usability, most broadband services are asymmetric. That means that upload and download speeds are not created equal; ADSL offers upload speeds of 400 kbps and download speeds of 1.4 Mbps, whereas cable offers upload speeds of 400- to 600 Kbps and download speeds of 1.5- to 3.0 Mbps. There are, however, a number of factors that will affect the actual upstream and downstream transfer rates, meaning that the speeds aren't as high as what's mentioned here.

NOTE

Most commercial ISPs limit (or *throttle*) upstream speeds to discourage home users from running servers (which is a violation of many cable and DSL contract terms of service).

Even with these limitations, however, upstream speed is generally at least twice that of an analog modem—a boon to hackers downloading data from your computer to their own.

The Problem with Low-Cost, 24/7, High-Speed Connectivity

The problems linked to high-speed, 24/7 connectivity and high-speed data rates associated with consumer broadband technologies also exist with traditional 24/7 high-speed business solutions such as T1. However, because most T1 lines are connected to companies that employ information technology (IT) professionals, it is more likely that security measures are in place to offset the security risk.

The problem with cable and DSL is that these technologies have brought high-speed, always-on access to home and small-office users who can't afford the high cost of T1. These less sophisticated users are also less likely to be aware of the security risk or to have the technical expertise or budget to implement the proper level of security.

Most small offices and a growing number of home users run network address translator (NAT) software of some type to share Internet access with multiple PCs on a small LAN. This provides a small measure of security to the systems on the local network because NAT assigns private IP addresses to the NAT client computers. These addresses are not visible on the Internet. However, the NAT host computer that is directly connected to the Internet is exposed.

How to Protect Your Broadband Connection

As we'll discuss in Chapters 12 and 13, many security measures can be implemented, regardless of the type of Internet connection being used. Some of these methods include:

- Ensuring that software on the computer has been patched to protect against known vulnerabilities. Security updates help to protect the operating system and other software running on the system so that bugs or issues related to the software won't be exploited.

- Having up-to-date antivirus (AV) software on your system.

- Using a firewall, which controls what can get to and what can be accessed from the computer.

There are, however, additional measures that you can take that are specific to computers with broadband connections. If you have a computer that uses a broadband Internet connection and the computer is *not* connected to a LAN and is not functioning as an Internet server, one step you can take is to be sure that file and print sharing is not enabled on that computer.

Some cable users have found that when the network interface card (NIC) used to connect to the cable modem was installed by the cable company (or by the user), Windows automatically binds the card to both TCP/IP and the Microsoft Networking service. Having this interface bound to Microsoft networking opens their systems to others on the cable segment.

NOTE

Chapter 13 provides details on how to disable file and print sharing on Windows, UNIX/Linux, and Macintosh computers, and how to check and change NIC bindings.

ISPs may also provide the option of having a static IP address, as opposed to one that is issued to the user when he or she logs on to the Internet. An *IP address* is a unique number that identifies a computer or device on a TCP/IP network, such as the Internet. A static IP address that never changes gives a fixed point for hackers to focus on. Conversely, with DHCP an address is assigned to a host computer each time the user logs on to the network or Internet. This essentially creates a moving target that is harder to hit.

Over the past decade, security has been in the forefront of computer use, so more products have become available that include security features built into them. Many DSL and cable modems include features such as packet filtering, NAT, and other elements that were previously unheard of for home use. In addition to this, software-based firewall, AV, and other solutions can be added to systems to provide enhanced security that can users can update on a routine basis.

Which Is More Secure?

A common question of debate concerns which is more secure: DSL or cable. Cable is a shared connection (that is, everyone in your neighborhood is part of the same network segment). In essence, this creates a LAN. That means that your neighbors have access to your system, much as neighboring computers on any LAN have access to one another.

As on a regular LAN, there are ways to protect yourself from your LAN-mates. The Data Over Cable Service Interface Specification (DOCSIS) standard for cable modems provides some measure of security because modems that comply with this specification support data encryption between the provider's hub and the user's computer. Data is *not* encrypted between the provider and the end destination (that is, when traveling over the Internet), but this standard does help to address the "neighborhood segment sharing" problem, because others on your cable segment will not be able to read your data if they intercept it. Cable networks that use DOCSIS standards also prevent your computer from announcing its shares to the network using NetBIOS protocols (which cause other computers on the network to show up in the Network Neighborhood or Network Places window on computers running Windows). Be aware, though, that a hacker could still connect to your computer if he or she knows your computer name or IP address.

DSL users are connected directly via their phone lines to the telephone company central office (CO). Thus, DSL provides fewer vulnerabilities to hackers—but this does not mean a DSL connection is a secure one.

As mentioned, no one should use a broadband Internet connection without also using a firewall to protect the network from outside intruders. Firewalls can filter both incoming and outgoing data and block open ports to cut hackers off from their usual entry points. A firewall can be either a hardware device or a software program that runs on the Internet-connected computer. Newer Microsoft operating systems even include a firewall with the OS. Windows Firewall, which was included with Windows XP Service Pack 2, only blocks incoming traffic to your computer. This meant that any malicious programs on your computer could connect to the Internet even though the firewall was running. This changed in Windows Vista, whose firewall will block both incoming and outgoing traffic, allowing you to decide which programs can connect to the Internet.

We discuss how firewalls work and the various types of firewalls that are available in Chapter 12.

Why Cybercriminals Love Wireless

Wireless technologies have emerged as a major change in how computers connect to the Internet, with many home and business-based users using wireless connections and/or devices. Wireless gives mobile computers the ability to boldly go where no Ethernet cable has gone before—and still stay connected to the local network and/or the Internet.

Windows XP and Vista include built-in support for 802.11 wireless networking. Setup of a wireless network is easy using the XP interface, as shown in Figure 2.1.

Figure 2.1 Setting Up Wireless Networking with Windows XP

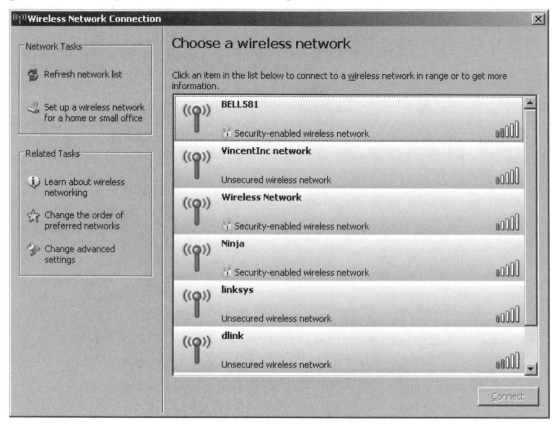

Standards and Standard Problems

Different types of wireless networks are available, the most common being 802.11 b/g. The first wireless standard developed for commercial use was 802.11b. It operates at 2.4 GHz and transfers data at a rate of 11 Mbps. Improving data transfer to 54 Mbps, 802.11 g was a welcome upgrade for consumers wanting faster throughput from their wireless infrastructure. Although the 2.4 GHz band would often lead to interference problems, backward compatibility and early adoption helped this combination become the standard for wireless devices.

For companies that required less interference or that could not adopt the 2.4 GHz band as an acceptable solution, 802.11a was released. This worked on the 5 GHz band, improving on wireless stability by reducing dropped connections while staying at the 54 Mbps transfer rate. The main downside of 802.11a is the expense of upgrading both the wireless access points and the client's wireless cards to devices that support this standard.

Wireless devices, such as those supporting Bluetooth, can also connect two remote locations by using line-of-sight antennas to send data from one location to another where the installation of cabling would not be feasible. A company that has a second building located less than a mile from the main building may choose to implement a line-of-sight wireless solution for Internet connectivity instead of spending the reoccurring cost of a traditional T1 line.

Bluetooth is a wireless technology designed to enable a wide variety of portable devices, such as personal digital assistants (PDAs) and mobile phones—as well as more traditional laptop and notebook computers—to connect to the Internet. In 2002, IEEE 802.15.1 was established as a standard for wireless personal area networks (PANs) based on Bluetooth Version 1.1 specifications.

Unfortunately, the ability to access a network without any physical connection makes it that much easier for hackers to do the same, as they don't have to worry about "plugging in" to the cable. If a network includes a wireless access point, it is vulnerable to outside intruders even if there is no remote access server or Internet connection on the network.

It's important to understand that most are based on radio transmissions that go out over the airwaves. For example, Bluetooth devices transmit in the 2.4 GHz spectrum. This is an unlicensed range, so anyone can transmit and receive on it. Transmissions over the airwaves can be intercepted, and 2.4 GHz antennas, amplifiers, and transceivers are readily available. The signals can be picked up hundreds of feet from the access point; high-gain antennas increase this distance. All of this is fodder for the cybercriminal.

The 802.11 wireless standards actually do provide for security measures, such as authentication and encryption. Unfortunately, the encryption these technologies use can be weak, and can be broken relatively easily. Older devices and small handheld devices, such as mobile phones, have limited memory and processing power. This means larger encryption algorithms that require heavy processing can't be used. Such older devices may use Wireless Equivalent Privacy (WEP), which is defined in IEEE 802.11b. A program named AirSnort that runs on Linux exploits the weaknesses of wireless encryption to discover the WEP encryption key simply by passively monitoring the wireless network. The fact that WEP uses static keys (rather than more secure dynamic keys that change at regular intervals) makes this technology especially dangerous.

Newer devices use Wi-Fi Protected Access (WPA) for encryption, which is stronger than WEP. One of the security problems that can occur with WPA, is that it allows short, dictionary-word-based passphrases. Programs such as Aircrack-ng can recover WEP and WPA keys by capturing packets of data.

The weakness of the encryption algorithms aside, wireless encryption covers only the transmission between a user's computer and the wireless gateway that connects the wireless network to the Internet. When the data reaches the Wireless Application Protocol (WAP) gateway, it must be transferred from the wireless network to the wired network. To do this, the wireless communication, which is in the form of encrypted Wireless Markup Language (WML), must be decrypted and then reencrypted to be transmitted on the cabled network. The data is vulnerable during this "encryption gap."

CyberStats

A World without Wires?

Pew Internet & American Life Project (www.pewinternet.org/pdfs/PIP_Wireless.Use.pdf) reports that 34 percent of Internet users have logged on using a wireless connection. Of those with PDAs, 13 percent are able to connect to the Internet using their PDA, and 25 percent of those with cell phones have the ability to connect to the Internet.

How to Protect Your Wireless Connection

Organizations and individuals who use wireless technologies don't want to give up the convenience, but they are recognizing that extra security precautions are necessary. One way to add security to wireless networks is to use hardware-based security devices such as smart cards; users are not able to access resources without swiping the issued card through a card reader.

NOTE

We discuss smart card authentication and access control in more detail in Chapter 12.

Other wireless security measures that can be implemented either by wireless device manufacturers or by wireless LAN (WLAN) administrators include:

- Moving wireless hubs away from windows and toward the center of buildings

- Ensuring that wireless encryption is enabled

- Disabling broadcasts on the network's hubs

- Changing default settings such as the service set identifier (SSID) set by the manufacturer and the default password on the wireless access point or router

- Limiting the number of wireless access points to make the WLAN less vulnerable to unauthorized access

- Assigning static IP addresses to wireless NICs and disabling DHCP on the wireless router

- Security auditing, in the form of a Media Access Control (MAC) address-tracking system that can be used to track the devices that access the wireless network

- Installing a firewall between the WLAN and the wired LAN

- Putting the wireless access points in what is known as a *demilitarized zone (DMZ)*, also referred to as a *perimeter network* or *screened subnet*, and configuring wireless users to use a virtual private network (VPN) to create a secure tunnel into the network

- Treating the wireless network as though it were a public network and not sending sensitive data over it without taking precautions (such as using another encryption method along with WEP)

Why Cybercriminals Love Mobile Computing

Over the past decade, the high price of portable computers—laptops, notebooks, and handhelds—has steadily dropped while the processing power has come to equal that of desktop machines. This trend has been great for on-the-go businesspeople, who can now continue to work when they're on the road, with little loss in productivity.

Often, getting the work done requires access to the corporate network, and accordingly, most of today's laptops come with built-in modems, wireless adapters, and Ethernet ports. Travelers can dial directly back to the remote access server on the company LAN or dial up a local ISP and "tunnel" back to the corporate network through the Internet. More hotels are now providing high-speed Internet services, to which you connect via your portable computer's Ethernet port or PC Card (PCMCIA) NIC.

Once you connect to the company's LAN via one of these remote access methods, your computer becomes another (temporary) node on that local network, and remote access technology allows you to perform any task you could perform from a wired workstation on-site. This is great for employees who must be away from the office—but it's also great for hackers looking to come in uninvited.

CyberStats

Telecommuting Numbers Continue to Grow

According to the WorldatWork report "Telework Trendlines for 2006" (www.working-fromanywhere.org/news/Trendlines_2006.pdf), 12.4 million Americans were allowed to work from home at least one day per month, and teleworkers were four times more likely to work while on vacation. The places in which they did work varied from their car to hotels and restaurants, and other locations where they would get sufficient time to perform some work on the go.

The Problem with Mobile Computing

Remember that every point of access on the network creates one more vulnerability. A remote access server provides a point of access, as does a VPN server.

Of course, mobile computing also provides an additional security consideration: the possibility that the entire computer will be stolen. You might think this isn't a security problem if you don't store sensitive information on the portable's hard disk—but what about your VPN or remote access software configuration, which would allow anyone in possession of the computer to connect to the company network? Although a password may be required for network logon, many users set up their systems to "remember" their passwords so that they won't have to take the time to type them in each time they connect, thus defeating the purpose of password security if someone else takes possession of the computer.

Mobile computing presents some special security concerns. User authentication is one of the biggest. Unlike the corporate environment, where there are security guards, surveillance cameras, and fellow employees to physically recognize the presence of suspicious strangers around the computer systems, a user connecting remotely to the network offers no assurance that he or she really is the person whose credentials are being used.

Oh, and there's one more reason cybercriminals love today's powerful, low-cost mobile computers: Now they *can* take it with them. Lightweight, compact computers are much easier to transport to a "secure" location such as a pay phone, from which a hacker can initiate a hard-to-trace online session, or to take on "drive-by hacking" expeditions to find wireless LANs to which they can connect surreptitiously.

On the Scene

Allowing Individuals to Use Their Own Equipment

Although many companies will provide laptops and other mobile devices to employees, some will take advantage of employees using their own computers and devices to get the job done. Unfortunately, when this is done, there is very little the company can do to enforce security policies on the employee's personally owned computer. From personal experience, a coworker had her laptop stolen, which contained work-related information and provided VPN access to the internal network. The computer wasn't locked down with startup passwords, so anyone who started the machine was able to access information on the machine.

How to Protect Your Mobile Computers and Remote Access Connections

The first line of defense in mobile security is physical security of the portable computer. Many laptop locking devices are on the market. Mobile users should be instructed to keep a close watch on their computers, especially in airports and other crowded public places. You can buy hardware devices that will emit a "homing" signal and software programs that you can set to automatically dial in or contact "home base" through the Internet the first time the computer goes online after someone uses an incorrect password.

Other measures that can improve the security of remote access connections include:

- Use of dedicated application access so that the remote user connects to a specific application on the network server using proprietary protocols. This means the connected user will not have access to any other network resources. This system works well in cases in which remote users need to perform only a specific task, such as checking e-mail.

- Use of two-factor authentication. In this system, two separate components are required to successfully access the network: something you know, and something you have. In addition to providing a password (something you know), you must also provide a hardware token, smart card, or biometric identifier such as a fingerprint (something you have).

- Deployment of callback security for telecommuters and other remote access users who connect from the same location all the time.

- Use of encryption for sensitive communications over public phone lines or through the Internet.

- Use of remote access policies to restrict what dial-in users can do on the network as well as the days and times of day they can connect and other parameters.

Remote access opens company networks to employees, partners, and customers—and to unwanted intruders. It is important to take extra security precautions at every point at which your network can be accessed from the outside.

Why Cybercriminals Love Sophisticated Web and E-Mail Technologies

Today's World Wide Web is a different "place" from its earlier years. In the early 1990s, most Web pages consisted of plain text and graphics. The limitations of HTML and the slow bandwidth of most Internet connections dictated that Web designers follow the "keep it simple, stupid" caveat.

Today it's a whole different ballgame. Web sites flash and dance. Increasingly sophisticated presentations and interaction are possible with technologies such as Java and Visual Basic scripting and ActiveX controls. New markup languages such as Dynamic HTML (DHTML) and XML provide opportunities for Web designers to push the envelope. The prevalence of high-speed connections makes bandwidth-intensive Web applications feasible.

But once again, one person's feature enhancement is another person's security hole. *Scripts* are programs that run when you access Web sites in which they are embedded. What the program does is up to the programmer. Most Web scripts serve useful, harmless purposes; for example, a Java script can produce visual effects such as falling snow or animated text. Applets and scripts can also create calculator tools, chat interfaces, games, or clocks.

Malicious programmers, however, can use these technologies for their own nefarious purposes. Although many kinds of attachments, Web page components, and other aspects of Web and e-mail technologies can present security risks, the most worrisome are those that can actually run code and do things on (or to) your computer. In most cases, this kind of material—sometimes known as *active content* because it can run itself on your machine—is benign and is designed to perform specific tasks to manage or update a page display, run an animation, perform a calculation, and so forth. But active content can also include malicious code that can do all kinds of nasty things to your PC if allowed to run unchecked. That's why most security experts recommend that users (and network administrators) screen active content. By far, the safest security policy is to refuse to accept active content. However, this alternative could also prevent you from being able to use features that you need that depend on active content. Other strategies include requiring the active content to show valid credentials before being allowed to run, or accepting active content only from specified (known safe) Internet locations or addresses. If written by a malicious programmer, active content can introduce viruses, worms, back doors, and all kinds of other questionable code and access points to your systems and networks.

This same problem (along with a few others) that applies to Web browsers also applies to today's sophisticated e-mail client programs that allow the display of HTML mail, running of scripts embedded in mail messages, and sending of attachments. Here again, active content—which makes sophisticated presentations and interaction work—opens the door to potential security breaches.

The Problem with Web Scripts and Controls

Scripts and controls can be used to perform tasks on your computer without your knowledge—including monitoring your communications with others or deleting key files on your hard disk. Java and ActiveX give programmers a way to run any program they like on your computer. Malicious code can emulate a login box request and send the password credentials you enter to the hacker, all without your knowledge.

Your Web browser can be exposed to malicious code in many ways. Following links from other Web sites or clicking on links in e-mail messages or newsgroup posts can take you to a page that runs a malicious script.

How to Protect Your Web Browser from Malicious Code

Because of these security concerns, a number of mechanisms have been developed to protect unwary Web users from potentially dangerous content. Code can be digitally signed to verify that it is from a legitimate vendor and thus is safe to download. Most modern Web browsers allow you to select the level of security you desire. You can disable Java and/or ActiveX, or you can set the browser to prompt you when a script is encountered so that you can decide whether to run it based on your trust (or lack thereof) in the site.

For example, the Microsoft Internet Explorer Web browser allows you to either select a predefined security level (Low, Medium Low, Medium, or High), as shown in Figure 2.2. The level selected determines whether unsigned ActiveX controls will be downloaded and whether you will be prompted before downloading any content that is considered potentially unsafe.

Figure 2.2 Microsoft Internet Explorer Web Browser Security Settings

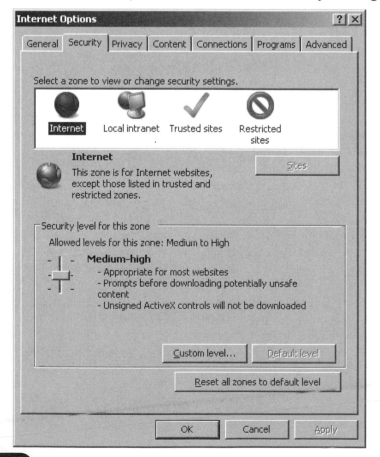

If none of the preset security levels works for you, you can also create your own customized security settings, as shown in Figure 2.3.

Figure 2.3 Custom Security Settings

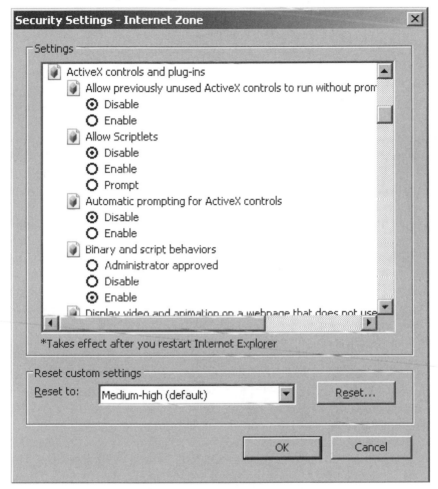

Because the Web is one of the most-used Internet applications, it is important to ensure that you don't expose your system and your network to a hack attack through the code that is run by your browser.

The Problem with Fancy E-Mail Clients

All of the same risks that are inherent in Web browsers that run scripts and controls surface again when you use an e-mail client that allows you to receive messages formatted in HTML, which can have the same sorts of malicious code embedded.

In the early days of e-mail, programs were simple and messages were basically text only. This system provided much less opportunity for security breaches, but it also limited the usefulness of e-mail communications. When it became possible to send files as attachments to messages, the doors opened to a new risk. Initially, attachments were usually photos (.jpg, .gif, etc.) or text files that were too large to include in the message itself. The problem arises when an attachment is or contains an executable program. Files with .exe, .com, or .bat extensions are obvious examples, but many other files can run code, infect your system with viruses, and otherwise do great damage. These files include screensaver files (.scr) and link files (.lnk). Registry (.reg) files can edit the Windows Registry, and .url files can open Web pages that run malicious code. Document files (such as Word .doc files) can include macros, which are simply small programs; virus writers have taken advantage of the powerful Visual Basic for Applications (VBA) support in Microsoft's Office applications to create macro viruses that can infect your system if you open the macro-containing document.

How to Protect Your E-Mail

To avoid the problems associated with modern e-mail programs, you might want to configure your e-mail client not to display a "preview pane" (which displays messages, including HTML messages, without you having to click on them to open them), install an AV package that checks both incoming and outgoing mail for viruses, and take care not to open e-mail attachments with suspicious extensions unless you are absolutely certain of their origin.

Note that once many e-mail-distributed viruses have infected a machine, they automatically send themselves to everyone in the victim's address book, appearing to be a message from the victim. This means that you can't assume that an attachment is safe just because you recognize the name in the message's "From" field.

In recognition of these problems, e-mail programs are building in more security—sometimes so much that the functionality of the mail client is severely crippled. For example, newer versions of Microsoft Outlook (such as Outlook 2002, 2003, and 2007) and Outlook Express will not allow you to open executable file attachments by default, even if you are 100 percent certain of the file's validity and safety. This restriction might be fine for the "average" user, but not for people such as software developers who need to send programs back and forth on a regular basis. When this feature was first included in Outlook, Microsoft offered such advice as renaming the file extension to something that isn't on the blocked file list, or using a ZIP program to compress the file. These suggestions were often useless if the firewall rules on a corporate network rejected ZIP attachments, or the user didn't understand how to change the extension. Luckily, add-on software allowed you to change this overprotective behavior, or you can change the default settings in Outlook Express to allow such files to be opened.

In many cases, the correct application configuration can save you a good deal of grief. For example, Microsoft Word now allows you to set security so that the system will prompt you before running any macros. If you open a document that shouldn't have macros and you get the dialog box asking you whether to disable macros, elect to do so and you can read the document itself without running the potentially dangerous code.

NOTE

We discuss Web and e-mail technologies in great detail in Chapter 9.

Why Cybercriminals Love E-Commerce and Online Banking

Most of us have heard the quote erroneously attributed to famous bank robber Willie Sutton in response to the question, "Why do you rob banks?" The answer: "That's where the money is." Regardless of who really said it, it makes sense.

It also makes sense that criminals are showing up in greater numbers online, because increasingly, that's where the money is. E-commerce, online banking, and related technologies have resulted in millions of dollars of financial transactions taking place across network connections.

The Problem with E-Commerce and Online Banking

The open nature and wide scope of the Internet make it a perfect forum for conducting business; transactions can be conducted between a business and a customer across the street or across the globe. Those wide-open cyberspaces also expose both seller and buyer to risks that aren't present, or at least not to the same extent, in face-to-face transactions.

When buyers must enter their credit card information to make a purchase, they are rightfully concerned that the information could fall into the wrong hands. Some would say that providing this information to a Web-based vendor is no different than giving it out over the telephone—but that philosophy doesn't take into account the difference between a telephone connection and an Internet transaction.

A phone call establishes a temporary dedicated private circuit directly between the caller and recipient; although it is possible to tap into a telephone line, it is relatively difficult and expensive. Information sent via e-mail or a Web form travels over the very public Internet and goes through a number of nodes (servers and routers) along the way. It is vulnerable to interception and, unless the information is encrypted, could then be used to make unauthorized purchases.

CyberStats

Fraudulent Online Transactions

The 2006 Annual Report of the FBI's Internet Crime Complaint Center stated that it received 207,492 complaints, with the vast majority of them involving online fraud. The total amount of money that was lost by everyone who filed a complaint in these fraud cases was $198.44 million. From this, e-mail and Web pages were the primary methods of contacting people, with e-mail being used in 73.9 percent of the cases and Web pages being involved in 36 percent of them. The full report is available at www.ic3.gov/media/annualreport/2006_IC3Report.pdf.

The Internet also makes it easy for criminals to exchange this illegally obtained information. Lists of stolen credit card numbers are posted in newsgroups that are frequented by criminally minded individuals. In fact, the incidence of credit card fraud in online transactions is significantly greater than that for more traditional purchase methods. According to a paper on credit card fraud published by the National White Collar Crime Center (NW3C) Research Section, estimates put the overall percentage of credit card fraud at about .08 percent of all credit card transactions, but the same source estimates fraud accounts for 3 percent to 5 percent of all transactions conducted online.

Credit card purchases are not the only online financial transactions that expose consumers to risk. An increasing number of busy professionals are turning to the convenience of online banking for depositing and transferring money and paying bills. Although one might assume that banks, of all businesses, would be certain to have adequate security measures in place, a number of serious security holes have been discovered in some online banking systems.

How to Protect Your E-Commerce and Online Banking Transactions

Protecting e-commerce and online banking transactions must be a joint effort involving everyone who participates. The "protection triad" includes:

- The IT professionals who run the e-commerce or bank servers

- The consumer who uses e-commerce or online banking services

- The law enforcement community

The role of the IT professional is to secure the servers that are used for financial transactions, using technologies such as firewalls to keep outsiders from breaking in and stealing confidential information and strong encryption to protect the data when it travels from customers through ISPs to the server. Chapters 10 and 12 discuss Web server security and protocols such as Secure Sockets Layer (SSL), Transport Layer Security (TLS), and Secure HTTP (S-HTTP) that can be used to transmit data securely through Web browsers.

Consumers must also be made aware of the dangers of online transactions so that they can take precautions, such as never giving credit card numbers and similar information online unless the Web site or form is a secure site. Consumers need to understand how to secure the home or office computers that they use to conduct online transactions, because their passwords and other personal information can be stored on their own local hard disks, and how to properly configure security options on their Web browsers.

Law enforcement agents must understand the scope and nature of the online fraud problem and should be educated in what information to gather, how to track down and preserve the evidence, and federal and private resources that can provide guidance and information in handling these types of cases.

Jurisdiction, as always, is an issue. The U.S. government established the Internet Fraud Complaint Center (IFCC) in May 2000, which is now the Internet Crime Complaint Center (IC3), to provide an avenue for victims of online crime to file complaints and submit information to a centralized source rather than having to figure out what law enforcement agency has jurisdiction in their particular situation. The I3C is operated by the FBI in partnership with the NW3C.

Why Cybercriminals Love Instant Messaging

Instant messaging (IM) is software that allows people to send text messages to one another. It gives Internet users the ability to communicate in near-real time with others anywhere in the world. It's an application that inspires a lot of passion: You either love it or hate it. Some people consider "IM'ing" a time waster and an intrusion, but others happily spend hours at home and work communicating this way. It does have advantages even in a business environment; you can get immediate questions answered without waiting for e-mail to go through or paying for long distance telephone calls.

IM is so popular that cell phones and PDAs such as the BlackBerry use their own versions of it. Short Message Service (SMS) allows people with cell phones to send short text messages to other cell phone users. Mobile Instant Messaging (MIM) extends the capabilities of SMS, offering features such as the use of aliases. It is so popular that some IM clients provide the option to send text messages directly to a cell phone, which subsequently makes it easier for spam and individuals such as online predators, cyberbullies, and other cybercriminals to reach you and your family.

Convenient as it might be, IM software (Google Talk, AOL's AIM and ICQ, Windows Live Messenger, Yahoo! Instant Messenger, Skype [see Figure 2.4], and others) poses serious security risks, along with providing criminals an easy way to communicate with one another to plan or discuss their crimes.

Figure 2.4 Skype IM Features

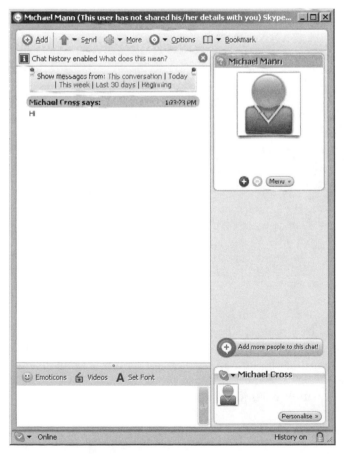

The Problem with Instant Messaging

In 2007, the SANS Institute identified IM as one of the top security risks (www.sans.org/top20.com). Some of the reasons given for this designation is that its widespread use could result in increased attacks. These attacks could include variants of e-mail worms, malware, and botnets (software running on collections of zombie computers that are used in coordinated attacks; we discuss botnets in greater depth in Chapter 10).

By default, most of the IM products are configured to stay active all the time, running in the background, and broadcast that the user is online even when the program interface is closed. This wouldn't be so bad except that the IM software also allows for sending of files among users, which means it's not that difficult for a knowledgeable hacker to use this open channel to transfer viruses hidden in Trojans or other unwanted "gifts."

Although IM vendors are pretty good about releasing fixes for these security flaws when they become known, new exploits are continuously being found, and many users don't update their software often. They could remain unaware of the problem until they are victimized. Network administrators and other IT professionals should stay current on these issues by subscribing to security newsletters and regularly visiting security bulletin Web sites. They should then work to educate the users in their organizations about security vulnerabilities and see that updates and fixes are installed when they become available.

CyberStats

The Popularity of Instant Messaging

In a 2006 report studying teens and the Internet (www.pewinternet.org/ppt/Pew Internet findings - teens and the internet - final.pdf), Pew Internet & American Life Project found that although IM is increasingly popular with all ages, IM use among teens overshadows that of their adult counterparts. Three-quarters of online teens use the Internet, as opposed to 42 percent of adults who are online, meaning that approximately 16 million teenagers have used IM.

Another possible security problem is the IM log that records the content of online discussions. These could be accessed by a hacker, exposing private conversations.

In fact, IM vendors generally admit that their products are not secure, and in their end-user agreements they recommend that you not use them for sensitive communication. Nevertheless, many business users discuss personnel matters, financial and budgeting decisions, marketing strategies, and other confidential information via instant messages.

Another problem with IM software is that there is no reliable authentication mechanism to verify that a person sending you a message across the Internet really is who he or she claims to be. Anyone can set up an IM account using a false name and information. For this reason, instant messages are also a popular way for pedophiles, scam artists, and other criminals to make contact with their victims and get to know those they target for their crimes.

How to Protect Your System from IM Security Flaws

The best way to avoid the security problems inherent in IM is to not use the programs or to use them only when necessary and never for sensitive or mission-critical communications. Many businesses block the ports used by IM software in their firewalls to prevent employees from using the programs.

If you must use IM, here are a few things you can do to reduce the risk:

- Administrators can block file transfers and game-playing capability at the firewall.

- If users only to communicate only with others within the company, administrators can install IM programs that run on the intranet, reducing exposure to the Internet.

- Users should close the program completely when not using it (just closing the interface can result in the program still running in the background—check the System Tray or the list of running processes to be sure).

- Users should not accept messages from people they don't know.

- Some IM programs allow you to block the display of your IP address to recipients. If you don't completely trust the person with whom you're conversing, you might want to enable this feature.

- Turn off message logging or, if you need to keep logs of your conversations, move the files to a location other than the default and encrypt them.

Like the other technologies we've discussed, IM software can be used for either good or evil. Because the programs were originally designed for recreational chatting, security hasn't been a high priority, but if you use IM in a business environment or on a home machine that has sensitive data stored on it, it's important to consider the security ramifications.

Why Cybercriminals Love New Operating Systems and Applications

User demands and rapidly increasing hardware capabilities result in new operating systems (or at least new versions) being released every few years. Each new incarnation includes nifty new features, and in many cases, the new versions are more stable and perform faster than their predecessors. It seems as though users hardly have time to learn one operating system before it's time to upgrade. The same goes for productivity applications; once you upgrade the operating system, you may also need a new version of your word processing or graphics software to go with it.

This system is great for the software vendors, which get to make a lot of new sales, of course. But it's also great for hackers, for a couple of reasons:

- New software, especially operating systems that include dramatic changes such as Microsoft's Windows Vista or Apple's Mac OS X, never comes out of the box perfect, regardless of how many tireless hours of beta testing went into it. It's commonplace for the manufacturer to know that possibly thousands of bugs exist in the operating system or software when it's released on the market, with plans to fix those vulnerabilities and glitches through follow-up patches and service packs. In the meantime, hackers can often exploit those bugs.

- Even if the software *is* perfect, users are not yet well acquainted with it and could misconfigure it in ways that open up security vulnerabilities.

Thus, cybercriminals are happy when you upgrade to the latest and greatest. It opens up a window of opportunity for them before bugs are reported and security patches are released—and before users learn to configure the new systems for best security.

There's not a lot you can do about this, other than perhaps foregoing the temptation to be an "early adopter" of every new software program that comes along. However, even if you wait, you'll still have to deal with users' learning curve. Network administrators should be especially wary and monitor closely for security breaches during the period immediately following major upgrades or the rollout of completely new software.

Why Cybercriminals Love Standardization

It might sound like a contradiction to say that cybercriminals love the new and different and then turn around and say that they love standardization, but it's really not. What we mean by standardization is everyone (or a vast majority) using the same operating systems, applications, protocols, and hardware.

Standardization makes things easier for hackers because they don't have to learn how to manipulate dozens of different types of systems. When a product becomes a standard, it also becomes a favorite target of hackers, crackers, and virus writers. Users of Windows operating systems are more vulnerable to attack than users of other systems in large part because the vast majority of computer users run Windows. It's common sense: If you want to do the largest amount of damage with a virus, you write one that targets the most popular operating system.

Standardization makes possible networking and computer communications on a large scale, but it also makes it possible for hackers to do their damage on a large scale. Standards are good in that they make computer hardware and software work more smoothly, but if your business deals with particularly sensitive information, one way to make your systems less vulnerable is to go with a proprietary rather than an industry-standard solution.

Looking to the Future

The evolution of the Internet has grown from an internetwork that required little to no security, to a massive infrastructure that supports how we do business and interact with others. It is a mainstay of modern economies, with numerous businesses depending on sales, banking, and other services. As the years pass, new Internet technologies will be developed, providing new ways to commit crimes.

This means that police, legislators, IT professionals, and other leaders in the fight against cybercrime must keep up-to-date with what technologies may be introduced in the near future, and make accommodations for what changes may be needed in legislation, investigation, and crime prevention.

The impact of laws becoming stagnant, and investigators and IT staff members failing to understand new ways that people are committing crimes, can be devastating. To effectively prepare for the future, however, project teams and focus groups would need to be created that understand new systems and software, and help identify what law enforcement needs to prepare for. Although law enforcement may distribute intelligence on new technologies, and ways they are being used internally, methods must be introduced that share this information globally among police and others in the criminal justice system.

Changes in Policing

As we'll discuss in Chapter 3, and other chapters throughout this book, cybercrime has forced police to change the way they do business. Medium to larger police departments commonly arrange training for officers, and set up specialized computer labs in which forensic recovery of digital evidence can be retrieved from computers, Universal Serial Bus (USB) storage devices, cell phones, and other technologies.

As mentioned in the previous chapter, frontline officers also need recurring training on seizing computer evidence, and what types of evidence may exist at a scene. Officers can inadvertently taint evidence or allow it to be destroyed completely by improperly securing a scene, and preventing others from accessing systems. In today's world, computers are as common a crime scene as filing cabinets were to a previous generation of officers. Unfortunately, whereas officers would never allow a suspect to start shredding documents, they might not think twice about someone fiddling with their BlackBerry and deleting a series of electronic files.

Because computers are so common, technological crime units are needed in almost every police department. Those who can't shoulder the financial burden of a computer forensic lab should at a minimum send detectives for some training and arrange computer forensic services to be performed by nearby police departments that are equipped for it.

Needless to say, the public must be prepared for the increased budgets that police will need to pay for the training, equipment, facilities, and personnel to perform these tasks. Implementing measures to investigate computer crime is not a one-time fee, and as anyone who has purchased a computer can testify, it does not get cheaper as old equipment and software need to be replaced.

Planning for the Future:
How to Thwart Tomorrow's Cybercriminal

What does all of the information we've discussed so far mean as we make plans for a future in which we will all be less likely to be victimized by cybercrime? Must we give up our fast, always-on connections and go back to dial-up modems? Must we forego the conveniences of wireless and mobile computing and go back to the Lynx text-based Web browser and the PINE e-mail program? Must we stop chatting online and start waiting in line at the drive-through bank again? Should we hang on to our ancient software once we've learned to use it, or should we switch to some exotic proprietary software that no one else has ever heard of?

Of course, we won't—probably can't—do any of this. What we *can* do is be aware of the dangers that each brave, new technological miracle poses and take steps that will protect us from criminal exploitation of these technologies while still allowing us to enjoy their benefits. Throughout this book, we'll provide very specific details of how we can achieve this goal.

Summary

Those who cannot remember the past are condemned to repeat it.

—*George Santayana*

Computers and networking have been around for only a few decades. Cybercrime thus far has a short but colorful history. What can we learn from that history that will help us build a more secure online future?

As we read through some of the events that brought us to where we are today, we can see that cyberspace is still much like the American West was in the 1800s: chaotic and unsettled, a new frontier that hasn't yet been tamed. The ARPA had its own agenda, the research universities that were involved in the Net's beginnings had their big dreams, the companies that flocked online in the 1990s had their marketing plans, the individuals who "live online" have their reasons, and the criminals who take advantage of the technology have their motives. However, there was no grand master plan by which the Internet evolved into the integral part of our lives that it occupies today. Rather, it "just grew that way," and the result is a hodgepodge of systems and technologies that work amazingly well in spite of its haphazard nature.

In the twenty-first century, the Internet has entered a new phase of existence. Law and order have come to the new frontier, making it a safer—and perhaps a less creative and less fun—"place" to work and play. Those who long for the "good old days" when the Net was the province of only an elite few and online crime wasn't—or didn't seem to be—a problem are missing the point: The genie won't go back into the bottle.

Law enforcement specialists know that the policing methods that work in rural areas are not necessarily appropriate in the inner city, and vice versa. Today's Internet is not the virtual small town that it used to be; it's now a bustling international urban environment. If we are to make it an environment that's safe for us and for our children, our cybercrime-fighting tactics will have to reflect that—much as we might wish it weren't so.

Frequently Asked Questions

Q: What about satellite Internet service? Does it suffer the same security vulnerabilities as DSL and cable?

A: Satellite Internet services such as HughesNet and StarBand use a dish-type antenna to transmit signals to and from a geostationary (fixed-position) satellite that is 22,300 miles above the Earth. Radio waves (which travel at the speed of light, or approximately 186,000 miles per second) must make this trip twice when you send a communication via satellite to a computer elsewhere in the world. During this journey, the radio waves are vulnerable to interception, just as other wireless technologies. Unlike a land-based wireless transmission, satellite transmission allows an attacker to eavesdrop from anywhere within a huge area (the satellite's reception range). Satellite systems use frequency hopping and multiple-access technologies that divide the signal, making it somewhat more difficult to intercept. In addition, some systems use a VPN for the connection, which prevents users from setting up their own VPNs to address security concerns. On the other hand, because satellite offers greater bandwidth than most wireless technologies, it is easier to deploy strong encryption and authentication methods.

Q: Does it matter whether I have a static or dynamic IP address?

A: Yes. Although there are advantages to having a static IP address (such as the ability to run a Web server, FTP site, or VPN), security isn't one of them. Many broadband providers issue a static IP, but others use technology that automatically changes your IP address on a regular basis (every day or even every hour), and some issue you several IP addresses so that you can manually change the address yourself when you want. This makes it more difficult for a hacker to continue attacking your site once he or she has found it.

Chapter 3

Understanding the People on the Scene

Topics we'll investigate in this chapter:

- Understanding Cybercriminals
- Understanding Cybervictims
- Understanding Cyberinvestigators

☑ Summary

☑ Frequently Asked Questions

Introduction

Cybercrime, by definition, involves computers and networks. However, as sophisticated as technology has become and as fascinating as the science of artificial intelligence (AI) might be, we are not yet at the point where computers can—by themselves—engage in criminal activity. The machines are wonderfully compliant (difficult as that sometimes might be to believe when we're struggling to make them work) and totally amoral. They do whatever we tell them to do, with no protests, no regrets, and no ulterior motives. A cybercrime always involves at least one human being who originates, plans, prepares, and initiates the criminal act.

The cybercriminal is usually not the only person (in body or presence) at the scene of the cybercrime, however. Some cybercrimes appear to be victimless, such as a network intrusion that occurs without anyone knowing about it, in which no files are harmed and no information is "stolen" or misused. In most cases, though, some person(s) is ultimately harmed by the cybercriminal's actions. These victims might be workers who lose productive time due to a denial-of-service (DoS) attack or have to redo their work because of cybervandalism. They might be company shareholders who lose money due to extra charges for the bandwidth that a hacker uses. They might be managers who lose "brownie points" in their bosses' eyes because of the impact on their budgets. They might be IT administrators who lose their jobs for "allowing" the attack to happen. In most cases of cybercrime, if you look hard enough, you'll find a victim.

When cybercrimes are reported to the police or other enforcement agencies, more people get involved. The investigators who collect clues to discover the identity of the cybercriminal and build up the evidence can spend days, weeks, or months on a single case. The skills, knowledge, perseverance, and determination of the investigator might have a profound impact on the outcome of the case.

When cybercrime occurs in the business environment, management personnel inevitably become involved as well. As we've mentioned in earlier chapters, the law enforcement personnel and the information technology (IT) professionals who need to cooperate in the investigative process often find themselves at odds. Managers, who know that cybercrime is hurting the company's bottom line and have a vested interest in minimizing the damage and seeing the cybercriminals brought to justice, are often in a unique position to facilitate cooperation among the other players.

In this chapter, we take a look—up close and personal—at all of the people on the scene of the cybercrime. We examine the roles of both cybercriminals and cybervictims and how they interact— sometimes in ways that mirror the "real-world" criminal–victim relationship and sometimes in ways that are quite different.

In this chapter's material, we try to get inside the heads of the cybercriminals and understand what motivates them. We show how cybercriminals can be divided into a number of different categories and how determining which category a cybercrook fits into can help you protect yourself from his or her actions. We also look for patterns that can help us predict who will be victimized by cybercrime, and we discuss ways of making potential victims less vulnerable.

Then we turn to the professionals on the scene: the law enforcement officers and private or corporate investigators and the IT professionals who are employed by the victimized companies or who are brought in as consultants. We discuss the characteristics of a good cybercrime investigator and the type of background and training that can give the aspiring cyberdetective a head start on the job. We also focus on the specific problems of IT and law enforcement pros when they try to work together and how they can overcome these problems.

Finally, we take a special look at the role of the chief executive officer (CEO) or manager in business-related cybercrimes. We examine what the IT team and the police need—and don't need—from upper management and how managers can become facilitators in the sometimes adversarial investigative process.

At this point, you could be wondering why this book seems to be suddenly stepping away from the technical topics of computer science and law to delve into a "soft science" such as psychology. Why do you—an IT professional or law enforcement officer—need to "understand" the cybercriminal? Why should you care what motivates such a person to break the law? What difference does it make to you if some personality types (and remember that companies have "personalities," too) are more likely than others to find themselves victims of cybercrimes? Isn't an investigator still an investigator, regardless of the type of crime that's been committed? Why are special skills or personal characteristics necessary for a cybercrime investigator?

We provide answers to these questions as you progress through this chapter. Specifically:

- We show you how an understanding of the basics of *criminal psychology* can put you one step ahead of the cybercriminal. You'll see how knowing what motivates a criminal can help you catch that criminal—or even help you take steps to prevent the next crime from occurring.

- You'll learn about *criminal profiling*, a subject that has been frequently discussed, and frequently misrepresented, in the popular media.

- We talk about the science of *victimology*—the study of crime victim characteristics—with the goal of determining why criminals target certain people as their victims.

- We discuss *career aptitude* as it applies to the criminal investigator. You'll find out why some people are better suited for this role than others. You'll learn why, in many cases, investigation is as much an art as it is a science.

The human element is not only an important component of every crime case, including cybercrimes, but it is often the most fascinating. We get down to the nitty-gritty technical details (and there will be plenty of those!) in upcoming chapters. But first, let's delve into the complex and often confusing issues surrounding the people who engage in, are victimized by, or devote their workdays to preventing, solving, and prosecuting cybercrime.

Understanding Cybercriminals

A number of scientific disciplines are devoted to gaining a better understanding of criminals and criminal behavior. *Criminal psychology* is the study of the criminal mind and what leads a person to engage in illegal or socially deviant behavior. You can think of criminal psychology as a subcategory of *forensic psychology*, which concerns itself with emotional and behavioral issues that pertain to the law and legal systems and includes police psychologists (who address emotional and behavioral issues with police officers), social psychologists (who study group behavior and broader societal implications of psychological issues), and others. The job of the criminal psychologist may also overlap with that of the *criminologist*, who studies criminals, crime, and the effect of the criminal justice system and societal factors on criminal behavior and crime rates.

NOTE

Forensic psychology is a different discipline from *forensic psychiatry*, which the American Academy of Psychiatry and the Law (AAPL) defines as "a medical subspecialty that includes research and clinical practice in the many areas in which psychiatry is applied to legal issues." (See www.aapl.org/org.htm.) Forensic psychiatrists are medical doctors and can treat patients, prescribe controlled drugs, and otherwise practice medicine. Forensic psychologists may also work directly with patients, but criminal psychologists often focus on studying the cases of criminals to detect patterns, analyze behaviors, and make predictions and profiles based on their analyses.

A new psychological specialty has evolved over the past few decades: that of the *investigative psychologist*. Investigative psychology involves applying knowledge of psychological principles to police work and criminal investigation.

On the Scene

At the FBI

Behavioral science is a broad term that refers to use of scientific methods to study the behavior of living creatures (including humans). *The behavioral sciences* is often used as a collective term referring to psychology, sociology, anthropology, and other sciences that study behavior of people or animals. The FBI uses the term much more specifically, as in the name of its Behavioral Science Unit (BSU) at its Quantico, Virginia, training academy.

The BSU focuses on the study of human behavior as it applies to criminals and crime. FBI personnel who work in the BSU are trained special agents who also have advanced degrees in psychology, sociology, criminology, and the like. The BSU is famous for its success in criminal profiling of serial killers and other violent criminals. The BSU uses a number of methodologies, such as computerized crime analysis, clinical forensic psychology, and applied criminal psychology, to provide assistance to other law enforcement agencies in solving crimes and capturing criminals.

Many of the FBI's behavioral science specialists have made names for themselves outside the agency. Robert Ressler, John E. Douglas, James T. Reese, and Roy Hazelwood all became famous for their work, as part of the BSU, on various high-profile cases. For more information on the BSU, you can visit its Web site at www.fbi.gov/hq/td/academy/bsu/bsu.htm.

Despite the FBI's and many large law enforcement agencies' focus on bringing scientific methods such as criminal psychology into police investigations, many police officers at the local level are still skeptical. "Why should I care about *understanding* criminals?" they ask. "All I want to do is catch them and put them behind bars."

This attitude is usually due to a misunderstanding about the meaning of the word *understanding*. One of its meanings is indeed "sympathetic, empathetic, or tolerant." Police (understandably!) see no reason to show this sort of feeling toward lawbreakers, especially people who cause harm to others in doing so. We're not asking them to exhibit this meaning of the word *understanding*.

The other meaning of the word is "to perceive and explain the meaning or nature of somebody or something." This is the kind of understanding you need as a law enforcement officer or IT professional involved in investigating cybercrimes as it relates to the cybercriminal's mindset and motivations. You need that kind of understanding because it will help you catch the criminal and put him or her behind bars.

Profiling Cybercriminals

Criminal profiling is the art and science of developing a description of a criminal's characteristics (physical, intellectual, and emotional) based on information collected at the scene(s) of the crime(s). A *criminal profile* is a psychological assessment made before the fact—that is, without knowing the identity of the criminal. The profile consists of a set of defined characteristics that are likely to be shared by criminals who commit a particular type of crime. The profile can be used to narrow the field of suspects or evaluate the likelihood that a particular suspect committed the crime.

Profiling by police has taken on a number of unfortunate connotations due to media focus on the term as it describes discriminatory police practices. In the minds of some members of the public, all police profiling has become associated with *racial* profiling, which in turn has come to mean treating people as criminal suspects based solely on their ethnicity or the appearance of ethnicity.

On the other hand, in some circles the perceived effectiveness of profiling has been elevated to almost mythical proportions. Movies and television series have glorified and glamorized the role of the criminal profiler, making it seem that profiling is almost akin to magic. Profilers in movies are able to take a look at the crime scene and unerringly describe the criminal's physical characteristics and background.

It's not quite that easy or certain in real life, but criminal profiling is a valuable tool that can give investigators many clues about the person who commits a specific crime or series of crimes. Nonetheless, it's important to understand that a profile—even one constructed by the top profilers in the field—will provide only an idea of the general *type* of person who committed a crime; a profile will *not* point to a specific person as the suspect. Although good profiles can be amazingly accurate as to the offender's occupation, educational background, childhood experiences, marital status, and even general physical appearance, there will always be many individuals who fit a given profile.

NOTE

Profiling has been in use in law enforcement for quite some time. Although the FBI is often credited with its "invention," a less sophisticated form of profiling and crime reconstruction was used in a number of historical cases, including that of the Jack the Ripper case in London in the 1880s.

Profiling is just one tool among many for conducting an investigation and building a criminal case. A profile is *not* evidence; rather, it is a starting point that can help investigators focus on the right suspect(s) and begin to gather evidence.

Understanding How Profiling Works

Criminal profiling is considered by some people—including, still, some law enforcement officers—to be an exotic "last resort" investigative tactic. Those skeptics equate the profiler's work with that of "forensic psychics" who offer their clairvoyant powers to assist in solving crimes. Profiling, however, is a process that is based on collecting information and then analyzing that information by applying logic.

Profilers draw inferences about the criminal's personality and other characteristics based on the following indicators:

- Their observations of the crime and crime scene

- The testimony of witnesses and victims

- Their knowledge of human psychology and criminal psychology

- The existence of patterns and correlations among different crimes

John E. Douglas, former FBI profiler, says in his book *Mindhunter*, "Behavior reflects personality." Profilers examine the criminal's behavior and develop a description of his or her personality.

Often, an important part of a criminal profiler's work involves comparing the facts and impressions from a group of crimes and determining whether it is likely that the crimes were committed by the same person. Repeat criminals are, not surprisingly, creatures of habit in ways other than the fact that they continue to commit crimes. They tend to do things in the same way each time; this is known in popular parlance as the criminal's *modus operandi* (method of operation, or MO). Behaviors that a criminal repeats at each crime scene, especially if the behavior seems to fulfill a psychological need (as opposed to being a matter of practicality), are also known as the criminal's *signature*. Cybercriminals, like other criminals, often give themselves away by their MOs or signatures.

There are two basic profiling methods: inductive and deductive. Each is based on a particular method of reasoning or logic. Generally, *inductive reasoning* works from the specific to the general, whereas *deductive reasoning* works from the more general to the more specific.

With inductive reasoning, you begin with observations or information, then come up with a theory that you apply to new circumstances. With deductive reasoning, you begin with a premise and then come up with specific conclusions based on the premise. For better understanding, see San Jose State University's exercises in inductive and deductive reasoning at www.sjsu.edu/depts/itl/graphics/induc/ind-ded.html.

Inductive Profiling

The *inductive profiling* method relies on statistics and comparative analysis to create a profile. Information is collected about criminals who have committed a specific type of crime. The information can take the form of formal studies of convicted criminals, informal observation of known criminals, clinical or other interviews with criminals known to have committed certain crimes, and data already available in databases.

By analyzing the data and establishing correlations, the profiler infers that characteristics common to a statistically significant number of offenders who commit a particular type of crime are applicable to other criminals who commit the same type of crime. The inductive-profiling model tends to produce results that are specific and generalized.

Deductive Profiling

According to Aristotle, a *deduction* is an argument in which, certain things being laid down, something other than these necessarily comes about through them.

The *deductive profiling* method relies on the application of deductive reasoning to the observable evidence. Investigators collect general information about the crime, and the profiler draws specific conclusions about the criminal's characteristics, based on the profiler's experience, knowledge, and critical thinking. Victimology, the crime scene, forensic evidence, and behavioral analysis are all components of the deductive process.

The deductive method involves several distinct steps:

1. A problem is stated.

2. Information is collected.

3. A working hypothesis is formulated.

4. The hypothesis is tested.

5. Results of the test are examined.

6. One or more conclusions are reached.

Hypotheses can be tested using *if/then thinking*. We might start with a hypothesis such as "Hackers are mostly harmless." If our hypothesis is correct, the data should show that the vast majority of hacking incidents cause no monetary loss or other harm to the companies or individuals whose systems are hacked. Finding one or two incidences of loss or harm would not disprove the hypothesis— but if we find large numbers of cases that are inconsistent with our hypothesis, we can consider it to be invalid. Our conclusion, then, could be the opposite of the hypothesis we started with: Hackers are *not* "mostly harmless."

Profilers using the deductive method often mention that success depends on being able to "get inside the mind" of the criminal, to think like the criminal thinks, to understand the criminal's motives and predict his future actions. The best deductive profilers might state that they rely on intuition or that they use common sense to develop profiles. However, close examination usually reveals that the "common sense" to which they refer is a process of logical thinking, applied to the hard evidence they've gathered and observed. This thinking process can take place subconsciously, leading to the "intuitive feelings" that don't really come out of nowhere but are instead the result of long hours or days of subconsciously processing masses of information.

Unlike the inductive process, which is based on statistical data (and which can be processed by a computer as well as or better than by a human being), deductive reasoning requires intelligence of a kind of which machines are not yet capable. Deductive thinking is not only a skill, but also a talent that some people seem to be born with and that other people can never learn. The most talented detectives tend to be masters of deductive reasoning. We discuss the qualifications and characteristics of a good investigator later in this chapter, in the "Understanding Cyberinvestigators" section.

> **NOTE**
>
> Perhaps one of the most famous proponents of deductive reasoning was Sir Arthur Conan Doyle, the Scottish writer and physician who created the Sherlock Holmes character in the 1880s. Doyle summed up the deductive method rather succinctly: "It is an old maxim of mine that when you have excluded the impossible, whatever remains, however improbable, must be the truth."

Uses of the Criminal Profile

A profile cannot, by itself, solve a criminal case. However, the profile can be used for several purposes:

- To narrow the field of suspects
- To link related crimes
- To give investigators valuable leads to follow

Although the profile is not itself evidence of a particular suspect's guilt, it can be used in court in conjunction with expert witness testimony. *Expert witnesses*, unlike other witnesses in a criminal case, are allowed to state opinions. An expert witness can reference a criminal profile as the basis of an opinion that there is a high probability of a link between a particular suspect and a particular crime scene. We discuss expert witnesses and expert testimony in more detail in Chapter 17.

Profiling that is based on collecting large amounts of data about cybercrime and those who commit it can serve another purpose. As a picture of the typical cybercriminal begins to come into focus, we could be forced to reexamine our own misconceptions about cybercriminals based on media myths and a few anecdotal cases.

Reexamining Myths and Misconceptions about Cybercriminals

Movies such as *The Matrix* and *Swordfish* have given us Hollywood's image of the cybercriminal, one that tends to be simplified and romanticized. In those movies, hackers are misunderstood geniuses with hearts of gold who are just trying to save the world, despite the interference of the big, bad government. News stories, on the other hand, often go overboard in the opposite direction. They paint anyone who believes in the distribution of open source software as a dangerous pirate who is determined to undermine the very foundations of our capitalistic society. The truth, as usual, lies somewhere in between these two extremes.

Now that Internet access is a mainstream activity, most members of the general public have heard of cybercrime, and many hold opinions at the extreme ends of the spectrum. Some of the most common misconceptions regarding cybercriminals include the following:

- All cybercriminals are "nerds"—bright but socially inept.
- All cybercriminals have very high IQs and a great deal of technical knowledge.

- All cybercriminals are male, usually teenage boys.

- All teenage boys with computers are dangerous cybercriminals.

- Cybercriminals aren't "real" criminals because they don't operate in the "real world."

- Cybercriminals are never violent.

- All cybercriminals neatly fit one profile.

Most of these misconceptions are based on stereotypes. We could argue that stereotyping is what profiling is all about. What is a stereotype, anyway? The dictionary defines the term as "an oversimplified standardized image or idea held by one person or group of another." The key here (and the difference between a stereotype and a profile) is *oversimplification*. A criminal profile is complex and based on hard data. A stereotype is a device that allows you to bypass collecting hard data and apply a "known" fact (or a statement widely accepted as such) to individual situations.

Are stereotypes always wrong? Of course they're not. If there were not some truth in a belief, at least some of the time, it would never become a stereotype. The danger of relying on stereotypes—especially in the context of investigating crime and enforcing the law—is that it puts blinders on the investigator and closes his or her mind to all the possibilities. Savvy criminals can take advantage of these stereotypes and literally "get away with murder" (and lesser crimes) simply by not fitting the known stereotype.

On the Scene

How and Why We Stereotype

The word *stereotype* is derived from the process of creating metal-engraved plates for printing. Once the plate is created, the image is "set" and cannot be easily changed. Thus, the word evolved into a description of the "set image" or opinion that people apply to an entire category of people.

Stereotypes often contain a grain of truth; women *do* tend to be more emotional than men, more Asians than Westerners *do* practice and master the martial arts, the rich *are* different from you and me and Ernest Hemingway (they have more money). The danger of stereotypes is that they provide a "quick and dirty"—and often misleading and inaccurate—way for us to judge people we don't know.

Stereotyping is a handy "shortcut," and the human brain is attracted to that. We all base some of our beliefs on stereotypes; when we simply don't have enough information to form an opinion, we tend to default to what we've heard from others, read in books, or seen on television. The media is one of the biggest perpetuators of stereotypes. Much comedy is based on common stereotypes. This is not necessarily out of any evil intent; when you have to tell a story in the space of a half-hour sitcom or a two-hour movie, shortcuts become a necessity. The more a particular stereotype is repeated, however, the more likely we are to believe it.

Let's take an up-close look at each misconception on our list and discuss how each came about and why each is generally an inaccurate assumption.

All Cybercriminals Are "Nerds"—Bright but Socially Inept

As with many misconceptions, this one grew out of a past when it was more often true than it is today. Recall from the history discussion in Chapter 2 that in the early days of computers and networking, few common folks had access to the huge, expensive, user-unfriendly mainframe systems that defined the word *computer*.

Who *did* have access? "Scientific types" at places such as MIT. These were the guys with crew cuts and slide rules in their pockets. Working with the first computers required extensive math skills. There were no computer "users" back then; if you wanted to interact with the machine, you needed to be a programmer. Programming was a painstaking process that required patience and the willingness to devote huge chunks of your time to coding. It was hardly conducive to cultivating opportunities to appear on the newspaper's society pages! When (if) you *did* get out into the world at night, what did you have to talk about after spending your days locked up with a bunch of vacuum tubes, poring over printouts of 1s and 0s? Not much that anyone else could understand or care about.

The word *nerd* has a couple of different meanings and even more connotations. The *MSN Encarta* dictionary (http://dictionary.msn.com) defines it as "somebody who is considered to be excessively interested in a subject or activity that is regarded as too technical or scientific." That's an apt description of a large proportion of the computer hobbyists of the 1950s, 1960s, and 1970s. Today, though, computers are almost ubiquitous. The skills needed to use the Net for mischievous or malicious purposes are far less complex than they used to be. The "nerd" stereotype still fits some people, but many of today's cybercriminals—especially computer scam artists and sexually motivated criminals who use the Internet to find victims—are smooth and charming and have highly developed social skills.

On the Scene

Cyber Serial Killer

In 2000, a Kansas man named John Robinson was arrested for sexual assault and became a suspect in the killings of several women over a span of 15 years. What made this case unique was the method of procuring victims: through Internet chat rooms, most of them dedicated to sadomasochism. In these forums, Robinson used the alias "The Slave Master." Although he had a criminal record (he had previously been arrested for theft and fraud), he represented himself to his victims as a rich, professional businessman.

In January 2003, he was sentenced to death for two of the murders, and life imprisonment for a third homicide. While Robinson was serving his sentence on death row, Missouri worked toward having him extradited to stand trial for three homicides that occurred in that state, and in October 2003, Robinson accepted plea bargains in which he was sentenced to life without the possibility of parole.

All Cybercriminals Have Very High IQs and a Great Deal of Technical Knowledge

Again, this is a stereotype based on outdated facts. Those early MIT math majors tended to fit it, but it bears little relevance to today's cybercriminal. The myth is further perpetuated by law enforcement itself, who all too often claim in the media that such unsolved cases involve criminals of high intelligence. After all, it would be embarrassing to say that the global village idiot has them stumped, and that anyone with a computer could have done the same.

Getting online now is as easy as pointing and clicking. Although some cybercrimes—such as writing and distributing new viruses or mounting intrusion attacks against highly protected networks—require technical expertise, many other cybercrimes can be (and are) committed by people of average or below-average intelligence with little or no technical training or skill. Cyber con games can be played by anyone who is capable of sending e-mail or using Internet chat programs. Data theft is often a simple matter of dragging and dropping. Even crimes that depend on complex technical exploits can be performed by unskilled hackers called *script kiddies*, who merely use the code written by others to do their mischief. Hundreds of Web sites and newsgroups provide technologically clueless "wannabe" hackers with these preconfigured or automated tools that can be used to crack systems.

Script kiddies, who use scripts written by others to break into networks, crack passwords, and wreak other mischief, must have at least enough technical ability to enter the proper commands to execute the script. However, even this isn't the case, as security applications and Web-based solutions provide point-and-click solutions to hacking a site. According to security expert David Rhoades, the latest phenomenon in the "devolution of hacking" is the *click kiddie*, who hacks simply by pointing and clicking, cutting and pasting. This is made possible by Web sites that do all the work for them. Rhoades included discussion of this type of hacker in his presentations "Hacking for the Masses" and "De-Evolution of the Hacker," which are available online at www.mavensecurity.com/presentations. As we'll discuss in other chapters of this book, security tools that are installed on computers and Web sites that analyze sites and systems for vulnerabilities are common tools for hackers, and are so user-friendly that they require minimal skill to use.

On the Scene

The World's Oldest Profession and the World's First Famous Female Hacker

A woman who used the pseudonym Susan Thunder evolved from a rock-star groupie and prostitute into a phone phreaker and computer hacker. She specialized in breaking into military computers and eventually became associated with infamous hackers Ron and Kevin Mitnick. She was, in fact, granted immunity from prosecution for testifying against them when they were arrested for their own hacking exploits.

Continued

> Given her background, it was only logical that Susan became adept at what is known in the hacking world as *social engineering*—that is, persuading authorized users to reveal their passwords. Legend has it that she often accomplished this goal by engaging in sexual relationships with the military personnel who had the information she sought.

All Cybercriminals Are Male, Usually Teenage Boys

This is a double stereotype. It makes assumptions about two groups: cybercriminals and women. Science and math in general, and computer technology in particular, have traditionally been predominantly male domains. Furthermore, law enforcement statistics show that males are more likely to commit crimes of almost all types than are females.

However, statistics also show that the gender gap is closing. Near the end of the 1990s, arrests of women comprised about 22 percent of all arrests (with women accounting for about 14 percent of violent offenders and about 29 percent of property-related crime offenders), according to the U.S. Department of Justice's (DOJ) Bureau of Justice Statistics (www.ojp.usdoj.gov/bjs/crimoff.htm# women). That same source states that during the 1990s, the number of female defendants convicted of felonies in the state courts increased at more than twice the rate of the increase of male convictions. This trend has continued into the twenty-first century; according to the FBI's Uniform Crime Reports for 2006 (www.fbi.gov/ucr/cius2006/data/table_33.html), 63,025 women were arrested for violent crimes (as opposed to 290,318 men), and 282,058 female offenders committed property crimes (as opposed to 614,088 men). In looking at this, you can see that although women are less frequently arrested, a suspect should never be overlooked on the basis of gender.

White-collar criminals have traditionally been male—but some experts theorize that this was because, until recent years, high-level corporate positions (which pose the greater opportunities and temptations) were almost exclusively held by men. Now that women have made it into the executive suite, more and more female offenders are being arrested on embezzlement, fraud, and other white-collar crime charges. See the paper "Integrity in the Corporate Suite: Predictors of Female Frauds" by Collins, Muchinsky, Mundfrom, and Collins, at www.cj.msu.edu/~faculty/collinsintegrity.html, for theoretical and statistical information.

Computer science is no longer an all-male occupation. The U.S. Department of Commerce statistics show that 28.5 percent of programmers are now female. Although only a small percentage of programmers (of either gender) use their skills for illegal purposes, women are definitely acquiring the means to commit computer crimes in greater numbers than ever before. Enrollment of women in computer security courses run by organizations such as the SANS Institute, and female attendance at hacking seminars and conventions such as DEFCON, are ever-increasing.

The "typical cybercriminal" profile of being male, white, and 19 to 30 years of age is still valid for speaking in generalities, but it is becoming less so every year. Increasingly, those who commit cybercrimes come from both genders, all races, and every age group.

On the Scene

Computer Crime Isn't Gender-Specific

Even though many types of cybercrime are gender-specific, that doesn't mean they are committed exclusively by male cybercriminals. For example, most cases of Internet luring or those involving child pornography are committed by males. However, the first cybercrime that I was subpoenaed to provide testimony against was a woman who was charged with possession of child pornography. The content of the digital images was serious and disturbing. Among the hundreds of other pictures on her computer and floppy disks were pornographic images of a 12-year-old girl and a horse. Once the woman's lawyer heard the testimony I was going to give about the evidence found on her computer, a plea bargain was quickly taken.

All Teenage Boys with Computers Are Dangerous Cybercriminals

Once again, the media is mostly responsible for this stereotype. After movies such as *WarGames* began to be shown in theatres, some parents worried less about their son hiding *Playboy* under the mattress and more him spending his nights hacking systems. Although it was irrational to worry about the family's Commodore 64 being used to break into the defense department computers in search of the codes to fire nuclear missiles, the same may be said 20 years from now about cave-dwelling terrorists hacking communication networks. In the 1980s, most parents could barely understand what the computer did, much less what their kid was doing on it. The media, feeding into the paranoia of the Cold War and fear of technology, added fuel to the fire with stories of nonsecure systems and young hackers at play. Since then, not much has changed.

This image is reinforced by stories that spread fear of teenage boys at keyboards, even when it is uncertain whether a cybercrime even took place. In 1999, the BBC reported on a 14-year-old boy named Nir Zigdon, who claimed to have taken down a Web site that was run by the Iraqi government of that time. Although he allegedly used a computer virus to take down the site (the U.S.-based site's operator claimed otherwise), the report explained how the boy was being hailed as a hero for destroying a site that contained anti–U.S. and anti-Israeli "propaganda." For further information, you can visit http://news.bbc.co.uk/2/hi/middle_east/269399.stm.

Even when crimes have obviously occurred, the media tend to stress the offender's age and connections to the Internet. Some of these reports are directly related to these issues, such as those dealing with the February 2000 script kiddie attacks against commercial Web sites by "Mafiaboy," who turned out to be a Canadian high school student. However, other news stories go to great lengths to shift the focus to technology. An example of this is the 1999 Columbine High School shootings, in which two students killed 12 students and a teacher and wounded 23 others before committing suicide. A short time after the massacre occurred, numerous news reports focused on teenaged Internet use and violence in computer games, as one of the shooters wrote levels for the video game Doom. As is the case with such coverage, every child was at risk.

No one can dispute that teenagers who get their kicks by vandalizing corporate Web sites or trying to penetrate government computer systems are criminals, and that such behavior constitutes a problem. Neither can anyone dispute that teenagers full of rage who open fire on their classmates and teachers are dangerous criminals. However, most of us realize that the vast majority of teens—even sullen, angry, rebellious teens—will never engage in such extreme behavior.

The same is true of the vast majority of teenage boys who have computer skills. The furthest most will go in using their computers for illegal activities is to download music or software for their own personal use. Although this activity might be "dangerous" to the record companies' and software vendors' bottom lines, it's a crime on the same level as taping music from the radio to share with a friend. It's hardly in the same category as bringing down the systems that run Wall Street or infiltrating the international banking system's computers.

Cybercriminals Aren't "Real" Criminals Because They Don't Operate in the "Real World"

Many cybercriminals buy into this myth themselves—or at least they use it to justify and rationalize their behavior. Even people who stop short of illegal activity often behave online in ways they would not think of behaving in their "real lives"—lying, cheating on their spouses via "virtual" relationships, or merely acting rude and obnoxious.

This phenomenon is so commonplace that an entire field of study, *cyberpsychology*, has grown up around it. Publications such as *CyberPsychology & Behavior* (www.liebertpub.com/publication. aspx?pub_id=10), professional mailing lists, and Web sites such as the Computer-Mediated Communication (CMC) Studies Center (www.december.com/cmc/mag/) have examined the double illusion of unreality and anonymity that leads people to behave differently (and often badly) in cyberspace.

Technology such as online chat, multiple-user dungeons (MUDs), and virtual reality programs have distorted some users' ability to distinguish between what is real and what is unreal. Many Internet users, especially those who are new to the online world, seem to see the people on the other end of their Internet connection as akin to characters in an interactive program, and they see the interactions and relationships they engage in with those people as nothing more than a game.

Because these people are not being their "real selves" in online interactions, they perhaps believe that no one else is, either. Hence, it becomes okay in their minds to concoct elaborate stories and deceptions, which might cross the line into illegal fraud. Furthermore, because they can sign on to chat rooms and other services using pseudonyms, they think nobody knows who they are or what they do online. For those people who have no real internal controls in the form of personal ethics and morals and who behave "properly" only out of fear of external consequences (societal disapproval or jail), this forum provides an excuse to throw off all inhibitions. Add to this the anecdotal evidence that many of those who frequent chat rooms lower their inhibitions even further by indulging in alcohol while they surf the Net, and you have a recipe for antisocial behavior.

Of course, this idea that nothing online is real and therefore nothing you do there "counts" is a fallacy. But it's an old trick of the criminal to depersonalize his or her victims; seeing them as something less than true human beings makes it easier to hurt them. This self-deception is made much easier in cyberspace because they never have to see the faces or hear the voices of the people they're victimizing; the people with whom the criminal deals can conveniently remain nothing more than words on a computer screen.

CyberLaw Review

When Rape Isn't Rape

Virtual communities provide a forum to interact with others online. Unfortunately, they can also be used to fuel the fantasies of sexual deviants and potential offenders. Chat rooms and text-based MUDs have been used to play out sexual fantasies, where several people will act out a rape fantasy by typing messages on what they are doing to a particular participant. Although these virtual worlds were originally text-based, many newer sites such as Second Life (www.secondlife.com) allow you to use 3D avatars, which are characters that people use to move through the community and interact with others. Users can even dress their characters in various clothing, appear naked, go to sex clubs or bordellos, and engage in virtual sex. As you might expect, even in the virtual world, real-world deviant fantasies will appear. In the case of one site called LamdaMOO, a user called Mr. Bungles ran a program that allowed his avatar to sexually assault the avatars of other users. Even though the concept may be disturbing, there are no laws preventing such activities or discussions to occur online. Although many virtual communities have imposed their own rules and have worked to police themselves, it is largely a situation of Internet user beware.

Cybercriminals Are Never Violent

Because the Internet is more a virtual than a physical medium, it seems logical to assume that even if cybercrime is real crime, it isn't *violent* crime. After all, it's the ability to commit their crimes from a distance that attracts many criminals to the Net in the first place.

It's true that a large percentage of reported cybercrimes are frauds, thefts, and cases of unauthorized access. However, it is interesting to note that the most frequently reported cybercrime in many reporting sites such as the Cybersnitch database (www.cybersnitch.net) is child pornography, which is generally classified as a violent or potentially violent crime for two reasons: the harm done to the children who are used to make the photographs, and the potential of the material to incite pedophiles to act out their fantasies with real children. Hacker intrusions are the second most frequently reported crime type; the third is electronic stalking, which can also be considered a violent crime because it terrorizes the victim, and cyberstalkers have often been known to progress to actually stalking their victims in real life.

Some people might argue that child porn and cyberstalking aren't in themselves physically violent crimes, but it would be difficult to make such a claim of the predators who use the Internet to find vulnerable people they can lure into a meeting to rape, assault, or kill them. In addition to these violent offenders who usually act alone, the terrorists who use the Internet to raise money, plan their activities, recruit new members, and communicate with one another are violent criminals of the most dangerous sort.

On the Scene

Cybercriminals Posing As Potential Victims

The case of one cybercriminal inspired New Jersey to adopt legislation making it illegal "via electronic or any other means, to lure or entice another person to meet or appear at any place, with a purpose to commit a criminal offense against any person." In 2002, Jonathan Gilberti posed online as a woman with a rape fantasy in a chat room. Posing as Trish Barteck (his in-law), he provided her name, address, physical description, and other information to others online, inviting men to come to her house and rape her. When one man arrived at her house and leered at her from his SUV, Barteck called the police and the subsequent investigation revealed Gilberti's role. Gilberti pleaded guilty to three counts of attempted sexual assault for this incident and others involving a different woman, but because there was no law directly dealing with this type of crime and future cases could be difficult to try, New Jersey approved the new law in 2005, which is available to view at www.njleg.state.nj.us/2004/Bills/PL05/1_.pdf.

Cybercriminals, like criminals in general, span a continuum that reaches from the kid whose curiosity causes him or her to try to hack into someone's network just to see if it can be done, with no intent to do damage, all the way up to those who use the Internet as a means to cause someone physical or emotional harm. This realization leads us to our last misconception.

All Cybercriminals Neatly Fit One Profile

We might be able to construct a profile of the type of person who commits a particular cybercrime, but it is impossible to create one profile that fits all cybercriminals, just as it is impossible to make an accurate profile of all traffic law violators. The casual speeder is likely to have a different personality and different motivations from the habitual drunk driver or the outraged motorist who uses his vehicle as a weapon to mow down pedestrians. Likewise, the computer scam artist is an entirely different creature from the cyberstalker, who is, in turn, nothing like the typical hacker.

Even within a particular category of cybercrime, the physiology, psychology, and motivations of each cybercriminal are different from every other. Nonetheless, some commonalities allow us to paint a very broad picture of the "typical" cybercriminal. We must keep in mind, however, that for a profile to be useful in our investigations, it must be based on the facts of an individual case.

Constructing a Profile of the Typical Cybercriminal

As a first step in building a profile (and remembering that it is *only* the first step), we can look at some generalities that, more often than not, apply to cybercriminals in all categories. It is important to see these characteristics as *probabilities*, not as absolute rules. There are exceptions to each case.

With that said, a majority of cybercriminals exhibit at least some of these characteristics:

- **At least a minimal amount of technical savvy** This assumption is based on common sense. Although, as we've mentioned before, it is easier than ever to get online without being a computer whiz, most people who use the Internet for illegal purposes are able to find their way around in cyberspace without a lot of assistance. People generally use the tools with which they feel comfortable, especially when engaging in high-risk activities such as committing crime. To use the Internet to carry out a planned act such as a crime, you must be capable of basic tasks such as sending e-mail, surfing the Web, or logging on to a chat line. Some crimes require a good deal more expertise. The typical cybercriminal isn't a computerphobe or someone who's just signed on to the Net for the first time.

- **Disregard for the law or a feeling of being above or beyond the law** Few people, including criminals, think of themselves as "bad." Most—though not all—lawbreakers justify their actions by instead seeing the laws themselves (at least the ones they break) as bad laws. Cybercriminals, like other habitual criminals, often exhibit disregard or disdain for the law. They are not the types of people who believe you should comply with the law just *because* it's the law. Rather, they tend to believe that laws they consider unreasonable are fair game to be broken. In some cases, they feel that they themselves, because of their special skills, intelligence, positions, or circumstances, are above the law. For example, an employee who regards the common thief as a crook might believe that embezzling money from his or her employer is okay because the company underpays and overworks its employees. Other cybercriminals believe that the law simply doesn't apply in cyberspace, hearkening back to the "unreality" aspect we mentioned earlier.

- **An active fantasy life** Many cybercriminals use the Internet as an outlet for their fantasies. They often construct entirely new personas that they use online—both to hide their true identities and avoid detection and because they enjoy "playing the part" of someone different from themselves. Con artists can concoct elaborate schemes based on their fantasies. Cyberstalkers build fantasies around their victims. Child pornographers deal in sexual fantasies. Hackers fantasize about "hacking the world," gaining control over other people by controlling their computer systems. This ties into the next common characteristic of cybercriminals.

- **A "control freak" and/or risk-taking nature** Criminals often expend more energy, for less practical return, in committing crimes than they would if they turned their efforts to more socially acceptable work. Why, then, do they engage in such high-risk behavior? For some, it is the risk of getting caught, the thrill of doing something that's forbidden, that makes a life of crime attractive. For others, it is the sense of control they get from manipulating or outwitting others. Although these two characteristics seem to conflict, they can exist simultaneously in the same person. The risk-taking element provides the "rush," while escaping detection one more time makes the cybercriminal feel safe and in control.

- **Strong motivations—but the motivations might be wildly different** As noted, it takes time and energy to commit most crimes. It takes extra effort, and a certain amount of skill, to commit cybercrimes. Most cybercriminals are strongly motivated, but the motivations range from just wanting to have fun to the need or desire for money, emotional or sexual impulses, political motives, or dark compulsions caused by mental illness or psychiatric conditions. Discerning the motivation for a particular crime is an important aspect of building a useful profile of the criminal who committed it.

Recognizing Criminal Motivations

In the words of one police academy instructor, "Why do criminals commit crimes? Because they're criminals." If only it were that simple. People break the law for many different reasons. Some of those reasons might even seem reasonable, such as the out-of-work mother with no money left who steals baby food to feed her child. On the other hand, many people in dire straits find solutions to their problems that don't involve breaking the law. Some cybercriminals—for example, the longtime loyal employee who suddenly embezzles company funds to pay unexpected medical bills or to get a relative out of trouble—might do so out of desperation, too. Most, though, are driven by far less noble motives: greed, anger, lust, or just plain boredom.

Why does motive matter? In many jurisdictions, motive is an important element of proving guilt to show that the accused possesses each component of the so-called *crime triangle*: means (a way to commit the crime), motive (a reason for committing the crime), and opportunity (being in the right place at the right time to commit the crime). Thus, understanding the criminal's motive is useful at two points in the investigation: when we are creating a profile to help us identify the correct suspect(s), and later, when we present the case against our suspect.

Common motives for committing cybercrimes include:

- For "fun"
- Monetary profit
- Anger, revenge, and other emotional needs
- Political motives
- Sexual impulses
- Serious psychiatric illness

Let's examine each motive individually and look at how each can apply to the cybercriminal.

For "Fun"

Young hackers are the cybercriminals most likely to fall into this category. According to J. Maxwell in the "Electronic Data Processing Audit, Control, and Security Newsletter," the hackers who do it for fun can be further broken down into several categories:

- *Pioneer types*, who are fascinated by the technology. They enjoy learning how the systems work via a trial-and-error process and hack as a learning experience.
- "*Scamps*," playful hackers who don't intend to do any harm. This is the type who might hack into a Web site and leave an innocuous message such as "J.B. was here."

- *Explorers*, who get their kicks out of "going where no hacker has gone before"—or at least, where they themselves have never been. Their curiosity leads them to break into networks just to look around and see what's there.

- *Game players*, who look at hacking into systems as a game, pitting themselves against the network's security measures and being motivated by the desire to "win" by breaking in.

Another of Maxwell's hacker personality types, the *addict*, might start as any of these character types but becomes psychologically dependent on the activity. At that point, the pioneer, scamp, explorer, or gamester is no longer really hacking just for fun, but because he or she *needs* to hack to feel okay or normal.

The distinguishing characteristic of the "for fun" hacker is enjoyment. Unlike other cybercriminals who use the computer and Internet as the means to an end, for these hackers, hacking is an end in itself. They might view the computer as a toy and the entire Internet as their playground.

These "for fun" hackers realize no practical or financial gain from their hacking; in fact, hacking could be an expensive hobby for those who are continually upgrading their own computer systems to make the hacking experience faster and more satisfying.

Monetary Profit

If love of money is the root of all evil, it's no surprise that many cybercrimes—like many offline crimes—are motivated by the desire for financial gain. "Hacking for dollars" can cover many different offenses, including embezzlement, corporate espionage, and selling one's hacking services to others who have monetary or nonmonetary motives (the "hacker for hire").

Most cyberscam artists are in it for the money. Their motive could be to get money into their own hands or obtain properties or services without paying for them.

Money-motivated cybercriminals come in all "flavors"—male, female, young, old, wealthy, poor, or middle class. Some never made it through high school; others have advanced degrees. *White-collar criminals* (embezzlers, trade-secret thieves, and the like) tend to be educated professionals, often in the midst of career stagnation or burnout. *Scam artists* are usually sociable and charming, able to persuade others to do what they want. *Hired hacks* are generally highly skilled technicians who, in their own eyes, are "just doing a job."

Anger, Revenge, and Other Emotional Needs

Money is not the only motive, or even the strongest one, for committing crimes. Many criminal offenses, especially those that involve violence (and threat of violence) or property destruction, are committed out of emotional motivations: anger, rage, or revenge for real or imagined wrongs.

Anger can drive people to do things they otherwise might not. Psychologists note that dealing with a person who is very angry, hurt, or emotionally distraught is like dealing with someone who is mentally disturbed or under the influence of alcohol or drugs. Indeed, strong emotions cause a release of adrenaline, which does act on the body and brain like a drug, resulting in both physiological and psychological changes (enhanced physical strength, heightened alertness, "tunnel vision," or obsession with the problem immediately at hand). A very angry person *is*—temporarily, at least—an emotionally disturbed person.

Cybercriminals who act out of anger might be spurned lovers or spouses, fired employees, business associates who feel they've been cheated or ripped off, or others who believe some great wrong has been done to them or someone they care about. Their crimes range from terrorist threats (for example, e-mail threatening to assault or kill someone) to defacing a company's Web site with profanities or bringing down an organization's network with DoS attacks or computer viruses, which we'll discuss in greater detail in Chapter 10.

Revenge differs from anger in that it is usually better planned and not an immediate response. This makes it a less emotional act; consequently, it could be more dangerous because the vengeance-motivated cybercriminal has more time to think through the plan, cover his or her tracks, and reduce the probability of being caught.

Almost anyone, if pushed hard enough and far enough, is capable of lashing out in anger. Thus, the anger-motivated cybercriminal can be someone who doesn't ordinarily engage in criminal activity. The crime could seem completely out of character. Just as an investigator asks, in the case of a money-motivated crime, "Who was in a position to benefit financially?" the investigator should approach a crime that appears to be motivated by anger with the question, "Who has been harmed or is close to someone who has been harmed by the victim?"

Anger and revenge are not the only motives that involve emotions. Cybercriminals commit crimes out of other emotional and psychological needs. For example, hackers could break into protected systems to prove themselves to their friends, to obtain a sense of belonging to the group. In fact, hackers can commit acts in groups that they would not commit individually. The "crowd mentality" (or *mob* mentality, in extreme cases) is a phenomenon with which psychologists are familiar and is something most law enforcement officers are aware of. Large groups can take on personalities of their own, becoming more or less than the sum of their parts. Hackers might egg one another on, daring each other to go further, with no one willing to be the first to say "no" and lose status in the eyes of his or her peers.

Hackers also commit crimes to gain attention. This is especially true of teenage hackers who want to embarrass their families or simply make family members or authority figures notice them.

Another emotional motivation for hacking is loyalty to a friend or the desire to "help" someone— for example, the high school hacker who doesn't want his girlfriend to flunk calculus and have to go to summer school, so he breaks into the school's computer system and changes her grade from an F to a C.

Political Motives

Politically motivated cybercriminals include members of extremist and radical groups at both ends of the political spectrum who use the Internet to spread propaganda, attack the Web sites and networks of their political enemies, steal money to fund their militant activities, or plan and coordinate their "real-world" crimes. Examples include:

- The 1996 case in which "hacktivists" infiltrated the U.S. DOJ through its Web site, deleted the DOJ's Web files, and replaced them with their own pages protesting the recently passed Communications Decency Act

- The rash of Web site defacements that included the message "Free Kevin" (in reference to Kevin Mitnick, who was arrested for computer crimes) in 1998

- The "cyberwars" between U.S. and Chinese hackers in summer 2000, following international disputes over the landing of a U.S. spy plane in China

- The use of botnets (which we'll discuss in Chapter 10) in 2007, which Russian hackers used to orchestrate DoS attacks against Estonian commercial and government sites

Cybercriminals with political motivations range from relatively benign hackers who just want to make a political statement, to organized terrorist groups such as Hezbollah, Hamas, and Al-Qaeda. *Cyberterrorism* refers to using the Internet and computer skills to disrupt or shut down the critical infrastructure and government services of a country. Although no such large-scale attacks have thus far been implemented, security experts warn that such attacks are or will be within the capabilities of some terrorist organizations and could pose a huge threat to government and business operations.

The politically motivated cybercriminal usually devotes a good deal of time to his or her cause and often (though by no means always) has a prior criminal record for offenses such as criminal trespass, rioting, and similar activities. True terrorists are especially dangerous because they are willing to die for their cause. They also often have large networks of likeminded people they can call on to help them carry out their missions and to hide them from law enforcement.

Sexual Impulses

Sex is one of the strongest instincts in any animal, including humans. Psychologists and psychiatrists argue over what causes normal sexual feelings to become perverted, but there is no question that sexual deviance (defined as sexual behavior that is out of the norm or breaks societal rules) is common among certain types of criminals.

Not all sexually deviant behavior is illegal or considered harmful. However, when sexual arousal becomes associated with violence or with inappropriate objects of desire, such as children, serious harm and criminal activity can result.

Sexually motivated cybercriminals include these types:

- *Passive pedophiles*, who use the Internet to access and download kiddie porn and use photos and stories of children engaging in sex (usually with adults) to feed their own fantasies. Even if they never act out those fantasies in real life, in the United States and many other countries it is illegal to even possess child pornography in photographic form. This law is based on the assumption that children were harmed in the making of the pictures. The pornography laws generally apply to visual depictions only; the written word (stories about child sex) is protected by the First Amendment. The issue of "virtual child pornography" that uses high-quality, computer-generated images instead of real photographs is a matter of intense debate. In April 2002, the Supreme Court struck down the federal laws making this form of kiddie porn illegal, although other countries have taken a stand against it.

- *Active pedophiles*, who use the Internet to find their victims. These criminals usually also collect child pornography, but they don't stop at fantasies. They often hang out in chat rooms that are frequented by children and engage them in virtual conversations, attempting to gain their trust and lure them into an in-person meeting. They might then rape the children, or they could simply "court" them, preferring to gradually seduce them into sexual relationships. Because children under a certain age (which varies from one state to another) are not considered capable of consenting to sex, sexual conduct with a minor is still a crime, even if the child agrees to it. Usually the offense is defined as *statutory rape* or some category of *sexual assault*. The crime of Internet luring is illegal under some state laws, and was introduced into Canada's Criminal Code in 2002.

- *Fans of S&M*, or sadomasochistic sex, who are aroused either by inflicting pain on others (sadists) or by having pain inflicted on them (masochists). Although S&M behavior between consenting adults is generally not considered a crime, some sadistic individuals hunt for partners on the Internet and then take the activities beyond the level that the partner bargained for or consented to, seriously injuring or sometimes even killing their victims.

■ *Serial rapists*, who develop relationships (hetero- or homosexual) online and then invite their victims to meet in real life, only to rape them. Serial rapists often have problems performing sexually in a normal, loving situation. They are able to become aroused only when the sex is violent and forced. Psychologists call rape an anger-motivated or power-motivated crime rather than a sexually motivated one, but sex is certainly an important element, if only as the "tool of the crime."

■ *Sexual serial killers*, who—like serial rapists—cruise Internet chat rooms and forums looking for victims. Psychiatric literature recognizes two types of serial killers: organized and disorganized. The *organized killer* is often of above-average intelligence, is socially gregarious and charming, and is usually married or living with a partner. *Disorganized killers* are almost exactly the opposite; their IQ levels are usually below average, and they are socially inadequate loners and are anxious during the commission of the crime. Organized killers tend to be very controlled and unemotional and are often diagnosed (as was Ted Bundy, one of the country's most famous sexual serial killers) as sociopaths. In fact, sexual serial killers, despite the sexual motivation for their crimes, belong in the next category of motivation: serious psychiatric illness.

Serious Psychiatric Illness

Criminal behavior is not, itself, indicative of mental illness. If it were, perhaps it could be treated medically. However, some criminals are motivated to engage in illegal and antisocial behavior by underlying psychiatric conditions, especially those conditions that manifest themselves in symptoms such as lack of impulse control and lack of inhibition, hallucinations and delusions, paranoia, hyperactivity, and inability to concentrate or possession of impaired communication skills.

Persons suffering from personality disorders, schizophrenia, bipolar affective disorder, aggression, depression, adjustment disorders, and sexual disorders such as paraphilias are prone to criminal behavior, according to "Psychiatric Illness Associated with Criminality," by William H. Wilson, MD, and Kathleen A. Trott, MD (www.emedicine.com/med/topic3485.htm). Illegal conduct can also stem from drug- or alcohol-induced psychosis or conditions caused by traumatic brain injury.

It might be easier for such persons to hide their mental illness in the online community, where they don't have to come into physical contact with others, than in the offline world. Cybercrime that is motivated by psychiatric illness can be difficult to investigate and solve, precisely because the criminal's motivations don't seem logical or rational. We can understand why a money-motivated offender commits crimes, even though we don't approve of the behavior. However, we might not be able to easily understand the actions of a mentally ill person.

Recognizing the Limitations of Statistical Analysis

According to author Samuel Clemens, writing under the famous pseudonym Mark Twain, "There are three kinds of lies: lies, damn lies, and statistics." Many members of the public are suspicious of statistical analysis and statistics-based arguments, and rightly so. Everyone who has worked with statistical data or has followed both sides in a political campaign knows that the same set of facts can be manipulated during presentation to support divergent conclusions.

Criminal profiles are based on probabilities. The probabilities are based on statistical patterns that have been discerned by studying similar past cases. As we've seen, profiling can be a useful tool, and cybercrime investigators—who face special challenges due to the complexity and global nature of the Internet—need all the tools they can get. However, it is important to remember that a carefully constructed profile can be completely wrong. The investigation should shape the profile; the profile should never shape the investigation.

Categorizing Cybercriminals

In Chapter 1, we discussed the importance of categorizing cybercrimes. In the previous section, we touched on one way that cybercriminals could be categorized, based on their motivations for committing crimes. There is another way to categorize Internet-using offenders: by the role the Internet plays in their criminal activity. This role generally breaks down into two broad categories:

- Criminals who use the Net as a tool of the crime
- Criminals who use the Net incidentally to the crime

In the following sections, we examine the differences between these two categories. We also take a look at a special category of cybercriminal: the one who would never engage in illegal activity in "real life" but who becomes a criminal via an online persona.

Criminals Who Use the Net As a Tool of the Crime

Many types of cybercrime depend on the use of a computer network to accomplish the criminal act. This doesn't mean that the same offense couldn't be committed without computers and networks; it means that in this instance, the network was directly used to commit the crime.

Here's an analogy to make it easier to understand this concept: A murder can be committed using any of a number of methods—a gun, a knife, poison, even a motor vehicle. Although the end result (death of the victim) is the same in all cases, the killing cannot be done in the same way if the tool is different. Likewise, an embezzler could steal company money without using a network, but it would be done in a different way. If the embezzler does use a network to divert funds, the network is a tool of that crime.

A network can be used as a crime tool by different types of cybercriminals. Most frequently, a network is used as a tool by:

- White-collar criminals
- Computer con artists
- Hackers, crackers, and network attackers

White-Collar Criminals

The term *white-collar criminal* is derived, of course, from the image of the office worker or professional who traditionally wears business attire (white shirt and tie) to work. White-collar cybercrimes can include many different offenses, such as:

- Changing company computer records to provide the criminal with an unauthorized pay raise or to eliminate or change bad employee evaluations or pad expense accounts

- Accessing and using insider information for purchasing stocks or securities, which are U.S. Securities and Exchange Commission (SEC) violations

- Selling company information to outsiders; using insider information to obtain kickbacks from clients, business partners, or competitors; or using confidential information for blackmail purposes

- Manipulating electronic accounts to appropriate the company's or clients' money or property for oneself

- "Cooking" the company books or financial statements to provide false information to creditors, investors, the Internal Revenue Service, internal auditors, and so on—often to cover other crimes

Studies of white-collar crime have shown that these offenders can fall into several subcategories, based on their underlying motivations:

- The *resentful* white-collar criminal cheats the company because he or she feels cheated *by* the company. This is often a long-time employee who has been passed over several times for a raise or promotion or has received a negative employee evaluation that, in the employee's eyes, is undeserved. These cybercriminals adopt something of a Robin Hood mentality, convinced that they are merely taking from the rich company—which can afford the loss and even deserves it—and giving to the poor (usually themselves).

- The *deliberate* white-collar criminal has no personal ethics that would prohibit stealing. Unlike the previously described offender, there is no period of building anger or resentment; this type begins criminal activity as soon as the opportunity arises. These cybercriminals can be quite bright and plan their crimes meticulously. They often have a timeline or monetary goal in mind; the master plan is to put the stolen money away in a safe place (such as an offshore bank account). After a certain number of years or after a specific amount of cash is built up, they plan to retire and live in luxury someplace beyond the jurisdiction of the law. They are often very disciplined and careful, taking only small amounts of money at a time so as not to be noticed.

- The *desperate* white-collar criminal steals in response to serious personal financial problems. These problems can be unpredictable, such as a medical or legal crisis in the family. More often, though, they are the result of bad judgment: gambling, alcohol, or drug problems, losing money in bad business investments, or living beyond their means to impress others. These cybercriminals are often careless, becoming more blatant as their situations worsen. Thus, they are the most likely type of white-collar cybercriminal to be caught.

White-collar criminals often give themselves away by leaving clues that arouse investigators' suspicions, such as:

- Unexplained income, property, or lifestyle that is far greater than the person's job makes feasible

- Many large cash transactions

- Multiple bank accounts in different banks, especially banks in different cities or countries

- Multiple businesses listed at the same address

- "Paper" corporations that have no physical assets and seem to make no product and provide no services

CyberCrimeStopper

The White-Collar Crime Fighter

White-Collar Crime Fighter magazine is a good source of information about white-collar crime, with tips and tricks on how to avoid being victimized and information for law enforcement officers and prosecutors who deal with white-collar offenses. A sample copy and subscription information are available on the magazine's Web site, at www.wccfighter.com.

A detailed list of types of white-collar crimes and scams is available at the National Check Fraud Center Web site, at www.ckfraud.org/whitecollar.html. Some of the crimes described in this list more appropriately belong in our next section, about computer con artists.

Computer Con Artists

Con artists use the Internet as a tool, to reach "marks" (their terminology for victims) that they could never reach otherwise. E-mail, Web sites, and chat rooms can all become tools for scammers to propagate their fraudulent schemes.

According to the Federal Trade Commission's (FTC) Consumer Fraud and Identity Theft Complaint Data (www.consumer.gov/sentinel/pubs/top10fraud2007.pdf), 87 percent of the complaints made about Internet-related fraud involved money being paid. In 2007, this involved 192,558 complainants paying a combined reported total of $525,743,643. In this same year, 64 percent of the fraud complaints involved companies soliciting the consumer by using the Internet as their initial method of contact, with 49 percent using e-mail and 15 percent using Web sites. Some of the most frequently reported online scams reported to the FTC include:

- **Internet auctions** Bidders send their money but do not receive the promised product, or they receive property that is not what it was represented to be.

- **Internet service scams** Customers prepay for access services and then companies fold and disappear, or customers are enticed into paying for services they don't want (for example, by official-looking notices that imply that you will lose your domain name registration if you don't send money to the scam artist). In another variation, an Internet service provider (ISP) mailed checks for $3.50 to people on a mailing list; unless the recipients read the fine print, they didn't realize that by cashing the check, they were agreeing to purchase Internet services that would be billed through their phone companies.

- **Identity theft** The top consumer complaint to the FTC for years has been identity theft, in which the personal or financial information of another person is obtained by a criminal, who then poses as that person. This can be as serious as someone using your information to obtain a loan under your name or a second mortgage on your house, to someone posing as you online to sully your reputation.

- **Credit card fraud** This type of fraud involves individuals and shady companies that pretend to (or actually do) sell a service or product via credit card, for the purpose of collecting the victim's credit card information and using it to make fraudulent purchases. Transferring the information from the card to another counterfeit card is a practice called *skimming*.

- **Web "cramming"** This crime involves offers for free services such as Web hosting for a trial period with no obligation, after which users are charged on their phone bills or credit cards, even though they never agreed to continue the service after the trial period.

- **Multilevel marketing (MLM) and pyramid schemes** Con artists play on users' greed and desire to get rich quick by signing recruits—for a hefty fee—and promising them huge profits if they recruit others. The *chain letter* is a variation on the pyramid scheme, as is the *Ponzi scheme* (named after Charles Ponzi, who successfully defrauded hundreds of people using this method in the 1920s). All of these con games were around long before the Internet, but today's ability to communicate quickly and easily with a huge number of people all over the world has given them new life. (See http://skepdic.com/pyramid.html for detailed explanations of how the pyramid, chain letter, Ponzi, and other MLM schemes work—and why they *don't* work for the naïve recruits who are their victims.)

- **Travel and vacation scams** These are the Internet-age variant of a time-honored telemarketing con. Travel "bargains" and "free" vacation scams (that include all manner of hidden costs) abound. These include selling frequent-flyer miles that are on the verge of expiration, selling travel vouchers in conjunction with pyramid schemes, bait-and-switch offers, and other too-good-to-be-true travel deals.

- **Business and investment "opportunities"** These range from work-at-home scams that require you to purchase an expensive starter kit and don't provide actual jobs to day-trading programs and solicitations for investment in worthless real estate. The SEC maintains a Web site on how to prevent Internet investment scams, at www.sec.gov/investor/pubs/cyberfraud.htm.

- **Scams involving healthcare products and services** These include weight loss, anti-aging, and alternative health products that are marketed under false or unproven claims; online prescription drug sales that don't require the patient to be seen by a physician; MLM of health products; and other con games that seek to take advantage of people who are ill or frightened about their health. A number of organizations and agencies exist to combat healthcare fraud, one of which is the National Council Against Health Fraud (www.ncahf.org).

(www.security-hacks.com), and Darknet (www.darknet.org.uk) provide information and software to discover vulnerabilities and access systems. Of course, almost any network security tool used for testing problems can be used for these purposes. In addition to this, there are newsgroups, mailing lists, online papers, and videos that provide guidance and detailed information. Hacker conferences such as DEFCON (www.defcon.org) and the Black Hat Briefings (www.blackhat.com) provide real-world opportunities for hackers to meet. Interestingly, the organizations that sponsor these meetings have become increasingly mainstream over the past few years, now attracting security professionals and government officials as well as hackers.

There is a definite hierarchy in the hacker community. "Real" hackers—expert programmers and networking wizards who write the code and discover the exploits—have disdain for the script kiddies who merely use software written by others to break into systems or launch attacks, without really understanding how it works. The hacker culture also divides itself into two groups:

- *Black hats* break into systems illegally, for personal gain, notoriety, or other less-than-legitimate purposes.

- *White hats* write and test open source software, work for corporations to help them beef up their security, work for the government to help catch and prosecute black-hat hackers, and otherwise use their hacking skills for noble and legal purposes.

There are also hackers who refer to themselves as *gray hats*, operating somewhere between the two primary groups. Gray-hat hackers might break the law, but they consider themselves to have a noble purpose in doing so. For example, they might crack systems without authorization and then notify the system owners of the systems' fallibility as a "public service," or find security holes in software and then publish them to force the software vendors to create patches or fixes for the problem.

NOTE

The white-hat/black-hat distinction has become more muddled as former criminal hackers have gone on the lecture circuit or attained corporate jobs as security experts, hacking sites have taken on a "security-conscious" angle, and conventions have acquired corporate sponsorship. Only in old Western movies can you rely on a person's hat color as a dependable indication of his character. In today's cyberworld, most people—including hackers—are neither all good nor all bad. A hacker who identifies him- or herself as a white-hat hacker might succumb to the temptation to engage in an illegal act, and a self-professed black hat can reform and become one of the "good guys."

Ethical hacking is a term used to describe hackers who use their skills to hack networks on behalf of the owners. Numerous courses train computer professionals in hacking systems, including the EC-Council's Certified Ethical Hacker (CEH) certification, courses, and even a master's of ethical hacking and countermeasures degree that's offered by the University of Abertay in Scotland. If a hacker has

CyberCrimeStopper

The FTC Scam Line

The FTC provides consumer information, takes complaints, and maintains a database of companies reported to engage in online fraud. Consumers who have been victims of fraud or deceptive or unfair business practices (online or offline) can contact the agency via its toll-free telephone help line at 1-877-FTC-HELP, or they can fill out the online complaint form through the FTC's Web site (www.ftc.gov). Internet fraud cases, telemarketing frauds, and identity theft cases are entered into a secure database called the Consumer Sentinel (www.consumer.gov/sentinel/). The database is made available to law enforcement agencies all over the world. The state attorney general's office in most states also handles these types of fraud cases.

There are a wide variety of sources for information on new and traditional types of scams. A good source of news, information, and links pertaining to all types of con games and fraud cases is Swindles (www.swindles.com). This site is updated daily. Scamwatch (www.scamwatch.com) is another good resource for reporting scams and other crimes, with a huge number of scams available to view and search for online.

Hackers, Crackers, and Network Attackers

The network is an important tool that makes white-collar criminals' and scam artists' "jobs" easier, but it is an absolutely essential tool for hackers. Unless a hacker has physical access to a computer, it would be impossible for him or her to commit a crime without the Net.

In Chapter 1, we discussed the types of crimes hackers commit: unauthorized access, theft of data or services, and destructive cybercrimes such as Web site defacement, release of viruses, and DoS and other attacks that bring down the server or network. In Chapter 10, you will learn the technical details of how most of these attacks work.

Hackers learn their "craft" in a number of ways: by trial and error, by studying network operating systems and protocols with an eye toward learning their vulnerabilities, and perhaps most significantly from other hackers. There is an enormous underground network (in the traditional, rather than technical, sense of the word) where those new to hacking can get information and learn from more experienced hackers.

There are numerous sites to meet hackers online, and many more that provide tools that can be used for hacking sites. Web sites such as the Ethical Hacker Network (www.ethicalhacker.net), Cult of the Dead Cow (www.cultdeadcow.com), Hacktivismo (www.hacktivismo.com), Security Hacks the requisite skills, including the social skills necessary to function in the corporate world, ethical hacking can be a lucrative business. Consultants charge companies $10,000 or more to test their security by attempting to hack into their systems and providing reports and recommendations on plugging the security holes that they find. (See www.research.ibm.com/journal/sj/403/palmer.html for more information about ethical hacking.)

Criminals Who Use the Net Incidentally to the Crime

Some criminals use the network in relation to their crimes, but the Net is not an actual tool of the crimes. That is, the network is not used to commit the *criminal* activity, although it can be used to prepare for or keep records of that criminal activity. Examples of this type of criminality include:

- Criminals who use the Net to find victims
- Criminals who use computers or networks for recordkeeping
- Criminals who use e-mail or chat services to correspond with accomplices

Even in cases in which the network is not a tool of the crime, it can still provide evidence of criminal intent and clues that help investigators track down the criminals. We discuss each situation in the following sections.

Criminals Who Use the Net to Find Victims

It might seem that using the Net to find victims would make the Net a tool of the crime. In some cases, the criminal goes on to use the Internet to actually commit the crime —for example, sending electronic chain letters, e-mailing fictitious notices purporting to be from the victims' ISPs that request their credit card information, or directing victims to a Web site that tries to sell them products under false pretenses). In those cases, the Internet *is* a tool of the crime, but the initial act of searching out potential victims is not, by itself, criminal. Thus, a pedophile or rapist or other criminal who uses the Net to find victims but then commits the criminal activity in the real world is using the Internet incidentally to the crime. However, the Internet can be used to set up a sting operation that will turn the tables and lure the criminal into revealing his or her identity to law enforcement.

Criminals Who Use Computers or Networks for Recordkeeping

People who engage in noncomputer-related criminal activity such as drug dealing, illegal gambling, or other illicit "businesses" can use computers to keep financial records, customer lists, and other information related to the criminal activity and use the Internet to transfer these files to an off-site location where they will be safer from law enforcement.

Transferring business records to a friend's computer or an Internet data storage service is not against the law, so Net use is incidental to this criminal activity, even though those files might be important evidence of the actual crime.

Criminals Who Use E-mail or Chat Services to Correspond with Accomplices

Criminals who work in groups—terrorist groups, theft rings, black-hat hackers—often use e-mail and chat in the same way that legitimate users do: to correspond with people they work with. The correspondence itself is not a crime; it is the illegal activity being planned or discussed that is criminal. However, the correspondence can be used not only to show the criminal's intent and help track him down, but also, in some cases, to prove the existence of a criminal conspiracy. This is important because if the elements of conspiracy exist, charges can be brought against all members of the conspiracy, not just the person(s) who physically committed the crime.

CyberLaw Review

Criminal Conspiracy

The wording of conspiracy statutes varies in different jurisdictions, but most states address conspiracy as an inchoate or preparatory offense. The conspiracy charge is a separate offense, but it must be charged in conjunction with another criminal offense. Generally, a criminal conspiracy exists when two or more persons agree that one or more of them will commit a felony offense *and* one or more of the conspirators perform some overt act in furtherance of the agreement. In other words, if in court the prosecution can show (for example, via e-mail collected pursuant to a search warrant or intercepted legally under court order) that such agreement was made and can further prove that at least one of the parties took some step toward committing the crime, *all* parties can be charged with criminal conspiracy, whether or not the crime was completed successfully.

Real-Life Noncriminals Who Commit Crimes Online

In some situations, people who are not criminals in real life engage in criminal conduct online. These include accidental cybercriminals and situational cybercriminals. *Accidental cybercriminals* have no criminal intent. They commit illegal acts online because of ignorance of the law or lack of familiarity with the technology. An example is someone who has a cable modem connection or is using the broadband Internet access available in some hotels and opens the Network Neighborhood folder on his computer (the network browse list) and sees other computers listed there. Curious, he might click one of the icons just to see what happens. If he has stumbled upon a computer on the network that is running a low-security operating system or doesn't require a username and password to log on, and it has network file sharing enabled, he might be able to access the shared files on that computer.

If our hypothetical user is not very technically or legally savvy, he might not even realize that those files are on someone else's private (or so the owner thought!) computer. Or he might think that because they're accessible, it is legal to look at them. However, depending on how the state's or country's unauthorized access statutes are written, it might be a crime to access any other computer across a network without permission, even if that computer's users have, perhaps unwittingly, made it technologically easy to do so.

The behavior of *situational cybercriminals* reflects an interesting phenomenon that we discussed earlier—the psychological dissociation experienced by some people when they go online. This dissociation can cause some people who, in real life, consider themselves upstanding, law-abiding citizens and would never deliberately commit a crime to engage in illegal activity when they done their "alternate persona" while online.

These people might have repressed desires to indulge in illicit conduct that they control through self-discipline but which they feel free to unleash when they log on to the Internet because there they can be (in their own minds) "someone else." They literally lead double lives, like a modern-day drjekyllandmrhyde@whoknows.com.

Understanding Cybervictims

The term *victim* is derived from the Latin word *victima*, which means "an animal offered as a sacrifice." Today the word is used to refer to someone or something that is harmed by some act or circumstance. The crime victim is the person *to whom* the crime happens, the one who is harmed by a criminal's illegal act.

The field of *victimology* involves collecting data about, and in effect profiling, the victims of crime. This information is useful for several reasons:

- It allows law enforcement officers to predict what people or personality types are likely to become victims of certain crimes and warn them. This in turn gives the potential victims the opportunity to take steps to protect themselves.

- It allows law enforcement officers to better profile the criminal, because patterns in victim choice are an important part of the criminal profile.

- It allows law enforcement officers to use the victim profile to bait criminals, to draw them out into the open.

On the Scene

Using Victimology to Develop a Sting

Officers had been investigating an online pedophile who was suspected of luring children into in-person meetings and raping them. An undercover office created an online persona—that of a 12-year-old girl—based on the characteristics of a pedophile's past victims. The officer then frequented the chat rooms where the offender was known to hang out, in hopes that the pedophile would try to set up a real-life meeting with the officer in her guise as a child. In this way, police could monitor the meeting place and positively identify the criminal.

It is very important, in any sting operation, to avoid committing entrapment, which will cause evidence against the offender to be thrown out of court. Generally, courts have held that officers can "provide a mere opportunity" for someone to commit a crime—as the officer in our example did by pretending to be a child who fit the profile of the pedophile's victims and waiting for the pedophile to initiate contact and pursue her. Entrapment occurs when officers go beyond providing the opportunity, overtly attempting to induce, entice, or persuade the suspect to commit the criminal act. For example, if our officer (playing the role of the child) had contacted the pedophile, had "come on" to him and asked him to meet her for sex, that could be held to constitute entrapment.

The victim of a crime is often the key witness against the offender. Using victimology techniques, even a deceased victim can provide important clues for investigators. Each aspect of the victim that's uncovered can reveal a greater understanding of the offender's mindset, interests, and patterns.

Categorizing Victims of Cybercrime

We can create categories of cybercrime victims, just as we were able to do with cybercriminals. Again, it is important to note that not all victims fit neatly into these categories, and some of the categories overlap at times. Some common victim characteristics include:

- People who are new to the Net
- People who are naturally naïve (sometimes including the young and the elderly)
- People who are disabled or disadvantaged
- The desperate, who are greedy, are lonely, or have other emotional needs
- Pseudo-victims who report having been victimized but actually were not
- People who are simply unlucky enough to be in the wrong (virtual) place at the wrong time

Let's take a moment to review each characteristic and understand why people in these groups are especially vulnerable to cybercrime.

New to the Net

Internet "newbies" might not yet be familiar with the common scams that would cause a Net veteran to sigh and say, "Ho, hum, not *that* sob story again." In addition, newbies are often unaware of common security practices and known software security holes. Newcomers might not realize that their systems can be infected with viruses simply by opening an e-mail attachment or visiting the wrong Web site, nor might they be aware that viruses can be sent from their own machines without their knowledge.

Computer users who have not had a lot of experience interacting online could be more trusting of those they "meet" via chat. They could believe that because *they* are honest in their online communications, everyone else is, too.

With huge numbers of people connecting to the Internet for the first time every year, cybercriminals always have a fresh crop of Net newbies on which to prey. In their efforts to educate the public about cybercrime, law enforcement and IT professionals should pay special attention to new Internet users, let them know that they can be the targets of scam artists and other offenders, and provide them with information on how to recognize and avoid questionable schemes.

Naturally Naïve

Some groups are naturally more naïve, as a whole, than others—although individual members of those groups might not be naïve at all. The very young and the elderly have long been the favorite marks of con artists, and that preference carries over to the online world.

Youngsters often have distorted world views, especially if they've led sheltered lives. They might not yet have internalized the idea—even if they've been told—that there are bad people who want to hurt others. They might think that if they are nice to others, everyone will be nice to them. Furthermore, kids are naturally curious and eager to please, which can be a dangerous combination of qualities when they come into contact with a cybercriminal. Children are, of course, *the* targets of some of the Internet's worst of the worst: pedophiles.

Many elderly people feel uncomfortable with new technology because they didn't grow up with it. They might enjoy helping people, a trait that scam artists can exploit. When elderly people do fall victim to criminal behavior, they might be hesitant to report it—even when they've been cheated out of thousands of dollars—because they feel that they were somehow to blame for being "dumb." Traditional mail-fraud schemes that targeted the elderly are being reborn in a new incarnation: e-mail fraud.

Schools, law enforcement, and other agencies are recognizing the growing problem faced by young and old victims, with many developing programs designed to help these "student drivers" ease onto the information superhighway without getting run down. Computers are taught in many schools as early as kindergarten, and many children are gaining an understanding of the dos and don'ts at an early age. Law enforcement and IT professionals can join together with schools and senior citizens' centers to increase awareness and educate these vulnerable groups.

Disabled and Disadvantaged

The mentally and physically disabled and the disadvantaged can also be targeted by particularly reprehensible cybercriminals who—with the goal of identifying potential victims—search online databases and join mailing lists that are intended as support groups for people with disabilities.

Online forums can be especially important as a means of social interaction and a source of friendship for people with certain disabilities that limit their mobility, such as paraplegia, or that make it inadvisable for them to be around groups of people, such as immune system disorders, or that have altered their appearance, such as traumatic injuries. Law enforcement agencies can partner with IT firms to provide a valuable service by helping these people develop a greater awareness of cybercrime while assisting them in learning to take full advantage of computer technology's ability to enhance their lives.

Desperate

Desperate people make excellent targets for cybercriminals. They could be looking for love in all the wrong online places, be desperately seeking salvation through Internet religious groups, be direly in need of money, or have some other immediate emotional or physical need. In any event, their desperation makes them vulnerable—to Lothario-style scam artists who enter romantic relationships with the intent to defraud the partner, or unethical online evangelists who are out to make money off others' spiritual longings, to get-rich-quick schemers, Internet loan sharks, or fraudulent job brokers.

Because desperation is usually a temporary or intermittent condition, and because, to paraphrase Henry David Thoreau, those suffering from it usually lead lives of *quiet* desperation, it might be more difficult to identify and warn these potential victims of their vulnerability. Investigators who detect this victimization pattern for a particular cybercriminal can, however, use the information in constructing stings, by posing as "marks" who fit the victim profile.

Pseudo-Victims

Sigmund Freud might have been right when he said that sometimes a cigar is just a cigar, but sometimes a victim is *not* just a victim. There are people who, for various reasons, report crimes that never occurred or represent themselves as victims when they are not (and could, in fact, actually be the perpetrator).

The motivations of these *pseudo-victims* run the gamut:

- People who take revenge or express their anger at another person by falsely accusing that person of a crime

- People who want attention; pretending to be a crime victim makes them feel "special"

- People who claim to be crime victims to cover up the fact that they themselves committed the crime

- People who pretend to be victims to claim money from victim relief funds, charitable organizations, or insurance companies

- People who honestly believe that a crime has been committed against them when they have been the victims of unethical or immoral—but not illegal—behavior

Although the vast majority of victim reports are genuine, when investigators interview crime victims they should always be cognizant of the possibility of pseudo-victimhood. In most states, statutes make it a criminal offense to file a false crime report; such charges might be appropriate in all except the last example.

The E-mail Threat That Wasn't

One investigation I assisted with involved a woman who had allegedly been threatened via e-mail by a female friend. The e-mail messages stated that the friendship was over, and included threats to the victim's life and safety. The victim provided copies of the e-mail messages to an officer, but upon investigating, the officer was met with a confusing defense: The suspect claimed she'd sent the messages but hadn't made the threats. After consulting me, I suggested that if the suspect was indeed innocent, analyzing her computer would quickly confirm it. After she surrendered her machine, I examined the e-mails sent from it, and saw the same messages without any threats. With this, the victim became suspect ... the person who had accused her friend had edited the e-mail messages, modifying the text and adding in the threats. Needless to say, Internet and computer-related crimes can have some unexpected twists.

In the Wrong (Virtual) Place at the Wrong Time

It is true that human predators, like their animal counterparts, often seek as prey the weakest members of the herd, or those they perceive to be weakest. However, not all crime victims are selected because they exhibit some vulnerability. Some criminals are indiscriminate and choose their victims at random—first come, first served. Sometimes ending up a cybercrime victim is just a matter of being in the wrong (virtual) place at the wrong time.

In building profiles, whether of criminals or of victims, just as profilers must be on the lookout for patterns, they must also take care not to imagine patterns where none exists. The fact that a criminal's victims *don't* fit a profile can also be valuable information for the investigator.

Making the Victim Part of the Crime-Fighting Team

When the field of victimology first emerged in the 1940s, those who studied victimization tended to see victims as objects of pity, weak people who were often viewed as contributing to their own bad fortune. This later became known as the "blame the victim" mentality and gave way to the more prevalent attitude today—that victims should be "empowered" through education and access to resources. In large part, the shift was in response to feminists who protested the denigrating and humiliating treatment that female crime victims—especially the victims of rape or sexual assault—sometimes suffered at the hands of law enforcement and the courts.

Many victims today prefer not to define themselves as victims because of the image of weakness and helplessness that implies. For that reason, the preferred term has become *survivor*, a word that implies strength.

Most states in the United States have enacted a set of legal rights for crime victims, often referred to as a Bill of Rights. Such legislation imposes requirements on law enforcement agencies to follow certain guidelines in dealing with crime victims. Many agencies now appoint crime victims' liaisons or utilize volunteers, who are trained to offer counseling and guidance to victims and in some cases to "protect" the victims from hostile or overeager law enforcement personnel.

Victims' rights granted by these laws often include:

- The right to be notified when the offender will come to trial

- The right to be present at the trial, either personally or through representation of an attorney

- The right to be informed of the disposition of the case

- If the suspect is convicted, the right to be informed and to give input when the suspect comes up for parole

- The right to be informed if and when the suspect is released from prison

- The right to be treated with dignity by the criminal justice system

- The right to be informed of victim social services and financial assistance that are available

- The right to be compensated for their loss, when possible

Victim compensation programs are usually state-funded programs designed to help pay medical and other expenses associated with being the victim of crime. In some cases, the courts require offenders to pay restitution directly to victims or to pay restitution into a compensation fund. These programs are usually administered by the state attorney general's office.

CyberLaw Review

Victim Services Programs

The U.S. DOJ operates the Office for Victims of Crime (OVC), which organizes events for National Crime Victims' Rights Week in April and provides news, research, and statistics and other resources at www.ojp.usdoj.gov/ovc. Information on the Crime Victims' Bill of Rights, with links to other sites, is also available to view at www.ojp.usdoj.gov/ovc/help/cvr.htm.

Understanding Cyberinvestigators

Are cybercrime investigations just the "same old stuff" for police detectives? Are the same personality characteristics, skills, and knowledge required for cyberinvestigations as for general criminal investigations? Do investigators who deal with cybercrime need special training? In the following sections, we address these questions and build a profile of an effective cyberinvestigator.

NOTE

There is generally no official job title or position called *cyberinvestigator*, although local agencies are usually free to create their own titles, so we can't say with certainty that such a title doesn't exist. We use the term here to refer to people whose investigative duties include cybercrimes.

Recognizing the Characteristics of a Good Cyberinvestigator

A good cyberinvestigator must possess the qualities that are necessary for any good criminal investigator, including:

- **Excellent observation skills** An investigator must notice things, including the "little things."

- **Good memory** To put together the many clues that pop up over the course of an investigation, a detective must be able to remember facts, names, places, and dates, or the investigator could miss a vital connection.

- **Organization skills** A good investigator not only remembers information, but also is able to organize it in a logical way so that patterns and correlations become apparent.

- **Documentation skills** A good investigator doesn't keep all this information in his or her head; instead, the investigator is able and willing to meticulously put it into writing so that it can be shared with others and used as a foundation for building the case.

- **Objectivity** The investigator must not allow personal prejudices, relationships, or feelings to affect his or her ability to evaluate the evidence objectively.

- **Knowledge** An effective investigator knows the criminal laws, the rules of evidence, victimology theory, criminal psychology, and investigative concepts and procedures and knows about scientific aids, lab services, and resources inside and outside the agency.

- **Ability to think like a criminal** The best investigators have a "native" awareness of criminal mental processes and can put themselves in the place of an offender and predict the offender's actions.

- **Intellectually controlled constructive imagination** The investigator must be creative enough to consider all possibilities, to examine facts and then extrapolate conclusions.

- **Curiosity** The best investigators are innately curious. They aren't satisfied with simply clearing the case. It's not enough for them to determine that the suspect committed the crime; they want to know why and exactly how the crime was committed.

- **Stamina** Investigation is hard work, often involving long hours. A good investigator must be physically up to the challenge.

- **Patience** Investigation is often a drawn-out process. Progress is frequently made one tiny step at a time. Leads lead to nowhere, prime suspects turn out to have airtight alibis, and the investigator must back up and start over from scratch.

- **Love of learning** Learning is really what investigation is all about—learning the facts of a case, learning about the people involved, sometimes even becoming an "instant expert" in another field, such as computer networking, to understand the technical aspects of the crime.

In addition to these generic qualities, an investigator who specializes in cybercrime needs a few additional characteristics:

- **A basic understanding of computer science** The more the investigator knows about how computers work (including both hardware and software), the better.

- **An understanding of computer networking protocols** Cybercrime, by definition, involves a network. Even if the investigator has a good grasp of computer technology in a stand-alone context, it doesn't mean he or she will understand how network intrusions and attacks work, what happens to e-mail when it leaves the sender's system, or how a Web browser requests and downloads pages, graphics, or scripts.

- **Knowledge of computer jargon** All vocations and most avocations have a unique *jargon*, terminology that has little meaning outside the field that members use as "shorthand" to communicate with one another. A good investigator must be able to "speak the language."

- **An understanding of hacker culture** It's been said that it takes a hacker to catch a hacker (usually by reformed hackers selling their services as security experts). There is a grain of truth in this axiom; it's much easier to track down hackers if you understand their mentality and the protocols (in the nontechnical sense this time) of interacting in the hacker community. Just as narcotics officers need to be intimately familiar with how drug dealers interact with each other, cybercrime investigators likewise should be experts in hacker culture.

- **Knowledge of computer and networking security issues** To investigate hacking or intrusion and network-attack crimes, the investigator should be familiar with common security "holes," security products (such as firewalls), and security policies and practices.

It should be apparent from the preceding list that cybercrime investigators usually need extensive training to operate effectively in this specialty area. This need is usually recognized in large law enforcement agencies, where IT professionals and computer science graduates might be recruited to handle cybercrime investigations or outside consultants might be called in to assist detectives with those investigations.

In small agencies, however, too often the detective on duty is assigned to the cybercrime case, whether or not he or she knows anything about computers. Almost as bad is the common situation in which the officer in the department who is considered the computer whiz (which can mean anything from "expert programmer" to "the only one in the department who knows how to burn information to a CD") is assigned to all cybercrime cases. Because the agency administrators perceive this officer to be a computer expert—even though he or she might be far from that—the newly anointed cybercrime investigator is expected to handle matters that are far beyond his or her capabilities.

Categorizing Cyberinvestigators by Skill Set

Although the skill *level* of those conducting cybercrime investigations varies tremendously, we can categorize most cyberinvestigators according to skill set, in one of four ways:

- **Investigators who specialize in computer/network crime** They are investigators first, with a secondary interest in technology. They are usually law enforcement officers or corporate security personnel.

- **Computer specialists who conduct investigations** They are IT professionals first, with a secondary interest in law enforcement/investigation. They often work as consultants to law enforcement agencies, are members of an IT department who assist officers in investigations, or are members of a technological crime unit within the law enforcement agency and perform much of the work involving acquisition of evidence from suspect machines.

- **Those who are equally skilled, trained, or interested in investigation and IT** They are involved in computers/cybercrime from the beginning of their careers; they may have parallel training in both fields, such as a double major in criminal justice and network engineering or programming. They may work for law enforcement agencies or as independent consultants and are generally in great demand and command high salaries.

- **Those who have no real skills or interest in either investigation or IT** These could be police officers who were "kicked upstairs" to the detective division and drew a cybercrime case randomly. They aren't really interested in investigative work and would prefer to be working patrol, and they have no training in or love of computers and networking. Another example of those who fall into this category are those who are more interested in getting promoted, and realize that being connected with high-tech projects or investigations is an asset to moving up the ladder.

Recruiting and Training Cyberinvestigators

The question has been asked before: Is investigation a skill or a talent? You might wonder what the difference is, and what difference the answer to that question makes.

A *skill* can be learned; a *talent* is inborn. Most creative activities involve both. Almost anyone can take piano lessons, learn to read music, and be able to play simple songs. That's a skill that can be developed through practice. Some people, however, are born with the ability to "play by ear," to sit down at a piano and perform any song they've ever heard, without sheet music, or to compose original pieces of their own. That's talent, and the best teacher can't teach you to do it if you don't have it.

Investigation is, as we've mentioned, a creative process. It requires certain skills that can be learned and developed, but the best investigators are also talented; they can be said to have "a nose for it" or can be thought to possess some quasi-magical sense of intuition. There are also people who seem to have a natural way with computers. The rare individual who is talented in both of these areas should be recruited vigorously by law enforcement agencies.

But raw talent is not enough to become a master cyberinvestigator, any more than it's enough to make you a concert pianist. Training is required to develop and perfect the skills that your talent brings you. Detectives who exclusively handle Internet and computer-related crimes require ongoing training, but officers should also get basic cybercrime training as part of their academy programs. Almost all officers working in today's world eventually encounter cybercrimes. As first responders, patrol officers need to know how to handle computer evidence, even if they won't be conducting the investigation. Advanced training in cybercrimes should be available—and mandatory—for those who actually handle the investigation. New technologies (and new ways to use them to commit crimes) are emerging constantly, so cybercrime investigators must stay up-to-date on the latest information. Organizations such as the International Association of Chiefs of Police (IACP; www.theiacp.org), the International High Technology Crime Investigation Association (HTCIA; www.htcia.org), and the International Association of Computer Investigative Specialists (IACIS; www.cops.org) can provide training guidelines and resources.

Incorporating Computer Professionals

Because the departments of any organization run on money, budgets are a major concern of law enforcement agencies. The training, facilities, forensic software, and other equipment necessary to have an adequate unit that can investigate computer and Internet-related crimes are expensive, but the benefits outweigh the costs. Often overlooked in the cost/benefit analysis is the fact that people already on staff can be an asset to these investigations.

As with any large organization, police departments commonly have an IT staff. These people usually have years of formal education and experience before ever being hired, and they often continue to upgrade their skills and knowledge throughout their careers. Ironically, it would take years to train an officer to reach this skill level, but law enforcement will often exclude computer professionals from the team because they don't have a badge.

Cyberinvestigators can benefit from using the existing IT resources available to them. For example, hardware specialists can provide information on the best way to open a particular model of laptop and remove its hard disk, whereas network administrators may be able to provide better insight into vulnerabilities that were exploited in a particular network operating system. Police departments can utilize these civilians as an information resource. In other cases, they would do well to hire a computer professional as part of a dedicated technology crime unit.

In law enforcement, officers commonly transfer from one branch or unit to another throughout their careers, giving them the widest possible range of experience. If they stay in one place too long, it will generally go against them when applying for promotions, so it is in their best interest to move on after a few years. Unfortunately, because cyberinvestigators require so much training, they move on once they gain any real expertise. For this reason, it is important that police departments take this into account, and not penalize officers for dedication to a specialized field of investigation. Also, because officers do rotate out of these units, it is wise to incorporate a civilian IT person as part of the technology crime unit. The computer professional would be an asset to performing computer forensics and other technology-driven duties while detectives focused on the actual investigation of the crimes, and they would become a permanent backbone or fixture of the unit as officers rotated through the unit over the decades.

Facilitating Cooperation: CEOs on the Scene

One more important person is involved in cybercrimes that victimize businesses and large organizations: the corporate chief executive officer (CEO) or manager. Corporate executives are finding their organizations increasingly exposed to the threat of criminal activity—and in some cases, criminal liability—from people both inside and outside the organization who use computers and networks to commit illegal acts.

The first step company executives must take upon discovering criminal activity is to report it to law enforcement. The choice to report the crime is not always as simple as it sounds. If every violation of the law were reported, investigated, and prosecuted, our criminal justice system would soon break down from the overload. For example, in many states it's a criminal offense to call someone a profane name in a public place. However, if this happens to you, unless the situation escalates, you probably won't call in the police. Why? Because consciously or subconsciously, you do a cost/benefit analysis and determine that the time and effort you would have to spend to give an official sworn statement and perhaps return to testify in court, along with the risk of making the offender *really* mad at you, isn't worth the benefit of pressing charges.

Similarly, if company officials discover that a hacker has broken into their network, but there has been little or no loss or damage, they might decide that the downtime of key personnel, the risk of bad publicity to the company if others find out they were hacked, and other factors make the cost of reporting outweigh the benefits.

Another reason that victimized companies hesitate to report cybercrime is the issue of their own liability. Even though the crime was committed against them, it is conceivable that their customers might sue them for negligence for allowing the crime to happen (as some of the victims of the terrorist attacks on New York City's World Trade Center sued the airlines that were also victimized). The perception today is that a company is legally responsible for preparing for every possible contingency to protect itself and its clients; this view has been upheld by juries, which have awarded big bucks to plaintiffs in many negligence cases. Even if clients don't sue, shareholders could be upset and investors might withhold funding if the company's network is seen as less than secure.

Managers could also be reluctant to open up the information stored on their network to government investigators. This is especially true if any less-than-legal activities are going on—"creative" tax strategies, for example. It's easier simply to absorb the costs accrued by the crime, if there are any, and spend the time and money to secure the network rather than pursue justice against those who breached it. In fact, in some cases, the discovery of unauthorized access could never make it up the management ladder at all; the network administrator or security specialist whose job is to prevent such incidents will not be eager to tell the bosses that hackers found their way around his or her security measures.

It is important for managers to realize that they have a vested interest in working with law enforcement to track down and bring charges against the cybercriminals who cost the company time and money and, in some cases, do irreparable damage to the business's reputation. Managers are more likely to cooperate with law enforcement if the investigative process isn't shrouded in mystery. Education, as always, is the key.

It is essential that managers, as well as their IT teams, understand how a criminal investigation works, their own roles in the investigation, and special issues that pertain to the collection, preservation, and presentation of digital evidence. We mentioned before that IT professionals and law enforcement officers often find themselves at odds in their efforts to reach a common goal: bringing the cybercriminal to justice. Managers, who see cybercrime hurting their bottom lines, can be in a unique position to facilitate cooperation between the two if they are made a part of the cybercrime-fighting team from the beginning.

Summary

Cybercrime is not just about computers. It is also about people. Understanding cybercrime is the first step in combating it. Understanding the people on the scene of the cybercrime—those who commit it, those who are injured by it, and those who work to stop it—is the first step toward understanding cybercrime.

Cybercriminals cannot be easily understood as a group because they engage in a wide range of very different criminal activities for very different reasons. However, we can gain more understanding if we categorize them and analyze each group separately. Understanding the motives, characteristics, and typical behaviors of criminals in each group, along with analyzing the evidence in each particular case, can help us develop a criminal profile that will assist in identifying and capturing offenders.

Part of the criminal profile involves studying the types of people criminals choose as victims. Victimology also serves other purposes; it allows us to predict where the cybercriminal might strike next and warn potential future victims. Victim profiles can also be used in concocting sting operations that lure the cybercriminal out of the virtual world and into the real one.

Investigators of cybercrime need all the characteristics that are required of any criminal investigator, plus a few extra ones to boot. Not only must cyberspace detectives be smart, logical, objective, patient, curious, and physically fit, but also they must have some knowledge and understanding of computers, networking, technical jargon, the hacker underground, and IT security issues. That's a tall order, and talented, skilled, well-trained cybercrime investigators are in high demand. Law enforcement agencies might have to pay premium salaries to get them—especially considering the discrepancy between compensation in the public sector and the corporate world for IT professionals. However, a professional cyberinvestigator can be invaluable to law enforcement agencies, which can expect to see the incidence of cybercrime continue to rise at an exponential rate for the foreseeable future.

Understanding the technology of cybercrime is easy compared with understanding the people who carry out the crimes. The human factor is often the most inexplicable component in an investigation.

Frequently Asked Questions

Q: Internet auctions are mentioned as one of the most frequently reported online crimes. Does this mean that all online auctions are con games?

A: No. Most online auctions are legitimate. Recognized auction sites such as eBay attempt to provide protections by publishing ratings of their sellers that are provided by people who have done business with them. The auction sites usually post security recommendations and guidelines that will help users protect themselves against fraud. However, the auctions do provide an opportunity for unscrupulous dealers to cheat their customers. It is important to be very careful when buying merchandise through an auction site.

Q: Why do con artists continue to engage in scams, even when they can make more money doing legitimate work, or even when the scam doesn't benefit them financially—or benefits them only minimally?

A: According to the study "Deceivers and Deceived: Observations on Confidence Men and Their Victims, Informants and Their Quarry, Political and Industrial Spies and Ordinary Citizens," by Richard Blum (see www.fraudaid.com/Why-Con-artists-Scam.htm), the typical con artist is both impulsive and compulsive and is addicted to the con games he plays because they give him the "high" of having put something over on someone. Blum concludes that most con artists exhibit the symptoms of antisocial personality disorder. According to the *Diagnostic and Statistical Manual of Mental Disorders*, Fourth Edition (DSM-IV), which is the primary diagnostic reference used by U.S. mental health professionals, characteristics of people with antisocial personality disorder include:

1. Failure to conform to social norms with respect to lawful behaviors, as indicated by repeatedly performing acts that are grounds for arrest

2. Deceitfulness, as indicated by repeated lying, use of aliases, or conning others for personal profit or pleasure

3. Impulsivity or failure to plan ahead

4. Irritability and aggressiveness, as indicated by repeated physical fights or assaults

5. Reckless disregard for safety of self or others

6. Consistent irresponsibility, as indicated by repeated failure to sustain consistent work behavior or to honor financial obligations

7. Lack of remorse, as indicated by being indifferent to or rationalizing the act of having hurt, mistreated, or stolen from another

Q: What factors should a company consider before recruiting hackers to work as corporate security specialists or computer crime specialists for law enforcement agencies?

A: This is a trend based on the notion that "it takes a hacker to catch a hacker" (or to protect a network from another hacker). It is certainly true that those who have committed the crimes are intimately familiar with how they are committed and with how they might be thwarted. Police have traditionally utilized the expertise of criminals, using studies made of people convicted of crimes. For example, questioning of professional burglars has indicated that certain homes are targeted—or avoided—based on such characteristics as whether a dog is present, whether exterior lighting illuminates windows and doors, and so forth. This information is useful in helping homeowners implement crime-prevention measures.

However, police agencies would not consider hiring former burglars as property-crime detectives or convicted murderers as homicide investigators. Hiring hackers who have broken the law in the past presents a number of problems that both private and public sector employers should keep in mind.

For one, many hacker types are philosophically opposed to big business. Although they could be persuaded to work for a corporation if tempted by enormous salaries to do what they do anyway—play with computers—they might not fit in well in the structured corporate environment. Hackers are often loners who do not conform to the corporate model, which stresses teamwork. Perhaps more important, a hacker who is guilty of criminal activity in the past can expose your company to substantial risks if he or she hasn't truly reformed. Your organization's network could be used to launch hack attacks when your "professional hacker" gets bored with assigned duties. This can leave the company open to serious liability issues. Your hacker could also build "back doors" into your system so that if you fire him or her or if he or she gets tired of playing the corporate game and leaves, he or she can get back in and have full access to your network.

Some computer security specialists are as skilled as the hackers but have never chosen to use their skills to go outside the law. Ethical-hacking courses, diploma programs, and degrees are available, allowing computer professionals to acquire the knowledge of a hacker without ever donning the "black hat."

Company officials should think long and hard and consider all the advantages and disadvantages before hiring a hacker just because it's currently the "thing to do." Law enforcement agencies, in most cases, are constrained by their own policies and their state commission rules from hiring people who have been convicted of serious criminal offenses. Many criminal hackers, however, have never been arrested or convicted. Agencies are finally realizing that it's in their interest to recruit people with computer skills. Most of them conduct thorough background investigations that reveal how those people acquired their skills and how they've used them in the past.

Chapter 4

Understanding the Technology

Topics we'll investigate in this chapter:

- **Understanding Computer Hardware**

- **The Language of the Machine**

- **Understanding Computer Operating Systems**

- **Understanding Network Basics**

☑ **Summary**

☑ **Frequently Asked Questions**

Introduction

In Chapter 3, we mentioned that, in addition to traditional investigative skills, a good cybercrime investigator needs a thorough understanding of the technology that is used to commit these crimes. Just as a homicide investigator must know something about basic human pathology to understand the significance of evidence provided by dead bodies—rigor mortis, lividity, blood-spatter patterns, and so forth—a cybercrime investigator needs to know how computers operate so as to recognize and preserve the evidence they offer.

A basic tenet of criminal investigation is that there is no "perfect crime." No matter how careful, a criminal always leaves something of him- or herself at the crime scene and/or takes something away from the scene. These clues can be obvious, or they can be well hidden or very subtle. Even though a cybercriminal usually never physically visits the location where the crime occurs (the destination computer or network), the same rule of thumb as for physical crimes applies: Everyone who accesses a network, a system, or a file leaves a track behind. Technically sophisticated criminals might be able to cover those tracks, just as sophisticated and careful criminals are able to do in the physical world. But in many cases, they don't completely destroy the evidence; they only make the evidence more difficult to find.

For example, a burglar might take care to wipe all fingerprints off everything he's touched while inside a residence, removing the most obvious evidence (and often the evidence that's the most helpful to police) that proves he was there. But if as he does so, tiny bits of fabric from the rag that he uses adhere to some of the surfaces, and if he takes that rag with him and it is later found in his possession, police could still have a way to link him to the crime scene. Likewise, the cybercriminal may take care to delete incriminating files from his hard disk, even going so far as to reformat the disk. It will appear to those who aren't technically savvy that the data is gone, but an investigator who understands how information is stored on disk will realize that evidence could still be on the disk, even though it's not immediately visible (much like latent fingerprints), and will take the proper steps to recover and preserve that evidence.

Information technology (IT) professionals who are reading this book and who already have a good understanding of technology might wonder whether they can skip this chapter. We recommend that they read the chapter. It might be useful for those who anticipate working with law enforcement officers and crime scene technicians to see computer technology from a new perspective: how it can serve as evidence and which technological details are most important to understand from the *investigative* point of view. Most IT professionals are used to looking at computer and networking hardware, software, and protocols in terms of *making things work*. Investigators see these items in terms of what they can reveal that is competent, relevant, and material to the case. A network administrator familiar with the Windows operating system, for example, knows that it can be made to display file modification dates, but he or she might not have considered how crucial this information could be in an investigation. Similarly, a police investigator who is not trained in the technology might realize the importance of the information but not realize that such information is available, because it isn't obvious when the operating system is using default settings. Once again, each side has only half of the pieces to the puzzle. If the two sides work together, the puzzle falls into place that much more quickly.

In this chapter, we provide an overview of how computers process and store information. First we look at the hardware, then we discuss the software (particularly the operating system) on which personal computers run. We will also discuss some basic issues of networks, and introduce you to some of the other devices that may be a source of evidence in an investigation. By introducing you to these technologies, we will be better able to expand on them in later chapters, where we discuss acquiring evidence from them.

Understanding Computer Hardware

It's commonplace for people who operate in the business world or in any administrative or clerical capacity in the public sector to have exposure to computers. The fact that they use computers every day doesn't mean that they understand them, however. This makes sense. Most of us drive cars every day without necessarily knowing anything about mechanics. Even people with enough mechanical aptitude to change their own car's oil and spark plugs might not really understand how an internal combustion engine works. Similarly, we can turn on our televisions and change the channels without really knowing how programs are broadcast over the airwaves or via cable.

Most casual users take it for granted that if they put gas in a car, it takes them where they want to go, and if they pay the cable bill, the show goes on. Even though we don't understand these technologies, they've been around long enough that we're comfortable with them. To "first-generation" users, though, the old Model T Ford must have seemed like quite a mysterious and scary machine, and pictures that somehow invisibly flew through the air and landed inside a little box in people's living rooms seemed nothing short of magic to early TV owners.

We must remember that many of the people using computers today are members of the "first generation" of computer users—people who didn't grow up with computers in every office, much less in almost every home. To them, computers still retain the flavor of something magical, something unexplainable. Some skilled crime investigators fit into this category. Just as effective cybercrime fighting requires that we acquaint IT professionals with the legal process, it also requires that we acquaint law enforcement personnel with computer processing—how the machines work "under the hood."

The first step toward this enlightenment is to open the case and look inside at all the computer's parts and pieces and what they do so that we can understand the role that each plays in creating and retaining electronic evidence.

NOTE

Police colleges and other training opportunities that provide courses on electronic search and seizure or computer forensics may have prerequisites that require a person to understand some of the specifics of how computers function and store information. Having a basic understanding of the topics covered in this chapter will be useful to officers or other individuals who plan to attend such courses.

Looking Inside the Machine

At its most basic level, all a computer really does is crunch numbers. As explained later in this chapter, all data—text, pictures, sounds, programs—must be reduced to numbers for the computer to "understand" it. According to the Merriam-Webster Online Dictionary (www.merriam-webster.com/dictionary/computer), a computer is "a programmable usually electronic device that can store, retrieve, and process data." To a allow a person to enter this data so that it can be processed, saved, and retrieved according to preprogrammed instructions, a combination of different kinds of hardware is required. Although we commonly think of the computer as a box with a keyboard, monitor, and mouse attached to it, it is actually an assembly of different parts.

Regardless of whether it is a tiny handheld model or a big mainframe system, computers consist of the same basic components:

- A control unit

- A processing unit

- A memory unit

- Input/output units

Of course, there must be a way for all these components to communicate with one another. PC architecture is fairly standardized, which makes it easy to interchange parts between different computers. The foundation of the system is a main circuit board, fondly referred to as the *motherboard*.

The Role of the Motherboard

As shown in Figure 4.1, most of the computer's components plug into the main board, and they all communicate via the electronic paths (circuits) that are imprinted into the board. Additional circuit boards can be added via *expansion slots*. The electronic interface between the motherboard and these additional boards, cards, and connectors is called the *bus*. The bus is the pathway on the motherboard that connects the components and allows them to interact with the processor.

The motherboard is the PC's control unit. The motherboard is actually made up of many subcomponents:

- The printed circuit board (PCB) itself, which may be made of several thin layers or a single planar surface onto which the circuitry is affixed

- Voltage regulators, which reduce the 5V signal from the power supply to the voltage needed by the processor (typically 3.3V or less)

- Capacitors that filter the signals

- The integrated chipset that controls the interface between the processor and all the other components

- Controllers for the keyboard and I/O devices (integrated SCSI, onboard sound and video, and so on)

- An erasable programmable read-only memory (EPROM) chip that contains the core software that directly drives the system hardware

- A battery-operated CMOS chip that contains the Basic Input Output System (BIOS) settings and the real-time clock that maintains the time and date

- Sockets and slots for attaching other components (processor, main memory, cache memory, expansion cards, power supply)

■ Ports and/or pins (headers) for connecting cables and devices (serial, parallel [ATA], SATA, USB, IDE, SCSI, IR, IEEE 1394/FireWire) and pin connectors for the case power switch, LED indicators, case speaker, and processor fan

Figure 4.1 Motherboard and Computer Components inside a Computer Case

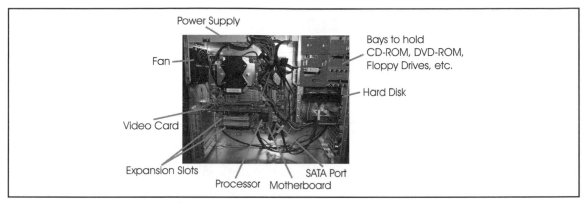

The layout and organization of the components on the motherboard is called its *form factor*. The form factor determines the size and shape of the board and where its integrated ports are located, as well as the type of power supply it is designed to use. The computer case type must match the motherboard form factor or the openings in the back of the case won't line up correctly with the slots and ports on the motherboard. Typical motherboard form factors include:

■ **ATX/mini ATX/microATX** Currently the most popular form factors; all current Intel motherboards are ATX or microATX. Port connectors and PS/2 mouse connectors are built in; access to components is generally more convenient, and the ATX power supply provides better air flow to reduce overheating problems. microATX provides a smaller motherboard size and smaller power supply, and supports AGP high-performance graphics. A subset of the microATX form factor is the FlexATX, which is a flexible form factor that allows various custom designs of the motherboard's shape.

■ **AT/Baby AT** The most common PC motherboard form factor prior to 1997. The power supply connects to the board with two connectors labeled P8 and P9; reversing them can destroy the motherboard.

■ **LPX/Mini LPX** Used by big brand-name computer manufacturers to save space in small cases. This form factor uses a "daughterboard" or riser card that plugs into the main board. Expansion cards then plug into the riser card.

■ **NLX** A modernized and improved version of LPX. This form factor is also used by name-brand vendors.

NOTE

For additional information and specifications of various form factors, you can visit www.formfactors.org.

The Roles of the Processor and Memory

Two of the most important components in a computer are the processor and memory. Let's take a brief look at what these components do.

The Processor

The *processor* (short for *microprocessor*) is an integrated circuit on a single chip that performs the basic computations in a computer. The processor is sometimes called the *CPU* (for *central processing unit*), although many computer users use that term to refer to the PC "box"—the case and its contents—without monitor, keyboard, and other external peripherals.

The processor is the part of the computer that does all the work of processing data. Processors receive input in the form of strings of 1s and 0s (called *binary communication*, which we discuss later in this chapter) and use logic circuits, or formulas, to create output (also in the form of 1s and 0s). This system is implemented via digital switches. In early computers, vacuum tubes were used as switches; they were later replaced by *transistors*, which were much smaller and faster and had no moving parts (making them *solid-state* switches). Transistors were then grouped together to form *integrated circuit* chips, made of materials (particularly silicon) that conduct electricity only under specific conditions (in other words, a *semiconductor*). As more and more transistors were included on a single chip, the chips became increasingly smaller and less expensive to make. In 1971, Intel was the first to use this technology to incorporate several separate logic components into one chip and call it a *microprocessor*.

Processors are able to perform different tasks using programmed instructions. Modern operating systems allow multiple applications to share the processor using a method known as *time slicing*, in which the processor works on data from one application, then switches to the next (and the next and the next) so quickly that it appears to the user as though all the applications are being processed simultaneously. This method is called *multitasking*, and there are a couple of different ways it can be accomplished. Some computers have more than one processor. To take advantage of multiple processors, the computer must run an operating system that supports multiprocessing. We discuss multitasking and multiprocessing in more depth later in this chapter.

The processor chip itself is an ultra-thin piece of silicon crystal, less than a single millimeter in thickness, that has millions of tiny electronic switches (transistors) embedded in it. This embedding is done via *photolithography*, which involves photographing the circuit pattern and chemically etching away the background. The chip is part of a *wafer*, which is a round piece of silicon substrate, on which 16 to 256 individual chips are etched (depending on wafer size). The chips are then *packaged*, which is the process of matching up the tiny connection points on the chip with the pins that will connect the processor to the motherboard socket and encasing the fragile chip in an outer cover.

Before they're packaged, the chips are tested to ensure that they perform their tasks properly and to determine their rated speed. Processor speed is dependent on the production quality, the processor design, the process technology, and the size of the circuit and die. Smaller chips generally can run faster because they generate less heat and use less power. As processor chips have shrunk in size, they've gotten faster. The circuit size of the original 8088 processor chip was 3 microns; modern Pentium chips are 0.25 microns or less. Overheating decreases performance, and the more power is used, the hotter the chip gets. For this reason, new processors run at lower voltages than older ones. They also are designed as dual voltage chips, in which the *core voltage* (the internal voltage) is lower than the *I/O voltage* (the external voltage). The same motherboard can support processors that use different voltages, because they have voltage regulators that convert the power supply voltage to the voltage needed by the processor that is installed.

Even running at lower voltages, modern high-speed processors get very hot. Heat sinks and processor fans help keep the temperature down. A practice popular with hackers and hardware aficionados—called *overclocking* (setting the processor to run faster than its rating)—causes processors to overheat easily. Elaborate—and expensive—water-cooling systems and Peltier coolers that work like tiny solid-state air conditioners are available to address this problem.

The System Memory

The term *memory* refers to a chip on which data is stored. Some novice computer users might confuse the terms *disk space* and *memory*; thus, you hear the question, "How much memory do I have left on my hard drive?" In one sense, the disk does indeed "remember" data. However, the term *memory* is more accurately used to describe a chip that stores data temporarily and is most commonly used to refer to the *system memory* or *random access memory (RAM)* that stores the instructions with which the processor is currently working and the data is currently being processed. Memory chips of various types are used in other parts of the computer; there's cache memory, video memory, and so on. It is called *random access* memory because data can be read from any location in memory, in any order.

The amount of RAM installed in your computer affects how many programs can run simultaneously and the speed of the computer's performance. Memory is a common system *bottleneck* (that is, the slowest component in the system that causes other components to work at less than their potential performance speed). The data that is stored in RAM, unlike data stored on disks or in some other types of memory, is *volatile*. That means the data is lost when the system is shut down or the power is lost.

Each RAM chip has a large number of memory *addresses* or *cells*, organized in rows and columns. A single chip can have millions of cells. Dynamic random access memory (DRAM) pairs a transistor and capacitor together to create a memory cell, which represents a single bit of data. Each address holds a specified number of bits of data. Multiple chips are combined on a *memory module*, which is a small circuit board that you insert in a memory slot on the computer's motherboard. The memory controller, which is part of the motherboard chipset, is the "traffic cop" that controls which memory chip is written to or read at a given time. How does the data get from the memory to the processor? It takes the bus—the memory bus (or data bus), that is. As mentioned earlier, a *bus* is a channel that carries the electronic signals representing the data within the PC from one component to another.

RAM can be both read and written. Computers use another type of memory, *read-only memory (ROM)*, for storing important programs that need to be permanently available. A special type of ROM mentioned earlier, erasable programmable ROM (EPROM), is used in situations in which you might need to occasionally, but not often, change the data. A common function of EPROM (or EEPROM, which is *electrically erasable PROM*) is to store "flashable" BIOS programs, which generally stay the same but might need to be updated occasionally. Technically, EPROM is not "read-only" 100 percent of the time, because it can be erased and rewritten, but most of the time it is only read, not written. The data stored in ROM (including EPROM) is *not* lost when the system is shut down.

Yet another type of memory used in PCs is *cache memory*. Cache memory is much faster than RAM but also much more expensive, so there is less of it. Cache memory holds recently accessed data. The cache is arranged in layers between the RAM and the processor. Primary, or Level 1 (L1), cache is fastest; when the processor needs a particular piece of data, the cache controller looks for it first in L1 cache. If it's not there, the controller moves on to the secondary, or L2, cache. If the controller still doesn't find the data, the controller looks to RAM for it. At this writing, L1 cache memory costs approximately 100 times as much as normal RAM or SDRAM, whereas L2 cache memory costs four to eight times the price of the most expensive available RAM. Cache speeds processing considerably because statistically, the data that is most recently used is likely to be needed again. Getting it from the faster cache memory instead of the slower RAM increases overall performance.

NOTE

There are other types of cache in addition to the processor's cache memory. For example, Web browsers create a cache on the hard disk where they store recently accessed Web pages, so if those same pages are requested again, the browser can access them from the local hard disk. This system is faster than going out over the Internet to download the same pages again. The word *cache* (pronounced "cash") originally meant "a secret page where things are stored," and appropriately, the Web cache can provide a treasure trove of information that might be useful to investigators, as we discuss in Chapter 15.

Cache memory uses static RAM (SRAM) instead of the dynamic RAM (DRAM) that is used for system memory. The difference is that SRAM doesn't require a periodic refresh to hold the data that is stored there, as DRAM does. This makes SRAM faster. Like DRAM, though, SRAM loses its data when the computer's power is turned off.

Storage Media

The term *storage media* is usually used to refer to a means of storing data permanently, and numerous media types can be used to store data more or less permanently, including those storing data magnetically or using optical disks. In this section, we'll look at a number of different digital media devices, as well as the most common method of storing data: hard disks.

Hard Disks

Hard disks are nonvolatile storage devices that are used to store and retrieve data quickly. *Nonvolatile storage* is physical media that retains data without electrical power. This means that no data is lost when the computer is powered off, making hard disks suitable for permanent storage of information. As we'll discuss in the sections that follow, hard disk drives write the digital data as magnetic patterns to rigid disks that are stored inside the hard disk drive (HDD). Because the HDD is installed in the computer, it is able to access and process the data faster than removable media such as floppy disks.

Although hard disks have been used for decades in computers, the use of them has expanded to other forms of technology. Today, you can find camcorders, game systems, and Digital Video Recorders that use hard disks to store data instead of magnetic tapes or other media. Regardless of their use, the hard disks and their related file systems all perform the same tasks of storing data so that it can be retrieved, processed, and viewed at a later time.

Overview of a Hard Disk

Although removable hard disks exist, most HDDs are designed for installation inside a computer, and for that reason were referred to as *fixed disks*. To avoid custom or proprietary hard disks needing to be purchased to fit inside different brands of computer, standards were developed early in the personal computer's history. These standards dictate the size and shape of the hard disk, as well as the interfaces used to attach them to the computer. As we saw when discussing motherboards, these standards are called form factors, and they refer to the physical external dimensions of the disk drive. The most common form factors that have been used over the past few decades are:

- 5.25-inch, which were the first hard drives that were used on PCs and were commonly installed in machines during the 1980s

- 3.5-inch, which is the common size form factor used in modern PCs

- 2.5-inch, which is the common size form factor used in laptop/notebook computers

NOTE

The two most common sizes of hard disk are the 2.5-inch form factor (used for laptops) and the 3.5-inch form factor (used for PCs). Although the numbers are generally associated with the width of the drive's platter (or sometimes the drive itself), this isn't necessarily the case. The 3.5-inch drives are generally 4 inches wide and use a platter that's 3.74 inches in width. They're called 3.5-inch form factor drives because they fit in the bay for a 3.5-inch floppy drive. Similarly, the obsolete 5.25-inch form factor was named as such because it fit in the 5.25-Inch floppy drive bay.

The 5.25-inch disk drive is obsolete, although you may still find some in legacy machines. The first of these drives appeared on the market in 1980, but were succeeded in 1983 when the 3.5-inch drives appeared. When these became available, they were either mounted into the computer case's 3.5-inch floppy drive bays, or screwed into frames that allowed the 3.5-inch form factor to fit into the larger 5.25-inch bays.

Even though the 3.5-inch form factor has been around for more than two decades, it continues to be the common size used in modern desktop computers. The other most popular form factor is the 2.5-inch disk, which is used in laptop computers. Figure 4.2 shows a 3.5-inch form factor hard disk on the left, and a 2.5-inch form factor drive on the right. When comparing the two, you can immediately see the difference in size between them, and see that both encase the internal mechanisms of the disk drive inside a sturdy metal case. This is to prevent dust and other foreign elements from coming into contact with the internal components, which (as we'll see later) would cause the disk to cease functioning.

Figure 4.2 Hard Disks

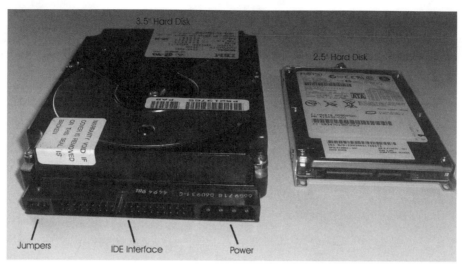

In looking at the 3.5-inch hard disk depicted on the left of Figure 4.2, you will see that the HDD has several connections that allow it to be installed in a computer. The 2.5-inch hard disk doesn't have these same components because it is installed differently in a laptop; a cover is removed from the laptop (generally on the back of the computer), where the 2.5-inch HDD is inserted into a slot. The 3.5-inch HDD needs to be installed in the computer using several different components outside the HDD:

- Jumpers
- Hard disk interface
- Power connector

Jumpers are a connector that works as an on/off switch for the hard disk. A small piece of plastic with metal connectors inside is placed over two of the metal pins to create an electrical circuit. The existence of the circuit lets the computer know whether the hard disk is configured in one of the following two roles:

- **Master** The primary hard disk that is installed on a computer. The master is the first hard disk that the computer will attempt to access when booting up (that is, starting), and it generally contains the operating system that will be loaded. If only one hard disk is installed on a machine, that hard disk is the master drive.

- **Slave** The secondary hard disk that is installed on a computer. Slave drives are generally used for additional data storage, and as a location where additional software is installed.

NOTE

The terms *master* and *slave* for hard disks have undergone some criticism in recent years, due to the political incorrectness of the terms. In reading material related to a hard disk's roles, you may see them referred to as *primary* and *secondary* hard disks instead.

The *power connector* on a hard disk used to plug the hard disk into the computer's power supply. A power cable running from the power supply is attached to the hard disk, allowing it to receive power when the computer is started.

The *hard disk interface* is used to attach the hard disk to the computer so that data can be accessed from the HDD. Although we'll discuss hard disk interfaces in greater detail later in this chapter, the one shown in Figure 4.2 is an IDE hard disk interface, which is one of the most popular interfaces used on HDDs. A thin, flat cable containing parallel wires called a *ribbon cable* is inserted into the interface on the HDD, while the other end of the ribbon cable is plugged into the disk drive controller. As a result of this configuration, the computer can communicate with the HDD and access its data.

On the Scene

The Evolution of Hard Disks

The hard disk is usually the primary permanent storage medium in a PC. However, the earliest PCs didn't have hard disks. In fact, early computers (prior to the PC) didn't have any sort of data storage medium. You had to type in every program that you wanted to run, each time you ran it. Later, punched cards or tape was used to store programs and data. The next advancement in technology brought us magnetic tape storage; large mainframes used big reels of tape, whereas early microcomputers used audiocassette tapes to store programs and data. By the time the IBM PC and its clones appeared, computers were using floppy disks (the 5.25-inch type that really was floppy). More expensive models had two floppy drives (which we'll discuss later in this chapter), one for loading programs and a second for saving data—but still no hard disk.

The first hard disks that came with PCs provided 5 megabytes (MB) of storage space—a huge amount, compared to floppies. The IBM PC XT came with a gigantic 10MB hard disk. Today's hard disks are generally measured in hundreds of gigabytes (GB), at prices far lower than those first comparatively tiny disks, with arrays of them measured in terabytes (TB). Despite the fact that they're much bigger, much faster, less fragile, and more reliable, the hard disks of today are designed basically the same way as those of years ago.

Disk Platter

Although there are a number of external elements to a hard disk, the major components are inside the HDD. As shown in Figure 4.3, hard disks comprise from one to several platters, which are flat, round disks that are mounted inside the disk. The platters are stacked one on top of another on a spindle that runs through a hole in the middle of each platter, like LPs on an old-time record player. A motor is attached to the spindle that rotates the platters, which are made of some rigid material (often aluminum alloy, glass, or a glass composite) and are coated with a magnetic substance. Electromagnetic heads write information onto the disks in the form of magnetic impulses and read the recorded information from them.

Figure 4.3 Inside Components of a Hard Disk

Data can be written to both sides of each platter. The information is recorded in tracks, which are concentric circles in which the data is written. The tracks are divided into sectors (smaller units). Thus, a particular bit of data resides in a specific sector of a specific track on a specific platter. Later in this chapter, when we discuss computer operating systems and file systems, you will see how the data is organized so that users can locate it on the disk.

The spindles of a hard disk spin the platters at high speeds, with the spindles on most IDE hard disks spinning platters at thousands of revolutions per minute (rpm). The read/write head moves over the platter and reads or writes data to the platter. When there is more than one platter in the hard disk, each platter usually has a read/write head on each of its sides. Smaller platter sizes do more than save space inside the computer; they also improve disk performance (seek time) because the heads don't have to move as far.

To read and write the magnetic information on the hard disk, the read/write head of the HDD is positioned incredibly close to the platter. It floats less than 0.1 micron over the surface of the platter.

A *micron* (or *micrometer*) is one one-millionth of a meter, meaning that the read/write is less than one-tenth of one one-millionth of a meter from the platter's surface. To illustrate this, Figure 4.4 compares the sizes of a read/write head and the sizes of an average dust particle (which is 2.5 microns) and an average human hair (which is 50 microns). In looking at the differences in size, it is easy to see how a simple piece of dust or hair on a platter could cause the hard disk to crash, and why the internal components are sealed inside the hard disk assembly.

Figure 4.4 Comparison of Objects to a Read/Write Head's Distance from the Platter

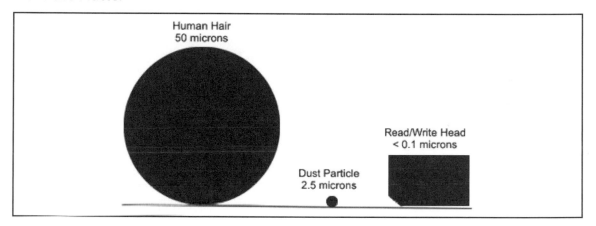

On the Scene

Hard Disk Sizes

IBM introduced its first hard disk in 1956, but the real "grandfather" of today's hard disks was the Winchester drive, which wasn't introduced until the 1970s. The standard physical size of disks at that time was 14 inches (the size of the platters that are stacked to make up the disk). In 1979, IBM made an 8-inch disk, and Seagate followed that in 1980 with the first 5.25-inch hard disk, which was used in early PCs. Three years later, disks got even smaller; the 3.5-inch disk was introduced. This became a standard for PCs. Much smaller disks (2.5 inches) were later developed for use in laptop and notebook computers. The IBM "microdrive" shrunk the diameter of the platter to 1 inch, connecting to a laptop computer via a PC Card (also called PCMCIA, for the Personal Computer Memory Card International Association that created the standard).

Tracks

While the platters in a hard disk spin, the read/write head moves into a position on the platter where it can read data. The part of the platter passing under the read/write head is called a track. *Tracks* are concentric circles on the disk where data is saved on the magnetic surface of the platter. These thin concentric rings or bands are shown in Figure 4.5, and although a full number of tracks aren't shown in this figure, a single 3.5-inch hard disk can have thousands of tracks. The tracks hold data, and pass beneath the stationary read/write head as the platter rotates.

Figure 4.5 Tracks on a Hard Disk

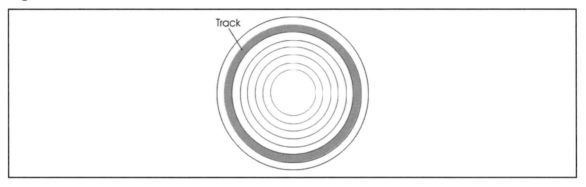

Tracks and sectors (which we'll discuss in the next section) are physically defined through the process of low-level formatting (LLF), which designates where the tracks and sectors are located on each disk. Although in the 1980s people would perform an LLF on their hard disk themselves, typically this is done at the factory where the hard disk is made. It is necessary for the tracks and sectors to be present so that the areas where data is written to are visible to the disk controller, and the operating system can perform a high-level format and generate the file structure.

Because there are so many tracks on a platter, they are numbered so that the computer can reference the correct one when reading and writing data. The tracks are numbered from zero to the highest numbered track (which is typically 1,023), starting from the outermost edge of the disk to the track nearest the center of the platter. In other words, the first track on the disk is the track on the outer edge of the platter, and the highest numbered disk is close to the center.

NOTE

Although we discuss tracks and sectors on hard disks here, other media also use these methods of formatting the surface of a disk to store data. For example, a 1.44MB floppy disk has 160 tracks.

Sectors

Sectors are segments of a track, and are the smallest physical storage unit on a disk. As mentioned, the hard disk comprises predefined tracks that form concentric rings on the disk. As seen in Figure 4.6, the disk is further organized by dividing the platter into pie slices, which also divide the tracks into smaller segments. These segments are called sectors, and are typically 512 bytes (0.5KB) in size. By knowing the track number and particular sector in which a piece of data is stored, a computer is able to locate where data is physically stored on the disk.

Figure 4.6 Sectors on a Hard Disk

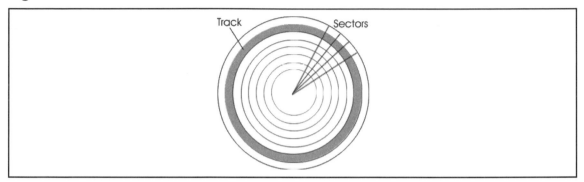

Just as tracks on a hard disk are numbered, an addressing scheme is also associated with sectors. When a low-level format is performed at the factory, a number is assigned to the sector by writing a number immediately before the sector's contents. This number in this header identifies the sector address, so it can be located on the disk.

Bad Sectors

At times, areas of a hard disk can be damaged, making them unusable. Bad sectors are sectors of a hard disk that cannot store data due to a manufacturing defect or accidental damage. When sectors become unusable, it only means that those areas of the disk cannot be used, not the entire disk itself. When you consider that an average 3.5-inch disk will have more than 1,000 tracks that are further segmented into millions of sectors, it isn't surprising that over the lifetime of a disk, a few sectors will eventually go bad.

Because bad sectors mean that damage has occurred at the surface of the disk, it cannot be repaired, and any data stored in that area of the hard disk is lost. It can, however, be marked as bad so that the operating system or other software doesn't write to this area again. To check and mark sectors as being unusable, special utilities are used. Programs such as Scandisk and Checkdisk (CHKDSK in DOS 8.3 notation) have been available under versions of Windows, and badblocks is a tool used on Linux systems. Each can detect a sector that has been damaged and mark it as bad.

Disk Partitions

Before a hard disk can be formatted to use a particular file system (which we'll discuss later in this chapter), the HDD needs to be partitioned. A partition is a logical division of the hard disk, allowing a single hard disk to function as though it were one or more hard disks on the computer. Even if different partitions aren't used, and the entire disk is set up as a single partition, a partition must be set so that the operating system knows the disk is going to be used in its entirety. Once a partition is set, it can be given a drive letter (such as C:, D:, and so on) and formatted to use a file system. When an area of the hard disk is formatted and issued a drive letter, it is referred to as a *volume*.

If more than one partition is set, multiple file systems supported by the operating system can be used on a single HDD. For example, on one volume of a Windows computer, you could have C: formatted as a FAT32 file system and D: formatted as a New Technology File System (NTFS). This allows you to use features unique to different file systems on the same computer.

On computers running Linux, DOS, or Windows operating systems, you can use different kinds of partitions. The two types of partitions are:

- Primary partition
- Extended partition

A *primary partition* is a partition on which you can install an operating system. A primary partition with an operating system installed on it is used when the computer starts to load the OS. Although a primary partition can exist without an operating system, on older Windows and DOS operating systems, the first partition installed had to be a primary partition. Modern versions of Windows allow up to four primary, or three primary and one extended partition (which we'll discuss next) on a single disk.

An *extended partition* is a partition that can be divided into additional logical drives. Unlike a primary partition, you don't need to assign it a drive letter and install a file system. Instead, you can use the operating system to create an additional number of logical drives within the extended partition. Each logical drive has its own drive letter and appears as a separate drive. Your only limitations to how many logical drives you create are the amount of free space available on the extended partition and the number of available drive letters you have left on your system.

System and Boot Partitions

When a partition is created, it can be designated as the boot partition, system partition, or both. A *system partition* stores files that are used to boot (start) the computer. These are used whenever a computer is powered on (cold boot) or restarted from within the operating system (warm boot). A *boot partition* is a volume of the computer that contains the system files used to start the operating system. Once the boot files on the system partition have been accessed and have started the computer, the system files on the boot partition are accessed to start the operating system. The *system partition* is where the operating system is installed. The system and boot partitions can exist as separate partitions on the same computer, or on separate volumes.

NOTE

Don't get too confused about the purposes of the boot and system partitions. The names are self-explanatory if you reverse their actual purposes. Remember that the system partition is used to store boot files, and the boot partition is used to store system files (that is, the operating system). On many machines, both of these are on the same volume of the computer.

Boot Sectors and the Master Boot Record

Although many sectors may exist on an HDD, the first sector (sector 0) on a hard disk is always the *boot sector*. This sector contains codes that the computer uses to start the machine. The boot sector is also referred to as the *Master Boot Record* (MBR). The MBR contains a partition table, which stores information on which primary partitions have be created on the hard disk so that it can then use this information to start the machine. By using the partition table in the MBR, the computer can understand how the hard disk is organized before actually starting the operating system that will interact with it. Once it determines how partitions are set up on the machine, it can then provide this information to the operating system.

NOTE

At times, you'll hear about boot viruses that infect your computer when it's started, which is why users have been warned never to leave a floppy disk or other media in a bootable drive when starting a machine. Because the MBR briefly has control of the computer when it starts, a boot virus will attempt to infect the boot sector to infect the machine immediately after it's started, and before any antivirus (AV) software is started.

NTFS Partition Boot Sector

One of the many file systems we'll discuss later in this chapter is NTFS, which is used on many computers running Windows. Because NTFS uses a Master File Table (MFT) that's used to store important information about the file system, information on the location of the MFT and MFT mirror file is stored in the boot sector. To prevent this information from being lost, a duplicate of the boot sector is stored at the disk's logical center, allowing it to be recovered if the original information in the boot sector was corrupted.

Clusters

Clusters are groups of two or more consecutive sectors on a hard disk, and they are the smallest amount of disk space that can be allocated to store a file. As we've mentioned, a sector is typically 512 bytes in size, but data saved to a hard disk is generally larger than this. As such, more than one sector is required to save the data to the disk. To access the data quickly, the computer will attempt to keep this data together by writing the data to a contiguous series of sectors on the disk. In doing so, the read/write head can access the data on a single track of the hard disk. As such, the head doesn't need to move from track to track, increasing the time it takes to read and write data.

Unlike tracks and sectors of the hard disk, clusters are logical units of file storage. Clusters are managed by the operating system, which assigns a unique number to each cluster so that it can keep track of files according to the clusters they use. Although the computer will try to store files in contiguous clusters on the disk, this isn't always possible, and so data belonging to a single file may be split across the disk in different clusters. This is invisible to the user of the computer, who will open the file without any knowledge of whether the data is stored in clusters that are scattered across various areas of the disk.

Cluster Size

Because clusters are controlled by the operating system, the size of the cluster is determined by a number of factors, including the file system being used. When a disk is formatted, the option may exist to specify the size of the cluster being used. For example, in Windows XP, right-clicking on a drive in Windows Explorer displays a context menu that provides a **Format** menu item. When you click on this menu item the screen shown in Figure 4.7 is displayed. As shown in this figure, the dialog box provides the ability to choose the file system in which the disk will be formatted, and it provides a drop-down list called **Allocation unit size**. This drop-down list is where you choose what size clusters will be created when the disk is formatted.

Figure 4.7 Specifying Cluster Size When Formatting a Disk

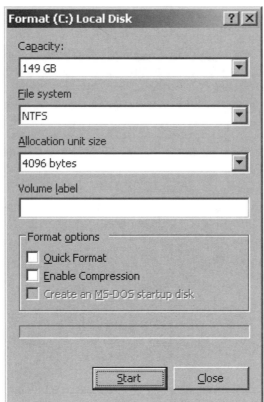

The dialog box in Figure 4.7 provides options to allocate clusters in sizes of 512 bytes, 1,024 bytes, 2,048 bytes, and 4,096 bytes. If a cluster size isn't specified, Windows will use the other option to use a default allocation size. On computers running Windows 2003 Server, the default cluster sizes are those shown in Table 4.1.

Table 4.1 Cluster Sizes on Windows 2003 Server

Volume Size	FAT	FAT32	NTFS
7MB – 16MB	2KB	Not supported	512 bytes
17MB – 32MB	512 bytes	Not supported	512 bytes
33MB – 64MB	1KB	512 bytes	512 bytes
65MB – 128MB	2KB	1KB	512 bytes
129MB – 256MB	4KB	2KB	512 bytes
257MB – 512MB	8KB	4KB	512 bytes
513MB – 1,024MB	16KB	4KB	1KB
1,025MB – 2GB	32KB	4KB	2KB
2GB – 4GB	64KB	4KB	4KB
4GB – 8GB	Not supported	4KB	4KB
8GB – 16GB	Not supported	8KB	4KB
16GB – 32GB	Not supported	16KB	4KB
32GB – 2TB	Not supported	Not supported	4KB

Slack Space

Because clusters are a fixed size, the data stored in a cluster will use the entire space, regardless of whether it needs the entire cluster. For example, if you allocated a cluster size of 4,096 bytes, and saved a 10-byte file to the disk, the entire 4KB cluster would be used even though 4,086 bytes of space are wasted. This wasted space is called *slack space* or *file slack*. Slack space is the area of space between the end of a file and the end of the last cluster used by that data.

Because an operating system will track where a file is located using the clusters used to store the data, clusters will always be used and potential storage space will always be wasted. Essentially, slack space is the same as pouring a bottle of cola into a series of glasses. As the bottle is emptied, the first glasses are filled to the top, but the final glass will be only partially filled. Because the glass has already been used, it can't be filled with something else as well. In the same way, once a cluster has been allocated to store a file, it can't be used to store data associated with other files.

Because extra space must be allocated to hold a file, it is better that the sizes of the clusters are lower. When clusters are smaller, the amount of space in the final cluster used to store a file will have less space that is unused. Smaller clusters will limit the amount of wasted space and will utilize disk space more effectively.

On any system, there will always be a certain amount of disk space that's wasted. You can calculate the amount of wasted space using the following formula:

(Cluster size/2)∗number of files

Although this formula isn't exact, it does give an estimate of how much disk space is wasted on a particular hard disk. The number of files includes the number of directories, and this amount is multiplied by half of the allocated cluster size. Therefore, if you had a cluster size of 2,048 bytes, you would divide this in half to make it 1,024 bytes (or 1KB). If there were 10,000 files on the hard disk, this would be multiplied by 1KB, making the amount of wasted space 10MB; that is, (2,048/2) * 10,000 = 10,000KB or 10MB.

Any tool used to acquire and analyze data on a hard disk should also examine the slack space. When a file is deleted from the disk, data will continue to reside in the unallocated disk space. Even if parts of the file are overwritten on the disk, data may be acquired from the slack space that could be crucial to your investigation.

Lost Clusters

As we mentioned, each cluster is given a unique number, and the operating system uses these to keep track of which files are stored in particular clusters on the hard disk. When you consider the thousands of files stored on a hard disk, and that each may be assigned to one or more clusters, it isn't surprising that occasionally a cluster gets mismarked. From time to time, an operating system will mark a cluster as being used, even though it hasn't been assigned to a file. This is known as a *lost cluster*.

Lost clusters are also known as *lost allocation units* or *lost file fragments*. In UNIX or Linux machines that refer to clusters as *blocks*, they are referred to as *lost blocks* or *orphans*. According to the operating system, these clusters don't belong to any particular file. They generally result from improperly shutting down the computer, loss of power, shutting down the computer without closing applications first, files not being closed properly, or ejecting removable storage such as floppy disks while the drive is reading or writing to the media. When these things occur, data in the cache may have been assigned a cluster, but it was never written because the machine lost power or shut down unexpectedly. Even though the cluster isn't actually used by a file, it isn't listed as being free to use by the operating system.

Although lost clusters are generally empty, such as when a cluster is allocated to a program but never released, lost clusters may contain data. If the system was incorrectly shut down (or some other activity occurred), the cluster may have had data written to it before the event occurred. This data may be a fragment of the file or other corrupted data.

Just as bad sectors can be marked as unusable using programs such as Scandisk or Checkdisk, these same programs can be used to identify lost clusters. These tools will find lost clusters, and can recover data that may have been stored in the cluster. The data is stored as files named *file####.chk*, and although most of the time they are empty and can be deleted, viewing the contents using Notepad or other tools to view text may reveal missing data that is important. In UNIX, you can use another program called Filesystem Check (fsck) to identify and fix orphans. With this tool, the lost blocks of data are saved in a directory called *lost+found*. If the data contained in these files doesn't have any useful information, it can simply be deleted. In doing so, the lost cluster is reassigned and disk space is freed up.

Disk Capacity

Disk capacity is the amount of data that a hard disk is capable of holding. The capacity is measured in bytes, which is 7 or 8 bits (depending on whether error correction is used). *Bit* is short for *binary digit*, and it is the smallest unit of measurement for data. It can have a value of 1 or 0, which respectively indicates on or off. A bit is abbreviated as *b*, whereas a byte is abbreviated as *B*. Because bits and bytes are incredibly small measurements of data, and the capacity of an HDD or other media is considerably larger, capacity is measured in increments of these values.

A *kilobyte* is abbreviated as KB, and although you might expect this to equal 1,000 bytes, it actually equals 1,024 bytes. This is because a kilobyte is calculated using binary (base 2) math instead of decimal (base 10) math. Because computers use this function to calculate the number of bytes used, a kilobyte is calculated as 2^{10} or 1,024. These values increase proportionally, but to make it easier for laypeople to understand, the terms associated with the number of bytes are incremented by thousands, millions, and larger amounts of bytes. The various units used to describe the capacity of disks are as follows:

- Kilobyte (KB), which is actually 1,024 bytes

- Megabyte (MB), which is 1,024KB or 1,048,576 bytes

- Gigabyte (GB), which is 1,024MB or 1,073,741,824 bytes

- Terabyte (TB), which is 1,024GB or 1,099,511,627,776 bytes

- Petabyte (PB), which is 1,024TB or 1,125,899,906,842,624 bytes

- Exabyte (EB), which is 1,024PB or 1,152,921,504,606,846,976 bytes

- Zettabyte (ZB), which is 1,024EB or 1,180,591,620,717,411,303,424 bytes

- Yottabyte (YB), which is 1,024 ZB or 1,208,925,819,614,629,174,706,176 bytes

To put these monumental sizes in terms that are fathomable, consider that a single terabyte can hold roughly the equivalent of 1,610 CDs of data, or approximately the same amount of data stored in all the books of a large library.

Hard Disk Interfaces

The *hard disk interface* is one of several standard technologies used to connect the hard disk to the computer so that the machine can then access data stored on the hard disk. The interface used by an HDD serves as a communication channel, allowing data to flow between the computer and the HDD. Over the years, a number of different interfaces have been developed, allowing the hard disk to be connected to a disk controller that's usually mounted directly on the computer's motherboard. The most common hard disk interfaces include:

- IDE/EIDE/ATA

- SATA

- SCSI

- USB

- Fibre Channel

IDE/EIDE/ATA

IDE is an acronym for Integrated Drive Electronics, and *EIDE* is an acronym for Enhanced IDE. Integrated Drive Electronics is so named because the disk controller is built into, or integrated with, the disk drive's logic board. It is also referred to as Advanced Technology Attachment (ATA), a standard of the American National Standards Institute (ANSI). Almost all modern PC motherboards include two EIDE connectors. Up to two ATA devices (hard disks or CD-ROM drives) can be connected to each connector, in a master/slave configuration. One drive functions as the "master," which responds first to probes or signals on the interrupt (a signal from a device or program to the operating system that causes the OS to stop briefly to determine what task to do next) that is shared with the other, "slave" drive that shares the same cable. User-configurable settings on the drives determine which will act as master and which as slave. Most drives have three settings: master, slave, and cable-controlled. If the latter is selected for both drives, the first drive in the chain will be the master drive.

SATA

SATA is an acronym for Serial Advanced Technology Attachment, and is the next generation that will probably replace ATA. It provides high data transfer rates between the motherboard and storage device, and uses thinner cables that can be used to hot-swap devices (plug in or unplug the devices while they're still operating). The ability to hot-swap devices has made SATA a possible successor to USB connections used with such things as external hard disks, which can be plugged into the computer to provide large removable storage or data.

SCSI

SCSI (pronounced "skuzzy") is an acronym for Small Computer System Interface. SCSI is another ANSI standard that provides faster data transfer than IDE/EIDE. Some motherboards have SCSI connectors and controllers built in; for those that don't, you can add SCSI disks by installing a SCSI controller card in one of the expansion slots. There are a number of different versions of SCSI; later forms provide faster transfer rates and other improvements. Devices can be "chained" on a SCSI bus, each with a different SCSI ID number. Depending on the SCSI version, either eight or 16 SCSI IDs can be attached to one controller (with the controller using one ID, thus allowing seven or 15 SCSI peripherals).

USB

USB is an acronym for Universal Serial Bus. As we'll discuss later in this chapter, USB is used for a variety of different peripherals, including keyboards, mice, and other devices that previously required serial and parallel ports, as well as newer technologies such as digital cameras and digital audio devices. Because USB uses a bus topology, the devices can be daisy-chained together or connected to a USB hub, allowing up to 127 devices to be connected to the computer at one time.

In addition to peripherals, USB provides an interface for external hard disks. Hard disks can be mounted in cases that provide a USB connection that plugs into a USB port on the computer. Once plugged into the port, the computer then detects the device and installs it, allowing you to access any data on the external hard disk. The current standard for USB is USB 2.0, which is backward compatible to earlier 1.0 and 1.1 standards, and supports bandwidths of 1.5Mbps (megabits per second), 12.5Mbps, and 480Mbps. Using an external USB hard disk that supports USB 2.0 provides a fast exchange of data between the computer and the HDD.

Fibre Channel

Fibre Channel is another ANSI standard that provides fast data transfer, and uses optical fiber to connect devices. Several different standards apply to fiber channels, but the one that primarily applies to storage is Fibre Channel Arbitrated Loop (FC-AL). FC-AL is designed for mass storage devices, and is used for storage area networks (SANs). A SAN is a network architecture in which computers attach to remote storage devices such as optical jukeboxes, disk arrays, tape libraries, and other mass storage devices. Because optical fiber is used to connect devices, FC-AL supports transfer rates of 100Mbps, and is expected to replace SCSI for network storage systems.

On the Scene

Hard Disk Sizes

There *are* ways to completely erase the data on a disk, but the average user (and the average cybercriminal) will not usually take these measures. Software programs that "zero out" the disk do so by overwriting all the 1s and 0s that make up the data on the disk, replacing them with 0s. These programs are often called "wiping" programs. Some of these programs make several passes, overwriting what was already overwritten in the previous pass, for added security. However, in some cases, the data tracks on the disk are wider than the data stream that is written on them. This means that some of the original data might still be visible and recoverable with sophisticated techniques.

A strong magnet can also erase or scramble the data on magnetic media. This process is called *degaussing*. It generally makes the disk unusable without restoring the factory-installed timing tracks. The platters might have to be disassembled to completely erase all the data on all of them, but equipment is available that will degauss all the platters while they remain intact.

In very high-security environments such as sensitive government operations, disks that have contained classified information are usually physically destroyed (pulverized, incinerated, or exposed to an abrasive or acid) to prevent recovery of the data.

Digital Media Devices

Although to this point we've focused on the most common method of storing data, it is important to realize there are other data storage methods besides hard disks. There are several popular types of removable media, so called because the disk itself is separate from the drive, the device that reads and writes to it. There are also devices that attach to a computer through a port, allowing data to be transferred between the machine and storage device. In the sections that follow, we'll look at a number of different digital media devices, including:

- Magnetic tape
- Floppy disk
- CDs and DVDs
- HD-DVD and Blu-ray

- iPod and Zune
- Flash memory
- USB

Magnetic Tape

In the early days of computing, magnetic tapes were one of the few methods used to store data. *Magnetic tapes* consist of a thin plastic strip that has a magnetic coating, on which data can be stored. Early systems throughout the 1950s to the 1970s used magnetic tape on 10.5-inch tape, whereas home computers in the early 1980s used audiocassette tapes for storing programs and data. Today, magnetic tape is still commonly used to back up data on network servers and individual computers.

Magnetic tape is a relatively inexpensive form of removable storage, especially for backing up data. It is less useful for data that needs to be accessed frequently, because it is a sequential access medium. You have to move back and forth through the tape to locate the particular data you want. In other words, to get from file 1 to file 20, you have to go through files 2 through 19. This is in contrast to direct access media such as disks, in which the heads can be moved directly to the location of the data you want to access without progressing in sequence through all the other files.

Floppy Disks

In the early days of personal computing, floppy disks were large (first 8 inches, then 5.25 inches in diameter), thin, and flexible. Today's "floppies," often and more accurately called diskettes, are smaller (3.5 inches), rigid, and less fragile. The disk inside the diskette housing is plastic and is coated with magnetic material. The drive into which you insert the diskette contains a motor to rotate the diskette so that the drive heads, made of tiny electromagnets, can read and write to different locations on the diskette. Standard diskettes today hold 1.44MB of data; SuperDisk technology (developed by Imation Corporation) provides for storing either 120MB or 240MB on diskettes of the same size. Although diskettes are still used, larger file sizes have created the need for removable media that store greater amounts of data.

Compact Discs and DVDs

CDs and DVDs are rigid disks a little less than 5 inches in diameter, made of hard plastic with a thin layer of coating. CDs and DVDs are called *optical media* because CD and DVD drives use a laser beam, along with an optoelectronic sensor, to write to and read the data that is "burned" into the coating material (a compound that changes from reflective to nonreflective when heated by the laser). The data is encoded in the form of incredibly tiny pits or bumps on the surface of the disc. CDs and DVDs work similarly, but the latter can store more data because the pits and tracks are smaller, because DVDs use a more efficient error correction method (that uses less space), and because DVDs can have two layers of storage on each side instead of just one.

CDs

The term *CD* originates from "Compact Disc" under which audio discs were marketed. Philips and Sony still hold the trademark to this name. Several different types of CDs have been developed over the years, with the first being CD Audio or Compact Disc Digital Audio (CDDA).

CD Audio discs are the first CDs that were used to record audio discs. Little has changed in CD physics since the origin of CD Audio discs in 1980. This is due in part to the desire to maintain physical compatibility with an established base of installed units, and because the structure of CD media was both groundbreaking and nearly ideal for this function.

CD-ROM

Until 1985, CDs were used only for audio. Then Philips and Sony introduced the CD-ROM standard. CD-ROM is an acronym for Compact Disc – Read Only Memory, and it refers to any data CD. However, the term has grown to refer to the CD-ROM drive used to read this optical storage medium. For example, when you buy software, the disc used to install the program is called an installation CD. Such a disc is capable of holding up to 700MB of data, and remains a common method of storing data.

DVDs

Originally, *DVD* was an acronym for *Digital Video Disc* and then later *Digital Versatile Disc*. Today it is generally agreed that DVD is not an acronym for anything. However, although these discs were originally meant to store video, they have become a common method of storing data. In fact, DVD-ROM drives are not only able to copy (rip) or create (burn) data on DVD discs, but also they are backward compatible and can copy and create CDs as well.

DVDs represent an evolutionary growth of CDs, with slight changes. Considering that the development of DVD follows the CD by 14 years, you can see that the CD was truly a revolutionary creation in its time. It is important to understand that both CDs and DVDs are electro optical devices, as opposed to nearly all other computer peripherals which are electromagnetic. No magnetic fields are involved in the reading or recording of these discs; therefore, they are immune to magnetic fields of any strength, unlike hard drives.

Due to their immunity to magnetic fields, CD and DVD media are unaffected by Electromagnetic Pulse (EMP) effects, X-rays, and other sources of electromagnetic radiation. The primary consideration with recordable CD media (and to a lesser extent, manufactured media) is energy transfer. It takes a significant amount of energy to affect the media that the writing laser transfers to the disc. Rewritable discs (which we'll discuss later) require even more energy to erase or rewrite data.

This is in direct contrast to floppy discs and hard drives, which can be affected by electromagnetic devices such as Magnetic Resonance Imaging (MRI) machines, some airport X-ray scanners, and other devices that create a strong magnetic field. CDs and DVDs are also immune to EMPs from nuclear detonations.

It is important to understand that CD and DVD media are *read with light* and that recordable discs are *written with heat*. Using an infrared (IR) laser, data is transferred to a CD or DVD onto a small, focused area that places all of the laser energy onto the target for transfer. It should be noted that all CD and DVD media are sensitive to heat (that is, higher than 120°F/49°C), and recordable media are sensitive to IR, ultraviolet (UV), and other potential intense light sources. Some rewritable media are affected by EPROM erasers, which use an intense UV light source. Various forensic alternative light sources can provide sufficient energy to affect optical media, especially if it is focused on a small area. It is not necessarily a question of heat but one of total energy transfer, which can result in heating.

Both CD and DVD media are organized as a single line of data in a spiral pattern. This spiral is more than 3.7 miles (or 6 kilometers [km]) in length on a CD, and 7.8 miles (or 12.5 km) for a DVD. The starting point for the spiral is toward the center of the disc, with the spiral extending outward. This means that the disc is read and written from the inside out, which is the opposite of how hard drives organize data.

With this spiral organization, there are no cylinders or tracks like those on a hard drive. The term *track* refers to a grouping of data for optical media. The information along the spiral is spaced linearly, thus following a predictable timing. This means that the spiral contains more information at the outer edge of the disc than at the beginning. It also means that if this information is to be read at a constant speed, the rotation of the disc must change between different points along the spiral.

As shown in Figure 4.8, all optical media are constructed of layers of different materials. This is similar to how all optical media discs are constructed. The differences between different types of discs are as follows:

- **CD-R** The dye layer can be written to once.

- **CD-ROM** The reflector has the information manufactured into it and there is no dye layer.

- **CD-RW** The dye is replaced with multiple layers of different metallic alloys. The alloy is bi-stable and can be changed many times between different states.

- **DVD** DVDs are constructed of two half-thickness discs bonded together, even when only one surface contains information. Each half disc contains the information layer 0.6 millimeters (mm) from the surface of the disc.

Figure 4.8 CD-R Construction

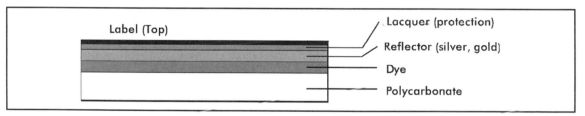

DVD media consist of two half-thickness polycarbonate discs; each half contains information and is constructed similarly to CD media. DVD write-once recordable media use a dye layer with slightly different dyes than those used for CD-R media, but otherwise they are very similar physically. Manufactured DVD media have the information manufactured into the reflector and no dye layer is present. Rewritable DVD media use bi-stable alloy layers similar to those for CD rewritable media. The differences between manufactured, write-once, and rewritable media are physically similar between CD and DVD media.

The key to all recordable media types is the presence of a reflector with the ability to reflect laser energy. Data is represented by blocking the path to the reflector either by dye or by a bi-stable metallic alloy. The bottom of a CD is made of a relatively thick piece of polycarbonate plastic. Alternatively, the top is protected by a thin coat of lacquer. Scratches on the polycarbonate are out of focus when the disc is read, and minor scratches are ignored completely. It takes a deep scratch in the polycarbonate to affect the readability of a disc. However, even a small scratch in the lacquer can damage the reflector. Scratching the top of a disc can render it unreadable, which is something to consider the next time you place a disc on your desk top-down "to protect it." A DVD has polycarbonate on both sides; therefore, it is difficult to scratch the reflector.

Types of DVDs

Just as several types of CDs are available for a variety of uses, a wide variety of DVDs are available as well. As mentioned previously, the storage capacity of a DVD is immense compared to that of a CD, and can range from 4.5GB on a single-layer, single-sided DVD to 17GB on a dual-layer, double-sided DVD. The various types of DVDs on the market include the following:

- **DVD-R** Stands for DVD minus Recordable. A DVD-R disc will hold up to 4.5GB of data, and is a write once-read many (WORM) medium. In other words, once it is written to, the data on the DVD cannot be modified.

- **DVD+R** Stands for DVD plus Recordable. A DVD+R disc will also hold up to 4.5GB of data, and is similar to the DVD-R. You should choose between DVD-R and DVD+R discs based on how you intend to use the disc. There is some evidence that DVD-R discs are more compatible with consumer DVD recorders than DVD+R discs; however, some consumer players that will only read DVD+R discs. DVD-R discs are often the best choice for compatibility if the disc being produced contains data files. Early DVD-ROM drives can generally read DVD-R discs but are incapable of reading DVD+R discs. DVD writers that only write DVD+R/RW discs will read DVD-R discs.

- **DVD-RW** Stands for DVD minus Read Write. This, like CD-RW discs, allows an average of 1,000 writes in each location on the disc before failing. A DVD-RW disc will hold up to 4.5GB of data and is recordable.

- **DVD+R DL** (dual-layer) Is an extension of the DVD standard to allow for dual-layer recording. Previously the only dual-layer discs were those manufactured that way. This allows up to 8.5GB of data to be written to a disc. Most current DVD drives support reading and writing DVD+R DL discs.

- **DVD+RW** Stands for DVD plus Read Write. This, like CD-RW discs, allows an average of 1,000 writes in each location on the disc before failing. A DVD+RW disc will hold up to 4.5GB of data and is recordable.

- **DVD-RAM** Is a relatively obsolete media format, which emphasized rewritable discs that could be written to more than 10,000 times. There were considerable interoperability issues with these discs and they never really caught on.

HD-DVD and Blu-ray

HD-DVD is an acronym for High Definition DVD, and is the high-density successor to DVD and a method of recording high-definition video to disc. Developed by Toshiba and NEC, a single-layer HD-DVD is capable of storing up to 15GB of data, whereas a dual-layer disc can store up to 30GB of data. Although developed for high-definition video, HD-DVD ROM drives for computers were released in 2006, allowing HD-DVD to be used as an optical storage medium for computers.

HD-DVDs require so much storage space because of the amount of data required to record high-definition television (HDTV) and video. A dual-layer HD-DVD can record eight hours of

HDTV or 48 hours of standard video. The difference between the two is that that HDTV uses 1,125 lines of digital video, which requires considerably more storage space. HD-DVD ROM drives are used much the same way that VCRs were used to record video onto VHS tapes, and have a transfer rate of 36Mbps, which is 12Mbps more than the rate at which HDTV signals are transmitted. Similar to the format wars between Betamax and VHS, HD-DVD has been less popular than Blu-ray.

Like HD-DVD, *Blu-ray* is a high-density optical storage method that was designed for recording high-definition video. The name of this technology comes from the blue-violet laser that is used to read and write to the discs. A single-layer Blu-ray disc can store up to 25GB of data, whereas a dual-layer Blu-ray disc can store up to 50GB of data.

Although stand-alone Blu-ray and HD-DVD players and recorders are available, ones that will play either technology are also available. Also, certain Blu-ray drives allow users to record and play data on computers. In 2007, Pioneer announced the release of a Blu-ray drive that can record data to Blu-ray discs, as well as DVDs and CDs. In addition to this, Sony has also released its own rewritable drive for computers.

iPod and Zune

iPod is the brand name of portable media players developed by Apple in 2001. iPods were originally designed to play audio files, with capability to play media files added in 2005. Apple has introduced variations of the iPod, with different capabilities. For example, the full-size iPod stores data on an internal hard disk, whereas the iPod Nano and iPod Shuffle both use flash memory, which we'll discuss later in this chapter. Although iPod is a device created by Apple, the term has come to apply in popular culture to any portable media player.

iPods store music and video by transferring the files from a computer. Audio and video files can be purchased from iTunes, or can be acquired illegally by downloading them from the Internet using peer-to-peer (P2P) software or other Internet sites and applications, or sharing them between devices.

Unless you're investigating the illegal download of music or video files, where iPods become an issue during an investigation is through their ability to store other data. iPods can be used to store and transfer photos, video files, calendars, and other data. As such, they can be used as storage devices to store any file that may be pertinent to an investigation. Using the Enable Disk Use option in iTunes activates this function, and allows you to transfer files to the iPod. Because any media files are stored in a hidden folder on the iPod, you will need to enable your computer to view hidden files to browse any files stored on the iPod.

iPods use a file system that is based on the computer formatting the iPod. When you plug an iPod into a computer, it will use the file system corresponding to the type of machine to which it's connecting. If you were formatting it on Windows XP, it would use a FAT32 file system format, but if you were formatting it on a machine running Macintosh OS X, it would be formatted to use the HFS Plus file system. The exception to this is the iPod Shuffle, which uses only the FAT32 file system.

Entering late in the portable digital media market is Microsoft, which developed its own version of the iPod in 2006. *Zune* is a portable media player that allows you to play both audio and video, as well as store images and other data. Another feature of this device is that you can share files wirelessly with others who use Zune. In addition to connecting to a computer, it can also be connected to an Xbox using USB. Ironically, although it is compatible with only Xbox 360 and Windows, it was incompatible with Windows Vista until late 2006.

Flash Memory Cards

Flash memory cards and sticks are popular for storing and transferring varying amounts of data. Memory cards have typically ranged from 8MB to 512MB, but new cards are capable of storing upward of 8GB of data. They are commonly used for storing photos in digital cameras (and transferring them to PCs) and for storing and transferring programs and data between handheld computers (Pocket PCs and Palm OS devices). Although called "memory," unlike RAM, flash media is nonvolatile storage; that means the data is retained until it is deliberately erased or overwritten. PC Card (PCMCIA) flash memory cards are also available. Flash memory readers/writers come in many handheld and some laptop/notebook computers, and external readers can be attached to PCs via USB or serial port. Flash memory cards include:

- Secure Digital (SD) Memory Card
- CompactFlash (CF) Memory Card
- Memory Stick (MS) Memory Card
- Multi Media Memory Card (MMC)
- xD-Picture Card (xD)
- SmartMedia (SM) Memory Card

USB Flash Drives

USB flash drives are small, portable storage devices that use a USB interface to connect to a computer. Like flash memory cards, they are removable and rewritable, and have become a common method of storing data. However, whereas flash memory cards require a reader to be installed, USB flash drives can be inserted into the USB ports found on most modern computers. The storage capacity of these drives ranges from 32MB to 64GB.

USB flash drives are constructed of a circuit board inside a plastic or metal casing, with a USB male connector protruding from one end. The connector is then covered with a cap that slips over it, allowing the device to be carried in a pocket or on a key fob without worry of damage. When you need it, you can insert the USB flash drive into the USB port on a computer, or into a USB hub that allows multiple devices to be connected to one machine.

USB flash drives often provide a switch that will set write protection on the device. In doing so, any data on the device cannot be modified, allowing it to be easily analyzed. This is similar to the write protection that could be used on floppy disks, making it impossible to modify or delete any existing data, or add additional files to the device.

Although USB flash drives offer limited options in terms of their hardware, a number of flash drives will come with software that you can use for additional features. Encryption may be used, protecting anyone from accessing data on the device without first entering a password. Compression may also be used, allowing more data to be stored on the device. Also, a number of programs are specifically designed to run from a USB flash drive rather than a hard disk. For example, Internet browsers may be used that will store any history and temporary files on the flash drive. This makes it more difficult to identify a person's browsing habits.

USB flash drives have been known by many other names over the years, including thumb drive and USB pen drive. Because these devices are so small, they can be packaged in almost any shape or item.

Some USB flash drives are hidden in pens, making them unidentifiable as a flash drive, unless one pulled each end of the pen to pop it open and saw the USB connector. The pen itself is completely usable, but contains a small flash drive that is fully functional. This allows the device to be hidden, and can be useful for carrying the drive around with you … unless you tend to forget your pen in places, or work in a place where others walk off with your pens.

Understanding Why These Technical Details Matter to the Investigator

Why does the cybercrime investigator need to know the difference between RAM and disk space, what a microprocessor does, or the function of cache memory? Understanding what each part of a computer does will ensure that you also understand where in the machine the evidence (data) you need might be—and where *not* to waste your time looking for it.

For example, if you know that information in RAM is lost when the machine is shut down, you'll be more careful about immediately turning off a computer being seized pursuant to warrant. You'll want to evaluate the situation; was the suspect "caught in the act" while at the computer? The information that the suspect is currently working on will *not* necessarily be saved if you shut down the system. The contents of open chat sessions, for example, could be lost forever if they're not automatically being logged. You will want to consider the best way to preserve this volatile data without compromising the integrity of the evidence. You might be able to save the current data, print current screens, or even have your crime scene photographer take photos of the screens to prevent information in RAM from being lost.

Understanding how data is stored on and accessed from hard disks and removable media will help you recognize why data can often be recovered even though the cybercriminal thinks he or she has "erased" it, either by merely deleting the files or by formatting the disk.

Investigators should also be aware of the many existing removable media options that allow cybercriminals to store evidentiary data in a location separate from the computer, easily transfer that data to another computer, or make copies of the data that can be used in case the original data on the computer's hard disk is destroyed. The presence of any removable media drive (diskette drive, CD-R, tape drive, or the like) means that there is definitely a possibility that data has been saved and taken away. Unfortunately, the absence of such a drive does not negate that possibility, because many removable media drives are external and portable; they can be quickly and easily moved from one computer to another, attaching to the machine by way of a serial, parallel, USB, or other port.

The Language of the Machine

Computer hardware and accessories, such as hard disks and removable media, might provide the physical evidence of cybercrime. However, in most cases the hardware itself is not really the evidence; it merely *contains* the evidence. Similarly, a letter written by a criminal might be entered into evidence, but it is not the physical page and ink that provide proof of guilt, it is the words written on the page that indicate the criminal's culpable mental state or that provide a written confession of the criminal's actions. If those words are in a language that the police, prosecutors, and jury can understand, using them as evidence is easy. On the other hand, if the words are written in a foreign language, using them as evidence might be more difficult because they will have to be interpreted by someone who understands both languages.

In a sense, most computer data is written in a foreign language. The data stored in computers is written in the "language" of 1s and 0s, or *binary language* (also called *machine language* or *machine code*). Although relatively few humans can program in pure machine language and few cybercrime investigators or programmers learn to translate the magnetic encoding representing 1s and 0s on a disk into "real" (understandable) data, it is helpful for investigators to understand how binary language works to anticipate questions that the defense can raise in a case that relies on computer data as evidence.

On the Scene

Getting Down to the Lowest Level

Machine language is the lowest level of programming language. The next step up is *assembly language*, which allows programmers to use names (or *mnemonics*) represented by ASCII characters, rather than just numbers. Code written in assembly language is translated into machine language by a program called an *assembler*.

Most programmers, however, write their code in *high-level languages* (for example, BASIC, C++, and so on). High-level languages are "friendlier" than other languages in that they are more like the languages that humans write and speak to communicate with one another and are less like the machine language that computers "understand." Although easier for people to work with, high-level languages must be converted into machine language for the computer to use the program. This is done by a program called a *compiler*, which reorganizes the instructions in the source code, or an *interpreter*, which immediately executes the source code. Because different computing platforms use different machine languages, there are different compilers for a single high-level language to enable the code to run on different platforms.

Wandering through a World of Numbers

Working with numbers, beyond the primitive method of simply representing each item counted as a one (for example, carving one notch on the investigator's wooden desktop for each case solved), requires that we use a *base system* to group items in an ordered fashion, making it easier for us to keep count.

Who's on Which Base?

Most of us are most familiar with the base-10 numbering system, also called the *decimal numbering system*. Many sources credit early Indian cultures with creating this numbering system approximately 5,000 years ago; it was later refined in the Arab world. This system uses 10 digits (0 through 9) to represent all possible numbers. Each digit's value depends on its *place*; as you move left in reading a number, each place represents 10 times the value to its right. Thus, the digit *1* can represent 1, 10, 100, 1,000, and so on, depending on its place as defined by the number of digits to its right. A *decimal point* is used to allow numbers less than 1 to be represented.

We use base 10 all the time; it is our day-to-day numbering system. When we see a decimal number such as *168*, we understand that the 1 represents one *hundred*, the 6 represents six *tens*, and the 8 represents eight *ones*, based on the place occupied by each digit in relation to the others.

Base 10 works great for human counting because we have 10 fingers (also called *digits*) that we can use to count on. Historians believe this explains the development and popularity of decimal numbering; primitive people found it easy to count to 10 on their fingers and then make a mark in the sand or on stone to represent each group of 10.

Computers, however, work with electrical impulses that have two discrete states. You can visualize this system by thinking of a standard light switch. The bulb can be in one of two possible states at a given time; it is either on or off. This is a *digital* signal. We don't have 10 different states to represent the 10 digits of the decimal system to the computer, but we can still represent all possible numbers using the base-2 numbering system, also called the *binary numbering system*.

Understanding the Binary Numbering System

Binary numbering uses only two digits, 0 and 1. Each binary digit (each 0 or 1) is called a *bit*. In binary numbering, as in decimal, the value of a digit is determined by its place. However, in binary, each place represents two times the value of the place to its right (instead of 10 times, as in base 10).

This means the binary number *1000* does not represent one thousand; instead, it represents eight (its decimal equivalent) because that's the value of the fourth place to the left. A zero is a placeholder that indicates that a place has no value, and a one indicates that a place has the value assigned to it. Thus, *1111* represents 15 in decimal, because each place (starting from the right) has a value of 1, 2, 4, and 8. Adding these values together gives us 15.

Converting between Binary and Decimal

Although computer processors must work with binary numbering, humans prefer to work with numbering systems that use more digits, because it is less confusing for us to deal with a number that looks like 139 than its binary equivalent of 10001011.

Table 4.2 shows the place values of the first 12 places of a binary number, starting from the right. If the binary digit is a 1, the value shown is assigned to it; if it's a 0, no value is assigned. The second line of the table shows the digits of a typical binary number.

Table 4.2 Place Values of Binary Digits

Value	2,048	1,024	512	256	128	64	32	16	8	4	2	1
Binary Digit	1	1	0	1	0	0	0	1	1	0	0	1

Looking at this binary number, 110100011001, we see that the bits that are "on" (represented by 1s) have values of 1, 8, 16, 256, 1,024, and 2,048. If we add those values together, we get 3,353. This is the decimal equivalent of the binary number.

Converting between Binary and Hexadecimal

Another numbering system that is sometimes used to make binary more palatable for humans is the *hexadecimal*, or *hex*, *system*, or base 16. Why not just use our familiar decimal system and convert it to binary instead of learning yet another numbering system? Hex is useful because it is easier to convert hex to binary. Because hex uses 16 digits, each byte (eight binary digits) can be represented by two hex digits. Hex also produces shorter numbers to work with than decimal.

Hex needs six more symbols than decimal to represent all its digits, so it uses the standard decimal digits 0 to 9 to represent the first 10 digits and then uses the first six letters of the alphabet, A to F, to represent the remaining six digits. Table 4.3 shows the hexadecimal digits and their decimal equivalents.

Table 4.3 Hexadecimal Digits and Their Decimal Equivalents

Hexadecimal	0	1	2	3	4	5	6	7	8	9	A	B	C	D	E	F
Decimal	0	1	2	3	4	5	6	7	8	9	10	11	12	13	14	15

Using this system, for example, the decimal number 11,085 is equivalent to the hex number 2B4D, and the decimal number 1,409 is equivalent to the hex number 581. In the first case, it's obvious that we're dealing with a hexadecimal number, but if we see the number 581, how do we know whether it's a decimal or a hexadecimal number? To solve this problem, hex numbers are indicated by either a prefix of *0x* or a suffix of *H*. Thus, our hex equivalent of 1,409 would be written as either *0x581* or *581H*.

In the computer world, you'll find that some numbers (such as Internet Protocol [IP] addresses) are traditionally represented by their decimal equivalents, whereas others (such as memory addresses and Media Access Control [MAC] addresses) are traditionally represented by their hexadecimal equivalents. We will discuss IP addresses and MAC addresses later in this chapter.

Converting Text to Binary

Computers "think" in binary, but people (aside from the rare mathematical genius) don't. We tend to work with words, and much of the data that we input to our computers is in the form of text. How does the computer process this data? Ultimately, it must be converted to the binary "language" that the computer understands.

Text files are commonly encoded in either ASCII (in UNIX and MS-DOS-based operating systems) or Unicode (in Windows). *ASCII* stands for *American Standard Code for Information Interchange*, which represents binary numbers as text. Assembly language uses ASCII characters for programming. Each character of the alphabet, numeric digit, or symbol is represented by a specific 1-byte string of binary digits. (In a binary file, there is no one-to-one correlation between characters and bytes.)

ASCII characters are used by text-based operating systems and programs such as MS-DOS and WordPerfect versions prior to 5.0. By contrast, graphical programs use bitmaps or geometrical shapes instead of characters to create display objects.

> **NOTE**
>
> The *extended ASCII* character set includes additional characters, such as shapes for drawing pictures so that graphics objects can be simulated. MS-DOS uses extended ASCII to display menus, bar charts, and other shapes that are based on straight lines.

Encoding Nontext Files

The original ASCII encoding scheme used 7-bit characters and is designed to handle plain text only. Then along came the Internet, and people wanted to send files to one another via e-mail. E-mail server software was designed to handle the ASCII character set and another 7-bit encoding scheme, Extended Binary Coded Decimal Interchange Code (EBCDIC), which IBM developed for its minicomputers and mainframes. This worked fine as long as everyone was sending plain text files. However, it was a problem if you wanted to send pictures, audio, programs, or files created in applications that did not produce plain text, because most nontext files use 8-bit characters. Even the documents created by word processors are usually not saved as ASCII files but as binary files (to preserve formatting information).

The answer to this problem was to use an encoding scheme that could represent nontext files as text. Programmers came up with solutions such as uuencode and *Multipurpose Internet Mail Extensions (MIME)* to convert nontext files into ASCII text. Thus, a photo or other nontext file could be sent across the Internet without a problem. An encoded file looks like a mass of meaningless ASCII characters to the human eye, but when it is decoded by software at the recipient's end, it is converted back into its original form. MIME provided a number of advantages over uuencode in that it supported sending multiple attachments and interactive multimedia content. Perhaps most important, it supports languages such as Japanese, Chinese, and Hebrew that don't use the Roman alphabet.

Another encoding scheme, called BinHex, is often used by Apple Macintosh software. Mac files differ from those created by Windows and some other operating systems in that Mac files consist of two parts, called *forks*—one that contains the actual data and one that contains attribute information and parametric values. Programs are available to convert the files into a single byte stream for sending over a network. Macintosh files can be sent via MIME, using the MIME encapsulation specifications outlined in RFC 1740.

Web browsers also support MIME so that they can display files that are not in Hypertext Markup Language (HTML) format. There is also a version of MIME called *S/MIME* that supports encryption of messages.

Understanding Why These Technical Details Matter to the Investigator

Investigators might not be capable of interpreting machine language, but they should understand what it is when they see it. The 1s and 0s of binary computation, the odd-looking hexadecimal numbers used in some types of addressing, and the indecipherable "gibberish" of MIME-encoded files might look meaningless, but when properly translated they can contain valuable evidence.

Just as an investigator should not throw away a letter found at the scene of a crime just because it happens to be written in Chinese, neither should computer data be dismissed as useless just because the investigators can't understand it. Pure binary data, or data that has been encoded for sending across a network, might be less convenient to work with than text or unencoded pictures, but often it can be converted to a readable form by the proper software.

It is also important for investigators to understand the difference between the type of encoding we are discussing here—which is done to make data recognizable and usable by a computer—and *encryption*, the purpose of which is to make data unrecognizable and unusable by unauthorized humans. Encoded data is intended to be easily decoded, and the software for doing so is widely available; encrypted data is intended to be difficult or impossible to decrypt without the proper key.

The very fact that a file has been encrypted can in some cases be a red flag that arouses suspicion or a building block of the probable cause needed to get a warrant or effect an arrest. Thus, knowing the difference between an encoded file and an encrypted file will save investigators time and strengthen their credibility before a judge.

On the Scene

Does File Encryption Create Probable Cause?

Investigators know that probable cause is usually not based on one fact or piece of evidence, but rather comprises multiple building blocks that, when taken together, would cause a reasonable and prudent person to believe that a crime has been committed by the suspect. Law enforcement professionals sometimes refer to these building blocks collectively as the *totality of the circumstances*. The Fourth Amendment to the U.S. Constitution requires that probable cause, based on the totality of the circumstances, be shown before a search warrant can be issued.

Does the existence of an encrypted file (or files) on a computer establish probable cause to seize that computer and examine the files, going on the theory that "only guilty people have something to hide"? In other words, if the girlfriend of a child-pornography suspect tells you that files on the family computer are encrypted so that she can't open them, is that enough cause for a search warrant? Given the nature of probable cause, the answer is no—at least, not by itself. Encryption alone generally would not be enough to satisfy the definition of probable cause. Use of encryption is not illegal in the United States (it is in some countries), and many people concerned with privacy use encryption to protect data that has nothing to do with criminal activity.

However, the fact that data is encrypted can be used as one of your building blocks of probable cause. If you have other evidence that indicates, for example, that a suspect regularly downloads pornographic photos of children (such as testimony of a known child pornographer that the suspect requested such photos from him, intercepted e-mail messages, or the like), the existence of encrypted files on the suspect's hard disk would add to the suspicion that illicit photos were stored there.

Other considerations include whether all the files on the disk are encrypted or only some select ones. The former situation is more indicative of someone who is just generally concerned about privacy, whereas the latter situation serves as a red flag that those particular files could contain something of interest to law enforcement. We'll discuss encryption more in this chapter, when we discuss file systems. We also discuss encryption in greater detail in Chapter 12, in the section on cryptography.

Understanding Computer Operating Systems

As a computer starts, the operating system is loaded into its memory and provides the foundation or *platform* on which application programs run. Although the vast majority of today's personal computers run some version of one of the three most popular PC operating systems (Windows, UNIX/Linux, or Macintosh OS), thousands of different computer operating systems exist. Some of these are network operating systems such as NetWare that run servers but don't function as desktop/client operating systems. Some run on mainframe or mini-mainframe computers, and some are designed for high-end workstations, such as Sun's Solaris. Others are proprietary operating systems used for specific devices, such as Cisco's Internet Operating System (IOS) that runs on Cisco routers, or SCOUT, which runs network appliances, whereas others are experimental operating systems such as GNU HURD and SkyOS. Some are used as embedded operating systems in a variety of devices, such as Windows Embedded CE or Windows XP Embedded, which is used in such devices as personal digital assistants (PDAs), Voice over IP (VoIP) phones, navigational devices, medical devices, and so on.

Understanding the Role of the Operating System Software

The operating system acts as a sort of liaison between the computer hardware and the application programs that are used to perform specific tasks (such as word processing or downloading and sending e-mail). It also provides file management, security, and coordination of application and utility programs that are running simultaneously. Operating systems can be classified in a number of different ways:

- *Text-based (or character-based) operating systems* such as MS-DOS and UNIX/Linux are faster performers because they don't have the overhead required to display complex graphics, but many people find them to be less user-friendly than *graphical user interface* (GUI) operating systems because you must learn and type commands to perform tasks. Most text-based operating systems can run shell programs to give them a graphical interface. Examples include Windows 3.*x* for MS-DOS and KDE for Linux.

- *Multiuser operating systems* generally run on mainframe systems and allow more than one user to log on, through terminals, and run programs simultaneously. The term is sometimes also used to refer to operating systems (such as Windows XP or Vista) that allow only one user at a time to log on but identify different users by a user account that is assigned a *profile* that defines settings, preferences, and documents that are specific to that user. Server operating systems (such as Windows Server 200*x*, Novell NetWare, and UNIX) allow multiple users to log on to the server over the network and access its resources, although only one user is logged on interactively (at the local machine).

- *Multitasking operating systems* are those that allow you to run more than one program at a time. MS-DOS is a *single-tasking* operating system; in other words, you have to close one application before you can start another. Shell programs (such as the Windows 3.1 shell) running on top of DOS allowed it to multitask. UNIX, and Windows 9x/ME/NT/2000, XP, and Vista are all true multitasking operating systems.

- *Multiprocessing operating systems* are able to use the capabilities of more than one microprocessor installed in the system, either by assigning different programs to run on different processors or by allowing different parts of a single program to run on different processors. For example, Windows 9x and ME operating systems do not recognize or use multiple processors, but Windows NT, 2000, XP, and Vista do. (The number of processors depends on the OS version.) UNIX and Macintosh also support multiple processors.

Differentiating between Multitasking and Multiprocessing Types

Different operating systems support such features as multitasking and multiprocessing in different ways. The type of multitasking or multiprocessing that a particular operating system uses depends on its *architecture*—that is, its design and structure.

Multitasking

Multitasking works by *time slicing*—that is, allowing multiple programs to use tiny slices of the processor's time, one after the other. PC operating systems use two basic types of multitasking: cooperative and preemptive. *Cooperative multitasking* was used by Windows 3.x and earlier, running on top of MS-DOS, as well as Macintosh operating systems prior to OS X. In this type of multitasking environment, each program must be written so that its *processes* (tasks or executing programs) use the processor for a short amount of time and then give up control of the processor to other processes. As long as the programs are written to cooperate, this system works. However, poorly written programs can take over the processor and refuse to relinquish control. When this happens, the system can freeze or crash.

Preemptive multitasking is more efficient. This method puts the operating system itself in charge of the processor. This way, a badly written program can't hog control of the processor; if it tries to do so, the operating system preempts its use of the processor and gives it to another process. A component in the operating system's kernel called the *scheduler* is responsible for allotting use of the processor to each process in turn. Some operating systems allow you to assign priorities to certain processes so that they come first when they need to use the processor. Preemptive processing is used by Windows 9x and later, UNIX, and Macintosh OS X.

Multiprocessing

Even if a computer has more than one processor physically installed, it might not be able to perform multiprocessing. To perform multiprocessing, the operating system must be capable of recognizing the presence of multiple processors and be able to use them. Some operating systems—such as Windows 9x—do not support multiprocessing. Even among those that do, not all multiprocessing operating systems are created equal.

There are three methods of supporting multiple processing:

- Asymmetric multiprocessing (AMP or ASMP)
- Symmetric multiprocessing (SMP)
- Massively parallel processing (MPP)

With *asymmetric multiprocessing*, each processor is assigned specific tasks. One primary processor acts as the "master" and controls the actions of the other, secondary processors.

Symmetric multiprocessing makes all the processors available to all individual processes. The processors share the workload, distributed more or less equally, thus increasing performance. Symmetric multiprocessing is also called *tightly coupled multiprocessing* because the multiple processors still use just one instance of the operating system and share the computer's memory and I/O resources.

Massively parallel processing is a means of crunching huge amounts of data by distributing the processing over hundreds or thousands of processors, which might be running in the same box or in separate, distantly located computers. Each processor in an MPP system has its own memory, disks, applications, and instances of the operating system. The problem being worked on is divided into many pieces, which are processed simultaneously by the multiple systems.

NOTE

MMP is generally used in research, academic, and government environments running large, complex computer systems. It is seldom used on desktop machines or typical business servers, although there is a type of parallel processing called *distributed computing* that uses large numbers of ordinary PCs on a network to work together on a problem, dividing the task among multiple machines. One of the best-known examples of this type of processing is done on Berkeley Open Infrastructure for Network Computing (BOINC), which expanded from the original Search for Extraterrestrial Intelligence (SETI) project called SETI@Home. BOINC recruits volunteers across the Internet who install software on their home computers that allows their systems, during idle time, to process a portion of the massive amount of data used for analyzing data from projects chosen by the user, which research such areas as biology, earth sciences, physics, and so on.

A paper that outlines the advantages of the distributed computing model of parallel processing used in SETI and other projects is available at http://roland.grc. nasa.gov/~mallman/papers/prime-delay.pdf.

Symmetric multiprocessing is the type supported by mainstream operating systems, including Windows XP and Vista, Linux, BSD, and other UNIX versions. To take advantage of the multiprocessing capabilities, the programs running on multiprocessor machines and operating systems must be *multithreaded*—that is, they must be written in a way that allows them to execute tasks in small executable parts called *threads*. Windows 2000/XP and later also support a feature called *processor affinity* that provides AMP-like functionality.

Differentiating between Proprietary and Open Source Operating Systems

Most commercial operating systems are *proprietary*—that is, the vendors keep the source code (the programming instructions) secret, and the licensing agreements prohibit "reverse engineering" (that is, dismantling the software's components and replicating them). However, some operating systems are distributed as *open source products*, meaning that the source code is made available to the public and developers at no cost. Anyone is free to modify the code to improve it. The only "catch" is that the license, although free, usually obligates programmers to disclose their improvements or even to make them available to the public at no cost.

The most notable (though not the only) open source operating system is Linux, which is based on the UNIX operating system. Many versions of UNIX, such as FreeBSD, are open source, with some such as HP-UX and Solaris originating as proprietary systems but moving to support open source. To confuse matters more, although the source code for Linux is free, vendors such as Red Hat market their own "distros" (Linux-speak for *distributions*) commercially. The term *open source* doesn't necessarily mean that the compiled version is free—only the source code is.

Linux was developed by and is named after Linus Torvalds, under the GNU General Public License (GPL). The licensing agreement makes it clear that developers who modify or distribute the software can charge for the service if they like; what they *can't* do is keep the source code secret or patent the products (unless the patent is licensed for everyone's free use).

NOTE

You can read all the terms of the entire GNU GPL on the GNU Web site, at www.gnu.org/licenses/gpl.html#SEC1. For information about the Open Source Initiative (OSI), visit www.opensource.org.

If open source software is free—or at least the source code is—why doesn't everyone use it instead of proprietary commercial software that costs big bucks? There are several reasons:

- There are dozens of different versions or distros of each open source operating system or application. This can be confusing to users, who don't know which one to select.

- Because anyone and everyone can make modifications to the operating system, you don't have the standardization that you have with proprietary software. In other words, one version of Linux might work fine with your hardware configuration, but another distro might not.

- Often, device drivers are not readily available for open source operating systems, so you must write your own. This is beyond the capabilities of many consumers and business users.

- Generally, no warranty is included with open source software, and no technical support is available (although some companies, such as Red Hat, package their distros of Linux and in essence sell the warranty/tech support services accompanied by the "free" software). This is especially important to business users, who generally will not use software that doesn't include tech support from the vendor.

The open source community has criticized vendors of proprietary software, such as Microsoft and Apple, for keeping their source code secret. As a result, Apple opened its source code for Darwin, the Mac OS X kernel, which is based on UNIX.

An Overview of Commonly Used Operating Systems

The most commonly used operating systems for computers include those made by Microsoft, Apple's Macintosh operating systems, and the various distros of Linux and other UNIX-based operating systems. In this section, we look briefly at these operating systems. In doing so, we'll see how some of these systems have evolved over the years, and we'll introduce you to some features that we'll discuss later in this chapter and expand upon in future chapters.

Understanding DOS

DOS is the Disk Operating System, which was the operating system first used on the original IBM PCs. Today, few computers still run some form of DOS. The most popular "flavor" of DOS is Microsoft's version, MS-DOS. IBM licensed DOS from Microsoft and marketed a version called PC-DOS that was bundled with its early PCs. Digital Research sold a version called DR-DOS that was later marketed by Caldera as DR-OpenDOS. There is also an open source version of DOS called FreeDOS; for more information on this product, see the FreeDOS Web site, at www.freedos.org.

The earliest versions of DOS used a file system called FAT12 (we'll discuss file systems in more detail in the next section). MS-DOS versions 3.*x* through 6.*x* supported the FAT16 file system along with the FAT12 file system and were used both as stand-alone operating systems and as the operating system on which Windows (through Version 3.11) was loaded, because early versions of Windows were not full-fledged operating systems, only graphical shells that required DOS underneath. MS-DOS Version 7.0, which also supported the FAT12 and FAT16 file systems, was part of the Windows 95 operating system. At that point in the evolution of Microsoft operating systems, the shell was integrated with the operating system, and users no longer installed MS-DOS and Windows as two separate products. Windows 95b (also called OEM Service Release 2, or OSR 2) was integrated with a new version of MS-DOS, Version 7.1, which supported the FAT32 file system.

MS-DOS as a stand-alone operating system is text-based and is not capable of multitasking. It has several limitations, such as the inability to work with disk partitions larger than 2GB or memory greater than 1MB (unless you use the Expanded Memory Scheme, or EMS, software). Windows 3.*x* used EMS to provide multitasking. DOS was built on the BASIC programming language, and most versions included a version of BASIC. The MS-DOS interface appears in Figure 4.9.

Figure 4.9 The Text-Based MS-DOS Interface

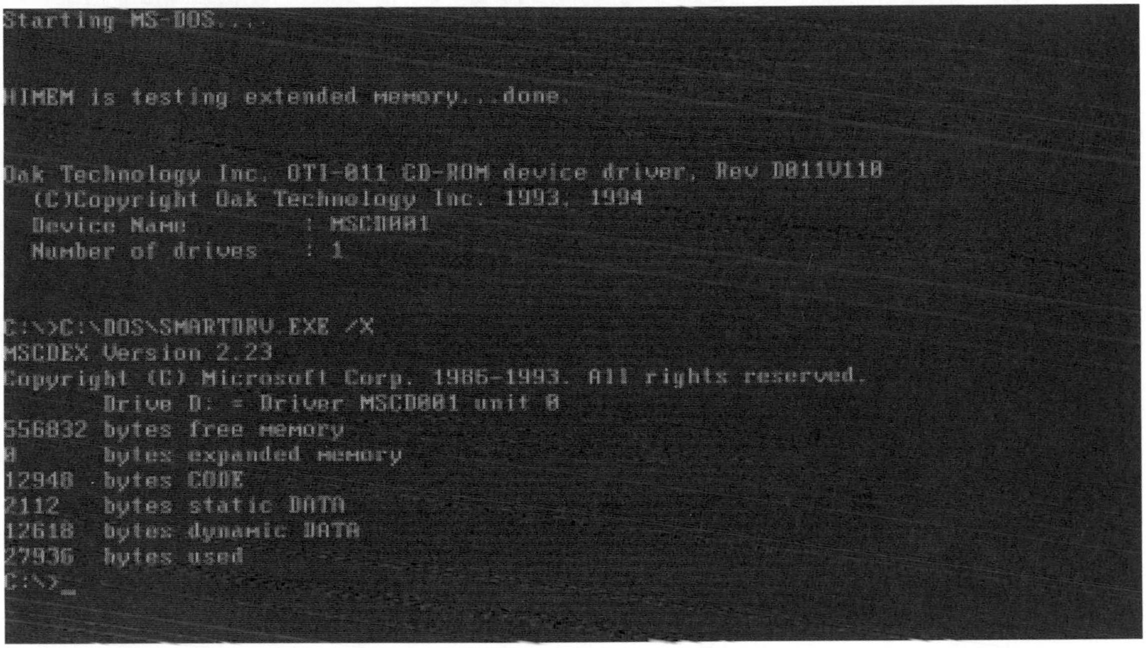

```
Starting MS-DOS...

HIMEM is testing extended memory...done.


Oak Technology Inc. OTI-011 CD-ROM device driver, Rev D011V110
  (C)Copyright Oak Technology Inc. 1993, 1994
  Device Name       : MSCD001
  Number of drives  : 1


C:\>C:\DOS\SMARTDRV.EXE /X
MSCDEX Version 2.23
Copyright (C) Microsoft Corp. 1986-1993. All rights reserved.
      Drive D: = Driver MSCD001 unit 0
556832 bytes free memory
0      bytes expanded memory
12948  bytes CODE
2112   bytes static DATA
12618  bytes dynamic DATA
27936  bytes used
C:\>_
```

Advantages of MS-DOS included size (Version 6.22 fits on three diskettes), relative simplicity, low cost, and the fact that it will run on older, low-powered hardware that doesn't have enough memory or disk space to support more modern operating systems.

Windows 1.x through 3.x

Not really operating systems in their own right, but rather add-ons to MS-DOS, Windows versions 1.*x* through 3.*x* were designed to bring a graphical environment to the Microsoft computing environment. Versions 1 and 2 were not very popular, but as the old adage says, the third time is a charm, and Windows 3.0, released in 1990, was the beginning of Microsoft's dominance in the operating system market.

On the Scene

Who "Stole" What from Whom?

It is a popular truism in the PC community that Microsoft "stole" (or at least derived) the idea of a graphical interface for Windows from its chief competitor at the time, Apple. Like most truisms, it is only partially true. It is true that Apple did develop a graphical operating system for its Local Integrated Software Architecture (LISA) computer, which

Continued

it officially released in 1983, just prior to Microsoft's announcement of Windows and almost two years before Windows 1.0 actually became available to the public. However, Apple didn't "invent" the idea of the mouse-driven GUI, as many people believe. The Xerox Alto (named after the Palo Alto Research Center, where it was developed) and Star computers were actually the first PCs to use these features, way back in the 1970s. Both Steve Jobs (of Apple) and Bill Gates (of Microsoft) visited Palo Alto and "borrowed" the ideas from Xerox, which later showed up in the Lisa (and later the Macintosh) and in Windows.

For more information about the Alto, see www.fortunecity.com/marina/reach/435/. To view the Lisa interface, see http://members.fortunecity.com/pcmuseum/lisadsk.htm. For a look at the interface on Windows 1.0 and subsequent versions of Windows (up through XP), visit www.infosatellite.com/news/2001/10/a251001windowshistory_screen-shots.html#win101.

Like DOS, you would be hard-pressed to find a computer running Windows 3.*x* in the world today. Like MS-DOS alone, it will run on older hardware, and many applications were made for it. Windows 3.*x* over MS-DOS is known as a *16-bit operating system*, meaning that it can process two bytes (which equals 16 bits) at a time. One of its limitations was the inability to handle filenames that have more than eight characters (with a three-character extension).

NOTE

The first microcomputer operating systems, used by the Commodore PET, Tandy TRS-80, Texas Instruments TI/99, and Apple II, were 8-bit operating systems.

Windows 3.11 added 32-bit file access (a new way of accessing the disk), updated device drivers, and bug fixes. Another popular version of Windows 3.1 and 3.11 was called Windows for Workgroups, which included integrated networking components for the first time. It included Microsoft Mail support and remote access services, and it claimed 50 percent to 150 percent faster disk I/O performance. Windows for Workgroups made peer-to-peer networking much easier and more convenient than earlier Microsoft operating systems and became very popular in small-business environments. Figure 4.10 shows the Windows 3.11 interface.

Figure 4.10 Windows 3.x Running on Top of MS-DOS, Providing a Graphical Interface

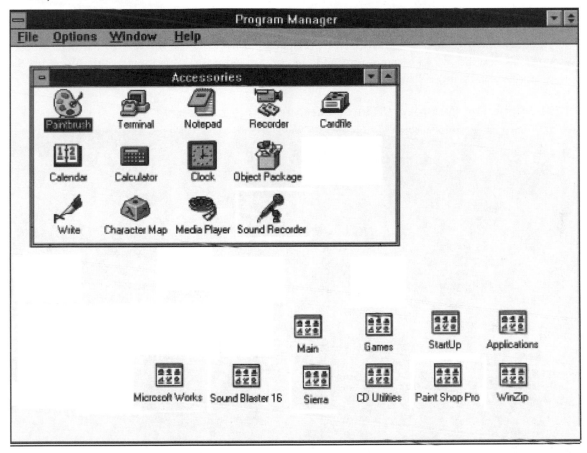

Windows 9x (95, 95b, 95c, 98, 98SE, and ME)

Windows 95 was a major new operating system release that was accompanied by heavy fanfare from Microsoft and the computing community. Released in August 1995, Windows 95 was Microsoft's first 32-bit consumer operating system; however, it is a *hybrid* operating system rather than a true 32-bit OS. For backward compatibility with older programs written for Windows 3.*x*, there was still a good deal of 16-bit code in Windows 95.

Windows 95 was designed to provide users with an entirely new interface (doing away with the old Program Manager and incorporating the now-familiar Start button and taskbar) and many enhanced features, such as:

- Preemptive multitasking (for 32-bit programs only)
- Support for long filenames (up to 256 characters) through the VFAT file system
- Plug and Play (which makes hardware installation easier)

- Power Management (a boon for laptop users)

- The Recycle Bin (which makes it easier to recover deleted files)

- Dial-up networking support built into the operating system

Although many computer enthusiasts were disappointed with the loss of DOS and changes to the Windows GUI, Windows 95 became tremendously popular and was the beginning of the Windows 9*x* family tree, which includes Windows 98 and ME. The Windows 95 interface appears in Figure 4.11.

Figure 4.11 The Windows 95 Interface

The second release of Windows 95, popularly called 95b and officially referred to as OSR 2, was not available to consumers on the shelves. It was released to original equipment manufacturers (OEMs, or PC hardware vendors) to install on the machines they sold. Version 95b added support for the FAT32 file system. A variant of 95b, called OSR 2.1, added rudimentary USB support. Another variant, OSR 2.5, which is often called Windows 95c, added the Internet Explorer 4.0 Web browser as an integrated component.

The next upgrade to Microsoft's 9*x* line of consumer operating systems was Windows 98, released, appropriately enough, in June 1998. This was the first version available as packaged software to consumers that supported the FAT32 file system (in addition to the "old" file systems FAT12 and FAT16). Windows 98 also added networking and dial-up enhancements, better hardware support, infrared (IrDA) support, and Advanced Configuration and Power Interface (ACPI) technology. It also included the Active Desktop (which you could add to Windows 95 by installing the Internet Explorer 4.0 browser) and provided for multiple-monitor support. Windows 98 replaced the old Help files with an indexed, searchable HTML system that is far more functional and added a number of interactive Troubleshooting Wizards, along with the Windows Update online driver/component update feature. Windows 98SE (second edition) added a few new features such as Internet Connection Sharing (ICS) and DVD-ROM support.

Next in the Windows 9x line was Windows ME, short for Millennium Edition, released in September 2000. ME added several multimedia features such as a video-editing program, and included better home networking support, but it was not a major upgrade. ME was presumably the last of the Windows operating systems exclusively geared to home users. The Windows 9x/ME line and the Windows NT/2000 line, geared toward businesses, were merged into one with the advent of Windows XP.

Windows NT

Microsoft designed Windows NT for the corporate desktop and server market. NT came in two versions: Workstation for desktops and Server for servers. NT was released in 1993 and was based in part on the work done jointly by Microsoft and IBM, before they parted ways, on OS/2. Thus, many of NT's features, such as its pure 32-bit code and its high-performance, secure file system, are similar to features in OS/2. NT was Microsoft's first operating system that was *not* based on MS-DOS. However, it could run MS-DOS programs by creating a virtual machine that emulated the DOS environment on which DOS applications can run.

NOTE

What does *NT* stand for? In its early days, Microsoft said the letters stood for *New Technology*. Later (when the technology could no longer be called "new"), Microsoft changed its story and said it doesn't stand for anything. David Cutler was the driving force behind the development of Windows NT.

The primary differences between Windows 9x and Windows NT were stability and security. The business environment requires an operating system that does not crash frequently, one that is secure enough to protect the sensitive data often stored on corporate computers. The architecture of Windows NT incorporated a hardware abstraction layer (referred to fondly as *HAL*) that prevented software applications from making direct calls to the hardware. This made NT more stable and less crash-prone but also meant that some applications written for Windows 9x wouldn't run on Windows NT.

NT 3.1 was released in 1993, a year prior to the release of Windows 95. The interface resembled Windows 3.x, but the kernel was completely different. A significant factor was the way NT handled memory. Unlike with Windows 3.x before it, each program ran in its own separate memory address. This meant that if one program crashed, it would not bring down with it the remaining programs that were currently running. Security features included mandatory logon (a user must have an account name and password to log on to the computer). NT also introduced support for a new file system, NTFS, which offers better performance as well as the ability to set permissions (called *NTFS permissions* or *file-level permissions*) on individual files and folders. NT 3.51 and earlier versions also included support for the native file system of IBM's OS/2, High Performance File System (HPFS).

NT 4.0 was a major upgrade released in 1996. The interface resembled that of Windows 95, and it included advanced user administration tools, wizards, a network monitor (a built-in protocol analyzer or "sniffer" software), a task manager (a tool that provides information on running applications and processes), and support for system policies and user profiles to allow administrators to more easily control the users' desktop environment. Remote access services and built-in virtual private network (VPN) support via Point-to-Point Tunneling Protocol (PPTP) were other improvements. NT 4.0 dropped support for HPFS. Figure 4.12 shows the Windows NT 4.0 interface.

Figure 4.12 The Windows NT 4.0 Interface

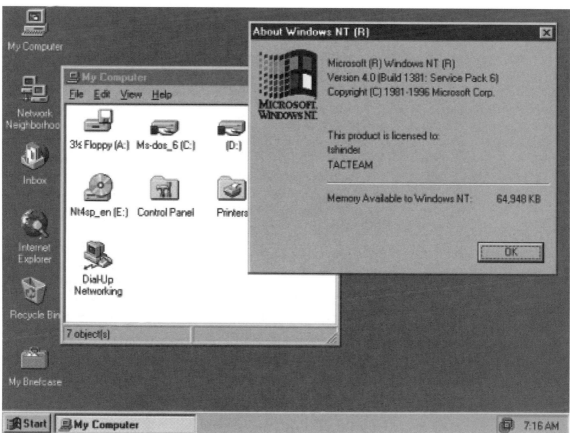

Although Windows NT Workstation had many advantages over the Windows 9*x* operating systems, it never became popular for home computing, for several reasons:

- NT does not support *Plug and Play* (a feature in which new hardware is automatically detected and the proper drivers are installed), so hardware installation is more difficult. NT was "pickier" about the hardware it supports.

- NT was not optimized for gaming; many popular Windows 9*x* and DOS games wouldn't run on NT, because the game software needs direct access to the hardware, which NT doesn't allow.

- NT Workstation cost about twice as much as Windows 9*x*.

- NT was more complex and less "user-friendly." Many home users considered its extra security measures unnecessary and inconvenient.

Despite its lack of popularity in the consumer market, Windows NT—both the Workstation and Server versions—became immensely popular in the business environment, with Microsoft's server product eventually overtaking and surpassing Novell's NetWare as a network authentication server. Windows NT made huge inroads into the Internet mail and Web server markets, which were previously dominated by UNIX.

On the Scene

OS/2

Operating System 2 (OS/2) began as a joint effort between IBM and Microsoft in the 1980s to replace DOS. The original OS/2 (Version 1) was text-based but was a 16-bit operating system, unlike the then-current version of DOS (Version 3.0), which was 8-bit. Version 2.0 included a graphical interface and was a true 32-bit operating system. OS/2 was designed to feature stability and multitasking capabilities that DOS didn't have.

After Microsoft's Windows 3.0 started to become popular, Microsoft dropped its support for OS/2, although it based the Windows NT kernel on the OS/2 kernel. IBM was really a hardware company rather than a software company, so when Microsoft left the project, IBM contracted with Commodore and borrowed from the Amiga for OS/2's object-oriented GUI. Version 2.11 added support for symmetric multiprocessing and was able to run Windows 3.*x* programs as well as applications written for OS/2. In 1994, IBM released OS/2 Warp 3.0. It included built-in Internet support (the first consumer OS to do so), and its successor, OS/2 Warp Connect, supported all the major networking protocols: Transmission Control Protocol/Internet Protocol (TCP/IP), Internetwork Packet Exchange (IPX), and NetBIOS.

In 1996, "Merlin" (OS/2 4.0) was released, with a more attractive interface and support for OpenGL and the Java virtual machine. Unfortunately for IBM, by this time Windows had gained momentum and most applications were written for it. OS/2 was unable to run 32-bit Windows applications, a limitation that severely hurt its popularity. Despite this, OS/2 continued to be popular in certain industries such as banking and IBM

Continued

continued to support it while also marketing OS/2 Warp Server for e-business. IBM's long fight to keep OS/2 as a marketable product ended December 23, 2005, when IBM withdrew all of its OS/2 products from the market, and stopped standard support of the product December 31, 2006.

If you think that OS/2 is gone forever, though, you're wrong. Serenity Systems manufactures an OEM upgrade to OS/2 called eComStation, which is available from www.ecomstation.com.

Windows 2000

Although Windows NT provided significantly more stability and security than the 9x operating systems, to continue to grow in market share among business customers, especially when competing with UNIX, Microsoft needed something better. Windows 2000 was released in February 2000, and although the interface hadn't really changed from NT, it represented at least as many changes as the upgrade from Windows 3.x to 95. Like NT, Windows 2000 is really a family of products: Professional (the desktop/client operating system that replaces NT Workstation) and three versions of the server software (Server, Advanced Server, and Datacenter Server).

The Windows 2000 operating systems are built on the NT kernel but with the Windows 98 interface and literally hundreds of enhancements and improvements. Many features that were missing in NT (although some of them could be added via third-party add-on software) such as file encryption, disk quotas, and—finally!—Plug and Play are included in Windows 2000. New security features included support for the Internet-standard Kerberos authentication protocol, IP Security (IPSec) for encrypting data that travels over the network, Group Policy (a much more robust and powerful replacement for system policies), and the Layer 2 Tunneling Protocol (L2TP) for more secure VPNs. The biggest difference between NT and Windows 2000 networking is the addition of *Active Directory*, a directory service similar in some ways to *Novell's eDirectory*, which was known as *Novell Directory Services* (NDS) at the time. Both Active Directory and eDirectory are used to provide a centralized database for managing security, user data, and distributed resources.

Windows XP

In October 2001, Microsoft released another semimajor desktop upgrade, this one called Windows XP. One thing that makes XP special is the fact that it is an upgrade to both the Windows 9x/ME line and the Windows NT/2000 line of desktop operating systems, which have been merged back together into one product line—sort of. Although both are based on the more stable NT kernel, XP comes in two different versions: XP Home Edition for consumers and XP Professional for business users.

The Home Edition of XP focuses on entertainment (digital photography, music, and video), gaming, and other consumer-oriented activities, along with features that make Internet connectivity and home networking easier than ever. The Professional Edition includes all the features of XP Home plus additional features that are geared toward the corporate user, such as Remote Desktop (a "lite" terminal server application that allows you to access your XP desktop from anywhere across the network), file encryption, support for multiple-processor systems, and advanced networking features. The Windows XP Professional interface is shown in Figure 4.13, and features increased use of themes to change the appearance of the taskbar, windows, and other objects running in the Windows environment.

Figure 4.13 Windows XP, Which Combines the Best of the 9x and NT/2000 Worlds

A Windows XP Pro computer, like NT Workstation and Windows 2000 Pro, can be a member of a Windows domain (a server-based network), whereas XP Home computers, like Windows 9x systems, can be used to access domain resources but cannot belong to the domain. Useful features included in both versions of XP are:

- A built-in Internet firewall for better security

- A Windows file protection feature that prevents accidentally changing the core operating system files

- Fast user switching that allows users to change the currently logged-on user account without closing applications (on nondomain computers)

- A number of new wizards that walk you through commonly performed tasks such as transferring files and settings from one computer to another, setting up a network, publishing to the Web, and so on

NOTE

You can find additional information on Windows XP at www.microsoft.com/windows/products/ windowsxp.

Windows Server 2003

Windows XP is a desktop/client operating system only. In the first few years after XP's release, Windows 2000 Server continued to be used as the server operating system on most Microsoft networks. Its successor, Windows Server 2003, was released in April 2003.

Like its predecessor, Windows Server 2003 comes in several different editions that are designed for different purposes on a network. These editions included Standard, Enterprise, Datacenter, Web, Storage, Small Business Server, and Cluster. Windows Server 2003 boasts a number of advancements over previous versions, including enhanced security, changes in Active Directory (such as the ability to run multiple instances of the directory server), and improvements in Group Policy and Internet Information Server (IIS). A major difference from previous Microsoft server operating systems was that the default installation of Windows Server 2003 doesn't have any server components enabled. This allows network administrators to choose and configure only the services they need, thereby reducing the possibility of attacks that exploit unnecessary services running on the server.

> **NOTE**
>
> Additional information on Windows Server 2003 is available at www.microsoft.com/windows server2003.

Windows Vista

In January 2007, the successor to Windows XP was released, to lackluster results. According to ZDNet (http://news.zdnet.com/2100-9593_22-6159700.html), the first week's sales of boxed copies of Vista were 59 percent lower than the first week's sales of XP sales. Added to this, *PC World* dubbed Windows Vista number 1 in "The 15 Biggest Tech Disappointments of 2007" (www.pcworld.com/article/id,140583-page,5-c,techindustrytrends/article.html). The complaints weren't exactly unmerited, as people found their existing hardware and software incompatible, and many manufacturers hadn't upgraded their products to work with Vista. The funny thing was, a number of Microsoft products were also incompatible with the new system.

Despite this, Vista does offer a number of improvements. It includes a new GUI, named Aero, that looks sleek and allows you to flip through the windows that you have open. It also provides improved security features, improvements in searching, speech recognition, and more efficient networking capabilities. Also new is the Windows Sidebar, which is used to access gadgets that allow you to access weather, a calculator, and other tools. For parents, one of the best features would probably be the parental control features, which you can use to control what Web sites and programs can be viewed and installed (a feature that isn't included in the Business or Enterprise edition of Vista).

Some of the security features available in Vista are directly related to cybercrime issues that we'll discuss in this book. Windows Defender is incorporated into Vista to provide protection against malware (*malicious programs*), which is software that can be installed without a person's knowledge and can damage systems. This antispyware product was previously available only as a download for Windows XP and Windows Server 2003.

Another new feature is BitLocker Drive Encryption, which you can use to encrypt entire volumes on machines running the Vista Enterprise or Ultimate edition or Windows Server 2008. Encrypting the data makes it unlikely that others will be able to access it if the computer is lost, stolen, or decommissioned (and the drive isn't properly wiped), or if someone attempts to steal data by accessing the files using hacking tools. We will discuss encryption further in Chapter 12.

NOTE

Additional information on Vista is available at www.microsoft.com/windows/ products/ windowsvista.

Windows Server 2008

In February 2008, Windows Server 2008 was released as the successor to Windows Server 2003. It comes in a number of different editions, including Standard, Enterprise, Web, and Datacenter. Unlike the release of Vista one year previous, there were no changes to the GUI, although there were a number of significant features, including:

- A scaled-back installation option called Server Core, which allows you to install a GUI-less version of the server. The "componentized" Server Core installation allows only the server roles and features that are necessary for a particular server. Because unnecessary services aren't installed, attackers can't use them to compromise a system.

- A Security Configuration Wizard that makes it easier for network administrators to properly configure security on servers.

- New cryptography features. A new cryptographic API called *Cryptography Next Generation* (CNG) is used for creation, storage, and retrieval of cryptographic keys, and the BitLocker Drive Encryption feature mentioned previously is used to encrypt volumes of data.

- The introduction of a new command-line shell and scripting language called Windows PowerShell.

- A self-healing feature to the NTFS file system. A service checks the file system for errors, and when one is found, it attempts to fix the error (meaning you don't have to take the system down to run CHKDSK).

NOTE

Additional information on Windows Server 2008 is available at www.microsoft.com/ windowsserver2008.

Linux/UNIX

UNIX has been around since the 1960s, when it was developed at Bell Labs in conjunction with MIT computer scientists and thus has a "head start" on most of the competition in the PC operating system market. Generally used for servers rather than desktop machines, UNIX is a very powerful operating system that runs many of the mail, Web, and other servers on the Internet. Traditionally, it has been a complex text-based operating system, although it has become more user-friendly with the addition of interfaces.

UNIX grew out of the Multiplexed Information and Computing Service (Multics) mainframe system developed at MIT but was a completely new operating system designed to create a multiuser computing environment that would support a large number of users. It originally ran on the huge PDP timesharing machines in use at universities and government facilities in the 1960s and 1970s. The first versions of UNIX were written in assembler language, but later versions were written in the high-level C programming language. In the late 1970s, the popularity of UNIX began to spread beyond the academic world, and in the early days of the Internet, it ran on most of the VAX computers that were connected to the internetwork. In the 1980s, more versions of UNIX were developed, and its use spread throughout the business world.

Today there are still a large number of different versions of UNIX, including IBM's AIX, Sun Microsystems' Solaris, Hewlett-Packard's HP-UX, Santa Cruz Operations' SCO OpenServer (which that company bought from Novell in 1995), and others. The X Window system was developed to add a graphical shell to UNIX and make it more user-friendly. It's not really a GUI but is instead a protocol that can be used to build a GUI, such as Common Desktop Environment (CDE). However, UNIX graphical interfaces tend to be somewhat clunky and ugly compared to Windows interfaces, and UNIX purists shun the GUI, preferring the higher-performance command-line environment.

In 1991, Finnish student Linus Torvalds wrote a UNIX-based operating system that he called Linux (mentioned briefly earlier in this chapter) and that he distributed free through Internet newsgroups. Linux caught on with programmers and then with users who were looking for an alternative to Microsoft Windows. Although Linux is often used to run servers (especially Web servers running the open source Apache Web server software), it is more suitable for the desktop than UNIX. Linux is a text-based operating system like UNIX, but when it became popular as a desktop operating system, developers soon created a variety of graphical shells that ran on top of it, much as Windows 3.x ran on MS-DOS.

In 1994, Red Hat released a commercial version of Linux, which was followed by a release from Caldera in 1997 called OpenLinux. A large number of versions of Linux are available today, with some of the most popular being:

- Red Hat (www.redhat.com)

- SUSE (www.novell.com/linux/)

- Ubuntu (www.ubuntu.com)

- openSUSE (www.opensuse.org)

- Debian (www.debian.org)

- Slackware (www.slackware.com)

- Turbolinux (www.turbolinux.com)

Dozens of distributions are available; you can find information and comparisons at the Linux Distrowatch Web site at www.distrowatch.com.

Apple

The Apple Macintosh computers differ from Intel-compatible PCs in many ways, one of which is the fact that they are proprietary. Until recently, Apple made both the hardware and the operating system software. In other words, Mac operating systems wouldn't run on PCs, and PC operating systems wouldn't run on Macs. The Apple–Intel architecture changed this, however, when computers developed by Apple began to use the Intel x86 processors that allowed multiple operating systems to run on a single Apple computer. Prior to this, running multiple operating systems on a Mac was limited to using software such as VMware (www.vmware.com), which is third-party software used to run other operating systems in a *virtual machine*. Using VMware allows you to run a PC operating system in a window on top of your Mac OS, or vice versa.

The latest version of the Mac OS, called OS X, is a big departure from prior versions because it is based on a version of UNIX called Darwin. Macintosh OS X combines the power of underlying UNIX code with a beautiful, user-friendly GUI called Aqua. The Mac has always been popular with educational institutions and graphic designers, but OS X gained popularity among both traditional UNIX users and die-hard Windows fans. A Mac OS X interface is shown in Figure 4.14.

Figure 4.14 The Macintosh OS X Interface on a UNIX OS

Unlike other operating systems that primarily use version numbers to designate new releases of the operating system, OS X uses the names of big cats for each new version. To date, these include:

- Puma (Version 10.1; released September 2001), which features support for writing CDs and DVDs, the ability to easily connect to a local area network (LAN) or the Internet, and built-in support to access files on Windows PCs across a network. It also includes software such as SAMBA, to allow you to share your Mac files with networked Windows machines. With OS X, the Mac finally added such advanced features as preemptive multitasking and protected memory and includes support for symmetric multiprocessing, USB, and FireWire (IEEE 1394).

- Jaguar (Version 10.2; released August 2002), which provides network support for Microsoft networks and iChat (instant messaging [IM]).

- Panther (Version 10.3; released October 2003), which provides the ability to switch between users (so that one user remains logged on while another user logs on), as well as improvements to iChat that allow audio and videoconferencing.

- Tiger (Version 10.4; released April 2005), which provides such new features as the Dashboard, which is used to run widgets (small applications that provide such functions as weather forecasts, a world clock, a calculator, calendars, and so on). This was the first release to run on Apple machines that used x86 processors.

- Leopard (Version 10.5; released October 2007), which provides a feature called Back to My Mac that allows remote access over the Internet to files on the computer, an automated backup utility called Time Machine, and the ability for Macs using Intel processors to install other operating systems such as Windows on separate partitions.

Apple also markets a server version, OS X Server, which supports clients running Mac, Windows, UNIX, and Linux. For more information about OS X, see the Apple Web site (www.apple.com).

File Systems

File systems or *file management systems* are systems that the operating system uses to organize and locate data stored on a hard disk. File systems can manage storage media such as hard disks, and control how sectors on the drive are used to store and access files. In doing so, a file system will keep track of which sectors are used to store files, and which are empty and available for use. In the complex world of networks, however, this isn't always the case. Network file systems aren't used to manage the HDD, but instead provide a way to present a client with access to data on a remote server.

Many file systems are *hierarchical file systems* in which the data is organized as a tree structure. As shown in Figure 4.15, a hierarchical file system looks like an inverted tree. At the base of the structure is a root directory, and directories (or *folders* as they're now called in Windows) branch out from the root. These directories are containers that can be used to store files or other directories. These directories within directories are called subdirectories (or subfolders). As we'll see later in this chapter, the file system will keep track of how this organization translates to directories and files that are stored on the disk so that when a particular directory is opened, the files in that directory are displayed properly and can be located on the hard disk.

Figure 4.15 A Hierarchical Directory Structure

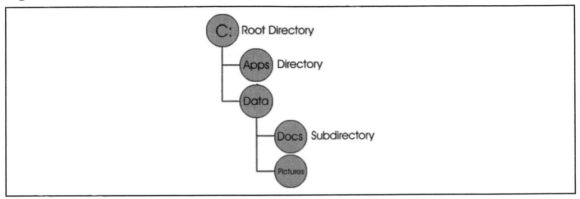

File systems will keep track of this structure (the directories and the files contained within those directories) using different methods. As we'll discuss in the next section, the FAT file system uses a File Allocation Table that will manage where the file is stored on the hard disk, and will also manage other aspects of how you name and can access the file. In earlier operating systems such as MS-DOS, the FAT file system only allowed files to be named with eight characters, with a period separating the name from a three-character extension. For example, a document might be named DOCUMENT.DOC using this 8.3 notation. When Windows 95 was developed, long file names (LFNs) were supported that allowed filenames to comprise up to 255 characters. This and other information is stored within the file by the file system, along with properties identifying the owner of a file, when it was created, and attributes that control access to the file (such as whether it is read only or can be modified).

Microsoft File Systems

Different operating systems use different file systems, and some operating systems support more than one file system. The most familiar are those used by the Microsoft operating systems:

- FAT12
- FAT16
- VFAT
- FAT32
- NTFS

In the following sections, we look at some of the characteristics of each file system, along with some less commonly encountered file systems used by networks and non-Microsoft operating systems.

FAT12

FAT stands for File Allocation Table; the FAT file system was developed for use by the DOS operating systems. The first version of the FAT file system was called FAT12 because its allocation tables used a 12-digit binary number (12 bits) for cluster information (which we'll discuss later in this chapter). The FAT12 file system was useful for the very small hard disks that came with the original IBM PC (less than 16MB in size). It is also used to format floppy diskettes.

FAT16

The *FAT16* file system was developed for disks larger than 16 MB, and for a long time it was the standard file system for formatting hard disks. As you can probably guess, it uses 16-bit allocation table entries. The FAT16 file system (often referred to as just the FAT file system) is supported by all Microsoft operating systems, from MS-DOS to Windows Vista. It is also supported by some non-Microsoft operating systems, such as Linux.

This support makes it the most universally compatible file system. However, it has many drawbacks, including the following:

- It doesn't scale well to large disks; because the cluster size increases as the disk partition size increases, a large disk (larger than about 2 GB) formatted with the FAT16 file system will have a lot of wasted space.

- It doesn't support file-level compression; the compression scheme that is used with the FAT16 file system, such as that implemented by DriveSpace, requires that the entire logical drive be compressed.

- It doesn't support file-level security (assignment of permissions to individual files and folders).

> **NOTE**
>
> You may read in some sources that the FAT16 file system is limited to 2 GB in size, but that's not really the case (although it does become inefficient at larger disk sizes). MS-DOS will not allow you to create a FAT16 partition larger than 2 GB, but you can create larger FAT16 partitions (up to 4 GB) in Windows NT/2000, XP, and Vista. These larger FAT16 partitions are not supported and recognized by MS-DOS or Windows 9*x*.

VFAT

Virtual FAT, or *VFAT*, is a file system driver that was introduced in Windows for Workgroups 3.11 and supported by Windows 95. Its advantages are that it operates in protected mode and provides the capability for using long filenames with the FAT16 file system. VFAT is not a file system; rather, it is a program extension that handles filenames over the 8.3 limitation imposed by the original FAT16 file system.

FAT32

The *FAT32* file system uses a 32-bit allocation table. It was first supported by the OSR 2 version of Windows 95 (95b) and was designed to improve on the functionality of the FAT16 file system by adding such features as:

- More efficient use of space with large hard disks by using smaller cluster sizes

- Support for larger partitions, up to 2 TB in size, in theory (Windows supports FAT32 partitions of up to 32 GB)

- Greater reliability, due to the inclusion of a backup copy of important data structure information in the boot record

The FAT32 file system also has its disadvantages, including the fact that it is incompatible with older Microsoft operating systems (for example, MS-DOS, Windows 3.x, Windows 95a, Windows NT), and some non-Microsoft operating systems (although FAT32 drivers are available from third-party vendors for Windows 95, NT, and even non-Microsoft operating systems such as Linux). Additionally, the overhead used by the FAT32 file system can slow performance slightly.

NTFS

NTFS is the most secure file system offered for computers running Microsoft Windows operating systems. NTFS was designed as a replacement for the FAT file system on Windows NT operating systems, including successive releases such as Windows 2000, Windows Server 2003, XP, and Vista. It was designed to be more robust and secure than other Microsoft file systems. Part of these features can be seen in how it handles partitions. As we'll see later in this chapter, partitions are logical divisions of a hard disk, allowing you to divide the space on a hard disk so that it functions as separate drives. For example, you could partition a hard disk to appear as C: or D: on the computer. NTFS supports very large partition sizes (up to 16EB, in theory) and allows you to create volumes that span two or more partitions.

NTFS is also more reliable because it supports a feature called *hot fixing*, a process by which the operating system detects a bad sector on the disk and automatically relocates the data stored on that sector to a good sector, and then marks the bad sector so that the system won't use it. This process is done on the fly, without the awareness or intervention of the user or applications.

Metadata and the Master File Table

Metadata is information about a particular set of data, and can include such information as who created a file, its size, and other technical information hidden from the common user. In other words, metadata is data about data. It can be used to describe a file, its format, when it was created, and other information. NTFS stores data about files, users, and other information the system uses in the form of special files that are hidden on the system. When a disk is formatted to use NTFS, these files are created, and their locations are stored in one of these files, called the Master File Table (MFT). The special system files that NTFS creates to store metadata, and their location in the MFT, are listed in Table 4.4.

Table 4.4 Special Files Created by NTFS, and Metadata Stored About Them in the Master File Table

MFT Record	System File	Filename	Description
0	MFT	$Mft	Stores information on files and folders on an NTFS volume
1	MFT 2	$MftMirr	Mirror of the first four records in the MFT
2	Log file	$LogFile	Transaction log that can be used for file recovery
3	Volume	$Volume	Stores information about the volume, including its label and version information
4	Attribute definitions	$AttrDef	Table of names, numbers, and descriptions of attributes used in NTFS
5	Root filename index	$	Root folder
6	Cluster bitmap	$Bitmap	Representation of which clusters are used on the volume
7	Boot cluster file	$Boot	Stores information needed to mount the volume. If the volume is bootable, it also contains bootstrap loader code
8	Bad cluster file	$BadClus	Stores information on bad clusters on a volume
9	Security file	$Secure	Stores unique security descriptors of files
10	Upcase table	$Upcase	Stores information used to convert lowercase characters to uppercase Unicode characters
11	NTFS extension file	$Extend	Stores information for optional extensions, such as quotas and object identifiers
12–15	Unused/reserved for future use		

Whereas the FAT file system uses a File Allocation Table to keep track of files, NTFS uses an MFT to perform similar (albeit more complex) functions. When a disk is formatted to use the NTFS file system, an MFT is created to keep track of each file on the volume. As shown in Table 4.4, the first record of the table describes the MFT itself, while a mirror of this information is stored in the second record in case the first record is corrupted. The third record in the MFT is a log that is used to recover files, while the bulk of the remaining records are used to keep track of each file and folder, the NTFS volume, and the attributes of those files. Keeping track of the files in a table allows them to be accessed quickly from the hard disk.

NTFS Attributes

One of the records stored in the MFT deals with NTFS attributes. NTFS views each file and directory as a set of file attributes, consisting of such information as its name, data, and security information. *Attributes* are data that define a file, and are used by the operating system and other software to determine how a file is accessed and used. In the MFT, a code is associated with each attribute, and may contain information on the attribute's name and description. In NTFS, two different kinds of attributes can be used:

- **Resident attributes** Attributes that can fit in an MFT record. The name of the file and timestamp are always included as a resident attribute.

- **Nonresident attributes** Allocated to one or more clusters elsewhere on the disk. These are used when information about a file is too large to fit in the MFT.

As shown in Table 4.5, a number of attributes can be associated with files and directories stored on an NTFS volume. To identify the location of all of the records associated with file attributes, NTFS uses an attribute list. The list contains attributes defined by NTFS, and also allows additional attributes to be added later.

Table 4.5 Common NTFS File Attributes

Attribute	Description
Attribute list	Locations of records that are not stored in the MFT record
Bitmap	Contains the cluster allocation bitmap, which is used by the $Bitmap file
Data	Contains data associated with the file. By default, all data is stored in a single attribute, even if it is split into separate pieces due to its size.
Filename	Name of the file. This includes its 8.3-character short name, 255-character long name, and other names or links required to identify the file.
Index Root	Index of files contained in a directory. If the index is small (that is, there are only a few files in a directory), the entire index will fit in this MFT attribute. If the index is large, an external index buffer may be used to store additional information.
Index Allocation	When an index is too large, this attribute is used to store pointers to index buffer entries. This allows the MFT to access the remaining index information for a directory.
Security Descriptor	Identifies the owner of the file, and who can access it. This attribute contains security information that controls access to a file or directory. Information on ownership, auditing, and access control lists (ACLs) is stored in this attribute.
Standard information	Basic information about the file, including whether a file is read-only, hidden and so on, and timestamps showing when a file was created, modified, and last accessed

Continued

Table 4.5 Continued. Common NTFS File Attributes

Attribute	Description
Object ID	Used to identify the file. The Object ID is a volume-unique file identifier, meaning that no two files on a volume will have the same Object ID.
Volume Name	Used to store information about the NTFS volume's name. Used by the $Volume file.
Volume Information	Attributes used to store information about the NTFS volume. Used by the $Volume file.
Volume Version	Attributes used to store version information about the NTFS volume. Used by the $Volume file.

From the administrator's and user's point of view, these attributes can be modified on the file or folder by using the file or accessing its properties. For example, by modifying the filename, you are modifying the *Filename* attribute. Similarly, opening a file will change timestamp information regarding when the file was last accessed. By accessing the properties of a file, you can set access permissions at the file level to control who can read, change, or otherwise access a file. This applies to users accessing the file from the local machine as well as over the network and is in addition to network share permissions that are set at the folder/directory level.

NTFS Compressed Files

NTFS allows files to be compressed to save space either by compressing an entire NTFS volume, or on a file-by-file basis. Using NTFS compression, you can compress individual folders or files, or everything on a particular drive using the NTFS file system. In doing so, a file is decompressed automatically when it is read, and compressed when it is saved or closed. Compressing data allows you to save disk space and archive folders, without having to rely on additional software to compress and decompress files.

When data is compressed on an NTFS drive, only the file system can read it. When a program attempts to open a file that's been compressed, the file system's compression drive must first decompress the file before making it available.

NTFS Encrypting File Systems

Encryption is the process of encoding a file so that it can't be read by anyone other than those who are authorized to open and view the data. Users who aren't authorized will be denied access to the file, and will be unable to open, copy, move, or rename a file or folder that's been encrypted. Encryption may be used on a single file or an entire disk.

Disk encryption refers to encrypting the entire contents of a hard disk, diskette, or removable disk. *File encryption* refers to encrypting data stored on disk on a file-by-file basis. In either case, the goal is to prevent unauthorized persons from opening and reading files that are stored on the disk. Support for disk/file encryption can be built into an operating system or file system. NTFS v5, the native file system for Windows 2000, Server 2003, XP, and Vista, includes the Encrypting File System (EFS), which can be used to protect data on a hard disk or large removable disk. EFS can't be used to protect data on floppy diskettes because they cannot be formatted in NTFS format, but it does allow encryption of individual files and/or folders. Because EFS is integrated with the operating system, the process of encryption and decryption is invisible to the user.

EFS relies on public key cryptography and digital certificates. Public key cryptography involves two mathematically related keys, one called the *public key* and another called the *private key*, which are generated to be used together. The private key is never shared; it is kept secret and used only by its owner. The public key is made available to anyone who wants it. Because of the time and amount of computer processing power required, it is considered "mathematically unfeasible" for anyone to be able to use the public key to re-create the private key, so this form of encryption is considered very secure.

Each file has a unique file encryption key, which is used to decrypt the file's data. Like the encrypted file or folder, the key is also encrypted, and must be decrypted by the user who has a private key that matches the public key. Because these keys match, the system can then determine that the person is authorized to view the data, and can then open the file.

Whether a person is permitted to access the data is based on the user account that is being used when opening the file. A digital certificate is used to identify the person logged on to the computer, and to provide credentials showing that the person is authorized to access certain data. EFS uses digital certificates that are associated with the user account. Although this requires less user interaction, it does have its drawbacks. It might not be possible to share encrypted files with others without decrypting them in cases where only one particular account is allowed access. In addition, there is a security risk if the user leaves the computer while logged on; then anyone who sits down at the machine can access the encrypted data.

Linux File Systems

Linux supports multiple file systems through the use of a *virtual file system* (VFS). VFS works as an abstract layer between the kernel and lower-level file systems. For a file system to work on Linux, it has to conform and provide an interface to VFS so that the upper levels of the operating system can communicate with the file systems used on the machine. Using VFS, Linux has been able to support a number of file systems, including the following:

- **ext** The first version of EFS, and the first file system created specifically for Linux. It was also the first file system to use the VFS that was added to the Linux kernel. It was replaced by ext2 and xiafs, which was based on the older Minix system and is not found in current systems due to its obsolescence. Minix was a file system originally used by Linux but was replaced by ext due to shortcomings such as a 14-character limit in naming files, and a 64 MB limitation on partition sizes.

- **ext2** Stands for Second Extended File System, and offers greater performance and support for up to 2 TB file sizes, and which continues to be a file system used on many Linux machines. This file system implemented a data structure that includes *inodes*, which store information about files, directories, and other system objects. ext2 stores files as blocks of data on the hard disk. As we'll see when we discuss clusters later in this chapter, *blocks* are the smallest unit of data used by the file system, and data is stored to one or more blocks on the HDD. A group of blocks containing information used by the operating system (which can contain such data as how to boot the system) is called a *superblock*.

- **ext3** Stands for Third Extended File System, and supersedes ext2. A major improvement to previous versions is that ext3 is a journaled file system, which makes it easier to recover. A journal is similar to transaction logs used in databases, where data is logged before being written. On ext3, the journal is updated before blocks of data are updated. If the computer crashed, the journal could be used to restore the file system by ensuring that any data that wasn't written to blocks before the crash are resolved so that the blocks are marked as being used when they are actually free (a concept we'll discuss later when we talk about clusters). On ext2, if a problem occurred, you would need to run Filesystem Check (fsck) to resolve issues with files and metadata on the system.

- **ext4** Short for Fourth Extended File System. In addition to improvements in performance, this version of the file system supports volumes of up to 1EB.

Mac OS X File System

Over the years, Macs have used several different file systems. When the original Macintosh computer was released January 24, 1984, it used the *Macintosh File System* (MFS), which was used to store data on 400KB floppy disks. Although archaic by today's standards, MFS offered a number of innovations, as is common with technology developed by Apple.

MFS saved files to hard disks in two parts. A *resource fork* was used to store structured information, and a *data fork* was used to store unstructured data. Whereas data used in a file would be stored in the data fork, information related to the file (including icons, menus and menu items, and other aspects of the file) would be stored in the resource fork. The resource fork allowed files to be opened by the correct application, without the need for a file extension, and could also be used to store metadata.

A year after MFS was released, the *Hierarchical File System* (HFS) replaced it. HFS continued to use multiple forks when storing data, but was designed to organize and manage data on both floppy disks and hard disks. Like its predecessor, it also supported filenames that were 255 characters in length, but where it was exceptional over MFS was in performance. MFS was designed for use on floppy disks, so it performed slowly on larger media. HFS was designed to perform well with hard disks, and it used a hierarchical design through a Catalog File to replace the flat table structure used by MFS.

In 1998, Apple introduced a new version of HFS called *HFS Plus*. In addition to better performance, improvements were made in how HFS Plus handled data. Like Linux machines, HFS and HFS Plus both store data in blocks on the hard disk, with volumes divided into logical blocks that are 512 bytes in size. HFS used 16-bit block addresses, but this was improved in HFS Plus, where 32-bit block addresses were supported. The 16-bit blocks used in HFS meant that only 65,536 blocks could be allocated to files on a volume. Although this wasn't an issue when hard disks were smaller, it resulted in a considerable amount of wasted space on larger volumes.

Mac OS X computers also support a number of other file systems, including the FAT16 and FAT32 file systems mentioned previously, and the UNIX File System (UFS) that's a variant of the BSD Fast File System.

CD-ROM/DVD File System

Not all file systems are developed for hard disks or accessing data over a network (as we'll discuss later in this chapter). File systems also exist that are specifically designed for organizing and accessing files stored on CDs and DVDs. As we discussed earlier in this chapter, although both are 5-inch optical discs that visually appear identical, CDs can contain up to 700MB of data whereas DVDs are able to store from 4.7GB to 17GB of data. Although CDs were designed to store an entire album of music and DVDs were designed to store an entire movie on one disc, both CDs and DVDs are capable of storing various kinds of data.

Universal Disk Format (UDF) is a file system that is used by both CDs and DVDs, and is a standard format the Optical Storage Technology Association (OSTA). UDF is based on the International Organization for Standardization (ISO) 13346 standard, and uses a file structure that's accessible by any computer or CD/DVD system. UDF was not initially supported by Microsoft operating systems, which was why Microsoft released a format called UDF Bridge with Windows 95 to provide support until the next release of Windows. Although UDF is compatible with ISO 9660 (which we'll discuss next), UDF was developed as a hybrid of both UDF and ISO 9660 standards. To allow DVDs to be played and burned (that is, recorded) on Windows computers, DVD-ROM vendors had to include support for both UDF and UDF Bridge.

ISO 9660 was introduced as a standard for CD-ROM media in 1988, and is commonly referred to as CDFS (Compact Disc File System). It allows CDs created on different operating systems to be accessed by other operating systems. Using this standard, CD data is stored as frames on the disc, with each frame being 24 bytes in length. Using ISO 9660 for recording, three different modes may be available in disc creation software:

- **CD-ROM Mode 1** Generally used to record computer data. Filenames are limited to eight characters with three additional characters for the extension (the standard 8.3 format).

- **CD-ROM Mode 2 Form 1** Also generally used for recording computer data. Although it uses the same format as Mode 1, it isn't compatible across all systems. It allows filenames of up to 180 characters (depending on how many extended attributes are used).

- **CD-ROM Mode 2 Form 2** Allows data to be fragmented so that data can be written in increments to the CD. It is commonly used for video CDs, and other fault-tolerant data, where any errors that occur would happen so fast that a person viewing the media would generally not detect it.

Because technology changed, extensions to the ISO 9660 standard were developed to address issues that the initial standard didn't address. These extensions include:

- **Joliet** Addresses limitations in the filenames as ISO 9660 didn't support long filenames. Joliet is still supported by disc creation software and all Windows operating systems since Windows 95, and allows filenames that are 64 characters in length.

- **Apple ISO9660 Extensions** Developed by Apple to address limitations in the properties of files stored on CDs. Because HFS supports more properties than the FAT file system and uses a resource fork and data fork to save files, Apple developed an extension that allows non–Macintosh systems to access data saved by Macintosh computers and view the properties of these files.

- **Rock Ridge Interchange Protocol** Abbreviated as RRIP and corresponds to IEEE P1282. RRIP is used for storing information that's specific to UNIX machines, and supports filenames that are up to 255 characters in length.

■ **El Torito** Developed by Phoenix Technologies (which manufactured the BIOS of computers) and IBM to allow computers to be booted from a CD. If a CD has already been inserted in a CD-ROM when the computer starts up and has a boot code on it, the BIOS assigns a drive number to the CD-ROM and allows the computer to boot from that device.

Understanding Network Basics

It wasn't so long ago that most computers were *stand-alone*, meaning they weren't connected to any type of network. If you wanted to share programs, pictures, or other data, you would copy it to a floppy disk and use *sneakernet* (put on your sneakers and walk it to another computer). Today that isn't the case. As we saw earlier in this chapter, operating systems over the past few years have added features that make it increasingly easier to connect to networks.

A *network* is two or more computers that are connected together so that they can share data and other resources. A network can be as small as a couple of computers connected with a hub in a home network, to a corporate network made up of thousands of computers, to the largest network on the planet—the Internet. From this, you can see that networks can be defined by their scale, as follows:

■ **Personal area network (PAN)** A network of two or more devices that exchange data within a few yards or so of one another. An example is a cell phone or PDA that is uses Bluetooth technology to exchange pictures or an address book with another laptop, cell phone, or PDA.

■ **Local area network (LAN)** A network of computers in a small geographic area, such as the computers networked together in a department, a floor of a building, an entire building, and so on.

■ **Metropolitan area network (MAN)** A network made up of smaller networks across the geographical span of a city. It may consist of several blocks of buildings, or smaller LANs that are connected across a city.

■ **Campus area network (CAN)** A network made up of several interconnected LANs, such as several buildings on a university campus. A CAN is a subset of a MAN, and the term is usually limited to describing the MAN of an educational institution.

■ **Wide area network (WAN)** A network that is spread across a large geographical area, such as in different cities, states, or countries. he largest (and best known) WAN is the Internet.

As we've already discussed in previous chapters, network connectivity opens up new opportunities for criminals as well as for legitimate computer users. Even for crimes that are less technical in nature, the network gives criminals an infinite number of additional locations for storing files that provide evidence of the crime. Investigators must be aware of this fact or they could overlook crucial pieces of evidence. For example, a child pornographer might be careful to upload all his illegal graphics files to a location someplace geographically far away from his home computer, deleting the originals from his hard disk. Examination of the suspect's own computer might reveal nothing incriminating. However, network logs could show when and to where the transmissions were made. The logs of File Transfer Protocol (FTP) clients or other programs used to transfer the data could reveal the site to which uploads were made. An investigator who doesn't understand how data is sent across networks or who is not aware of the existence of log files or the significance of program settings would not even know how to begin to look for this evidence.

Network Operating Systems

Modern operating systems have networking capabilities built in. Early PC operating systems such as DOS (and the Windows shell that ran on it) did not; it wasn't until Version 3.11, with Windows for Workgroups, that Microsoft included networking components. As the name implied, that version of Windows was designed to function in a small peer-to-peer local network. Windows NT added authentication server functionality (Microsoft called the authentication server a *domain controller*), but with the early versions of NT, the focus was still on the LAN, not the WAN. At that time, Microsoft operating systems were not considered scalable enough for enterprise networking, and most Web servers on the Internet were UNIX machines. With Windows 95, it became easier for users to connect to the Internet, and NT 4.0 supported Web services (IIS) that made it easy to host Web sites on the Internet or intranets. Windows 2000 built more heavily on Internet connectivity and added features to the server products that made it more suitable for enterprise-level computing, including a robust directory service (Active Directory), industry-standard security protocols such as Kerberos and IPSec, and load-balancing and clustering support. The next generation of Windows servers, 2003 and 2008, continued this trend and embrace the idea that "the network *is* the computer" to a larger extent than ever.

The term *network operating system (NOS)* is used in three different ways:

- It is sometimes used to refer to any computer operating system that has built-in networking components, as do all of today's popular PC operating systems. Thus, Windows 9*x*, NT, 200*x*, XP, and Vista, along with most distros of Linux, UNIX, and Macintosh, are considered NOSes, whereas MS-DOS and Windows 3.1 and earlier are not.

- It is sometimes used to refer to the components of the operating system that make networking possible. For example, today's Windows operating systems include file and print sharing services, which allow the computer to act as a server and share its resources with other systems, and the Client for Microsoft Networks (known as the Workstation service in NT) which allows the computer to connect to and access the shared resources of other systems. These components, along with the protocol stacks on which the network operates, are sometimes referred to as the NOS.

- It is sometimes used to refer to the server operating system software—such as Windows NT Server, Windows 200*x* Server, UNIX, Apple OS X Server, or NetWare—especially when functioning as an authentication server that maintains a security accounts database for the network.

In the following sections, we look at how client/server computing works and discuss both the server software and the client software that work together to enable network communications. We will also take a look at network file systems and how they differ from local file systems as well as the protocols that govern the network communication process.

Understanding Client/Server Computing

The term *client/server computing* has different meanings, depending on the context in which it is used. Some documentation uses the term narrowly, to refer to applications in which the bulk of the processing is performed on a server. For example, SQL Server is a database application that uses the server's power to sort the data in response to a query and then returns only the results to the client. Contrast this system with Microsoft's Access, in which database files are stored on a server, but a client query results in the entire file being transferred to the client machine, where the sorting takes place.

Using this meaning of the term, *thin client computing* is the ultimate form of client/server computing. With thin client software such as Microsoft's terminal services, the operating system runs on the server, and all applications run there; only the graphical representation of the desktop screen runs on the client machine. This means client machines can be low-power systems with modest processors and small amounts of RAM—machines that are not capable of running the operating system themselves. Thus, a user can work in Windows XP using an old 80486 system that has only 16MB of RAM, because the operating system isn't really running on that old system—it's being used only as a terminal to access the OS on the server.

Authentication Server-Based Networks

A second, broader meaning of the term *client/server computing* refers to a network that is based on an authentication server. This is a server that controls access to the network, storing a security accounts database that holds users' network-wide account information. When a user wants to log on to the network the client computer contacts this authentication server. The server checks its database to ensure that the user is authorized and to determine the level of access allowed to that user (usually based on security groups to which the user belongs). The authentication server is a centralized point of security and network resource management and must run special (and usually expensive) server software. In Microsoft networking, this type of network is called a *domain* and the authentication server is called a *domain controller*. UNIX and NetWare servers also provide network authentication services.

NOTE

We discuss *authentication*, which refers to the verification of a user's or computer's identity, in much more detail in Chapter 12, when we discuss security concepts.

Authentication server operating systems such as NT Server used a flat accounts database, but the trend quickly changed toward the use of hierarchical databases called *directory services*, such as Novell's eDirectory, Apple's Open Directory implantation, and Microsoft's Active Directory. All these services have something in common: They are compatible with the *Lightweight Directory Access Protocol (LDAP)* standards. This is an industry standard based on the ISO's X.500 specifications, and adherence to the standards allows directory services from different vendors to interoperate on a network.

These client/server (or server-based) networks provide many advantages, especially for large networks. Because security and management are centralized, this type of network can be more easily secured and managed than the alternative network model.

Peer-to-Peer Networks

Networks without an authentication server are called *workgroups* or *peer-to-peer networks*. This model is appropriate for small networks with only a few computers, in environments where high security is not required. They are common to small offices or home networks. In a workgroup, all computers can provide both client and server services.

NOTE

In this context, the term *server services* means only that the computers make their resources accessible to (share them with) other computers on the network. The computers in a workgroup do not have to run expensive server software, although a workgroup can have machines running such software as Windows Server 2008, operating as *member servers* instead of domain controllers. The key differentiating factor is that in a workgroup, there is no *authentication* server, although there can be other types of servers (file and print servers, remote access servers, fax servers, and the like).

Workgroups are less expensive to implement than server-based networks, for several reasons:

- Server operating system software is costly, and must be purchased to implement a server-based network.

- Server software generally requires more powerful hardware than do desktop operating systems, so you might need to purchase more expensive machinery to run it.

- Server-based networks generally require a dedicated network administrator to perform the many tasks involved in network administration and maintenance, necessitating hiring additional personnel or extra work on the part of an existing employee.

Despite the cost advantage of workgroups, they are less secure, because the user of each computer must manage its resources. To access resources on any other computer in the workgroup, a user must have a local account created on that machine, or alternatively, each individual shared resource can be protected by a password. Either of these methods gets very cumbersome when there are more than a handful of users and/or more than a few shared resources.

With the first method, a user might need accounts on a dozen or more computers; with the second method, that user would have to keep track of dozens or even hundreds of different passwords to access different shared folders or printers. Contrast this scenario with the authentication server-based network, where each user has a single username and password for logging on to the entire network. The user can then access any resource on any machine in the network for which the appropriate permissions have been assigned. Although administrators do have to assign permissions to each shared resource, from the user's point of view this is a much simpler system. When workgroups grow beyond 20 or 25 computers, it is usually advantageous to convert to a centralized (server-based) model.

Server Software

Remember that all modern operating systems, even consumer and home editions, have a *server component* (such as file and print sharing for Microsoft Networks) that allows them to share their resources. When we refer to server software here, we're talking about operating systems capable of providing network authentication services (as well as other server services such as domain name system [DNS], Web services, or remote access services). There are also many server *applications* (such as the SQL database server, the ISA proxy/firewall server, the Exchange mail server, and the like) that can be installed only on a system running a server operating system.

Earlier in this chapter, we discussed the major computer operating systems, as well as a number of the major server operating systems. Windows NT and Windows Server 200*x* are higher-level products that provide services on most corporate networks. Previous to Windows NT 4.0, the major network operating system was Novell NetWare, which is still used on many networks. However, when Windows 2000 was released, Novell lost significant ground to Microsoft. As we mentioned previously, Windows 2000 Server provided a directory service called Active Directory that was similar to Novell's NDS (later called eDirectory). Using the directory service, user accounts and access to resources could be easily managed, controlling who had access to what.

Active Directory (AD) catalogs information about the network as objects. These objects include the users (people who use the network), computers, printers, and other resources that make up the network. Each object has attributes associated with it, such as a person's attributes including his or her first and last names, logon name, and other information. To organize the objects, network administrators can arrange them into containers, much in the same way that you might organize files into folders on your hard disk. When a person logs on to the network, Active Directory compares the logon information to the password associated with that user account. After authenticating the user, appropriate access is given.

Another popular server is UNIX, which has been around since the beginning of networking and the Internet. UNIX is a very powerful server operating system, but it is considered to have a steep learning curve. It is a character-based OS, but GUI interfaces are available. There are dozens of different popular commercial and free distributions of UNIX.

Apple also makes its OS X in a server version, which supports Macintosh, Windows, UNIX, and Linux clients and includes Apache Web server, Post Office Protocol (POP) and Internet Message Access Protocol (IMAP) mail, and DNS and Dynamic Host Configuration Protocol (DHCP) services. OS X Server runs only on Macintosh systems, and isn't widely implemented. The server version of OS X is less costly than Microsoft's and Novell's products and much more user-friendly than other versions of UNIX.

Client Software

Most modern operating systems can also function as network clients. For example, if you were running Windows 2008 on your computer, you could log on to the network as a user, run programs, and use it as you would Windows Vista. With the exception of NetWare, this is common among many server operating systems. However, it would be inefficient and costly to run Windows Server 2008, for example, as a desktop client as it costs considerably more than the desktop operating system. UNIX is most often used as a server, but Linux has grown in popularity as a desktop/client OS. Mac OS X comes in both client and server forms. Novell doesn't make a client OS of its own; NetWare clients generally run Windows or UNIX operating systems with NetWare client software installed.

This brings up an important point: Client machines don't necessarily have to run an operating system made by the vendor of the network's server software. Macintosh and UNIX-based clients can access Windows servers, Windows and Macintosh clients can access UNIX servers, and so forth. As shown in the Figure 4.16, the Novell client for Windows is used to supply a username and password, which is then sent to a Novell server. The Novell server then uses eDirectory to authenticate the user and to determine what the user is permitted to access, and may access a script to map drives to locations on the network. As a result, the user will see a variety of new drive letters, which allow the user to store files on network servers.

Figure 4.16 The Novell Client

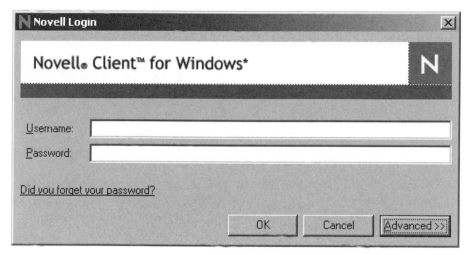

Understanding Network Hardware

Just as operating systems commonly have the features necessary to connect to a network easily, so do computers. Although a person used to have to buy and install a network card in his or her computer to connect to an existing network, laptops and desktops are now sold with Ethernet cards included as a basic feature. Even if the computer isn't used for a home or organization's network, manufacturers know that they will still be used to connect to the Internet, as in the case of users who use Digital Subscriber Line (DSL) technology.

Just as you need a working knowledge of the hardware that makes up a PC to understand how a computer works, you need to be familiar with the hardware that enables network communication to understand how that communication process works. Networks range from very small (two directly linked computers) to very large (WANs that rely on complex hardware devices to link entire local networks in distant locations). Thus, the number and types of network hardware devices on a network will vary. However, all computer networking begins with an *interface* connecting each networked computer to the network.

The Role of the NIC

The *network interface card (NIC)* or *network card* is the hardware device most essential to establishing communication between computers. Although there are ways to connect computers without a NIC (by modem over phone lines or via a serial "null modem" cable, for instance), in most cases where there is a network, there is a NIC for each participating computer.

The NIC is responsible for preparing the data to be sent over the network medium. Exactly how that preparation is done depends on the medium being used. Most networks today use Ethernet.

Ethernet was developed in the 1960s with specifications developed by Digital, Intel, and Xerox (governed by IEEE 802.3 standards). It uses a method of accessing the network called Carrier Sense Multiple Access/Collision Detection (CSMA/CD), in which each computer monitors the network to ensure that no one else is sending data along the same line of cabling. If two computers send data at the same time, it causes a collision that's detected by the other workstations, and the computers will wait a random time interval to send the data again.

Understanding How Data Is Sent across a Network

On a network, data is sent across the cables as signals that represent the binary 1s and 0s that represent the data. Signals represent individual bits, and those bits are often grouped together in bytes for convenience, but computers send data across the network in larger units: packets, segments, datagrams, or frames. A *packet* is a generic term, generally defined as a "chunk" of data of a size that is convenient for transmitting. Rather than sending an entire, large file as one long stream of bits, the system divides the file into blocks, and each block is transmitted individually. This system allows for more efficient network communications, because one computer doesn't "hog" the network bandwidth while sending a large amount of data. On an internetwork, where there are multiple routes from a particular sender to a particular destination, this system also allows the separate blocks of data to take different routes.

Most networks, including the Internet, run on the TCP/IP protocols. At the transport level, a unit of data is called a *segment* when TCP is the transport layer protocol. To further confuse an already confusing issue, it's called a *user datagram* when User Datagram Protocol (UDP) is used. One step down, at the network (IP) level, the chunks of data that are routed across the network are called *datagrams*. When we move down to the data link level (at which Ethernet and other link layer protocols operate), the unit of data we work with is called a *frame*.

The Internet uses *packet-switching technology* to most effectively move large amounts of data being transmitted by multiple computers along the best pathways toward their destinations. Each packet travels independently; when all the packets that make up a communication arrive at the destination computer, they are reassembled in proper order using information contained in their *headers*. You can think of a packet as an electronic envelope that contains the data as well as addressing and other relevant information (such as sequencing and checksum information).

The Role of the Network Media

The *network media* are the cable or wireless technologies on which the signal is sent. Cable types include thin and thick coaxial cable (similar to but not the same as cable TV media), twisted-pair cable (such as that used for modern telephone lines, available in both shielded and unshielded types), and fiber optic cable, which sends pulses of light through thin strands of glass or plastic for fast, reliable communication but is expensive and difficult to work with. Wireless media include radio waves, laser, infrared, and microwave.

Unauthorized people can capture data directly from the media, by "tapping into" the cable and using a protocol analyzer to open packets and view the data inside. Copper cables are especially easy to compromise in this way, but data can also be intercepted on fiber optic cabling using a device called an *optical splitter*. Wireless transmissions are also easy to intercept; the practice of "war driving" is popular with hackers, who set up laptop systems with wireless network cards and then drive around looking for open wireless networks to connect to. Because many businesses leave the default settings on their wireless access points and don't elect to use wireless encryption protocols, their networks are wide open to anyone with a portable computer, a wireless NIC, and a small amount of technical knowledge. We address wireless security in detail in Chapter 10, when we discuss network intrusions and attacks, and again in Chapter 13.

The Roles of Network Connectivity Devices

Network connectivity devices do exactly what the name implies: They connect two or more segments of cable. Complex connectivity devices can serve two seemingly opposite purposes: They are used to divide large networks into smaller parts (called *subnets* or *segments*, depending on the device type), and they are used to combine small networks into a larger network called an *internetwork* or *internet*. Less complex connectivity devices do neither; they are used merely as connection points for the computers on a network (or network segment) or to amplify the signals of networked computers, which extends the distance over which transmissions can be sent. They can also:

- Connect network segments that use different media types (for instance, thin coax and unshielded twisted pair [UTP])

- Segment the network to reduce traffic without dividing the network into separate IP subnets

We look briefly at some of these devices in the following subsections. In looking at these various devices, it is important to realize that newer corporate networks use *switches* that combine many of the features of different devices into a single device. This isn't uncommon, as network devices commonly incorporate many features that were previously available only in separate network components.

Repeaters and Hubs

Repeaters and *hubs* are connection devices. We discuss them together because, in many cases, they are the same thing. In fact, you will hear hubs referred to as *multiport repeaters*. Repeaters connect two network segments (usually thin or thick coax) and boost the signal so that the distance of the cabling can be extended past the normal limits at which attenuation, or weakening, interferes with the reliable transmission of the data.

A repeater is used to extend the usable length of a given type of cable. For instance, a 10Base5 Ethernet network, using thick coax cable, has a maximum cable segment length of 500 meters, or 1,640 feet. At that distance, *attenuation* (signal loss due to distance) begins to take place. But when you place a repeater at the end of the cable and attach another length to the repeater's second port, the signal is boosted and the data can travel farther without damage or loss.

Hubs are different from basic repeaters in that the repeater generally has only two ports, whereas the hub can have many more (typically from five to 64 or more). Hubs can also be connected to one another and stacked, providing even more ports. Hubs are generally used with Ethernet twisted-pair cable, and most modern hubs are repeaters with multiple ports; they also strengthen the signal before passing it back to the computers attached to it. Hubs can be categorized as follows:

- **Passive hubs** These hubs serve as connection points only; they do not boost the signal. Passive hubs do not require electricity and thus don't use a power cord as active hubs do.

- **Active hubs** These hubs serve as both a connection point and a signal booster. Data that comes in is passed back out on all ports. Active hubs require electrical power.

■   **Intelligent or "smart" hubs** These are active hubs that include a microprocessor chip with diagnostic capabilities so that you can monitor the transmission on individual ports.

Another type of hub, called a *switching hub* and is more commonly called simply a *switch*.

Bridges

Bridges can separate a network into segments, but they don't *subnet* the network as routers do. In other words, if you use a bridge to physically separate two areas of the network, it still appears to higher-level protocols to be one network.

A bridge monitors the data frames it receives to construct a table of *MAC addresses*, which are unique addresses that are assigned to the NIC to identify it on the network. The bridge determines which NIC sent the data using the source addresses on the frames. This is a simple table that tells the bridge on which side a particular address resides. Then the bridge can look at the destination address on a frame and, if it is in the table, determine whether to let it cross the bridge (if the address is on the other side) or not (if the address is on the side from which it was received).

In this way, less unnecessary traffic is generated. Let's say a computer in the HR department sends a message to another computer that is also in that department, and the signal goes only to those computers on that side of the bridge. The computers in Finance, on the other side of the bridge, go blithely on with their business and never have to deal with the message. Bridges can cut network congestion because they can do some basic filtering of data traffic based on the destination computer's MAC address. When a transmission reaches the bridge, the bridge will not pass it to the other side of the network if the destination computer's MAC address is known to be on the same side of the network as the sending computer.

Switches

Switching hubs are installed in place of the active hubs that have been more typically used to connect computers on a UTP-cabled network. Switches cost a bit more than hubs, but offer several important advantages.

A switch combines the characteristics of hubs and bridges. Like a bridge, a switch constructs a table of MAC addresses. The switch knows which computer network interface (identified by its physical address) is attached to which of its ports. It can then determine the destination address for a particular packet and route it only to the port to which that NIC is attached. Obviously, this system cuts down a great deal on unnecessary bandwidth usage because the packet is not sent out to all the remaining ports, where it will be disregarded when those computers determine that it is not intended for them. Figure 4.17 illustrates this process.

Figure 4.17 Switches Reducing Traffic by Sending Data Out the Port with Which the Destination MAC Address Is Associated

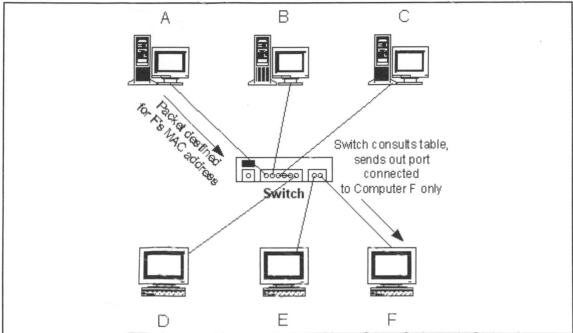

Using switches instead of hubs creates individual "collision domains" for each segment (the cable length between the switch and each node). This means a particular computer receives only the packets addressed to it, or to a multicast address to which it belongs, or to the broadcast address (when messages are being sent to every computer). You increase potential bandwidth in this way by the number of devices connected to the switch, because each computer can send and receive at the same time that one or more other nodes are doing so.

Switches can forward data frames more quickly than bridges because instead of reading the entire incoming Ethernet frame before forwarding it to the destination segment, the switch typically reads only the destination address in the frame, then retransmits it to the correct segment. This is why switches can offer fewer and shorter delays throughout the network, resulting in better performance.

A type of switch that operates at the network layer, or on Layer 3 of the Open Systems Interconnection model (OSI model), has become a popular connectivity option. A Layer 3 switch, sometimes referred to as a *switch router*, is in fact a type of router. Although a Layer 2 switch (switching hub) is unable to distinguish between protocols, a Layer 3 switch actually performs the functions of a router. A Layer 3 switch can filter the packets of a particular protocol to allow you to further reduce network traffic.

Layer 3 switches perform the same tasks as routers and can be deployed in the same locations in which a router is traditionally used. Yet the Layer 3 switch overcomes the performance disadvantage of routers, layering routing on top of switching technology. Layer 3 switches have become the solution of choice for enterprise network connectivity.

Routers

Routers are multiport connectivity devices that are used on large, complex networks because they are able to use the logical IP address to determine where packets need to go. How does using the IP address help to simplify the routing process? s we'll discuss later in this chapter, an IP address is used to identify each computer on a network. The IP address is divided into two parts: the network ID and the host ID. The network ID is a group of numbers that identifies which network the computer is on, and the host ID is used to identify which of the computers (or host as it's called on TCP/IP networks) sent or is meant to receive a particular message. The network ID is the key here because it "narrows down" the location of the particular destination computer by acting somewhat the way a ZIP Code does for the post office.

Routers are used to handle complex routing tasks. Routers also reduce network congestion by confining broadcast messages to a single subnet. A router can be either a dedicated device or a computer running an operating system that is capable of acting as a router. A Windows server can function as a router when two network cards are installed and IP forwarding is enabled.

Routers are capable of filtering so that you can, for instance, block inbound traffic. This capability allows the router to act as a *firewall*, creating a barrier that prevents undesirable packets from either entering or leaving a particular designated area of the network. However, in general, the more filtering a router is configured to do, the slower its performance.

Gateways

Gateways are usually not implemented as "devices" (although they can be). Rather, they are implemented as software programs running on servers. However, because they are also used to connect disparate networks, we touch briefly on what they are and why they are implemented in many networks.

Gateways can be used to connect two networks that use entirely different protocols. For instance, Microsoft's Host Integration Server allows PCs running Windows to communicate with an IBM mainframe computer, even though the two systems are "alien" to one another. There are many other different types of gateways, such as e-mail gateways, which translate between e-mail protocols.

NOTE

Additional information on Microsoft's Host Integration Servers is available at www.microsoft.com/hiserver/default.mspx.

Protocols

A protocol is a set of rules that determine how computers connect, communicate, and exchange data over a network. To illustrate how a protocol works, consider what happens when you make a phone call. You dial a number that identifies the person being called. When the phone rings and the person answers, he or she says "Hello"; when one person finishes talking the other can begin; and when communication terminates, you say "Goodbye." These rules serve as a protocol for communications between two people, just as network protocols dictate how computers communicate.

Many different kinds of protocols are available, each providing different functions on a network. In some cases, these protocols are combined into a protocol suite, as in the case of TCP/IP. The TCP/IP protocol suite includes such individual protocols as the following:

- **TCP** (Transmission Control Protocol) Used to coordinate the transmission, reception, and retransmission (if necessary) of packets of data on a network. It is a connection-oriented protocol that provides reliable communication between two hosts on a network so that transmission of data between them is guaranteed.

- **IP** (Internet Protocol) Used to specify the format of packets and provides connectionless delivery of packets.

- **UDP** (User Datagram Protocol) Used for one-way transmission of data, and doesn't guarantee that every bit of data will make it to its destination. This is used for streaming video or other media being sent that doesn't require every bit of data to display the information.

- **HTTP** (Hypertext Transfer Protocol) Used to transfer data over a TCP/IP network, and primarily used by Internet browsers to access HTML files (also known as Web pages) on intranets and the Internet.

- **FTP** (File Transfer Protocol) Commonly used to transfer files over a TCP/IP network.

Although numerous individual protocols are installed with TCP/IP, which protocol a particular program uses is often invisible to the user. For example, someone sending a video message over the Internet wouldn't know whether UDP was the protocol being used, whereas the average person wouldn't care that HTTP was a protocol being used to access a Web page.

Understanding IP Addresses

All law enforcement investigators need to understand the basics of IP addressing to trace users of the Internet to a physical location. Much like a phone number that shows up on a caller ID box from a threatening phone call can provide an investigator with a specific starting location for his or her investigation, an IP address can provide that same type of lead. By understanding what IP addresses are, how they're assigned, and who has control over them, an investigator can develop workable case leads.

IP addresses provide a connection point through which communication can occur between two computers. Without getting into too much detail about them, it is important that you understand how to identify an IP address when you see one. These addresses are made up of four 8-bit numbers divided by a dot (.), much like this one: 155.212.56.73. Currently, the Internet operates under the Internet Protocol Version 4 (IPv4) standard. In IPv4, approximately 4 billion IP addresses are available for use over the Internet. That number will be expanding in the near future to about 16 billion times that number when transition is made to IPv6.

During the birth and initial development of today's Internet, IP addresses primarily were assigned to computers for them to pass network traffic over the Internet. Computers were physically very large, extremely expensive, and pretty much limited to the organizations that controlled the primary networks that were part of the primordial Internet. During this time, an IP address most likely could be traced back to a specific computer. A limited number of large organizations own and control most of the IP addresses available with IPv4. Therefore, if an investigator has been able to ascertain the IP address of an illegal communication, he or she will also be able to determine which organization owns the network space within which that address is contained. That information in and of itself will often not be enough because many of these organizations sublease blocks of the IP addresses they own to smaller companies, such as Internet service providers (ISPs). The investigative follow-up with the ISP is therefore likely to provide the best results. Using an analogy, we can think about IP addresses much like phone numbers, where the major corporations are states and ISPs are towns or calling districts. If an investigator was following up on a case involving a phone number, the area code would narrow down the search to a particular state, and the remaining numbers would identify a particular account.

Remember that for Internet traffic to occur, an external IP address must be available to the device. An ISP provides access to an external IP address. ISPs sublease blocks of IP addresses from one or more of the larger corporations that control address space, and in return they will in essence sublease one of those addresses to the individual customer. This connection to the Internet is most often done through a modem. Modems come in varying configurations, such as dial-up, cable, and DSL. Depending on when you began to use the Internet, you may already be familiar with these devices. The older of the three listed is the dial-up modem, which required the use of a telephone line. When users wanted to connect to the Internet, they would plug the modem installed in their computer to their phone line and then dial one of the access numbers provided by the ISP. The dial-up modem is the slowest of the available devices and can make the transfer of large files a painful process. Therefore, when dealing with cases that require large file transfers such as child pornography, it is less likely that a dial-up connection would be used. A distinct advantage of the dial-up modem, though, is portability, because the connection can be made on any phone line by dialing an appropriate access number and providing valid account information.

More common today is Internet service provided through TV cable or through DSL; both of these services provide higher connection speeds, making the transfer of large files relatively easy. When a consumer contacts an ISP about Internet access, typically the consumer is assigned an installation date when a technician comes to the residence to connect the necessary wiring to the home through either the consumer's cable provider (cable modem) or phone provider (DSL). With the appropriate wiring in place, an external modem is connected to the line provided through which the computer in the home will connect. The modem provides the interface through which the home computer can be physically connected to the Internet.

When the home user is connected to the ISP's physical connection to the Internet, the ISP must still assign the home user's computer an IP address for the computer to communicate over the Internet. IP addresses are assigned in two ways: statically and dynamically. If static addressing was to be used, the install technician would configure the computer's NIC with the specific IP address during install. Static assignment by an ISP would limit the total number of customers an ISP could have by the total number of external addresses it controls. Let's say that XYZ ISP had subleased a block of 1,000 unique and valid IP addresses from a large corporation. If that ISP statically assigned addresses to its customers, the total number of customers it could have on the Internet would be limited to 1,000. Leasing blocks of external IP addresses is very expensive as the demand is high compared to availability. ISPs realize that it is unlikely that all of their customers will be on the Internet at the same time, so to get the largest return on their investment, they use an addressing scheme called *dynamic addressing*, which allows for computers that are actively connected to the Internet to be assigned an unused IP address.

Here's how dynamic addressing works. XYZ ISP has 1,000 addresses available to its customers. It sets up a server, referred to as a DHCP server, which maintains a list of the available addresses. At installation, the technician sets the consumer's computer NIC to get an address assignment through DHCP. When the consumer's computer is turned on and connected to the network, the NIC puts out a broadcast requesting an IP address assignment. The DHCP server responsible for the assignment responds to the request by providing an IP address from the pool of available addresses to the computer's NIC. The length of time that the computer will use that assigned address is based on the "lease" time set by the DHCP server. Remember that the ISP wants to have the maximum number of customers using the smallest number of addresses, so the ISP wants to ensure that any unused addresses are made available to other computers. The lease time determines how long that address will be used before the NIC will be required to send out another broadcast for an IP address. The IP address returned after the reassignment could be the same address used previously or an entirely new address, depending on what's available in the server pool.

You can determine a number of details about the configuration of a computer's NIC(s) in Windows by using a tool called ipconfig. As shown in Figure 4.18, when you enter the command *ipconfig /all* at a computer's command prompt, the IP address assigned to different NICs on the computer is displayed with other networking information.

Figure 4.18 The ipconfig /all Command

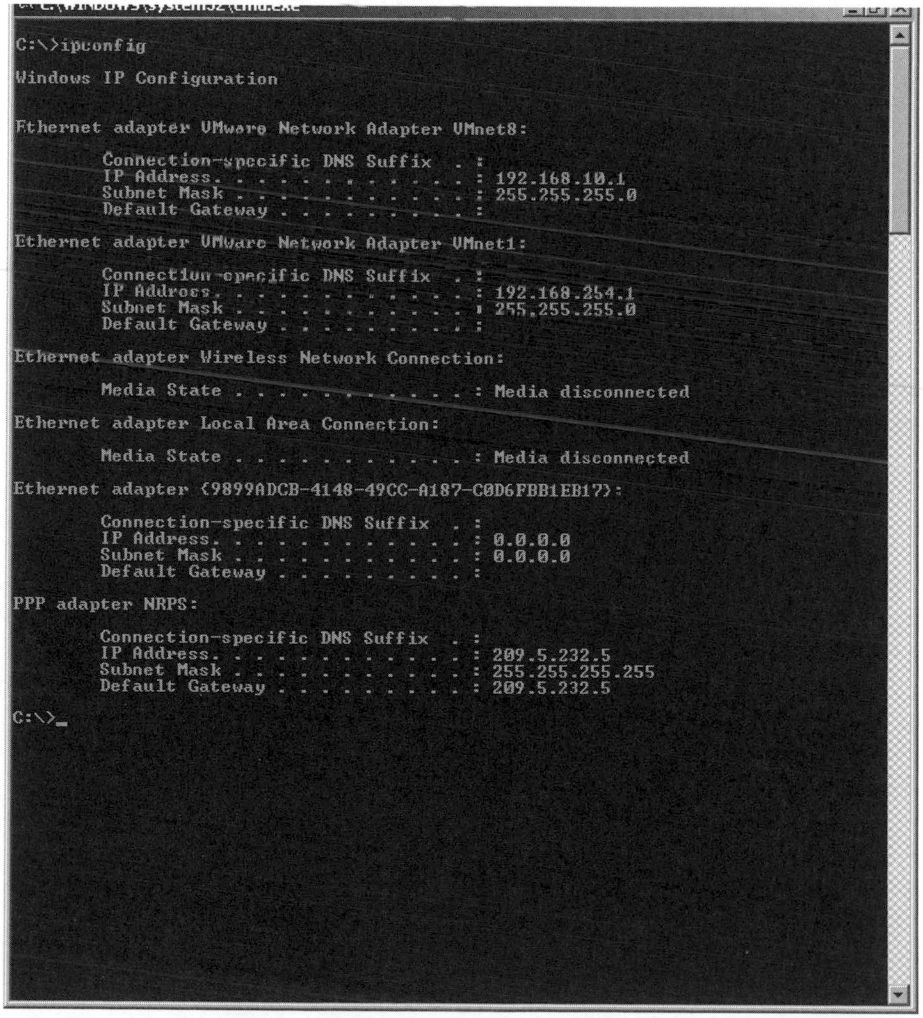

Note that this example provides details on several different NICs; a physical Ethernet port is identified by the Local Area Connection designation, a wireless network connection, virtual network adapters used by VMware, and a dial-up connection to the Internet that is associated with a modem. Each NIC can possess a different IP address. IP addresses are important because each device that communicates over a TPC/IP network and the Internet must have an address. In a computer crime investigation involving the Internet, it is very likely that the investigator will need to track an IP address to a location—preferably a person. As discussed earlier, ISPs control the assignment of IP addresses, and ISPs can provide the link between the IP address and the account holder. Understanding the distinction between static and dynamic IP assignment is very important because the investigator must record the date/time that IP address was captured. If the ISP uses DHCP, the IP address assignments can change—investigators need to be sure that the account holder identified by the ISP was actually assigned the IP address in question when the illicit activity occurred.

Let's take a moment and think about this. You're investigating an e-mail-based criminal threatening case where you were able to determine the originating IP address of the illegal communication. You were able to determine which ISP controls the address space that includes the IP address in question. If ISPs use dynamic addressing, how are you going to be able to determine which subscriber account used that address if any of a thousand or more could have been assigned to the suspect's computer? In this case, it would be extremely important for you to also record and note the date and time of the originating communication. The date/timestamp can be matched against the logs for the DHCP server to determine which subscriber account was assigned the IP address in question at that time.

Summary

Cybercrime investigators need to be as intimately familiar with the internal workings of computers and the software that runs on them as homicide investigators must be with basic human pathology. That includes understanding the function of all the hardware components that go together to make up a computer and how these components interact with one another.

It would be difficult for an investigator to conduct a proper investigation in a foreign country where he or she does not speak the local language, because many clues might go unnoticed if the investigator cannot understand the information being collected. Likewise, a cybercrime investigator must have a basic understanding of the "language" used by the machines to process data and communicate with each another. Even though an investigator in the field might not be able to speak all human languages, it is helpful to at least be able to recognize what language written evidence is in, because this evidence might be significant and will certainly help the investigator find someone who can translate it. Similarly, even though a cybercrime investigator is not expected to be able to program in binary, it helps to recognize the significance of data that is in binary or hexadecimal format and when it can or can't be valuable as evidence.

Computers today run a variety of operating systems and file systems, and the investigator's job of locating evidence will be performed differently depending on the system being used. A good cybercrime investigator is familiar with the most common operating systems and how their file systems organize the data on disk.

Regardless of operating system or hardware platform, the majority of networks today run on the TCP/IP protocols. TCP/IP is the most routable protocol stack and thus the most appropriate for large routed networks, it is required for connecting to the Internet. This chapter provided a basic overview of networking hardware and software and how TCP/IP communications are accomplished.

Frequently Asked Questions

Q: What is meant by terms such as *data transfer rate* and *seek time* in relation to hard disks?

A: These are ways to measure the performance of a hard disk. The *data transfer rate* refers to the number of bytes per second (bps) that the disk drive is able to transfer to the processor. This is usually measured for today's disks in megabytes per second, and rates between 5 and 40 are common. The higher this number is, the better the disk performance. *Seek time* refers to the time interval between the time the processor makes a request for a file from disk and the time at which the first byte of that file is received by the processor. This time is measured in milliseconds (typically between 7 and 20), and the lower this number is, the better the performance.

Q: How does a CD-R drive write data on a CD?

A: CD-Recordable, or CD-R, discs, unlike regular read-only CDs, have a layer of dye (usually a greenish color) on the disk that is then covered with a reflective gold layer. Both of these thin layers sit on top of a rigid piece of plastic called the *substrate*. The CD-R drive has a *writing laser* that is more powerful than the reading laser in a regular CD-ROM drive. This more powerful laser heats the layer of dye from the bottom, going through the substrate. The heating process changes the transparency of the dye at that spot, creating a "bump" that is not reflective. This bump forms a readable mark that is then read by the CD drive as data. The same encoding scheme is used as for regular CDs; that's why a regular CD-ROM drive can read CD-R discs.

Q: How does virtual memory work?

A: When an operating system supports the use of virtual memory, it creates a file on the hard disk (called a *swap file* or a *page file*) in which it can "swap out" data between the RAM and the disk. The system detects which areas of the physical memory (RAM) haven't been used recently. Then it copies the data from that location in memory to the file on the hard disk. This means there will be more free space in RAM, which allows you to run additional applications or speed the performance of applications that are currently running. When the processor needs the data stored in the swap/page file, it can be loaded from the hard disk back to RAM. The data is stored in units called *pages*. Using virtual memory can degrade performance if the system has to frequently swap the data in and out of RAM. This is because the hard disk is much slower than the RAM. Frequent swapping results in *disk thrashing*, which is usually a sign that you need to add more physical memory to the computer.

Chapter 5

The Computer Investigation Process

Topics we'll investigate in this chapter:

- **Demystifying Computer/Cybercrime**

- **Investigating Computer Crime**

- **Investigating Company Policy Violations**

- **Conducting a Computer Forensic Investigation**

☑ **Summary**

☑ **Frequently Asked Questions**

Introduction

The word *forensics* is derived from a Latin term meaning a forum in which legal disputes are settled, but no one in ancient Rome could have ever imagined how the term applies to today's legal system. As with other areas of forensics, *computer forensics* refers to an investigation process of gathering and examining evidence to establish facts so that accurate testimony and evidence can later be presented in court or other hearings. The key to this definition is that any work an investigator performs may be scrutinized and used as evidence in court.

Where computer forensics differs from other forensic sciences is that electronic evidence is collected and examined. Although fingerprints or other evidence may also be obtained from the devices collected at a crime scene, a computer forensic technician will use specialized methods, techniques, and tools to acquire data stored on hard disks, Universal Serial Bus (USB) flash drives, or other devices. Once the data is acquired from a device, he or she will then examine it to identify which files, folders, or information may be useful as evidence, and can provide facts about the case.

Although computer forensics is commonly used in criminal cases, it may also be used in civil disputes or corporate investigations, such as when internal policies have been violated. When an employee is suspected of using a computer to perform some action that violates policies, the files, e-mail, and other data on the computer may be inspected. Because it is possible that the violations could lead to criminal charges or civil actions against the employee, it is important that forensic procedures are followed.

Collecting such evidence requires following established procedures, and it can take a considerable amount of time to ensure that it is collected correctly. Because it may establish the identity of a culprit and may be used to establish the guilt or innocence of people, it is vital that the data isn't modified as it's acquired, or afterward when the data is examined. In addition to this, any actions and results are documented in case this information is required in court. By following such methodologies, you can investigate a computer crime effectively, and can collect and process evidence with a higher degree of success.

Demystifying Computer/Cybercrime

We often fear most what we don't understand. That could be said about computers and the investigation of computer crimes. In terms of policing, many investigators cringe at the mention of a computer and seek to offload any computer-related crime to the "computer crime guy" in their office. When you consider the number of technologies we discussed in the previous chapter, it is understandable why this occurs. Unlike new officers who grew up with computers, aspects of these technologies can seem overwhelming to veterans of the force. However, just as older officers had to make the transition from using a typewriter to using computers to fill out their reports, the same transition must be made in realizing that computers are yet another source of evidence—nothing more, nothing less.

Although computers have been readily available to the general public for a few decades, they've finally reached levels where it is feasible to expect that everyone has access to a computer. The computer is no longer a "nice to have," it is a "must have." Those who don't own their own computers can walk into a public library or cyber café to gain access to one. Similarly, access to the Internet is becoming ubiquitous through connections provided by libraries, coffee shops, computer stores, and even fast food restaurants.

This explosion of computer technology and acceptance has opened a new world of opportunity to the criminal element that constantly looks for new ways to exploit people through time-proven scams and tactics. As computers become more deeply integrated within society, it is likely that a computer or similar device will play a greater role in criminal activity.

As we discussed in Chapter 1, computers start to play a role in crime in situations where the capabilities of the computer allow a person to commit that crime or store information related to the crime. An e-mail phishing scam is a common example where the bad guy generates a fictitious e-mail for the sole purpose of enticing people to a spoofed site where they are conned into entering sensitive personal information. That sensitive information is then available to the bad guy to perpetrate an identity theft. In another example, a suspect might use the computer to scan and generate fake bank checks, or create fake identification. In both of these cases, the crime required the inherent capabilities of the computer for its commission.

In many cases, the crimes that are being committed haven't changed; only the manner in which they're being committed has changed. Think about it. Before the Internet, the telephone, the telegraph, and the Pony Express, if a person wanted to threaten to kill someone, it was likely that he or she would have to physically place him- or herself in proximity to the person and speak that threat. As services and technologies developed, new ways emerged through which a person could commit that same threatening act. The person could send a letter, send a telegram, or even better, make a phone call. Now we can send an e-mail or instant message (IM). Same crime; same underlying elements and facts to be proven. They change only in the manner of delivery. The key to a successful investigation of a computer crime is the development and follow-up of case leads. Although many leads will dead-end, the lead that continues to develop into further leads can end up solving your case. Many investigators believe that investigations involving computers are above their capabilities, but that is often not the case. By learning and adapting some basic computer knowledge and skills, today's investigator can react to new technologies and still develop workable old-school leads.

Because computers are so pervasive, it is an absolute necessity that investigators learn how to investigate crimes that involve a computer. The basic design of computers—including vast amounts of storage and meticulous file timestamping—can make them a wealth of evidence as traces of the crime can often be retrieved by an experienced investigator. This does not mean that every investigator needs to become an expert in computer technology, but there are basic concepts and methods that must be learned to develop old-school leads. *The key is to gain at least some basic computer knowledge and skills to put you ahead of the average computer user; skills that allow you to apply traditional policing skills and procedures to the case.*

As we'll see in the sections that follow, computer investigations can involve a wide variety of people. This includes not only law enforcement, but also the complainant who may have in-depth knowledge of the systems involved, the managers of a company who are familiar with policies and procedures, and others (such as information technology [IT] staff members) who can assist in effectively investigating the crime. In many cases, investigations may not even involve police, but rather may be conducted by those who perform investigations on behalf of the company for which they work. From this, you can see that investigators require good old-fashioned people skills and policing skills. Not only must they know how to secure a computer crime scene, but they also must also know how to deal with all those who may be involved. Essentially, this is no different from any other investigation. The investigative qualities needed to battle crime haven't changed; just the battlefield has changed.

Investigating Computer Crime

Computer forensics may be used in any crime that involves a computer. Because computers are so commonly used in homes and businesses, they are increasingly a source of evidence. Files stored on computers are often used in place of other record systems, and may contain a significant amount of information that can be used to convict a suspect or prove his or her innocence. For example, in a homicide investigation, a suspect may have written about his or her plans in a diary on the computer, or in a blog on the Internet. Conversely, if a person was accused of sending e-mail threats, a simple check of the messages on his or her machine could establish whether the accusations were false. Almost any type of crime may result in some type of evidence being stored on a computer, but a number of cybercrimes commonly require a computer forensic examination. These include:

- Threatening e-mail
- Harassment
- Fraud
- Hacking and/or dissemination of viruses
- Theft of intellectual property
- Child pornography

When crimes are committed using computers, often the only evidence available to prosecute the person who committed the offence is in a digital format. Illegal images will be stored only on a hard disk or other medium, proof of an intruder's activities may be stored in logs, and documents containing evidence of the crime are available only by investigating computers used in the crime, or ones that were subjected to the crime. By examining the digital contents of these computers, an investigator can reach a successful conclusion; prosecuting the culprit, and using information acquired from the investigation to make existing systems more secure.

On the Scene

When Bad Situations Are Used to Improve Current Systems

When a computer system is hacked or used in the commission of a crime, the victim is often unaware of vulnerabilities in the system that left him or her open to attack. A person who had malicious software installed might not know of antivirus (AV) or antispyware software, or the need to update signature files regularly. Similarly, a company might not know that its current firewall failed to prevent certain kinds of

Continued

intrusions, or was configured incorrectly. To prevent future intrusions or attacks, victims of computer crime can learn from the experience, and improve current systems.

An example of this is a crime that occurred against a major university in October 2006. Brock University experienced the embarrassing situation of its systems being hacked, and the personal information of upward of 70,000 alumni and other donators being stolen. The information of possibly every person who had ever donated to the university was accessed, including credit card and banking information. The university contacted police to investigate the incident, and contacted those people whose information may have been stolen. Within 24 hours, people were contacted via telephone and thousands of letters were sent to inform donators of this breach in security. The university followed by having the security of its systems reviewed and improvements made. Damage control also involved responding to the media, and informing the public that steps were being taken to repair vulnerabilities and improve security. Although the university was caught in a bad situation, its actions represent a textbook case of how to properly respond to an incident, and use the situation to review and revise current systems.

How an Investigation Starts

Investigations always start with a crime being committed, and someone noticing it. As insipid as this sounds, if these two factors aren't in place, an investigation will never occur. To illustrate this, let us look at a situation where a man has downloaded pornography to his computer. If the people posing in these images are of legal age, it is not illegal for this man to save the images to his hard disk and view them later, but if the images depict minors engaged in sex, the pictures are illegal and a crime has been committed. However, even though a crime has been committed, this doesn't mean this man will ever be investigated. For an investigation to occur, someone must notice that the crime has happened, and report it to the appropriate authorities. If no complaint is made, the person gets away with the crime.

The complainant plays a key role in any investigation. In addition to making authorities aware of the criminal activity, the complainant provides essential information about what he or she has discovered. The complainant may have seen a threatening e-mail or other illegal materials displayed on a coworker's computer, and can identify which computer contained the evidence. If the complainant was repairing a computer and found illegal files in a particular directory, he or she can hasten an investigation by indicating where the files are stored. The statements made by a complainant can also be used to acquire search warrants (as we'll discuss later in this chapter), and as the basis for further testimony in court. As the catalyst of an investigation, the role of a complainant is vital.

Who the complainant contacts often depends on the environment in which the crime has taken place, and the computer(s) involved. In a computer crime, the computer may play one of two roles:

- It may be the target of a crime.
- It may be used to commit crime.

If the complainant notices that his or her home computer has been involved in a criminal offense, chances are that the complainant is the victim and the computer was a target of a crime.

After all, few people confess to their involvement, or would subject themselves to being suspected. In situations involving home computers, the police are generally called first. This is also the case when someone notices illegal content on another person's home computer, or in small-business environments that have a limited staff. In larger companies, a complainant may first contact his or her supervisor or the IT department. This is especially the case if the crime involves a person's ability to work, such as when a server is compromised or a workstation has been infected by a virus or hacked. If the organization's IT staff has someone who has been trained to properly respond to incidents, this person may take some actions him- or herself before eventually contacting police.

What Is Your Role?

In a corporate environment, a network administrator or members of an incident response team will generally be the first people to respond to the incident. An incident response team consists of members of the IT staff, and has the training and expertise to respond to various types of incidents. Members of this team may work with police investigators to provide access to systems and expertise, if needed. Senior staff members should be notified to deal with the effects of the incident, and any inability to conduct normal business. In some cases, the company's public information officer may be involved, if the incident becomes known to the media and is deemed newsworthy.

If police aren't called in and the matter is to be handled internally, the incident response team will deal with a much broader range of roles. Team members will not only deal with the initial response to the incident, but also will conduct the investigation and provide evidence to an internal authority. This authority may be senior staff members, or in the case of a law enforcement agency, an internal affairs department. Even though no police may be involved in the situation, the procedures used in the forensic examination should be the same.

When conducting the investigation, a person must be designated as being in charge of the scene. This person should be knowledgeable in forensics, and be directly involved in the investigation. In other words, just because the owner of the company is available, that person should not be in charge if he or she is computer-illiterate and/or is unfamiliar with procedures. The person in charge should have the authority to make final decisions on how the scene is secured, and how evidence is searched, handled, and processed.

People may perform the following three major roles when conducting an investigation:

- First responder
- Investigator
- Crime scene technician

As we'll see in the paragraphs that follow, and as shown in Figure 5.1, each role has specific duties associated with it, which are vital to a successful investigation. In certain situations, such as those involving an internal investigation within a company, a person may perform more than one of these roles.

Figure 5.1 Primary Roles in an Investigation Involving Computer Forensics

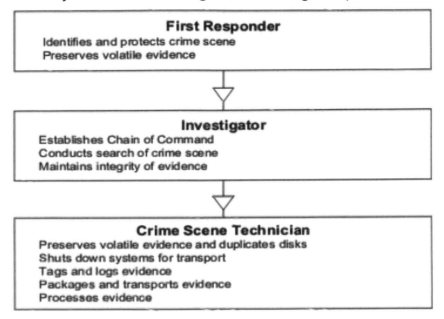

The Role of First Responder

First responders should follow the same edict to which aspiring physicians swear when they take the Hippocratic oath: *First, do no harm.* Unless specifically trained in computer forensics, people who are first on the scene should not attempt to do anything with or to the computers other than protect them from tampering or damage. It is very easy for technically astute criminals to plant Trojan horses or otherwise "rig" their computers to automatically destroy evidence when shut down or restarted by anyone other than themselves. The first responder should *not* attempt to shut down or unplug the computer or access it to look for evidence. The first responder *should* be concerned with the following tasks:

- **Identifying the crime scene** Officers or incident response team members who arrive first at a scene should identify the scope of the crime scene and establish a perimeter. This might include only one area of a room or it might include several rooms or even multiple buildings if the suspect is working with a complex setup of networked computers. First responders can begin to compile a list of systems that might have been involved in the criminal incident and from which evidence will be collected.

- **Protecting the crime scene** In a cybercrime case where digital evidence is sought, all computer systems—including those that appear to be powered off or nonfunctional—should be considered part of the crime scene, as should laptop, notebook, and other portable computers (including handheld computers and personal digital assistants [PDAs]). The items subject to seizure may be limited by the wording of the applicable search warrant, but first responders should cordon off and protect as much of the computer and electronic equipment as possible and wait for the investigator in charge of the case to determine what equipment, if any, will be excluded.

- **Preserving temporary and fragile evidence** In the case of evidence that could disappear before investigators arrive (such as information that is on the monitor and changing), first responders should take any possible steps to preserve or record it. If a camera is available, photos of the screen will preserve a record of what was there. If no camera is available, officers should take detailed notes and be prepared to testify in court as to what they saw.

NOTE

Protecting the crime scene could also involve disconnecting the computers from the network so as to remove a way for the suspect or an accomplice to deliberately alter the evidence or for someone else to unintentionally do so.

The Role of Investigators

The IT incident response team might have already begun to collect evidence in some cases. If so, the best practice is to have one person from the IT team coordinate the hand-over (and explanation, if necessary) of that evidence with one person from the police investigative team. The investigator (or the investigative team) is generally responsible for coordinating the activities of all others at the scene and will be responsible for the following:

- **Establishing the chain of command** The investigator in charge of the scene should ensure that everyone else is aware of the chain of command and that important decisions are filtered through him or her. Computers and related equipment should not be accessed, moved, or removed without explicit instructions from the senior investigator. The investigators shape and control the investigation. If the investigator in charge has to leave the scene, he or she should designate a person remaining on the scene to be in charge of the scene and stay in close contact with that person until all evidence has been collected and moved to secure storage.

- **Conducting the crime scene search** An investigator should direct the search of the crime scene, which may be carried out by investigators or by other officers. If the search warrant allows, officers should look for all computer hardware, software, manuals, written notes, and logs related to the operation of the computers. This includes printers, scanners, and all storage media: diskettes, optical discs (CDs, DVDs, and so on), tapes, any other removable disks, and any "extra" hard disks that might be lying around.

- **Maintaining integrity of the evidence** Investigators should continue to protect the evidence as preparations are made to preserve volatile evidence, duplicate the disks, and properly shut down the system. The investigator should oversee the actions of the crime scene technicians and convey any special considerations that should be taken based on the nature of the case and knowledge of the suspect(s).

The Role of Crime Scene Technicians

Crime scene technicians responding to a cybercrime case should, if at all possible, be specifically trained in computer forensics. Computer forensic specialists must have a strong background in computer technology with an understanding of how disks are structured, how file systems work, and how and where data is recorded. Generally, crime scene technicians will be responsible for the following tasks (although these may overlap with those of the investigators):

- **Preserving volatile evidence and duplicating disks** Volatile data is that which is in the computer's memory and consists of processes that are running. (See the "Preserving Volatile Data" section in Chapter 15 for instructions on how to deal with it.) Disks should be duplicated prior to shutdown, in case the system is rigged to wipe the disks on startup. We'll briefly discuss disk imaging later in this chapter, and more thoroughly in the next chapter when we discuss computer forensic hardware and software.

- **Shutting down the systems for transport** Proper shutdown is important to maintain the integrity of the original evidence. One school of thought says the computer should be shut down through the standard method (closing all programs and so on) to avoid corrupting files. Another says that after ensuring that no defragmentation or disk-checking program is running, you should shut down the computer by disconnecting the power cord, to prevent the running of self-destruct programs that are set to run on shutdown. UNIX computers usually should not be abruptly shut down this way while the root user is logged on because doing so can damage data.

NOTE

If the system is turned off, the investigative team generally should seize the computer and boot it in a controlled environment. When you do bring up the system, you should not boot from the computer's hard disk, but instead from a controlled boot disk to prevent the operating system from writing to the hard disk, so crucial data won't be overwritten.

- **Tagging and logging the evidence** All evidence should be tagged and/or marked with the initials of the officer or technician, time and date collected, case number, and identifying information. The evidence on the tag or mark should also be entered in the evidence log. We'll discuss documentation in great detail in Chapter 15.

- **Packaging the evidence** Computer evidence, especially any containing exposed circuit boards (such as hard disks), should be placed in antistatic bags for transport. Paper documentation such as manuals and books should be placed in plastic bags or otherwise protected from damage.

- **Transporting the evidence** All evidence should be transported as directly as possible to the secure evidence storage locker or room. During transport, the evidence should not be allowed to come into contact with any equipment that generates a magnetic field (including police radios and other electronic equipment in the squad car) nor left in the sun or in a vehicle or other place where the temperature rises above about 75°F. The chain of custody must be meticulously maintained during transport.

- **Processing the evidence** When the duplicate disk is brought back to the lab, the disk image can be reconstructed and the data analyzed using special forensic software.

Investigation Methodology

Investigation methodology is the practices, procedures, and techniques used to collect, store, analyze, and present information and evidence that is obtained through a computer forensic investigation. Although the individual steps to perform these tasks may vary from case to case and may depend on the types of software and equipment being used, many common practices will always be consistent. You can break down the methodology of a computer forensic investigation into three basic stages:

- Acquisition

- Authentication

- Analysis

Acquisition is the act or process of gathering information and evidence. As we've mentioned, the evidence pertains not only to a computer that's been seized, but also to the data stored on that computer. It is the data on a computer that will be used to provide insight into the details of a crime or other incident, and be used as evidence to convict a suspect. Computer forensic software can be used to acquire data from a machine, and make an exact copy of everything stored on the hard disks. Because the investigator is studying this image of the computer's data, the machine's original data is unaltered during later examination. The computer forensic technician can then study the suspect computer's contents through an image of the data, leaving the original data untouched.

To guarantee that the data acquired from a computer is a correct duplicate, it must be authenticated. *Authentication* is a process of ensuring that the acquired evidence is the same as the data that was originally seized. If the data that's been acquired from a computer was corrupted, modified, or missing from the imaging process, it would not only affect your ability to accurately examine the machine's contents, but also could make all of the evidence you find on the computer inadmissible in court. After all, if it was not a perfect duplicate, how would the court know that anything you found was really on the original machine? To authenticate the data that's acquired from a suspect computer, features included in forensic software can be used to compare the data that's duplicated in the imaging process to the original data on a suspect's computer.

Once these steps have been completed, the content of the computer can then be inspected for individual pieces of evidence that will later be used in court or other disciplinary processes. When a duplicate is made of a computer's data, an image is made of everything on the machine. This includes system and configuration files, executable programs, and other files that are installed with the operating system and other software. In addition to this, you'd find innocuous documents and pictures that the computer's users have saved, but wouldn't be useful to an investigation. Needless to say, most of what you'd find on any computer would not be evidence. The person examining the machine must sift through these files to find evidence related to his or her investigation, or evidence that is are illegal and may result in additional charges.

Analysis is the process of examining and evaluating information. When examining computer files, it is vital that they aren't modified in any way. This refers to not only changing the information in the file itself (such as by accidentally changing the values entered in a spreadsheet), but also modifying the properties of the file. For example, opening a JPEG or other picture could change the date and time property that shows when the file was last accessed. If you wanted to prove when a suspect last viewed this image, that information would be lost to you, and a suspect could then argue that he or she never saw the file. It is important to use tools that won't modify data in any way, and that analysis occurs after the data is acquired and authenticated by imaging the hard disk. If any data that was duplicated is damaged or modified, the original data on the suspect computer can still be used to create another duplicate.

Securing Evidence

If data and equipment are to be used as evidence, you will need to ensure that their integrity hasn't been compromised. Preservation of data involves practices that protect data and equipment from harm so that original evidence is preserved in a state as close as possible to when it was initially acquired. If data is lost, altered, or damaged, you may not be able to even mention it in court. This means inadmissible evidence might as well have never existed at all. Worse yet, the credibility of how evidence was collected and examined may be called into question, making other pieces of evidence inadmissible as well.

Evidence must be secure throughout the investigation. Securing evidence is a process that begins when a crime is first suspected, and continues after the examination has been completed. If a trial, civil suit, or disciplinary hearing has ended, the evidence must remain secure in case of an appeal or other legal processes. Because of this, a retention date should be set for all equipment and data that is retained as evidence. For example, the police may retain evidence files acquired from forensic software for many years after a person has been convicted. Similarly, a company may retain such files for a few years after firing an employee, in case the person attempts to sue for wrongful dismissal. The retention date provides a guideline as to how long a forensic technician should retain the data before deleting it, or allowing equipment to be released or destroyed. To determine specified dates, a company should consult legal counsel, and continue to be in contact with the investigator to determine whether the data acquired from an examination can be deleted or may still be needed.

Securing the Crime Scene

As mentioned earlier in this chapter, the first responder is responsible for establishing the scale of the crime scene, and then securing that area. In some situations, this may be as simple as securing a server closet or server room, whereas in other situations it may be as complex as dealing with computers and devices spread across a network. Once the suspected systems have been identified, it is important to prevent individuals from entering the area, and protecting systems so that equipment isn't touched and data isn't manipulated or lost.

At face value, it may seem difficult to prevent others from accessing systems. However, in many cases, people will respect the difficulty of the situation, or will not want to get involved for fear of having to testify later. The fact is that anyone who does have access to affected systems may be required to testify or at least explain his or her presence at the scene. In worst-case scenarios, they may even be considered suspects. As part of securing the crime scene, a list of anyone who has attempted to or has achieved access to the area should be developed. This should include the name of the person, the time he or she entered and left the area, and the purpose of his or her presence.

During the Investigation of a Machine

Disk imaging software will create an exact duplicate of a disk's contents, and can be used to make copies of hard disks, CDs, DVDs, floppies, and other media. Disk imaging creates a bitstream copy, whereby each physical sector of the original disk is duplicated. To make it easier to store and analyze, the image is compressed into an image file, which is also called an *evidence file*.

Once an image of the disk has been made, you should confirm that it's an exact duplicate. As we mentioned earlier in this chapter, authentication is vital to ensuring that the data that's been acquired is identical to that of the suspect's or victim's computer. Many computer forensic programs that create images of a disk have the built-in ability to perform integrity checks, whereas others will require you to perform checks using separate programs. Such software may use a cyclic redundancy check (CRC), using a checksum or hashing algorithm to verify the accuracy and reliability of the image.

When you're ready to perform an examination, copies of data should be made on media that's *forensically sterile*. This means that the disk has no other data on it, and has no viruses or defects. This will prevent mistakes involving data from one case mixing with other data, as can happen with cross-linked files or when copies of files are mixed with others on a disk. When providing copies of data to investigators, defense lawyers, or the prosecution, the media used to distribute copies of evidence should also be forensically sterile.

Although the situations in each case involving computer equipment will be different, there are a number of common steps you can follow to protect the integrity and prevent loss of evidence. These procedures assume that the computer has been shut down when you encounter it.

1. Photograph the computer screen(s) to capture the data displayed there at the time of seizure. Be aware that more than one monitor can be connected to a single computer; modern operating systems such as Windows XP support spreading the display across as many as 10 monitors. Monitors attached to the computer but turned off could still be displaying parts of the desktop and open applications.

2. Take steps to preserve volatile data.

3. Make an image of the disk(s) to work with so that the integrity of the original can be preserved. You should take this step *before* the system is shut down, in case the owner has installed a self-destruct program to activate on shutdown or startup.

4. Check the integrity of the image to confirm that it is an exact duplicate, using a CRC or other program that uses a checksum or hashing algorithm to verify that the image is accurate and reliable.

5. Shut down the system safely according to the procedures for the operating system that is running.

6. Photograph the system setup before moving anything, including the back and front of the computer showing cables and wires attached.

7. Unplug the system and all peripherals, marking/tagging each piece as it is collected.

8. Use an antistatic wrist strap or other grounding method before handling equipment, especially circuit cards, disks, and other similar items.

9. Place circuit cards, disks, and the like in antistatic bags for transport. Keep all equipment away from heat sources and magnetic fields.

When the Computer Is Not Being Examined

Anytime a computer is not being examined, it must be stored in a secure location. Once the computer has been transported from the original crime scene, it should be stored in a locked room or closet that has limited access. In police departments, this may be a property room or an area of the lab in which electronic evidence is acquired and examined. For internal investigations conducted in a corporate environment, it should be treated with the same level of respect, and also stored in a location with limited access.

Data acquired from a computer should be stored on a server or another computer that has limited access. Because any images of the computer that have been acquired using forensic software will be used to examine the computer's contents, and will be used in court as evidence, it is important that few people ever have access to these files. If an unintended individual were able to access the files, it could be argued that the files were tampered with, and this could result in the case being thrown out of court or could seriously undermine the case.

However, in any organization, there are those that will need to access a room that contains evidence. Lawyers, police investigators, and members of the IT staff fixing a computer, printer, or other device in the room may need to access the secure location from time to time. To keep track of those entering the room, you should maintain a log showing who entered the room or secure are a, the dates and times they were there, and any other information (such as their purpose for being there). By having people sign in and sign out, you can keep track of who had access should it ever come into question.

From the time an incident or crime has been identified, it is important that any evidence that may exist in an area be protected from tampering, accidents, or other potential damage. By keeping the crime scene, evidence, and any items transported to another location secure, you are preventing the validity of evidence from coming into question, and protecting any devices in your care from coming to harm.

On the Scene

Treating Every Investigation As Though It Were Going to Court

Every case must be treated as though it would eventually go to court, and be subject to the scrutiny of lawyers and others involved in the trial process. Although it may seem that a computer isn't part of a criminal case, examination of the computer may present materials that are illegal. In addition, those who are suspected of breaking the law or policies may eventually sue the company and others involved in the investigation. By following computer forensic procedures, keeping detailed documentation on what was done, and maintaining a log of who had access to the computer and its data, you can protect the integrity of the case and protect those involved in the investigation from civil litigation.

Before the Investigation

Contrary to what's seen in the movies and television, a significant amount of work goes into investigating computer crimes before they occur. The training and tools used in this type of investigation must be in place prior to examining any computer. Because it is so specialized, the person examining the computer must be knowledgeable in computer forensics and different areas of IT, and the equipment and software used to perform the examination of a machine must already be available to him or her.

When a crime does occur, certain actions must also be taken before attempting to acquire evidence from a machine. Interviews must be conducted and search warrants may need to be obtained. If this isn't done, time may be wasted searching for evidence that doesn't exist, or is located in other areas of a hard disk or even a different computer. Worse yet, if certain steps aren't followed, any evidence that is acquired may be inadmissible in court, making the entire process a waste of time.

Preparing for an Investigation

Preparation is one of the most important aspects of any investigation. Regardless of whether it is the police or part of an incident response team performing the investigation, it is important that a proactive approach is taken. It is important that those involved in investigations are properly trained, and that they have the necessary resources and tools available to them. The more that is done before an investigation, the fewer problems you'll have when conducting the investigation.

Training is crucial to every part of an investigation. Computer forensics requires knowledge of procedures, and expertise with forensic software and hardware that's being used to acquire and study the data. You can obtain this not only through courses, but also by studying under those with more experience in performing investigations. Additional experience with network components and technologies such as Transmission Control Protocol/Internet Protocol (TCP/IP) are also essential, as is knowledge of computer hardware, as it's common to remove hard disks or other devices before connecting them to the investigator's computer to duplicate the data. As you might expect, certification in these various areas is often useful, especially when providing testimony as an expert witness in court. The more training a person has in various aspects of computers, the better.

Because no one can know everything about computers, it is important to maintain reference materials that can be consulted as needed. A library of manuals and other books dealing with software and hardware that is commonly used can be useful in looking up infrequently used commands or features, but resources can also include maintaining hyperlinks and electronic documents. Links to the manufacturers of computers, cell phones, hard disks, and other devices will enable you to look up information on how to properly remove a hard disk from a particular make and model of computer, how to access the Basic Input Output System (BIOS) Setup, and how to bypass certain security features or access information stored in the device. These links will allow you to refer to manuals, knowledge bases, and other online resources quickly during an investigation.

Other resources that should be maintained are prepared documents that may be used during an investigation. As we'll discuss in Chapter 15, chain of custody forms may be used to keep track of who had possession of evidence at any given time, and property forms may also be used to maintain information on who is ultimately responsible for evidence that's stored in a secure location. Contact lists are also useful, providing a listing of individuals with specific skills (such as the hardware technician in the company where you work, or an expert in Linux or Macintosh machines that can be contacted as needed). Such lists should also contain information on how to contact certain legal departments or individuals in charge of abusing services at certain Web sites or companies. For example, if a case involved a free e-mail account at Hotmail, it would be useful to keep a request form that can be completed when requesting information on a particular account, and phone numbers to contact Hotmail during the investigation. In many cases, these documents can be stored on a computer or server that's used for forensic examinations so that the information is always handy in an electronic format.

It is also important to have a computer forensic lab set up prior to conducting an investigation. The lab should be of adequate size, and should have a server or media (such as CDs and DVDs) on which to store evidence files, with storage facilities that allow computers to be locked in a secure location when not being examined. In addition to this, you will need to outfit the lab with equipment that can be used in the facility or taken in the field to locations where the crime has taken place. This would include such items as:

- **Laptop computer** The laptop should have forensic software installed on it, and should include additional hardware that may be used to acquire data. We'll discuss different types of computer forensic hardware and software in Chapter 6.

- **Boot disk and CD or USB flash drive or tools** The boot disk is used to start a computer from a floppy disk or CD so that files aren't modified when the computer starts. A CD or other medium containing various utilities can also be useful to acquire data from a machine. Any tools that are included should not unknowingly modify data.

- **Digital camera** This can be used to photograph what's displayed on a computer screen, and to photograph the scene of the crime. Before taking the computer from the crime scene, the back of the computer should be photographed to show where cables were plugged into the machine so that it can be set up the same way once the investigation is over.

- **Evidence and antistatic bags, tags, and stickers** Evidence bags are tamperproof bags in which items can be stored to prevent unauthorized handling or contamination by fingerprints, DNA, or other taint evidence. Once sealed, the bag must be ripped open to access the contents. To safely transport hard disks and any circuit boards, they should also be stored in antistatic bags. Tags and stickers can also be used to identify the contents of the bag, showing the incident number or other information that associates items with a particular criminal case or incident.

- **Pens, notepad, and masking tape** It is important to document the actions taken in removing keyboards, monitors, and other peripherals attached to the computer prior to transporting it. You can use masking tape to mark which cables were attached to the suspect computer and where they were connected.

Conducting Interviews

It is important to always remember that a complainant can provide a wealth of information necessary to the successfully investigation of an incident. It is also important to identify and document who had access to affected systems, what they observed, and any other information they can provide. When interviewing people at a crime scene, it is important to record their names and contact information, in case they need to be contacted at a later time. Not only can their information be useful in identifying what the problem is and which systems were affected, but also their statements can be used to obtain search warrants and to provide testimony in court if criminal charges are laid on a suspect.

Obtaining Search Warrants

A *search warrant* is a legal document that permits members of law enforcement to search a specific location for evidence related to a criminal investigation, and seize that evidence so that it may be analyzed and possibly used in court. For the warrant to be legal, it must be signed by a judge or magistrate, such as a justice of the peace or another type of judicial officer. To obtain this signature, the police officer or government agent must present good reasons as to why a search warrant should be granted. This requires law enforcement officials to provide a sworn statement in which the location to be searched is identified, and may list the type of property being sought. The statement may also be accompanied by documentation on the complaint that initiated an investigation, and other written information that would validate the request. The key point of this process is to protect the rights of the individual, and to provide reasonable grounds for why permission should be given to invade a person's privacy and property.

Many countries use search warrants to protect the privacy of their citizens by requiring authorities to prove the necessity for the search and seizure of a person's property. An example of legislation that's used to prevent unreasonable searches and seizures of property is the Fourth Amendment of the U.S. Constitution, which states:

"The right of the people to be secure in their persons, houses, papers, and effects, against unreasonable searches and seizures, shall not be violated, and no Warrants shall issue, but upon probable cause, supported by Oath or affirmation, and particularly describing the place to be searched, and the persons or things to be seized."

In looking at this quote, you will notice that probable cause is the primary basis for issuing a search warrant. *Probable cause* is a standard of proof that must be shown, in which a cautious person would find reasonable grounds for suspicion. This places the burden of proof on the government so that investigations aren't conducted in an authoritarian or oppressive manner. Without probable cause, the request for a search warrant is denied.

If the search warrant is issued, its use is limited. After all, it would go against the philosophy of protecting the individual's rights if a warrant allowed police to search a person's home indefinitely, as many times as they like. The warrant can be executed only within a set amount of time (generally three days), so if a search warrant wasn't used in that time, a new one would need to be obtained. Also, an officer may search only those areas that are outlined in the court order, and generally cannot seize items that aren't included in the document. For example, if the warrant specified that a person's home could be searched, the police could not search other properties (such as a cabin) also owned by the person. By being specific in what can be searched, the conditions of the warrant protect both the rights of the individual and the integrity of the investigation.

Searching without Warrants

Warrants are not necessary in every situation where evidence could be obtained. Despite appearances at times, legislation is often constructed from common sense needs and well-thought-out arguments, balancing the needs of society against the government's ability to manage its citizens. Requesting a search warrant to acquire every piece of evidence in every criminal and civil case would become an administrative nightmare, so exclusions to needing a warrant are provided in statutes that address investigative procedures and requirements.

For law enforcement, there are a number of exceptions to where a search warrant is needed, although few apply to computer forensics. For example, an officer can frisk a suspect, checking his or her clothes for weapons or contraband, but there is no way this search would include an examination of the person's computer. In terms of computer forensics, a primary reason why a search warrant could be excluded is when the evidence is in plain view, and an officer can see it from a reasonable vantage point. For example, if an officer approached a car and saw the passenger viewing child pornography on a laptop computer, the laptop would be seized for later analysis. Similarly, let's say an officer had a warrant to search the home of a suspect and seize computer equipment believed to contain child pornography. If the officer saw a collection of photographs displaying naked children in various acts, the officer could then seize the pictures as evidence even though they may not have been specifically mentioned in the warrant. When illegal items or other evidence is in plain view, it is often reasonable for the officer to seize the item immediately, rather than leave it and take the risk of it being hidden, altered, or destroyed.

The need for a search warrant is also excluded when consent is given by the owner, or by an authorized person who is in charge of the area or item being searched. In other words, if the victim of a cybercrime wanted to have his or her own computer searched for evidence, a search warrant wouldn't be necessary. Similarly, the senior staff members of a company or the manager of an IT department could give permission to have servers and workstations in a company examined. The key is whether the person owns the property or has proper authorization, which can sometimes be less than clear. For example, on a college campus, a student in residence might be able to give permission to search the room he or she occupies, but wouldn't be able to give permission to search his or her roommate's computer. Similarly, a parent would be able to give permission to search a family computer, but may not have the authority to permit a search of an adult child's PC. Because a search conducted on a computer without a warrant or proper permission could make any evidence that's collected inadmissible in court, it's vital to determine who can give permission before seizing or examining a computer.

Legal differences exist between how a private citizen and law enforcement can gather evidence. There are stricter guidelines and legislation controlling how agents of the government may obtain evidence. Because of this, evidence that is collected prior to involving law enforcement is less vulnerable to being excluded in court. If the IT staff of a company acquired files from a server or workstation before calling the police, the files would probably be admitted as evidence in a trial, even though the same actions taken by law enforcement without permission or a warrant could make those files inadmissible.

Constitutional protection against illegal search and seizure applies to government agents (such as the police), but may not apply to private citizens. Before a government agent can search and seize computers and other evidence, a search warrant, consent, or statutory authority (along with probable cause) must be obtained. This does not apply to private citizens, unless they are acting as an "agent of the government" and working under the direction or advice of law enforcement or other government parties. However, although fewer restrictions apply to private citizens, forensic procedures should still be followed. Failing to follow forensic procedures may result in lost or unusable evidence. The procedures outlined in this section will help to preserve evidence and ensure that it is considered admissible in court.

Preparing for Searches

Because search warrants aren't required in all situations, you should try to identify whether one is needed early in the investigation. In doing so, you should ask the following questions:

- Does the company or complainant own the computer? If so, permission can be given to search the machine.

- Does the company have a legitimate reason for searching the computer? If not, the employee using the computer could have reason for civil litigation.

■ Have employees been warned that the company has the right to search the machine? As we'll discuss later in this chapter, by warning employees that computers may be searched at any time, the employee has little to no recourse if anything has been found on his or her machine.

If there are no legal grounds to search the computer without a warrant, statements and any documented evidence pertaining to the incident should be collected. Statements should include as many details as possible, providing a timeline of when events took place and what occurred. Statements should be gathered from anyone associated with the incident, and this should be done as soon as possible so that memories of the event aren't diluted over time. Gathering statements in this manner provides information that can be used to obtain a search warrant, and can be used as evidence later on if the case goes to trial.

Professional Conduct

At all times in an investigation, it is important to maintain professional conduct. Whether you are working as a member of the police force or as an employee of a company, you are acting as a representative of the organization, and the level of ethical behavior that's displayed will indicate how you're handling the case as a whole. By reflecting the ethics adopted by the organization, you are also showing that the investigation will be handled with integrity.

A balance of morality and objectivity must be maintained throughout the investigation. If potentially offensive materials are found on the computer, showing interest in the material is unprofessional and could be used to undermine the findings in court. In the same way, you should also display objectivity, and not make judgments on what is found during an examination of evidence, or when interviewing those involved in the investigation. You should avoid making any kinds of jokes or comments about what is found, and focus on the tasks involved in performing the investigation with professionalism.

In performing these tasks, it is important to remain somewhat detached from the incident. Although it is important to display a level of compassion toward any victims in the case, you should remain disconnected from anything but the tasks that must be performed. By showing disgust or other negative emotions toward what has occurred, you could be perceived as being judgmental, or as though you have a vendetta against the person who committed the crime. Professional detachment involves placing all of your attention on the work, rather than the emotional or psychological stress factors that may be involved.

Confidentiality is another important component of professional conduct. Throughout the investigation, it is important to keep information about the case private, and to not reveal information to those who aren't directly involved in investigating the incident. Information should not be shared with witnesses, coworkers, or others outside the case, especially if they show interest in what has occurred. This can be difficult, as friends or family may often ask about higher-profile cases that are being reported in the media. However, it is important that information is limited to those who need it. You don't want to accidentally reveal what's going on to someone who may later be a suspect, or who will pass information on even further.

The investigator may also work with public relations or a media representative in the company or police to determine what will be revealed to the public. In such situations, crime technicians and anyone else involved in the investigation should limit their comments to information that has been approved for public release, and keep any additional facts to themselves.

Investigating Company Policy Violations

Corporate investigations are often different from other types of investigations. When criminal activity occurs on a home computer, generally the police are called to conduct an investigation. In companies where an IT staff is available, policies may exist that designate a person or team of people with specialized skills to initially respond to the incident. The incident response team may contact police eventually, but this will often depend on the type of incident and what is found in their investigation.

Investigations in corporations can also be different from others involving computer forensics, as a crime might never have been committed even though an investigation is required. Anyone who has worked for a company knows that employers will impose certain rules and practices that must be followed by employees as conditions of their employment. A number of regulations may be implemented to address how computers and other equipment are to be used in the workplace, and breaking these rules could result in an investigation and in having computers and other devices used by the employee undergo a forensic examination.

Policy and Procedure Development

A *policy* is used to address concerns and identify risks to a company, whereas *procedures* are used to provide information on how to perform specific tasks and/or deal with a problem. For example, a policy may be created to deal with the potential threat of unauthorized access to restricted areas of a building, and procedures may be implemented that state how a visitor should be signed into a building and escorted to a particular department. Through the policy, an issue that is pertinent to the organization is explained and dealt with. Through the procedure, people are shown how to abide by policies by following specific instructions.

When you consider the sheer number of issues an organization may face, you can see that many different types of policies and procedures may be implemented. Regardless of the type, however, each should have the following features:

- It should be straightforward, stating points clearly and understandably. If areas of a policy can be interpreted in different ways, it can be disputed when attempting to enforce it.

- It must define what actions should be taken. Procedures must lay out the steps needed to complete a task, and policies must outline the actions that may be taken if the policy is violated.

- It cannot violate any applicable law. If a policy does violate any existing legislation, it cannot be adequately enforced. In addition, the company may face civil or criminal charges, because it implemented a policy that forced employees to break the law.

- It must be enforceable. If a policy isn't enforced each time it is violated, or if it can't be enforced for some reason (such as because it violates contractual agreements with individuals or unions), the policy becomes worthless to the company. A policy must be fairly and equally enforced whenever it is violated, or any disciplinary actions dictated in the policy can be disputed.

When implementing policies, companies should also devise methods to confirm that employees have read and agreed to comply with them. One method is to have employees read and sign copies of certain policies when they are hired. However, if there are changes to the policy, each person already hired must be approached, and must reread and sign the policy. Another method is to implement one policy that employees sign upon being hired, which states that part of their employment relies on reading and acknowledging compliance with all policies. The policies can then be posted on the corporate intranet, enabling employees to read them at their convenience. Still another method is to e-mail copies of policies to all of the employees' internal e-mail addresses, and requesting them to respond stating they have read and agree with the terms of the policies. Whatever method is implemented, it is important that some process is in place. If employees are unaware of the policies, they can't realistically be expected to comply with them.

Acceptable Use Policy

A policy that employees should be required to acknowledge as having read and one with which they should comply is an acceptable use policy. This type of policy establishes guidelines on the appropriate use of technology. It is used to outline what types of activities are permissible when using a computer or network, and what an organization considers proper behavior. Acceptable use policies not only protect an organization from liability, but also provide employees with an understanding of what they can and cannot do using company resources.

Acceptable use policies will restrict certain actions, including what types of Web sites or e-mail an employee is allowed to access on the Internet at work. You may have read news articles about employees who access pornography over the Internet. Not only does this use up bandwidth and fill hard disk space on nonwork-related activities, but others seeing the employee view the material can create an uncomfortable work environment. Worse yet, a company can be liable for creating or allowing a hostile work environment under the Civil Rights Act of 1964 or other legislation. For these reasons, businesses commonly include sections in their acceptable use policies that deal with these issues.

Acceptable use policies would also specify methods of how information can be distributed to the public, to avoid sensitive information from being "leaked." Imposing rules on the dissemination of information might include:

- Specifications that prohibit classified information from being transmitted via the Internet (for example, via e-mail or File Transfer Protocol [FTP])
- Provisions on how content for the Web site is approved
- Rules on printing confidential materials
- Restrictions on who can create media releases, and so on

Through this, important information is protected, and employees have an understanding of what files they can or cannot e-mail, print, or distribute to other parties.

Incident Response Policy

Incident response policies are implemented to provide an understanding of how certain incidents are to be dealt with. The policy should identify an incident response team, who is to be notified of issues, and who has the knowledge and skills to deal with them effectively. Members of the team should be experienced in handling issues relating to unauthorized access, denial or disruptions of service, viruses, unauthorized changes to systems or data, critical system failures, or attempts to breach the policies and/or security of an organization. If the incident is of a criminal nature, the policy should specify at what point law enforcement should be contacted to take control of the investigation.

A good incident response policy will outline who is responsible for specific tasks when a crisis occurs. It will include such information as:

- Who will investigate or analyze incidents to determine how an incident occurred and what problems are faced because of it

- Which individuals or departments are to fix particular problems and restore the system to a secure state

- How certain incidents are to be handled, and references to other documentation

Incident response policies should also provide steps on what users are supposed to do when identifying a possible threat. These steps should be clearly defined so that there will be no confusion regarding how to deal with an incident. Upon realizing that an issue exists, an individual should notify his or her supervisor, a designated person, or a department that can then contact the incident response team. While awaiting the team's arrival, the scene of the incident should be vacated and any technologies involved should be left as they were. In other words, those on the scene shouldn't touch anything, as this could alter the evidence. The users should also document what they observed when the incident occurred, and list anyone who was in the area when the incident occurred.

To address how a company should handle intrusions and other incidents, it is important that the incident response policy includes a contingency plan. The contingency plan will address how the company will continue to function during the investigation, such as when critical servers are taken offline during forensic examinations. Backup equipment may be used to replace these servers or other devices so that employees can still perform their jobs and (in such cases as e-commerce sites) customers can still make purchases. By having such practices in place, any investigation can avoid (as much as possible) negatively impacting normal business practices.

Policy Violations

When policies are violated, it doesn't necessarily mean that a full police investigation is required. In many situations, the violation may require disciplinary actions against the employee, whether it is a reprimand, fine, demotion, or termination. The severity of the actions will often depend on the past performance and current conduct of the person. Despite the end result, computer forensics may still be incorporated. Using forensic procedures to investigate the incident creates a tighter case against the employee, thereby making it difficult for the employee to argue the facts.

In any investigation, it is important to treat the case as though it were going to court, as you never know what you'll find. For example, an employee may have violated a company's acceptable use policy by viewing questionable Web sites during work hours. However, if it was found that the person was downloading child pornography, the internal investigation becomes a criminal one. Any actions taken in the investigation would be scrutinized, and anything found could be evidence in a criminal trial.

Policy violations can also extend beyond the machines owned by a company. Many people have their own blogs or personal Web sites, or enjoy social networks such as Facebook (http://www.facebook.com), Friendster ((http://www.friendster.com), and others. On such sites, people can publish text and pictures to the Internet. If the person mentions where he or she works, and makes derogatory comments about coworkers or portrays the company in a negative manner, it may seem that little can be done. After all, the information isn't on a corporate computer, but on another server entirely. However, depending on policies implemented in the organization, this may not always be the case. In 2007, an eleventh grade student in Abbotsford, BC, named Amanda Bunn created a page on Facebook titled "If 200 people sign this, I'll kick (teacher Pat Mullaney) in the box." Because the threat was made to her teacher, the student was suspended for three weeks before ultimately being expelled from the school. Other schools have taken similar actions against students in cases of cyberbullying. Because school policies exist in many schools that prohibit threatening teachers and students, the students are held accountable for their actions, even though the incidents never occurred on school property.

In the same way that schools are realizing that cyberbullying can escalate into more violent actions, fewer and fewer organizations are tolerating hostile working environments. *Hostile working environments* are workplaces where a person fears intimidation, harassment, physical threats, humiliation, or other experiences that create an offensive or oppressive atmosphere. One common example of a hostile working environment is sexual harassment. If a person had to view sexual images displayed on a computer, or received messages sent through e-mail, Short Message Service (SMS) or IM that had undertones or blatant sexual remarks, he or she could feel objectified and humiliated by the atmosphere. In such cases, internal disciplinary tribunals, criminal charges, or civil suits may be the only way to stop such actions. When these activities are received, transmitted, or displayed using technologies issued by the company, it is simple to acquire evidence by looking at information stored on the devices or on hard disks.

One of the most devastating types of policy violation is industrial espionage, which is also a criminal act. *Industrial espionage* is the selling of trade secrets, intellectual property, or other classified information to competitors. If the wrong person has access to such information, it could be detrimental to the organization, as releasing it to the public or competitors could undermine confidence in the organization, and even jeopardize its ability to remain solvent. Source code for programs, secret recipes, and other knowledge that is often limited to the most trusted insiders could be devastating if released. Information must be kept secure, and any suspected leaks must be dealt with swiftly.

On the Scene

The Cola Wars and Industrial Espionage

When you think of Coca-Cola and Pepsi, you probably think of staunch competitors in the Cola Wars, with each trying to get an advantage over the other in the marketplace. The last thing you'd imagine is the two of them working together to stop a Coke employee from selling secrets to Pepsi. However, because such companies rely on

Continued

secret recipes and other trade secrets to remain in business, the threat of industrial espionage is one that can't be tolerated and is considered one of their greatest risks to security.

In May 2006, PepsiCo Inc. received a letter offering to sell them trade secrets of the Coca-Cola Co. Pepsi immediately contacted Coke, who in turn contacted the FBI. The FBI worked with both companies to create a sting operation that led to the arrest of Joya Williams, a secretary who worked at Coca-Cola, and two others working with her to sell the secrets. Williams had stolen not only confidential information, but also a sample of a new soft drink the company was developing, which she, Ibrahim Dimson, and Edmund Duhaney tried to sell to Pepsi for $1.5 million.

In 2007, Williams was convicted and received a prison sentence of eight years; Dimson entered a guilty plea and was sentenced to five years in prison. Both were also sentenced to an additional three years of supervised release, and each was ordered to pay $40,000 in restitution. Duhaney also entered a guilty plea, thereby closing the cap on this case.

Warning Banners

Warning banners are brief messages that are used to inform users of policies and legislation regarding the use of a system and the information it contains. They are generally displayed at the startup of programs and operating systems, or when accessing the default page of intranets and public Web sites. Because the warning banner advises a user about key elements of proper usage, and may even provide references to existing laws and policies, it serves as a legal notice to users of the system.

Warning banners can come in different formats, including splash screens or message boxes that pop up when software is started, or information appearing in graphics or other content on Web sites. As shown in Figure 5.2, the Goddard Space Flight Center (webmaster.gsfc.nasa.gov/warning.html) has a simple textual warning that outlines the purpose of the site, and stating that any attempts to modify the site may be punishable under the Computer Fraud and Abuse Act of 1986. It also informs the user that any activities on the site may be monitored to the degree that keystrokes may be recorded. By using the Web site, the user agrees to these actions, so anyone committing a criminal act has consented to having information gathered in logs, which could then be used against him or her as evidence.

Figure 5.2 Warning Banner on the Goddard Space Flight Center Web Site

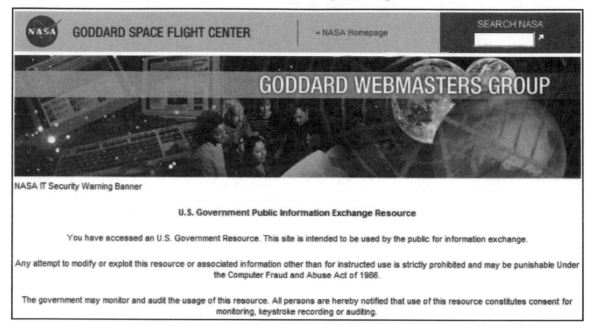

Warning banners should be implemented at any access point to a system in the event an organization seeks to discipline an employee or prosecute an unauthorized user. By providing a clear and strong message, the warning banner essentially dissolves any excuse of a user not knowing that what he or she did was wrong. The user is given a warning, so any violations of it can be proven as being intentional. The message should provide the following points of information, and should correspond with any security policies the user may have read and agreed to as part of his or her employment:

- A brief outline of what is considered proper usage of the system

- Expectations of privacy, and that the system may be monitored for illegal or improper activity

- Any penalties or possible punishment that may result from noncompliance

Adding such messages when users log on to an operating system is relatively simple, and should be implemented on any computers that are part of a corporate network. Computers running Windows can have information added to the Registry that will cause a message box to appear with a warning before the user logs on. This feature has been included in Windows operating systems since Windows 95 and Windows NT 3.1, and presents the warning banner after pressing Ctrl + Alt + Del and before being presented with a login dialog box. It requires the user to agree to the warning by clicking an OK button before he or she is able to use Windows.

Conducting a Computer Forensic Investigation

Although investigations will often vary in the type of incident or crime that has occurred, the evidence that's available, and the environment in which evidence is collected, many elements are common in any investigation. As we've seen throughout this chapter, it is important that you assume that any investigation will invariably wind up in court, where the evidence and process in which it was collected may be challenged. Because of this, it is important to always follow the procedures in the investigative process.

Once you've gone through the process of securing a crime scene and interviewing witnesses, you must collect, preserve, and transport the evidence. Each piece of evidence must then be assessed, with digital evidence acquired from hard disks and other media, before being examined. Throughout this process, documentation is essential, as any actions that are taken should be included in a statement and/or final report. As we'll see in the sections that follow, this can be a lengthy process with procedures that must be followed to prevent any evidence from becoming inadmissible, or important pieces of evidence being overlooked altogether.

The Investigation Process

The process of conducting a computer forensic investigation can be a hectic experience, especially in a business environment where it is essential that systems are online to maintain the business. For example, if the company used an e-commerce site to make sales, taking the system down to perform an examination could cost thousands upon thousands of dollars. During such instances, you want to ensure that you follow forensic procedures, but not waste time wondering which steps should be performed next.

Although we've primarily discussed the investigation process from law enforcement's side in this chapter, the subsections that follow will provide information related to the roles of the incident response team and IT staff in the investigation. To perform an investigation properly, it is important that sets of procedures are followed that detail the steps to be taken. Following these guidelines will help you to meet the goals of an incident investigation, and provide information that can be used to handle the incident so that it doesn't escalate into a more significant problem. In the investigation process, you need to follow these six steps:

- Preparation
- Detection
- Containment
- Eradication
- Recovery
- Follow-up

Preparation

As with anything dealing with security, it is important that threats are dealt with proactively, with safeguards and other measures in place before problems occur. If the necessary policies, procedures, and tools aren't available when responding to an incident, an incident response team can waste valuable time trying to get organized. Preparation is the key to handling and investigating incidents.

As we've stressed throughout this chapter, it is important that people are properly trained in how to identify and report problems, and that they have a thorough understanding of the tasks they're expected to perform. In addition, companies should develop communication plans. Part of this policy should include or reference a communication plan that provides contact information on who will need to be called when problems are first reported. This includes members of the incident response team, other IT staff members, third-party vendors and support personnel, senior management, department managers, public relations personnel, and anyone else who may need to be conferred with the incident. The contact list should include the names of anyone who may need to be called during an incident, and his or her phone number, pager number, address, and any other relevant information.

In an emergency, it is important that people aren't scrambling to find contact information, so such information should be left with a centralized source. Some options might be the company switchboard, dispatch, Help Desk, or other departments of the company. If an incident needed to be reported, employees could notify the switchboard operator or dispatcher, who in turn could contact incident response team members.

Passwords are another piece of information that should be available in emergencies. Members of the IT staff or the incident response team may have varying levels of security, and may be unable to get into certain areas of the network or certain systems. For example, they may not have passwords to access administrative functions in certain systems, or workstations and servers may be locked down and can't be accessed without an administrator password. To allow them entry in extreme situations, copies of passwords should be written down, sealed in an envelope, and stored in a locked container (such as a safe). Any encrypted keys needed to access critical data should also be stored with these passwords. In an emergency, if the person who knows the passwords is unavailable, a member of the team can access the passwords and keys.

A company will need to do business after an incident has occurred, but in some incidents data may be altered, corrupted, or deleted. When this happens, the data may be irrevocably lost, unless backups have been regularly performed beforehand. By performing regular backups, you can restore the data on a server or workstation as needed. This is especially important if a particular machine is seized as evidence or data prior to the investigation date needs to be reviewed. To make it easier for members of the team to restore the data, recovery procedures should be documented thoroughly, allowing members to follow the understandable steps to restore systems to their previous state.

To aid in the detection process of an incident investigation (which we'll discuss next), preparation also requires that logging is activated on systems. Logging information to a file is a feature that's commonly provided for operating systems, and for certain software and equipment. Logs can provide a great deal of information, revealing indicators that may show whether an incident has occurred. The more information that's provided in these logs, the more evidence you'll have for discovering incidents and dealing with them accordingly.

Baselines should also be created by recording data on how the system behaves normally. The metrics recorded in a baseline would include measurements of network traffic, memory usage, and other information that provides a clear understanding of how systems normally run. The incident response team can compare the baseline to measurements taken when a problem is suspected, and thereby detect whether an incident has occurred.

Detection

Determining whether an incident has actually occurred is the next step of the incident investigation process. After all, just because someone reported that something doesn't seem right doesn't mean that the company's at risk or that a crime has occurred. A user could report that files have been deleted, and although it could be indicative of hacking, it could just mean the user is too embarrassed to admit he or she deleted them by accident. The detection phase of incident investigation examines such reports, and determines what further actions (if any) are required.

Detection requires looking at the safeguards and auditing controls that have previously been set up, and determining whether anomalies exist. For example, logs may provide a great deal of information that can confirm or discard any notions of unwanted activity. Members of the IT staff or information security personnel should check logs on a regular basis, and determine whether indications of problems have been recorded. System logs may show errors related to security violations, impending hardware failure, or other potential problems. Firewall logs should also be analyzed to identify indications of attempted hacking from the Internet, policy breaches, or other damaging events. By not checking logs regularly, an incident may be avoided early, preventing more significant problems from occurring.

Software specifically designed to deal with certain incidents, or elements of an incident, can be used in the detection process. AV software packages can be used to detect viruses, and can be configured to automatically deal with them upon detection. Intrusion detection systems can also be used to identify whether system security has been violated, systems have been misused, or accounts have been used or modified. Implementation of such software not only aids in protecting the network, but also allows you to detect incidents early.

In addition to the logs created by systems on the network, the IT staff should also keep a manual logbook. This will provide a record of dates, times, observations, system names, error messages, actions taken, and other details that may be considered valuable. The name of the person who reported the incident and the names of people who had access to systems should also be recorded. Creating a log should be done as early as possible. Information recorded in the log may be vital to solving problems, and may be needed for reference purposes if you're later required to testify in court.

Another reason for maintaining a logbook is that it can reveal patterns. Hackers may make several attempts to hack into a network, and being able to reference information on these previous occurrences can be valuable in identifying vulnerabilities, finding who is making these attempts, and may be used in the prosecution of that person. It can also be useful in identifying training issues, such as when multiple mistakes by the same person result in damaged data, invalid data entry, or erroneous reporting of incidents. Without a log of previous incident investigations, such patterns may be unidentifiable.

When an incident is confirmed, it is important that an image of the affected system is made as soon as possible. As we'll discuss later in this chapter and again in Chapter 6, computer forensic software can be used to create an image of the data, creating an exact duplicate of a hard disk. This allows you to examine data on the disk, while leaving the original computer untouched. This is important, because examinations of the original computer's data could modify data on the disk. Even opening a file can alter information (such as the date/time of when it was last opened), and can negatively affect any further investigation or future prosecution. It is important to make an image of the system as soon as possible, because further intrusions into the system or malicious programs could delete evidence used to identify a suspect. Rather than giving the suspect a chance to cover his or her tracks, it is important to preserve that evidence quickly.

Containment

It is important to limit the extent and significance of an incident so that it doesn't spread to other systems and continue doing damage. It makes no sense to identify a hacker's entry into a server, and then allow him or her to continue entering other servers on the network. In the same light, allowing viruses to spread across the network increases the level of damage. Containment limits the scope of such incidents, preventing the damage from spreading.

How an incident is contained will depend on the type of incident that has occurred, what is affected, and the importance of systems to the business. If someone had hacked into a network file server, it might be prudent to remove that server from the network, such as by unplugging the network cable from the adapter. In doing so, the hacker would be unable to do further harm, and would be unable to modify or delete any evidence he or she left behind. In other situations, such as an employee sending threatening e-mails, it would be overkill to prevent everyone from using network resources. In this case, having a member of the incident response team stay with that person until the police arrive, so as to prevent them from using a computer, would probably suffice.

Eradication

Just as it's important to prevent further damage by containing an incident, it is equally important to remove its cause. Eradication removes the source of a threat so that further damage isn't caused or repeated. In doing so, the system is left more secure, and further incidents may be prevented.

Eradication may occur through a variety of methods. For example, if a virus were detected on systems, eradication would require removing the virus from all media and systems by using AV software. In situations involving violations of law or policy, the eradication phase of incident investigation might require disciplinary action (such as terminating the employee) or pressing criminal charges. As you can see by this, the appropriate method of eradicating an incident depends on what or who is being dealt with.

Recovery

Once an incident has been handled, the company's IT staff will need to ensure that any data, software, and other systems are back to normal. The recovery phase is where these are restored to a normal state. Here it is determined that the incident did not permanently affect elements of the network, and everything is as it was previous to the incident.

Recovery is important because data may be modified, deleted, or corrupted during incidents, and configurations of systems may be changed. Other problems that may result include malicious code that was planted on systems. Such code may be triggered by certain events, or may activate at a later date when everything is presumed to be okay. Because of the possibility of future threats, you need to determine whether any remnants of an attack exist, and what may have been damaged by the incident.

Systems may be restored in a variety of ways. Certain systems may need to be reconfigured to the way they were before the incident, data may need to be validated to verify that it is correct, or in other cases, the system may need to be completely restored from backups. If data has been modified or destroyed, and a backup is restored, any work that took place since the backup was performed will need to be redone.

Follow-up

The follow-up to an incident investigation is where you determine whether improvements can be made to incident handling procedures. At this point, you examine the previous phases of the investigation, and review what was done and why. The follow-up requires an analysis of such details as:

- Preparation for the investigation, and whether additional preparation is needed
- Whether communication was effective, or if information was not conveyed in a timely fashion
- Steps taken during the investigation, and problems identified
- Determining whether the incident was detected quickly and accurately
- Whether the incident was adequately contained or spread to different systems
- Evaluating tools used in the investigation and whether new tools would result in improvements

It is also important for companies to identify how much the incident cost, so changes to budgets can be made to effectively manage the risks associated with certain incidents. This includes the cost of downtime, personnel costs, the value of data that was lost, hardware that was damaged, and other costs related to the investigation. By determining the financial costs associated with an incident, insurance claims can then be filed to reimburse the company and cost/benefit analyses can be updated. This information may also be included in Victim Impact Statements provided to the police.

Assessing Evidence

Earlier in this chapter, we discussed how the crime scene technician is responsible for processing digital evidence that is collected during an investigation. Although this may involve the technician being called directly to a crime scene and forced to deal with the situation on the fly, often this will entail assisting in obtaining a search warrant and assisting in technical aspects of the case before any evidence is ready to be searched and seized. As we'll see in the sections that follow, processing evidence is a four-part set of procedures consisting of assessment, acquisition, examination, and documentation.

Evidence assessment is the first part of this process, and it involves evaluating issues related to the case and the digital evidence that's being sought. It requires reviewing the search warrant or details of legal authorization to obtain the evidence, the details of the case, hardware and software that may be involved, and the evidence you hope to acquire for later evaluation. After completing these steps, you should be able to determine the best course of action to take in obtaining the evidence, based on the scope of the case.

Case Assessment

When an incident occurs that requires a computer forensic investigation, the investigator for the case will request the services of the crime scene technician. The request for forensic services should not be taken at face value so that the technician simply walks blindly into the case. It is important that the technician reviews the request and identifies the legal authority for his for her participation. This request for assistance should be in writing, and it should include such information as:

- Who is making the request for service, and contact information to call, page, and/or e-mail this person

- The incident or case number

- The name and other information regarding the suspect

- Who owns the machine

- Whether the data has been viewed or accessed by anyone prior to your examination

- What kind(s) of forensic services are being requested

A request for service form that allows an investigator to provide this information is useful for several reasons. First and foremost, it provides an easy reference that connects evidence to a particular case. The form will provide information on whether a search warrant is required (based on who owns the computer), and can be useful in identifying information to search for. For example, if you were interested in searching for documents containing the suspect's name, you could simply refer to the form to get the correct spelling. If you were unsure whether all of the services requested have been fulfilled, you could look at the list of services the investigator wanted you to perform. Also, if the request for services was illegitimate and the request was made for personal reasons, you have an official form that will protect you from disciplinary actions.

Because the computer may have been accessed prior to your acquiring the data and examining it, you should also request the complete chain of evidence documentation. This is especially important if a computer has already been seized and is being delivered to the forensic lab. If there are any questions regarding data, you can then contact any parties who previously had custody of the machine to determine whether they accessed any files or performed any actions with the machine.

Although an investigator may be adept at interviewing suspects, following leads, and performing other tasks necessary to an investigation, he or she may not fully understand what is involved with computer forensics. It is important to discuss what you can and cannot do in an investigation, and what may or may not be discovered. In addition to this, you should discuss whether other attempts to acquire evidence or certain avenues of investigation have already been acted upon, such as the following:

- Is there a need for the use of other types of forensics? Has the evidence been checked for fingerprints, DNA, trace evidence, or other forensic evidence? If there is a need for this, you should wait before touching the computer until this has been completed.

- Has an attempt been made to acquire evidence from noncomputer sources? Because evidence is so often found on computers, it is possible that other sources of evidence have been overlooked. For example, digital cameras and cell phones that take pictures can be useful in child pornography cases, whereas check paper, paper files, and other items may be useful in financial crimes.

- Is there a need to acquire evidence from other systems? In cases involving the Internet, you may wish to obtain logs and account information from Internet service providers (ISPs), who may have logged when the person connected to the Internet, what sites he or she visited, e-mails that were sent and received, remote storage locations, and other information.

You should also discuss specific details of the case that can be used to narrow your search for information on a computer. If you understand why a person is being investigated, and the type of evidence the investigator is searching for, it can decrease the amount of time required in finding that evidence. For example, fraud cases will often involve searching for spreadsheets and financial records, child pornography cases will require looking for photographs, and hacking cases will often require looking at source code and specific applications. In addition to this, certain information about the suspect should be available to you, such as the suspect's name, e-mail address, aliases, and user account information. By having this information beforehand, you will spend less time attempting to identify it when examining the computer.

In identifying aspects about the suspect who uses or owns a machine being examined, it can be useful to determine the person's computer skills. Different suspects will have varying levels of expertise with computers, with more advanced users possibly incorporating encryption or booby traps that will delete data if certain actions are performed. The more you know about a suspect and the case prior to dealing with the evidence, the better position you'll be in to successfully acquire and evaluate pertinent evidence.

Processing Location Assessment

Although the thought of where you'll collect or examine evidence may not be the first thought in an investigation, it is important to identify this early in the investigation. In many cases, the evidence will be examined in a forensic lab, where you'll be working with equipment in your own work area. In other situations, you'll have to visit the scene of the crime. Sometimes this will be an easily controlled environment, such as a server room that limits the number of people who can enter and have access to evidence. Other situations may require you to collect evidence from a kiosk, a computer in a public Internet café, or the scene of a homicide where other forensic professionals are still gathering their own evidence. By understanding where the evidence needs to be gathered, you'll be better prepared to determine the type of equipment you'll need to bring, or whether other personnel (such as police officers) will need to be present.

On the Scene

Computer Forensics in the Field

In most situations, computers that are seized as evidence are delivered to the person(s) who will perform a forensic examination of the digital evidence. This examination is then done in the (relative) comfort of a forensic lab setting. This isn't always the case, though, as situations may dictate a need for you to attend a crime scene to process and transport computers for later analysis.

One of my early forays into the field involved a multiple homicide, in which an entire family had been murdered (after which the killer committed suicide). Although everyone involved was deceased, there was a need to determine why the tragedy had occurred. The detective in charge of the case requested that I attend the crime scene so that I could seize the computer (properly package and transport it) and later perform

Continued

a forensic examination of the data. While I was there, the Forensic Unit was still processing the crime scene. Afterward, I made a second trip to the family business, where another computer was seized. While I was there, the employees of the murdered family were grieving and were understandably distraught.

Although this was an unusual situation, it does illustrate the diverse locations one may visit in the field. Each location was also disturbing for different reasons. The first was a grisly crime scene, whereas the second was a business environment that was emotionally charged. It is also important that those planning to work in computer forensics are aware that the circumstances requiring your services can be unusual and disquieting.

When assessing the location, you should consider a number of factors. It may take considerably longer to collect evidence from some scenes compared to others, so an estimate should be provided to the investigator. If it will take awhile to collect the evidence, you should try to determine how your presence will impact the business. In some situations, it is better to remove a hard disk from a server, and to allow members of the company's IT staff to restore systems as swiftly as possible. However, even in the best of circumstances, a computer may be unavailable for some time, requiring personnel at the company to use other systems. If you will be on-site for some time, considerations may need to be made regarding who will perform other forensic examinations while you're unavailable.

Equipment and training may also be an issue in certain circumstances. In our previous example of a homicide scene, you may be exposed to blood spatters or other biological matter. In such cases, you may need to work in a suit that will protect you from biological hazards, or at the very least wear a mask and latex or vinyl gloves. The same could also apply if a computer is located in a marijuana grow operation, or a scene with chemicals or allergens present. By understanding the location in which an investigation will take place, you can better prepare for factors that will impact your ability to collect and examine evidence.

Evidence Assessment

The final step in evidence assessment specifically deals with the evidence itself. You should identify the stability of the evidence, and collect the most volatile evidence first before moving to nonvolatile evidence. In doing so, you should prioritize the collection and acquisition of evidence so that the evidence that is most likely to contain what you're searching for is examined first. For example, if a border guard discovered that someone had child pornography as the wallpaper on a laptop, you would obviously want to acquire evidence from the laptop and examine it first, before moving on to any CDs, DVDs, and other media that may also have been collected. Throughout this process, you should document any actions taken, and determine the best methods of relating that information. This may include taking notes, making diagrams, photographing items, or utilizing features available through forensic software.

When evidence needs to be transported, you should evaluate the condition and vulnerability of the items. Certain devices such as PDAs, cell phones, and laptops could simply be packaged in an evidence bag, whereas circuit boards and individual hard disks should first be stored in antistatic bags. In some cases, an investigator may also need to provide continuous electric power to battery-operated devices such as laptops that are low in power so that any volatile evidence isn't lost before it is delivered to you. Once the evidence has been acquired, you should then place the evidence in a secure location that is free of electromagnetic interference.

Acquiring Evidence

The next phase of processing evidence is acquisition. As we mentioned earlier in this chapter, acquiring evidence is the process of obtaining digital evidence from its original source. In doing so, it is vital that the original data isn't altered, damaged, or destroyed when making a copy from which the forensic technician can work.

The first step in acquiring evidence from a computer is to document as much information about the machine as possible. You should note the serial number and any identifying information on the computer so that you can prove that the computer that was taken from a crime scene was actually the one that evidence was acquired from at a later time. This is especially important when there is a backlog of cases, and the computer may have been stored until the examiner had time to work on the machine. In documenting information, you should also review information on any hardware and software configurations that were noted when the machine was seized, in case this needs to be duplicated on the examiner's machine.

If you are dealing with a hard disk that has already been removed from a computer, the tasks in acquiring evidence are considerably easier. You would simply attach the hard disk to the examiner's workstation in a forensic lab, or to a write protection device such as FastBloc (used with EnCase software that we'll discuss in Chapter 6), and then use forensic software to acquire its contents. However, generally you will be dealing with an entire computer or laptop, and not with individual components that have been seized. In such cases, you'll need to take steps to remove storage devices yourself. Disassembling the computer case will provide you with physical access to these devices, so you should ensure that you have taken precautions against static discharge and that you do not have the equipment close to any strong magnetic fields. Either of these can seriously damage computer components, so during the disassembly you should wear an antistatic wristband or stand on an antistatic mat.

Once the case has been opened, you can identify what hard disks and other components (for example, PC Card, network card, and so on) are installed, and you can begin to take steps to remove the storage devices. Before removing any storage devices, you should note how they are installed and configured so that they can later be reinstalled exactly as they were before. This could include taking a picture of the inside of the computer so that a visual reference is available for later. Once you've noted this, you should then remove the power connector or data cable from the back of the drive or motherboard. Doing so will prevent the destruction, damage, or modification of any data that is stored on the device in steps that follow. After disconnecting the storage device, you should make a note of the make, model, size, jumper settings, location, drive interface, and any other information you can see that will identify the hard disk and its settings.

Once you've removed the power connector or data cable from the hard disk, you can then take steps to retrieve information stored on the computer through a series of controlled boots. To perform a controlled boot and capture data stored in the CMOS/BIOS, you would start the computer and press the particular key on the keyboard that allows you to access the BIOS Setup for that particular machine. This is often displayed on the screen when the computer is first powered on, and is generally the Del or F10 key that accesses this program. However, you should check the manufacturer's Web site if it's not evident which key to press, as it can vary from system to system. Once you've entered the BIOS Setup, you can view the configuration information for that machine. You should note the date and time of the system, whether power on passwords has been set up, and the boot sequence of the machine. If the boot order of the machine isn't configured to first try and boot from a floppy disk or the CD-ROM, you may need to change this. However, before modifying these settings, document what the original settings were, and what you changed them to afterward.

After ensuring that the system is configured to first boot from a floppy or CD-ROM, you would then test your forensic boot disk to make sure the computer will boot from that drive properly. With the power connector or data cable still removed from the storage devices, you would insert the boot disk, and then boot the computer. If it boots from the floppy or CD-ROM, you would then reconnect the storage devices to prepare for a third boot. When the computer boots this time, document the drive configuration information, including the logical block addressing (LBA), large disk, cylinders, heads, and sectors (CHS), and whether the computer is configured to auto-detect any hard disks that are installed. Once this is documented, power the system down.

If possible, it is best to physically remove the hard disk from the computer that's been seized and connect it to a workstation in a forensic lab, or to a device such as FastBloc that prevents disk writes and works between the examiner's computer and the hard disk. If it is attached to the machine that will perform the acquisition, you can then use information acquired earlier from the CMOS/BIOS to properly configure the storage device so that it will be recognized. In some situations, such as those that follow, it may be easier or possible to read the hard disk only by leaving it installed on the suspect's machine:

- Laptop computers use different hard disks from desktop computers, although adapters can be purchased that will connect the hard disk to a desktop system. In some cases, removing the disk from the laptop may be difficult, and reading the disk may not be possible if the appropriate adapter to connect the drive to a ribbon cable is unavailable.

- Equipment requirements, such as when the disk is used for network storage and network equipment is needed to access the data, or when other equipment (such as the adapters mentioned previously) are not available to the technician performing the examination.

- Redundant Array of Inexpensive Disks (RAID) technology may need to be left in an array, as attempting to acquire data from such disks individually may not provide results that are usable.

- Legacy equipment. In some cases, older drives may not work with newer systems, making it impossible to read the data.

If the hard disk isn't going to be connected to the examiner's machine, you will need to leave it installed on the suspect's machine. Depending on the forensic software being used, the examiner could then attach a CD-RW or other storage device to the machine, or connect to the machine using a network cable, null modem cable, or other method of allowing communication between the two machines. Regardless of the method used to connect the machines, the data that's acquired and saved as image files should be stored on forensically clean media.

Write protection is an important part of acquiring data, as it will prevent any data from being written to the suspect hard disk. If hardware-based write protection is used, it should be installed prior to starting the computer, whereas software-based write protection should be activated immediately after booting the system with the examiner's operating system or boot disk. Once it is started, you should then attempt to capture and document any electronic identifiers the disk might have, such as its electronic serial number. Once these facts about the disk have been recorded, you are then ready to begin to acquire the data using methods that won't modify data on the disk, such as by using disk-imaging software to duplicate the data.

Disk Imaging

Disk imaging is accepted as standard practice in computer forensics to preserve the integrity of the original evidence. Disk imaging differs from creating a standard backup of a disk (for fault-tolerance purposes) in that ambient data is not copied to a backup; only active files are copied. Because a backup created with popular backup programs such as the Windows built-in backup utility is not an exact duplicate (in other words, a physical bitstream image), these programs should not be used for disk imaging. Programs such as Norton Ghost include switches that allow you to make a bitstream copy, but these programs were not originally designed for forensic use and do not include the features and analysis tools that are included with imaging programs and stand-alone imaging systems designed especially for forensic examination.

Bitstream Copies

Digital evidence is, by its nature, fragile. Some data is *volatile*—that is, it is transient in nature and, unlike data stored on disk, will be lost when the computer is shut down. Data on a computer disk can be easily damaged, destroyed, or changed either deliberately or accidentally. The first step in handling such digital evidence is to protect it from any sort of manipulation or accident. The best way to do this is to immediately make a complete bitstream image of the media on which the evidence is stored.

A *bitstream image* is a copy that records every data bit that was recorded to the original storage device, including all hidden files, temp files, corrupted files, file fragments, and erased files that have not yet been overwritten. In other words, every binary digit is duplicated exactly onto the copy media. Bitstream copies (sometimes called *bitstream backups*) use CRC computations to validate that the copy is the same as the original source data. The "mirror image" should be an exact duplicate of the original, and the original should then be stored in a safe place where its integrity can be maintained. The copy is made via a process called *disk imaging*. In some cases, evidence could be limited to a few data files that can be copied individually rather than creating a copy of the entire disk.

Using Disk Imaging to Create Duplicate Copies

Disk imaging refers to the process of making an exact copy of a disk. Imaging is sometimes also called *disk cloning* or *ghosting*, but the latter terms usually refer to images created for purposes other than evidence preservation. Disk imaging differs from just copying all the files on a disk in that the disk structure and relative location of data on the disk are preserved. When you copy all the data on a disk to another disk, that data will usually be stored on the new disk in contiguous clusters as there is room to store it. That way, all the data on the two disks will be identical, but the way that the data is distributed on the disks will not. When you create a disk image (a bitstream copy), each physical sector of the disk is copied so that the data is distributed in the same way, and then the image is compressed into a file called an *image file*. This image is exactly like the original, both physically and logically. There are a number of different ways to create a bit-level duplicate of a disk, including:

■ Removing the hard disk from the suspect computer and attaching it to another computer (preferably a forensic workstation) to make the copy

- Attaching another hard disk to the suspect computer and making the copy

- Using a stand-alone imaging device such as the DIBS Rapid Action Imaging Device

- Using a network connection (Ethernet connection, crossover cable, null modem cable, USB, or the like) to transfer the contents of the disk to another computer or forensic workstation

Which of these methods you choose will usually depend on the equipment that you have at hand. A portable forensic workstation or stand-alone imaging device is probably the best solution, but it's also the most expensive.

Examining Evidence

The examination of evidence occurs after it has been acquired using forensic software. Working from an image of the original machine, you can extract files and other data from the image to separate files, which the examiner can then review. For example, a Microsoft Word document found in the image of the suspect machine could be extracted, allowing it to be opened and viewed in Word without modifying the original data or that available through the disk image. In this example, the file is first extracted and then analyzed to determine what value it holds as evidence. Although every file may not be individually examined in this manner, the process of analyzing data does require a repeated process of extracting data stored in different areas of the machine, and then determining its value to the investigation.

Extracting data from the machine isn't limited only to files that are available to the operating system, file system, or other software that may have been installed on the machine. By viewing various areas of the disk, you can access and examine file fragments and data that has been corrupted or deleted. Extraction of evidence from a hard disk can occur at either of two levels:

- Logical extraction

- Physical extraction

A *logical extraction* is used to identify and recover files based on the operating system(s), file system(s), and application(s) installed on the computer. This type of extraction allows you to identify what data is stored in active files, deleted files, slack space, and unallocated file space. This type of examination would find information that is available to the operating system, and/or is visible to the file system on the suspect's computer. When this type of extraction occurs, any or all of the following actions might be performed:

- Extraction of file system information. This is done to identify the structure of folders, as well as the names, locations, sizes, attributes, dates, and timestamps of files.

- Extraction of files relevant to the investigation, which would be based on the name, extension, header/footer, content, and/or location of the file on the drive.

- Extraction of data that is encrypted, password-protected, and/or compressed.

- Extraction of data in the file slack. As we discussed in Chapter 4, a cluster is a group of disk sectors where data is stored, and to which the operating system assigned a unique number to keep track of files. Because the cluster is a fixed size in operating systems such as

Windows, the entire cluster is reserved for a file even if the file doesn't fill that amount of space. This unused space is referred to as slack space.

- Extraction of data in unallocated space. Unallocated disk space is the part of a hard disk that is not part of any partition. For example, if you had a single 1GB partition that was assigned a drive letter (such as C:), this would be allocated space. However, if the drive was larger than 1GB, the remaining space on the drive would be unallocated space. Even though it hasn't been allocated to a partition, it may still contain damaged or deleted data.

- Recovery of deleted files. As we'll see in Chapter 6, you can use various techniques and tools to recover data that been deleted.

- Reduction of data, which would reduce the number of files returned by eliminating known files.

A *physical extraction* is used to identify and recover files and data across the entire physical hard drive. Because it occurs at the physical level, the file system used on the hard disk doesn't matter. A physical extraction may involve a number of different methods to find data that is stored on the computer, including:

- **Keyword searching** Extracting data in this way involves searching for specific data using specific keywords. Because the search occurs at a physical level, it can find data that is stored anywhere on the hard disk.

- **File carving** In this case, utilities will recover files or file fragments by looking for file headers/footers and other identifiers in the data. This is particularly useful when attempting to find data that has been damaged or deleted, was located in corrupt directories on the disk, or was stored on damaged media.

- **Partition table and unused space examinations** Examining the partition structure can help you to identify the file system being used and determine whether the physical size of the hard disk is accounted for.

Once the data has been extracted from the computer, it can then be analyzed. This involves looking at the data and determining whether it's relevant and significant to the case. Although an investigator may analyze data such as pictures that have been found on the machine, or may perform subsequent analysis on various files that have been recovered, the person examining the machine will perform a significant amount of this work to limit the amount of information that is later provided to the investigator of the case. Various types of analysis include:

- Time frame analysis
- Data hiding analysis
- Application and file analysis
- Ownership and possession analysis

Time Frame Analysis

Timeframe analysis is used to determine when files were downloaded, viewed, or modified on a machine. It can be useful in constructing a sequence of events, or associating a particular user to a time period. Using the date and timestamps on files, which show when a file was created, last accessed, or modified, a time frame can be established that shows when particular events occurred. In addition to this, dates and times stored in logs and other system files can show when a particular user logged on to a system or performed some action.

Data Hiding Analysis

Data hiding analysis involves looking for data that may be hidden on the hard disk. By concealing the information, the person who hid the information hopes it will avoid detection from casual or forensic detection. Although some techniques for hiding data may require special tools, others may be simple to detect if you're aware of the methods being used. In Chapter 7, we'll discuss a number of these tools and methods in great detail.

Steganography

Steganography (from the Greek word for *covered writing*) refers to a method of hiding data—not just concealing its contents as encryption does, but concealing its very existence. Steganography is usually used in conjunction with encryption for added protection of sensitive data. This method ameliorates one of the biggest problems of encrypting data—the fact that it is encrypted draws the attention of people who are looking for confidential or sensitive information. For more information on steganography, see Chapter 7.

Application and File Analysis

Application and file analysis is used to identify what kinds of programs the suspect is using, to identify common file types used for specific purposes relevant to the investigation, and to associate files that have been located on the drive with particular software. Often, people will use certain patterns to name files or directories, whether it is to be as specific and detailed as possible (for example, TaxReturn2007.q07) or to hide the contents by using a specific code (for example, cp13yf.jpg to indicate child pornography depicting a 13-year-old girl). By identifying these patterns and their relevance, you can expand your search to look for other files with these features.

Some files can be associated with specific applications, to identify what programs are commonly being used. For example, you could identify files in a Temporary Internet Files directory to those used with Internet Explorer, whereas other files could be associated with e-mail programs. In doing so, you can determine what programs are being used. Similarly, by reviewing the Internet history and messages in the e-mail software, you could correlate files that have been saved to those sent or received via e-mail, or downloaded from a particular Web site.

The most direct method of determining what's in a file is, of course, to examine the contents. To identify what is depicted in an image, or the data in a spreadsheet or document, you will need to view the contents and determine their relevance to the case. To reduce the number of files you'll need to review, you should perform other actions mentioned in previous sections to narrow down what needs to be viewed.

Ownership and Possession Analysis

Ownership and possession analysis is used to identify who created, modified, or accessed files on a computer. By identifying the individual who created, viewed, or downloaded a particular file, you can associate the existence of a file to the actions of a person. For example, if a person said that he or she hadn't seen a file, you could show that the file's ownership belonged to that person's user account, and by identifying the last time it was accessed, you could show that the person had reasonable knowledge of its existence. In this example, you can see that this type of analysis can easily be used with time frame analysis to show when a particular person used the computer and had access to a particular file.

Ownership of a file can be displayed through the properties of a file. In looking at the properties of a file, you can view who the current owner of a file is. If multiple users are on a machine, you can associate who owns the file with the person who uses that particular account. In knowing this, you can then peruse firewall logs or other resources to obtain additional information about the user's actions.

Documenting and Reporting Evidence

Because any evidence may be used in possible criminal proceedings, thorough documentation cannot be stressed enough. Documentation provides a clear understanding of what occurred to obtain the evidence, and what the evidence represents. No matter what role you play in an investigation, you must document any observations and actions that were made. Information should include the date, time, conversations pertinent to the investigation, tasks that were performed to obtain evidence, names of those present or who assisted, and anything else that was relevant to the forensic procedures that took place. We will discuss documentation in depth in Chapter 15.

Closing the Case

Regardless of what the investigation entails, there comes a time where every case must be closed. Once the analysis has been completed and a sufficient amount of time has passed, you will need to accept what has been found and move on to another case. If certain evidence has been found, it may even be decided that additional evidence on the computer isn't necessary for the case. For example, if you've found the smoking gun in the case (such as dozens of child pornography pictures), additional evidence may be unnecessary if enough has been found to pursue a conviction. Once you're satisfied that based on the search parameters you have, the analyses you've performed are complete and there's little to nothing else to find, it is usually time to stop. After all, no one makes a career of a single case.

After a final report has been prepared and submitted to the investigator and/or prosecutor, you should follow up to identify what actions (if any) are being taken regarding the case. In some situations, new information that can be used to search for evidence may become available, and you may be asked to revisit the machine or examine new sources of data (such as other machines, devices, or storage sites) and try to find more. Other times, you will find that the person has taken a plea bargain (ending your role in the process), or that a trial will be underway at some point in the future. By following up with investigators, you will be able to determine what will occur next in the case.

At some point, any evidence you've acquired and analyzed will no longer be needed. Policies dealing with the destruction and disposal of evidence should be in place, to provide a guideline for how long you should keep property that's been seized, and disk images that have been acquired from machines, media, and devices. When the date approaches, you should contact the investigator, as he or she will be able to inform you whether the evidence should be retained longer. In some situations, evidence will be retained in the event of an appeal or delays in hearing the case in court or other hearings.

Summary

Computer forensics is used to collect, examine, preserve, and present data that is stored or transmitted in an electronic format. This branch of forensics uses scientific methods to retrieve and document evidence located on computers and other electronic devices. Using specialized tools and techniques, digital evidence may be retrieved in a variety of ways. Such evidence may reside on hard disks and other devices, even if it has been deleted so that it's no longer visible through the normal functions of the computer, or hidden in other ways. Forensic software can reveal this data that is invisible through normal channels, and restore it to a previous state. Because the purpose of computer forensics is its possible use in court, strict procedures must be followed for evidence to be admissible.

For evidence to be used in court, numerous standards must be met to ensure that the evidence isn't compromised and that information has been obtained correctly. If you don't follow forensic procedures, judges may deem evidence inadmissible, defense lawyers may argue its validity, and the case may be damaged significantly. In many cases, the only evidence available is that which exists in a digital format. This could mean that the ability to punish an offender rests with the quality of the evidence you've acquired, authenticated, examined, and presented to the court through thorough documentation and testimony.

Frequently Asked Questions

Q: How should I prepare evidence to be transported in a forensic investigation?

A: Before transporting evidence, you should ensure that it is protected from risks of being damaged. Hard disks and other components should be packed in antistatic bags, and other components should be packaged to reduce the risk of damage from being jostled. All evidence should be sealed in a bag and/or tagged to identify it as a particular piece of evidence, and information about the evidence should be included in an evidence log.

Q: I'm new to cybercrime, but I really want to get involved. Should I jump right into doing forensics?

A: Although a plethora of training is available in the field of digital forensics, you may want to consider getting acclimated to crimes with a cyber component before jumping into forensics with both feet. Much of what we discussed in this chapter reflects the belief that most cybercrime is just plain old crime. Whereas we may hold this belief to help those who dislike technology realize that they can still work computer crime cases without having a thorough knowledge of computers, we may suggest the same train of thought to you; there is plenty of crime to investigate that has a cyber component which does not require a forensic examination. Tracing e-mail harassments, responding to threats over chat, and investigating sexual solicitations over IM are but a few of the types of crimes that can be investigated without immediately requiring a forensic exam. Our recommendation is to find a training course that focuses on the investigation of Internet-related crime—the skills you learn in a class such as this won't be wasted if you choose to go the forensics route in the future. By the way, focusing on crimes that you can investigate without requiring a forensic examination will make your chief a lot happier than your request to purchase $20,000 of software equipment to start processing forensic cases.

Q: I want to get involved with catching predators online. I've seen the TV shows and there doesn't appear to be anything to it. Why should I bother to learn all the technology junk if I don't need to?

A: Little technical knowledge is required to "chat" with a potential suspect, and if everything goes according to plan, the suspect shows up at your door and you take him or her into custody. But what happens when things don't go according to plan? Are you aware of the underlying software or process that makes the chatting possible? Is your machine configured correctly and protected appropriately? (Naming the computer DetectiveDesk22 may show up during a scan of your computer and may blow your cover.) Are you knowledgeable about how the particular chatting software works? Does it use a proxy? Will it provide you with a direct connection during a file transfer or Webcam stream—and if so, do you have the skills to capture the bad guy's IP address during that exact moment of transfer? Do you have the skills to properly set up an online identity and protect it from discovery? Although the initial setup of the identity may be trivial, the long-term maintenance and believability of the profile may affect your investigations.

In principle, it sounds like a good idea to get a screen name together to begin enticing predators into the stationhouse, but obtaining basic computer investigative skills will go a long way toward conducting more successful and productive investigations. Further, these skills may prove critical one day when a predator shoots you a Webcam image of a child held hostage—that exact moment is not the time to begin learning about the underlying technology. You need to acquire and practice these skills before you're employed in active operations.

Chapter 6

Computer Forensic Software and Hardware

Topics we'll investigate in this chapter:

- Disk Imaging
- Forensic Software Tools
- Forensic Hardware Tools

☑ Summary

☑ Frequently Asked Questions

Introduction

The quality of work in computer forensics is often based on the tools used during the investigation. To acquire and examine the data on a suspect machine or device, you must use specialized hardware and software. In this way, you can create an image of the data on the machine, allowing you to review the data without modifying it. In doing so, any evidence is protected, and is less likely to be brought into question during a trial.

In this chapter, we discuss disk imaging and introduce hardware- and software-based forensic tools. Due to the large number of hardware and software tools available, we can cover only a few in detail. Also, we will discuss a number of different types of tools in later chapters, so if you don't see one that you're familiar with here, don't presume that we didn't include it in the book. To aid you in identifying the wide variety of tools available for specific uses, we have included tables within the chapter that supply a brief description of the salient features of each tool.

Disk Imaging

Disk imaging refers to the process of making an exact copy of a disk. Imaging is sometimes also called *disk cloning* or *ghosting*, but the latter terms usually refer to images created for purposes other than evidence preservation. Disk imaging differs from just copying all the files on a disk in that the disk structure and relative location of data on the disk are preserved. When you copy all the data on one disk to another disk the data is usually stored on the new disk in contiguous clusters as space permits. That way, all the data on the two disks will be identical, but the way the data is distributed on the disks will not. When you create a disk image (a bitstream copy), each physical sector of the disk is copied so that the data is distributed in the same way, and then the image is compressed into a file called an *image file*. This image is exactly like the original, both physically and logically.

You can create a bit-level duplicate of a disk in a number of different ways, including:

- Removing the hard disk from the suspect computer and attaching it to another computer (preferably a forensic workstation) to make the copy

- Attaching another hard disk to the suspect computer and making the copy

- Using a stand-alone imaging device such as the DIBS Rapid Action Imaging Device

- Using a network connection (Ethernet connection, crossover cable, null modem cable, Universal Serial Bus [USB], or the like) to transfer the contents of the disk to another computer or forensic workstation

Which of these methods you choose will usually depend on the equipment you have at hand. A portable forensic workstation or stand-alone imaging device is probably the best solution, but it's also the most expensive.

A History of Disk Imaging

Disk imaging can serve a number of purposes and was initially used for purposes other than computer forensics and digital evidence collection. Computer virus researchers used disk imaging in the 1980s when studying new computer viruses so that they could execute the virus code without destroying or damaging the data on the original disk. Copying just the virus files didn't always work because some viruses had to be on specific parts of the disk to do what they were written to do. For this reason, a program was developed that would copy the data exactly as it was located on the disk, duplicating sector addresses and creating an exact duplication or disk "image."

The usefulness of such a program did not go unnoticed to computer crime investigators. Detective Inspector John Austen at London's Scotland Yard was the first to recognize the investigative applications of the tool, and the concept of computer forensic imaging equipment was born shortly thereafter.

Meanwhile, disk imaging has come to be used for creating backups that can be put into place quickly and easily if the original disk fails, by simply swapping out the imaged disk for the original. Another popular use of imaging is to speed up the process of rolling out operating systems and software on a large number of computers simultaneously, with the same configuration. Norton Ghost is one of the most popular programs used for this purpose. For more information on Ghost, investigate the Product menus at www.symantec.com.

It is important for investigators to understand the differences between these imaging purposes and the products that are designed for different purposes. Cloning products such as Ghost are not designed to preserve the user data on a disk; the purpose is to create a standard installation configuration that can be distributed to multiple computers. Although these products can be used on a disk with user data, there is another problem: The images they create are not exact bit-by-bit copies of the originals. According to the Symantec Knowledge Base, "Normally, Ghost does not create an exact duplicate of a disk. Instead, Ghost re-creates the partition information as needed and copies the contents of the files." Thus, a checksum of the image disk almost always results in a value that is different from the checksum value of the original disk. This could be why such evidence is excluded in some courts, because rules of evidence generally require that when a duplicate is admitted as evidence in place of the original, it must be an *exact* duplicate of the original. Although investigators sometimes use Ghost to create a disk image, and some versions of Ghost have switches and options that can be used to force it to create a bitstream copy, it is usually best to use software specifically designed for forensic purposes. On the other hand, if Ghost is the only duplication program you have, a ghosted image is better than no image.

Imaging Software

A number of disk-imaging programs are popular with law enforcement computer forensic specialists. These programs were developed specifically for the purpose of creating duplicate disks to be used in processing computer evidence and analyzing that evidence. Examples of products that we'll discuss later in this chapter include SafeBack, EnCase, and ProDiscover.

NOTE

The National Institute of Standards and Technology (NIST) developed a disk-imaging tool specification as part of its Computer Forensics Tool Testing (CFTT) project, the objective of which was to provide for standardization of automated tools used in investigations involving computer forensics.

Stand-Alone Imaging Tools

Stand-alone imaging tools such as the DIBS Portable Evidence Recovery Unit and Rapid Action Imaging Device eliminate the need for a second computer while maintaining the integrity of the suspect computer. These portable units can make duplicates of the suspect computer's disk(s) onto another clean hard disk or optical media without the need to remove the original disk from the suspect computer.

The Role of Imaging in Computer Forensics

Disk imaging is accepted as standard practice in computer forensics to preserve the integrity of the original evidence. Disk imaging differs from creating a standard backup of a disk (for fault-tolerance purposes) in that ambient data is not copied to a backup; only active files are copied. Because a backup created with popular backup programs such as the Windows built-in backup utility, Backup Exec, ARCserve, and the like is not an exact duplicate (in other words, a physical bitstream image), these programs should not be used for disk imaging. Programs such as Norton Ghost include switches that allow you to make a bitstream copy, but these programs were not originally designed for forensic use and do not include the features and analysis tools that are included with imaging programs and stand-alone imaging systems designed especially for forensic examination.

Despite this, network administrators may have created regular backups of servers and workstations on a network, or individuals may have backed up data on their home computers. These may also contain important data, as they contain a snapshot of data from a specific point in time, and you shouldn't overlook them as potential sources of evidence.

"Snapshot" Tools and File Copying

Sometimes it is not possible or desirable to make a full bitstream image of a disk. This could be because the system is mission-critical and management does not want to have it out of commission during an investigation, or because the decision has already been made not to pursue prosecution. However, there are still ways to collect data about the intrusion or other crime for the purpose of analyzing what happened and preventing it from happening again.

One set of software tools designed to allow administrators to create a "snapshot" of the state of a machine that has been compromised is The Coroner's Toolkit, written by the authors of the once popular UNIX utility called the System Administrator Tools for Analyzing Networks (SATAN). Running these tools on a UNIX system that has been breached is very helpful in performing a forensic analysis, because it will provide information on running processes, the state of the network, deleted files, user information, and much more.

In some cases, when evidence is documentary in nature, it might be possible to introduce copies of individual files rather than copying the entire disk. You should use this method only when you need specific identifiable documents and there's no need to search for ambient data or other hidden data.

Forensic Software Tools

This section summarizes the features and advantages of a large number of software forensic tools. For detailed information and technical reports it is always best to view the vendor Web sites as well as organizations that conduct technical reviews and evaluations, such as NIST. The CFTT project Web site contains additional valuable information:

- www.cftt.nist.gov/disk_imaging.htm

- www.cftt.nist.gov/presentations.htm

- www.cftt.nist.gov/software_write_block.htm

Although information based on experience is presented in the subsections that follow, much of the information is based on the assertions of the various vendors who make the products listed in the chapter. The CFTT project is a good source of comparative data when deciding among these vendors.

Visual TimeAnalyzer

Visual TimeAnalyzer, shown in Figure 6.1, is a tool designed to track and control computer usage. It provides its results through detailed reports, and allows you to track individual users or projects, including monitoring working hours and breaks, identifying what software is being used on the PC, and controlling Internet usage and time spent online. The software has some privacy safeguards and does not monitor all user data, such as passwords and personal documents. Unlike spyware, it does not record specific keystrokes or run screen captures as a background process. Visual TimeAnalyzer is available at www.neuber.com/timeanalyzer/index.html.

Figure 6.1 Visual TimeAnalyzer

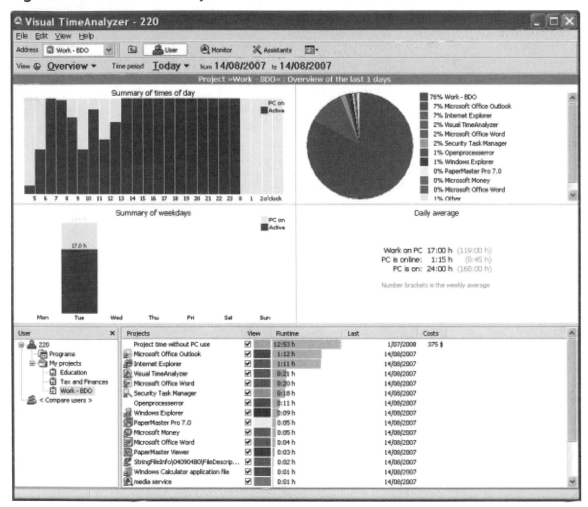

X-Ways Forensics

X-Ways Forensics is based on WinHex (which we'll discuss later in this chapter) and is designed to be an advanced work environment for the digital forensic analyst. It is available at www.x-ways.net/ forensics/, and it provides a number of features for computer forensic investigations, including:

- Forensic cloning and imaging of sound disks

- Examination of the complete directory structure inside raw image files, even if the directory spans segments

- Native support for FAT, NTFS, Ext2, Ext3, Ext4, CDFS, and UDF file systems; built-in interpretation of RAID 0 and RAID 5 systems and dynamic disks; and support for the HFS, HFS+, ReiserFS, Reiser4, UFS, and UFS2 file systems

- Viewing and dumping of physical RAM and the virtual memory space of running processes

- Hard disk cleansing to produce forensically sterile media

- Gathering of slack space, free space, interpartition space, and generic text from drives and images

- Creation of file and directory catalogs for all computer media

- Calculation for mass hash-file encryption (CRC32, MD5, SHA1, and SHA256)

- Examination of e-mail extracted from Outlook (PST)*, Outlook Express (DBX), Mozilla (including Netscape and Thunderbird), generic mailbox (mbox, Berkeley, BSD, UNIX), Eudora, PocoMail, Barca, Opera, Forte Agent, The Bat!, Pegasus, PMMail, FoxMail, and local copies of maildir folders

- Automatic identification of encrypted Microsoft Office and PDF documents

- Automatic identification of pictures embedded in documents (for example, Microsoft Word, PDF, and PowerPoint)

- Skin color detection (that is, a gallery view sorted by skin color percentage that greatly accelerates searches for traces of child pornography and obscene images)

X-Ways Forensics can also write-protect data to ensure authenticity and integrity. It has a case management function integrated with automated activity logging (audit logs) and automated reporting. The generated reports can be imported and further processed by any application that processes Hypertext Markup Language (HTML)—for example, Microsoft Word. It also associates comments about files for inclusion in the generated reports or for filtering.

Evidor

Evidor is a tool for searching drives for occurrences of keywords provided by the investigator. It searches for all occurrences of keywords within text files in digital media such as hard disks, and retrieves the context. It examines all files in the entire allocated space—including Windows swap/paging and hibernate files—along with unallocated and slack space. It will find data files that have been deleted if they still physically exist on the hard disk. Evidor is a small subset of the search functionality included in X-Ways Forensics, but it cannot access remote networked hard disks. It is available from www.x-ways.net/evidor/index-m.html.

Slack Space and Data Recovery Tools

Slack space and data recovery tools aid in the recovery of deleted files and data, including file fragments in slack space on file systems supported by Windows. For more information on slack space, refer to the information we previously discussed in Chapter 4.

Ontrack

Ontrack Data Recovery is a simple-to-use tool for recovering lost, remote, and deleted data. It comes with a file repair capability for files in Microsoft Word and ZIP formats. It also recovers deleted files, folders, and entire partitions. It uses an emergency boot diskette to retrieve data from systems that cannot boot Windows. The user can start, stop, or resume the recovery process and select an FTP location as the destination for the recovered data. The user can configure the file filter for a quick or full scan.

The analyst can use this application to perform an enhanced search using options such as find, find next, and find previous. Ontrack can filter and sort data according to the file date, time, name, status, and size. It can scan the media for lost and remote data and lets the user specify the locations to which to copy the recovered files and folders.

DriveSpy

DriveSpy is another DOS-based data acquisition tool developed by Digital Intelligence Forensic Solutions, and is available from www.digitalintelligence.com. If you're familiar with DOS commands, it is an easy-to-use tool, as it uses a DOS prompt and many of the commands used in DOS to navigate through the directory structure of a system being analyzed. In addition to these commands, you can use other special commands to invoke features of DriveSpy.

Even though it is a DOS-based tool, it can acquire evidence from partitions using the File Transfer Protocol (FAT) file system, non-DOS partitions, and hidden DOS partitions. This not only includes files that are visible to the file system, but also data that has been deleted, and data that exists in slack space and in unallocated space on the disk. It supports acquisition from hard drives that are larger than 8.4 GB, as well as floppy disks and other storage media. It provides a built-in sector and cluster Hex Viewer to view data, and can create and restore compressed forensic images of partitions.

A beneficial feature of this tool to an investigation is its logging capabilities. You can configure DriveSpy to document how the acquisition of evidence is conducted, including logging every keystroke that you made. The software writes these to a log file, and you can use them later in a report of what actions you took to acquire the evidence.

Additional Data Recovery Tools

You can use the following tools to recover information from many sources, including cameras and disk drives.

Forensic Sorter

Forensic Sorter is a tool developed by Paraben Corp. (www.paraben-forensics.com) that's designed to organize and speed up the examination of a hard drive's contents. It sorts the contents of hard drives into categories such as video, audio, and spreadsheets so that you can easily find what you're looking for. It will filter common Windows files as well as recover deleted files, or file fragments in slack, deleted, and unallocated space.

The application supports drive images in RAW, PFR (Forensic Replicator), SafeBack, and EnCase image files and is compatible with Paraben's P2 Forensic Examination Technology. It sorts files by header rather than file extension for accuracy, and it sorts files located in unpartitioned space. Forensic Sorter identifies encrypted files for easy recovery using Paraben's Decryption Collection. All data output is nonproprietary, so you can use any tool for analysis after sorting. It is designed for use with Paraben's Case Agent Companion. It features:

- Encrypting File System (EFS) file detection
- New Technology File System (NTFS) compressed file read operations and stream operations
- HTML reporting
- Ext2 and Ext3 partition operations
- Compressed archive (ZIP, RAR, etc.) sorting
- Sorting of drives with bad sectors
- Unicode support
- Removable disk support
- OLE storage support
- Palm OS file detection
- Chat log file detection
- E-mail Examiner and Network E-mail Examiner-supported file detection
- XML output validation

Directory Snoop

Directory Snoop is a product developed by Briggs Softworks and is available at www.briggsoft.com/dsnoop.htm. This program is a cluster-level search tool that allows Windows users to analyze and view files in FAT- and NTFS-formatted disk drives to see what data can be recovered. It can recover deleted files or permanently erase sensitive files. Supported media include hard drives, floppy disks, ZIP disks, magneto-optical drives, and flashcard devices. Its features include:

- FAT and NTFS modules
- Recovering deleted files, including those emptied from the Recycle Bin
- Destroying sensitive files with its secure wiping functionality which provides up to 35 wipe passes
- Secure wiping slack and free drive space
- Purging sensitive filenames left behind after normal erasing
- Copying open and locked files with the cluster copy function
- Searching, filtering, and sorting files globally by name and other parameters
- Viewing, searching, printing, and copying raw cluster data

- Dynamically linking clusters with cluster chains and the files that use them

- Examining the FAT and Master File Tables (MFTs)

- Viewing files through external applications

- Verifying the effectiveness of other file wiping programs

PHOTORECOVERY

PHOTORECOVERY, by LC Technology, Inc., was developed for recovering images, movies, and media files from a variety of digital media types. You can use it with memory sticks, Smart Media, Connect Flash I and II, Micro Drives, SD and XD Cards, multimedia chips, floppy disks, and almost all other forms of digital film. When you put the digital media in the external reading device, PHOTORECOVERY will save the pictures in specified locations. It is available at www.lc-tech.com/software/prwindetail.html.

File Integrity Checkers

Failing to maintain the integrity of a file or drive image could mean the end of a forensic examination. File integrity checkers help you to prove that the file you copied into evidence has not subsequently been altered. They make possible a quick and reliable diagnosis of a system image for the purpose of determining whether any changes have occurred. The following sections highlight some of the most popular file integrity checkers available.

File Date Time Extractor

File Date Time Extractor (FDTE) from Digital Detective (www.digital-detective.co.uk) is designed to search through binary files to uncover hidden, embedded, 64-bit date and time data. Windows files, such as Word documents, contain several timestamp formats. It is important to note that false positives are common due to data patterns in files that look like timestamps but are not.

Decode – Forensic Date/Time Decoder

Decode is another tool developed by Digital Detective, and is available to download for free from www.digital-detective.co.uk/freetools/decode.asp. It was designed to decode date/time values that are found embedded within binary and other file types. It supports the following date/time formats and will allow you to specify the offset from GMT.

Date and time values are stored within Windows in various formats. For example, Internet history (index.dat) files, Recycle Bin (INFO) files, Windows link files, and Microsoft Office documents contain a 64-bit date/time structure. Decode can take a decimal hexadecimal value and convert it into a date and time value in a variety of formats.

Disk Imaging Tools and Toolkits

The following tools are used to create a bit-image copy of a drive or other media. Toolkits and additional tools are also available to extend the functionality of the primary tools in these software packages.

SnapBack DatArrest

SnapBack DatArrest can obtain the mirror images of different operating systems, and is available from www.snapback.com. It can back up data present in a system's hard disk and is specially designed to create backups of mission-critical data.

The captured image contains all system and networking software with associated drivers, software applications, and configurations, and all the files including deleted files, slack space, and data files, as well as the CMOS settings for the system.

The data gathering takes place in several modes, such as copying server hard drives to tape, PC hard drives to tape, server or PC hard drives to removable media, hard drives to hard drives, or tape to tape. It obtains a bit-level backup of data present in a hard disk. The DatArrest Suite provides the ability to copy:

- Server hard drives to tape

- PC hard drives to tape

- Server or PC hard drives to removable media

- Hard drives to hard drives

- Tape to tape

DatArrest backs up any hard drive (Small Computer System Interface [SCSI], Integrated Drive Electronics [IDE], etc.) to any SCSI tape drive, removable drive, and even SCSI or IDE hard drives.

ProDiscover

This Windows-based application, designed by the Technology Pathways forensic team, creates bitstream copies saved as compressed image files on the forensic workstation. It can recover deleted files from slack space, analyze the Windows alternate data streams for hidden data, and analyze images created with the UNIX *dd* utility and then generate reports. The vendor hosts an e-mail discussion list for exchange of tips and techniques and peer support for users of computer forensic products (see www.techpathways.com).

ProDiscover DFT reads the disk at the sector level, circumventing the standard file system while it recovers files, looks in slack data and in the Host Protected Area (HPA) section of a disk, and examines alternate data streams in Windows systems. This unique approach also allows you to examine files without altering valuable metadata, such as the date the data was last accessed.

Its main features are as follows:

- Conforms to NIST's disk-imaging tool specification 3.1.6 to ensure high quality

- Creates a bitstream copy of the evidence disk

- Supports FAT12, FAT16, FAT32, and NTFS file systems

- Analyzes data in a protected area (Advanced Technology Attachment [ATA]) by identifying the partitions in the protected area

- Calculates the file checksum using either SHA1 or MD5

- Analyzes data in alternate data streams of NTFS partitions
- Is capable of analyzing dynamic disks

NTI Tools

NTI Tools offer a variety of product suites that are compilations of its various software forensic tools. It is available from www.forensics-intl.com/tools.html. The products in this tool set include:

- Stealth Suite, which people without a forensic background can use to assess activity on a computer hard disk. These tools can help identify whether a targeted computer system was used to access inappropriate information.

- Computer Incident Response Suite, which is often used in corporate and government investigations and security risk reviews. It is optimized for MS-DOS, which is the lowest-cost forensic platform for MS-DOS and Windows processing. Many of the tools also come in a Windows version. This should be one of your first forensic tool sets. It also is an excellent set of tools for cross-validating your findings before going to court.

- Data Elimination Suite, which is used for computer data elimination and validation. It allows you to remove information from a drive and cross-validate that the information has been removed. It eliminates classified data "leakage" and verifies that the data was properly eliminated.

- TextSearch Suite, which is used to process Windows NT/2000/XP-based computer systems from an MS-DOS command line. TextSearch Suite provides the same interface and features as its predecessor, TextSearch Plus, and also identifies many compressed and graphics files using the file header signature, giving the investigator a list of files that could store information in a compressed or graphics format. The suite also includes the HexSearch utility, which provides a similar interface as TextSearch Plus while allowing the user to search for hexadecimal strings, such as file headers, nonprinting characters, and more.

- NTI Secure ToolKit, which is used to secure sensitive files stored on portable and desktop computers. Because it uses NIST-tested and approved Advanced Encryption Standard (AES) 256-bit encryption, it qualifies for government use with classified *'Secret'* level data. This software exceeds commercial security requirements and it is much easier to use than Pretty Good Privacy (PGP). It includes a management tool so that corporate information is not lost to the corporation. An export license may be required for locations outside the United States.

SafeBack

SafeBack was one of the earliest DOS-based tools for acquiring evidence from a computer sector by sector. It is developed by NTI, and is available from www.forensics-intl.com/safeback.html. SafeBack has been marketed to law enforcement agencies since 1990 and has been used by the FBI and the Criminal Investigation Division of the IRS to create image files for forensic examination and evidentiary purposes. Booting from a floppy disk, it can make a duplicate image of everything on a hard disk, preserving data integrity and allowing you to analyze evidence without worrying about modifying it.

SafeBack is capable of duplicating individual partitions or entire disks of virtually any size, and the image files can be transferred to SCSI tape units or almost any other magnetic storage media.

The product contains cyclic redundancy check (CRC) functions to check the integrity of the copies, and date and timestamps to maintain an audit trail of the software's operations. The vendor provides a three-day computer forensic course to train forensic specialists in the use of the software. (In fact, the company does not provide technical support to individuals who have not undergone this training.) Although it is a DOS-based tool, you can use it to copy DOS, Windows, and UNIX disks (including Windows NT/2000 RAID drives) on Intel-compatible systems. Images can be saved as multiple files for storage on CDs or other small-capacity media. To avoid legal concerns about possible alteration, no compression or translation is used in creating the image.

R-Studio

R-Studio is a family of powerful and cost-effective data recovery software. It recovers files from FAT12, FAT16, FAT32, NTFS, NTFS 5 (created or updated by Windows 2000/XP/2003/Vista), HFS/HFS+ (Macintosh), little- and big-endian variants of UFS1/UFS2 (FreeBSD, OpenBSD, NetBSD, and Solaris), Ext2FS (Linux), and Ext3FS (Linux) partitions. It functions on local and network disks, even if such partitions are formatted, damaged, or deleted. The suite includes a variety of different tools, and is available from www.data-recovery-software.net.

The Forensic Toolkit (FTK)

The Forensic Toolkit (FTK) is a product developed by AccessData (www.accessdata.com), and is a fully integrated forensic data acquisition and analysis program. It provides a number of features, including support for full text indexing of image files without needing to extract them to a hard disk, and it includes a file viewer to preview files. It also has an imaging component (derived from the shareware ISOBuster product) that does a good job of collecting data from CDs and DVDs with any of the commonly supported file systems. We'll discuss FTK in greater detail in Chapter 7.

EnCase

EnCase is developed by Guidance Software (www.guidancesoftware.com), and has a friendly graphical interface that makes it easier for many forensic technicians to use. It provides for previewing evidence, copying targeted drives (creating a bitstream image), and searching and analyzing data. Documents, zipped files, and e-mail attachments can be automatically searched and analyzed, and Registry and graphics viewers are included. The software supports multiple platforms and file systems. The software calls the bitstream drive image an Evidence File and mounts it as a virtual drive (a read-only file) that you can search and examine using the GUI tools. Timestamps and other data remain unchanged during the examination. The "preview" mode allows the investigator to use a null modem cable or Ethernet connection to view data on the subject machine without changing anything; the vendor says it is impossible to make any alterations to the evidence during this process.

Web Site History and Favorites

FavURLView – Favourite Viewer

FavURLView is another tool from Digital Detective, and is available as a free download from www.digital-detective.co.uk/freetools/favurlview.asp. It is designed to decode Internet Shortcut

(URL) files (including their modified date and time) so that you can then compare a shortcut description with the associated link. Other forensic software that supports external viewers (such as EnCase and ILook) can run this program, although it has been designed to accept data from EnCase through the command line.

NetAnalysis

NetAnalysis is another tool for viewing Internet-related information. It is developed by Digital Detective, and is available from www.digital-detective.co.uk/netanalysis.asp. This product allows you to analyze a Web browser's history data. It is commonly used by law enforcement in child pornography cases. The forensic examination and analysis of user activity on the Internet can be the pivotal evidence in any case. With the increase in the use of computers by pedophiles and other Internet criminals, it is vital for a forensic investigator to be able to extract this data and analyze it quickly and present the evidence in an understandable format.

NetAnalysis includes the following functionality:

- Viewing Web history, manually or automatically
- Viewing browser cache data
- Extraction of browser data from unallocated space

The history extractor will also extract history records in a straightforward manner from a write-protected physical or logical device.

Linux/UNIX Tools: LTools and MTools

LTools

The LTools application is equipped with many command-line applications, which are executed from an MS-DOS window in Windows 9*x*, Me, NT, 2000, or XP. These applications provide the same functionality as the Linux *ls*, *cp*, *rm*, *chmod*, *chown*, and *ln* commands. Therefore, the MS-DOS and Windows operating systems allow users to list Linux files and directories to copy files from Linux to Windows. Supported command sets include those for:

- Deleting or renaming files in Linux (*ldel* and *lren*)
- Creating symbolic links (*lln*)
- Creating new Linux directories (*lmkdir*)
- Modifying a Linux file's access rights (*lchange*)
- Changing the Linux default directory (*lcd*)
- Setting the Linux default drive (*ldrive*)

Many of the tools present in UNIX operating systems have functions that are built into a single executable file. These functions are called a *bundle* of command-line parameters.

MTools

The MTools application is a group of tools that allow the user to manipulate UNIX systems. MTools can perform read, write, and other operations on MS-DOS files. Each application copies the commands that are present in MS-DOS. MTools also allows the user to unload and mount floppy disks.

The Coroner's Toolkit and Tctutils

Dan Farmer and Wietse Venema developed The Coroner's Toolkit. This is a group of applications that can be used to aid a forensic investigation on UNIX systems. This system can be executed in most UNIX/Linux operating systems.

The Coroner's Toolkit has a collection of applications and plug-ins that give the program additional functionality. The Coroner's Toolkit was first put into use for the purpose of a postmortem analysis of a UNIX operating system after a break-in. The application was first given to a computer forensic class for real-life applications in the field in 1999. This tool is mainly designed to help in a forensic investigation and is one of the tools forensic investigators use most frequently.

Other Tools

WinHex Specialist Edition

WinHex began as a disk-editing program and has developed into a forensic tool that is useful to digital evidence examiners of all skill levels. You can use WinHex Specialist Edition to validate the results of other tools and to perform specialized tasks such as file comparison and text extraction. This program can also teach novice analysts about disk layout, file system structures, data recovery, and other fundamental concepts of digital forensics.

WinHex is primarily a hexadecimal editor. It inspects and edits all types of files and can also recover deleted files and lost data from hard drives. It can do this on hard drives with corrupt file systems or from digital camera cards. It includes a RAM editor that provides access to the virtual memory of other processes, and is useful in concatenating and splitting files and in unifying and dividing odd and even bytes and words. It also has the ability to analyze, examine, and compare files, and it can create a drive image and make backups of drives. In addition, it can import all clipboard formats including ASCII hexadecimal values.

AutoRuns

AutoRuns is a utility used to view autostart locations, and to display programs that are configured to run at system boot or logon. It displays the entries in the order in which Windows processes them, and includes any programs that are in the startup folder, or Registry keys such as Run and RunOnce. It can also be configured to show Explorer shell extensions, toolbars, WINLOGON notifications, autostart services, and more. This product is available from Microsoft at http://technet.microsoft.com/en-us/sysinternals/default.aspx.

Forensic Software Reference

In looking at the number of programs we've discussed so far, you can see that a vast number of utilities and programs are available to assist in computer forensic investigations. To provide a more comprehensive overview of the tools that can be used, Table 6.1 is offered as a list of forensic software tools.

Table 6.1 Forensic Software

Program	Description
AOL PW Extractor	Reveals all AOL passwords on your computer
Accent Access Password Recovery	Recovers forgotten or lost passwords for Microsoft Access documents
Accent Excel Password Recovery	Recovers forgotten or lost passwords for Microsoft Excel documents
Accent Money Password Recovery	Recovers forgotten or lost passwords for Microsoft Money documents
Accent Office Password Recovery	Recovers forgotten or lost passwords for Microsoft Office documents. If you have lost or forgotten a password for opening a Microsoft Office document (Access, Excel, or Word), or a password for saving changes to a Word document, you can use this software. It will help you search for a password more effectively via the following methods: a dictionary-based attack, a brute force attack, or a brute force attack with a mask.
ACDSee	Fast photo viewer and manager. Enables you to easily find, view, manage, print, edit, and share images.
Active Partition Recovery	Recovers deleted partitions (FAT and NTFS file systems). Restores deleted FAT and NTFS logical drives, creates an image of a drive for backup purposes, scans hard drives and detects deleted FAT and NTFS partitions or logical drives, and enables you to preview files and folders on a deleted partition or drive to recover data. This is a very small, easy-to-use MS-DOS program (only 150 kb in size).
Active Ports	Shows all open Transmission Control Protocol/Internet Protocol (TCP/IP) and User Datagram Protocol (UDP) ports on Windows NT/2000/XP computers and maps them to the parent application
Active UNDELETE	Restores deleted files and directories

Continued

Table 6.1 Continued. Forensic Software

Program	Description
Active Uneraser for MS-DOS	Data recovery (undelete) software for MS-DOS. Recovers deleted files on FAT16, FAT32, and NTFS partitions.
Adobe Reader	PDF reader
Advanced Attachments Processor	Extracts attachments from e-mail client message databases, and makes an archive of the extracted files
Advanced Email Extractor	Extracts e-mail addresses from Web pages on the Internet (using Hypertext Transfer Protocol [HTTP] and HTTPS protocols) and from HTML and text files on local disks
Advanced Mailbox Processor	Extracts owners' names and e-mail addresses from local files to create a list
Advanced Forensics Format (AFF)	An extensible open format for the storage of disk images and related forensic information
Afind	Lists files by their last access time without altering the data. Afind searches for access times between specified time frames, and coordinates the results with logon information provided from ntlast. This enables you to determine user activity even if file logging has not been enabled.
Automated Image and Restore (AIR)	A GUI front end to dd/dcfldd. Creates forensic bit images.
Allin1 for Sleuth Kit	Runs time-consuming tasks in Sleuth Kit/Autopsy in batch mode
APDFPRP	PDF file cracker
ASP	ZIP file cracker
Autopsy Forensic Browser	HTML front end for TCT and TCTUtils. It has a file-manager-style interface, can display the contents of a file as raw data or in ASCII, and generates reports.

Continued

Table 6.1 Continued. Forensic Software

Program	Description
AutoStart Viewer	When you start Windows, dozens of programs are already running—many of them are invisible and are running in the background. This software identifies what is running and why, and determines whether the running applications are Trojans. AutoStart Viewer allows you to see every AutoStart on your system on one screen. In addition, it gives you complete control over the AutoStart references, and allows you to modify or delete them at will.
AVIPreview	A program capable of playing partially downloaded AVI movies
Back2Life	Simple undelete utility for Windows
BadCopyPro	Data recovery software for floppy disk, CD, DVD, memory card, ZIP disk, flash drive, and other storage media
BCWipe	Disk wiper (DoD – seven-pass wipe tool)
Belkasoft Forensic IM Extractor	Supports various instant messengers (IMs): ICQ versions 99a up to ICQ5, MSN Messenger, Yahoo! Messenger, &RQ, and Miranda. Supports deep ICQ analysis using different methods (with and without usage of the index file) that allow the user to extract even deleted and overwritten messages.
BinText	Finds ASCII, Unicode, and resource strings in a file
BitForm Discover	Analyzes and reports information about metadata and hidden information within document collections
Black Bag Macintosh Forensic Software	A suite of forensic solutions and a Macintosh boot CD which boots any system capable of running Mac OS X
bmap	Stores data in slack space on Ext2 file systems, among other features. Forensic examiners can use bmap to detect used slack space and to recover data.
Browser History Viewer	Examines the contents of Web browser history files and exports the data

Continued

Table 6.1 Continued. Forensic Software

Program	Description
BXDR	Will display the full sector count on a hard disk drive, including protected areas that utilities such as SafeBack and EnCase miss when imaging
ByteBack	Data recovery and forensic software program that accesses media at the physical level
Cache Reader	Reads the index.dat file in the Temporary Internet Files (TIF) folder of Internet Explorer versions 5 and 6
Cache View	Opens cached files for viewing and copies or moves them out of the cache. It will even reconstruct the names and directory paths of Web sites so that you can view the HTML files. Supports all versions of Netscape, Mozilla (Gecko), and Internet Explorer.
CacheInf	Displays a browser's cache, and provides the option to delete it. Additionally, searches the cache for filenames and URLs and saves the search results into a comma-separated value (CSV) file.
Cache View	A viewer for the Netscape Navigator, Mozilla, and Internet Explorer caches. It displays cached files, and gives you the option to copy them or move them out of the cache. It can reconstruct the names and directory paths of the files. Cache View extracts the following information about cached files: URL, size (in bytes), Multipurpose Internet Mail Extensions (MIME) type, last modified date, the date the file was downloaded, and the expiration date.
CacheX for IE	Displays a browser cache with a Windows Explorer-like user interface. To view a file offline with your browser, double-click it.
Captain Nemo	Connects a drive containing a UNIX/Linux, Windows NT, or Novell operating system directly to a computer running Windows for accessing, viewing, printing, and copying the files as though they were on another Windows drive on the computer. This product supports only Ext2 file systems on Linux.

Continued

Table 6.1 Continued. Forensic Software

Program	Description
Captive	The first free NTFS read/write file system for GNU/Linux
Catalogue	File metadata miner. This file cataloging utility enables quick creation of HTML page listing files and associated metadata, and manages and updates document properties associated with such files.
CD Roller	Retrieves data from a hard disk created by drag-and-drop CD and DVD writing software, such as Adaptec's Roxio, Ahead's Nero, CeQuadrat's PacketCD, Instant Write, and B's CliP
CD/DVD Inspector	Analyzes and extracts data on CD-R, CD-RW, and DVD media. Tailored for use by professionals in data recovery, forensics, and law enforcement.
CDRoller	Tool set for CD and DVD data recovery
Chip-it	Extracts phone numbers from a variety of mobile phones. Freeware.
chrootkit	Checks for evidence of modification of the system binaries by a rootkit on a local machine
CMOS Recovery Tools	Recovers CMOS passwords. Works with the following Basic Input Output Systems (BIOSes): ACER/IBM, AMI, AMI WinBIOS 2.5, Award 4.5x/4.6x, Compaq (1992), Compaq (new version), IBM (PS/2, Activa, Thinkpad), Packard-Bell, Phoenix 1.00.09.AC0 (1994), Phoenix a486 1.03, Phoenix 1.04, Phoenix 1.10 A03, Phoenix 4.05 rev 1.02.943, Phoenix 4.06 rev 1.13.1107, Phoenix 4 Release 6 (user), Gateway Solo, Phoenix 4.0 Release 6, Toshiba, and Zenith AMI.
CookieView – Cookie Decoder	Decodes the internal cookie data, such as the dates and times, and splits the data into separate cookie records. This software was originally written as an external viewer for EnCase and ILook. Either drag and drop a cookie onto the main window or set it as an external viewer.
Coreography	Browses memory images. Coreography is an open source utility.

Continued

Table 6.1 Continued. Forensic Software

Program	Description
Creed (Cisco Router Evidence Extraction Disk) – Raw Image (Freeware)	Creates and restores disk images, even non-PC formatted disks. This software was created by New Technologies. Once you have downloaded the ZIP file, unzip it into its own directory. This is an MS-DOS application, so no further installation is required.
Crucial ADS	Finds hidden data streams in NTFS file systems
Digital Investigation Manager (D.I.M.)	Manages incident response and forensic acquisition procedures. D.I.M. allows operations to be organized by case. Each case may contain an unlimited number of hosts (for example, workstations, servers, laptops, and PDAs). Items of evidence (hard disks, CD/DVD-ROMs, memory cards, log files, network dumps) are associated with each host.
DataGrab	Investigates Internet Relay Chat (IRC) communications
Davory	Recovers files from logically damaged or formatted drives. Created by the maker of WinHex.
DbExtract	Extracts mail messages from Outlook Express Version 5 DBX files. It requires the existence of the Visual Basic 6 runtime DLL, msvbvm60.dll.
DBXanalyzer	Reads, analyzes, and manages e-mail data files created by Microsoft Outlook Express versions 5 and 6
DBXpress	A faster, more accurate, and more powerful version of DBXtract. It requires that .NET Framework Version 1.1 be installed.
DBXtract	Extracts all e-mail and news messages from individual DBX files
DCFL-DD	An enhanced dd with MD5 hashing
dd for Windows	Flexibly copies data within a Win32 environment
dd rescue	Copies data from one file or block device to another

Continued

Table 6.1 Continued. Forensic Software

Program	Description
DecExt	Recovers Base64 pictures
Declasfy	Wipes drives according to DoD specifications. Drive wiping with Declasfy can serve many purposes where information security is a concern—for example, preparing drives for internal reuse; securing private information prior to retirement or donation of a drive; securing private information for compliance with HIPAA; and other regulatory requirements.
Decode	Decodes the date/time values embedded within binary and other file types
DFSee	A generic partition and file system utility. It supports the following partition tables: FDISK, LVM, (V)FAT, FAT32, HPFS, NTFS, and JFS.
Digital AudioRescue Professional	Recovers lost data from multimedia devices, including digital audio recorders, MP3 and WMA players, PDAs, and mobile phones. This program supports recovery from hard drives, CompactFlash cards, IBM Microdrives, SmartMedia cards, MultiMedia cards, Secure Digital cards, and Memory Sticks.
Digital Image Recovery	Reconstructs deleted images, videos, and audio files from formatted media, even if the media was ejected during a write process
Directory Snoop	Snoops FAT- and NTFS-formatted disk drives to see what data may be hiding in the cracks. This is a cluster-level search tool. Use Directory Snoop to recover deleted files or permanently erase sensitive files. Supported media includes local hard drives, floppy disks, ZIP disks, MO disks, and flashcard devices.

Continued

Table 6.1 Continued. Forensic Software

Program	Description
DIRV	A filter for the *DIR /S* command. Dirv is a program for those who still use *DIR /S* to obtain a recursive directory list of all the files on a system. The DIR /S program produces output that is difficult to import into a database for additional processing. Dirv takes the output generated on file systems supported by Windows NT or Windows 9*x* and converts it to one-line records that contain the appropriate path and filename, merged.
Disable	Disables a computer keyboard. Best used on a boot disk for evidence protection, which is often called an *evidence disk*.
Disk Investigator	Helps you to discover all hidden data on a hard disk
DiskCat	Catalogs all files on hard or floppy disks. DiskCat is short for "disk cataloger." It is customizable and is especially useful for forensic purposes and file maintenance. Its output is a fixed-length record and database for further analysis and sorting.
DiskPatch	Repairs Master Boot Records (MBRs), partitions, and boot sectors. It also clones and wipes disks and scans for errors.
disktype	Detects the format of a disk or disk image. It detects common file systems, partition tables, and boot codes.
DivX Player	The DivX codec plays any DivX video data, including DivX VOD movies.
DNA Manager	Distributed network password cracker from Access Data. Harnesses networked PCs to do this.

Continued

Table 6.1 Continued. Forensic Software

Program	Description
DriveLook	Scans a drive or partition for text strings and stores them in a table. You can browse this table and view the locations where the words have been found. The search function enables fast inquiries for combinations of words. The program also enables you to index all of the text on a hard drive, browse a list of all words stored on the drive, search for words or combinations of words, view the location of words in a disk editor, switch between several views (such as hexadecimal and text), use physical drives or logical drives as input, use image files as input, and access remote drives over a serial cable or TCP/IP connection. DriveLook is used for forensic drive investigation and data searches.
dtSearch	Provides more than two dozen indexed and unindexed text search options for all popular file types
dumpautocomplete	Dumps Firefox AutoComplete files into XML files
e2recover	Undeletes data on Ext2 file systems
e2Salvage	Recovers lost Ext2 partitions
Eindeutig	Parses Outlook Express DBX files
E-Mail Detective	Extracts all e-mail data (including graphics) from America Online databases stored on a disk drive
EMF Printer Spool File Viewer	Displays the contents of an EMF spool file
EnCase	Performs most digital forensic analysis operations

Continued

Table 6.1 Continued. Forensic Software

Program	Description
Ethereal	Analyzes network packets. A network packet analyzer will try to capture network packets and display the packet data in as much detail as possible. Data can be captured "off the wire" from a live network connection or read from a capture file. It runs on all major operating systems, including UNIX, Linux, and Windows. Live data can be read from the following network types: Ethernet, FDDI, PPP, Token-Ring, IEEE 802.11, and Classical IP over ATM. Loopback interfaces are also supported. However, not all of these network types are supported on all operating systems.
Event Analysis and Reconstruction in Lisp (EARL)	Reconstructs finite state machine events. This is experimental software.
Event Log Explorer	Views, monitors, and analyzes events recorded in the security, system, application, and other logs produced by the Windows operating system
Eventlog	Takes the output of a Windows NT security event log and reformats it to single lines containing pipes. These can be easily imported into a database or spreadsheet.
Evidence Mover	Automates the transfer of evidentiary data from one location to another with 100 percent accuracy
Evidor: The Evidence Collector	Retrieves the context of keywords found on computer media, Windows swap/paging files, Hibernate files, and unallocated space and slack space. Created by the maker of WinHex.
EXIF Image Viewer	Reads EXIF information embedded in photos and thumbnails
EXIF Reader	Analyzes and displays the shutter speed, flash condition, focal length, and other image information included in the EXIF image format, which is supported in many digital cameras
Exifer	Recovers and displays the metadata (EXIF/IPTC) included in pictures taken by digital cameras

Continued

Table 6.1 Continued. Forensic Software

Program	Description
EXIFRead	Utility that extracts image information from EXIF/JPG files
Explore2fs	The Win32 explorer for Linux ex2fs partitions; reads ex2fs filesystems under NT 4.0 (and Windows 95). It is a separate program, not a file system driver.
Extract 2.10	Extracts files from a disk image created using WinImage, FDFormat, or compatible tools running under MS-DOS, Windows 95, Windows 98, or the Windows NT console
Fatback	Undeletes files from FAT file systems
faust	Analyzes files found after an intrusion or the compromising of a honey pot. faust is a Perl script.
File Date & Time Extractor (FDTE)	Searches binary files for hidden, embedded, 64-bit dates and times
File Disk	A virtual disk driver for Windows NT/2000/XP that uses one or more files to emulate physical disks. A console application is included for dynamically mounting and unmounting files.
File Investigator	Identifies files by content and extensions. Supports 1,806 file formats.
File Juicer	Extracts images from binary files on the Macintosh
File Scavenger	Undeletes files on NTFS volumes. Runs on Windows NT/2000/XP. Reformatted volumes or broken hardware/software RAID volumes can also be recovered.
FileSystem Investigator	Views and extracts file system data. Platform-independent.
Final E-mail	Scans Outlook Express, Eudora, and Netscape Mail e-mail database files and recovers messages. Also, locates lost e-mails that do not have data location information associated with them.
FINAL Photo Retriever	Recovers image files, video files, and audio files from hard disks and removable media
FinalData	Recovers data. Runs on Windows NT 4.0/2000/XP.

Continued

Table 6.1 Continued. Forensic Software

Program	Description
FINALdBase 2.0 for Oracle	Recovers Oracle databases. Runs on UNIX systems.
FinalEmail	Recovers the e-mail database file and locates lost e-mails that do not have data location information associated with them
Forensic and Log Analysis GUI (FLAG)	Analyzes log files for use in forensic investigations. Often, when investigating a large case, a great deal of data needs to be analyzed and correlated. FLAG uses a database as a back end to assist in managing large volumes of data.
Flash Retriever Forensic	Recovers pictures, movies, and sounds from a variety of media
Floppy Image	Creates image files of floppy disks and back (for backup, shipping, or transfer). Saves the image file compressed, uncompressed, or as a self-extracting .exe file. Users can add descriptions to or convert their old image files.
Foremost	Recovers files based on their headers and footers. Runs on Linux systems. Foremost can process image files, such as those generated by dd, SafeBack, and EnCase.
Forensic Acquisition Utilities	A collection of utilities and libraries used in forensic-related investigations
Forensic Analysis Toolkit (FATKit)	Analyzes volatile system memory. A cross-platform, modular, and extensible digital investigation framework.
Forensic Internet Explorer (Beta)	Parses the index.dat file, which identifies host sites that have been visited
Forensic Script	Modified version of a script from "Forensic Analysis of a Live Linux System, Part One," by Mariusz Burdach, as well as a server-side script for Netcat, and a description of the relationship between a specified set of ports and files
Forensic Tools on the Mac (by M. Dornseif)	Compiles various forensic tools on the Macintosh

Continued

Table 6.1 Continued. Forensic Software

Program	Description
Foundstone's Forensic Toolkit	Examines the NTFS file system for unauthorized activity
FSDEXT2	Transparently mounts Linux ext2fs partitions on Windows 9x systems
FS-TST	Tests disk-imaging tools typically used in forensic investigations. This package includes programs that use the Int13 BIOS disk interface to initialize disk drives, detect changes in disk contents, compare pairs of disks, and simulate bad sectors on a disk.
FTimes	Creates system baselines and assists in collecting evidence. Its primary purpose is to gather or develop information about specified directories and files in a manner conducive to intrusion analysis.
AccessData Forensic Toolkit (FTK)	A complete forensic toolkit
ftrace	Performs fast traceroutes on Win32-based systems
Galleta	Reconstructs a subject's Internet Explorer cookie files
Gargoyle Forensic Pro	Determines whether malware is present on a system under investigation
Gemulator Explorer	Reads Atari ST- and Apple Macintosh-formatted disks. Runs on Windows systems.
Symantec's Norton Ghost	Performs advanced backup and recovery operations
GNU utilities for Win32	Native Win32 ports of several GNU utilities
gpart	Attempts to determine the primary partition table of a PC hard disk when the primary partition table in sector 0 is damaged, incorrect, or deleted. If identified, the table can be written to a file or device.
GRAB	Acquires image data. Runs on Linux systems. Created by the developer of Helix.
Handle	Displays information about open handles for any process in the system. You can use it to see the programs that have a file open, or to see the object types and names of all the handles allocated by a program.
Hard Disk Copy	Backs up and copies hard disk sectors

Continued

Table 6.1 Continued. Forensic Software

Program	Description
Hard Drive Mechanic Deluxe	Repairs hard disk drives
HD95Copy	Copies a hard drive to an image file on a network server, another hard disk, or any medium you can access using a logical drive letter. The hard disk is copied sector by sector, provided that filenames and hidden files and directories are backed up also. It also supports removable media.
HD98Copy	Same functionality as HD95Copy. Documentation in German and English.
hfsutils	Manipulates HFS volumes on UNIX and other systems. HFS is the Hierarchical File System, the native volume format used on modern Macintosh computers.
History Inspector	Reads Internet Explorer versions 5 and 6 history database (index.dat) files and presents the data as a synoptical table. It also supports link browsing, adding Favorites, copying URLs, adding personal notes, searching and replacing text items, and printing.
History Inspector for Internet Explorer	Reads all of the information in the history database and presents a list in chronological or alphabetical order
Host Protected Area (HPA)	Identifies the following information about a disk drive: the manufacturer, serial number, total number of sectors on the drive, and number of sectors set aside in the HPA if one exists on the drive. HPA is very useful on a forensic boot disk because it can capture key information about any IDE drives in the system. This information can be sent to an output log file for future reference. HPA is a 16-bit program designed to work only on IDE drives.
HTTrack Website Copier	Downloads the contents of a Web site to a local directory, and recursively builds all directories, getting the HTML code, images, and all other files from the server to your computer
Hurricane Search (formerly WinGrep)	Displays the results of a search in a hierarchical tree of the files that contain a match

Continued

Table 6.1 Continued. Forensic Software

Program	Description
IE Forensic Tool	Generates an easy-to-read report showing all of the cookies, as well as the Web browsing history of the current user
IECacheList (Lite, Free, or Pro; Commercial)	Displays the contents of Internet Explorer's index.dat files, including "lost" and hidden content
IECookiesView	A small utility that displays the details of all cookies that Internet Explorer stores on your computer
IEhist	Dumps the Web browsing history from Internet Explorer index.dat files into delimited files suitable for import into other tools
IEHistoryView	Reads all information from a history file and generates the list of all URLs that you have visited in the last few days, and displays it
Incident Response Collection Report (IRCR)	A collection of tools that gathers or analyzes forensic data on a Windows system. This product is similar to The Coroner's Toolkit by Dan Farmer and Wietse Venema.
Index Dat Spy	Exposes the contents of any index.dat file, even if the file is currently in use by Windows. It translates binary data into a human-readable form.
Inforenz Forager	Analyzes the hidden history of computer files
Innovision USB WriteBlocker	Examines USB devices in Windows
Inquire	Issues a SCSI Inquiry command and lists any hard disk drives found along with model number, product revision level, and serial number (ESN). This is a Windows application.
Internet Cache Explorer	Displays the contents of a browser cache. It comes with many additional features, such as a search function that you can use to find URLs or text within visited pages and an option to save complete Web pages (including images) for later use.
IrfanView	Displays 32-bit image data. Supports many file formats, and can be used as an external viewer for forensic analysis.

Continued

Table 6.1 Continued. Forensic Software

Program	Description
JAFAT – Archive of Forensic Analysis Tools	Obtains the Safari browsing and download history on a Mac OS X system. Also, the archive contains a link parser, a cookie tool, and "dumpster dive."
Karen's Power Tools	A variety of utilities
KaZAlyzer	Performs the following operations: lists all database entries in a tabular form, displays the file integrity tag, enables tagging and commenting on each record, identifies files that appear from titles, keywords, or other evidence to be child pornography, identifies files that have a known child pornography hash value, identifies all graphics and movie files, sorts by individual columns, exports the contents of a database to a CSV file, and produces summary reports. KaZAlyser can open one or more database files from any FastTrack-based installation, such as Kazaa, iMesh, or Grokster, and can display the contents in a tabular form. Once loaded into KaZAlyser, filters can be applied to the database entries to limit the display to particular records such as "all graphics files" or "identify known child pornography." KaZAlyser is the successor to the popular P2Pview Kazaa and Morpheus database viewer. KaZAlyser provides significant enhancements to the forensic investigation process.
KnTTools with KnTList	Acquires physical memory evidence from select Windows operating systems
List Alternate Data Streams (LADS)	Lists all ADS of an NTFS directory. It shows the ADS of encrypted files, even when these files were encrypted with another copy of Windows 2000. It can recursively search through subdirectories and displays a byte total.
LDE	A disk editor for Linux, originally written to help recover deleted files. It is free under the GNU public license.

Continued

Table 6.1 Continued. Forensic Software

Program	Description
LibPST	A set of functions in library form for accessing Outlook's Personal folders. Included with this library is the readpst utility that converts a PST file to mbox format. This program is part of the ol2mbox project.
Legal Imager and reaSsembly Application (LISA)	An MS-DOS-based disk-imaging tool, suitable for taking images of hard disk drives for the purpose of forensic analysis
ListDLLs	Displays the full pathnames of loaded modules. Also, ListDLLs will flag loaded DLLs that have different version numbers from their corresponding on-disk files (which occurs when the file is updated after a program loads the DLL), and can determine which DLLs were relocated because they are not loaded at their base address.
Live View	Creates a VMware virtual machine out of a raw (dd-style) disk image or physical disk. This tool is Java-based.
Lookout	Performs lightning-fast searches for e-mail and files. Works with Microsoft Outlook.
M2CFG USB WriteBlock	Toggles write protection for USB devices on and off. This utility requires Windows XP Service Pack 2.
M2CFG Yahoo! Email/Text Parser	Reads a Yahoo! e-mail text file, and writes each e-mail message with its respective attachment(s) to a separate file. Yahoo! returns the contents of each screen name as one text file. This file contains all e-mail content and Base64 attachments as plain text.
Mac Emulator	Macintosh emulator for Window XP
MACMatch	Searches for files by their last write date, last access date, or creation date without changing any of this data
MacOpener 2000	Accesses Macintosh-formatted disks from a Windows PC. Enables access to Macintosh disks from the Windows desktop. You can also format disks as Macintosh disks.

Continued

Table 6.1 Continued. Forensic Software

Program	Description
mac-robber	Collects data from allocated files in a mounted file system. The data can be used by the mactime tool in the Sleuth Kit to make a timeline of file activity.
Magic Rescue	Scans a block device for all recoverable file types and calls an external program to extract them. It looks at the "magic bytes" within the contents of a file, so it can be used both as an undelete utility and for recovering a corrupted drive or partition.
Mailbag Assistant	Supports Outlook Express, Eudora, Netscape, Mozilla, Pegasus, The Bat!, Forte Agent, Calypso, PocoMail, FoxMail, Juno 3.*x*, UNIX mail (Pine, Elm, mbox, etc.), and EML message files
MailMeter Forensic	E-mail management and investigative solution for organizations that need to perform in-depth forensic analysis and evidentiary discovery on corporate e-mail data
MAK_HTML	Links all files in a folder to an index.htm file that can be used to "browse" the identified files. A program from Dane Mares.
MD5	MD5 hashing algorithm
MD5 and Hashing Utilities	Calculate the 128-bit MD5 hash value of any file or block of text
MD5Deep	Computes MD5 message digests on an arbitrary number of files
md5summer	Generates and verifies MD5 checksums. md5summer is an application for Microsoft Windows 9*x*/NT/Me/2000/XP.
Media Merge/PC	Reads a tape in any format and looks at any part of the tape in unprocessed mode. To do forensic analysis on data from a tape, first it is essential to read the tape. Often with an investigation, tapes may be obtained but there is no knowledge of how they were written. With Media Merge/PC, the raw data may always be read provided a compatible tape drive is available, and the chances are extremely high that the logical tape format will automatically be detected and the files restored just as on the host system.

Continued

Table 6.1 Continued. Forensic Software

Program	Description
memdump	Dumps main memory (/dev/mem) on Solaris, BSD UNIX, and Linux systems
memfetch	Dumps the memory of a running process, either immediately or when an error condition occurs. It recovers information that would otherwise be lost, making it easier to check the internals of a running process.
Metadata Assistant	Analyzes Word, Excel, PowerPoint 97, PowerPoint 2000, PowerPoint 2002 (XP), and PowerPoint 2003 documents to determine what hidden metadata a client might see, display its findings, and then offers the ability to clean the document by selecting a variety of options
MiTeC Tools	Includes an EXIF reader, Windows Registry recovery, a portable executable reader, and other utilities
Mod Com	Alters the operating system files on a floppy boot disk so that, when booted, it will not alter anything on the C: drive. This is what is done manually in the basic forensic classes when you alter boot disks to disable access to the C: drive. This program creates a forensically sound boot disk.
Mount Image Pro	Enables the mounting of EnCase, UNIX DD, or SMART forensic images as a drive letter on your file system
MS Access Database Cracker	Decrypts the master password stored in a Microsoft Access database. There are two utilities in the ZIP for decoding Access 95/97/2000/XP.
MTools	A collection of utilities to access MS-DOS disks from UNIX without mounting them. It supports Windows 95-style long filenames, OS/2 XDF disks, and 2 m disks (stores up to 1992 KB on a high-density 3.5-inch disk).
NASA Tools	Fatback and Enhanced Loopback.
NCFS Software Write-block XP	Blocks write operations.
Nero Express	Burns CDs and DVDs

Continued

Table 6.1 Continued. Forensic Software

Program	Description
NetAnalysis – Forensic Internet History Analyser	Forensically analyzes Internet user activity. It can also extract Web browser history from unallocated disk space.
NetIntercept – Network Forensics Analysis Tool	Captures, analyzes, and discovers network traffic. The Forensic View uncovers malicious activity. It also searches connections by several customizable criteria.
Nigilant32	An incident response tool that captures as much information as possible from a running system with the smallest potential impact
NirSoft Web site	Provides a unique collection of small and useful freeware forensic analysis utilities
NT SAMs	Linux boot disk that accesses the Windows partition and then resets account passwords by exploiting that SAM file
NTLast	Performs security audits on Windows NT systems. NTLast is specifically targeted for security and Internet Information Server (IIS) administration. It performs scheduled reviews of NT event logs to uncover server breaches, and identifies and tracks users who have gained system access and documents the details. It reports on the status of IIS users as well as filters Web server logons from console logons.
ntpasswd	Edits Registry entries and NT passwords. An image disk to boot to recover (reset) passwords by modifying the encrypted password in the Registry's SAM file. You'll need the rewrite to create the boot disk ou with any UNIX dd if=bootdisk.bin of=/dev/fd0 bs=1024.
ntreg	Mounts NT Registry files such as SAM and SECURITY on Linux file systems. This is a file system driver for Linux that accesses the NT Registry file format. Supports only read-only mounts.
Open Digital Evidence Search and Seizure Architecture (ODESSA)	A cross-platform framework for performing computer forensics and incident response
OE-Mail Recovery	Recovers Outlook Express e-mail

Continued

Table 6.1 Continued. Forensic Software

Program	Description
Offline Registry Parser	A Perl script that parses the raw Registry files in binary mode, and prints out the data to include last-write information
Online Digital Forensic Suite (OnlineDFS)	Applies digital forensic technology to the investigation of operational computer systems
Ontrack PowerControls	Copies and searches mailbox data in Microsoft Exchange Server backups, unmounted databases (EDB files), and information store files
Open Ports	Detects all open TCP and UDP ports on a computer system, including the owner process. Using advanced port-to-process mapping technology developed for Port Explorer, OpenPorts displays results in five different styles, allowing for easy interpretation by both scripts and human eyes. This is a command line interface/console (CLI) tool.
OST to PST	Creates a PST from an orphaned OST file
Outindex E-Discovery & Compliance	Extracts e-mails from Microsoft Outlook PST files and writes them to databases such as Oracle and SQL Server
Outlook Recovery	Recovers data from corrupted Microsoft Outlook Personal Storage (PST) files
Oxygen	Forensically analyzes mobile phones. The software does not change any data on the phone. Oxygen runs on any version of the Windows operating system.
P2 Power Pack	Contains the following items from Paraben Forensics: Case Agent Companion Version 1.0, Decryption Collection Enterprise Version 2.5, E-mail Examiner Version 4.01, Forensic Replicator Version 3.1, Forensic Sorter Version 1.0, Network E-mail Examiner Version 1.9, PDA Seizure Version 3.0.1.35, Text Searcher Version 1.0, and Chat Examiner Version1.0
Paraben Case Agent Companion	Optimizes the time of the examiner and the agent working the case. Includes viewers for more than 225 file formats and is compatible with Paraben's P2.

Continued

Table 6.1 Continued. Forensic Software

Program	Description
Paraben Cell Seizure	Enables the forensic acquisition of user data and portions of unallocated storage on some devices. Cell phone forensics is not to be compared with traditional bitstream forensics. Cell phone data storage is proprietary, based on the manufacturer, model, and system. Each device is unique and should be dealt with caution as each cell phone has unique considerations. Continual advances will be made to Cell Seizure in reference to acquiring proprietary data. Cell Seizure currently supports certain models of Nokia, Sony-Ericcson, Motorola, and Siemens cell phones. It also supports GSM SIM cards with the use of a SIM card reader, which can be found in the Cell Seizure Toolbox.
Paraben Decryption Collection	A suite of programs that recover passwords. Includes EFS support, Windows Server 2003 support, and Lotus Notes support along with support for everything included in the Standard Edition. It also includes QuickBooks 2003 support and Peachtree 2004 support.
Paraben E-mail Examiner	Examines e-mail messages. E-mail Examiner claims to recover more active and deleted mail messages than the leading competitor.
Paraben Forensic Replicator	Replicates exact copies of drives and media. Forensic Replicator can acquire a wide range of electronic media, from floppies to hard disks. Forensic Replicator images can be compressed and segmented and easily read into the most popular forensic analysis programs.
Paraben Forensic Sorter	Classifies data into more than 14 different categories, recovers deleted files, and filters common hashes (for example, FOCH), making examinations easier to manage and faster to process
Paraben NetAnalysis	Interrogates Web browser cache and history data with powerful searching, filtering, and evidence identification

Continued

Table 6.1 Continued. Forensic Software

Program	Description
Paraben Network Email Examiner	Examines a variety of network e-mail archives. Network E-mail Examiner is compatible with E-mail Examiner and can easily be configured for more complex tasks.
Paraben PDA Seizure	Captures data and reports on data from a PDA. Runs in a Windows environment. Includes USB support.
Paraben Text Searcher	Searches text
Paragon Ext2FS Anywhere	Mounts Linux partitions on Windows file systems as normal logical drives with appropriate drive letters
Partition Image	Saves partitions in many formats to an image file. Runs on Linux and other versions of UNIX.
Partition Magic	Formats and manages partitions on a hard drive
Pasco	Examines the contents of Internet Explorer's cache files. Pasco parses the information in an index.dat file and outputs the results in a field-delimited manner so that they may be imported into your favorite spreadsheet program. Pasco runs Windows, Mac OS X, Linux, and BSD UNIX operating systems.
PC Inspector File Recovery	Recovers data on FAT12, FAT16, FAT32, and NTFS file systems. Some of the features in PC INSPECTOR File Recovery 3.*x* include finding partitions automatically, even if the boot sector or FAT file system has been erased or damaged. This feature does not work with the NTFS file system.
PC Inspector Smart Recovery	Recovers data from Flash Card, Smart Media, SONY Memory Stick, IBM MicroDrive, Multimedia Card, Secure Digital Card, or other storage media for digital cameras
Palm dd (pdd)	Images memory and forensically acquires data from the Palm OS family of PDAs. pdd will preserve the crime scene by obtaining a bit-for-bit image or "snapshot" of the Palm device's memory contents. Runs on all versions of the Windows operating system.

Continued

Table 6.1 Continued. Forensic Software

Program	Description
PDU spy	Another mobile phone examination program. The site has a number of interesting recovery programs and useful bits for investigating phones. Freeware.
PenguinBackup	A PalmPilot single-floppy backup system
PERKEO++	Locates pornography on any type of digital media
PFC Viewer	Displays and exports the contents of the AOL Filing Cabinet, also known as the Personal Filing Cabinet. PFC Viewer is a Java application.
Phonebase	Reports on the contents of SIM cards and phone memories. These are typically lists of phone numbers and associated names, recently made calls, and text messages.
Photo Rescue	Retrieves deleted data on Compact Flash cards
PhotoRec	Recovers lost pictures from digital camera memory
Picalo	Forensically analyzes data. Data Analysis and Fraud Detection, a collaborative, open source effort to produce a data analysis application suitable for auditors, fraud examiners, data miners, and other data analysts. Comes in Windows, Macintosh, and UNIX/Linux versions.
Pictuate	Finds and analyzes images for pornographic content; scans computer disks to find all image files, then scores those images based on their content. The results are sorted in descending order and viewed in a panel of thumbnail images. The user sees the images most likely to be pornographic (target images) first, and progresses to less likely candidates in subsequent panels.
Pilot-Link	Retrieves the contents of ROM and RAM from Palm devices. Additionally, pilot link allows acquisition.
Pinpoint Labs Free Tools	Pinpoint FileMatch, Pinpoint Hash, Pinpoint Metaviewer.

Continued

Table 6.1 Continued. Forensic Software

Program	Description
Port Explorer	Displays all open ports on a system and the programs that own them. Also called port-to-process mapping. Additional functionality includes packet sniffing, bandwidth throttling, and country detection. Port Explorer has an intuitive GUI that displays all network activity on your computer.
POSE	Emulates Palm devices on the desktop
Private Eyec	Displays the entire contents of an area on your PC referred to as *protected storage*
Process Dumper & Memory Parser (MMP)	Creates a dump of a running process for forensic purposes. MMP parses the metainformation stored within process dumps made with Process Dumper (pd) and extracts the different process mappings to disk.
Process Explorer	Identifies the handles and DLLs that have been opened by processes or loaded into process space. The Process Explorer display consists of two subwindows. The top window always shows a list of the currently active processes, including the names of their owning accounts, whereas the information displayed in the bottom window depends on the mode that Process Explorer is in. If it is in handle mode you'll see the handles that the process selected in the top window has opened; if Process Explorer is in DLL mode you'll see the DLLs and memory-mapped files that the process has loaded. Process Explorer also has a powerful search capability that will quickly show you which processes have handles opened or DLLs loaded. Process Explorer can track down DLL-version problems or handle leaks, and provide insight into the way Windows and applications work.
Process Viewer for Windows (PrcView)	Displays detailed information about processes running under Windows
procshow	Displays information about a running process

Continued

Table 6.1 Continued. Forensic Software

Program	Description
Protected Storage Explorer	Displays saved data from the Protected Storage Service, including passwords for e-mail accounts in Microsoft Outlook, Microsoft Outlook Express, MSN Messenger, saved Internet Explorer form data such as phone numbers, credit card numbers, Web e-mail, search engine queries, usernames and passwords on Web pages, and cached logon credentials of sites that require authentication, including FTP sites
Password Recovery Toolkit (PRTK)	Recovers passwords. Developed by Access Data.
PTfinder Collection	A collection of PTfinders for Windows 2000/ XP/XP SP1/XP SP2/Server 2003
PurgeIE	Allows you either to manage your cookies and cache files in a logical manner or, for complete privacy, to eliminate them altogether, complete with all references, tracks, trails and strays
PuTTY	A free implementation of Telnet and SSH for Win32 and UNIX platforms, along with an xterm terminal emulator
PyFlag	The Python implementation of Flag that includes additional improvements
QuickTime	Plays video, audio, QuickTime VR, and graphics files. Freeware.
Remote Data Acquisition (RDA)	Remotely acquires data—such as disk cloning or disk/partition imaging data—and verifies the transfer using MD5 or CRC32 checksums. The program is both the server and the client and is a command-line tool that runs on Linux.
R-Drive Image	Creates disk image files for backup or duplication purposes. The image file contains an exact, byte-by-byte copy of a hard drive, partition, or logical disk.
RealPlayer	Plays every major media format, including DVDs
Recover	Automates some steps of recovering deleted files on an Ext2 file system
Recover CHK Files	Renames CHK files to the correct extension

Continued

Table 6.1 Continued. Forensic Software

Program	Description
Recover4all	After downloading the utility, run the self-extracting EXE file and choose the *unzip* option. You should not save anything to the drive where your deleted files are to prevent the deleted files from being overwritten. For example, if your deleted files are on the C: drive, do not install any software and do not download anything to C:. Download Recover4all to A:. Recover4all does not require installation and can be run from a floppy disk.
Red Cliff Web Historian	Reviews Web sites stored in the history files of the most commonly used browsers, including Microsoft Internet Explorer, Mozilla, Firefox, Netscape, Opera, and Safari
Regdat and RegdatXP	Display the contents of copies of the Windows 9*x* and Windows Me Registry files System.dat, Classes.dat, and User.dat, and displays the contents in a Regedit-like interface. You can search for keys and values and export them. Also, functions for comparing the file with the current Registry are provided, as well as tools to edit the file.
Registry Information Extractor (RIE)	Extracts Registry information on Windows 95/98/Me operating systems. It will be updated to extract a lot more information from the Registry, including Windows NT/2000/XP support. Currently, it can extract the following information: registered owner, registered organization, Windows version, Windows version number, Windows installed date, and the computer name. RIE can also be used as a file viewer from within EnCase. This is a test release of a software utility that is in development and under testing.
RegMon	Determines the applications that are accessing the Windows Registry, which keys they are accessing, and the Registry data they are reading and writing, all in real time

Continued

Table 6.1 Continued. Forensic Software

Program	Description
RegTools	Contains the following applications: RegDACL, a permissions manager for Registry keys; RegOwner, an ownership manager for Registry keys; RegAudit, an audit manager for Registry keys; and RegLast, which lists or queries the last write data of Registry keys
Resource Hacker	Views, modifies, renames, adds, deletes, and extracts resources in 32-bit Windows executables and resource files (RES files). Freeware.
Resplendent Registrar	Reviews the Registry in Windows NT/2000/9x/ Me systems. It searches the Registry extremely quickly, and presents the search results in a usable fashion.
Restorer2000	Undeletes files deleted accidentally in NTFS partitions, and recovers data on formatted or corrupted drives
Rifiuti	Examines the contents of the INFO2 file in the Recycle Bin, and produces field-delimited output that you can import into your favorite spreadsheet program. Rifiuti runs on Windows, Mac OS X, Linux, and BSD UNIX platforms.
RKDetect	Finds services hidden by generic Windows rootkits such as Hacker Defender
R-Linux	Recovers data on Ext2 file system partitions used in several UNIX operating systems. Supported host operating systems include Windows 9x/Me/NT/2000/XP. Recovered data can be written to any disk visible by the host operating system. R-Linux also can create disk images that can be later processed by the more powerful R-Studio. Freeware.

Continued

Table 6.1 Continued. Forensic Software

Program	Description
R-Mail	Recovers accidentally deleted e-mail messages and damaged DBX files where Outlook Express stores folders with e-mail messages. The new e-mail data recovery technology IntelligentRebuild allows R-Mail users to quickly reconstruct damaged DBX files created by Outlook Express and easily restore the lost messages. The messages are recovered in EML format and can be imported into Outlook Express e-mail and Internet news databases.
RootkitRevealer	Detects rootkits. Processes files produced by Windows NT 4 and later.
R-Studio	Recovers and undeletes data. Supports the FAT12, FAT16, FAT32, NTFS, NTFS 5, and Ext2 file systems and recovers files both on local logical and physical disks and disks on remote computers over networks, even if their partition structures are damaged or deleted.
R-Undelete	Undeletes data on the FAT, NTFS, NTFS 5, and Ext2 file systems. R-Undelete can undelete files on any valid logical disks accessible by the host OS. It cannot undelete files on damaged or deleted volumes, or if the hard drive has been repartitioned.
R-Word	Recovers Microsoft Word documents
SafeBack	Creates mirror-image (bitstream) backup copies of hard disks or partitions
SagePass	Retrieves passwords from Sage Sterling, Line 100, and Instant accounting systems
Scalpel: A Frugal, High Performance File Carver	Reads a database of header and footer definitions and extracts matching files from a set of image files or raw device files
sdd	A replacement for the dd utility
SecCheck	Detects and removes malicious applications, back doors, Trojans, worms, and viruses
SecReport – Click Toolbox	Collects security-related information from Windows-based systems (SecReport) and compares any two reports from different systems or the same system after a specified delta of time. A suite of two command-line tools.

Continued

Table 6.1 Continued. Forensic Software

Program	Description
SecretExplorer	Views, analyzes, edits, imports, and exports protected storage, retrieves AutoComplete passwords and data, recovers passwords, and transfers passwords and settings from one computer to another
Secure Hash Signature Generator	Creates signatures that are unique to the data stored on a disk drive. These signatures are used to verify intentional or accidental tampering with the drive image.
SHA verify	Calculates the MD5 (128-bit), SHA1 (160-bit), SHA2 (256-bit), SHA2 (384-bit), and SHA2 (512-bit) hashes of files
ShoWin	Displays information about Windows, such as account passwords. ShoWin displays the information when you drag your cursor over it. One of the most popular uses of this program is to display hidden password Editbox fields (the text behind the asterisks). This will work in many programs, although Microsoft has changed the way things work in some of its applications, most notably the Office suite and Windows 2000. ShoWin will not work in these cases. Neither will it work for password entry boxes on Web pages, at least with most Web browsers. Additional features include the ability to enable windows that have been disabled, unhide hidden windows, and force a window to stay on top or be placed below others.
SIM Manager	Recovers phone numbers and Short Message Service (SMS) messages from a range of mobile phones
SIM Scan	Investigates the contents of SIM cards. Freeware.
SIMCon	Provides forensic imaging and analysis of the contents of SIM cards, including recovery of deleted items. Free for law enforcement.
Sleuth Kit Windows Executables	Microsoft Windows executables for The Sleuth Kit. Full source code and documentation can be downloaded.
Sleuth Kit/Autopsy Foremost patch	Integrates Foremost into Autopsy and enables the configuration file to be edited. Created by P. Bakker.

Continued

Table 6.1 Continued. Forensic Software

Program	Description
Sleuth Kit/Autopsy Searchtools patch	Performs indexed searching capabilities for Sleuth Kit/Autopsy tools. Created by P. Bakker.
SMART	Monitors hard disk drives and performs failure prediction operations. It uses S.M.A.R.T. technology to monitor the health status of hard disk drives, prevents data loss, and predicts possible drive failures.
SnapView HTML Viewer	Examines recovered HTML pages stored in unallocated space. This viewer is built on the same technology as that used by Internet Explorer, and loads pages quickly. It can also toggle between page and source views. It can use any available Internet Explorer plug-ins, giving it a large selection of supported file formats, among them HTML, JPEG, GIF, ICO, Flash Move, Adobe Acrobat, Word, Excel, PowerPoint, Bitmap, PNG, and ART.
SNIFFER	Extracts files from the free space of computer hard disks, from a series of disk image files, or directly from the hard disk device. Run on MS-DOS.
SomarSoft Utilities	Contains the following programs: DumpSec, a security auditing program for Windows NT and 2000; DumpEvt, a Windows NT program for dumping the event log in a format suitable for importing into a database; and DumpReg, a program for Windows NT and Windows 95 that dumps the contents of the Registry.
Spam CSI	Performs forensic analysis of e-mail data
Spector CNE	Records everything employees do online, including IM, chats, sending and receiving e-mails, visiting Web sites, launching applications, downloading files, and typing keys
Spider	Displays all of the URLs and cookies stored in the index.dat file, and removes them

Continued

Table 6.1 Continued. Forensic Software

Program	Description
ssdeep	Creates a short text signature for each input file. The signatures can be used to match other files against the original. Unlike MD5 and SHA1, however, this algorithm can match two input files even if they are not exactly the same. Files match if they have significant homologies, or if the same sequences of bytes are in the same order. Functions in a manner similar to md5deep.
Stealer	Extracts the machine name, usernames, and dial-up user accounts and passwords. It also identifies passwords and usernames on secure Web sites and password-protected shared folders on a network. Most of this information is stored within the PWL file. You must run Stealer on a restored drive if you are using it to identify information on a seized computer. One law enforcement agency used it to gain access to encrypted data as the password for the encrypted material had been duplicated. This utility can save you weeks of waiting if you are contemplating a brute force attack. Runs on Windows 9x and Me.
StegAlyzerAS	Performs digital forensic analysis. This utility is designed to extend the scope of traditional digital forensic examinations by allowing the examiner to scan suspect media for artifacts of steganography applications.
StegDetect	Automatically detects steganographic content in image files. It is capable of detecting several different steganographic methods for embedding information in JPEG images. Supported methods are jsteg, jphide (UNIX and Windows), invisible secrets, and outguess 01.3b.

Continued

Table 6.1 Continued. Forensic Software

Program	Description
StegHide	Embeds a secret message in a cover file by replacing some of the least significant bits of the cover file with parts of the secret message. After that, the secret message is imperceptible and can be extracted only with the correct pass phrase. Features include support for JPEG, BMP, WAV, and AU files; encryption of plain data before embedding (Blowfish encryption algorithm); pseudo-random distribution of hidden bits in the stego file; and embedding a CRC32 checksum in the data.
Stego Suite 4.1	Investigates, detects, analyzes, and recovers digital steganography. Stego Suite 4.1 includes Stego Watch, an automated steganography investigation scanning software package; nine steganography detection algorithms covering all common digital image file types and audio WAV files; Stego Analyst, a visual image analysis package for in-depth digital image and audio file analysis; and Stego Break, an automated steganography cracking tool.
Stellar Phoenix FAT	Recovers data on FAT file systems. It does not need to be installed prior to a data loss. Stellar Phoenix FAT provides easy recovery after the partition table, boot sector, and root directory have been corrupted and data has been lost. This software runs on MS-DOS as well as Windows 95/98/Me, NT (FAT file systems), and 2000 (FAT file systems). Supports all variants of the FAT file system.
Stellar Phoenix Novell	Recovers vital data from corrupt volumes resulting from a crashed server. It accesses data when the volumes cannot be mounted. This software can save recovered data to a disk drive after cases of corrupt or missing volumes, deleted files, allocation errors, and partition loss.

Continued

Table 6.1 Continued. Forensic Software

Program	Description
Stellar Phoenix NTFS	Recovers data after disk crashes caused by accidental formatting, viruses, software malfunctions, file or directory deletion, or sabotage. Stellar Phoenix NT Data Recovery software examines an inaccessible hard drive and displays the stored data. The disk recovery process requires only a selection of the target files and directories to copy to a working drive.
Sterilize	Sterilizes media for use as working/examination data copies
STG Cache Audit	Displays the contents of browser caches, cookies, and history information
STrace for NT	Examines the system calls made by a process running on Windows NT. It is meant to be used like the strace (or truss) UNIX operating system variants. Runs on Windows NT.
Stream Explorer	Reveals alternate file streams on NTFS file systems. Runs on Windows NT 4.0 as well as Windows 2000/XP/2003.
Streams	Reveals NTFS alternate streams
Strings	Searches for ANSI and Unicode strings in binary images
SuperDIR	Lists all files and directories on FAT file systems, and dumps the results into a database. It will calculate a CRC32 for every file. Very fast.
SuperSCAB	Analyzes seized computers
Swapper	Swaps all byte pairs in a file. This is required for forensic research of disks, mobile phones, and copiers.
Symantec	Antivirus (AV) program
TAFT – The ATA Forensics Tool	Communicates directly with the ATA controller to retrieve information about a hard disk, and to examine and change HPA and DCO settings
TaFWeb Whois	A version of the whois utility. It can report Internet Protocol (IP) numbers as well as domain names.
TapeCat	Forensically analyzes tapes. Runs on all versions of Windows.

Continued

Table 6.1 Continued. Forensic Software

Program	Description
TASK	Performs a comprehensive forensic analysis of Windows and UNIX file systems. Open source from @stake.
Tcpflow	Captures data transmitted as part of TCP connections (flows), and stores it in a way that is convenient for protocol analysis or debugging. The Tcpdump utility shows a summary of the packets transmitted on the wire but usually doesn't store the data. In contrast, Tcpflow reconstructs the actual data streams and stores each flow in a separate file for later analysis. Tcpflow processes sequence numbers and correctly reconstructs data streams regardless of retransmissions or out-of-order delivery. However, it currently does not process IP fragments—flows containing IP fragments will not be recorded properly.
Tcptrace	Analyzes TCP dump files. It takes as input the files produced by several popular packet-capture programs, including Tcpdump, Snoop, Etherpeek, HP Net Metrix, and WinDump. Tcptrace can produce several different types of output containing information on each connection seen, such as elapsed time, bytes and segments sent and received, retransmissions, round-trip times, window advertisements, and throughput. It can also produce a number of graphs for further analysis.
TCTUtils	An enhancement to The Coroner's Toolkit utility. TCTUtils can list directory inode contents, can find the inode that is using a given block, and enables the viewing of inode and block details in various formats.
TestDisk	Checks and undeletes partitions
Text2Hex	Will convert ASCII characters to hexadecimal values. This is particularly useful when performing searches using software that can accept hexadecimal values as search criteria.
ThumbsDisplay	Displays all thumbnail images with original filenames and timestamps

Continued

Table 6.1 Continued. Forensic Software

Program	Description
ThumbsPlus	Displays thumbnail images and displays, edits, and batch-converts regular image files
TNEF	Unpacks Microsoft MS-TNEF MIME attachment files
Tree Browser (TB)/KDE Tree Browser (KTB)	Displays file hierarchies
True Time	Prompts the user for the correct date and time, and obtains the system date and time from the system BIOS. The output can be redirected to a file for use in forensic investigations. Excellent addition to a forensic boot disk.
TULP2G	Extracts and decodes data stored in electronic devices. Based on Windows .NET technology.
UDP Cast	A Netcat substitute.
UndeleteSMS	Recovers deleted SMS messages from a GSM SIM card
Unique	Eliminates duplicate records in a file. This program will take a sorted input file and copy records to the output for which it finds a unique occurrence of the sort key. The program passes the input file, and when it finds a new and unique sort key in a record it copies that record to the output, and disregards all subsequent records that contain that same sort key. Therefore, only a single record per sort key is copied to the output file.
URLSearch	Extracts Web addresses and other text strings from local and remote files. Results can be edited and exported in various ways. Web addresses can be sorted by domains and exported to your browser's bookmarks (supported browsers are Netscape, Internet Explorer, and Opera). UrlSearch can also be used as a download agent and can view history and cookie files, edit typed URLs, and calculate hit rates.
USB Blocker	Designed to meet the needs of write-blocking USB devices

Continued

Table 6.1 Continued. Forensic Software

Program	Description
UTF-8 output patch for task-1.60/Sleuth Kit-1.6*x*	Displays foreign characters in the names of files located in an NTFS image. By default, Sleuth Kit converts the Unicode NTFS file system structures into ASCII. This patch changes that behavior, but doesn't change the keyword searching ability. That is still done with the strings and grep utilities, which do not easily support Unicode.
Ultimate Toolkit (UTK)	The complete AccessData software kit
VFC – Virtual Forensic Computing	Rapidly boots a forensic image of a suspect's computer, or boots a write-blocked physical hard drive
Viesoft Forensic Scan	Scans index.dat files
vinetto	Extracts thumbnail images and associated metadata from the thumbs.db files generated by Windows. A console-based program that runs under Cygwin or Linux.
Vision	Reports all open TCP and UDP ports and maps them to the process or application accessing them
Web Cache Illuminator	Creates a meaningful list that displays all filenames in the Web browser cache and the title of the Web page
WebDate	Returns the last modified date and time of a Web site, Web page, or individual file
Webtracer	Determines the owner of a Web site, the location of a server, the sender of an e-mail, and other evidence of Internet identity
WhatFormat	Analyzes the first bytes of a file for signatures (or magic numbers) and determines the format of the file from this evidence
Win32 Analyzer	Creates a forensic snapshot of a computer. Uses Windows and third-party tools.
Win32 First Responder's Analyzer Toolkit	Performs basic security tasks. A self-extracting Windows executable designed to be run from a floppy disk.

Continued

Table 6.1 Continued. Forensic Software

Program	Description
Windows Forensic Toolchest (WFT)	Provides automated incident response on a Windows system and collects security-relevant information from the system
Windows Forensics and Incident Recovery tools	A set of tools produced by the Forensic Server Project for incident response and computer forensic activities on Windows systems
Windows Memory Forensic Toolkit (WMFT)	A collection of proof-of-concept tools, used for forensic analysis of physical memory images gathered from compromised Windows machines
Windows NT/2000 Incident Response Tools	Gathers and analyzes forensic data on a Windows system and produces snapshots of past states of the system. This program is a collection of tools, and like The Coroner's Toolkit, most of the tools are oriented toward data collection rather than analysis.
WinDump	Creates dump files of network traffic data. WinDump prints the headers of packets on a network interface that match a specified Boolean expression. It can also be run with the *–w* flag, which causes it to save the packet data to a file for later analysis, and with the *–b* flag, which causes it to read from a saved packet file rather than read packets from a network interface. In all cases, only packets that match the specified expression will be processed by WinDump.
WinGREP	Searches files for specified text strings
WinHex	Edits hexadecimal data
WinImage	Creates disk images from a floppy and vice versa, among other functions. Developed because Windows lacks a native *dd* command.

Continued

Table 6.1 Continued. Forensic Software

Program	Description
Wininterrogate	Recursively scans a directory structure and obtains the following information: filename and size, complete path of files and directories, directory name, creation time, last access time, last write time, and MD5 checksum. Additional information gathered from DLL, VBX, DRV, EXE, OCX, BIN, SCR files includes CompanyName, FileDescription, FileVersion, InternalName, LegalCopyright, OriginalFilename, ProductName, ProductVersion, Comments, LegalTrademarks, PrivateBuild, and SpecialBuild.
WinOra	Converts the installation time format used in the Windows Registry
WinPcap 3.1	Used in several network investigation tools
WinRAR	Compresses and uncompresses RAR-format files. Also processes other compression formats. Runs on all versions of Windows.
WinZip	Compresses and uncompresses ZIP-format files. Runs on all versions of Windows.
Wipe	Securely wipes files from storage media. It is based on work by Peter Gutmann.
X1 Search	Searches for information, previews it in its native format, and takes action on it regardless of type or location
XANALYS Forensic Analyzer	Automatically examines an EnCase file. Extends EnCase functionality.
XnView	Views and browses multimedia files, and converts the format
X-Ways Trace	Tracks and examines past Web browsing activity on a computer
Yahoo! Message Archive Decoder	Accesses Yahoo! Messenger archive files (DAT files) and presents them in a readable format
ZefrJPG	Recovers JPG files destroyed by the Love Letter worm and its variants on FAT or NTFS file systems (thanks to Robert Green @ http://personal.atl.bellsouth.net/~lasrpro)

Continued

Table 6.1 Continued. Forensic Software

Program	Description
Zeitline	Edits timelines for computer forensic purposes
Zero Assumption Digital Image Recovery	Recovers digital image data produced by a digital camera. It allows you to recover digital photos accidentally deleted from digital camera memory. Freeware.

Forensic Hardware Tools

Although thus far we've discussed ways to use software for data acquisition and other forensic services, these aren't the only methods of duplicating data. Using forensic hardware tools in a forensic lab or in the field, you can create forensic images that you can later analyze for potential evidence. In some cases, these tools serve as portable forensic labs, allowing you to perform acquisition and analysis before the computer is even removed from the crime scene.

A number of these tools will store data directly on a hard disk inside the device, and provide the ability to transfer image files from the device to another computer in a forensic lab; you can then wipe the device's drive to make it forensically sterile. This ensures that there is no contamination from other data on the drive each time data is acquired from a new machine.

In the following sections, we provide details on some of the more popular forensic hardware tools available today.

ImageMASSter Solo-3 Forensic

ImageMASSter Solo-3 Forensic is a hardware tool developed by Intelligent Computer Solutions (ICS) and available from www.icsforensic.com. It is a portable, hand-held device that can acquire data from suspect machines at speeds exceeding 4 GB per minute. By connecting the hard disks directly to the machine using a drive-to-drive interface or external FireWire/USB interface, you can create an exact replica of data from one or two drives simultaneously without any reduction in speed. Specifically designed for computer forensic purposes, it can acquire data from IDE, Serial Advanced Technology Attachment (SATA), and SCSI hard drives.

LinkMASSter-2 Forensic

LinkMASSter-2 Forensic is another hardware tool developed by ICS and available from www. icsforensic.com. The device attaches to a computer through a FireWire or USB port, and can then create an image of any data on the machine. Software is used to boot the machine and connect to the LinkMASSter, allowing it to acquire data using the FireWire or USB ports. Data on the original machine is protected during acquisition due to write-blocking features in the device.

ImageMASSter 6007SAS

ImageMASSter 6007SAS is a powerful tool for creating images of data from suspect machines, and is a useful part of any forensic lab. It is developed by ICS, and is available from www.icsforensic.com. It duplicates IDE, SAS, SATA, and IDE hard drives, and can migrate server data from SCSI to SAS/SATA. ImageMASSter can also acquire data from multiple hard disks, and store multiple images on one hard drive. It is the only duplication system on the market that supports SAS (Serial Attach SCSI) hard drives, and can copy multiple drives simultaneously at high speeds. It also includes a 1 GB network connection that can then be used to transfer files to and from a network drive. To acquire and analyze data, the system provides a Windows XP-based interface that allows you to copy data from Windows, Macintosh, and UNIX file systems.

RoadMASSter-3

Whereas many tools are developed for use inside a forensic lab, the RoadMASSter-3 is a data acquisition and analysis tool designed for use in the field. The RoadMASSter-3 is developed by ICS, is available from www.icsforensic.com, and is designed to create and image and analyze data acquired from suspect hard drives. It can connect to an unopened computer using FireWire and USB ports, and can connect directly to IDE, SATA, SAS, and SCSI hard drives. It can also acquire data from multiple drives to a single target drive, making acquisition faster.

The RoadMASSter-3 also allows you to analyze data immediately. It provides a 15-inch color display in its case that allows you to view the data stored in the image file, meaning you can determine whether any evidence exists on the machine while you're still in the field.

Disk Jockey IT

Disk Jockey IT is a portable, hand-held hardware tool developed by Diskology, and is available from www.diskology.com. It is actually the smallest write-blocking and disk copy device available for computer forensics. You can use it as a write-blocking device for data acquired using FireWire and USB connections to a suspect computer. You can then connect the device to a Macintosh or Windows computer in write-protect mode to analyze the data without fear of altering the data.

FastBloc

FastBloc LE (formerly FastBlocIDE) is a data acquisition and write protection device that is commonly used with EnCase. As such, it should come as no surprise that it is also manufactured by Guidance Software (www.guidancesoftware.com). FastBloc installs on any PC with a spare 5.25-inch drive bay, but FastBloc is also available as a separate device that connects to laptops or desktop machines. It supports the following connections:

- A 40-pin IDE interface connection
- A host controller connection
- A 40-pin and a 44-pin IDE connection
- A suspect drive connection

- An ATA-6 support

- An ATA-6-compliant host controller

FastBloc LE is a common piece of equipment in a forensic lab environment, as it reliably prevents writing to a suspect drive while data is being acquired. It is also easy to use. A connection is established between FastBloc LE and other devices using a direct IDE-to-IDE device so that the data can be acquired remarkably quickly, and it does not require any other complicated or expensive hardware. You can use this tool to acquire drives without physically opening the forensic computer. When you use it with an ATA 6 controller, it can transfer data up to a rate of 133 MB per second, and it can also support drives bigger than 128 GB. FastBloc's main features are as follows:

- It uses IDE controllers and doesn't require SCSI controller card drivers.

- It is similar in height and width as the internal CD-ROM drive.

- Its small size (5.75 x 3 x 1.625 inches) allows for complete portability and ease of use in the field.

- It has ports for desktop IDE as well as laptop IDE media.

Forensic Hardware Tools Reference

As was the case with software-based tools, a wide variety of different forensic hardware tools are available on the market. Table 6.2 lists a number of popular forensic hardware tools that you can use. We will cover some of them in more detail and will discuss others in various sections of this book.

Table 6.2 Forensic Hardware Devices

Hardware Device	Description
NoWrite	Prevents data from being written to the hard disk. It supports hard disk drives with high capacities and is compatible with all kinds of devices, including USB and FireWire boxes, adapters, and cables belonging to IDE. It supports communication between common IDE interfaces.
FireWire DriveDock	A forensic instrument designed to load hard drives on computer systems. It comprises a 3.5-inch hard drive that is used along with a single device to give complete FireWire desktop storage. It is a compact device of about 4 cubic inches that can control everything in a 3.5-inch hard drive.

Continued

Table 6.2 Continued. Forensic Hardware Device

Hardware Device	Description
LockDown	An advanced FireWire or USB to IDE write blocker that combines swiftness and portability to allow IDE media to be acquired quickly and safely in Windows-based systems. Available from Paraben.
Write Protect Card Reader	Transfers data to a computer system from digital cameras, digital camcorders, PDAs, MP3 players, and digital voice recorders. It can read multiple types of flash memory while blocking any writes to it. It is a small, palm-size package with a simple USB 2.0/1.1 connection and requires no external power.
Drive Lock IDE	Is designed to completely prevent write commands from being accidentally sent to hard disk drives connected through the IDE or PATA hard drive interface. This write-protect device also blocks Serial ATA hard drives using the SATA option. It is designed to block write commands sent to the hard drive while previewed or duplicated.
Serial-ATA DriveLock Kit	A hardware write-protect device designed to prevent data writes to SATA, IDE, and PATA hard disk drives. The tool is connected to a computer's PATA interface to block write commands sent to the hard drive while being previewed or duplicated.
Wipe MASSter	A commercial drive wiper
ImageMASSter Solo-3 IT	Designed exclusively for forensic data acquisition. This data imaging tool is a lightweight, portable, hand-held device that can acquire data to one or two evidence drives at high speeds, exceeding 3 GB per minute.
ImageMASSter 4002i	Loads two IDE hard drives at speeds exceeding 1.94 GB per minute
ImageMASSter 3002SCSI	A high-speed disk imager with operating speeds that can exceed 3.9 GB per minute. No speed degradation occurs when copying to four hard drives.
Image MASSter 3004SATA	Can duplicate four Serial ATA hard drives simultaneously

Summary

In this chapter, we learned that computer forensics requires specialized tools to duplicate data from a hard disk or other media. In some cases, the tools are software-based, but you can also use hardware to acquire evidence from suspect machines. The hardware- and software-based solutions will create bitstream images of the disk, and include any data that is visible to the file system, as well as hidden and deleted files and fragments of files, the MBR, the partition table, and any number of other items on a disk. You can then use software to mount these images and view the data in a variety of ways. Many tools will even allow you to preview the data without extracting it from the forensic image file.

The primary purpose of this chapter was to give you a level of familiarity with the wide range of hardware and software forensic tools that are available. It is not possible to detail in this chapter all of the features and functions of these tools; therefore, it is important that you investigate the features and functions required by your incident response team or computer forensic lab prior to purchasing and using these tools in an actual investigation.

Frequently Asked Questions

Q: If software is available to create a forensic image of a hard disk or other media, what is the benefit of forensic hardware?

A: Different types of forensic hardware are available. You can use write-blocking tools to prevent data from being written to a suspect hard disk or other media. Forensic tools are also available that you can connect to an unopened computer or hard disk to acquire data from it. In some cases, some tools even enable you to analyze the acquired data in the field. Many of these tools are portable, allowing you to carry them to a crime scene, and can enable you to acquire data from multiple hard drives at high speeds.

Q: Why is it important that all the software used by law enforcement officers be licensed and registered? Law enforcement budgets are often tight; why not use freeware as much as possible?

A: Some freeware and shareware tools that are available on the Internet are good tools, and the price is certainly right. However, there are some dangers in using these programs for forensic purposes. First, you never know exactly what you're getting when you download a free program (and you certainly can't ask for your money back if it doesn't work properly). Downloads can be infected with viruses or Trojans that can damage the systems on which you use them. Using unlicensed software (illegal copies) is even worse. The opposing attorney(s) will have a field day if they discover that the police used pirated or "borrowed" software in the investigation. This behavior can destroy the credibility of the people who conducted the forensic examination and even result in losing the case. In addition, with properly purchased and registered software, you will be able to get technical support from the vendor if necessary. Makers of computer forensic software often offer discounts to law enforcement agencies, making it easier to afford the proper tools for the job. After all, officers and agencies probably wouldn't suggest saving money by buying their duty weapons from a pawnshop; that's because these are essential tools of the trade and must be as reliable as possible. For the cybercrime investigator or technician, the same is true of the forensic software that is used to collect and preserve evidence that can make or break a criminal case.

Q: There are so many tools. Do we need them all?

A: It is important to become familiar with a wide range of tools. It is not necessary to have all the tools.

Q: Many of the tools run on an operating system I am not familiar with. Do I need to become familiar with these operating systems?

A: Although it is good to have some level of familiarity with a wide range of systems, these tools are available for most operating systems. Whether you are familiar with Linux, Windows, or another operating system, it is likely that you will be able to find a tool that functions on your system.

Q: What types of evidence can digital forensic tools provide?

A: Computers store large amounts of data to a network or system of hard disks. Much of this information is stored without the user being conscious of its existence. This data may be in the form of tangible files or information that the computer used to carry out a specific task. A few examples are user files, system files, deleted files, and system data that enable the computer to perform its tasks.

Q: Do I need to scan a drive for malware if I have a read-only image?

A: Any forensic image file with a capture containing 100 percent of the information on a hard drive has the potential to be a virus pathway into a secure computer system. Any forensic investigation must exercise appropriate care in ensuring that none of these pathways exist.

Chapter 7

Acquiring Data, Duplicating Data, and Recovering Deleted Files

Topics we'll investigate in this chapter:

- **Recovering Deleted Files and Deleted Partitions**

- **Data Acquisition and Duplication**

☑ **Summary**

☑ **Frequently Asked Questions**

Introduction

Before you can analyze data, you need to acquire it. This means the data needs to be duplicated so that the person performing the analysis can work from it without modifying the data. As we saw in Chapter 6, this can require using any number of tools to duplicate the data so that an exact, sector-by-sector mirror image of the disk is generated. This enables the forensic analyst to view any data that is hidden, fragmented, or deleted. Whether data is being duplicated as part of a computer forensic investigation, or backed up for other purposes, it is vital that the original data isn't modified or corrupted during the duplication process.

Deleted data can be an issue for any situation dealing with computers. A file may be deleted on purpose or by accident, as a normal process of an application, or as the result of a virus, intrusion, or malicious software. In some cases, an entire partition may be lost, causing everything on a volume to appear unrecoverable. However, this isn't necessarily the case. When data is deleted, various tools may be used to recover the data from a hard disk or other storage media. In some cases, the files may be corrupted or damaged in some way, and additional software may be needed to repair the file. As we'll see in the sections that follow, regardless of the cause, there are many ways to recover data.

Recovering Deleted Files and Deleted Partitions

In the organization where you work, there is probably an inventory of assets. It may be as simple as a typed out list for insurance purposes, or a database containing records of every desk, computer, printer, and every other asset owned by the organization. On your computer, a similar table of records is used to maintain information about the files saved on your hard disk. In the same way that deleting a record from an inventory doesn't make your desk disappear, deleting a file on your hard disk doesn't necessarily make the data disappear.

In Chapter 4, we discussed how files are stored on hard disks and other media. *Clusters* are two or more sectors of a hard disk, and are the smallest unit of disk space that can be allocated to store a file. When a file is saved, information on which clusters are used to store the file is kept in another kind of table. A *file allocation table* is used to keep track of files on FAT and FAT32 file systems, whereas on New Technology File System (NTFS) volumes a *Master File Table* (MFT) is used. Using such tables, the operating system can maintain where files are located. When a file is deleted, the record of the file is removed from the table, thereby making it appear as though it doesn't exist anymore. The clusters used by the file are marked as being free, and can now be used to store other data. However, although the record is gone, the data may still reside in the clusters of the hard disk.

Also in Chapter 4, we discussed how *partitions* are used to create a logical division of a hard disk. Even if multiple partitions aren't used, the entire disk can be set as a single partition, formatted to use a particular file system (such as FAT or NTFS) and given a drive letter (such as C:, D:, etc.). Information about how partitions are set up on a machine is stored in a *partition table*, which is stored in the Master Boot Record (MBR). When the computer is booted, the partition table allows the computer to understand how the hard disk is organized, and then passes this information to the operating system when it is started. When a partition is deleted, the entry in the partition table is removed, making the data inaccessible. However, even though the partition entry has been removed, the data still resides on the hard disk.

As we'll see in the sections that follow, you can use many different tools to recover deleted files and deleted partitions from a hard disk. Depending on how the data was deleted, and whether it was overwritten before it could be recovered, there is the possibility that files and partitions can be restored.

Recovering "Deleted" and "Erased" Data

Every operating system provides a way to remove data from a hard disk. If it didn't, a hard disk would fill up quickly from all of the temporary files, backup files, and other data written to a disk by the operating system or other software installed on a computer. Although the OS and applications on a machine will generally clean these up when they are no longer needed, this isn't always the case (as we'll see in a later section of this chapter). In addition to all the files created and deleted by programs on your computer, there are also the ones that users of the computer have created and no longer need anymore.

A *deleted file* is any file that has been logically erased from the file system, but may still remain physically on storage media. How a file is deleted can vary. Whereas for many people, deleting a file means selecting a file and pressing the Del or Delete key on their keyboard, there are other ways in which a file may be deleted.

Command-Line Delete

In the days before the graphical user interface (GUI), the only way to delete a file was from a command prompt. When DOS (Disk Operating System) was one of the major operating systems of choice, you would enter textual commands from a prompt, which was generally a symbol following the drive letter you were currently using. In Windows, the *Command Prompt* is a window that provides an interface to enter the commands to perform certain actions. As shown in Figure 7.1, the Command Prompt allows you to enter commands that can be used to delete files and directories from a partition.

Figure 7.1 Command Prompt Delete

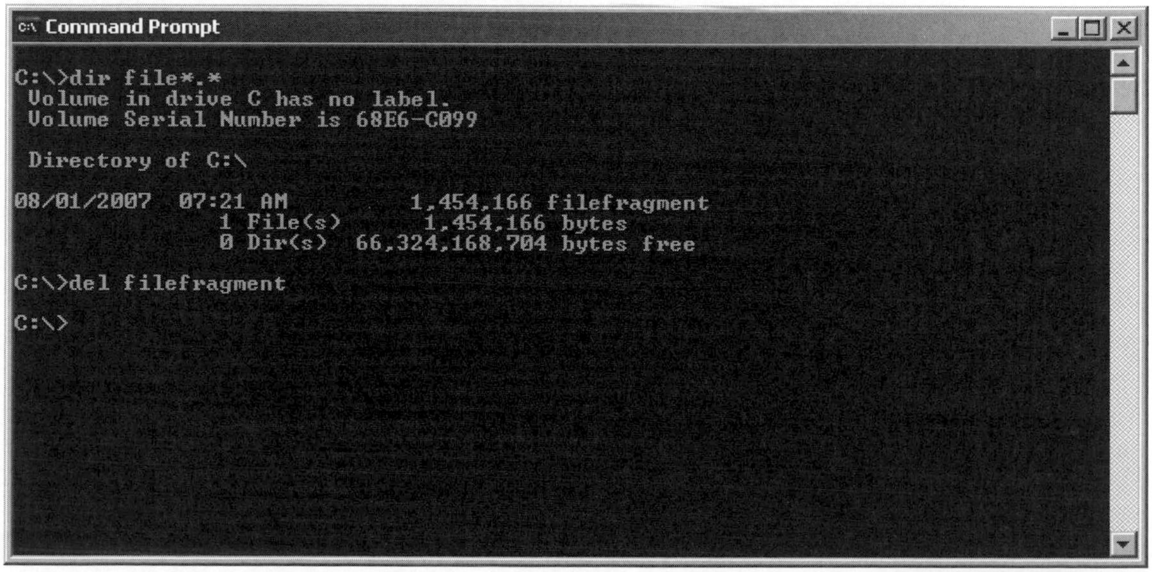

You can use two commands to delete files or directories from the command line:

- *DEL*

- *ERASE*

Each command has been available on Microsoft operating systems since DOS, and is used to remove a file from any writeable storage media. They perform the same function, and have the same *switches*, which are options that control what actions are taken by a command. Table 7.1 lists the switches available on systems running Windows 2000, XP, and higher.

Table 7.1 DEL/ERASE Switches

Switch	Description
/p	Prompts you for confirmation as to whether you want to delete the file
/f	Forces the deletion of read-only files
/s	Deletes the specified files from the current directory and any subdirectories
/q	Specifies not to prompt for confirmation before deleting files. This is called *quiet* mode.
/a:	Deletes files based on the following attributes: *r* Read-only *a* Archive *s* System *h* Hidden – Prefix used with any of the preceding attributes, indicating "not"
/?	Displays help

In using this command, you can specify a particular filename or use wildcards. For example, if you wanted to delete a file called filename.txt in the root directory of C:, you would type **DEL C:\filename.txt**. However, if you wanted to deleted all files in the current directory, you could type **DEL *.***, which indicates to delete files with any filename or extension.

As we discussed, the FAT file system uses a file allocation table to keep track of files, whereas NTFS uses an MFT. In using this command, the file that is deleted will have the pointer to that file removed from the table, but the data will remain on the hard disk. This gives you the opportunity to acquire the data using file recovery or forensic tools that we'll discuss later in this chapter.

Moving Files

Another method of deleting a file involves moving it. If the file is moved from one directory to another on the same partition, the table used to keep track of where files are stored is updated. Because the file still resides on the same partition, a pointer to the file's location is updated. The record showing the file's location is modified to reflect that it's now in another directory, but nothing else about the file changes. Any attributes on the file (such as whether the file is compressed) remain the same.

However, when a file is moved from one hard disk or partition to another, it is actually a multistep process of copying and deleting the file. First, a new copy of the file is created on the target partition. Once the file has been copied, the original file is then deleted. This process also requires some house-keeping in the FAT or MFT tables. A new entry is created in the table on the partition where it has been copied, while the record for the deleted file is removed from the table on its partition.

When a file is moved from one partition to another, it can offer greater possibilities for recovering a file that has been deleted. If a file is moved to another partition and then deleted later, the file has essentially been deleted twice. As such, you may be able to recover it from the partition on which it was deleted, and you may also be able to recover it from the partition from which it was moved.

Disk Cleanup

Another way in which files are deleted is when software does it for you. Software will generally clean up after itself by deleting old setup, temporary, and backup files when they're no longer needed. However, sometimes files are not properly removed, and a considerable number of files may continue to reside on a hard disk. This is the reason for tools such as Disk Cleanup, which removes files and programs from a Windows XP or Windows Vista computer. Disk Cleanup will check for files that can be safely removed so that more disk space is available for use and performance is improved.

The Recycle Bin

So far, we've looked at various ways of how files can be deleted by using commands and utilities, and performing actions such as moving files. With each method, the files are no longer visible to the operating system, and are considered "permanently" deleted. However, this doesn't mean the data is completely gone. Until the data is overwritten or destroyed using the methods we'll discuss later in this chapter, it may still be recovered. The operating system considers the file "permanently" deleted because there are no programs native to the OS that will allow you to restore the files. For most people, this means the file is simply gone.

To give users a second chance of restoring a file before "permanently" deleting it, a number of operating systems provide an easy-to-use method of restoring deleted files. A *Recycle Bin* or *Trash Can* is a repository where files are temporarily stored after they are deleted. On machines running Windows 95 and later, this container for deleted items is called a Recycle Bin, whereas Macintosh OS uses a Trash Can.

The Trash Can available in Macintosh OS X allows items to be dragged and dropped into the Trash Can icon on the desktop. By opening the Trash, you can browse previously deleted items, and manually drag and drop items out of the trash, or delete all of the items you want to get rid of. Macintosh OS X doesn't provide the ability to delete individual items in the trash, and can only empty everything.

The Recycle Bin has been available in every Microsoft operating system since Windows 95, and also allows items to be dragged and dropped into the Recycle Bin icon on the desktop. When a file is deleted from the desktop or by using Windows Explorer, the file is moved to the Recycle Bin with a record of its original location. The file hasn't actually been deleted; its pointer has simply been changed to show that it now resides in the Recycle Bin. Whereas Macintosh OS X expects you to remember where a file was deleted from, Windows will automatically restore an item to its original location.

Another similarity between the two is that you can open the Recycle Bin and browse previously deleted files and directories. Unfortunately, you can't browse the contents of deleted directories in the Recycle Bin. If a file or directory was deleted and you tried to open it in the Recycle Bin to view its contents, double-clicking on it would display only the properties of the deleted item. The option of double-clicking on an item to view its properties isn't available in the Trash Can, nor is the ability to delete individual items from the Trash. In the Recycle Bin, however, you can restore or "permanently" delete individual items so that the space can be made available for storing other files.

What Gets Deleted

Even though the Recycle Bin is a repository for deleted items, this isn't to say that everything that's deleted will wind up in there. Any items stored on local hard drives that were deleted using Windows Explorer or the desktop will appear in the Recycle Bin. In addition to this, any items you delete using software that is Windows-compliant will send a deleted item to the Recycle Bin. For example, if you were opening a file using Microsoft Word and noticed a file listed in the Open dialog box that you wanted to get rid of, selecting the item and pressing the Delete key on your keyboard would send the item to the Recycle Bin. However, many programs are not compliant and will simply delete the item, never to be seen again without the use of data recovery or forensic software.

As we saw in previous sections, when you use utilities such as Disk Cleanup, or the command-line *DEL* and *ERASE* commands, the files bypass the Recycle Bin and are simply deleted. The same may occur if software on your machine was cleaning up files after an installation or shutting down. This is because these programs may delete so many files that the Recycle Bin would fill up quickly. For example, if you used Windows Update to apply a number of fixes or upgrades, the files used to install programs, patches, and service packs would be deleted and would never appear in the Recycle Bin. If they did, you would have a hard time finding the files you mistakenly deleted when browsing the Recycle Bin.

Files are also not deleted if they are not on the local hard drives. If you were to delete a file on a mapped network drive, a compressed folder, a floppy disk, or any other form of removable storage media, the file would not be sent to the Recycle Bin. The same may occur if a file that is too large for the Recycle Bin is deleted. If there isn't enough space in the Recycle Bin for a file or directory that's deleted, a warning message will appear informing you that it will be deleted. If you agree to the deletion, it bypasses the Recycle Bin and is deleted from the system.

Storage Locations of the Recycle Bin

When files are deleted, they are stored in a special hidden directory, which is located in the root directory. Because one Recycle Bin is allocated for each partition on a computer, there is one of these folders on each partition of a hard disk. The name of this folder depends on the file system and operating system being used:

- On FAT file systems, the folder is named *RECYCLED*. For example, on your C: drive the storage location of the Recycle Bin would be C:\RECYCLED.

- On NTFS file systems used by Windows NT, 2000, and XP, this folder is named *RECYCLER*. For example, on your C: drive the storage location of the Recycle Bin would be C:\RECYCLER.

- On NTFS file systems used on Windows Vista, this folder is named *$Recycle.Bin*. For example, on your C: drive the storage location of the Recycle Bin would be C:\RECYCLE.BIN.

If you were to look for these directories on a partition of your hard disk, you might be surprised to find that none of these appears. The reason is probably because they are hidden folders. We'll discuss hidden data and how to view it later in this chapter.

On NTFS partitions, a Recycle Bin is created in the RECYCLER folder for each user who logs on to the computer. Because the RECYCLER directory contains Recycle Bins for each user of the computer, a number of subdirectories will exist under this folder. Each subdirectory is named after the *Security Identifier* (SID) that identifies the user. The SID is a unique number that identifies users and groups in Windows, appearing similar to S-1-5-21-191058668-193157475-1542849698-500. Although opening the Recycle Bin will automatically show the contents of a directory related to the account with which you logged on, looking at the subdirectories in the RECYCLER folder will require you to find which SID corresponds to your account.

NOTE

For a listing of well-known SIDs in Windows, you can visit http://support.microsoft.com/kb/243330. This will provide you with information on SIDs associated with particular groups and users. For example, if you were analyzing the Administrator account, this would be a well-known SID, and could be identified as S-1-5-*domain*-500.

Undeleting or Permanently Deleting a File

Before we discuss how to undelete or remove a file from the Recycle Bin, let's review exactly what happens when the file is deleted. When you delete a file from the desktop or using Windows Explorer, My Computer, or a compliant application, the entry in the file allocation table or MFT is removed, and the file is indicated as being located in the Recycle Bin directory in the root drive of the partition on which it was deleted. The file is then renamed, using the following syntax:

D<original drive letter><#>.<original extension>

To illustrate how the renaming works, let's say you deleted C:\myfile.txt, and this was the second file that was deleted and residing in the Recycle Bin. In using the preceding syntax, the file would be renamed Dc2.txt. In looking at this, you can see that it starts with the letter D, followed by the original drive letter (c), that it was the second file deleted, and that it uses a .txt extension. Its original name and location are stored in a hidden index file named INFO, which is located in the Recycle Bin folder in the root directory. On Windows 95 machines and partitions using NTFS, this file is called INFO2.

The information stored in the INFO file is important, because it allows the file to be automatically restored to its original location. You can view information on the files that have been deleted and stored in the Recycle Bin by double-clicking on the Recycle Bin icon on the Windows desktop. In doing so, a screen similar to that shown in Figure 7.2 will appear. In looking at this figure, you can see that the Recycle Bin allows you to view such information as when a file was deleted, as well as its original location. By right-clicking on a file, you can then click on the **Restore** menu item in the context menu that appears. By restoring a file, the original path to be read from the INFO file, and the file to be renamed and restored to its original path and filename.

Figure 7.2 Recycle Bin

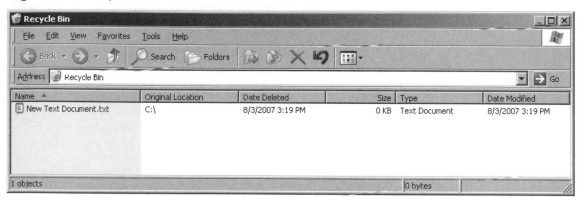

Deleting or emptying files from the Recycle Bin permanently deletes them from the system, and makes it so that they can be recovered only with data recovery or forensic software. To delete a file from the Recycle Bin, you can select the file and then press the **Del** or **Delete** key on your keyboard. You could also delete all of the files from the Recycle Bin by right-clicking on the desktop icon and then clicking **Empty Recycle Bin** from the context menu that appears.

Although the Recycle Bin can be configured so that files are immediately deleted, you can also delete a file and not have it go to the Recycle Bin on a file-by-file basis. If you wanted to bypass the Recycle Bin and simply delete the file, you would select the file you want to delete, and then hold down **Shift + Del** (that is, the Shift key and Delete key at the same time). When doing this, a prompt will appear asking you to confirm the deletion; when you choose **Yes**, the Recycle Bin is bypassed and the file is deleted.

Data Recovery in Linux

Just as you can remove files in Windows and Macintosh operating systems by selecting a file and pressing the Delete key on the keyboard, you also can delete Linux files from a hard disk in this way. And you can delete files in Linux and UNIX machines by using commands. To delete a file in Linux or UNIX, you would use the *rm* command. Deleting a file with this command won't prompt you for any confirmation by default, so once it's deleted you'll have to rely on data recovery software to restore the file. Like the *DEL* and *ERASE* commands we discussed earlier in this chapter, you can use a number of switches with the *rm* command, as shown in Table 7.2.

Table 7.2 rm Switches

Switch	Description
–f	Forces deletion of files, and ignores nonexistent files, without prompting
–I	Interactive mode, where confirmation is required before files are deleted
–r	Contents of a directory are removed recursively.
–v	Verbose. Provides details of what is done.

A more secure way of deleting files in Linux and UNIX is to use the *shred* command. With this command, the file is deleted and overwritten to ensure that it can't be recovered. As we mentioned, by overwriting the data on a disk, the file cannot be recovered. As such, it is important that you use this command only when you're absolutely sure you want the file to be destroyed. You can use a number of options with this command, as listed in Table 7.3.

Table 7.3 shred Switches

Switch	Description
–f	Forces deletion of files, and will change permissions to allow writing if necessary
–n	Iterations in which the file will be overwritten. By default, it is overwritten 25 times, but with this command, you can specify a number.
–s	Shreds a specific number of bytes
–u	Truncates and removes the file after writing
–v	Verbose. Provides details of what is done.
–x	Indicates not to round file sizes to the nearest block
–z	Adds a final overwrite with all zeros to hide that the file was shredded

A number of Linux desktops provide a Recycle Bin that you can use to restore files that were deleted by selecting a file and pressing the Del key on your keyboard. As we mentioned earlier, Recycle Bins are part of the desktop environment, and on Linux and other operating systems, a number of desktop environments can be used, such as GNOME and Xfce. These desktop environments provide a Recycle Bin, allowing files to be restored or permanently deleted. However, any files deleted using the *rm* or *shred* command bypass the Recycle Bin. Although the *shred* command overwrites the data so that it can't be restored, the *rm* command doesn't modify the data after deleting it. This means that any files deleted using the *rm* command could have data restored using recovery tools.

Recovering Deleted Files

When a file is deleted, it doesn't necessarily mean that the data cannot be completely or partially recovered. Data written on a hard disk generally stays there unless it is overwritten or destroyed using methods we'll discuss later in this chapter. Simply deleting the data using operating system file management utilities does not get rid of the data. It only removes the pointer the file system uses to locate that data physically on the disk. The data itself (in the form of the physical changes to the disk's magnetic surface) is still there and can be recovered using special recovery software.

Many people also think that formatting a hard disk erases all its data, but this isn't necessarily so. *Formatting* defines the structure of the disk. *Low-level formatting* (LLF), which physically defines where the tracks and sectors are on the disk, does erase data. However, modern disks are formatted at the low level at the factory; users do not perform LLF on today's Integrated Drive Electronics (IDE) and Small Computer System Interface (SCSI) disks. So, when we discuss formatting, we are generally talking about *high-level formatting* (HLF). This term refers to the process of defining the file system structure. Thus, we say a disk is formatted in FAT or formatted in NTFS.

Assuming a file hasn't been overwritten or damaged in some way, there is always the chance that tools can be used to restore the data. The question that will determine which tools you use is: *Why am I recovering it?* This question in itself will decide whether you will need to perform data recovery or computer forensics.

Although the two terms are often used interchangeably, there is a difference. *Data recovery* is a process of salvaging data that was lost or deleted to make it available again. *Computer forensics* is a process of gathering and examining evidence to establish facts so that accurate testimony and evidence can later be presented in court or other hearings. In looking at these definitions, you will notice that there is a difference in why the data is being acquired; data recovery seeks to restore the data, whereas computer forensics seeks to obtain data to be used as evidence in court.

Data recovery software is extremely useful in situations where someone has accidentally deleted files from his or her computer or other media, such as when an officer has deleted his or her curriculum vitae, notes that were stored in a Microsoft Word document, or other data that isn't evidence in a case. However, although extremely useful, such software isn't suitable for obtaining evidence from a suspect computer. Standard data recovery software may not guarantee that the file won't be modified when it is recovered, or the software may generate temporary files that could damage other data on the disk. To preserve data, computer forensic software is necessary.

As we discussed in Chapter 5, if you are investigating an incident, always assume that the case will eventually go to court. If you used software that wasn't designed for forensic use, you could alter or damage data on the disk, and compromise the investigation. In addition to this, any data that you retrieved could be deemed inadmissible in court. In any situation where you are investigating an intrusion, policy violations, cybercrimes, or other incidents in which data could be used as evidence you should always take the side of caution and use computer forensic tools.

Regardless of which type of tool you use, you should never install the software on the drive containing the data you wish to recover. For example, if you accidentally deleted a file on your C: drive and then downloaded and installed data recovery software to your C: drive, you could overwrite the data that you were trying to recover in the first place. Computer forensic software may use bootable disks to access the drive, or connect to the machine using a network cable. By sharing the drive and connecting to it over a network or using a network cable to connect two machines, you could restore the data without worrying about corrupting data on the disk. If the computer has two drives and you are performing data recovery, you could also install the software on another drive. However, if you deleted the file on a boot partition, files may be installed in your operating system's directory or other directories used to store common files. Whenever you are using these tools, remember that the integrity of the data you are seeking to recover is paramount, and take whatever actions necessary to keep it from being damaged or destroyed.

Deleted File Recovery Tools

Data recovery tools are designed to restore data that has been deleted or corrupted from any number of sources, including hard disks, CDs, DVDs, Blu-ray discs, HD-DVDs, floppy disks, memory cards used in digital cameras, and other storage media. Depending on the capabilities of the software, it will scan the media and look for any damaged, corrupted, or deleted files and display which ones are available for recovery, allowing you to pick and choose which ones will be restored. In some cases, the tools will even repair damaged files so that data can be accessible again.

On the Scene

Computer Forensic Tools versus Data Recovery Tools

Even though many deleted file recovery tools aren't suitable for computer forensics, it is important that officers and security professionals realize these tools are available on the Internet or are included with operating systems. It is possible that before a forensic examination of the computer is performed, the user of the computer or a member of the information technology (IT) staff may attempt to use such tools. Also, in cases where data needs to be recovered but isn't part of an investigation, disk imaging software that we discussed in Chapter 6 may be more time-consuming and overkill to what's needed to restore the data.

Undelete Tools

As we mentioned earlier in this chapter, using commands such as *DEL* and *ERASE* from the command line or holding down the Shift key when deleting a file will bypass the Recycle Bin. To restore the file, you need to use tools that will search the hard disk for deleted files and allow you to undelete them. Fortunately, a number of tools are available that perform this task, with various features that make undeleting files easier. They should be used as soon as possible, however, to avoid any other data overwriting the file.

Undelete

In discussing tools that undelete files, we should start with one of the most basic ones which were used in MS-DOS 5.00 to 6.22. Undelete is a command-line tool that you can use on these old systems, allowing you to simply type **UNDELETE** followed by the path to the file you wish to restore. For example, if you wanted to undelete a file named mytext.txt from your root directory, you would simply type **UNDELETE C:\MYTEXT.TXT**. Doing so would restore the file.

People who have been using computers since the days of MS-DOS tend to automatically think of this program when mentioning Undelete. However, it was designed to work only on systems running MS-DOS 5-6.22, and it can cause problems when run on later systems running Windows 9*x* or later. However, a number of other programs use this name, but are designed for newer operating systems. These include:

- Active@ UNDELETE (www.active-undelete.com), which can recover data from basic and dynamic volumes, including RAID volumes, and large hard disks that are more than 500GB in size. It also supports recovery form removable storage media such as USB Flash Drives, ZIP drives, memory sticks and cards, and so forth.

- Active@ UNERASER (www.uneraser.com), which can access deleted files before Windows even starts, and supports local files, compressed files, and MBR backups, and can access sectors of the disk drive via a Disk Viewer feature. The Active@ UNERASER tool can run from either a bootable floppy disk or a CD. Just to make things even easier, it provides a Bootable ISO CD-Image and Bootable Floppy Creator to create the disk or CD that can then be used to recover files.

- R-Undelete from r-Tools Technology (www.r-undelete.com), which restores deleted files, but also provides an easy-to-use wizard that takes you through the steps of recovering a file. It also provides features that allow you to reconstruct damaged graphics, audio, and video files. Before recovering files, you can preview the file to determine whether you actually want to restore it or leave it deleted.

- Easy-Undelete (www.easy-undelete.com), which will restore not only files from hard disks using FAT12, FAT16, FAT32, and NTFS file systems, but also non-Microsoft partitions such as Linux and Macintosh OS X. It also supports other storage media, such as memory cards used in digital cameras, and it includes a preview feature that allows you to view images before restoring them. In addition, it provides a hexadecimal preview feature that allows you to view the contents of clusters.

- WinUndelete (www.winundelete.com), which allows you to recover files from Microsoft file systems with the original created and modified storage dates. It provides a search feature to scan for specific files, and allows you to filter results by extensions and file types. It also allows you to preview certain types of data before restoring them, such as Microsoft Office documents, images, and plain text.

- Mycroft V3, which is computer forensic software that is developed by DIBS USA, and is available from www.dibsusa.com. The software runs from a bootable floppy disk, and provides a search engine that is used to scan a computer for data on the disk. Using this tool, an investigator can determine whether there is evidence on the computer. By using this tool to provide a cursory search of a computer's hard disk, you can determine whether additional investigation and acquisition of evidence is necessary.

Recycle Bin Replacements

Earlier we discussed how the Recycle Bin stores deleted files in certain locations on the hard disk. However, other tools are available that you can install to replace the existing Recycle Bin on Windows machines. These tools are often used because they provide increased functionality over the Windows Recycle Bin. When these tools are installed, the deleted file is sent to the tool and not to the Windows Recycle Bin. As such, you should try to identify whether these tools have been installed on a suspect machine so that you can determine whether deleted files may exist in alternative locations. Two popular replacements for the Recycle Bin include:

- Undelete from Diskeeper Corporation (www.undelete.com), which replaces the Recycle Bin with a *Recovery Bin*. Once you install Undelete, any file that's deleted is sent to the Recovery Bin, allowing you to search the bin and restore any files that were accidentally deleted. It even provides the ability to view versions of files that were deleted, to select the correct version to restore. If you had a Microsoft Word, Excel, or PowerPoint file that was overwritten, you could use the Recovery Bin to restore a previous version. You can use versions of the Undelete software to protect local files, and use the Server Edition to protect and restore files deleted by network clients.

■ Fundelete is a tool that replaces the Recycle Bin on systems running Windows NT, Me, 2000, and XP so that any files that are deleted from the Command Prompt, using Shift + Del command or within a program can be recovered. It also provides filter options so that files with specific file extensions aren't sent to the Fundelete Bin.

NOTE

Fundelete was created by Sysinternals, which was acquired by Microsoft in 2006. As such, visiting the Sysinternals site will redirect you to Microsoft's Web site. You can find information on the Sysinternals products on Microsoft's TechNet Web site, at www.microsoft.com/technet/sysinternals/default.mspx, whereas copies of Fundelete are still available from sites such as http://fundelete.en.softonic.com.

CD/DVD Data Recovery

As you're well aware at this point in the book, not all data is stored on hard disks, so it follows suit that certain data recovery software would be specifically designed to restore damaged and deleted files stored on CDs and DVDs. When data is stored on CDs and DVDs, the data can be deleted from rewriteable discs, and can be damaged by scratches, damage, and defects in the media. Some of the more popular programs that you can use to restore this data include:

■ CDRoller

■ IsoBuster

■ CD Data Rescue

■ InDisk Recovery

CDRoller

Despite its name, CDRoller recovers data written to CDs and DVDs, and is available from www.cdroller.com. It not only allows you to recover data from CD-ROM, CD-R, and a variety of other CD and DVD formats, but it will also allow you to recover data recorded directly onto the discs, such as that written by stand-alone DVD recorders, camcorders, and other products. It provides the ability to split recovered VOB and VRO files into separate clips, and can convert raw video into MPEG files, allowing you to create a new video from damaged data.

This tool also provides software to burn data onto CDs and DVDs, allowing you to back up any data before there is a problem or once it has been recovered. It supports the ISO 9660 file system, Joliet extensions for long filename support, and discs formatted in the Universal Disk Format (UDF) file system.

ISOBuster

IsoBuster is another tool that supports a wide range of discs, and is available from www.isobuster.com. It recovers data from CDs and DVDs as well as from Blu-ray and HD-DVD discs. It also supports ISO 9660, Joliet, and UDF; will scan for IFO, BUP, and VOB file systems on audio and video DVDs; and supports Mount Rainier CD-RW and DVD+RW discs. IsoBuster is also one of the few tools that provide support for discs created using Macintosh file systems. It has an HFS Reader to support HFS and HFS Plus file systems, and built-in support for Resource Fork extensions in ISO 9660 and UDF file systems.

CD Data Rescue

CD Data Rescue is a tool developed by Naltech Software (www.naltech.com) and is designed to recover data from damaged, scratched, and defective CD-ROM, CD-R, and CD-RW discs. It supports Mount Rainier/EasyWrite MRW discs, and can recover data created by CD writing software in ISO and UDF formats.

InDisk Recovery

InDisk Recovery, developed by OctaneSoft (www.octanesoft.com), is designed to recover data from damaged, scratched, defective, or otherwise unreadable CD and DVD discs. It supports the ISO-9660, UDF, and Joliet file systems.

Microsoft Office Repair and Recovery

Data recovery doesn't just mean restoring deleted files. On occasion, any previously deleted data may be incomplete or corrupt once it is recovered. Even if the file hasn't been deleted and restored, a file may be corrupted from improperly shutting down the application or computer, or records within a database may be deleted accidentally. To restore the data within these files, you can use any of the following products:

- OfficeFIX
- Repair My Excel
- Repair My Word

OfficeFIX

OfficeFIX is a suite of products from Cimaware Software (www.cimaware.com) that is designed to repair and recover data from damaged files that were created with Microsoft Office products. The following tools are included in the suite:

- **AccessFIX** A tool with features to recover, repair, and undelete Access databases. It recovers the data stored in tables, as well as forms, reports, macros, and other data and elements of the database. It has functions that will restore deleted records from tables, and restores password-protected files regardless of whether you have the password.

- **ExcelFIX** A tool used to recover corrupted Excel files. It will extract the information from a damaged Excel spreadsheet and store it in a new file, complete with any data, formulas, and other content.

- **WordFIX** A tool used to recover Word files. This not only includes files created with the PC version of Microsoft Word, but also those created with any version of Word for Macintosh. Not only can it recover the text, but higher editions of this tool can also recover formatting, tables of contents, embedded images, and other data.

- **OutlookFIX** A tool used to repair files used in Microsoft Outlook. It provides the ability to recover damaged or deleted e-mail, calendars, notes, attachments, and other elements in Outlook. It also provides an inbox repair tool, and has the ability to split large files into smaller ones to solve the 2 GB limitation on Personal Folders Files (PST).

Repair My Excel and Repair My Word

A number of other products are designed to repair Microsoft Office products. GetData Software Development (www.getdata.com) provides a number of recovery tools, including:

- **Repair My Excel** (www.repairmyexcel.com) Used to recover spreadsheets created in Excel, including formulas, formatting, and other elements of the file's contents.

- **Repair My Word** A free tool available from www.repairmyword.com that is used to recover text from corrupt or damaged Word files. Once recovered, it can then be saved in another Word document.

Compressed Files

Compressed files are files on which a compression algorithm has been used to reduce file size. Because the compressed file may be damaged, it means that any files stored inside it are inaccessible. This means that before you can recover a Word document, image, or other file, you must first repair the compressed file created with a tool such as PKZIP, WinZip, RAR, or other compression software.

Zip Repair

Zip Repair is another tool developed by GetData Software Development (www.getdata.com), and can be downloaded from www.ziprepair.com. It is used to repair corrupted ZIP files that have been compressed using WinZip or other software. It supports large file sizes of 2GB or more, and can even repair and extract data from spanned ZIP volumes that have been split into smaller sets of data. Spanned ZIP files are often used to make large ZIP files into smaller pieces, allowing them to be e-mailed without worry of any e-mail size limitations.

Deleted Images

Of the various types of data you will try to recover, deleted images are common. Images may be corrupted or deleted from hard disks, or directly from the memory card used in a digital camera. At times, the image may have been damaged, and repair of the file is necessary. As we'll see from the tools that follow, a number of different tools are available for recovering lost images.

eIMAGE Recovery

eIMAGE Recovery, developed by OctaneSoft (www.octanesoft.com), is designed to recover any digital images or media that may have been lost or deleted from memory cards used by digital cameras.

It can restore files from any number of different media, including Compact Flash, SmartMedia, memory sticks, mmd, XD, multimedia, or secure digital memory cards.

Canon RAW File Recovery Software

Canon RAW File Recovery Software (CRW Repair), a free tool developed by GetData Software Development (www.getdata.com), can be downloaded from www.crwrepair.com. Canon cameras usually store images in a JPEG format, with RAW images stored inside a file with a .crw extension. The CRW file is generally used for processing photos, and allows the photo's exposure, white balance, and other elements to be manipulated. The CRW file also allows users of the camera to access the JPEG quickly. Unfortunately, because it is a complex file, it can easily be corrupted by such things as a change in file size. CRW Repair will examine the file size to ensure that it's correct, and has the ability to access and extract the JPEG image.

ImageRecall

ImageRecall Software (www.imagerecall.com) provides several editions of software that could be used to retrieve corrupted or deleted files. Don't Panic – Photo Edition allows you to recover pictures and video that have been damaged or deleted from digital cameras. Using this software, you can obtain and restore data from memory cards, USB storage devices, and other storage media. The tool also provides a Thumbnail viewer that allows you to view small images of the pictures available to recover. Initially, the software is available only for Windows 2000, XP, and Vista, but added support for Macintosh OS X is forthcoming.

RecoverPlus Pro

RecoverPlus Pro is a tool that allows you to recover digital images that may have been damaged or deleted, and is available from www.arcksoft.com. It provides recovery of a wide variety of graphics formats, and will attempt to adjust the image to improve it during recovery. It will attempt to repair any images that are unreadable, and will repair RAW files such as Canon CRW, CR2, and Nikon NEF. It provides a preview pane, which allows you to view a full-size image as well as thumbnails that are rendered from the image file. RecoverPlus Pro also provides a number of options for how files are scanned and undeleted, including performing a deep level scan on damaged media.

Zero Assumption Digital Image Recovery

Zero Assumption Digital Image Recovery was a free stand-alone digital image recovery tool developed by Zero Assumption Recovery (www.z-a-recovery.com). However, the stand-alone version of this tool is discontinued, as its features are included in the trial and full versions of ZAR. As part of ZAR, Digital Image Recovery is designed to restore pictures from digital memory cards. The types of images it can restore are GIF, JPEG, TIFF, CRW, CR2, MOV, and WAV files.

DiskInternals Flash Recovery

As we saw earlier in this chapter, DiskInternals (www.diskinternals.com) provides a number of data recovery solutions, including DiskInternals Flash Recovery. It is designed to recover deleted or corrupted pictures from memory cards, including those that have been reformatted or lost due to a hardware malfunction. It provides an easy-to-use interface that allows images to be recovered using a wizard that takes the user step by step through the recovery process.

PC Inspector Smart Recovery

PC Inspector Smart Recovery is a free tool developed by CONVAR that can be used to restore files from memory cards and memory sticks used with digital cameras. It acquires read-only access to the memory card, ensuring that the data isn't altered. Once recovered, you can then specify where you would like the files saved. It is available from www.pcinspector.de/smart_media_recovery/uk/ welcome.htm.

Recovering Deleted Partitions

Partitioning a hard disk involves dividing the disk into volumes, which generally appear to the operating system as logical drives, identified by different drive letters. The disk is divided into logical drives for the purposes of performance and organization of the data. Each logical drive can be formatted separately so that each one uses a different file system. Of course, you can partition the disk as a single partition. Partitioning schemes and tools differ depending on the operating system and file system.

Contrary to popular belief, partitioning utilities do not erase the data on a disk; they only delete and manipulate the partition tables. Even though tools such as Partition Magic warn that their use will erase the data on a disk, this is not true; the warning is intended for the average user who will not be able to recover the data after using the utility. Generally, partition utilities will delete the entry for that partition in the partition table so that any space associated with the partition becomes unallocated. Even if the tool overwrites the first sector (sector 0) of the partition before removing it, a backup of the boot sector may still be available and can be restored. Professional data recovery techniques can still recover the data, although the data might be fragmented—that is, the contents of a file could be spread out in different areas of the disk and recoverable in bits and pieces.

Deleting Partitions Using Windows

You can create and delete partitions in Windows using the *Computer Management (Local)* console, which is used to control various aspects of your computer. To open the console, you can right-click on the **My Computer** icon on your desktop, and then click the **Manage** menu item on the context menu that appears. Alternatively, you can open the console through the Control Panel. From the Windows **Start** menu, select **Settings** and click the **Control Panel** menu item. When the Control Panel opens, you would then double-click **Administrative Tools**, and then double-click **Computer Management**. It is important to note, however, that to access this tool, you need to use an Administrator account or be a member of the Administrators group.

As shown in Figure 7.3, the Computer Management console provides access to a variety of tools that you can use to manage your computer. By expanding the **Storage** node in the left pane, you can then click on the **Disk Management** item in the console tree. When you select this item, information about the hard disks and other storage (such as DVD or CD-ROM drives) installed on your computer appears in the right portion of the screen.

Figure 7.3 Disk Management in the Computer Management Console

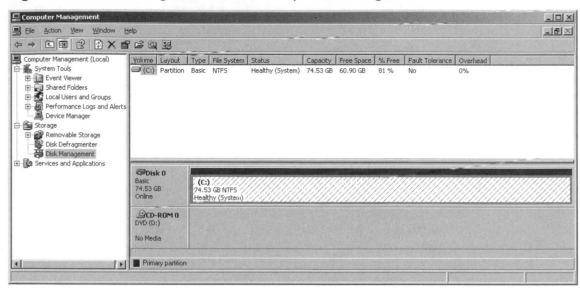

When you right-click on a partition, logical drive, or volume in the lower-right pane of the console, a context menu will appear with a **Delete Partition** menu item. If this item is enabled, clicking it will delete the partition. However, the Delete Partition menu item will not be enabled in certain circumstances, where it is impossible to delete the partition:

- A system volume (which contains files to boot the computer), boot volume (which contains system files), or a volume with an active paging file or crash dump (memory dump).

- An extended partition that isn't empty. Before deleting an extended partition, all of the logical drives in that partition must be deleted first.

Deleting Partitions from the Command Line

You also can delete partitions from the command line, using disk partitioning utilities that require you to type commands from a prompt. You can use two commands on different versions of Windows:

- *FDISK*
- *DISKPART*

Using either of these tools, you can view a listing of partitions, determine the number or drive letter of the disk, and delete any existing partitions. This practice does, however, have the same limitations that we saw previously, when discussing deleting a partition with the Computer Management console. You must be an Administrator or a member of the Administrators group, and you can't delete a system volume, a boot volume, or a volume with an active paging file or crash dump. In addition, any logical drives need to be deleted before deleting an extended partition.

FDISK

FDISK is a command line interpreter that is used to create and delete partitions on computers running MS-DOS, Windows 9*x*, Windows NT, or Windows Me. As shown in Table 7.4, you can use a number of switches with this command to view information and perform various actions on a hard disk. When you type **FDISK** without any of these switches, a series of screens will enable you to navigate through the process of partitioning the disk.

Table 7.4 FDISK Switches

Switch	Description
/MBR	Rewrites the MBR
/CMBR <disk>	Re-creates the MBR on a specific disk
/PRI: <size>	Creates a primary partition
/EXT: <size>	Creates an extended partition
/LOG: <size>	Creates a logical drive
/Q	Prevents rebooting the computer automatically after exiting FDISK
/STATUS	Shows the current status of hard drives
/ACTOK	Forces FDISK not to check disk integrity
/FPRMT	Disables prompt for FAT32 support

DISKPART

DISKPART is a command-line interpreter that is used to create and delete partitions on computers running Windows 2000, XP, or Vista. Unlike FDISK, it doesn't provide a series of menus that can be navigated to delete partitions. Instead, as shown in Figure 7.4, typing **DISKPART** at the prompt will activate the command-line interpreter, allowing you to enter different commands.

Figure 7.4 DISKPART

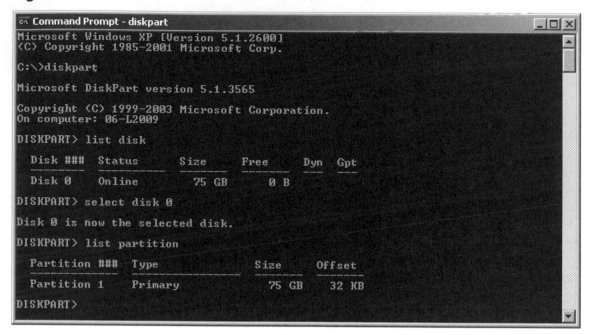

You can use a number of commands to view information on disks and partitions on your hard disk, as well as perform tasks such as creating and deleting partitions. Table 7.5 lists the commands available through DISKPART.

Table 7.5 DISKPART Commands

Switch	Description
ADD	Adds a mirror to a simple volume
ACTIVE	Marks the current partition as being the active boot partition
ASSIGN	Assigns a drive letter or mount point to the selected volume
BREAK	Breaks a mirror set
CLEAN	Clears the configuration information or all information off the disk
CONVERT	Converts the disk from one format to another. This will allow you to convert the disk from dynamic to basic, basic to dynamic, MBR to GPT, or GPT to MBR.
CREATE	Creates a volume or partition
DELETE	Deletes a missing disk, selected volume, or selected partition
DETAIL	Provides details about a disk, partition, or volume

Continued

Table 7.5 Continued. DISKPART Commands

Switch	Description
EXIT	Exits the program
EXTEND	Extends a volume
HELP	Prints a listing of Help commands
IMPORT	Imports a disk group
LIST	Prints a list of disks, partitions, or volumes
INACTIVE	Marks the current partition as an inactive partition
ONLINE	Marks as online a disk that is currently marked as offline
REM	Used to comment scripts
REMOVE	Removes a drive letter or mount point
REPAIR	Repairs a RAID-5 volume
RESCAN	Forces DISKPART to rescan the computer for disks and volumes
RETAIN	Places a retainer partition under a simple volume
SELECT	Moves the focus on an object

Using a combination of these commands, you can delete a partition from a computer, allowing you to later create and format it in a particular file format.

Deleted Partition Recovery Tools

When a partition is deleted, its entry in the partition table is removed. Although it can appear quite imposing that an entire partition of information is no longer visible, the data hasn't been destroyed from the disk. Essentially, deleting the partition is similar to removing the table of contents from a book; none of the information outside the table is missing, it just requires other methods to find it. This is where partition recovery tools come into play.

Partition recovery tools perform a number of automated tasks that will attempt to restore a damaged or deleted partition, and/or restore data from that partition. Some of the automated tasks these tools will use to locate and recover data include:

- Determining the error on the disk, and allowing the user to choose another partition and make it active.

- Scanning the disk space for a partition boot sector or damaged partition information, and then attempting to reconstruct the partition table entry. By finding the partition boot sector, it will have all the information necessary to reconstruct the entry in the partition table. Because both NTFS and FAT32 volumes maintain backup boot sectors, you can recover the volume by restoring the boot sector.

- Scanning the disk space for a partition boot sector or data from deleted partition information, and then attempting to reconstruct the partition table entry.

A number of tools are available for partition recovery, each of which has various features that can make it easier to restore data that may have been lost from accidental deletion or damage to the partition. Damaged partitions can occur from power or software failure, a root directory being damaged by a virus, formatting, and being deleted with tools such as FDISK, DISKPART, or the Disk Management tool in the Computer Management console. Problems can also occur when the partition table, MFT, root directory, or boot record is lost or corrupt. Each of these can cause Windows not to recognize the hard disk, requiring partition recovery tools to be used to recover the partition and data.

Active@ Partition Recovery

Active@ Partition Recovery is a tool developed by Active@ Data Recovery Software, and is available from www.partition-recovery.com. It recovers FAT12, FAT16, FAT32, and NTFS partitions and logical drives. It also provides the ability to create an image file of the drive to back up data on a disk, as well as back up MBR, partition table, and boot sectors, which can be restored after a problem occurs.

Active@ Partition Recovery will scan the hard disk to locate deleted partitions and logical drives. In doing so, a SuperScan (which does an extensive scan of the hard disk) may even detect partitions after new ones have been created. Even if you've formatted and used these new partitions, the old ones may still be detected. Once they are detected, you can then undelete primary and extended partitions or logical drives to restore the data. If you're unsure whether the data on the partition is something you want to recover, this tool provides the ability to preview files and folders located on the deleted partition or drive before it's recovered.

Different versions of Active@ Partition Recovery software are available to use, including:

- Active@ Partition Recovery for DOS, which is a DOS-based version of the tool and is used if the system partition has been lost, or if the computer doesn't boot in Windows. It can't recover a partition if it's been overwritten. It is small enough to run from a bootable floppy, and supports IDE, ATA, and SCSI hard drives.

- Active@ Partition Recovery for Windows, which is the Windows-based version of the tool and is used if a nonsystem partition is lost, or when the computer boots in Windows. It can also be used to restore a deleted partition on a USB Flash Drive or memory card. It supports IDE, ATA, SATA, and SCSI drives.

Active@ Disk Image

Whereas Active@ Partition allows you to create a raw image of a logical or physical drive, Active@ Disk Image is a DOS-based tool designed to completely back up and restore an image of your entire hard disk, FAT12, FAT16, FAT32, and NTFS partitions and logical drives. This tool allows you to create compressed and uncompressed images that contain a mirror of the drive's surface, or compressed data images that contain data stored in the clusters. As with other tools from this developer, you can preview the data stored in one or more image files before restoring them. The software is available from www.disk-image.net.

DiskInternals Partition Recovery

DiskInternals Partition Recovery is a tool that is used to recover deleted and damaged partitions, and is available from www.diskinternals.com. It supports FAT12, FAT16, FAT32, and NTFS volumes, and provides features to recover deleted files. Even if files were deleted before the partition was lost, they can still be recovered.

DiskInternals Partition Recovery also provides the ability to create snapshot files of logical drives, allowing any data on a drive to be stored in files that can be kept on another machine until needed. By creating an image of the drive, you can restore the data in case of a problem.

DiskInternals Partition Recovery also provides features to recover the MBR, and unformat NTFS and FAT drives. In addition to this, it can provide recovery for other storage media such as USB Flash Drives, memory cards, and other media.

One of the major features of this tool is that it provides a number of wizards that take you step by step through the process of recovering partitions. Because it walks you through the process, this means you can recover a partition without any previous experience.

GetDataBack

GetDataBack is a partition recovery tool developed by RunTime Software, and is available from www.runtime.org. It will restore data from a variety of sources, including hard disks, memory cards, USB Flash Drives, iPods, and other media. Two versions of this software are available from this site:

- GetDataBack for NTFS, which is used to recover data from an NTFS file system
- GetDataBack for FAT, which is used to recover data from a FAT file system

Each tool can be used on a remote computer, allowing you to connect over a network or serial cable to restore a damaged or deleted partition. This can be useful if you don't want to remove the drive and attach it to another computer, or use DOS-based tools to recover the partition.

It provides a wizard-like interface that allows you to specify settings to optimize the recovery process, selecting whether to use default settings, whether damage was caused by partitioning software such as FDISK or by formatting the drive, or whether a new operating system was installed. If there is no problem with the partition, you can also set the tool to simply recover deleted files.

NTFS Deleted Partition Recovery

NTFS Deleted Partition Recovery is a tool that is designed to recover partitions and perform other tasks to restore data that may have resulted in a loss of data. It can retrieve data from formatted, corrupted, or otherwise damaged partitions, as well as from other storage media such as ZIP drives, USB Flash Drives, memory cards, and so forth. It is available from www.techddi.com.

Handy Recovery

Handy Recovery is a tool for recovering deleted, damaged, and formatted partitions, and is available from www.handyrecovery.com. Using this tool, you can search for files by name or by using a mask, and restore entire folders and their contents. You can browse data on the disk, allowing you to see deleted files and folders with ones that haven't been deleted. It supports FAT12, FAT16, FAT32, and NTFS file systems, and will recover compressed and encrypted files stored on drives formatted as NTFS. It can also recover data from memory cards and other media. Each file that is displayed provides information on to the probability of successfully recovering it.

Acronis Recovery Expert

Acronis Recovery Expert is another easy-to-use tool that recovers deleted or lost partitions. It is available from www.acronis.com, it provides a series of wizards that take you step by step through the process of recovering data, and it supports FAT16, FAT32, NTFS, HPFS, Linux Ext2, Ext3, ReiserFS, and Linux Swap file systems. It also provides features that allow you to work from bootable CDs and floppy disks, so you can recover system partitions or systems that fail to boot.

TestDisk

TestDisk is a free tool that can be used to recover data and partitions that have been deleted or lost, and can run on a number of different systems including Windows NT/2000/XP/2003, Linux, FreeBSD, NetBSD, OpenBSD, SunOS, and Macintosh OS X. It has features to fix partition tables, recover FAT32 and NTFS boot sectors from a backup, and rebuild FAT12, FAT16, FAT32, and NTFS boot sectors. It can also locate Ext2 and Ext3 backup SuperBlocks and fix MFTs using an MFT mirror, and it provides other features that make it possible to recover partitions from a number of different systems. It is available from www.cgsecurity.org.

Scaven

Scaven is a partition recovery tool that can perform unattended multistring searches on hard disks, and recover deleted and lost data. It can recover data from accidentally formatted drives, drives with bad sectors, damaged MBRs, and lost partitions. It is available from http://pjwalczak.com/scaven/index.php.

Recover It All!

Recover It All! is a tool developed by DTIData, and is available from www.dtidata.com/recover_it_all.htm. It is designed to restore data lost from accidentally formatting the disk, deleted files, and deleted or damaged partitions and boot sectors. It also provides an executable that will run from a floppy disk, allowing you to restore the partition even if the computer's operating system won't start, and will prevent overwriting data on the disk by installing the software.

Partition Table Doctor

Partition Table Doctor is a partition recovery tool that checks and repairs the MBR, partition table, and boot sector, and recovers damaged or deleted data from FAT16, FAT32, NTFS, Ext2, Ext3, and Linux Swap partitions on IDE, ATA, SATA, SCSI, and removable hard disk drives. It provides features to browse the contents of a disk, and allows you to back up and restore the MBR, partition table, and boot sector. It is available from www.ptdd.com.

Data Acquisition and Duplication

Electronic evidence is fragile by nature, and can easily be modified, damaged, or destroyed. Even booting a computer can erase temporary files, modify timestamps, or alter other data in addition to writing data and creating new files to the drive using the boot process. Beyond this, a computer could be booby trapped so that if a set of keys wasn't pressed at bootup or an incorrect password was entered, a program or script could run to reformat the hard disk or overwrite certain data, making retrieval of evidence more difficult or impossible. Because of this, data must be acquired or duplicated from a hard disk before any analysis takes place.

As we discussed in Chapter 5, *data acquisition* is the act or process of gathering information and evidence. In computer forensics, this means using established methods to acquire data from a suspect computer or storage medium to gain insight into a crime or other incident, and potentially use it as evidence to convict a suspect. The goal of data acquisition is to preserve evidence, so any tools that are used should not alter the data in any way, and should provide an exact duplicate. To prevent contamination, any data that is duplicated should be stored on forensically sterile medium, meaning that the disk has no other data on it, and has no viruses or defects.

Duplication of data is a critical part of any computer forensic investigation. As we saw in Chapter 6, a number of tools are available that can create a copy of data. To effectively examine data on a suspect machine, a person performing a forensic examination of a machine needs to create an *image* of the disk. As we discussed in the previous chapter, when you create a disk image (a bitstream copy), each physical sector of the disk is copied so that the data is distributed in the same way, and then the image is compressed into a file called an *image file*. This image is exactly like the original, both physically and logically. As an exact duplicate of the data on a suspect machine or storage medium, the mirror image includes hidden files, temp files, corrupted files, file fragments, and erased files that have not yet been overwritten. In other words, every binary digit is duplicated exactly.

This is different from other methods that may be used to duplicate data for disaster recovery or other purposes where every scrap of data isn't necessary. For example, when you use tools to back up a hard disk, the only data duplicated is that which is visible to the file system. Similarly, a disk image may be created as a method of backing up a system, including only files that haven't been deleted. The backup or clone of the disk contents wouldn't include any data that was hidden, deleted, or lost on the disk. If a disaster occurred and/or data needed to be restored, the backup or image could be used to recover data and get systems back online quickly.

From the perspective of someone performing an investigation, backups on magnetic tape or image files stored to disks can be a useful source of evidence. Most organizations will have a regimen of nightly backups, in which data stored on servers and certain other computers on the network will be copied to magnetic tape or other storage media. Even individuals may back up important data to a disk or location on the network, creating an image of any data that was saved to the disk over a period of time. This can be important to an investigation, as an investigator can provide a timeline of what data was saved to certain files at what time. For example, if someone was embezzling from a company, you could see what entries that person added, deleted, and modified in a spreadsheet or database on a given day by restoring versions of the file from different backups. You can use a number of tools to duplicate data stored on magnetic tapes, and other tools to mount an image file created with various types of software. By analyzing a duplicate of the image or backup, you may find important evidence without altering the original media or file.

In an investigation, however, most of the time you'll need to use software to create an image of a hard disk, CDs, DVDs, floppy disks, USB Flash Drives, memory cards from digital cameras, and other storage media. The bitstream copy will contain all of the data stored on the device or removable media, and can later be analyzed for potential evidence.

Because you don't boot from the hard disk of a computer you're investigating, you need to connect the computer you're using (with forensic software installed) to the suspect's machine via a network cable or serial cable. Once you've created a physical connection to the computer, you can then run the forensic software and create an image of the machine's hard disk.

Forensic software may include a special program that can run from a bootable floppy, or be small enough to fit on a bootable CD or floppy. Upon booting from the CD or floppy, the program on the floppy or CD is run. Depending on the program, it may connect to the forensic software on your computer so that it can then make an exact image of the disk, or it may simply write the image file to your computer.

Alternatively, you could also remove the hard disk from a suspect computer and connect it to your computer or to a device that provides write protection. Write protection prevents data from being written to the disk that you're duplicating. When using any forensic software, it is always advisable to use hardware-based write-blocking software. The hardware prevents the forensic software and the operating system you're using from altering data on the suspect hard disk when you attach the hard drive to your computer. Once the hard disk is connected to your computer in this way, you can then begin running the forensic software so that a duplicate of the data is written to an image file on your machine.

Once the image is created, you can then use the forensic software or other tools that we'll discuss in this chapter to mount the image. This allows the software to display the contents of the machine, and will allow you to view any data that exists on the machine from which it was acquired. Any software being used should mount the image as a read-only volume, so there is no way that any changes can be made to the data. This allows you to view data in areas of the disk, including partition information, sectors, files stored on the machine, the directory structure, and other information. Because it is read-only, any files you view won't be altered, and will retain their original timestamps and other attributes.

Because the data you're analyzing is a duplicate of the original source, this means the original hard disk or storage medium is preserved in its original state. If a situation occurred where the image file or duplicated magnetic media was damaged or destroyed, you could reacquire the data as you did the first time. Of course, any machine used to store forensic image files should be backed up regularly. This will ensure that if a problem did occur that damaged or deleted the image file you're working from, you could then restore it from an existing backup.

Notes from the Underground

Booby Traps

Booby trap is military slang for a trap that's set off by a foolish or unsuspecting person. In computers, many different kinds of traps can be set for people whom you don't want to have access. A simple trap is to create an icon on the desktop that someone may want to activate. For example, if a suspect created an icon named "Kiddie Porn," an investigator might be tempted to double-click on it. The trap is that the shortcut actually points to a script or program that will overwrite selected files, encrypt the hard disk, or perform other actions that make analyzing the disk impossible. If you didn't want to use an icon, you could configure your computer to run a particular script or program at startup or shutdown. This could be as simple as adding a batch file to the Windows Startup menu, or adding a few lines to an AUTOEXEC.BAT file.

Many applications on the Internet are designed to wipe data from your computer, by overwriting deleted files. A simple batch file could delete a folder, and then invoke such a program that would overwrite any deleted files with a series of 1s and 0s or other data. It could even initiate an LLF that would erase everything on the disk sector by sector.

The danger of booby traps is another reason why it's so important to analyze a computer using an image of its data. By working from an image file, you won't need to worry about such programs executing and damaging evidence on a machine. The original data remains preserved, and because the forensic software mounts the image as a read-only file, there is no chance that such scripts or programs will modify any data in the image file.

Data Acquisition Tools

Although the number of tools for forensic acquisition and analysis was limited several years ago, quite a few options are available today. As mentioned, in choosing which tools to use, you should ensure that they do not modify data. You should also evaluate the reputations of these tools, and whether they have previously been accepted in court. For example, EnCase has been widely accepted, so there would be less of a chance of it being heavily scrutinized. Because testifying in court can be stressful enough, you don't want to waste time justifying the tools you used to acquire evidence. Although you may still need to validate the tool that was used, using tools that are widely accepted and previously accepted can make the process easier.

In the sections that follow, we'll take a closer look at one of the tools we discussed in Chapter 6, FTK Imager. As we'll see, this tool allows you to create image files that may be mounted and analyzed afterward. In discussing this tool, you'll gain a better understanding of how disk imaging tools are used to acquire data from a suspect machine.

FTK Imager

FTK Imager is an imaging tool developed by AccessData (www.accessdata.com) that allows you to preview data and assess potential evidence on a machine. Using this tool, you can make a forensic image of the data, duplicating everything on the machine so that there is no chance of modifying the original data. By previewing the contents of the image and reviewing the duplicated data, you can then determine whether additional analysis is required using the Forensic Toolkit (FTK).

Using FTK, you can view forensic images of hard disks, floppy disks, CDs, DVDs, and other storage media that was created with FTK Imager, or you can view images created with other tools. It will read image files created with ICS, SafeBack, and forensic, uncompressed images created with Ghost, and read or write image files in EnCase, dd Raw, SMART, and FTK image formats. This means that even if another organization or person with different software created a forensic image, you could still view the image file and determine whether it contained any evidence. This is particularly useful in situations such as when an internal investigation was conducted, a forensic image was created from a suspect computer, and police now need to view the evidence that was acquired.

In addition to the image file formats that can be made for analyzing disks, there are also a number of file formats that can be read and created for CD and DVD forensics. These include ISOBuster CUE, CloneCD, Alcohol, PlexTools, Virtual CD, and many others.

As shown in Figure 7.5, FTK Imager provides an easy-to-use interface. Once an evidence file is opened, you can view the folder structure in the Evidence Tree, located in the upper left-hand pane. By selecting a folder, you can then view files stored in that folder in the File List, located in the upper-right pane. To preview a particular file, you can select it in the upper pane, and view an image of pictures, hexadecimal data, text, and previews of other data in the lower right-hand pane. You can view additional information on the file, including any DOS attributes the file might have, in the Properties pane in the lower left-hand side of the screen.

Figure 7.5 FTK Imager

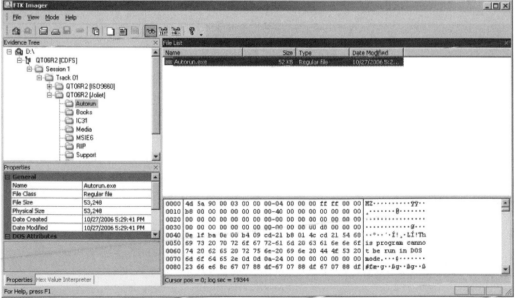

Using FTK imager to create a forensic image is relatively easy, as seen in the step-by-step instructions provided here, which outline how to acquire data from a CD/DVD or floppy. You would follow similar steps to acquire data from other media.

1. Once FTK Imager has been installed, from the Windows **Start** menu, select **Programs | AccessData | FTK Imager** and then click on the **FTK Imager** menu item.

2. When the programs open, click on the **File** menu, and then click on the **Add Evidence Item** menu item.

3. When the **Select Source** dialog box appears, click on the option labeled **Logical Drive**. Click the **Next** button.

4. When the **Select Drive** dialog box appears, select the drive containing your floppy disk or CD. Click **Finish**.

5. When the **Create Image** dialog box appears, click **Add**.

6. When the **Select Image Destination** dialog box appears, specify where the image file will be stored by entering a path into the field labeled **Image destination folder**.

7. In the field labeled **Image filename**, enter the name you'd like to give the file without an extension. Click **Finish**.

8. When the **Create Image** dialog box appears again, click **Start**.

9. Wait while FTK Imager creates a forensic image file of the data on the drive you specified. This may take several minutes. Once the **Status** field indicates *Image created successfully*, click the **Close** button.

Recovering Data from Backups

An often-overlooked source of data recovery can be especially useful in cases where the cybercriminal might have been savvy enough to destroy data completely (as we'll discuss later in this chapter). This source is the backup(s) that the suspect or (if the suspect's computer is on a network) the system administrator might have made for fault-tolerance purposes. In many cases in which suspects have destroyed incriminating files, copies of those files still existed on the backup media. This is especially true in a corporate situation, where system administrators often automatically back up user data to a server each day.

Even when the suspect uses a home computer, it's worth checking for the existence of backups. Many people who have home computers, having been the victims of system failure in the past and having lost valuable data because of it, regularly back up their important files. Child pornographers often are emotionally attached to their kiddie porn collections and might have made extra copies in case of a disk failure. If a tape drive is attached to the system, there's a good chance it's used for backups. If a CD or DVD writer is installed, the suspect might have used it for archiving. You should request that the search warrant specify seizure of any tapes, disks, CD-ROMs, or other media commonly used to back up files, in addition to the computer equipment itself. Backups have saved the day in many cases when no evidence could be found on the computer's hard disk.

Finding Hidden Data

In many instances, data hidden on the hard disk can be very useful to investigators in building a case against a cybercrime suspect. Some of this data might be ambient data that was left behind when files were deleted or disks were repartitioned. There are also a number of places where data can be deliberately hidden by technically savvy criminals using a disk editor, steganographic software, and other methods. Finding, retrieving, and reconstructing this hidden data can be an extremely tedious process, but it's worth the effort if it results in evidence that can make or break a case.

Where Data Hides

A *disk sector* is a unit of space of a fixed size (such as 512 bytes). Older hard disks could have some wasted storage space on the outside tracks because of the way the disks are divided into sectors that contain an equal number of sectors per track. The discrepancy in circumference between the inside and outside tracks causes this wasted space. It is possible in some cases to hide data in the space between sectors on the larger outside tracks. This space is called the *sector gap*. Some data recovery services might be able to locate and retrieve data that is hidden in this gap.

Another place that data can be hidden is in the *slack area* caused by file sizes that don't exactly match the size of the clusters in which they are stored. Cluster sizes can vary, but anytime a file or portion of a file is smaller than the cluster size, the "leftover" bits in that cluster go unused. In file systems such as FAT16, where cluster sizes increase based on the partition size, this can result in a very large amount of "empty" space, and that space can be used to covertly store other bits of data. Data can be hidden here, unbeknownst to the user. Clusters are made up of sectors. When the file is too small to fill up the last sector in a file, DOS and Windows use random data from the system's memory buffers to make up the difference. This is called *RAM slack* and can result in data from the work session (the time since the computer was last booted) being stored on the disk in this slack space to "pad" the final sector. All sorts of data dumped from memory can be lurking in the slack space and could prove useful to the investigator. Any kind of disk (diskette, hard disk, and removable disk) is subject to slack. Computer forensic analysis tools such as those marketed by NTI can recover data hidden in slack areas.

Shadow data is created because the vertical and horizontal alignments of the mechanical heads that write to the disk are not exactly the same each time a write operation is performed. This means that even when data is overwritten, remnants of the old data could still be there. It is sometimes possible (although very time-consuming and expensive) to reconstruct the data from these remnants.

Detecting Steganographic Data

Steganography software hides files within other files, using empty space or the least significant bit to encode messages. For example, data can be hidden within an image file by slightly altering a single bit related to a particular pixel. If one pixel in the photo has a red component, represented by the binary number 10001100, the least significant bit (the last one) can be changed to a 1, making the binary 10001101. This will make that one pixel a tiny bit redder, which will not be noticeable to viewers. This creates one "hidden" bit, a 1. To create a 0, you would leave the least significant bit as it was. The entire file that you want to hide is broken up into its binary components, and these are then concealed in different parts of the photo image. Determining which pixels contain the hidden bits, and in what order, can be done by a random number generator that uses a key so that only someone who knows the key will be able to reconstruct the hidden message by retrieving the hidden bits in the correct order.

Several "antisteganography" programs on the market allow you to detect the presence of data that is hidden within other files using steganographic techniques. Examples of such software include Stego Suite, marketed by WetStone Technologies; for more information, see www.wetstonetech.com/pdf/DS_SS.pdf.

Detecting the presence of steganographic data is much easier than extracting the message itself. This is usually done by software that checks the statistical profile of an image and looks for statistical artifacts left by steganographic software. *Steganalysis* is the process of detecting steganography in files and rendering the covert messages useless.

For more information on this topic, see "Steganalysis: The Investigation of Hidden Information" at www.jjtc.com/pub/it98a.htm.

Methods for Hiding Files

Files can be hidden on a system in a number of ways. On DOS/Windows file systems, setting the hidden attribute (*–h* at the command line, or set in the File Properties dialog box in the GUI) will prevent the file from showing up in response to the *DIR* command at the command line or in the files list in Explorer if the default settings are in place in Folder Options | View. However, if the Show Hidden Files and Folders option button is enabled, these hidden files will still be displayed. On UNIX systems, files and directories with names that begin with a dot are hidden and are not displayed in response to the *ls* command unless you use the *–a* switch.

Another method for hiding files is known as *hiding in plain view*. Using this method, a cyber-criminal gives a file a name that makes it appear to be something it isn't—and something that the investigator would not be interested in. For example, a graphics file containing child pornography could be renamed to something like window.sys and stored in the Windows system directory. To the casual observer, it looks like just another operating system file. When the criminal wants to access it, he merely has to change the file extension back to .jpg or .gif and open it in any graphics viewer program.

Another way to hide files is to use areas of the hard disk that normally aren't visible. The Host Protected Area or Hidden Protected Area (HPA) is an area of the hard disk that normally isn't visible to an operating system. An HPA may be used to store utilities, diagnostic tools, or programs used when the computer is first powered up. Although it may seem insidious, many computer manufacturers use this space to store software. For example, IBM and LG notebooks both use an HPA to store system restore and recovery software. If this hidden partition of the hard disk exists, and is known to the user of the computer, it may be used to store illegal or sensitive materials that may be relevant to your case. Tools such as X-Ways Forensics, which we discussed in the previous chapter, will detect these protected areas, allowing you to access any data that may be stored there.

The Recycle Bin

Although it might seem obvious to technical experts that moving a file to the Recycle Bin or Trash does not even remove the file's pointers as deleting it does, many cybercriminals are not technical experts and could think that they have deleted evidence, when in fact it is still intact in the Recycle Bin. Of course, this is more likely to be true in the case of "nontechnical" cybercrimes such as child pornography or con-artist scams than network intrusions and other hacker activities. However, considering the level of technical knowledge required (or rather, not required) to launch attacks using the script- and click-kiddie methods, it never hurts to check. The evidence you need could be sitting right there waiting for you, easily restored with a single click of the mouse.

Locating Forgotten Evidence

A great deal of data is stored on computers automatically by application programs and/or the operating system. Some users are unaware of this stored data; others know about it but might forget to get rid of it when they are destroying evidence on a system. Depending on the nature of the offense, some of this data could be useful to the cybercrime investigator. Sources of forgotten evidence include Web caches, temporary (temp) files, swap/page files, and application logs. In the next sections, we look at how each of these sources can provide valuable evidentiary information in some cybercrime cases.

Web Caches and URL Histories

Web browsers are designed with performance in mind. Users want their Web pages to pop up in the browser as quickly as possible. One way to speed up access is to provide a way for the browser to get the file from the local computer's hard disk, rather than downloading it over a much slower Internet connection. For this reason, Web browsers by default *cache* the pages that a user visits, along with related graphics, sounds, and other embedded files. In other words, all this data is stored on the computer's hard disk so that if you visit the same page again, it can be quickly retrieved from the disk. These files are usually called *temporary Internet files* and are stored in a special folder, usually under the user's profile name, as shown in Figure 7.6. They provide a visual record of the sites that the user has visited recently. This information can be especially useful in child pornography cases or cases of terrorists who frequent certain Web sites.

Figure 7.6 Temporary Internet Files (the Web Cache), Which Can Provide Clues to the Web Sites a Computer User Has Recently Visited

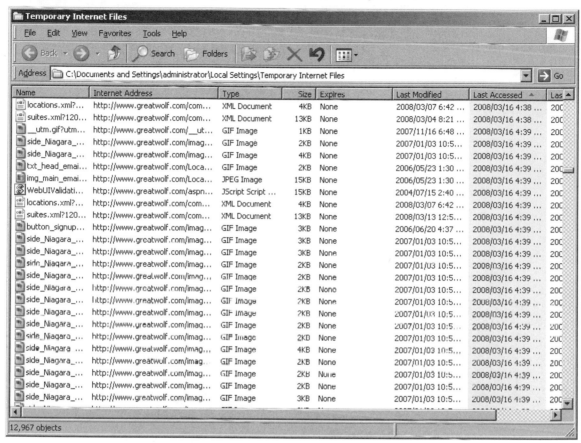

Another source of information about Web sites that have been visited is the History folder. Cybercriminals sometimes delete their temporary Internet files but forget to clear the history records. Unlike the Web cache, the History folder doesn't contain actual copies of the Web pages; instead, it contains a list of links (URLs) to those sites. On Windows machines using the Internet Explorer browser, these links are usually located in a folder named History under the user's profile name, as shown in Figure 7.7. (Separate Web caches and histories are maintained for every user who has a local account on the computer.)

Figure 7.7 The History Folder, Which Contains URLs for Recently Visited Web Sites

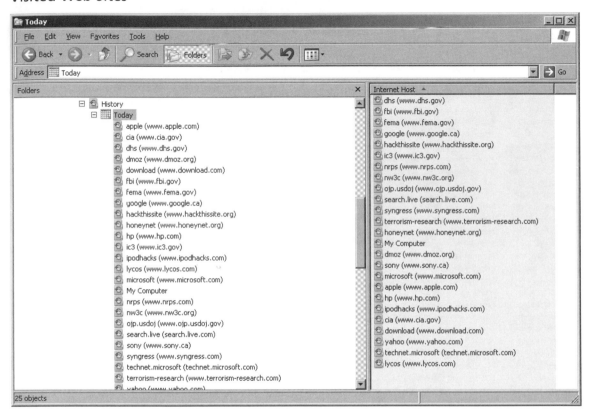

Temp Files

Applications such as Microsoft Word create temporary (temp) files on a system. These files are used for tracking changes made to the original and for recovery if the program crashes. Working on a Word document can result in dozens of temp files, usually stored in the same directory as the original .doc file. In theory, when you close the document or application, these temporary files are deleted, but this doesn't always happen. Even when they are "deleted" by the system, they are still on the disk until overwritten, like other "deleted" files, and can be recovered using tools designed for that purpose.

Other temporary files include those that are downloaded from the Internet or e-mail attachments that have been opened and saved in a Temp directory, usually located in the system root directory (the directory where the operating system files are located, such as WINDOWS or WINNT). These temporary files can be deleted when the system shuts down or reboots, which is another reason to image the disk *before* shutting down the system if at all possible.

NOTE

Temporary files often have the .tmp extension. A search for files with this extension can turn up a wealth of forgotten data, some of which might be useful as evidence.

Swap and Page Files

Most modern operating systems utilize a feature called *virtual memory*, which allows the system to "fool" applications into thinking the computer has more RAM than is actually installed. A portion of the hard disk is used to emulate additional memory and data is "swapped" from real physical memory to this holding space on disk as it's needed by the processor. On Windows *9x*, this data is held in a file called the *swap file*. On Windows NT, 2000, XP and Vista systems, it is called the *page file* because data is swapped in units called *pages*. Linux systems create a swap partition on the disk for this same purpose. These files are generally created automatically by the operating system.

These files contain all sorts of data, including e-mail, Web pages, word processing documents, and any other work that has been performed on the computer during the work session. Many computer users are either unaware of the existence of these files or don't really understand what they are, what they do, and what kind of data they contain. Some swap files are temporary and others are permanent, depending on the operating system in use and how it is configured. The files might be marked with the hidden attribute, which makes them invisible in the directory structure under default settings. Swap files are created by the operating system in a default location. Table 7.6 shows the swap filename and its default location for different Microsoft operating systems. Note that technically savvy users can change the location of the swap file or create additional swap/page files so that there are multiple virtual memory locations on a system.

Table 7.6 Swap Filenames and Locations

Operating System	Filename	Default Location
Windows 3.*x*	386SPART.PAR	Windows\System subdirectory or root directory of the drive designated in the virtual memory dialog box
Windows 9*x*	WIN386.SWP	Root directory of the drive designated in the virtual memory dialog box
Windows NT/2000/XP	PAGEFILE.SYS	Root directory of the drive on which the system root directory (WINNT by default) is installed

To find the location of the swap or page file, open the Virtual Memory dialog box. (This is also where a user can change the file's location.) For example, in Windows XP Professional, open the **System** applet from the **Control Panel**, click the **Advanced** tab, click the **Settings** button under **Performance**, then click the **Advanced** tab again, and click the **Change** button at the bottom of the page under **Virtual Memory**. This series of steps brings you to the Virtual Memory dialog box (at last!), and you can see the location of one or more page files, as shown in Figure 7.8.

Figure 7.8 Viewing the Location, Size, and Status of the Page File(s) on Windows XP Using the Virtual Memory Dialog Box

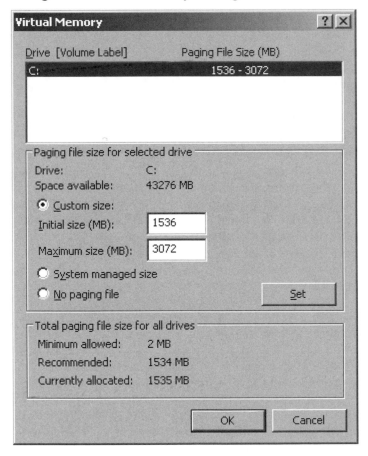

You can then navigate to the drive on which the file is stored and locate it there. Note, however, that the page file will not be visible unless you have unchecked the **Hide protected operating system files (recommended)** checkbox in the **Tools | Folder Options | View** advanced settings in Windows Explorer.

You can view the swap/page file with a utility such as DiskEdit, but much of the information is binary (0s and 1s) and not very usable. Special programs such as NTA Stealth and the Filter I "intelligent forensic editor" are designed to read swap file data and other *ambient* computer data.

Filter I uses a type of artificial intelligence (AI) to locate fragments of various types of files, including e-mail, chat conversations, newsgroup posts, and even network passwords and credit card and Social Security numbers. NTA Stealth is an upgrade to the Net Threat Analyzer tool, and is used to evaluate Internet browsing, download activity, and e-mail communications in ambient data for evidence related to illegal activities. Both of these software packages are marketed by NTI (www.forensics-intl.com). The company also makes text search and disk search programs that can search storage devices at the physical level and locate data that is stored between allocated partitions or text strings that are in unallocated space.

Defeating Data Recovery Techniques

At this point, some law enforcement officers might be wondering about the security of their own sensitive data, whether these same recovery techniques pose security threats to them, and whether and how they can protect against such threats. The bad news is that all this data lurking in unsuspected places can, indeed, pose a risk to the agency in the event that the wrong person gets control of law enforcement computers. The good news—in terms of protecting sensitive law enforcement data—is that there *are* ways to defeat data recovery methods. On the other hand, suspects can use the same techniques to cover their tracks and destroy evidence of their crimes. Thus, for both reasons, investigators need to be aware of the ways that data *can* be removed from a disk "once and for all."

Some of these data recovery techniques require physical access to the system, but others can be initiated over the network. In addition to the security methods that we discuss in Chapters 12 and 13, what can you do to ensure that confidential data doesn't remain on a disk after you're finished with it? In general, there are three ways to do this: overwriting, degaussing (demagnetizing), and physically destroying the disk.

NOTE

If disks that have been used as target disks for making bitstream copies of suspect disks in forensic examinations are to be reused, it is very important to completely wipe the disks between uses to prevent remnants of data from prior cases "bleeding" through and appearing to be evidence in the current case.

Overwriting the Disk

The term *data remanence* refers to the residual physical manifestations of data that have supposedly been deleted or erased. Many "disk-wiping" utilities available commercially and as freeware or shareware on the Internet claim to remove this remanence, from which the data can be reconstructed. These utilities work by writing over the unallocated space on the disk. Windows 2000, XP, and Vista include a command-line utility called CIPHER.EXE that, in addition to encrypting, decrypting, and managing encrypted files using the Encrypting File System (EFS), has a switch that overwrites data in unallocated clusters. These utilities attempt to fill the unallocated space with random binary values and can overwrite several times (which is necessary to overwrite the shadow data).

Tests of many of these utilities show that they often don't affect the data in file slack or alternate data streams and can leave remnants of shadow data. To be effective, overwriting must be done many times using alternating patterns, and still could leave some types of data behind. If you're serious about eliminating data remanence by the overwriting method, you should use a program that meets or exceeds the U.S. Department of Defense (DoD) security standards. Under these standards, the overwrite process must undergo at least three passes: One pass overwrites data with a character, another overwrites that pass with the complement of the first character overwrite, and a third write uses a random character. The process must also be verified.

An example of a disk-wiping program that meets DoD standards is Active@ KillDisk (www.killdisk.com). It is a popular product that companies use to overwrite any data on hard disks and other media, especially those that are being disposed of or resold. Other important products that meet DoD standards are DiskScrub and M-Sweep Pro Data Eliminator from NTI. M-Sweep Pro Data Eliminator was designed specifically for use on notebook systems but can also be used on desktop hard disks and removable disks. It overwrites the ambient data storage areas (file slack, unallocated file space, and so on). The sale of these products is restricted to law enforcement, U.S. medical facilities and hospitals, U.S. financial institutions, law and accounting firms, government agencies, and Fortune 1000 corporations.

NOTE

The best disk-wiping programs for FAT and NTFS file systems are DOS-based (command-line programs); Windows-based programs cannot generally eliminate the ambient data in obscure areas of the storage space.

Permanently Deleting Files

Drive wiping is a crucial component of all digital forensic examinations. Any drive that is not thoroughly wiped has to be considered suspect. Although many different tools are available to aid in this goal, we will explore the features of a couple of these in more detail.

PDWipe

PDWipe is capable of wiping large hard drives (in excess of 8.4 GB) in just less than 11 minutes. It will perform a declassification drive wipe in accordance with the NAVSO P5239-10 security standard. This wiping algorithm exceeds that specified by the DoD 5220.22-M specification for both "clearing" and "purging" sensitive information on hard drives.

PDWipe provides the option of specifying a character code other than 0x00 when wiping a drive. It also offers the ability to wipe the drive using a random pattern. PDWipe can also record Logical Sector Addresses, and cylinder-head-sector (CHS) addresses for Int13 and Int13x geometries at the beginning of the sectors being wiped. This is useful when diagnosing architectural discrepancies when moving a drive between systems or validating imaging utilities.

PDWipe can process all drives in a system such that *all* drives can be wiped with a single program operation. If desired, PDWipe will generate a report of the wiping activity performed on a system. PDWipe can also verify that the contents of a specified number of randomly chosen sectors have been wiped. If wipe verification is requested, PDWipe will also automatically verify the first and last sectors on the drive.

PDWipe will support any drive which is accessible to your system through the Int13 or the Microsoft/IBM Int13 extensions. Basic Input Output Systems (BIOSes) typically provide this capability for all attached IDE or EIDE devices. In addition, most SCSI adapters offer the ability to support attached devices through Int13 as well.

Darik's Boot and Nuke (DBAN)

Darik's Boot and Nuke (DBAN) is a free tool available from http://dban.sourceforge.net. It is a self-contained boot floppy that securely wipes the hard disks of most computers. DBAN will automatically and completely delete the contents of any hard disk that it can detect, which makes it an appropriate utility for bulk or emergency data destruction.

DBAN can ensure due diligence in computer recycling, a way of preventing identity theft if you want to sell a computer, and a good way to totally clean a Microsoft Windows installation of viruses and spyware. DBAN prevents or thoroughly hinders all known techniques of hard disk forensic analysis.

Degaussing or Demagnetizing

Another way to get rid of the data remaining on a disk is to create a very strong magnetic field that is capable of reducing the magnetic state of the media to zero. This process is called *degaussing*, and the device that generates the magnetic field is called a *degausser*. Degaussers work either by applying an alternating magnetic field using AC power or by applying a unidirectional field using DC power. Handheld permanent magnets can also be used to degauss some types of magnetic media (diskettes and hard disk platters; they are not usually used to degauss magnetic tapes). There are different types of magnetic tape, based on the coercivity of the media. It is important to have the proper type of degausser that matches the tape type, to purge all the data from the tape.

NOTE

When magnetic media is exposed to extreme temperatures or stored for long periods of time, it becomes more resistant to degaussing.

Physically Destroying the Disk

In cases where it is extremely important that there be no possibility that data remaining on a disk could ever be reconstructed—for example, in a national security situation in which classified data was stored on the disk—it might be preferable to physically destroy the disk. This can be done in several ways. The most effective include:

- Pulverization (completely crushing or grinding the disk down to powder)
- Incineration (burning the disk to ashes)
- Abrasion (using a sander or emery wheel to completely remove the surface of the disk)
- Acid (applying a concentrated solution of hydriodic acid to the surface of the disk)

Destroying CDs and DVDs

The fear of identity theft has increased the number of people who shred their bills and other paperwork in shredders. However, although many people shred their documents, they will simply throw away the CDs and DVDs containing their data. As a result, anyone who wants to access the data can simply pull the CD/DVD out of the trash. To prevent others from gaining access to programs, financial information, or other data stored on this media, CD/DVD shredders can be used to destroy the disks.

Although once considered business equipment, the cost of shredders has dropped to the point where any security-minded person can afford a CD/DVD shredder for home use. As shown in Figure 7.9, the DVD/CD Shredder Plus DS from Aleratec (www.aleratec.com) is a crosscut paper shredder, but is also a DVD, CD, and credit card strip cut shredder. Using this tool, a person or business can cut credit cards, ID cards, or other plastic cards into strips to prevent identity theft, destroy documents, and slice CDs/DVDs into pieces. Although you might think using this device would be noisy and disruptive to an office or home, it destroys unwanted CDs and DVDs quickly, quietly, and efficiently.

Figure 7.9 Aleratec DVD/CD Shredder Plus DS Destroying a CD

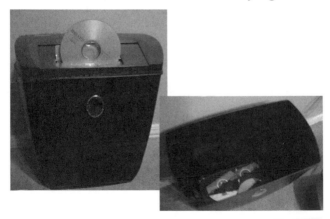

Summary

As we saw in this chapter, you can delete data from a system in a number of ways. Operating systems provide commands to remove data from a hard disk or other media, such as menu items or commands used from a Command Prompt. When a file is deleted using the Del key or commands in compliant programs, it will generally be sent to the Recycle Bin. When this occurs, the user can recover the file him- or herself. If the file has been emptied from the Recycle Bin or deleted using other methods, you may need to use tools to recover the file. Even if an entire partition is deleted, and the volume is formatted, this doesn't mean the data is gone. As we discussed, data recovery and computer forensic tools may still be able to retrieve the data from a system.

Although many data recovery tools are available on the market, not all of them should be used for computer forensics. Disk imaging software that creates a bitstream image of the disk should be used so that an exact duplicate of the data is created. As a result, computer forensic software can be used to analyze the data, without worry of modifying the original data.

Any image files that are created should be made on forensically sterile media, and any disks that are reused should be overwritten using special software or demagnetized using a degausser. Hard disks that are to be disposed of should similarly have their data overwritten or destroyed. To ensure that the image files stored on CDs or DVDs are properly destroyed, they should be destroyed using a CD/DVD shredder once a retention date has been met.

Frequently Asked Questions

Q: I have restored a deleted file, but when I open it, the file is empty. What happened?

A: The file is probably zero length. Because the file size is zero, an empty file is created. If clusters were used by other files, so that it was overwritten. Because so much data was overwritten by another file, there was nothing to recover.

Q: I am preparing to back up data on my hard disk using a partition recovery tool. What data should I back up?

A: You should make an image of all data on the disk so that this can be restored in the event of a problem. The image file could be stored on a network server or another disk, where it will be safe until you need it. You should also back up the MBR, partition table, and boot sectors, which can be restored after a problem occurs.

Q: If I am unsure what has occurred and think that the case may never go to court. Do I still need to image the drive?

A: You never know what may occur. Imaging the drive is useful if something does turn out to be wrong. Also, being able to demonstrate that you use imaging tools as a standard practice will make it more difficult for your procedures to be attacked in court, even on other unrelated cases.

Chapter 8

iPod, Cell Phone, PDA, and BlackBerry Forensics

Topics we'll investigate in this chapter:

- iPod/MP3 Forensics
- Cell Phone Forensics
- PDA Forensics
- BlackBerry Forensics

☑ Summary

☑ Frequently Asked Questions

Introduction

Consider any popular technology, and most likely it was introduced as an expensive status symbol, but within a few years became something so affordable that almost everyone had one…or at least wanted one. Today, portable music players, cell phones, and devices such as personal digital assistants (PDAs) have become commonplace. However, just as your friends, colleagues, and family may have one or more of these devices, criminals also use them for more illicit purposes. Increasingly, drug dealers and other criminals use these communication devices to store information about customers and associates. As we'll see, the iPod is becoming a medium to store much more than just music.

Because cell phones, PDAs, and BlackBerry devices also provide the ability to access the Internet, they are as much a source of evidence in cybercrime cases as a computer is. Although a laptop or desktop computer may not have any illicit e-mails or illegal files downloaded from the Internet, these other technologies may have been used to transmit or receive the evidence.

This chapter will demonstrate how iPods and other MP3 players can be used to store any type of data or information that can be stored on a regular personal computer. The data can be encrypted, hidden, and easily manipulated by the user. In this chapter, we will explore the ways to store, access, and find data stored on iPods, and the tricks people use to hide malicious data. We will also discuss the concept of conducting a forensic investigation on data that has been read, stored, or manipulated on some type of mobile device. The techniques for investigating a mobile device are similar to those we would use to investigate more traditional storage devices; however, there are some notable differences that we need to be aware of while collecting potential evidence.

iPod/MP3 Forensics

In the late 1990s, digital music began to gain in popularity. The MP3 music format was portable and the sound quality was closer to that of compact discs than the analog tapes that had been used for decades prior could ever be. The MP3 format used compression so that the files were small in size and you could easily store and listen to them on a personal computer.

Before the paint had even dried on MP3 technology, people had figured out ways to cheat the system. The new MP3 technology led to two of the first file-transferring networks: Napster and Gnutella, which allowed users to share and download music without purchasing it, leading to government and retail industry outrage and uproar. This was a gray area at first, because there were no laws on the books about file transferring or sharing from peer-to-peer (P2P) networks and individual users. Eventually Napster, Gnutella, and most other similar networks were shut down by government authority.

Soon after MP3 technology caught on, the first digital media players became available, but there was still not a commercially viable way to legally purchase and download MP3s until 2000–2001, when Apple released the iPod and its iTunes online retail download service. Suddenly consumers had a very good way to legally purchase music and transfer it to their iPods or other digital media players. The digital music industry boomed, and since then it has become a powerful segment of the music business as a whole.

Although there are many different brands and types of digital media devices, Apple's iPod accounts for more than 80 percent of the digital media market. Far be it to say that there aren't other MP3 players on the market. Many are available, holding the equivalent of a CD's worth of music to dozens of gigabytes of data. The storage capacities of these devices increase every year or so, with the price constantly dropping. An example of this is the MP3 player depicted in Figure 8.1, which holds 512 MB of data and was purchased at a toy store for $15.

Figure 8.1 The Nextar Digital MP3 Player

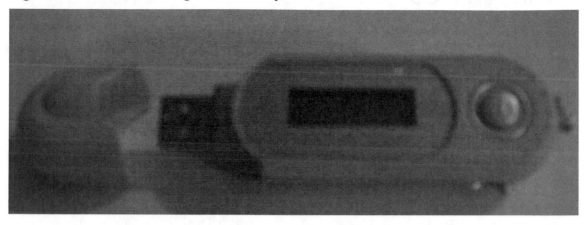

As shown in Figure 8.2, when you plug the MP3 player into a computer's Universal Serial Bus (USB) port, you can view the data as any other type of removable media. Plus, you can store files on the MP3 player, even if they aren't music files. Saving such files on the MP3 player won't affect the ability for other music files to play on the device. The exception, of course, would be if you modified the names and extensions of the files, making them appear as MP3 files, even if they are documents or image files (as in the case of renaming a JPEG to MUSIC.MP3).

Figure 8.2 Files Stored on an MP3 Player

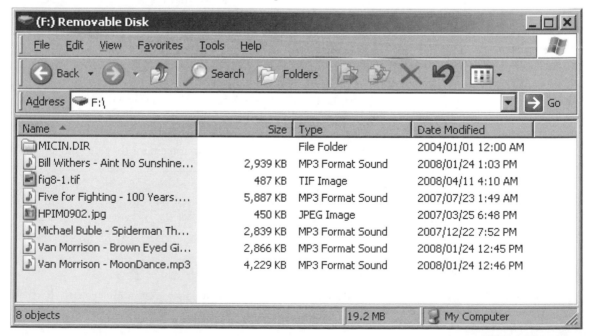

Why Is an iPod Considered Alternative Media?

iPods have standard file systems of either Apple's HFS+ or Microsoft's FAT32, which we will explore in greater detail later. These file systems are static because they are not continually transferring data like other types of file systems, such as cell phones, for instance. Because of their static nature, performing forensics on MP3 players is not substantially different from performing forensics on a regular computer hard drive. The difference between the two that makes an MP3 player an alternative media device is that its primary function is that of a music player. Even though MP3 players have always been able to store files like USB flash drives have, only recently have iPods evolved into photo storage and video player devices. Because they are used for entertainment purposes, iPods might not be thought of as data repositories containing evidence.

Imaging and Hashing

The first step in iPod forensics is to create an image of a device and hash it to ensure integrity. As we've discussed in previous chapters, with digital evidence, we do not work on original evidence. Instead, we attempt to create a duplicate of the evidence. This duplicate can be an exact replica of all data contained on the device. There are two types of images: physical images and logical images. A *physical image* is a bit-for-bit copy of all data contained on a device, and a *logical image* is an image of the file system exactly as it appears on a device. For forensic purposes, a physical image is always the preferred type.

To preserve the integrity of the data, forensic examiners perform what is called a "hash" at every step of the way. A *hash* is a one-way mathematical algorithm that acts as a "fingerprint" of all data contained on a device. This ensures that the data has not been altered from its original state at any point during the imaging process. You can perform a hash by using a tool such as md5sum. First you apply the tool to a file, and it returns a number that corresponds to a particular algorithm. Then the imaging is performed and you rerun the md5sum tool. If any part of that file is altered after you rerun the md5sum tool, the number will change, signifying a potential loss of evidence integrity. This will ensure that the data you are working on has not been altered.

Another way to preserve the data is to use a write blocker. Write-blocking a device will protect the device from any manipulation. It will essentially guard your evidence from being written to during imaging. This way, if you happen to make an error, your evidence will be protected. A write blocker typically comprises visible external hardware, such as Logicube's Forensic Talon or Intelligent Computer Solutions' (ICS) Solo III. A hard drive is physically attached to one of these devices, which will ensure that no writes can be made to the evidence contained on that drive.

Because iPods do not have Integrated Drive Electronics (IDE) interfaces and they use FireWire or USB, they cannot be synced to standard IDE imaging devices such as the Solo III without a USB adapter. Similarly, an iPod should not be synced into a forensic tower and imaged using a Windows-based tool. When you plug any USB or FireWire device into a Windows machine, Windows will "touch" the device and change the files contained on the device. One of the most important rules that forensic examiners must follow is not to alter evidence, including date and time stamps on evidence.

Hardware versus Nonhardware Imaging

As we saw in Chapter 6, you can image data using hardware and software operating systems. It is highly recommended that if you have a hardware device that has a USB and/or FireWire interface, you should image the data using the hardware device. Hardware devices write-block very well and they leave little room for error. An excellent hardware device is the Tableau Forensic USB Bridge, but others like it are available on the market. They are relatively inexpensive and user-friendly. A nonhardware solution, such as an operating system like Linux or DOS, can be configured to not automatically mount a device when imaging. Linux is not a substitution for a write blocker, and it is susceptible to human error.

Removing the Hard Drive

It is possible to obtain an image by removing the hard drive from an iPod if the iPod does not use flash memory. See the section "Types of iPods," later in this chapter, to see which ones contain hard drives. You can remove a hard drive from an iPod, but this is prohibitive because removing a hard drive could break the device.

Acquiring Data

Once you have write-protected the device, you can then use any number of tools to create an image. You also can use on the device EnCase and other software used to create a forensic image of hard disks. Another method you can use, but only if absolutely necessary, is to employ an operating system such as Linux for imaging. You can configure Linux to not automatically mount a USB device when the device is plugged into your forensic tower. This means that in theory, an iPod would remain untouched with files being unaffected when plugged in. This method allows for no write protection, however. If you make a mistake, you could destroy your evidence. We suggest that if you use this method, you employ the Linux command *dd* or the DCFL lab version, called *DCFLDD*, to image the device.

DD

The *dd* command is a common UNIX command that is also used in Linux, and is used to convert and copy data. A version of DD is also available for systems running Windows, which is available from either http://unxutils.sourceforge.net or www.cygwin.com. It allows you to copy a hard disk to another disk drive or to magnetic tape, or vice versa. In doing so, data is transferred byte for byte, creating an exact mirror image. The syntax for using this command is:

```
dd <options>
```

As you can see from this syntax, options are used with this command to specify different aspects of converting and copying data. For example, if you wanted to copy the contents of one disk to another, you would use the command with the *if* (input file) and *of* (output file) options:

```
dd if=/dev/hda of=/dev/hdy
```

Similarly, if you were going to back up the disk to an image on a hard disk, you could use the following example:

```
dd if=/dev/hda of=/path/to/image
```

You can use additional options with the *dd* command to specify the size of blocks to copy, whether data is to be converted when copying, and other options, as shown in Table 8.1.

Table 8.1 dd Options

Option	Description
If=inputfile	Specifies where to input data from (file or device)
of=outputfile	Specifies where to output data to (file or device)
ibs=bytes	Number of bytes to read at a time
obs=bytes	Number of bytes to write at a time
bs=bytes	Number of bytes to read and write. This is used instead of *ibs* and *obs*, and specifies the same number of bytes to use for both input and output.
bs=bytes	Number of bytes to convert at a time
skip=blocks	Specifies to skip blocks in the input file before copying
seek=blocks	Specifies to skip blocks in the output file before copying
count=blocks	Copies blocks from the input file, instead of everything at the end of the file
conv=conversion	Specifies to convert the input file before copying to an output file. Conversion methods include: *ascii,* which converts EBCDIC to ASCII ebcdic, which converts ASCII to EBCDIC ibm, ASCII to alternate EBCDIC *block,* which replaces the input newline with a padding of spaces to fit the size of *cbs* *unblock,* which replaces trailing-space characters in data sets of size *cbs* with newline characters *lcase,* which converts uppercase characters to lowercase *ucase,* which converts lowercase characters to uppercase *swap,* which swaps every pair of input bytes *noerror,* which ignores read errors *notrunc,* which specifies not to truncate the output file *sync,* which pads every input block to the size of *ibs* with null bytes if it's shorter than the specified size

Using DD to Create an Image

Using DD to create an image of an iPod or MP3 player involves several steps. The steps to perform this method follow.

The first thing that you see is the *fdisk* output of the device, with two partitions. In this case, the device /dev/sdd corresponds to the iPod device which is the target of the imaging process. The first entry in fdisk's output for /dev/hda corresponds to the hard drive of the host computer used in the imaging operation and can be safely ignored (see Figure 8.3).

Figure 8.3 fdisk Output

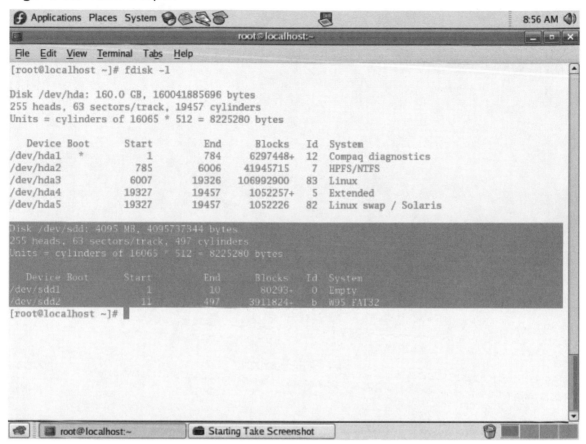

It is important to remember that the whole point of imaging in this way is to not mount the device. You can do everything you need to image the device without mounting.

The next step is to collect the MD5 hash of the device. You can perform this step in multiple ways, such as using another hashing tool or outputting an MD5 file to another directory. Figure 8.4 shows the command syntax for running the MD5 checksum utility md5sum on the target device /dev/sdd and storing the result in the file /root/ipod.before.md5.

Figure 8.4 Collecting an MD5 Hash

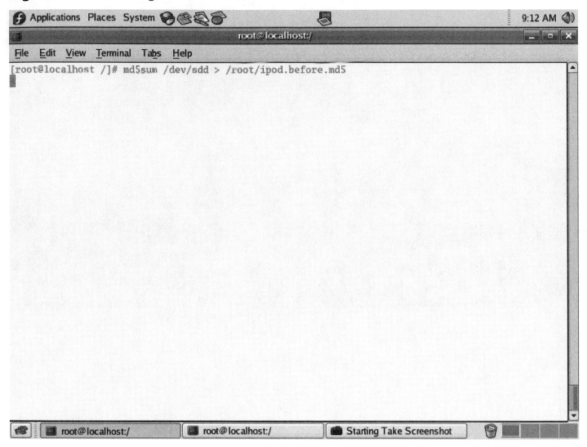

Next, you view the /root/ipod.md5 file to make sure the hash is valid (see Figure 8.5). In forensics, it is good to double-check your work at every point, especially when there is no hardware write protection.

Figure 8.5 The more Command Displaying the Contents of the File to the Screen

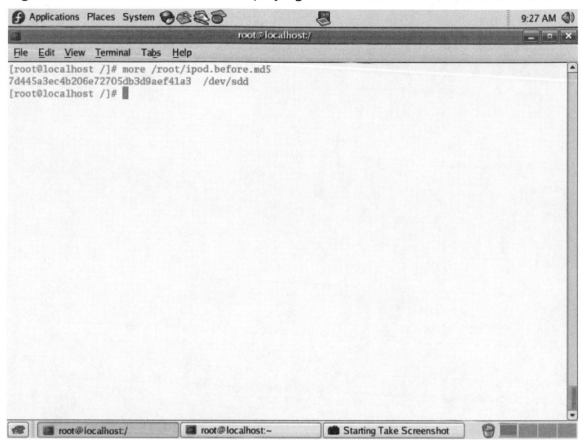

The next step is to create an image file from the device. This example uses the Linux *dd* command to image the data (see Figure 8.6). The *BS* option stands for "block size." Block size can change as desired, and has no impact on the data copied, except to optimize the throughput rate of the copy by copying that many bytes on each copy operation. The next two commands are the input file and the output file. It is important to double-check that an iPod device is the input file and not the output file. Putting the iPod device as the *of* parameter could alter the contents of the evidence drive!

Figure 8.6 Imaging a Device

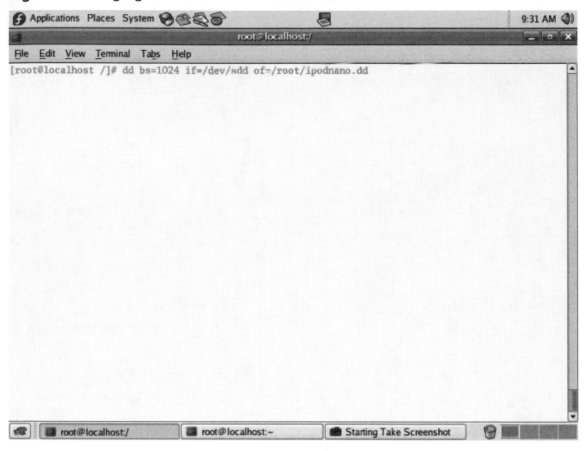

Figure 8.7 is an example of a completed *dd* function.

Figure 8.7 A Completed dd Function

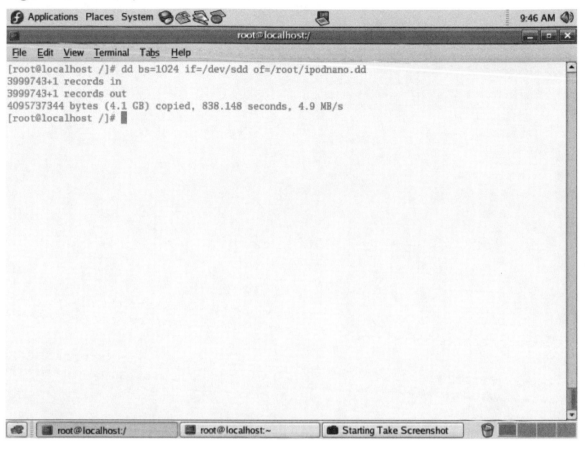

After the image is complete, you would then perform another hash to ensure that the data has not been changed. As shown in Figure 8.8, by comparing the two hashes, you can then see that the data has not changed.

Figure 8.8 Comparing the Two Hashes

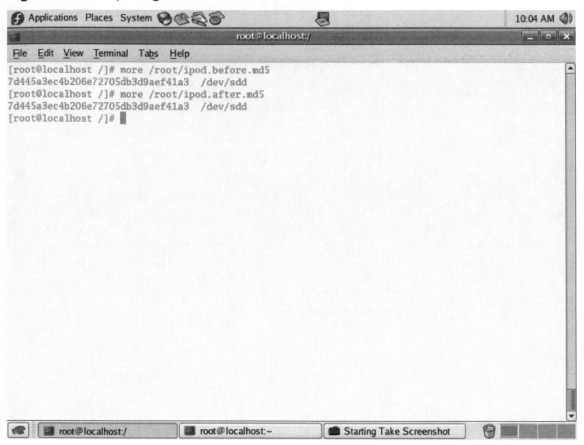

As the previous example shows, the before and after hashes of the iPod device are the same, which means nothing on the evidence drive was altered. Additionally, a hash of the forensic copy should be made to ensure that the hash of the image file is the same as that of the iPod. This proves that the image contains the exact same data as the iPod and that the "dd" of the drive worked correctly.

Registry Keys

If you are using a Windows-based imaging tool such as Guidance Software's EnCase, you can use a key in the Windows Registry to write-block a USB device that is plugged into a forensic tower. This will keep Windows from writing to evidence. Doing a Web search on "write-blocking USB device" will give further information on the steps necessary to carry out this procedure.

It is important to remember that using Linux or a Registry key edit for imaging is a last resort. It is always better to use a hardware write-blocking device. You can find many guides online that will detail the steps you need to follow if you choose to take this route. You can also go to www.windowsitpro.com/windowsstorage/Article/ArticleID/44380/44380.html.

Types of iPods

iPods come in many different physical and firmware versions. The first generation of iPods became available to consumers in October 2001. They had a storage capacity of up to 10 GB. Apple has introduced many subsequent generations of the iPod. With each new generation, features became enhanced, including the addition of color screens, and video storage and playback capability. The storage capacity increased as well. Newer iPods can have storage capacities of up to 80 GB, using a Toshiba 1.8 hard drive.

The iPod Mini debuted in January 2004. The Mini was the first iPod available in various colors and was substantially smaller than other models. Storage capacity for the Mini was up to 6 GB, using a 1-inch Hitachi Microdrive.

The iPod Nano was the new version of the Mini. It was even sleeker and smaller and came in either black or white. Current Nano models have a storage capacity of up to 8 GB, using flash memory. The Nano has the ability to store and show digital photographs and video via a color screen.

The iPod Shuffle appeared in January 2005. The Shuffle used flash memory instead of a hard drive. The first Shuffle was smaller than a pack of gum. Unlike the other iPod models, it had no LCD display. The second-generation Shuffle was even smaller than its predecessor.

File Types Supported

Currently, iPods support the following file types: Advanced Audio Coding (AAC), Protected AAC, MPEG Audio Layer III (MP#), Variable bit rate MP# (MP# VBR), Audible Audiobook, Apple Lossless, Audio Interchange File Format (AIFF), Windows Audio, and Compact Disc Digital Audio, JPG, JPEG, TIF, TIFF, GIF, PNG, BMP, PSD, SGI, MPEG-4, and H.264.

File Systems

A file system is what organizes the files that are accessed by a computer's operating system and other software installed on the machine. We discussed file systems at length in Chapter 4. Just as computers may use different file systems, devices such as MP3 players also use various file systems to access files. The file system used needs to be one that's supported by the computer that will be used to copy music and other files to the MP3 player.

The iPod uses two standard file systems: Microsoft's FAT32 and Apple's HFS+. The FAT32 file system is compatible with Apple Macintoshes and Windows PCs. HFS+ is writeable only with Macintoshes. If a user has an iPod formatted with FAT32 and both a Macintosh and a Windows-based PC, he can read and write to the iPod using both file systems. Such a user can also write and read to the iPod using Linux. The iPod is essentially a storage device and you can configure it to use almost any file system. I have used the extended 2 and 3, as well as FAT16 file systems on my iPods.

"Hacking Tools" and Encrypted Home Directories

Because an iPod or other MP3 players can be used to store data other than music files, it follows suit that they can also be loaded with hacking tools or malicious software. For example, by repartitioning an iPod Shuffle, you can create enough space to install a bootable Linux distribution that contains various "hacking tools," including the popular Metasploit. The iPod control folder is left intact, along with all of the other folders needed for the iPod to function normally. By plugging the iPod into another machine, you can then boot it into Linux and use Metasploit or another hacking tool to break into another machine and access its data. Even if an iPod appears to act like it should, it may not in fact be what it seems.

Mojopac is another hacking tool for use with the Windows operating system. Mojopac allows a hacker to use an iPod as a virtual Windows desktop. Plugging an iPod into the USB port on a Windows computer copies the applications on that computer's desktop and allows the iPod to become a working virtual machine. For more information or to purchase this tool, go to www.mojopac.com.

Another hacking technique using iPods is called "slurping." Slurping uses a tool called Slurp that captures documents, spreadsheets, and other files from the desktop of a computer using an iPod via the computer's USB port. This can be useful or malicious. For example, a malicious user could ask you whether she can use your computer to charge up her iPod using a USB port on your computer. Once the iPod is synced to the computer, Slurp captures all the documents and spreadsheets on your computer's desktop. You can find the original article and code at www.sharp-ideas.net/pod_slurping.php.

Evidence: Normal versus Not Normal

When conducting an exam, forensic examiners need to know the distinction between normal data files and evidence that is not normal. Depending on the firmware and version of a particular iPod, there may be some variance in this determination throughout an analysis. For example, on older iPods, the song-naming convention displays the entire name of a song plus the music file extension, whereas on newer iPods songs are displayed with a four-letter code in addition to the file extension.

In Figure 8.9, you see the main directory structure of an iPod Nano, which contains the iPod_Control, Device, iTunes, Music, and Artwork main directories. The New Folder icon is not typical.

Figure 8.9 An iPod Nano's Directory Structure

The Device folder contains files with some important information about the iPod, such as the firmware version and serial number. One of the files that forensic examiners should note is the iTunes DB file, which provides information about music files, including their file type, their music category, and the location on the device. This file is controlled by the iTunes software (see Figure 8.10). If a user manually moved a file onto an iPod, it would not be listed in the iTunes DB file. The file is found in the iPod_Control/iTunes directory.

Figure 8.10 An Example of the iTunes DB

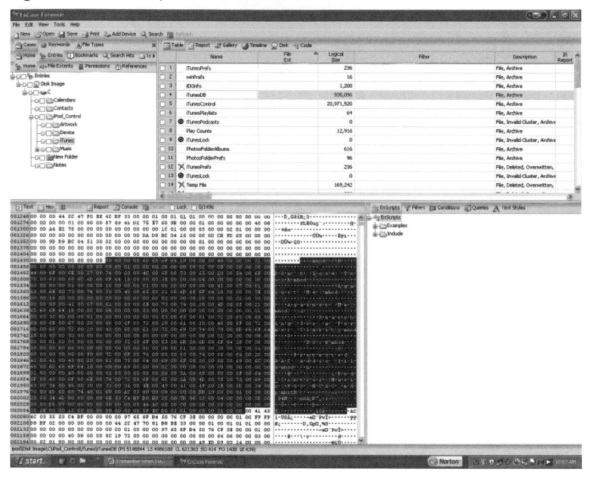

The iPod Shuffle has a file called iTunes SD, which provides MP3 location and song title information. The shuffle is the only iPod which contains this file. The iPod_Control directory is the control center of an iPod. It contains the Music and iTunes directories. This is where all music files are stored by default. All music files are dispersed into various directories, each named F##. Further investigation of the directories reveals the actual music files themselves. Newer versions of iTunes will condense MP3 or other digital-music-formatted songs into four-letter codes followed by an extension, as shown in Figure 8.11, and as discussed earlier.

Figure 8.11 An Example of an MP3 File on an iPod

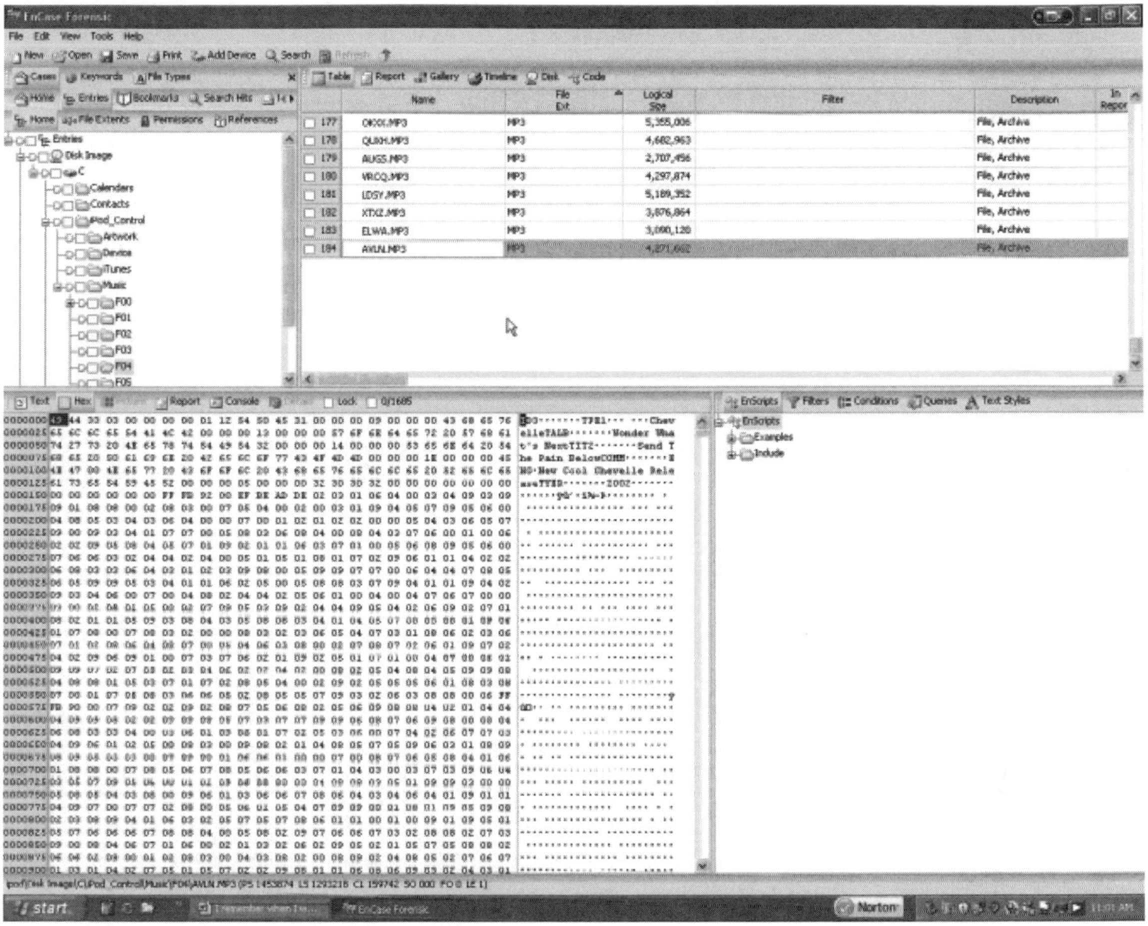

When you are looking at digital photos or video files on an iPod, it is important to understand that the photos or videos themselves may be important evidence. The evidence could reside in plain sight on the iPod, or it could be hidden inside folders. For example, in a child pornography case, photo or video evidence might be in the default photo and video directories. Further investigation might be necessary to uncover hidden evidence.

Other directories are the Contacts, Podcasts, and Notes directories. Different versions of iPods have slightly different directories. For example, the iPod Shuffle has the Shuffle DB but does not have a picture-viewing directory. If there are photos in a Shuffle directory, those photos were placed on the device manually, not using the iTunes software.

Uncovering What Should Not Be There

Just because an iPod has been manipulated or changed from its factory configuration does not necessarily mean that suspicious activity is occurring. Many people like to change or hack their iPods. Sometimes it can be innocent, but other times it can be a telltale sign of malicious activity.

Suspicious items to look for are things such as mismatched file extensions. An example is a .jpeg file with an .mp3 extension. Most forensic tools are able to detect such discrepancies by using signature analysis tools. These tools find files that have a header that is different from the extension. You can configure most forensic tools to add custom file signatures.

Other suspicious items are hidden or improperly named files, which include files named something innocuous—for example, a photo that is named to look like an MP3 file. Additionally, files that should arouse suspicion could include those with blatantly outrageous names, such as "hax0r."

Too many partitions indicate that an iPod is not set to the factory default and should be looked at carefully. A file system other than the standard FAT32 or HFS+ installed on an iPod could indicate suspicious activity.

For example, the image in Figure 8.12 appears to contain a normal iPod directory structure. However, there are a few unusual items that bear notice, such as a Knoppix directory and the syslinux.cfg and ldlinux.sys files, which indicate that this iPod has some form of Linux on it. Also of note is the framework-2.5 directory. This directory contains the Metasploit hacking tool which you can find at www.metasploit.com. In this case, it happens to be Damn Small Linux (DSL), a very small, bootable version of the Linux operating system. There is also a slurp-audit directory, which is very suspicious.

Figure 8.12 A Suspicious iPod

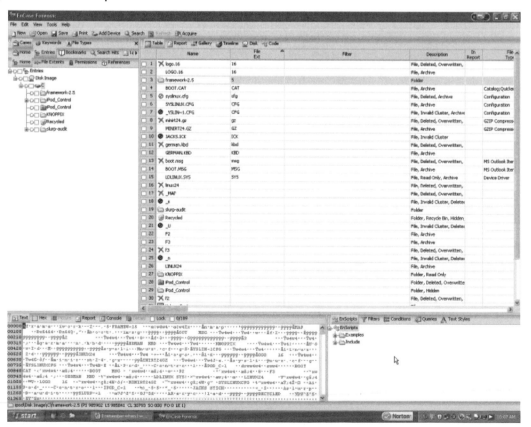

Another tactic that users employ to disguise files is to insert text within a music file. A hidden message such as "The cow jumps over the moon at noon" might be inserted into an MP3 file. The MP3 will still play normally, which makes it difficult to detect. In this case, the best way to detect text within an MP3 file is through keyword searches. It is also possible to get hashes of songs from Apple and compare them to the song hashes on the suspect device. This will not show up on signature analysis because the actual file header will still match its extension.

Yet another way to hide photos is to make them cover art. With the color iPods, users can match cover art to music files. Default cover art is often included in songs purchased from iTunes. There are also Web sites that have current cover art. Users have the option of changing the cover art to suit their preferences, making it a good place to hide bad photos.

On the Scene

iPods for Storing Illegal Material

At a conference, a colleague had a conversation with a federal agent about a child pornography case that he had worked on. He and his colleagues had raided the suspect's home as usual, but noticed that the suspect was strangely unalarmed and even smirking as the agents copied all the data from his computers. He continuously proclaimed his innocence. The agent remembered a presentation about iPods being used to store data and noticed that the suspect had an iPod on his desk. According to the warrant served on the suspect, the agents were permitted to seize all electronic equipment capable of storing data. The agent picked up the iPod, and suddenly the suspect's demeanor and attitude changed—he turned pale and became agitated. Before the raid was finished, the suspect had confessed that he routinely erased his computers' hard drives after transferring all of his child pornography photographs to his iPod. The evidence resulted in a conviction.

Analysis Tools

Forensic examiners can use almost any forensic tool that supports FAT32 or HFS+ for analyzing iPods, including Guidance Software's EnCase, AccessData's FTK, Brian Carrier's Sleuth Kit, and Paraben's P2. All of these tools utilize similar functionality to carry out analyses. All have a relatively intuitive user interface. The Sleuth Kit is primarily for more advanced users and runs only on the UNIX/Linux platform. All of these tools are commercially available; the Sleuth Kit is downloadable free of charge. Not all of these tools will support the HFS+ file system, so users may be limited by particular file system parameters. All of these tools are capable of rendering image files and text files, and they have keyword search capability. A forensic examiner would use these tools in the same manner as he or she would in performing a static hard-drive analysis.

Cell Phone Forensics

The terms *mobile phones*, *cellular phones*, and *wireless phones* are interchangeable terms for the portable handheld devices that allow for wireless communication, and that have become common household items in the twenty-first century. They are so common that according to a 2006 survey by Pew Research Center (http://pcwsocialtrends.org/pubs/?chartid=203), 74 percent of people had a cell phone, with equal numbers (49 percent) considering them a necessity or a luxury. More people considered this a necessity than other technologies such as cable or satellite TV (33 percent) or high-speed Internet (29 percent), and slightly less (51 percent) than a home computer. In fact, according to this survey, the number of people who had a cell phone was 1 percent higher than those who had a home computer! When you consider these statistics, it makes sense that performing forensic services on cell phones is a must for modern computer forensic technicians.

In addition to the primary function of providing voice communication, cell phones can also provide a wide variety of other features, including:

- Video calling (communication with live video)
- E-mail
- Internet access
- Text messaging using Short Message Service (SMS)
- The ability to send photos and video using Multimedia Message Service (MMS)
- Built-in digital cameras and camcorders
- MP3 player features

How Cell Phones Work

Cell phones work by connecting to a cellular network, which people pay a subscription fee to join. The cellular network is a wireless digital/radio network that is made up of cells that are served by transceivers called *base stations*. These base stations are connected to the public switched telephone network (PSTN) the same as a normal landline phone, allowing the calls to and from your wireless phone to be sent to any phone, regardless of whether it's part of the cellular network.

Cell phones use *Subscriber Identity Modules* (SIM) or *SIM cards*, which are smart cards, to store information about the subscriber to the cellular network. Because the card stores information about the cell phone subscriber, it allows cell phone users to switch phones by removing the card and placing it in a new phone. The information in the card is used to authenticate the user to the network.

Cell phones may also use memory storage cards called *flash media*, which allow pictures, video, music, applications, and other data to be stored on the cell phone. Some of the most common cards are Compact Flash, Smart Media, and Memory Stick cards.

Acquiring Evidence from Cell Phones

You can acquire data from cell phones using a combination of software and hardware. Readers are used to access data from flash cards and SIM cards, and are relatively inexpensive. Forensic software such as EnCase can then be used to acquire evidence from the card as it would other types of media.

In addition to this, other products are available that are specifically designed for cell phones and other mobile devices, such as PDAs and BlackBerry devices (which we'll discuss later in this chapter).

Readers, readers, readers!

Many of the card types inherent to cell phone technology (notably SIM) are proprietary—to decipher SIM contents, custom forensic software/hardware packages are usually required. For the more common data storage card types (common form factors for PDAs, cameras, cell phones, and so on) a high-quality 15-in-one card reader is a good tool to add to a forensic toolkit; forensically sound card media readers are distributed via forensic vendors such as Digital Intelligence.

Write Protect Card Reader

An example of one such card reader is the Write Protect Card Reader from ICS. It transfers data from digital cameras, digital camcorders, PDAs, MP3 players, and digital voice recorders to a laptop or desktop computer. It can read several types of flash memory while blocking any writes to it. It is a small, palm-size package with a simple USB 1.1/2.0 connection and requires no external power.

Forensic Software

Because of the increasing need to acquire data from cell phones and other mobile devices, a variety of different forensic software solutions are available. By accessing the data on the cell phone, you can acquire evidence for criminal cases, internal investigations, and civil litigations, or view information that may be useful for intelligence purposes. We discuss some of the more popular products used for obtaining such data from cell phones in the subsections that follow.

Device Seizure

Device Seizure is covert surveillance software developed by Paraben Corporation. It can aid in forensically analyzing and recovering mobile phone and PDA data including deleted text messages, photos, and call logs. It supports Palm, Windows CE, Windows Mobile, BlackBerry, and Psion devices as well as certain Nokia, Sony Ericsson, Motorola, iDen, Siemens, LG, Samsung, and Symbian-based phone models. It also supports GSM SIM card acquisition and deleted data recovery using SIMCon technology. Device Seizure is supported on Windows 98, XP, and Vista.

Oxygen Phone Manager

Oxygen Phone Manager II for Nokia phones provides a simple and convenient way to control mobile phones from a PC. Oxygen Phone Manager II offers management for the phonebook, the call register, the calendar, to-do lists, SMS and MMS messages, logos, tones, General Packet Radio Service (GPRS) and Wireless Application Protocol (WAP) settings, profiles, Dictaphones, FM stations, Java games, and applications.

SIM Card Seizure

Paraben acquired SIMCon and integrated it into SIM Card Seizure and Device Seizure. You can use SIM Card Seizure to recover deleted SMS messages and perform comprehensive analysis of SIM card data. It is a combination of the SIM card acquisition and analysis components in Paraben's Device

Seizure utility and a specialized SIM card forensic acquisition and analysis tool. SIM Card Seizure includes the software and a forensic SIM card reader. Its features are included in Device Seizure and the Device Seizure Toolbox.

Cellebrite for Forensics and Law Enforcement

The Cellebrite Universal Forensic Extraction Device (UFED) system is a tool developed by Cellebrite Mobile Synchronization, and is available at www.cellebrite.com/cellebrite-for-forensics-law-enforcement.html. It is a stand-alone device that allows you to connect 95 percent of the cell phones on the market to the device using a cable, and then extract such data as the phonebook, pictures, videos, text messages, logs of calls, and other information from the handset. When used in the field, the data acquired from the cell phone can be stored on an SD card or USB flash drive, whereas in the forensic lab it can be transferred to a computer for analysis. You use Cellebrite with standard cell phones, as well as with smartphones and PDAs such as the Palm OS, BlackBerry, and Symbian.

Storage of Cell Phones and Other Wireless Devices

Wireless devices such as cell phones, PDAs, pagers, and so on require additional measures for storage, as they can receive unwanted signals that can corrupt or modify the evidence on these devices. Because they can accept incoming transmissions, it is possible for a suspect to access a device that's been seized from him or her remotely, and delete or modify any incriminating evidence. For example, many devices store a limited log of incoming calls, where the oldest phone numbers are purged to make room for new calls received by the device. By repeatedly calling the cell phone, a suspect could remove evidence of calls received by people.

Similarly, if pagers, cell phones, or other equipment that contains possible evidence and runs on battery is involved, they need to be preserved for immediate examination. Phone numbers, pages received by the person, and other evidence could be lost once the battery power runs out. As such, it's important to document anything that is visible through the display of a device, and to photograph it if possible.

To preserve the evidence on these devices, it's important to store them in special bags and boxes that prevent unwanted signals from reaching them. Some of these boxes even provide outlets to allow power to be provided to the devices while they are being stored. Examples of two such products are the StrongHold Bag and StrongHold Box developed by Paraben (www.paraben-forensics.com).

As shown in Figure 8.13, Paraben's Wireless StrongHold Bag is an evidence bag that is made of nickel, copper, and silver-plated nylon woven fabric. Because of this amalgam of materials, signals are prevented from penetrating the bag.

Figure 8.13 The Paraben Wireless StrongHold Bag

As shown in Figure 8.14, Paraben's StrongHold Box is a portable faraday cage that allows you to store wireless devices inside, and work on them inside the box through signal blocking gloves. The box has shielded power, light, and data connections, and is constructed of materials that prevent signals from reaching any wireless devices stored inside.

Figure 8.14 The Paraben StrongHold Box

> **NOTE**
>
> You can obtain additional information on cell phone forensics from the National Institute of Standards and Technology (NIST), which published the "Guidelines on Cell Phone Forensics." You can obtain a copy of this document from the NIST Web site, at http://csrc.nist.gov/publications/nistpubs/800-101/SP800-101.pdf.

PDA Forensics

A personal digital assistant (PDA) is a handheld computing device that combines a multitude of functions and features including computing, telephone, fax, and Internet. Additionally, the PDA can and most often contains some form of networking or other form of connectivity capabilities. Today, a PDA is a powerful device that can function as a cellular phone, a fax sender, a Web browser, and a personal organizer. These devices have reached such a level of power and functionality that they are in essence minicomputers.

Components of a PDA

The PDA device has several components. Our intent here is to discuss some of the more common ones. The first component of the PDA is the microprocessor, which is similar to any other microprocessor except that there is a restriction on its size. Another component of the PDA is some form of input device, such as a touch screen. In addition to these components, an essential component is the operating system that is running the software for the PDA device.

Investigative Methods

As discussed previously, the concept of PDA forensics is very similar to the procedures and methodologies that are used with any form of forensics. When we discuss PDA forensics, there are investigative methods that you should use when performing a forensic investigation of a PDA. The four main steps when it comes to performing a forensic investigation of a PDA are:

1. Examination
2. Identification
3. Collection
4. Documentation

   We start off by securing the evidence. It is essential that you follow a process that has been approved by legal counsel to secure the PDA. When you seize the PDA you have to ensure that you take the PDA, the docking cradle, and the external memory cards. This is probably one of the most difficult things to control and requires that you conduct a thorough search for any and all memory cards. With the size of memory cards today, there is an extensive amount of evidence that you would be missing if you missed just one memory card. Once you secure the evidence, the next step is to create an exact image to preserve the crime scene. Once you have acquired the image it is time to examine the evidence. Once you have examined the evidence, you have to present it, which is usually done by compiling an extensive report based on the investigation thus far. It is also your responsibility as the examiner to maintain the evidence, which consists of keeping it in a secure location. You also have to ensure that the PDA remains charged so that the data and information are maintained in a constant state.

Step 1: Examination

In the examination step of PDA forensics, you first need to understand the potential sources of the evidence, which can be the device, the device cradle, the power supply, and any other peripherals or media that the device being examined has come into contact with. In addition to these sources, you should also investigate any device that has synchronized with the PDA you are examining.

Step 2: Identification

In the identification step of PDA forensics, you start the process by identifying the type of device you are investigating. Once you have identified the device, you then have to identify the operating system that the device is using. It is critical to the investigative process that you determine the operating system. Furthermore, once you have identified the operating system, it is important to note that it is possible that the device could be running two operating systems. During the identification process, there are several interfaces that can assist you, including the cradle interface, the manufacturer serial number, the cradle type, and the power supply itself.

Step 3: Collection

During this part of the forensic investigation, it is imperative that you collect data and potential evidence from the memory devices that are part of or are suspected to be part of the PDA you are investigating. There are a multitude of these types of devices, so we will limit our discussion to just a few, including the SD, the MMC semiconductor cards, the micro-drives, and the USB tokens. The SD cards range in size from a few megabytes to several gigabytes, and the USB tokens can range from a few megabytes to multiple gigabytes. In addition to seizing and collecting the memory devices, you also have to collect the power leads, cables, and any cradles that exist for the PDA. Extending the investigation process further, it is imperative that you collect all of the types of information consisting of both volatile and dynamic information. Consequently, it is imperative that you give the volatile information priority while you collect evidence. The reason for giving this information priority is because anything that is classified as volatile information will not survive if the machine is powered off or reset. Once you have captured the information, it is imperative that you place the PDA into an evidence bag and maintain it at stable power support throughout the investigation.

Step 4: Documentation

As with any component in the forensic process, it is critical that you maintain your documentation and "chain of custody." As you collect information and potential evidence, you need to record all visible data. Your records must document the case number and the date and time it was collected. Additionally, the entire investigation area needs to be photographed, which includes any devices that can be connected to the PDA or currently are connected to the PDA. Another part of the documentation process is to generate a report that consists of the detailed information that describes the entire forensic process you are performing. Within this report you need to annotate the state and status of the device in question during your collection process. The final step of the collection process consists of accumulating all of the information and storing it in a secure and safe location.

PDA Investigative Tips

When it comes to the PDA device, you need to consider several things while carrying out an investigation. These devices can be managed and maintained at all times. Adding further complication is the fact that with PDA devices, a suspect can have immediate access 24 hours a day, seven days a week. Another thing that makes your job as an investigator more challenging is that PDAs are immediate boot cycle devices. Accordingly, it is important to remember that these devices typically contain a plethora of information and are a vault of evidence for the forensic examiner.

Device Switched On

When you are beginning your investigation process, and you discover that the PDA you want to process for evidence is in the "on" mode, it is imperative that you act immediately and get power to the PDA so that it will not lose the volatile information that could quite possibly be essential to your evidence collection process.

Device Switched Off

If the device is in the "off" state, you should leave the device in this state and then switch the device on and take a picture of it. Additionally, you need to note and record the current battery charge.

Device in Its Cradle

Avoid any further communication activities with the device and remove any connections from the PC device. It is important to note that there is a possibility that a sophisticated suspect might have a "tripwire" device, and once you disconnect the PC this could activate the device, which in turn could run a script that might erase potential evidence. Despite this possibility, you have to disconnect the device to continue the investigation.

Device Not in Its Cradle

If the device is not in the cradle, your investigative requirements are made much simpler, because there is no danger of a "tripwire" being triggered. With the device being out of its cradle, you simply seize the cradle and any cords associated with it.

Wireless Connection

Avoid any further communication activities if possible. Eliminate any wireless activity by placing the device into an envelope that can isolate it. This envelope also needs to provide antistatic protection so that the device is not damaged.

Expansion Card in Slot

Do not initiate any contact that requires taking components off the device, or that requires you to open the device in any way. This includes any and all peripheral devices and/or media types of cards.

Expansion Sleeve Removed

The first thing to accomplish is to seize the sleeve itself, and also seize any and all related peripherals and media cards.

On the Scene

Impact of Mishandling PDA Devices

While conducting an investigation of a potential crime scene, our team discovered a sticky note with a password written on it. The team member entered the password, but it did not work, so he continued to try to get access, but after the tenth attempt the BlackBerry did a complete data wipe, and whatever information was on that device was lost. This is because there is software that will log the attempts at entry and will do a complete wipe after a certain number of invalid login attempts.

Deploying PDA Forensic Tools

Whereas several tools are available for conducting a forensic investigation, fewer tools are available when investigating handheld or PDA devices.

PDA Secure

The first tool to discuss is the PDA Secure tool. This tool offers enhanced password protection, along with encryption, device locking, and data wiping. The PDA Secure tool allows administrators greater control over how handheld devices are used on networks. Additionally, it allows you to set a time and date range to monitor information such as network logon traffic, infrared transmissions, and any applications being used.

PDA Seizure

PDA Seizure is a comprehensive tool that assists in seizing the PDA. It allows the data to be acquired, viewed, and reported on. PDA Seizure works within a Windows environment and can extract the random access memory (RAM) and read only memory (ROM). It has an easy-to-use graphical user interface (GUI), and includes the tools that are needed to investigate the files that are contained within the PDA.

PDA Seizure provides multiplatform support, where the forensic examiner can acquire and examine information on PDAs for both the Pocket PC and Palm OS platforms. The PDA Seizure tool has a significant number of features, including forensic imaging tools, searches on data within acquired files, hashing for integrity protection of acquired files, and bookmarking capability to assist the examiner in the organization of information.

EnCase

EnCase is one of the most popular commercial forensic tools available, and you can use it to acquire information and evidence from a PDA. The EnCase tool can acquire images, and also consists of tools that allow you to conduct complex investigations efficiently and accurately.

BlackBerry Forensics

The BlackBerry is also known as a RIM device and is equipped with the RIM software implementation of proprietary wireless-oriented protocols. Furthermore, the device is supported by the RIM BlackBerry Message Center. The BlackBerry shares similarities with the PDA devices discussed earlier; however, it is always on and participating in some form of wireless push technology. As a result of this, the BlackBerry does not require some form of desktop synchronization like the PDA does. This unique component of the BlackBerry adds a different dimension to the process of forensic examination, and in essence this portability can be the examiner's greatest ally.

Operating System of the BlackBerry

The current version of the BlackBerry OS has numerous capabilities and features, including over-the-air activation, the ability to synchronize contacts and appointments with Microsoft Outlook, a password keeper program to store sensitive information, and the ability to customize your BlackBerry display data.

BlackBerry Operation and Security

The BlackBerry device has an integrated wireless modem, which allows it to communicate over the BellSouth Intelligent Wireless Network. The BlackBerry uses the BlackBerry Serial Protocol, which is used to back up, restore, and synchronize the data that is communicated between the BlackBerry handheld unit and the desktop software. This protocol comprises simple packets and single byte return codes. The device uses a strong encryption scheme that safeguards confidentiality and authenticity of data. It keeps data encrypted while in transit between the enterprise server and the device itself.

Wireless Security

The BlackBerry has a couple of transport encryption options, which are the Triple Data Encryption Standard (DES) and the Advanced Encryption Standard (AES). Those who want to implement the most secure method will elect to encrypt with the AES algorithm. The BlackBerry has another feature that is referred to as the Password Keeper, which offers the capability of securely storing password entries on the devices, which could consist of banking passwords, PINs, and so on. This important information is protected by AES encryption.

Security for Stored Data

Several capabilities are available on the BlackBerry when it comes to securing the data that is stored there. The first option we will discuss is the capability to make password authentication mandatory through the customizable information technology (IT) policies on the BlackBerry Enterprise Server. An additional method of protection from unauthorized parties is the fact that there is no staging of data between the server and the BlackBerry where data is decrypted.

Forensic Examination of a BlackBerry

Because the BlackBerry is an always-on, push messaging device, information can be pushed to it at any time. It is important to note that the information that is pushed has the potential of overwriting any data that was previously deleted. The problem is compounded by the fact that, without warning, a multitude of applications may receive information and make the attempts by the forensic investigator to recover information and an unaltered file system much more difficult. The first step in preserving the information is to eliminate the ability of the device to receive this data push. If possible, you can turn the radio off, or a better solution is to take the device to an area where the signal cannot be received, such as putting the device inside a filing cabinet drawer. One might think, "I'll just turn it off." This would be a serious mistake! The BlackBerry is not really "off" unless power is removed for an extended period, or the unit is placed in storage mode. Furthermore, once the unit is powered back on, any items that were in the queue waiting to be pushed to the device could possibly be pushed before you could stop them. As mentioned previously, it is quite possible that a change to state such as a power-off of the BlackBerry could result in a program being run on the unit that will allow the device to accept remote commands via e-mail.

Acquisition of Information Considerations

The considerations for the BlackBerry are similar in some ways to the PDA devices, but there are some differences. Let's look at the considerations you have to make when acquiring evidence from the BlackBerry.

Device Is in the "Off" State

If the unit is off at the time of acquisition, the investigator needs to take it to a shielded location before attempting to switch it on. If a shielded location is not readily available, you might have success using a safe or other room that can block the signal well enough to prevent the data push. One thing to consider is having a unit available that you can use to walk the network and look for weak coverage areas to use.

Device Is in the "On" State

If the device you are examining is in the "on" state, then as outlined and detailed above, you need to take the device to a secure location and disable or turn off the radio before beginning the examination.

Password-Protected

One thing to consider when it comes to password protection is the fact that the password itself is not stored on the device. The only thing that is stored on the device is a hashing of the plain text password. This storage is similar to the storage used by the majority of operating systems.

Evidence Collection

To collect evidence from the BlackBerry you have to violate the traditional forensic methods by requiring the investigator to record logs kept on the unit that will be wiped after an image is taken. You want to collect evidence from several different log files, including:

- **Radio Status** This log lets you enumerate the state of the device's radio functions.
- **Roam and Radio** This log has a buffer of up to 16 entries, records information concerning the tower, channel, and so on, and will not survive a reset.
- **Transmit/Receive** This log records gateway information and the type and size of data transmitted.
- **Profile String** This log contains the negotiation with the last utilized radio tower.

Once the log information is extracted and enumerated, the image will be taken. If you do not require or need the log information, the image can be acquired immediately.

Unit Control Functions

You review the logs by using the unit control functions. The first function is the Mobitex2 Radio Status, which provides information on the Radio Status, Roam and Radio Transmit, or Receive and Profile String. The second control function is the Device Status, which provides information on memory allocation, port status, file system allocation, and central processing unit (CPU) WatchPuppy. The third control function is the Battery Status, which provides information on the battery type, load, status, and temperature. The last control function we will discuss is the Free Mem, which provides information on memory allocation, Common Port File System, WatchPuppy, OTA status, Halt, and Reset.

Imaging and Profiling

When you are conducting a forensic examination of a BlackBerry, you need to conduct imaging and profiling. You accomplish this by extracting the logs from a developed image and acquiring an image of a bit-by-bit backup using the BlackBerry Software Development Kit (SDK). The SDK is available from www.blackberry.com and is essential for the forensic examiner when investigating a BlackBerry. The SDK utility dumps the contents of the Flash RAM into a file. Once the Flash RAM is dumped, you can examine and review it using traditional methods with your favorite hex editor or other tool. In addition to reviewing the evidence with traditional methods, you can use the Simulator from the SDK to match the network and model of the investigated unit.

Attacking the BlackBerry

Several tools and methods are available that allow you to attack a BlackBerry. The first tool is the BlackBerry Attack Toolkit, which you can use along with the BBProxy software to exploit Web site vulnerabilities. The second tool is the Attack Vector, which links and tricks users by downloading malicious software to the BlackBerry. The last method we will discuss is the method of hijacks (or blackjacks). As the name implies, this allows someone to hijack a legal user's BlackBerry and replace him or her on the network with potentially harmful devices.

Securing the BlackBerry

You can do several things to secure the information on a BlackBerry. The first thing you can do is clean the BlackBerry memory, and protect stored messages on the messaging server. You can encrypt the application password as well as the storage of it on the BlackBerry. Furthermore, you can protect storage of user data on a locked BlackBerry by limiting the password authentication attempts. It is possible to set a maximum of 10 attempts to gain access to the device. Additionally, you can use AES technology to secure the storage of the password keeper and password entries on the BlackBerry.

Information Hiding in a BlackBerry

You can hide information in several places in a Blackberry. You can create hidden databases and hide information in partition gaps. You can also hide data in the gap between the OS/application and file partitions.

BlackBerry Signing Authority Tool

The Signing Authority tool helps developers protect data and intellectual property, and enables them to handle access to their sensitive application program interfaces (APIs). The tool provides this protection by using public and private signature keys. It does this by using asymmetric cryptography to validate the authenticity of the request. Furthermore, the signing tool allows developers to exchange API information in a secure manner and environment.

Summary

In this chapter, we discussed a number of technologies that an investigator may not immediately think of when conducting an investigation. We introduced you to iPods and MP3 players, and we saw how they can be used to store more than just music files. We explained the file structure of the iPod and showed how evidence can be hidden within the iPod. From a law enforcement standpoint, it is very important that search warrants specify that all data storage devices, including iPods and MP3 players, should be acquired as potential evidence. The iPod might be the sole source of evidence that makes or breaks a case.

We also looked at cell phones, and saw how modern cell phones allow for Internet access and other features that were previously available only with computers. As with any wireless device that can be connected to remotely, certain storage requirements must be considered to preserve possible evidence. By properly storing them, the possibility that evidence on the mobile phone will be damaged or destroyed by unwanted signals is dramatically decreased.

We then discussed the methods of investigating a PDA. We talked about securing the evidence, and how the PDA, docking cradle, and any external memory cards should be seized. The next method we discussed was acquiring the evidence. We covered how you have to create an exact image of the evidence, and once the evidence is secured and acquired, the need to go on and examine the evidence that was acquired.

We then talked about the forensic examination considerations when confronted with a BlackBerry (RIM) device. We concentrated on how the BlackBerry has similarities to the PDA, but one way that they differ is that the BlackBerry does not require synchronization to receive a significant amount of information. The BlackBerry is always on, and to make the task a little more difficult, it is in a state where it is susceptible to receiving push technology updates at any time. Therefore, we discussed how it is imperative that we take this into account when preparing to examine a BlackBerry. We also discussed the software that is available to assist us when we are examining a BlackBerry.

Frequently Asked Questions

Q: When conducting a forensic investigation of a PDA, what is the first step in the process?

A: As with any forensic examination, the first step is to have permission to seize the evidence that is required for your investigation.

Q: What sort of tools do I use to conduct a forensic examination of a PDA?

A: Most of the forensic tools that work with images will create an image of a PDA file system. The commercial software product EnCase has this capability, as do many others.

Q: If I am preparing to conduct an investigation of a PDA, why must I maintain the charge to the device?

A: Similar to a regular PC, the PDA device has both volatile and nonvolatile information, and if the power is not maintained, there is a possibility you could lose information.

Q: Aren't a PDA and a BlackBerry the same thing?

A: It is not uncommon to make this assumption, and there are similarities, but there are also many differences. The BlackBerry is an always-on device that can have information pushed to it at any time, and unlike the PDA, the BlackBerry does not require synchronization with a PC.

Q: How would I get access to log files on a BlackBerry?

A: Some of the best tools for conducting an investigation of a BlackBerry come from the BlackBerry itself. There is an SDK that can access and collect log files and other information.

Chapter 9

Understanding E-mail and Internet Crimes

Topics we'll investigate in this chapter:

- **Understanding E-mail and E-mail Forensics**
- **Tracing a Domain Name or IP Address**
- **Understanding Browser Security**
- **Investigating Child Pornography and Other Crimes That Victimize Children**
- **Cyberterrorism**

☑ **Summary**

☑ **Frequently Asked Questions**

Introduction

A number of tools are used to access resources on the Internet, and each of them can be used to commit a crime or potentially become a victim. By accessing the Internet, e-mail clients and Internet browsers can expose computers to viruses and spam, and can expose the people using those computers to various forms of cybercrime.

The Internet is widely used as a source of information and enjoyment, but it is as susceptible to crime as any community. There are online predators who attempt to coerce or seduce children into having sex, and child pornography is rampantly downloaded and traded online. These images may be acquired using home computers or in the workplace. Just as hackers can access systems and cause damage, so can terrorists. Cyberterrorism can involve damaging key systems, accessing sensitive intelligence, or performing other acts that could cause harm on a widespread level.

In this chapter, we'll look at a wide range of tools that are used to access illegal materials and expose victims to cybercriminals and illegal materials. Obviously, the most common tools used on the Internet are e-mail clients and Internet browsers. E-mail clients are used to send and receive messages, and they can be used as a source of evidence to see who a person has contacted, what was said, and what files were sent and received by that person. Internet browsers allow people to access both legitimate and illegal materials, and can expose a machine to a wide range of threats. As such, we'll look at how poor security in Internet browsers can be exploited, and simple measures to secure the browser.

Understanding E-mail and E-mail Forensics

E-mail is short for "electronic mail," and it is used to send messages to others on the Internet. According to the Pew Internet & American Life Project, in a February–March 2007 survey, 71 percent of American adults use the Internet and 91 percent of them send or read e-mail. Because sending an e-mail is more common today than writing a letter was a few decades ago, it should come as no surprise that e-mail is also used for illegal purposes.

Most people send and receive e-mails using *e-mail client* software such as Microsoft Outlook, Outlook Express, Thunderbird, Eudora, or others. These programs are installed on a computer, and they store the messages in files on the local hard disk. Online services, including free e-mail services, are also available, in which a person accesses his or her e-mail through a Web site. These messages are stored on the e-mail service's servers. Some of the most popular services include Hotmail (www.hotmail.com) and Gmail (http://mail.google.com). More secure services such as Hushmail (www.hushmail.com) are also available that will encrypt messages before they're sent.

E-mail Terminology

Before you can start to examine e-mail archives, you have to understand the special language that is used when talking about e-mail. Just like the police and other professions use acronyms in everyday jargon, e-mail technology has unique words that are used to describe the smaller-scale ingredients of an e-mail. These terms include the following:

- **IMAP** Internet Message Access Protocol is a method for accessing e-mail or bulletin board messages that are kept on a mail server, making them appear and act as though they were stored locally.

- **MAPI** Messaging Application Program Interface is a Microsoft Windows interface that allows you to send e-mail from inside an application. Typical applications that work with this option are word processors, spreadsheets, and graphics applications.

- **SMTP** Simple Mail Transfer Protocol receives outgoing mail from clients and validates source and destination addresses. It also sends and receives e-mail to and from other SMTP servers. The standard SMTP port is 25.

- **HTTP** Hypertext Transfer Protocol is typically used in Web mail and the message remains on the Web mail server.

- **ESMTP** Enhanced SMTP is a set of protocol extensions to the SMTP standard.

- **POP3** Post Office Protocol 3 is a standard protocol for receiving e-mail that deletes mail on the server as soon as the user has downloaded the e-mail. The standard port for POP3 is 110.

- **Cc** Carbon Copy is a field in the e-mail header that directs a copy of the message to go to another recipient e-mail address.

- **Bcc** Blind Carbon Copy is a field that is hidden from the receiver but allows for a copy of the message to be sent to the e-mail address in this field.

- **HELO** This is a communication command from the client to the server in SMTP e-mail delivery.

- **EHLO** This is the HELO command in ESMTP clients.

- **NNTP** Network News Transfer Protocol is used for newsgroups similar to standard e-mail. Headers are usually downloaded first in groups. The bodies are downloaded when the message is opened.

Each of these items will help you to understand e-mail, and they provide an easy reference for some of the topics we'll discuss in the sections that follow.

Understanding E-mail Headers

There's more to managing information security than dealing with boundary devices and various types of logs. E-mail can open the doors for all kinds of attacks and infections in an organization. Besides making sure to install and use antivirus (AV) software that inspects all e-mail payloads (and hopefully blocks all potential sources of such attacks), it's also necessary for users and administrators to deal with unsolicited e-mail (also called *spam*) or with e-mail-based denial-of-service (DoS) attacks (so-called *mail bombs*). To deal properly with spam and e-mail-based DoS attacks, it's absolutely essential to understand how to read e-mail headers. Such knowledge will not only permit administrators and investigators to determine at least a putative (if not the actual) source for the attack or spam, but it will also help them to define a strategy for dealing with such behavior.

The ability to track e-mail messages is important in many different types of cybercrime cases. It is not unusual for criminals to use e-mail in the following ways:

- To harass victims (cyberstalking)

- To send extortion demands or threats

- To contact potential victims (pedophiles, serial rapists)

- To solicit "marks" for con games (Nigerian scam, pyramid schemes)

- To coax people to visit Web sites and provide personal information that can be used for identity theft and other purposes (phishing)

- To communicate with accomplices

In all of these situations and others, e-mail may be one (or the only) clue to the criminal's identity and may become evidence at trial. Unless the criminal is kind enough to sign the message with a full (and accurate) name, address, and phone number, the only way to determine where a message originated is to examine the message "headers." E-mail generally goes through a number of different computers on the way from the sender to the intended recipient. Header information is added to the message at each machine along the way, until it reaches its destination. (The workstation on which the recipient reads the mail generally doesn't add header info.) It is important for investigators to know what information can—and can't—be discerned from e-mail headers and to understand that headers can be spoofed (forged).

Breaking down and understanding e-mail headers requires some knowledge of how to recognize and decode the fields in those headers. This level of structure is well documented and is primarily defined in Request for Comments (RFC) 822, which documents the layout and structure of SMTP message header fields. Although there are more fields than the ones we discuss here, Table 9.1 lists the most important fields as well as all the fields you'll need to check to try to trace messages back to their origins and to identify the route they took from their putative original sender to reach the recipient's e-mail server.

Table 9.1 Important RFC 822 E-mail Header Fields

Field Name	Explanation
Source/Sender Header Fields	
From	Identifies e-mail sender, usually by name and e-mail address
Sender	Identifies actual sender of e-mail (may differ from the From field in some e-mail systems)
Reply-to	E-mail address to which replies should be sent
Return-path	Path (address) back to sender
Received	Except when users reside on the same server, known as a *message transfer agent,* or *MTA*, every e-mail goes through at least one intermediary server as it's routed from sender to receiver. Each such intermediary appears on its own Received line.
Resent-*xxx*	Applies to re-sent messages, for From, Sender, and Reply-to fields

Continued

Table 9.1 Continued. Important RFC 822 E-mail Header Fields

Field Name	Explanation
Destination Header Fields	
To	Identifies name and/or e-mail address for recipient
Cc	Secondary message recipients
Bcc	Blind carbon-copy message recipients. (Message is delivered to all Bcc designees, but no Bcc designee information is included in the header itself.)
Resent-*xxx*	Applies to re-sent messages for To, Cc, and Bcc fields
Date Headers	
Date	Date and time original message was sent
Resent-date	Date and time re-sent message was sent
Optional Headers	
Subject	Topic for message
Message-ID	Unique message identifier (handled by MTA from originating system); also supplied for re-sent messages
In-reply-to	Identifies message being replied to
References	Identifies other messages to which this message applies
Keywords	Keywords to help sort and organize message contents (seldom used)
Comments	Text comments about message (seldom used)
Encrypted	Indicates message content is encrypted
X-xxx	Identifies user-defined fields

The fields of greatest interest when dealing with malicious e-mail or spam are those that identify the putative sender (From, Reply-to, Sender, Return-path, and so forth), as well as all the various *received* fields that indicate the mail servers involved in routing the message(s) from the sender to your server. Although those Received lines that don't include a From field do not actually identify a sender, users can report that spam is being routed through those servers to the Internet service providers (ISPs) or organizations that operate them. In many cases, the provider will be able to filter out the unwanted e-mail rather than forwarding it to the complaining user or some other hapless victim. In fact, it's best to concentrate on the Internet Protocol (IP) address reported on these lines, because clever e-mail attackers can forge much of this information. For more information on dealing with unwanted e-mail, including detailed instructions on creating and issuing spam complaints to forwarding server operators, see the excellent article "Reporting SPAM" at www.freelabs.com/~whitis/spam_reporting.html. (This site also contains a useful Links section with further pointers to spam investigation and reporting.)

Unfortunately, e-mail messages are far too easy to spoof, in the sense that knowledgeable individuals can either use software tools or construct entirely bogus RFC 822 e-mail headers by hand. Thus, not all reports of unwanted forwarding may produce the desired results of eliminating or reducing unwanted mail traffic. Some service providers operate special e-mail services known as *anonymous* or *pseudo remailers*. These so-called "anonymizer" services are deliberately designed to shield users from outright or personal identification; many operate outside the United States.

CyberCrimeStopper

Dealing with Anonymizer Service Providers

In some cases, the companies or organizations that operate anonymizer services will respond favorably to requests for assistance from law enforcement professionals who seek to identify their customers who are using the service for criminal purposes. In other cases, a company may refuse to cooperate in any way at all; such lack of cooperation is more likely to occur when anonymizer service providers operate offshore. Nevertheless, some of the most notorious anonymizer services (for example, anon. penet.fi, originally based in Finland) have ceased operation, primarily in response to frequent repeated requests to identify their customers to law enforcement professionals all over the world. An old Internet saying applies when seeking cooperation from anonymous remailers: YMMV ("Your mileage may vary"). This is a polite euphemism for the very real situation in which things do not work exactly as described or advertised, or assistance with (or from) a service may simply not be available. It's worth a try (or a warrant, where one can be obtained), but seeking cooperation from these services may not always produce the desired results!

For more information about e-mail header fields and how to interpret them, consult the text for RFC 822 at www.faqs.org/rfcs/rfc822.html, or the article "Reading Email Headers" on the StopSpam Web site at www.stopspam.org/email/headers/headers.html. You'll also find valuable e-mail resources online at http://everythingemail.net and through the Internet Mail Consortium at www.imc.org.

Looking at E-mail Headers

Many e-mail programs don't show the full e-mail headers by default in the message, but you can view the headers if you drill down through the interface. In Outlook Express, you can view e-mail headers by right-clicking on a message in the message list, and then clicking on the **Properties** menu item in the context menu that appears. As shown in Figure 9.1, clicking on the Details tab allows you to view the e-mail headers associated with that message. In looking at the information in the header, please note that the e-mail addresses have been changed to fictious ones. To view the full HTML code in the e-mail message, you could then click on the **Message Source** button.

Figure 9.1 A Microsoft Outlook Express E-mail Header

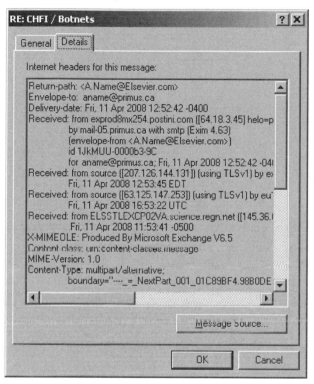

If this message were part of a mail bomb attack or spam, you'd want to contact the operators of the various servers identified in the Return-path and From fields, and inside the various Received fields in the header. But first, it would also be useful to employ the *whois* command at your command line to check the domain names reported against the IP addresses used. *Whois* allows you find out to whom a domain name is registered.

Windows does not typically include built-in whois capabilities, but numerous sources for Windows-compatible whois utilities are available, such as those at www.tatumweb.com/iptools.htm. Or you can use the services at www.samspade.org to perform the necessary lookups through its Web pages without using a whois tool on your Windows PC. Likewise, if you have access to a UNIX shell account, you should be able to use the *whois* command at the command line. Mac OS X has a useful graphical version of whois, as shown in Figure 9.2.

Figure 9.2 The Mac OS X Graphical Whois Utility

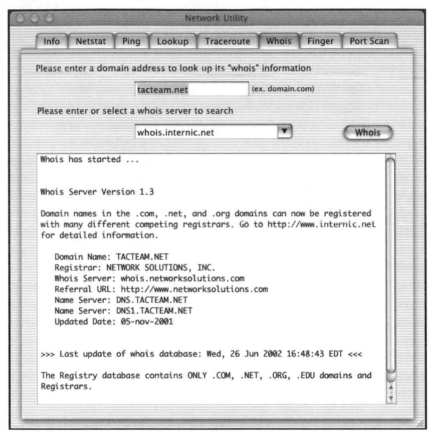

> **NOTE**
>
> Other useful commands include *nslookup* and *dig*, to map from domain names to IP addresses.

E-mail Forensics

Numerous e-mail recovery and e-mail forensic tools are available to view the files where e-mails are archived on a hard disk. For example, e-mail is stored in .dbx files, and those files are named after the folder in which the e-mails are stored (that is, Inbox.dbx, Deleted Items.dbx, and so on). Typically, you would create a traditional bitstream image of the entire drive and then extract these files from the drive image. Many good virtual mounting programs are available that allow you to mount the image file and extract a copy of the data from that drive. Some of the e-mail forensic and recovery tools available include the following:

- **Paraben's E-mail Examiner** Designed to process a wide variety of active and deleted e-mail archives. This includes Outlook Exchange, Outlook Express, Eudora, Pegasus Mail, EML message files, and many others.

- **Paraben's Network E-mail Examiner (NEMX)** Can be used to process Microsoft Exchange archives as well as Lotus Notes and GroupWise files. Built into the tool is a corruption repair utility that will also save some time in processing by attempting to bypass corruption and move on to read the rest of the archive, allowing you to keep the data in its original state.

- **Ontrack PowerControls** A tool for copying, searching, recovering, and analyzing e-mail and other mailbox items from Microsoft Exchange server backups, Information Store files, and unmounted databases (EDB).

Tracing a Domain Name or IP Address

The *domain name system* (DNS) is responsible for maintaining domain-name-to-IP-address mappings on the Internet. Numerous boundary devices, such as firewalls and screening routers, can perform reverse DNS lookups to make sure that reported domain names match actual IP destination addresses in inbound traffic. When these do not match up properly—that is, when looking up the domain name produces an IP address that is different from the one in the destination address—the sender may be attempting to spoof a domain name without making sure the IP address matches. This is a sign of a less-than-savvy hacker. Hackers who know what they're doing generally make an effort to match the IP addresses from which they claim to originate with the domain names they use.

Nevertheless, the "reverse DNS lookup" technique permits a device to query the DNS server for an IP address to go along with a domain name, as well as to perform the more standard name-to-address translations that DNS typically provides whenever a computer attempts to connect to another machine using a "friendly" DNS name instead of the IP address. You can configure most boundary equipment, and many IP servers, to perform a reverse DNS lookup before granting access even to anonymous users, and to deny access to users whose reported domain names and IP addresses don't match up. Although this is not an entirely foolproof technique for blocking spoofed traffic completely, it is highly recommended for networks that permit traffic to enter from outside their local networks (especially from the Internet).

In general, DNS queries that use reverse lookup work backward through the IP address to the domain name, using a special file on the DNS server called *in-addr-arpa*. For example, if a Web server has an Internet address of 206.224.64.194, the lookup proceeds in reverse order into a file named 64.224.206-in-addr-arpa on some DNS server where individual addresses on that subnet can be resolved (such as the Web server named www.lanw.com at 206.224.64.194). Most network boundary devices and servers perform such lookups automatically and write them to their log files. Nevertheless, investigators should also know how to get from domain names to IP addresses and from IP addresses to domain names manually, if only to confirm the results they find in firewall, router, or server log files.

Table 9.2 summarizes key commands you can use to obtain domain name and IP address-related information. Rather than providing complete syntax information, we provide pointers to Windows and UNIX/Linux commands, with help files where you can find such details and numerous examples. Please note also that www.tatumweb.com/iptools.htm offers access to numerous Web-based lookup tools with the same functionality. The benefit of this latter approach is that you can simply enter a domain name or IP address and other arguments as needed, and observe the results without mastering the underlying command syntax or details.

Table 9.2 Domain Name/IP Address Lookup Utilities

Command	Explanation	Windows Help	UNIX/Linux Help File
Nslookup	Inspects contents of DNS server files, including forward and reverse lookups	Enter **nslookup**, then type **help**.	man nslookup
DiG	Provides information from DNS servers about domain names and/or IP addresses	Not available on Windows by default	man DiG
Whois	Maps hostnames to IP addresses and vice versa	Not available on Windows by default	man Whois

NOTE

A useful Web site for obtaining DNS information is at www.dnsreport.com. Administrators can use it to find out about problems and vulnerabilities with their DNS servers.

The tools listed in Table 9.2 are vital to properly investigating the source of an e-mail or the owner of a Web site. By using the whois tool at www.samspade.org, we could enter the URL of a Web site and get information that was provided when the domain name was registered. As shown in Figure 9.3, the results of entering the URL www.microsoft.com produce the name and address of the registrant, contact e-mail, and other information that can be useful in an investigation.

Figure 9.3 Whois Output for www.microsoft.com

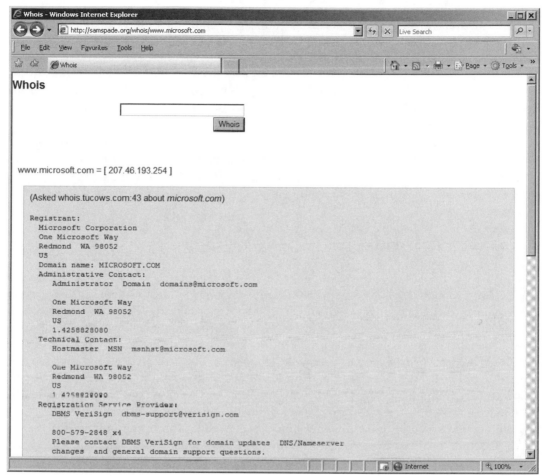

Similarly, by performing a reverse lookup using *Nslookup* or using *whois* to identify the owner of a mail server (found in the header of an e-mail), an investigator could then request or serve the ISP with a warrant to provide account information on the person who sent the e-mail. For example, by viewing the e-mail header and seeing the IP address from which the e-mail was received, you can then use the Nslookup.exe tool in Windows or an online Nslookup tool such as the one at www. zoneedit.com/lookup.html to view the contact information for the ISP to which the IP address is registered. The ISP can then check its logs to see to whom the IP address was issued when the e-mail was sent.

Understanding Browser Security

No matter what type of Internet connection a company or individual uses, whether broadband, dial-up, or local area network (LAN), it is important to address the security vulnerabilities that Web browsers introduce to the systems and network. Many of the most commonly used Internet service client software programs, such as Web browsers and e-mail utilities, are vulnerable to an ever-expanding list of malicious attacks. Most of these attacks are made possible by the dynamic and automated capabilities that these tools have acquired over the years. The inclusion of scripting and programming languages in these utilities (for example, JavaScript, Java, and ActiveX) has introduced new and easily exploited security vulnerabilities to an already imperfect environment. In an effort to maintain browser market share by offering the widest range of capabilities and features, Microsoft's Web browser Internet Explorer and e-mail clients Outlook and Outlook Express have become immensely popular and consequently are the most commonly attacked Internet service clients.

It is important to remember that Microsoft is not the only vendor whose Internet service products are susceptible to attacks—it's merely because this company's products are the most popular that they have become the favorite target of attackers. Some users—including networking professionals who should know better—operate under a false sense of security because they use non-Microsoft products. Each time a security flaw in Internet Explorer, Outlook, or a Microsoft operating system is announced, they proudly boast that they would never use such an insecure product. Meanwhile, a Web search for UNIX or Linux security vulnerabilities turns up thousands of pages detailing security holes in various UNIX/Linux versions. It bears repeating that there is *no* truly secure network-connected computer.

When it comes to Web browsers, the truth is that any utility that supports the execution of scripts or programming code downloaded from a Web page or an e-mail message is vulnerable. This includes not only Internet Explorer, but also other browsers such as Firefox, Opera, Safari, and so on. The proliferation of these vulnerabilities is the result of pursuing functionality in hopes of obtaining market share instead of thoroughly investigating and dealing with the security implications.

Most vulnerabilities found in Web and e-mail clients relate to buffer overflow errors or arbitrary code execution. Both of these vulnerabilities enable a remote system, whether a Web site or a sender of an e-mail message, to execute malicious code on your computer. In most cases, the executed code is granted system-level privileges, meaning that there are literally no restrictions on what actions such code can take.

The same technologies that create vulnerabilities in Web browsers can also be used in HTML e-mail. Many popular e-mail clients, including Outlook and Outlook Express, allow active content to run, leaving a system open to malicious coders.

> ### Crimestoppers
>
> ## Securing E-mail Clients
>
> The following Web resources give you more specific information about securing various e-mail clients:
>
> - Outlook/Outlook Express: http://antivirus.about.com/library/bloutlook.htm
> - Pegasus: http://antivirus.about.com/library/blpegasus.htm
> - Eudora: http://antivirus.about.com/library/bleudora.htm

In the next sections, we look at the technologies that create security risks in Web browsers and e-mail, and then we discuss how to make each of the popular browser programs more secure.

Types of Dangerous Code

Several different types of code can be used to enhance Web pages and e-mail and to perform unwanted and even dangerous actions on a computer. The following sections provide an overview of the most popular of these types of code: JavaScript, ActiveX, and Java.

JavaScript

JavaScript is a scripting language developed by Netscape to allow executable code to be embedded in Web pages. All major Web browsers support JavaScript. JavaScript is used to manipulate browser window size, open and close windows, manage forms, and alter browser settings. JavaScript itself is relatively secure. However, improper implementations (such as vendor programming errors) have enabled numerous attacks. Each vendor has patched most of these vulnerabilities, but it is still possible to use JavaScript to perform a malicious activity if you can trick Web surfers into doing something they shouldn't. Unfortunately, it is usually easy for a malicious Web site to trick visitors into providing access or enabling code execution when they shouldn't.

ActiveX

ActiveX is a code-embedding technology developed by Microsoft. It employs a security control known as *code signing*. Each ActiveX program is called a *control*. When a control is downloaded to a Web browser, it is scanned for a digital signature using the Authenticode technology to verify the signature with a certificate authority (CA) and ensure that it hasn't been altered before downloading the control. A dialog box is displayed, indicating that the ActiveX control is signed by a specific company or individual and prompting the user to indicate whether to accept this control, always accept controls from this entity, or deny this control. Once an ActiveX control is on a system, it can do anything it is programmed to do, whether benign or malicious. Just because you know who are the authors of a control doesn't guarantee that the control is secure or that its interactions with other controls will not introduce new vulnerabilities to your system.

Java

Java is a programming language developed by Sun Microsystems. It is fundamentally different from JavaScript in that it uses a technique known as *sandboxing* to restrict its capabilities. Java programs that execute locally are called *applets*. Each applet is checked to make sure it is coded properly and is not corrupted before it is allowed to execute. Then a security monitor oversees the applet's activity to prevent it from performing actions that it should not be able to perform, such as reading data, opening network connections, or deleting files.

Unfortunately, some implementations of Java have been compromised using various exploits. Hostile applets can also crash browsers and systems, kill other applets, extract your e-mail address and send it to the applet's distributor, and perform other nasty acts.

Making Browsers and E-mail Clients More Secure

Network administrators and users can take several steps to make Web browsers and e-mail clients more secure and protect against malicious code or unauthorized use of information. These steps include restricting the use of programming languages, keeping security patches current, and becoming aware of the function of cookies.

Restricting Programming Languages

Most Web browsers have optional settings that allow users to restrict or deny the use of Web-based programming languages. For example, Internet Explorer can be set to always allow, always deny, or prompt for user input when a JavaScript, Java, or ActiveX element appears on a Web page. Restricting all executable code from Web sites, or at least forcing the user to make choices each time such code is downloaded, reduces security breaches caused by malicious downloaded components.

A side benefit of restricting these programming languages for a Web browser is that those restrictions often apply to the e-mail client as well. The same malicious code that can be downloaded from a Web site could just as easily be sent to a person's e-mail account. If you don't have such restrictions in place, your mail client could automatically execute downloaded code.

Keeping Security Patches Current

New exploits for Web browsers and e-mail clients seem to appear daily. Product vendors usually address significant threats promptly by releasing a patch for their products. To maintain a secure system, you must remain informed about your software and apply patches for vulnerabilities when they become available.

However, you must consider a few caveats when working with software patches:

- Patches are often released quickly, in response to an immediate problem, so they may not have been thoroughly tested. This can result in failed installations, crashed systems, inoperable programs, or additional security vulnerabilities.

- It is extremely important to test new patches on nonproduction systems before deploying them throughout your network.

- If a patch cannot be deemed safe for deployment, you should weigh the consequences of not deploying it and remaining vulnerable to the threat against the possibility that the patch might itself cause system damage. If the threat is minimal, it is often safer to wait until you experience the problem a patch is designed to address before deploying such a questionable patch.

Cookie Awareness

A *cookie* is a kind of token or message that a Web site hands off to a Web browser to help track a visitor between clicks. The browser stores the message on the visitor's local hard disk in a text file. The file contains information that identifies the user and his or her preferences or previous activities at that Web site. If the user revisits the same Web site, the user's browser sends the cookie back to the Web server. Cookies are extremely useful in allowing a Web site to provide a seemingly continuous communications session with a visitor, such as maintaining a shopping cart, remembering search keywords, or customizing displayed data based on the user's preferences. However, because cookies contain identifying information, they might be used for less noble purposes.

Cookies have been discussed extensively in the popular press. These stories sometimes grant cookies more power than they really have and assign them more regard than they deserve. Cookies raise questions about privacy, but they are unable to execute code or access files. Instead, cookies simply store data from Web browsing sessions and send that same data back to a Web server. Cookies can be delivered to a computer via Web pages or HTML-enabled e-mail. Malicious, or at least unscrupulous, use of cookies occurs when they are used to track a user's surfing habits from one system to another, to grab a user's logon information from one site and send it to another, or even to capture a user's e-mail address and add the user to mailing lists without the user's knowledge. Fortunately, cookies can be disabled in the same manner as programming languages.

Securing Web Browser Software

Although the same general principles apply, each of the popular Web browser programs has a slightly different method to configure its security options. Securing Web browser software involves applying the latest updates and patches, modifying a few settings, and practicing intelligent surfing. Microsoft seems to release an Internet Explorer-specific security patch just about every week. This constant flow of patches is due to both the oversights of the programmers who wrote the code and the focused attacks on Microsoft products by the malevolent cracker community. In spite of this negative attention, you can still employ Internet Explorer as a relatively secure Web browser—when it is configured correctly.

The first step in securing Internet Explorer is to install the latest patches and updates. Users can do this automatically through Windows Update, or they can do it manually. Either way, only through patch application will most of the known vulnerabilities of Internet Explorer programming be resolved.

The second step is to configure Internet Explorer for secure surfing. Users can do this through the Internet Options applet. In Internet Explorer 7, you can access this applet through the Windows Control Panel or through the Tools menu of Internet Explorer. If the default settings are altered on the Security, Privacy, Content, and Advanced tabs, as shown in Figure 9.4, Internet Explorer security is improved significantly.

Figure 9.4 Settings on the Security Tab in Internet Explorer's Internet Options, Used to Define Security Zones

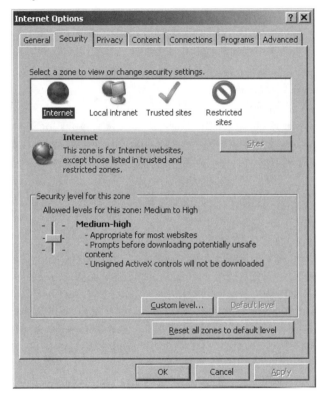

Zones are defined on the Security tab. A *zone* is nothing more than a named collection of Web sites (from the Internet or a local intranet) that can be assigned a specific security level. Internet Explorer uses zones to define the threat level a specific Web site poses to the system. Internet Explorer offers four security zone options:

- **Internet** Contains all sites not assigned to other zones.
- **Local intranet** Contains all sites within the local intranet or on the local system. The operating system maintains this zone automatically.
- **Trusted sites** Contains only sites manually added to this zone. Users should add only fully trusted sites to this zone.
- **Restricted sites** Contains only sites manually added to this zone. Users should add any sites that are specifically not trusted or that are known to be malicious to this zone.

Each zone is assigned a predefined security level, or a custom level can be created. The pre-defined security levels are offered on a slide controller with a description of the content that will be downloaded under particular conditions. You can also define custom security levels to exactly fit the security restrictions of your environment. There are security controls related to how ActiveX, down-loads, Java, data management, data handling, scripting, and logon are handled. The most secure configuration is to set all zones to the High security level. However, keep in mind that increased security means less functionality and capability.

The Privacy tab, shown in Figure 9.5, defines how Internet Explorer manages personal information through cookies.

Figure 9.5 The Privacy Tab in Internet Explorer's Internet Options, Where You Can Set Cookie Options

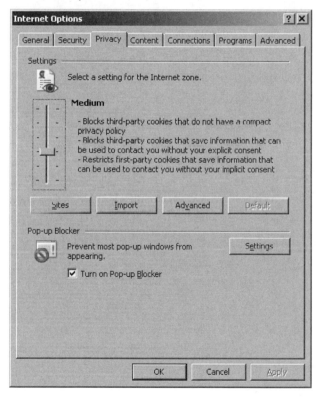

The Privacy tab offers a slide controller with six settings ranging from full disclosure to complete isolation. You can also define a custom set of cookie controls by deciding whether first-party and third-party cookies are allowed, are denied, or initiate a prompt, and whether session cookies are allowed. You can define individual Web sites whose cookies are either always allowed or always blocked. Preventing all use of cookies is the most secure configuration, but it is also the least functional. Many Web sites will not function properly under this setting, and some will not even allow you to visit them when cookies are disabled.

The Content tab, shown in Figure 9.6, gives you access to the certificates that Internet Explorer trusts and accepts. If you've accepted a certificate that you no longer trust, you can peruse this storehouse and remove it.

Figure 9.6 The Content Tab in Internet Explorer's Internet Options, Where You Can Configure Certificate Options

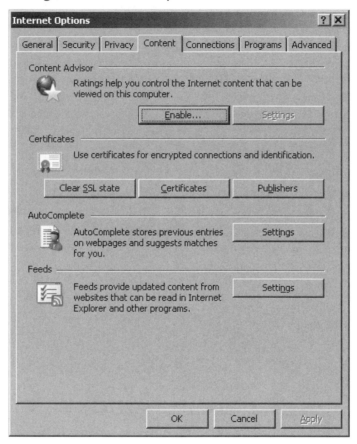

The Content tab also gives you access to Internet Explorer's AutoComplete capability. This feature is useful in many circumstances, but when it is used to remember usernames and passwords to Internet sites, it becomes a security risk. The most secure configuration requires that AutoComplete be turned off for usernames and passwords, that prompting to save passwords is disabled, and that the current password cache is cleared.

On the Advanced tab, shown in Figure 9.7, several security-specific controls are included at the bottom of a lengthy list of functional controls. These security controls include checking for certificate revocation, not saving encrypted pages to disk, deleting temporary Internet files when the browser is closed, using Secure Shell/Transport Layer Security (SSL/TLS), and warning when forms are submitted insecurely. The most secure configuration has all of these settings enabled.

Figure 9.7 The Advanced Tab in Internet Explorer's Internet Options, Where You Can Configure Security Settings

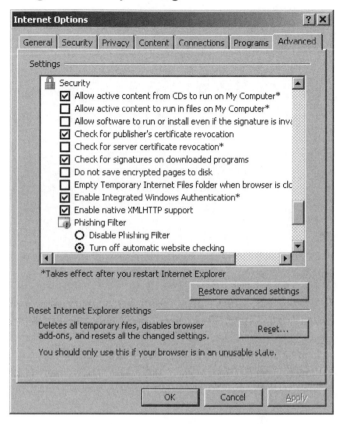

Another option that is available through the Advanced tab is turning on the Phishing Filter. *Phishing* is a method of tricking computer users to reveal personal information to fraudulent Web sites that appear authentic. When the Phishing Filter is enabled, Internet Explorer will analyze the sites you visit to check for features that are common to phishing sites. It will compare the address of a Web site to a list of sites, reported to Microsoft, which is stored on your computer. If the site is on the list, a warning will appear, notifying you whether the site has characteristics of a phishing site.

A final step in maintaining a secure Internet Explorer deployment is to practice safe surfing habits. Common sense should determine what users do, both online and offline. Unfortunately, as many law enforcement officers have observed in the course of their duties, common sense isn't all that common. Most of us wouldn't walk down a dark alley in the middle of the city at 3:00 A.M., but people do it—and unfortunately, they sometimes learn a lesson the hard way. Visiting Web sites of questionable design is the virtual equivalent of putting oneself in harm's way in a dark alley, but Internet users do it all the time. Here are some guidelines that should be followed to ensure safe surfing:

- Download software only from original vendor Web sites.

- Always attempt to verify the origin or ownership of a Web site before downloading materials from it.

www.syngress.com

- Never assume that anything presented online is 100 percent accurate.

- Avoid visiting suspect Web sites—especially those that offer cracking tools, pirated programs, or pornography—from a system that needs to remain secure.

- Always reject certificates or other dialog box prompts by clicking **No**, **Cancel**, or **Close** when prompted by Web sites or vendors with which you are unfamiliar.

Investigating Child Pornography and Other Crimes That Victimize Children

Child pornography is the sexually explicit depiction of anyone under the age of legal consent. When most people think of child pornography, which is also called *kiddie porn*, they think it relates to photos of prepubescent children involved in sexual activity. Although this is an example of child pornography, it can also include stories and other written passages, drawings, digitally manipulated images, video, or any number of other media. Also, because the legal definitions of a child and laws related to consent vary, a picture may be legal in one region or country and illegal in another.

In addition to child pornography, numerous other crimes have gained worldwide notice due to the Internet, thereby creating new terms to describe the crimes. *Internet luring* is the act of using a computer and the Internet to lure a child for sexual purposes. The people who accost children online are referred to as *online predators*, and they may even travel to other states or countries to visit children for the purpose of having sex. As we'll see in the sections that follow, a number of laws in different countries have been developed to protect children from exploitation. Because the Internet allows distribution of these materials across jurisdictions, this often requires law enforcement to work together and may require joint operations that are coordinated by government agencies or special projects that focus on eliminating child pornography, prosecuting offenders, and rescuing children.

Defining a Child

The age that a person progresses from childhood to adulthood varies depending on culture, religion, and legal designations. For example, in Jewish law, the age of maturity is 13 for a boy and 12 for a girl. However, Israeli law dictates that children cannot have consensual sex until 16, marry until 17, or reach the age of majority until 18. In looking at these ages, you can see that the differential of a child and adult varies dramatically. In terms of determining an age of consent for sexual activities, it can be even more convoluted.

Many people believe that the age of consent for sex is the same age used to determine whether a person is of legal age to pose or perform sexual acts in pornography. However, separate ages are often set for exploitive situations, such as prostitution and pornography. For example, although the legal age for consensual sex in Canada is 14, it is illegal to be in pornography until age 18. Similarly, although 12 is the minimum age for consensual sex in Mexico, a prostitute is underage if he or she is younger than 16. As you can see by this, the age in which a child is considered to be mature enough to handle sex or participate in sexually exploitive situations is neither agreed upon nor internationally recognized.

NOTE

You can view the latest information on ages of sexual consent at the World Ages of Consent for Sex and Marriage Web site at http://aoc.puellula.com/, or by visiting the Interpol Web page on sexual offenses against children at www.interpol.int/Public/Children/SexualAbuse/NationalLaws/.

The varying ages of sexual consent have also caused another problem: *child sex tourism*, in which pedophiles travel to countries with low ages of consent to have sex with children, who are under the age of 18. A *pedophile* is someone whose primary sexual interest is in children. Some professionals make the distinction that pedophiles are interested in children and *hebophiles* are interested in adolescents; however, for the purposes of this chapter, we will use the term *pedophile* to refer to a person whose sexual interest is with a minor (that is, below the age of legal consent). Because such individuals are fearful of being arrested in their own country, they will travel to countries such as Thailand, where the legal age of consent is 13 and child prostitutes are plentiful. Even if a person is arrested in that country, often he or she can avoid prosecution by bribing officials.

Over the past few years, reforms in child exploitation laws throughout the world have established higher ages of consent, or in some cases have helped to establish an age of consent where there was none before. However, an international standard age of consent for areas of sexual consent, pornography, and other sexual exploitive activities is needed.

Understanding Child Pornography

Although we provided a clear definition of child pornography earlier, many countries have found it difficult to create a clear legal definition ... or create any kind of legislation at all. In a report developed by the International Centre for Missing & Exploited Children in 2006 (www.icmec.org/en_X1/pdf/ModelLegislationFINAL.pdf), a review of 184 countries that were members of Interpol found that 95 countries had no legislation specifically addressing child pornography. Of those that did:

- Fifty-four countries had no definition of child pornography in their legislation.

- Twenty-seven countries didn't provide for computer-facilitated offenses (that is, digital images and media, and downloading or distributing over the Internet).

- Forty-one countries didn't criminalize the possession of child pornography.

Of the countries that do have laws that address these issues, child pornography is generally defined as having sexually explicit content. This may include such acts as lascivious exhibition of genitals, masturbation, fellatio, and/or cunnilingus (oral sex), intercourse, anal sex, or other graphic content. In countries where child pornography laws exist, it is generally illegal to possess, distribute, or produce such images or depictions. However, exceptions may exist if it is for specific circumstances, such as artistic or medical purposes. For example, a photo in a medical book may show a child's genitals, but would not be considered child pornography.

Child Pornography without the Pornography

Because of wordings in the law, some photos and depictions of children don't meet the legal definitions of child pornography. These photos are widely available on the Internet, and in art books and other media. In some cases, they are even available in mainstream bookstores.

Child erotica is a term applied to photos or depictions of naked children, which may or may not be also categorized as art. The images don't fall under standard definitions of pornography, as the photos of the children are natural poses and are not sexually explicit. In other words, there is no lascivious exhibition of genitalia, such as a child spreading his or her legs or posing lewdly. In many cases, the distinction between whether it is deemed as art is in the way it's presented.

Also, many sites on the Internet operate under the thin guise of promoting nudism, even though the images predominantly show teenage or prepubescent children. Many sites operate by charging money for access to more revealing images of children or the bulk of their photos. The photos are often taken at nudist resorts or other locations where nudity is legal, allowing amateur photographers to take photos of naked boys and girls without worry of immediate repercussions. By skirting the line between what is legal and illegal, these sites are able to operate.

Another type of photography that skirts the issue of child pornography is Web sites featuring child models. These *child model* or *glamour* sites feature young girls posing in bikinis, miniskirts, sheer lingerie, and other outfits. The photos of girls on such sites may not contain any nudity, but they are provocative and show scantily clad girls in suggestive poses. For good reason, such sites have undergone serious scrutiny over the past few years, with many being shut down.

Determining Whether Something is Legally Child Pornography

In the 1996 case *United States v. Dost*, a federal judge suggested a six-step method of evaluating images to determine whether the nude image of a child could be considered legal or illegal. The criteria were as follows:

- If the focal point was the child's genitalia or pubic area
- If the setting of the visual depiction was sexually suggestive
- If the child was in inappropriate attire or an unnatural pose
- If the child was fully, partially, or completely nude
- If the visual depiction suggested coyness or a willingness to engage in sexual activity
- If the visual depiction was intended or designed to elicit a sexual response from the person viewing it

Although the list of factors isn't comprehensive, and other aspects of an image may be relevant, the Dost factors do provide a good measurement for determining whether an image is illegal. They address the fact that just because nudity is present, labeling it child pornography may not be applicable.

On the Scene

Child Modeling Sites

As with most child modeling sites, children appear with permission of the parent or legal guardian, because the child is too young to consent. The rationale for parents allowing the photographs has ranged from raising money for college (as in the case of the now defunct Lil' Amber site that featured a 9-year-old girl) to gaining exposure for legitimate modeling jobs—neither being a particularly good reason for creating sexualized images of a child. In 2002, Representative Mark Foley took on combating this type of exploitation and introduced a bill called the Child Modeling Exploitation Prevention Act, which would ban selling photographs of minors. Needless to say, doing so would impact legitimate modeling companies and other businesses, and due to opposition the bill never left committee. As for Rep. Mark Foley, he resigned in 2006 after ABC News reported on his inappropriate e-mails and sexually explicit instant messages (IMs) to teenaged pages.

Child Pornography without the Child

Laws against child pornography are based on the assumption that children are harmed in the making of the pictures. The pornography laws generally apply to visual depictions only, with the written word (stories about child sex) being protected by the First Amendment in the United States. However, even though no child is harmed in the generation of certain types of pornography, it is viewed by those who abuse children sexually or by those who are intrigued by the idea of having sex with a child. Many different types of child pornography don't involve actual children.

Virtual child pornography is a type of digital fakery in which the images appear to be of children having sex or posing nude, but they are actually digitally manipulated or *morphed* images. Such images can be created via simple cut and paste or via extensive digital editing. Superimposing a child's face onto a body of a minor, or showing someone with a body type similar to that of an underage child, gives the illusion that a child is actually posing nude or having sex.

CyberLaw Review

Virtual Pornography Being Virtually Legal

In the United Kingdom, under the Protection of Children Act (1978) and Section 160 of the Criminal Justice Act of 1988, it is a criminal offense for a person to possess either a photograph or a "pseudophotograph" of a child that is considered indecent. The term *pseudophotograph* is defined as an image made by computer graphics or that otherwise appears to be a photograph. Typically, this is a photograph that is created using a graphics manipulation software program such as Adobe Photoshop to superimpose a child's head onto a different body.

The issue of "virtual child pornography" that uses high-quality, computer-generated images instead of real photographs is a matter of intense debate. It is illegal in some countries, such as Germany, where it is punishable by up to five years' imprisonment, but it is legal in other countries, such as the United States. In April 2002, the Supreme Court struck down the federal laws making this form of kiddie porn illegal. At the time of this writing, the Justice Department and members of Congress were intent on rewriting those laws more narrowly, in a way that would outlaw virtual child pornography which is indistinguishable from the real thing while still allowing the law to pass constitutional muster.

The Motives of Those Who View Child Pornography

People view child pornography with different intentions or purposes. Although some women do access or produce child pornography, most of those who create, access, and disseminate this type of material are men. Those who are sexually attracted to this type of pornography will often fall into one of these categories:

- Passive pedophiles, who use the Internet to access and download kiddie porn and use photos and stories of children engaging in sex (usually with adults) to feed their own fantasies. Even if they never act out those fantasies in real life, in the United States and many other countries, it is illegal to even possess child pornography in photographic form.

- Active pedophiles, who use the Internet to find their victims. These criminals usually also collect child pornography, but they don't stop at fantasies. They often hang out in chat rooms that are frequented by children and engage them in virtual conversations, attempting to gain their trust and lure them into an in-person meeting. They might then rape the children, or they could simply "court" them, preferring to gradually seduce them into sexual relationships. Because children under a certain age (which varies from one state to another) are not considered capable of consenting to sex, sexual conduct with a minor is still a crime, even if the child agrees to it. Usually the offense is defined as statutory rape or some category of sexual assault.

- Sexually indiscriminate, in which the person is looking for new kinds of sexual stimuli.

- Sexually curious, in which the person is accessing the images out of curiosity. For example, people under the age of 18 may access child pornography to view people within their own age range, whereas adults may visit a site because they are curious as to what kiddie porn is.

In some cases, people have viewed a considerable amount of pornography, and then they move on to forms of pornography by which they would have initially been offended. In other words, they have viewed so much porn that they have become desensitized to it. Such people will visit sites and possibly download images with little regard to its implications, because to them, porn is porn. When analyzing a computer, it is easy to identify such people because the computer contains a diverse range of different types of pornography. For example, images may include erotic images from men's magazines, amateur adult porn, images of older women or men (possibly even senior citizens) posing or engaged in sex, as well as a number of other genres. Regardless of whether the computer contains a prevalent amount of child pornography, it is important to remember that even a single image of child pornography can result in criminal charges.

The Victims of Child Pornography

According to the National Centre for Missing & Exploited Children's report mentioned previously, of those arrested for possession of child pornography:

- Eighty-three percent had images involving children between the ages of six and 12

- Thirty-nine percent had images involving children between the ages of three and five

- Nineteen percent had images of infants and toddlers under the age of three

As previously mentioned, most of the children used in child pornography are female victims, and although these figures do not account for adolescents, you can see that most of the children involved in child pornography are between the ages of six and 12. Although the gender is agreed upon by most studies, an article available from the Computer Crime Research Center (www.crime-research.org/articles/536/) states that "Federal Bureau of Investigation (FBI) personnel estimate that over 50% of all child pornography seized in the United States depicts boys rather than girls. Canadian Customs puts that figure at 75% for Canada." Regardless of gender, the children may be required to pose nude for softcore images, or they may be used for hardcore pictures and videos in which they perform various sex acts.

How they become victims of this crime varies, but sufficient information shows that it is an international problem. Children may be exploited in countries with low ages of consent, where there are no child pornography laws, or where existing laws aren't enforced. Poverty is also an issue, as children who are impoverished and/or living on the street are often targeted for prostitution or pornography.

As mentioned earlier in this chapter, countries with low ages of consent for exploitive activities such as prostitution, or where underage prostitution is not enforced, can be destinations for child sex tourism and child pornography. In a report from Save the Children, titled "Position paper on child pornography and Internet-related sexual exploitation of Children" (www.inhope.org/doc/stc-pp-cp.pdf), it was reported that up to 50 percent of child prostitutes were also subjects of child pornography. As such, child prostitution provides an avenue for pedophiles and pornographers to acquire children to abuse.

The areas of the world where the production of child pornography is most prevalent have changed over the years, ranging from Japan, Taiwan, Russia, and other countries. According to a 2004 report by the Russian National Consultation on the Commercial Sexual Exploitation of Children (www.ecpat.net/eng/Russia.asp), child pornography makes up 25 percent of the pornography on Internet Web sites, and more than 50 percent of these contain child pornography from Russia. It is estimated that pornography from this country involves tens of thousands of children being exploited.

Child pornography created in Russia, the Ukraine, and other areas of the former Eastern Europe has also become a problem over the past number of years. Although not limited to these parts of the world, young women or girls may be offered modeling jobs that are actually child pornography. They may be required to pose nude or while engaged in sex acts. The images are then sold over the Internet or through various magazines in countries where the legal age is low enough to make publishing legal.

In some cases, the level at which children are procured is highly organized and insidious. In Russia, businesses involved in child pornography will pose as modeling and fitness schools, where children are actually groomed for participation in pornographic films. One such institution was the "Aphrodite School" that operated as a school for young models. It had an enrollment procedure that should have seemed odd to parents, whereby the girls had to show themselves naked before they were accepted. Although this may seem inconceivable to most people, in many cases the parents involved were living in destitution with no chance for a better life. Poverty mixed with opportunity can create an atmosphere in which children appear in pornography with their parents' permission or endorsement.

Regardless of the situation, a child is powerless and cannot give consent to appearing in pornography, and thereby doesn't have a choice. As stated in the Save the Children report mentioned previously, "German police estimate that 130.000 children in 1993 were forced by parents or other acquaintances to participate in the production of pornography." Beyond commercial pornographers and child sex tourists, children may become victims of the very people they believe are there to protect them.

The Role of the Internet in Promoting Child Pornography

When the Internet began to become popular in the mid-1990s, child pornography began to appear on various sites. In these early years, most of the pornography came in the form of photographs or pictures from magazines that were converted into an electronic format using scanners. These were often photographs of children taken by child abusers, or magazines from the Netherlands featuring adolescent girls. Another common source was nudist magazines, showing naked minors playing sports or other activities. In some cases, these scanned images were more than a decade old, but the amateur production of child porn soon increased with newer photos. Once digital cameras become more affordable, higher-quality images began to appear more frequently on Web sites located in countries where child pornography laws were nonexistent or not enforced.

The Internet has created a new marketplace that makes the distribution of child pornography easier. According to the Save the Children report cited earlier, "Child pornography on the Internet has expanded dramatically in recent years and appears to have largely overtaken and absorbed previous production and distribution methods of child pornographic material." As with any other kind of pornography, anything a pedophile wants is just a mouse-click away.

By being part of the global village, pedophiles have been able to establish international child pornography rings. The Internet can be used to make connections with others who possess child pornography, allowing them to trade and sell it with one another as well as learn the dos and don'ts to avoid getting caught. Not only is the Internet a resource for porn, but it is also an educational tool.

Driven from Back Alleys to the Information Superhighway

The Internet provided a relative safe haven for those who sought child pornography. Prior to the Internet, the availability of child porn was often limited to behind-the-counter purchases at adult bookstores or to ordering magazines and films from other countries and receiving them through the mail. In the 1970s, adult bookstores began to sell child porn openly, which incited new laws and police crackdowns, making the availability of these items more difficult to purchase. This lasted until the 1980s, when computers provided a new method of exchanging data. *Bulletin board systems* (BBSes) are programs that can be installed on a computer, allowing other computers to dial in and access e-mail, exchange messages, download files, and perform other functions that became commonplace on the Internet. During the 1980s, those who sought child pornography no longer had to travel to unsafe neighborhoods; they could now download child porn to a computer.

Because BBSes were privately run, what was allowed on the board depended on the person who owned the computer on which the BBS was installed. Individuals could start their own BBSes, and create private areas that limited access to anything they wanted, ranging from illegal software to child pornography. However, although BBSes did exist that provided access to folders filled with child pornography, many of those who ran these boards discouraged such activities and commonly banned people from their BBS. Another reason they were self-policed was that most of those in law enforcement were computer-illiterate—remember that computers were relatively new at this time. By the time the police took a serious interest in BBSes, many of them were shutting down from lack of use, because most people had discovered the Internet.

Whereas BBSes provided access to a local community of computer users, the Internet provided availability to international sources. In terms of child pornography, it opened up the market. It allowed pedophiles from around the world the chance to communicate with one another and share pictures and videos, with a greater degree of anonymity than they'd ever had before.

The ability to download more pornography and save it to a computer also stemmed from advances in connectivity and storage media. The sizes of hard disks on computers increased and their prices dropped during the early 1990s, allowing them to acquire more files in less time. A 500 KB file would have taken more than 35 minutes to download from a BBS using a 2400-baud modem, but when the Internet became popular, ISPs required people to have a modem that could connect at 28.8- or 33.6 Kbps. This same 500 KB file now took less than three minutes to download. Today, people commonly have high-speed connections to the Internet, meaning that it now takes a few seconds to download this same file. The advances in speed and storage made it possible for higher-quality images and full videos to be distributed over the Internet.

As we'll see in the next section, the Internet provided a number of features and areas where child porn could easily be obtained. In many cases, the pornography could be acquired at no additional cost, making it significantly cheaper than previous methods. Consider that in the 1970s, kiddie porn would have to be ordered through the mail. The postal service was the main distribution source for child pornography at that time. Whenever child porn was identified, the package would be delivered to the intended recipient, meaning that he or she would have to sign for it. Postal inspectors and police would execute a search warrant and arrest the person who signed. Using information associated with the order, the evidence in a single case could include the order form, the check or money order to pay for the porn, the signature provided by the person who accepted the order, and the porn itself. The paper trail was easy to follow, making the risks associated with manufacturing and possessing child pornography extreme. The risks were less so with the Internet, and because the costs of those risks weren't passed on to the consumer, it was cheap to pay for the porn when required to do so.

Tools of the Trade

A number of tools and services are used to acquire child pornography. Basically, any Internet tool that has the capability of sending and receiving a file can be used to exchange images, videos, and other files containing pornographic images. If these tools also have the capability of communicating with other people, online predators may use them to meet children online.

E-mail

Because e-mail allows you to attach files to a message, any images, videos, audio, or other files can be sent with a message. E-mail is used to distribute child pornography in small quantities, attaching one or a few files to any message. A person may send child pornography to others who have an interest, or a pedophile may send messages to a child with these images attached to seduce or groom the child into having sex or sending back pictures of him- or herself. Because a message can be associated with the image, the predator can tell the child that this is what he'd like to do, and possibly pique the child's interest or desensitize him or her and loosen any inhibitions.

Mailing Lists

Mailing lists are lists of e-mail addresses that are subscribed to, allowing you to join a group that shares a common interest or a need to exchange information. When you send an e-mail to the group's e-mail address, everyone in the group receives it. Numerous mailing lists are available on the Internet, and you can subscribe to them by sending an e-mail to either an automated program or a moderator. The moderator's purpose is to ensure that any rules pertaining to the group are observed, and to facilitate adding new members to the list. Because mailing lists may consist of any type of group with a shared interest, it follows suit that there are those available for sharing child pornography, or information on how to obtain it (for example, lists of sites, and so on).

E-Groups

An *e-group* is a service that allows users to send e-mails to members, post messages, share pictures, and chat with other members, among other things. One popular site for e-groups is Yahoo! Groups (http://groups.yahoo.com). By searching such sites, you can find groups dealing with everything you can imagine, and a number of things you can't. Once you find a site, you subscribe to it much like a message list. Certain people can even have different access from others, controlling whether certain trusted users have access to specific photos or other items that the rest of the group can't see.

Newsgroups

Newsgroups or *discussion groups* are used to exchange messages and files through *Usenet*, which was established in 1980 and continues as one of the oldest computer networks. These groups allow people to post publicly accessible messages, which are distributed across *news servers* on the Internet. Each group may contain thousands of messages from people, and there are tens of thousands of newsgroups that you can view or subscribe to. You access newsgroups using a newsreader or features in e-mail programs such as Outlook Express, which connect to the news server to download groups and their messages.

There are newsgroups that address specific interests and topics, which may or may not be monitored by a moderator. By accessing a group, you can post text or binary files, including images, videos, audio, software, and other files. This makes newsgroups one of the largest possible sources of pornography on the Internet, with specific groups geared toward child porn. As shown in Figure 9.8, some newsreaders allow you to filter the listing of groups (which in this case exceeded 60,000) so that you can find ones with specific subject matter. The names of these groups reflect their content, with some of them providing free downloads of pornographic images and videos featuring adolescents and prepubescent children.

Figure 9.8 A Listing of Available Newsgroups Using the Forte Agent Newsreader

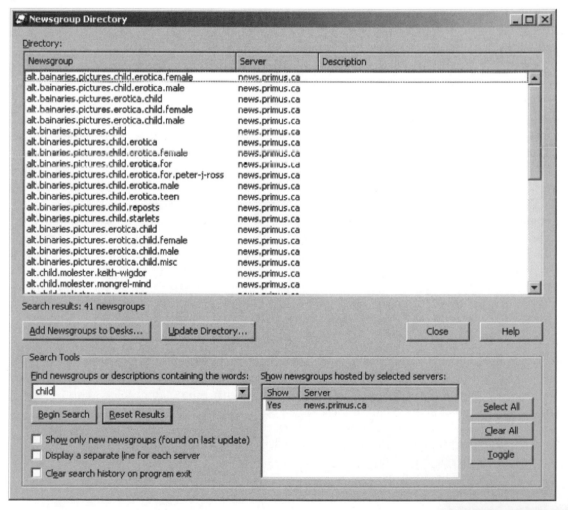

Peer-to-Peer Applications

Peer-to-peer (P2P) applications are used to network different computers together over the Internet so that people can share files on one another's hard drives. Examples of P2P networks include Kazaa, Morpheus, FreeNet, and Gnutella. Users access the distributed network of computers using P2P software, which allows them to share files and have a shared directory on their hard drive searched. These tools can be used to search the computers making up the network for specific types of files or files that match a certain criterion.

When you've heard of file sharing, you've probably heard it in the context of people sharing copies of music files with one another. However, more than simply music is available on these networks. Using them, you can download literature, programs, videos, images, and other items. However, although the music industry has made an issue of file sharing, a more important issue of P2P is that it is also used to exchange child pornography. In fact, according to the Internet Pornography Statistics Web page at Top Ten Reviews (http://internet-filter-review.toptenreviews.com/internet-pornography-statistics.html), in 2006 there were 116,000 Gnutella requests daily for child pornography.

Web Sites

Web sites are a popular method of providing access to child pornography. *Web sites* are collections of files called *Web pages*, which are documents written in HTML that may contain scripts, Java applets, or other programmed features which make the site automated or interactive. These pages may consist of text, pictures, audio, video, or other content that Internet users can access using *Web browsers* such as Internet Explorer, Opera, Safari, and Firefox. These browsers access the site and their pages using a unique address, called a Uniform Resource Locator (URL). As mentioned, many of the sites providing access to child pornography may also charge a fee. The owners of these sites may create their own porn to sell online, or collect it from other sources on the Internet.

A new twist to being able to find such sites is the image search features in search engines. *Search engines* are used to find specific sites via keywords or phrases that you enter. Sites such as Google also have features to look for images that are on sites, allowing you to find sites that have specific names or content. For example, by going to http://images.google.ca, you could type in "child porn" and preview images from sites around the world. By clicking on one of these images, you are then taken to the site. Not only is this useful to pedophiles interested in child pornography, but it can also be a useful tool for investigators trying to find these sites.

Chat Rooms and Instant Messaging

Chat rooms are Web sites or programs that allow people to send text messages to one another in real time. The chat room works as a virtual room, where groups of people send messages that others can read instantaneously. Often, people in chat rooms will use aliases or nicknames to provide some anonymity, and will use the chat room to meet others. If individual visitors to the chat room wish to talk privately, they can enter a private chat room, which allows two or more people to send messages privately to one another. Some examples of chat rooms are Internet Relay Chat (IRC) and Web sites such as Talk City (www.talkcity.com).

Among other groups, chat rooms appeal to adolescents and teenagers, who communicate with others and use features to send files to one another online. Because of this, online predators will use chat rooms to meet young people and attempt to engage in *sex chat*, where individuals in a private chat room will tell one another what they like to do sexually to one another. Basically, sex chat is the textual equivalent of a dirty phone call. In addition to this, features in chat programs allow people to send pictures to one another, enabling pedophiles to exchange child pornography, or groom potential victims with pictures.

Instant messaging is similar to the function of a private chat room. It is a service that allows two or more clients to send messages to one another in real time using IM software. Generally, each IM client ties into a service that transfers messages between other users with the same client software. However, there are programs such as Trillian that allow users to consolidate their accounts on different IM networks and connect to AIM, Yahoo! Messenger, Windows Live Messenger, ICQ (I Seek You), and IRC all within a single interface. In recent years, such features have also been folded into other IM software, such as Windows Live Messenger supporting messages exchanged with Yahoo! Messenger clients.

Because so many young people enjoy chat rooms and instant messaging, these features are also being incorporated into other tools. For example, a game used on an Xbox or PlayStation may provide features so that you can chat with people you're playing against online. Although this can be fun for those with a real interest in the game, it can also be used by pedophiles to connect with children and adolescents who are trying to connect with young people in new ways.

Challenges in Controlling Child Pornography

Cybercrime cases often have more challenges than other, more traditional types of crime. To effectively combat computer-related crimes, those directly involved in investigating these crimes need specialized training and equipment, which (as with anything dealing with computers) needs to be upgraded every few years, at least. This can be difficult for many police organizations, as the costs for implementing specialized units can be quite high. This can limit the ability to investigate computer crimes at its most basic level.

In many cases, a crime might originate in one country where legislation differs from that of your own country or where the act is not a crime at all. For example, although child pornography might be defined as pornographic images of persons younger than 18 years of age in North America, the legal age to pose for such images in other countries might be considerably younger. This difference can cause a dilemma for law enforcement officers, because it is legal for a Web site in one country to distribute the images but illegal for people in other countries to download them. Investigators can arrest people in possession of the pornographic files, but they might be powerless to shut down the Web site distributing the pornography.

In Cyprus, police face the obstacle of conflicting laws. As did most European countries, the Cypriot government signed the Budapest Convention on Cybercrime in 2001, and agreed to take action against such crimes as child pornography. However, existing laws protect privacy, and state that communication services are prohibited from disclosing personal information. Under Chapter 17 of the Cyprus Constitution, a person's right to privacy can't be infringed by listening in on private telephone conversations, which means that any data transmitted over the phone line (such as child pornography) also can't be used as evidence. Unless the material is found on the hard disk of a computer or other media, Cypriot authorities can't investigate incidents in which a person is downloading or distributing child porn.

Not all countries view a child in the same way, such as Norway which considers the sexual maturity of a child. Norway considers that child pornography is sexually explicit material with a child under the age of 16, but if the child's sexual maturity is obviously over, under paragraph 204 of the Penal Code he or she isn't considered a minor in terms of child pornography. Whether a child has reached a certain level of sexual maturity is determined on a case-by-case basis by the court. However, this doesn't mean that a person can't be punished in such situations, as charges against someone producing child pornography could still be filed under other laws dealing with assault or exploitation.

The ability to perform investigations that go outside jurisdictional boundaries almost always relies on cooperation with law enforcement entities in those areas. Police in one country generally have no official jurisdiction in other countries. However, when police in different countries work together their impact on crime can be significant. This impact is seen in a number of collaborative efforts between police and other law enforcement agencies in various countries.

As nations cooperate with one another in various endeavors, a global vision of what is considered right and wrong has been established on a variety of subjects. Because numerous countries don't have laws or adequate legislation dealing with child pornography, cyberterrorism, and other activities related to cybercrime, international consortiums saw a need to provide a legal framework for updating the laws of these countries. International organizations and political coalitions have influenced legal changes in many countries, pressuring some countries to create new laws or revise existing ones to deal with crimes that the majority of the world considers abhorrent or potentially devastating.

Anti-Child Pornography Initiatives and Organizations

Because a simple cybercrime case can quickly expand to involve law enforcement in other areas, there is a need for initiatives and organizations to aid in coordinating and assisting in these investigations. In the sections that follow, we'll look at a few of these initiatives and organizations, including:

- Innocent Images National Initiative

- Internet Crimes Against Children

- Project Safe Childhood

- Child Exploitation Tracking System

Innocent Images National Initiative

The FBI developed the *Innocent Images National Initiative* (IINI) as part of its Cyber Crimes Program for the purpose of identifying, investigating, and prosecuting those who use computers for child sexual exploitation and child pornography. In performing these tasks, the FBI also attempts to identify and rescue children being exploited or appearing in these images.

Originally, the IINI provided one of the few online presences of law enforcement, although this is no longer the case due to the volume of police and other agencies that pose undercover in chat rooms and other forums, attempt to identify online predators, or are involved in cybercrime investigations. Because of the involvement of local, state, and international law enforcement officials in these endeavors, the IINI provides training and assistance, as well as coordinating national or international investigations.

Over the years, the IINI has expanded its mission to include sexual tourism, in which American citizens or residents travel for the purpose of having sex with minors. Several federal statutes in the United States deal with sex tourism and trafficking (18 U.S.C. §§ 1591, 2421, 2422, and 2423), and make interstate and international sex tourism and sex trafficking within a state illegal. Although its focus now includes these types of illegal activities, this hasn't deterred the IINI from attempting to identify, investigate, and prosecute those who produce, distribute, or possess child pornography.

Additional information on the IINI is available on the FBI's Web site at www.fbi.gov/publications/ innocent.htm. By visiting this Web page, you can view the latest statistics on the IINI, and also view information on individuals the IINI has added to the FBI's Ten Most Wanted Fugitives.

Internet Crimes Against Children

The *Internet Crimes Against Children* (ICAC) Program is a network of 46 regional task forces that are funded by the U.S. Department of Justice (DOJ). It was created to provide federal assistance to state and local law enforcement so that they could better investigate computer and Internet-based crimes that sexually exploit children.

The program is funded through the United States Office of Juvenile Justice and Delinquency Prevention, and provides a variety of different resources that are useful to organizations and law enforcement officials dealing with crimes against children, including the following:

■ The Training & Technical Assistance program provided by ICAC (www.icactraining.org) offers information and resources for training ICAC initiatives, as well as contact information for technical support. This trains law enforcement officials on how to perform undercover chats, investigative techniques, and a variety of other topics and technologies. It also provides presentation material to teach students ranging from kindergarten to high school, parents, and other interested parties.

■ The ICAC Research Center (www.unh.edu/ccrc/) provides up-to-date statistics, publications, and other resources on sexual abuse, exploitation, and other crimes and issues dealing with children.

■ The e-mail distribution list provided by ICAC allows individuals affiliated with ICAC to communicate with one another and share information.

Project Safe Childhood

Project Safe Childhood (PSC) is an initiative developed by the U.S. DOJ to provide a coordinated effort in combating child pornography and sexual exploitation. It is designed to help local communities create programs and develop strategies to investigate child exploitation, and identify and rescue victims. PSC is based on Project Safe Neighborhoods, and focuses on providing a framework to better investigate and prosecute crimes that involve and target children through the Internet and other methods of communication and media. It involves U.S. attorneys partnering with ICAC task forces, nonprofit organizations, and federal, state, and local law enforcement officials to develop strategies to combat these issues and assist child victims.

By coordinating efforts, local law enforcement officials are better able to access services provided at a federal level. PSC works in conjunction with the Innocent Images National Initiative so that PSC task forces can pursue local leads. Once an arrest is made, federal agencies can then charge the person under federal law, which generally involves harsher penalties than laws at the state level.

Part of the PSC initiative involves developing programs to provide training and education, and to promote awareness. This includes educating communities as well as law enforcement. Training programs are provided a variety of resources, including ICAC and the National Center for Missing and Exploited Children (www.missingkids.com), which provides information about missing children on its Web site, online resources, and a CyberTipline to report child pornography and sexual exploitation.

The PSC Web site at www.projectsafechildhood.gov provides information on legislation that is used to prosecute offenders, as well as online resources such as publications, links to related Web sites, and information on training and technical assistance.

Child Exploitation Tracking System

The *Child Exploitation Tracking System* (CETS) is a tool developed for law enforcement to organize, analyze, share, and search information related to child exploitation cases, such as cases involving child pornography. Developed as a partnership project between Canadian police services, the National Child Exploitation Coordination Centre (NCECC; www.ncecc.ca), and Microsoft, CETS is used to track cases and reveal common factors among them. Using this tool, authorities can identify links between different cases, even if they're being investigated by law enforcement officials in different jurisdictions.

The success of CETS was seen even before it was officially unveiled in April 2005. An example of how well it works is a 2004 arrest of a man who took photographs of himself sexually assaulting a 4-year-old girl and then distributed them on the Internet. The man was identified by CETS, which linked information in Operation Falcon (a U.S. Department of Homeland Security investigation) to an FBI investigation. This link was discovered while the program was still in its beta version, and since then has been used to assisted in the arrests of dozens of other people, including the March 2006 arrests of 27 people located in four different countries who ran a private chat room designed to groom children.

CETS works by allowing different police to access a centralized database, which is located at the NCECC in Ottawa, Ontario. By entering information into CETS, an investigator can then determine whether aspects of his or her case match with other investigations that involve the same people. It will search for similar e-mail addresses, online identities (aliases, nicknames, and so on), or other aspects that can match a person to multiple cases. By finding matches between such information, law enforcement officials are better able to make arrests and identify victims.

Although CETS was initially available to Canadian law enforcement, it is now used in other countries, with additional countries looking to deploy CETS in the future. It is used in the United Kingdom, and in October 2006 it assisted police in identifying and arresting 37 suspects and rescuing five children. Indonesia, Italy, and Brazil also began to use CETS in 2006, with 13 other countries planning to deploy it as well.

Cyberterrorism

In the wake of the events of September 11, 2001, the North American public has become more concerned with the potential for disasters caused by cyberterrorism. Cyberterrorism involves using common hacking methods (such as unauthorized access to computers, viruses, e-mail bombs, and so forth) for the purpose of causing damage, especially to critical national infrastructure (water supplies, electrical grids, telephone switches) or national security and military defense systems. As with other forms of terrorism, cyberterrorism is generally politically motivated and is directed against noncombatant targets (civilians). An act of cyberterrorism can result in damage to a country's economy and infrastructure as well as loss of life. We can only imagine the devastation that could be caused by a hacker taking down an air traffic control system, a government computer system that controls nuclear missile targeting, or a 911 emergency system. The threat is exacerbated by the fact that traditional counterterrorism tactics are useless against an enemy who can use technology to strike from thousands of miles away.

The more dependent a society becomes on its computer systems, the more vulnerable it becomes to cyberterrorists. Food processing and pharmaceutical plants, electrical and natural gas utilities, traffic control systems, medical facilities, and military, public safety, and civilian communications systems are all areas of great vulnerability. The terrorist generally aims for destruction on a large scale, and that is certainly possible for someone who manages to take control of one or more of these crucial systems. For discussion of possible scenarios involving cyberterrorism, see http://afgen.com/terrorism1.html.

Cyberterrorism is an issue that has been a concern for law enforcement agencies in many countries over the past several years. Computer and network security has been a major focus for both information technology (IT) departments and police management throughout the world. Regulations and internal policies dealing with connectivity to the Internet and securing information have become commonplace. IT specialists in corporations and small-business networks have shown increased diligence by implementing firewalls and applying security updates, AV software, and numerous other measures.

The threat of cyberterrorism isn't new. On October 1, 1997, Arnaud de Borchgrave, director of the Global Organized Crime Project of the Center for Strategic and International Studies, testified before the U.S. House of Representatives Committee on International Relations. During this testimony, he stated that "already eight hostile or potentially hostile nations have developed the required technology and skills to wage information warfare by means of electronic sabotage and lethal destruction, and 120 nations have developed computer attack capabilities." Information warfare could include not only acts of cyberterrorism, but also espionage and intelligence gathering. You can find further information on this testimony at the Web site for the Center for Strategic & International Studies (CSIS) at www.csis.org/hill/ts100197.html.

The difficulties with imposing legislation dealing with cyberterrorism and its impact on citizens are in many ways similar to the problems of imposing security measures within an organization. For years, companies have had to balance security with accessibility when new policies were used to limit staff members' activities. With every new policy, members of an organization would find that their ability to access certain information was reduced. Too much security could result in people being unable to do their jobs, whereas too little resulted in vulnerabilities that left the company at risk. The impact of cyberterrorism and other cybercrime legislation can pose similar risks, affecting the freedom of people to access certain information or perform actions that are commonplace to their online activities. Freedom and security are, by definition, on opposite ends of a continuum. The more you have of one, the less you have of the other. Balancing the need for governmental control to provide protection of its citizenry with that citizenry's desire to be free from oppressive overregulation is a political dilemma faced by democratic countries founded on the principles of liberty and human rights.

Another category of cybercrime related to but different from cyberterrorism is "hacktivism," which generally involves damage to property without risk of injury to people. During the Kosovo conflict, many "hacktivists" used the Internet to spread propaganda, taking over Web sites of government agencies and changing them to reflect the hackers' political views. Hacktivism shouldn't be confused with simple political activism that involves using the Internet. The latter includes such activities as constructing a Web site of your own and posting your political opinions there. Hacktivism is a criminal activity in that it involves hacking into someone else's site without permission or disrupting the network activities of organizations or governments whose policies you dislike. Hacktivists use e-mail bombs, DoS attacks, viruses and worms, and other common hacker ploys for political purposes. However, when hacktivists cross over the line to disrupt services (such as those of medical facilities or utility companies) in a way that poses a threat to human life or livelihood, they become cyberterrorists.

Summary

In this chapter, we discussed a number of issues related to e-mail and Internet crimes. We saw how e-mail and Web sites can be used for criminal purposes such as acquiring child pornography, phishing, luring children for sex, distributing viruses, and other acts that are harmful to people and systems. To commit these and other acts, a wide range of tools are available.

We also discussed how information may be acquired from e-mails during an investigation, and that certain tools may be used to review e-mails and track them to their source. By tracing e-mails and Web sites to the people who own them, you can arrest the culprits and stop their involvement in cybercrime.

Individuals and organizations can protect themselves in a number of ways. Security settings can be configured to prevent someone from being victimized by phishing scams, malicious code, or vulnerabilities that can be exploited in browsers and e-mail clients. By doing as much as possible to secure systems, the likelihood of being victimized is lessened.

Frequently Asked Questions

Q: I am trying to trace the origin of an e-mail, but Nslookup doesn't work on my computer due to network firewall restrictions. What can I do?

A: Online services provide Nslookup and whois tools. By entering the IP address into an online Nslookup tool, you'll receive the same information that you would by using the Nslookup tool on your computer.

Q: I have made an image of a computer, but I am unable to access the e-mail on the computer using forensic software. What should I do?

A: You can extract the e-mail archive files from the computer, and then use e-mail forensic software to access the e-mail stored in these files.

Q: I work for an ISP in the United States, and I have discovered child pornography on a Web site we host. What should I do?

A: Under the Protection of Children from Sexual Predators Act of 1998 (Sexual Predators Act), ISPs are required to notify law enforcement of Web sites containing child pornography on their server(s). Failing to report it could mean that the ISP will be fined.

Q: I am investigating an incident where child pornography was found on a computer. The person who used the computer claims he received a pop up containing a link to child pornography and clicked on it. How can I determine whether the person's story is true?

A: Always remember that just because a questionable site or image is found on a computer, it doesn't mean the person is surfing for kiddie porn. E-mail messages and pop ups are distributed with images and links to child pornography Web sites, and because the pop up, e-mail, or Web site contained images of child pornography, this means they are also on the person's hard drive. When analyzing a computer, it is easy to identify such situations as the computer contains only images and Web site history relating to an e-mail, pop up, or Web page that was visited. In other words, the person's browsing behavior doesn't indicate that he was trolling for kiddie porn sites. In addition, firewall logs may show that the person accessed the site or pop up for only a moment, indicating that he closed the pop up or Web browser immediately after identifying the illegal material.

Chapter 10

Understanding Network Intrusions and Attacks

Topics we'll investigate in this chapter:

- **Understanding Network Intrusions and Attacks**

- **Recognizing Preintrusion/Attack Activities**

- **Understanding Technical Exploits**

- **Attacking with Trojans, Viruses, and Worms**

- **Hacking for Nontechies**

- **Understanding Wireless Attacks**

Introduction

As we've discussed in earlier chapters, there are many different types of cybercrime, committed by all kinds of cybercriminals—some of whom have very little technical knowledge or skill. However, thanks to the news media and a few popular movies, most people associate the term *cybercrime* with a particular type of offense: hacking into a system or network from outside an organization. Included in this narrow definition are malicious attacks designed to crash computers and congest networks, even when no actual "illegal entry" takes place. In either case, the criminal is presumed to have a high level of knowledge about computers and networking.

Unlike the cyberscam artist who needs to know only enough about computers to send mass e-mailings, or the child pornographer whose technical know-how is limited to uploading and downloading files, the network intruder or attacker has traditionally been able to boast of a certain amount of skill. It takes knowledge (and sometimes talent) to circumvent security measures and slip through the holes programmers leave in applications and operating systems to gain access to someone else's servers. It takes a thorough understanding of how network protocols work to exploit their characteristics and bring down systems or entire networks. Or at least, it once did.

Dedicated hackers spend hundreds or even thousands of hours perfecting intrusion techniques and attacks. Today, however, many hackers who break into or bring down networks aren't really hackers at all—at least, not in the original sense of the word (which referred to computer "whiz kids" whose mastery of the technology was the key to their ability to penetrate and crack systems). This is because the "real" hackers have generously made available the fruits of their knowledge and labor in the form of scripts and executable programs that do all the work. The "script kiddies" who use them might be scorned as hacker "wannabes" by those with technical knowledge, but hacking tools still continue to proliferate, shared freely through "warez" newsgroups and Web sites, making intrusions and attacks easy. Beyond this, many of the same tools used by information technology (IT) professionals to test security and identify issues can also be used to hack the network. No longer does a would-be intruder or attack have to bother to learn the technical aspects of Windows vulnerabilities or Transmission Control Protocol/Internet Protocol (TCP/IP) security flaws. Now anyone, with no training at all, can "worm" his way into the network of a competing business or launch a massive denial-of-service (DoS) attack against a company whose politics he doesn't like.

It is important for cybercrime investigators who build cases charging unauthorized access or breach of network integrity to understand the basics of how intrusion techniques and system attacks work, even though intruders and attackers need not necessarily understand the technicalities of what they're doing. After all, the investigator could be required to testify in court about an important issue that must be established in every criminal case: whether probable cause existed to make the arrest. It could be difficult to convince a jury that you had enough evidence to believe the accused committed a crime if you're unable to explain exactly *what* the crime is and exactly *how* it was committed.

In this chapter, we provide overviews of the technical aspects of various types of intrusions and attacks. We start with a discussion of an intruder's preparatory activities that might precede an attack:

- Scanning for open ports on the targeted network

- Disguising the attacker's Internet Protocol (IP) address and other identifying information

- Placing software constructs or hardware devices (such as Trojan programs or keystroke monitors) to gather preliminary data that will help the attacker carry out the attack

Whereas in Chapter 11 we look at how intruders crack passwords and software exploits to gain access to systems and networks, in this chapter we'll discuss the many types of technical exploits that hackers use to access or attack networked computers. We also address the "script kiddie" and "click kiddie" phenomenon and show you how people with almost no technical expertise can use readily available tools to jumpstart their hacking careers. Finally, we discuss wireless networks, and some of the differences that make them prone to attacks.

> ### NOTE
>
> Some of the attacks and exploits discussed in this chapter might be considered by some to be "obsolete." However, this is true only if we assume that all systems are running the latest versions of software and that all security patches have been applied. Unfortunately, this is not the case; in a world where a substantial number of business and government computers still run older versions of Windows, it would be naïve to assume that the vulnerabilities of older operating systems and applications are no longer relevant.

Understanding Network Intrusions and Attacks

Network intrusions and attacks come in many forms and from all directions. Although external threats (usually from across the Internet) get the most attention, attacks and intrusions can—and often do—come from employees, contractors, and others on-site or within a local network. Remember that just because someone is authorized to access a network doesn't mean that he or she has authorization to access *all* its resources.

We can no longer assume that attackers are particularly knowledgeable about computers. At one time, an attacker had to have a minimal level of skill to launch an attack, but today readily available tools completely automate the attack process. An attack really can come from just about anyone who has the motivation and the mindset to launch it.

Some intrusions and "attacks" can even be unintentional. Users with just enough technical knowledge to be dangerous could experiment with changing settings and crash the system or network; curious people could stumble on unsecured resources to which they shouldn't have access; and employees attempting to make things more convenient for themselves (for example, by installing wireless access points so that they'll have network connectivity when they take their laptops to the conference room for meetings) can unknowingly open up security holes.

In the following sections, we examine the difference between an intrusion and an attack; discuss various types of attacks, including accidental ones; and provide some guidelines for preventing intentional internal security breaches.

On the Scene

Considering Internal Threats

All cybercrime by its very definition involves using a network to access systems. However, when investigators are confronted with theft or destruction of data or attacks that crash servers, the possibility of an "inside job" shouldn't be discounted. Not all attacks or unauthorized entries into systems come from the Internet; they can also come from somewhere on the local area network (LAN) or via physical access to the affected machines.

Intrusions versus Attacks

It is important for investigators to understand the difference between an intrusion and an attack because whether there was an actual unauthorized entry to the network or system can be an important factor in proving the elements of a criminal offense. Attacks can be committed without gaining entry to the network or system, as in the case of DoS attacks. These attacks overload network resources to make the network unavailable to legitimate users, but the attacker never gains access to any computer on the network.

If investigators and prosecutors don't understand this difference (which they can do only by understanding the technical aspects of how the attack works), they could file charges that won't stand up in court or bring the wrong charges against a cybercriminal. This would be similar to a situation in which no one on the law enforcement team understood the difference between the offenses of robbery and burglary. Robbery requires that a physical assault or threat of serious bodily injury takes place during the commission or attempted commission of a theft. Burglary requires that the offender unlawfully enters the premises of another person to commit a theft. If law enforcement officers arrest a suspect for breaking into a home and stealing a television set while the residents are gone, and they charge the suspect with robbery (and if the prosecutor brings such a case to trial), the suspect will almost certainly be found not guilty, because the state doesn't have proof of the elements of the offense of robbery. This situation would never happen, because law enforcement officers are drilled in the technical differences between robbery and burglary from the time they attend the police academy, and all prosecuting attorneys are well versed in these differences. However, it's entirely plausible to imagine the wrong charges being filed in a computer crime case simply because no one involved understands the technical aspects of these types of crimes.

It's important, then, to be precise when we refer to specific computer crimes. DoS attackers should not be referred to as *intruders* when no intrusion occurs. Likewise, not all intruders can accurately be classified as *attackers*—although those who gain access and then destroy data or plant viruses are properly called by both names.

CyberLaw Review

Analyzing the Law

As an example of how important it is to understand the elements of the offense, which vary from statute to statute and jurisdiction to jurisdiction, Texas Penal Code section 33.02 defines "Breach of Computer Security" as follows:

"A person commits an offense if the person knowingly accesses a computer, computer network, or computer system without the effective consent of the owner."

At first glance, it would appear that this offense would not apply to attacks in which there is no entry to the network. The statute requires "access" as an element of the offense, and a standard dictionary definition of that word is "a means of entry." However, to understand what the legislature intended when this statute was passed, we have to look back to the *legal* definitions that apply to this particular chapter of the Penal Code, which are contained in section 33.01. There, the term *access* is defined as follows:

"To approach, instruct, communicate with, store data in, retrieve or intercept data from, alter data or computer software in, or *otherwise make use of any resource of a computer, computer network, computer program, or computer system.*"

As you can see, this definition is broader. The key to bringing this charge against a DoS attacker is the phrase in italics. Because network bandwidth is a resource of a computer network, and because the attacker does indeed make use of that resource, the attacker could be charged under section 33.02.

It is very important for law enforcement officers to carefully analyze the statutes under which they intend to file charges and, if in doubt, to consult the district attorney or state attorney general for clarification of the language in the statute.

Recognizing Direct versus Distributed Attacks

Attackers can launch their attacks against a system or network in two different ways. A *direct attack* is launched from a computer used by the attacker (often after preintrusion/attack tools, such as port scanners, are used to find potential victims).

A *distributed attack* is more complex. Distributed attacks use someone else's system(s), rather than the attacker's, to perform the tasks that directly launch the attack. In this type of attack, there are multiple victims, which include not only the target of the attack but also intermediary remote systems from which the attack is launched that are controlled by the attacker. The intermediaries are referred to as *agents* or *zombies*. Software robots called *botnets* or *bots* are installed on the zombie computers, and can run autonomously and automatically. The bots can be configured to attack at a specific time, or take commands from the attacker on a remote computer. This type of attack, of course, makes it more difficult to track down the perpetrator, because the attack packets that reach the victim have multiple source addresses, and none of these is the address of the attack's originator. Commands from attacker to intermediary are often encrypted to further thwart tracing. Encrypted transmissions can't be read by a packet sniffer (a protocol analyzer).

A distributed attack works a little like the practical joke in which the jokester calls numerous pizza parlors, pretending to be a customer, and requests that pizzas be delivered to someone else's address. The primary victim is the resident at the target address who ends up with a flood of unwanted pizzas, but the pizza vendors are victims as well because their resources are used, without their prior knowledge or consent, to carry out the attack.

> **NOTE**
>
> To better understand the concept of DoS, the technicalities of which we discuss later in this chapter, let's take the pizza prank scenario described in this section a step further. If our attacker is really determined, he might call not only pizza parlors, but also all the Chinese restaurants, florists, and other "we deliver" businesses in the area, coordinating the requests so that all the delivery persons converge on the victim at the same time. If there are so many delivery vans parked on the street that the victim's family members are unable to get to their own driveway, this results in a *denial of service* to legitimate users of the driveway.

Attackers using the distributed method can launch their attacks simultaneously from dozens, hundreds, or even thousands of Internet hosts all over the world. This means that far more traffic can be generated than is possible with standard one-source attacks. A typical distributed attack model using UNIX-based computers, according to the CERT Distributed Systems Intruder Tools Workshop, has the attacker controlling several systems called *masters*. Each master controls a larger number of agents running *daemons*—the software that is used to launch the attack. The daemons are installed on the agent machines by exploiting operating system or protocol vulnerabilities. This entire process can be automated so that potential agents are discovered and penetrated and the daemon is installed on all of them, then steps are taken to hide the fact that an intrusion occurred, using batch scripts. (We discuss attack automation in more detail in the next section.) Table 10.1 outlines the distributed attack process (after installation of the daemons).

Table 10.1 The Distributed Attack Process

Step	Component	Action
1	Daemon (or agent)	Announces itself to the "masters" that have been predefined
2	Master	Lists the daemon as "ready and willing" to be used for the attack

Continued

Table 10.1 Continued. The Distributed Attack Process

Step	Component	Action
3	Attacker	Issues the command to the masters to launch the attack
4	Master	Issues the command to the daemons on the agents to launch the attack (with specific parameters such as identity of target and duration of attack)
5	Daemon	Launches the attack on the specified victim

Because this model's components are arranged in a pyramid form, with one attacker controlling several masters, which in turn control numerous agents/daemons, it is easier to disable the attack system closer to the top, where there are fewer systems to deal with. If the masters are disabled, the agents and their daemon software will not be able to function. Of course, the most efficient disabling technique is to find the attacker, thus disabling the entire attack sequence.

Automated Attacks

An *automated attack* is one that's performed by a computer program rather than the attacker manually performing the steps in the attack sequence. For quite some time, hackers have distributed attack tools that make it easier to launch network attacks. However, prior to 2000, most of these tools would initiate only one attack sequence; launching additional attack sequences required the intervention of the human attacker. However, newer tools are able to continually initiate new attack cycles on their own. This was the case with worms such as Nimda and Code Red, which we'll discuss later in this chapter. This increasing level of automation makes these attacks more dangerous and more widespread. According to CERT, the increasing automation and sophistication of attack tools is one of the most significant trends in the "Black Hat" hacking community.

Today's attack tools can perform the entire attack process. Instead of a hacker being required to perform a port scan with one tool to identify vulnerable systems, then using a different tool to penetrate the victim network and yet another tool to propagate the attack, now one tool can do it all. This speeds up the process as well as makes it easier for hackers who lack technical skills to mount a successful attack. Some attack tools are executed at the command line, but many of them have user-friendly graphical interfaces as well as detailed help files to instruct attackers in their use. Configuration files might also allow users to customize the attack.

To avoid detection by intrusion detection system (IDS) software that relies on pattern recognition, modern tools can employ different techniques—such as random selection—to interrupt patterns that would trigger detection by the IDS. In addition, many of the tools use common protocols such as Hypertext Transfer Protocol (HTTP) and Internet Relay Chat (IRC), which disguise their packets by making them look like normal Internet traffic. These tools are widely available through anonymous File Transfer Protocol (FTP) sites and hacker newsgroups on the Internet. Hackers can also modify legitimate network analysis tools if they have the source code, turning them into attack tools by adding code to exploit the vulnerabilities that they find.

> **NOTE**
>
> It is ironic that hackers make their attack tools available on anonymous FTP sites, because anonymous FTP and Trivial File Transfer Protocol (TFTP) are themselves often exploited by attackers. Knowledgeable hackers can easily create tools and scripts that attempt an anonymous logon; try various commands such as *pwd*, *mkdir*, and *rmdir* (to print the working directory, make a directory, and remove a directory on UNIX/ Linux systems, respectively); and plant a Trojan in the FTP site that then enables the hacker to access the system remotely, without a password.

Botnets

Botnets are one of the biggest and best hidden threats on the Internet. Often, a botnet will be installed on a machine as a worm or Trojan horse, and will run silently on a person's machine. The person who controls the botnets is referred to as the *bot herder*, and he or she can send commands to the bots and receive data (such as passwords or access to other resources) from them. The reason the bot herder does this can vary, ranging from using the bots to store files on other people's machines, to instruct them to send simultaneous requests to a single site in a DoS attack, or to send out spam mail.

To illustrate how a bot may be used, consider a bot herder who wishes to send spam to large numbers of users. These e-mail messages may claim they are from eBay or another popular site, and may ask the person to update his or her personal and credit card information. The bot herder sends out a Trojan horse that infects computers with the botnet. These infected computers are now referred to as agents or zombies, and will automatically log on to a Web server or IRC server, which is referred to as the *Command and Control* (C&C) server. The bot herder can now send messages to the botnets through the C&C server, instructing each zombie machine to send out the spam.

This creates a new problem for investigators. Although in the previous chapter we discussed how to trace an IP address back to its source, such an e-mail would lead back to the zombie computer, and not the actual bot herder. In other words, if a bot on your computer had sent out the e-mail, it would appear that it came from you. Investigators need to keep this in mind when tracing the source of a cybercrime as such e-mails may not appear in the Sent Items of the e-mail program on the zombie computer. Scanning for Trojans on the machine may identify the existence of known bots that have infected the machine.

On the Scene

Botnets

In 2005, Dutch police arrested three suspects (ages 19, 22, and 27) who had threatened a U.S. company with a DoS attack. The three had used the Toxbot Trojan to infect computers in preparation of the attack. However, when the Netherlands Computer Emergency Response Team and several Internet service providers (ISPs) began to dismantle the C&C and investigate the technical aspects of the botnet, they found that 1.5 million computers had been made into zombies.

Accidental "Attacks"

Some intrusions and "attacks" might actually be unintentional. Server or network crashes can be caused by users experimenting, visiting Web sites that run malicious code, or unknowingly downloading and introducing a virus into the system. In fact, a large number of virus attacks are initiated accidentally or unknowingly. The user who appears to have sent the virus via e-mail is often a victim of the attack him- or herself, because many viruses and worms are written to spread themselves by accessing the victim's address book and sending infected mail to all the addresses found there.

Accidental attacks can be just as destructive as deliberate ones, and network security personnel must be just as vigilant in protecting against them. However, from the law enforcement perspective, the perpetrator's *intent* matters very much. Most criminal offenses require that an act be committed intentionally or at least knowingly, so the elements of the offense might not be present if an employee causes an intrusion or attack without intending to—even if his or her actions were careless. On the other hand, some acts are still considered criminal when a lower state of culpability (recklessness or negligence) is present. It is very important for investigators to be aware of the culpable mental state that is specified as an element of each offense to be charged. If no level of culpability is specified, the criminal code usually defines a "default" level of culpability that applies.

Preventing Intentional Internal Security Breaches

Users inside the network are in the best position to gain access to information or sabotage the network's integrity. According to most computer security studies, as documented in Request for Comments (RFC) 2196, actual loss (in terms of money, productivity, computer reputation, and other tangible and intangible harm) is greater for internal security breaches than for those from the outside. Internal attackers are more dangerous for several reasons:

- People inside the network generally know more about the company, the network, the layout of the building(s), normal operating procedure, and other information that makes it easier for them to gain access without detection.

- Internal attackers usually have at least some degree of legitimate access and could find it easy to discover passwords and holes in the current security system.

- Internal hackers know what information is on the network and what actions will cause the most damage.

Preventing such problems begins with the same methods used to prevent unintentional security compromises, but it goes a step further. To a large extent, unintended breaches can be prevented through education. This obviously will not have the same effect on network users who intend to breach security. The best way to prevent such breaches depends, in part, on the motivations of the employee(s) concerned.

Implementing auditing helps detect internal breaches of security by recording specified security events. Administrators are then able to track when objects such as files or folders are accessed, the user account used to access them, when users exercise user rights, and when users log on or off the computer or network. Modern network operating systems include built-in auditing functionality. We discuss methods of auditing security events in Chapter 13. We discuss interpreting and using security audit log files in Chapter 14.

Firewalls are helpful in keeping basically compliant employees from accidentally (or out of ignorance of security considerations) visiting dangerous Web sites or sending specific types of packets outside the local network. However, firewalls are of more limited use in preventing intentional internal security breaches. Simply limiting users' access to the external network cannot thwart insiders who are determined to destroy, modify, or copy data. Because they have physical access, insiders can copy data to removable media or to a portable computer, or perhaps even print it to paper and remove it from the premises. They can change the format of the data to disguise it, or they can even employ steganography to hide it inside seemingly innocent files and then upload the files to Web-based data storage services.

In a high-security environment, measures should be taken to prevent this sort of theft. For example:

- Install computers without diskette drives and CD/DVD writers, and disable Universal Serial Bus (USB) ports so that external hard disks or flash drives can't be used. In situations where high security is necessary, it may even be prudent to use diskless workstations.

- Apply system or Group Policy that prevents users from installing software (such as that needed for a desktop computer to communicate with a BlackBerry or Palm OS device).

- Lock PC cases and cover physical access to serial ports, USB ports, and other connection points so that removable media devices can't be attached.

Intentional internal breaches of security constitute a serious problem, and company policies should treat them as such. We discuss this topic in more detail in Chapter 12, in the section "Designing and Implementing Security Policies."

Preventing Unauthorized External Intrusions

External intrusions and attacks are the major concerns of many companies when it comes to network security issues. In a number of high-profile cases in recent years, the Web servers of prominent organizations have been hacked. Attempts to penetrate sensitive government networks, such as the Pentagon's systems, occur on a regular basis. Distributed denial-of-service (DDoS) attacks make front-page news when they crash servers and prevent Internet users from accessing popular sites.

> **NOTE**
>
> Psychological factors affect the ways in which companies handle various types of security breaches. Companies usually see internal breaches as personnel problems and handle them in an administrative manner. External breaches might seem more like violations and are more often prosecuted as criminal actions. Because the external intruder can come from anywhere, at any time, the sense of uncertainty and fear of the unknown can cause organizations to react in a much stronger way to this type of threat. Thus, law enforcement officers are more likely to become involved when the breach is external. Officers might then (erroneously) conclude that the ratio of external to internal breaches is greater than it really is.

The good news about external intrusions is that the area(s) that must be controlled are much more focused than with internal attacks. There are usually only a limited number of points of entry to the network from the outside. This is where a properly configured firewall can be invaluable, allowing authorized traffic into the network while keeping unauthorized traffic out. On the other hand, the popularity of firewalls ensures that dedicated hackers know how they work and spend a great deal of time and effort devising ways to defeat them.

Planning for Firewall Failures

Organizations should never depend on the firewall to provide 100 percent protection, even against outside intruders. To be effective, a security plan must be both multifaceted and multilayered. Although administrators can hope that a firewall will keep intruders out of the network completely, their planning must take into consideration the possibility that the firewall will fail and address such questions as:

- If intruders *do* get in, what is the contingency plan?
- How can we reduce the amount of damage attackers can cause?
- How can the most sensitive or valuable data be protected?

External Intruders with Internal Access

A special type of external intruder is the outsider who *physically* breaks into your facility to gain access to your network. Although not a true insider because he or she is not authorized to be there and does not have a valid account on the network, this intruder enjoys many of the same advantages as the true insider. In Chapter 13, we'll discuss physical security and its importance to securing a network.

On the Scene

Tactical Planning

In dealing with network intruders, network administrators should practice what police officers in defensive tactics training call *if/then thinking*. This strategy involves considering every possible outcome of a given situation and then posing the question: "*If* this happens, *then* what could be done to protect us from the consequences?" The answers to these questions should form the basis of the organization's security policy.

This tactic requires that administrators be able to plan responses in detail, which means thinking in specifics rather than generalities. The security threat assessment must be based in part on understanding the motivations of people initiating the attack and in part on the technical aspects of the type of attack that is initiated. In a high-security environment, these tasks should be the responsibility of an *incident response team*.

Recognizing the "Fact of the Attack"

If preventive measures don't work (and it's likely that sometimes they won't), the next step for network administrators is to shift into reactive mode and attempt to minimize the damage. Before they can do that, they must have a way to recognize that an attack is taking place.

IDSes use two methods to identify that an attack is occurring:

- **Pattern recognition** Analyzing files, network traffic, sequences in random access memory (RAM), or other data for repeated or recognizable signs of attack, such as unexplained increases in file size or particular character strings

- **Effect recognition** Identifying the results of an attack, such as a system crash caused by overload or a sudden reboot for no reason

It's easy to program an IDS to recognize specific patterns, but attackers can defeat it by making small changes to the pattern or by fragmenting the attack packets—that is, dividing the attack messages or code into fragmented packets. A number of TCP/IP exploits use fragmented packets; these exploits are called *frag attacks*. Effect recognition is more difficult because the "effects" often resemble normal network traffic or problems caused by hardware or software faults.

The problem with any IDS—indeed, with all computer software—is that it does only exactly what it is told to do. Thus far, true artificial intelligence (programs that can "think") hasn't been achieved. Law enforcement officers know that the human factor—intuition and the ability to make great leaps of logic—can be very important in detecting and solving crimes. Unfortunately, no device or program is able to observe the behavior of computer systems and network components and intuitively recognize that there's something wrong. Very specific criteria must be set and met before an IDS will recognize an attack. This explains why human administrators will always remain an important ingredient in creating a proper security posture in any organization and why eternal vigilance is more than just a watchword for people with security responsibilities.

Identifying and Categorizing Attack Types

The *attack type* refers to *how* an intruder gains entry to your computer or network (if, indeed, entry is actually gained at all) and *what the attacker does* once he or she has gained entry (or without gaining entry). Some of the more common types of hack attacks include social engineering attacks, DoS attacks, scanning and spoofing, "nuke" attacks, and dissemination of malicious code. When you have a basic understanding of how each type of attack works, you will be better armed to guard against them.

It is useful for us to sort these different intrusions and attacks into categories such as the following:

- Preintrusion/attack activities.

- Password-cracking methods, which we discussed in detail in Chapter 11.

- Technical exploits (taking advantage of characteristics of the equipment or protocols). We'll discuss exploits involving operating systems and applications in Chapter 11.

- Malicious code attacks (Trojans, viruses, worms).

The following sections discuss specific types of attacks that fit into each category.

Recognizing Preintrusion/Attack Activities

Hacker how-to documents often break the hack/attack process into steps, as follows:

1. Preattack
2. Initial access
3. Full system access
4. Planting "back doors" for future access
5. Covering tracks

The preattack phase focuses on gathering information. Experienced hackers tell newbies to learn as much about the targeted victim as they can before initiating an attack. This "intel" information is vitally important for a hacker who has a concrete goal, such as corporate espionage.

On the Scene

Planning the Hack and Hacking the Plan

The most successful hackers plan their attack strategies in almost as much detail as a military unit or police SWAT team plans a strike or raid. Then they carry out the hack exactly according to plan. These are the real pros, and they are the most difficult to defend against or apprehend. The hackers who get caught are usually careless, hurried, or inexperienced. In contrast, amateur hackers "play it by ear," breaking into systems and wandering around looking for something of interest. The term *amateur* refers to someone who does something for fun, just for the love of it. Professional hackers (hackers for hire) know exactly what they're after, and they get in, get it, and get out quickly, like a master thief. The planning phase can last many times longer than the actual execution of the hack. When professional hackers get caught, it's usually because they're egotistical and brag about their exploits to the wrong people.

Preattack information gathering and planning involve determining the goal of the hack, determining the target of the attack (the network or system that must be compromised to achieve the goal), and identifying the weaknesses of the target that can be exploited to carry out the hack. Preattack planning can also include taking steps to disguise the attacker's identity or putting preliminary programs or devices in place to gather information or to make it easier to get into the system when the time comes to carry out the attack. Some specific preattack activities include:

- Port scanning to identify potential targets and their weaknesses
- IP spoofing to disguise the attacker's identity
- Placing Trojans on the target system
- Placing tracking devices and software (such as keystroke loggers) on the target system
- Putting protocol analyzers (sniffers) in place to capture transmissions to and from the target system

In the following sections, we look at each of these activities in more detail.

Port Scans

A *port* is, in its simplest meaning, a point where information enters or leaves a computer. Transmission Control Protocol (TCP) and User Datagram Protocol (UDP) use port numbers to provide separate "subaddresses" to identify what service or application incoming information is destined for, or from which outgoing information originates.

The term *port scanner*, in the context of network security, refers to a software program that hackers use to remotely determine what TCP/UDP ports are open on a given system and thus are vulnerable to attack. Scanners are also used by administrators to detect vulnerabilities in their own systems, to correct them before an intruder finds them.

Scanning is used for several purposes prior to penetration and/or attack:

- **Target enumeration** Locating host systems that are open to attack
- **Target identification** Identifying the target system
- **Service identification** Identifying the vulnerable services or ports on the target system

---

NOTE

A common saying among hackers is "A good port scanner is worth a thousand passwords."

A good scanning program can locate a target computer on the Internet (one that is vulnerable to attack), determine what TCP/IP services are running on the machine, and probe those services for security weaknesses. Many scanning programs are available as freeware on the Internet, but numerous security tools are also available for purchase with greater reliability and functions.

Port scanning refers to a means of locating "listening" TCP or UDP ports on a computer or router and obtaining as much information as possible about the device from the listening ports. TCP and UDP services and applications use a number of *well-known ports* (see the "Who's Listening?" sidebar in this section), which are widely published. The hacker uses his or her knowledge of these commonly used ports to extrapolate information.

For example, Telnet normally uses port 23. If the hacker finds that port open and listening, he or she knows that Telnet is probably enabled on the machine. The hacker can then try to infiltrate the system by, for example, guessing the appropriate password in a brute force attack.

On the Scene

Who's Listening?

The official well-known port assignments are documented in RFC 1700, available on the Web at www.freesoft.org/CIE/RFC/1700/index.htm. The port assignments are made by the Internet Assigned Numbers Authority (IANA). In general, a service uses the same port number with UDP as with TCP, although there are some exceptions. The assigned ports were originally those from 0–255, but the number was later expanded to 0–1,023.

Continued

Some of the most used well-known ports include:

- TCP/UDP port 20: FTP (data)
- TCP/UDP port 21: FTP (control)
- TCP/UDP port 23: Telnet
- TCP/UDP port 25: Simple Mail Transfer Protocol (SMTP)
- TCP/UDP port 53: Domain name system (DNS)
- TCP/UDP port 67: BOOTP server
- TCP/UDP port 68: BOOTP client
- TCP/UDP port 69: TFTP
- TCP/UDP port 80: HTTP
- TCP/UDP port 88: Kerberos
- TCP/UDP port 110: Post Office Protocol 3 (POP3)
- TCP/UDP port 119: Network News Transfer Protocol (NNTP)
- TCP/UDP port 137: NetBIOS name service
- TCP/UDP port 138: NetBIOS datagram service
- TCP/UDP port 139: NetBIOS session service
- TCP/UDP port 194: IRC
- TCP/UDP port 220: Internet Message Access Protocol (IMAP) v3
- TCP/UDP port 389: Lightweight Directory Access Protocol (LDAP)

Ports 1,024–65,535 are called *registered ports*; these numbers are not controlled by IANA and can be used by user processes or applications. Some of these are traditionally used by specific applications (for example, SQL uses port 1,433) and could be of interest to hackers.

A total of 65,535 TCP ports (and the same number of UDP ports) are used for various services and applications. If a port is open, it responds when another computer attempts to contact it over the network. Port-scanning programs such as Nmap are used to determine which ports are open on a particular machine. The program sends packets for a wide variety of protocols, and by examining which messages receive responses and which don't it creates a map of the computer's listening ports.

Port scanning does no harm to a network or system, but it provides hackers with information they can use to penetrate the network. Because people conducting port scans are often up to no good, they frequently forge the source IP address to hide their identity.

CyberLaw Review

Should Scanning Be Illegal?

Some in the IT industry argue that port scanning should not be illegal, because "no harm is done." They say port scanning is similar to ringing someone's doorbell to see if anybody is home—not in itself a crime. However, laws are enacted not just to protect from actual physical harm, but also to protect people's privacy and their interests in their own property. Those on the other side of the argument say that port scanning is really more like the virtual equivalent of someone who goes from door to door in an apartment building, trying each one to find out whether it's locked and whether there is an easy way in. Although this practice might do no actual harm if the "door scanner" only collects information and doesn't enter the premises, and although the person might have the right to be in the public hallway, in most jurisdictions such behavior would, at the very least, cause discomfort to the building's residents and attract the attention of the police.

In 2000, in *Moulton v. VC3*, a U.S. District Court in Georgia ruled that port scanning does not damage a network and thus does not constitute a crime or create a cause of action for civil suit. Although the federal laws in regard to computer fraud and abuse have changed since then, there is still a requirement that loss or damage must occur to charge a violation.

Half scans (also called *half open scans* or *FIN scans*) attempt to avoid detection by sending only initial or final packets rather than establishing a connection. A half scan starts the SYN/ACK process with a targeted computer but does not complete it. (See the description of this process in the following section on TCP/IP exploits.) Software that conducts half scans, such as Jakal, is called a *stealth scanner*. Many port-scanning detectors are unable to detect half scans.

Address Spoofing

The Merriam-Webster Online Dictionary (www.merriam-webster.com) defines a *spoof* as a "light humorous parody" or hoax, but also defines it as being synonymous with a less benign action of deception. Hackers use spoofed addresses to deceive other computers and fool them into thinking a message originated from a different machine. Although IP spoofing is probably the most popular, it is not the only spoofing method used by hackers. Others include ARP spoofing, Web spoofing (which we'll discuss in Chapter 11), and DNS spoofing. Let's take a quick look at how each of these works.

IP Spoofing

IP spoofing involves changing the packet headers of a message to indicate that it came from an IP address other than the true source. In essence, the sending computer impersonates another machine, fooling the recipient into accepting its messages. The spoofed address is normally a trusted port, which allows a hacker to get a message through a firewall or router that would otherwise be filtered out. When configured properly, modern firewalls protect against IP spoofing.

Spoofing is used whenever it is beneficial for one machine to impersonate another. It is often used in combination with one of the other types of attacks. For example, a spoofed address is used to hide the true IP address of the attacker in Ping of Death, Teardrop, and other attacks. Any service that uses IP address authentication is susceptible to IP spoofing.

After deciding on the targeted victim, the next step in spoofing is to find out the address of a trusted host. Legitimate communications between the trusted host and the target can be intercepted and examined. Often, hackers use a DoS attack against the trusted host to prevent it from communicating on the network. Then the packet headers can be modified to make it look as though the attacker's messages are coming from the trusted host, and the packets are sent to a service or port that uses address authentication. One of the most difficult aspects of IP spoofing is the necessity of correctly guessing the sequence numbers of the trusted machine. This process is made easy for the attacker by the numerous spoofing tools that are available on the Web.

ARP Spoofing

The Address Resolution Protocol (ARP) maintains the *ARP cache*. This is a table that maps IP addresses to Media Access Control (MAC) or physical addresses of computers on the network. This cache is necessary because the MAC address is used at the physical level to locate the destination computer to which a message should be delivered. If there is no cache entry for a particular IP address, ARP sends a broadcast message to all the computers on the subnet, requesting that the machine with the IP address in question respond with its MAC address. This mapping then gets added to the ARP cache. *ARP spoofing*, also called *ARP poisoning*, is a method of sending forged replies which result in incorrect entries in the cache. This results in subsequent messages being sent to the wrong computer (the machine whose MAC address is incorrectly matched with the IP address). Once again, this process has been automated b hacker tools such as ARPoison and Parasite have automated this process.

DNS Spoofing

DNS spoofing refers to two methods of causing a DNS server to direct users incorrectly:

- "Poisoning" of the DNS cache (similar to ARP poisoning in that incorrect information is entered into the cache) of name resolution servers, resulting in those servers directing users to the wrong Web sites or e-mail being sent to the wrong mail servers

- Using the recursive mechanism of DNS to predict the request that a DNS server will send and responding with forged information

Either of these methods allows the attacker to intercept the victim's mail or to set up spoofed Web pages that give users inaccurate information. This method can even be used to con the victim into providing personal information through Web forms. (See the section on Web spoofing in the discussion of browser exploits in Chapter 11.)

On the Scene

What Makes DNS Spoofing So Dangerous?

Because the DNS is responsible for managing the resolution of domain names (such as www.microsoft.com) into an equivalent IP address (for example, 206.122.10.6), any successful replacement of a valid address with an alternate address causes people attempting to access the domain name to visit the wrong TCP/IP address. This gives attackers the chance to create their own Web site that masquerades as a legitimate site and to attempt to steal all kinds of information by getting between the user and the real site. Alternatively, the attackers can completely take over the apparent role of the real site. Because DNS helps mediate access to Web, FTP, e-mail, and other services, the opportunities for mischief inherent in DNS spoofing are serious and powerful.

Placement of Trojans

Trojans, or *Trojan horse software*, are programs that appear to be legitimate or innocent but actually do something else in addition to or instead of their ostensible purposes. We discuss Trojans in general later in this chapter, in the section "Attacking with Trojans, Viruses, and Worms." As part of the preattack phase, a hacker can plant on the victim's computer a Trojan program that installs keystroke-logging programs to gather information for the main attack or that sets up the means by which the attacker will later get into the system. An infamous case of the latter was the Back Orifice Trojan, which could be disguised as a component of some other innocuous software program and, once installed, created a "back door" for attackers to take over control of the victim PC. For more information about the updated Back Orifice 2000 (BO2K), you can visit www.bo2k.com.

Placement of Tracking Devices and Software

If an attacker has on-site access to the victim system, one way to collect passwords and other information prior to an attack is to place a physical tracking device (a *keystroke logger*) on the system. This is a very small device, about 2 inches long and a half-inch in diameter, which you can install in less than a minute; you simply unplug the keyboard from the PC and plug the keyboard into the logger, and then plug the logger into the PC's keyboard port. It is not noticeable to most users.

Inside the logger are a microchip and a nonvolatile memory chip (similar to a CompactFlash card or memory stick). Depending on the amount of memory in the device, it can record anywhere from a few to dozens of pages of keystrokes; for example, 64 KB of memory will store about 32 pages. No software needs to be installed on the computer for the loggers to work, and they are compatible with a variety of PC operating systems. No battery or outside power source is required; the device draws power from the computer. Once the strokes have been captured, the attacker removes the device and attaches it to a different PC. The captured data can be password-protected; once the correct password is entered, it can be read in Notepad or another text editor. Afterward, the data can be saved to a file and the memory in the device can be erased. An example of a keystroke-logging device is the KeyGhost (see www.keyghost.com).

On the Scene

Keystroke Logging As an Investigative or Monitoring Tool

Keystroke loggers and spyware programs are not used exclusively by criminals. Law enforcement investigators use logging devices and software to gather evidence of offenses. In early 2000, Nicodemo S. Scarfo, Jr., was charged with illegal gambling, racketeering, and loan shark activities based on evidence in a file on his computer, which had been encrypted with Pretty Good Privacy (PGP). Investigators used a keystroke logger to get the information needed to break the encryption. Defense attorneys tried to get the evidence suppressed, arguing that the use of the tool represented an unconstitutional search. However, the court ruled against the petition to suppress, and Scarfo eventually pled guilty.

Keystroke loggers and spyware have other legitimate purposes. Companies may use them to monitor employees' computer and Internet activities (according to company policy), and parents can use them to oversee what their children are doing on the Net.

Software programs can also perform keystroke logging, but the attacker needs to be able to log on to the system to install the software; the advantage of the physical device is that it can capture the passwords necessary to log on. Software-based loggers capture only the keystrokes made after booting into the operating system, whereas the hardware device can capture keystrokes made before the OS loads—for example, changes made to the Basic Input Output System (BIOS).

Other spyware programs can do much more than just log keystrokes. Many of these programs allow the person who installs and configures the software to specify criteria that will trigger the capture of screenshots. Some of the programs can even rename themselves and change their locations on the disk to avoid detection. One such example of these monitoring programs is Spector Pro (www.spectorsoft.com).

Placement of Packet Capture and Protocol Analyzer Software

Network monitors, also called *protocol analyzers*, allow administrators to capture and analyze the traffic on their networks for troubleshooting purposes or to monitor network activity. Hackers can use these same tools to capture packets surreptitiously and read the information in those packets. Analyzers that allow for placing the network adapter in promiscuous mode are especially useful to hackers. In this mode, the adapter can capture traffic sent to or from any computer on the network segment. Some analyzers, such as the Network Monitor built into Microsoft Windows 2000 Server and Windows Server 2003, limit capture to packets sent to or from the machine that is running the analyzer software. However, a version of Microsoft's NetMon comes with the company's Systems Management Server product and permits the use of promiscuous mode.

These programs are network *sniffers*. Any person with Administrative privileges can install the Network Monitor on a Windows Server and start "listening" to activity on the wire. Administrators—or hackers who have compromised an administrative account—can use the tool to collect network data and analyze it on the spot, or they can save the recorded activities to review at a later time. It is possible to set triggers for when certain events or data cross the wire, so the tool can be used, for example, when certain keywords in e-mail communications move through the network. The Network Monitor program allows its users to capture only those frames that they are interested in based on protocol or the source or destination computer. Even more detailed and exacting filters can be applied to data that has been collected, allowing the monitoring person to pinpoint the precise elements that he or she is looking for in the captured data.

Figure 10.1 shows the contents of a captured packet. You can see the text message ("Windows 2003 is great!") that was sent across the network.

Figure 10.1 The Contents of a Captured Packet

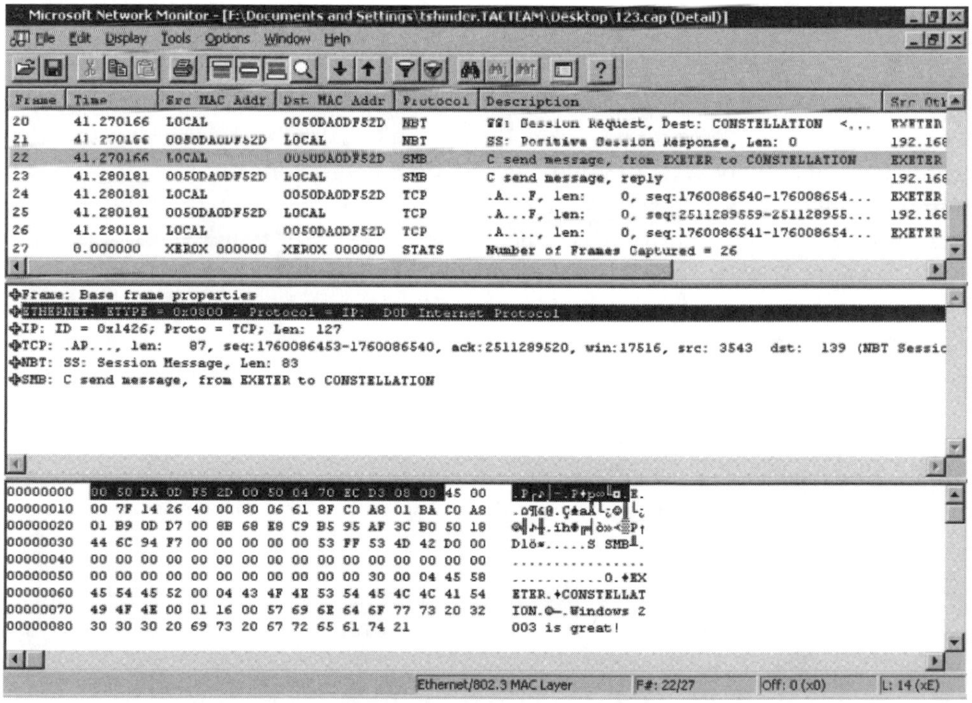

Some commercial products provide greater functionality than the Network Monitor tool for Windows servers. You can use network information-gathering tools to obtain network data for forensic analysis and identify network issues; of course, malicious users also can use these tools for hacking purposes. These tools generally offer the functionality of a sniffer and an IDS combined. As we mentioned, sniffers are powerful programs that work by placing the host system's network card into promiscuous mode. A network card in promiscuous mode can receive all the data it can see, not just packets addressed to it. Switches segment traffic and know which particular port to send traffic to and block it from all the rest. Although this feature adds much needed performance gains, it does raise a barrier when attempting to sniff all potential switched ports. Forensic analysis will usually require the switch to be configured to mirror a port. Some common network monitoring tools include:

- **NetWitness** Designed to analyze network traffic and monitor it.

- **NetResident** Considered an advanced network content monitoring program that captures, stores, analyzes, and reconstructs network events such as e-mail messages, Web pages, downloaded files, and other types of network traffic.

- **InfiniStream Security Forensics** A commercial product that builds on sniffer technology by providing high-end tracking of absolutely everything.

- **CA Network Forensics** Allows the user to uncover and investigate network traffic. This program captures raw network data and uses forensic analysis to check for exploitation, internal data theft, and security violations.

- **WireShark** An open source protocol analyzer that can capture traffic in real time. Not only is it free to use, but it also works well in both a Windows and Linux environment. You can find more details about the program at the official site, www.wireshark.com.

Prevention and Response

There is no way to prevent port scanning—but IT professionals can control whether the scanner finds open doors to their networks. An important security step for administrators is to use port-scanning software themselves to learn about their own networks' vulnerabilities and then plug the openings so that others will be unable to use them to gain access. Most firewalls log port-scanning attempts, and freeware or shareware such as Lockdown2000 or NukeNabber can be downloaded and installed to notify the administrator that ports are being scanned and provide the IP address from which the scan originates.

You can prevent IP spoofing using source address verification on the router, if it supports this function. Other steps you can take to protect against spoofing include:

- Using encrypted authentication

- Configuring the router to reject any messages from outside that appear to come from an internal (local) address

Administrators can prevent ARP spoofing using static ARP tables. A static table is manually configured by the administrator, so broadcast responses don't result in an automatic update of the cache. The problem with this solution is that it doesn't work well with large networks; the burden on the administrator to keep the tables current would be overwhelming. Another solution is *MAC binding*. This method is enabled on the network switches and allows automatic updating, but when a particular IP address has been associated with a MAC address, that association can't be changed except by an administrative action. Furthermore, some tools monitor changes to the cache, with automatic notification to administrators so that they will be aware of any attempts to use ARP spoofing.

Administrators can prevent DNS spoofing by securing the DNS servers on the Internet and by using the latest version of the DNS software. As vulnerabilities are identified, they are generally addressed in the next version.

Properly configured firewalls can help keep Trojans out of the network, and software such as Trojan Remover claims to be able to eliminate Trojan programs even when antivirus (AV) software cannot detect them. The usual virus protection guidelines (don't open unsolicited attachments, download files only from reputable sites, apply security patches diligently) can also help protect against Trojans.

Keystroke logging devices are impossible to detect via software. Physical examination of the cable connecting the keyboard to the computer reveals the presence of such devices. Antikeystroke logger programs can scan for keystroke logging activity and detect software-based loggers. An example is Anti-Keylogger, which is available from www.anti-keyloggers.com.

Protective measures against sniffers include limiting physical access to the network (because the sniffer software must be installed on a computer on the local subnet), using switches instead of hubs to prevent all packets from going to all the systems on the network, and using encryption. This last solution won't prevent sniffers from capturing network packets, but it will prevent the hacker from being able to read the data inside them. "Antisniffing" software can be used to scan the network for sniffers or for computers whose network adapters are running in promiscuous mode.

Understanding Technical Exploits

If a cyberintruder or attacker is unable to come up with passwords to get into the network posing as a legitimate user, he or she has numerous methods for breaking in without credentials. Generally, these methods exploit the characteristics of the protocols, operating system, or application software used on the targeted system or network. In the following sections, we discuss some popular technical exploits hackers use to gain access or to interrupt communications on networks. We will continue this discussion in Chapter 11, when we focus on exploits and vulnerabilities in operating systems and applications. Investigators should have a basic understanding of how these techniques work. Knowledge of how a cybercriminal commits the crime often provides valuable information for profiling that leads to apprehension.

Protocol Exploits

Protocol exploits use the characteristics of a protocol, such as the "handshake" method that TCP uses to establish a communications session, to obtain a result that was never intended—for example, over-whelming the targeted system to the point where it is unable to communicate with legitimate users. There are many ways that the normal behavior of network protocols can be manipulated to congest the network or server to the point where no legitimate communications can get through. In this section, we discuss in detail what a DoS attack is and the many ways that the characteristics of TCP/IP can be used to launch DoS attacks. We also discuss source routing attacks and other protocol exploits.

DoS Attacks That Exploit TCP/IP

DoS attacks, mentioned previously in this chapter, are one of the most popular choices of Internet hackers who want to disrupt a network's operations. In February 2000, massive DoS attacks brought down several of the world's biggest Web sites, including Yahoo.com and Buy.com. Many such attacks exploit various characteristics of the TCP/IP protocol suite. This section goes into detail on how various DoS attacks work. Attack types we discuss include:

- DNS DoS attacks, which exploit the DNS protocols

- SYN/LAND attacks, which exploit the way the TCP handshake process works

- The Ping of Death, which uses a "killer packet" to overwhelm a system

- Ping flood, fraggle, and smurf attacks, which use various methods to "flood" the network or server

- UDP bomb and UDP snork, which exploit User Datagram Protocol

- Teardrop attacks, which exploit the IP packet header fields

- Exploits of Simple Network Management Protocol (SNMP), which is included with most TCP/IP implementations

What Is Denial of Service?

Although they do not destroy or steal data like some other types of attacks, DoS attackers aim to bring down a network, denying service to its legitimate users. DoS attacks are easy to initiate; software is readily available from hacker Web sites and warez newsgroups that allow anyone to launch a DoS attack with little or no technical expertise.

The purpose of a DoS attack is to render a network inaccessible by generating a type or amount of network traffic that crashes the servers, overwhelms the routers, or otherwise prevents the network's devices from functioning properly. DoS can be accomplished by tying up the server's resources by, for example, overwhelming the CPU and memory resources. In other cases, a particular user or machine can be the target of DoS attacks that hang up the client machine and require it to be rebooted.

As we mentioned earlier in this chapter, *distributed DoS*, or *DDoS*, attacks use intermediary computers, called *agents*, on which programs called *zombies* have previously been surreptitiously installed. The hacker activates these zombie programs remotely, causing the intermediary computers (which can number in the hundreds or even thousands) to simultaneously launch the actual attack. Because the attack comes from the computers running the zombie programs, which could be on networks anywhere in the world, the hacker is able to conceal the true origin of the attack.

Examples of DDoS tools hackers use are Tribe FloodNet (TFN), TFN2K, Trinoo, and Stacheldraht (German for *barbed wire*). Early versions of DDoS tools targeted UNIX and Solaris systems, but TFN2K can run on both UNIX and Windows systems. Tools and information regarding DDoS attacks are available from http://packetstormsecurity.org/distributed/.

Because DDoS attacks are so popular, many tools have been developed to help you detect, eliminate, and analyze DDoS software that could be installed on your network. It is important to note that DDoS attacks pose a two-layer threat. Not only could your network be the target of a DoS attack that crashes your servers and prevents incoming and outgoing traffic, but also your computers could be used as the "innocent middlemen" to launch a DoS attack against another network or site.

DoS/DDoS attacks can be accomplished in a number of ways. Application exploits, operating system exploits, and protocol exploits can all be used to overload systems and create a denial of service. In the following sections, we address specific types of DoS and DDoS attacks and explain how they work.

On the Scene

DoS As a Weapon of Cyberwar

In November 2000, Lucent Technologies announced that a pro-Palestinian group named Unity had attacked its Web site using a tool called Defend, which creates a flood of messages designed to overwhelm the system and create a denial of service. Lucent was said to be targeted because it did business in Israel.

DNS DoS

The DNS DoS attack exploits the difference in size between a DNS query and a DNS response, in which all of the network's bandwidth is tied up by bogus DNS queries. The attacker uses the DNS servers as "amplifiers" to multiply the DNS traffic.

The attacker begins by sending small DNS queries to each DNS server that contains the spoofed IP address (see the "IP Spoofing" section earlier in this chapter) of the intended victim. The responses returned to the small queries are much larger in size so that if a large number of responses are returned at the same time, the link becomes congested and a denial of service will take place.

One solution to this problem is for administrators to configure DNS servers to respond with a "refused" response, which is much smaller in size than a name resolution response, when they receive DNS queries from suspicious or unexpected sources.

SYN/LAND Attacks

SYN attacks exploit the TCP "three-way handshake," the process by which a communications session is established between two computers. Because TCP (unlike UDP) is connection-oriented, a *session*, or direct one-to-one communication link, must be created prior to sending data. The client computer initiates the communication with the server (the computer whose resources it wants to access).

The "handshake" includes the following steps:

1. The client machine sends a synchronization request (SYN) segment.

2. The server sends an acknowledgment (ACK) message and a SYN, which acknowledges the client machine's request that was sent in step 1, and sends the client a synchronization request of its own. The client and server machines must synchronize each other's sequence numbers.

3. The client sends an ACK back to the server, acknowledging the server's request for synchronization. When both machines have acknowledged each other's requests, the handshake has been successfully completed and a connection is established between the two computers.

Figure 10.2 illustrates how the process works.

Figure 10.2 TCP Using a "Three-Way Handshake" to Establish a Connection

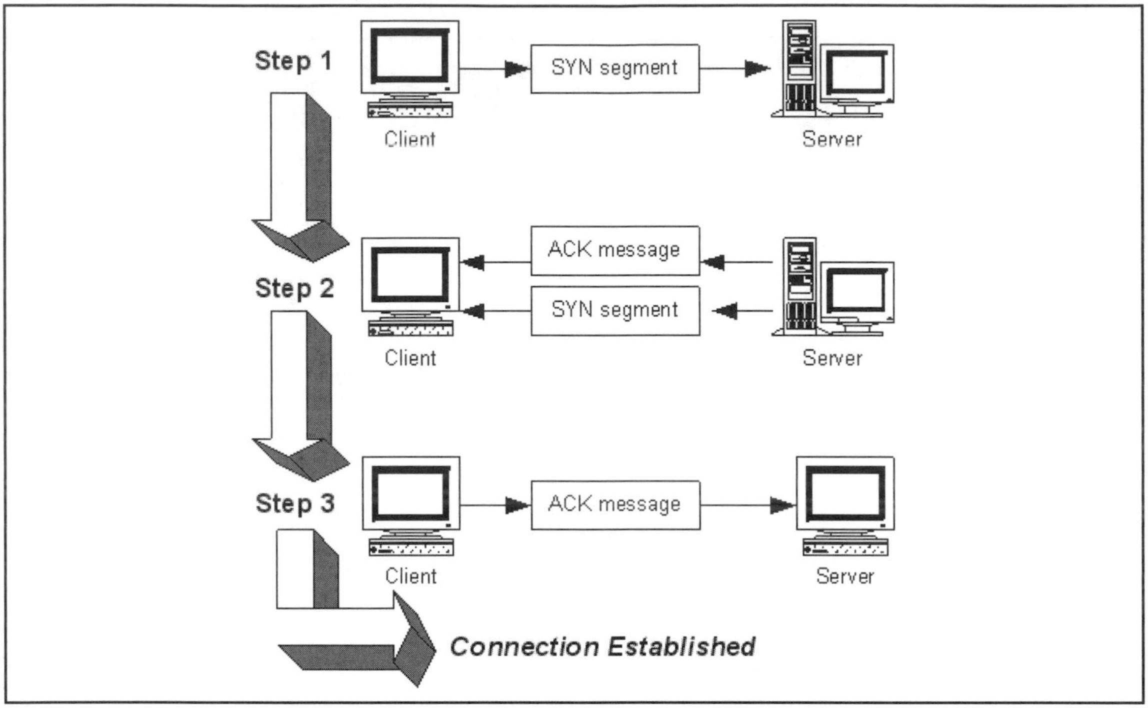

A SYN attack uses this process to flood the system targeted as the victim of the attack with multiple SYN packets that have bad source IP addresses. This causes the system to respond with SYN/ACK messages. The problem comes in when the system, waiting for the ACK message from the client that normally comes in response to its SYN/ACK, puts the waiting SYN/ACK messages into a queue. This is a problem because the queue is limited in the number of messages it can handle. When the queue is full, all subsequent incoming SYN packets will be ignored. For a SYN/ACK to be removed from the queue the client must return an ACK or an interval timer must run out and terminate the three-way handshake process.

Because the source IP addresses for the SYN packets sent by the attacker are no good, the ACKs that the server is waiting for never come. The queue stays full, and there is no room for valid SYN requests to be processed. Thus, service is denied to legitimate clients attempting to establish communications with the server.

The LAND attack is a variation on the SYN attack. In the LAND attack, instead of sending SYN packets with IP addresses that do not exist, the flood of SYN packets all have the same spoof IP address—that of the targeted computer.

You can prevent a LAND attack by filtering out incoming packets whose source IP addresses appear to be from computers on the internal network.

The Ping of Death

Another type of DoS attack is the so-called *Ping of Death* (also known as the *large packet ping*). The Ping of Death attack is launched by creating an IP packet larger than 65,536 bytes, which is the maximum allowed by the IP specification (sometimes referred to as a *killer packet*). This packet can cause the target system to crash, hang, or reboot.

Ping Flood/Fraggle/Smurf

The *ping flood* or *ICMP flood* is a means of tying up a specific client machine. It is caused by an attacker sending a large number of ping packets (ICMP echo request packets) to the victim. This flood prevents the software from responding to server ping activity requests, which causes the server to eventually time out the connection. A symptom of a ping flood is a huge amount of modem activity. This type of attack is also referred to as a *ping storm.*

The *fraggle attack* is related to the ping storm. Using a spoofed IP address (which is the address of the targeted victim), an attacker sends ping packets to a subnet, causing all computers on the subnet to respond to the spoofed address and flood it with echo reply messages.

On the Scene

Fraggle Attacks in Action

During the Kosovo crisis, pro-Serbian hackers frequently used the fraggle attack against U.S. and NATO sites to overload them and bring them down.

The *smurf* attack is a form of brute force attack that uses the same method as the ping flood, but directs the flood of Internet Control Message Protocol (ICMP) echo request packets at the network's router. The destination address of the ping packets is the broadcast address of the network, which causes the router to broadcast the packet to every computer on the network or segment. This can result in a very large amount of network traffic if there are many host computers, and it can create congestion that causes a denial of service to legitimate users.

NOTE

The broadcast address is normally represented by all 1s in the host ID (in the binary form of the address). This means, for example, that on Class C network 192.168.1.0, the broadcast address would be 192.168.1.255. The number 255 in decimal represents 11111111 in binary, and in a Class C network, the last, or *z*, octet represents the host ID. A message sent to the broadcast address is sent simultaneously to all hosts on the network.

In its most insidious form, the smurf attacker spoofs the source IP address of the ping packet. Then both the network to which the packets are sent *and* the network of the spoofed source IP address will be overwhelmed with traffic. The network to which the spoofed source address belongs will be deluged with responses to the ping when all the hosts to which the ping was sent answer the echo request with an echo reply.

Smurf attacks can generally do more damage than some other forms of DoS, such as SYN floods. The SYN flood affects only the ability of other computers to establish a TCP connection to the flooded server, but a smurf attack can bring an entire ISP down for minutes or hours. This is because a single attacker can easily send 40 to 50 ping packets per second, even using a slow modem connection. Because each packet is broadcast to every computer on the destination network, the number of responses per second is 40 to 50 times the number of computers on the network—which could be hundreds or thousands. This is enough data to congest even a T1 link.

One way to prevent a smurf attack from using a network as the broadcast target is to turn off the capability to transmit broadcast traffic on the router. Most routers allow you to do this. To prevent the network from being the victim of the spoofed IP address, you should configure the firewall to filter out incoming ping packets.

UDP Bomb/UDP Snork

An attacker can use UDP and one of several services that echo packets on receipt to create service-denying network congestion by generating a flood of UDP packets between two target systems. For example, the UDP chargen service on the first computer, which is a testing tool that generates a series of characters for every packet that it receives, sends packets to another system's UDP echo service, which echoes every character it receives. UDP chargen is on port 19. By exploiting these testing tools, an endless flow of echoes goes back and forth between the two systems, congesting the network. This is sometimes called a *UDP packet storm* or *UDP bomb*.

In addition to port 7, the echo port, an attacker can use port 17, the quote of the day service (quotd), or the daytime service on port 13. These services also echo packets they receive. Disabling unnecessary UDP services on each computer (especially those mentioned earlier) or using a firewall to filter those ports or services protects you from this type of attack.

The *snork attack* is similar to the UDP bomb. It uses a UDP frame that has a source port of either 7 (echo) or 9 (chargen), with a destination port of 135 (Microsoft location service). The result is the same as the UDP bomb—a flood of unnecessary transmissions that can slow performance or crash the systems that are involved.

Teardrop Attacks

The *Teardrop attack* works a little differently from the Ping of Death, but with similar results. The Teardrop program creates IP fragments, which are pieces of an IP packet into which an original packet can be divided as it travels through the Internet. The problem is that the offset fields on these fragments, which are supposed to indicate the portion (in bytes) of the original packet that is contained in the fragment, overlap.

For example, normally two fragments' offset fields might appear as shown here:

```
Fragment 1: (offset) 100 - 300
Fragment 2: (offset) 301 - 600
```

This indicates that the first fragment contains bytes 100 through 300 of the original packet and the second fragment contains bytes 301 through 600.

Overlapping offset fields appear something like this:

```
Fragment 1: (offset) 100 - 300
Fragment 2: (offset) 200 - 400
```

When the destination computer tries to reassemble these packets, it is unable to do so and could crash, hang, or reboot.

Variations include:

- NewTear
- Teardrop2
- SynDrop
- Boink

All of these programs generate some sort of fragment overlap.

SNMP Exploits

SNMP is used to monitor network devices and manage networks. It is a set of protocols that uses messages called *Protocol Data Units (PDUs)* over the network to various machines or devices that have SNMP *agent* software installed. These agents maintain Management Information Bases (MIBs) that contain information about the device. When agents receive the PDUs, they respond with information from the MIB. Vulnerabilities have been discovered in some implementations of SNMP that provide a means for attackers to disable the devices or create a DoS.

Source Routing Attacks

TCP/IP supports *source routing*, which is a means to permit the sender of network data to route the packets through a specific point on the network. There are two types of source routing:

- **Strict source routing** The data's sender can specify the exact route (rarely used).
- **Loose source record route (LSRR)** The sender can specify certain routers (hops) through which the packet must pass.

The source route is an option in the IP header that allows the sender to override routing decisions that are normally made by the routers between the source and destination machines. Network administrators use source routing to map the network or for troubleshooting routing and communications problems. You can also use it to force traffic through a route that will provide the best performance. Unfortunately, hackers can exploit source routing.

If the system allows source routing, an intruder can use it to reach private internal addresses on the LAN that normally would not be reachable from the Internet, by routing the traffic through another machine that is reachable from both the Internet and the internal machine. Source routing can be disabled on most routers to prevent this type of attack.

Other Protocol Exploits

The attacks we have discussed so far involve exploiting some feature or weakness of the TCP/IP protocols. Hackers can also exploit vulnerabilities of other common protocols, such as HTTP, DNS, Common Gateway Interface (CGI), and other commonly used protocols.

Router Exploits

Many hackers now target routers instead of computers for their attacks. The popularity of DSL and cable Internet connectivity has brought routers to home networks as well as business networks. This, in turn, has created a new point of vulnerability.

Many of the new, relatively inexpensive routers designed for broadband connections come with default administrator passwords that can be used on any of the vendor's devices if the administrator does not change the password. This means a hacker with knowledge of the default password could log on and make changes to the routing table or router configuration. This differs from most operating systems that do not come with a default password but require the user to create one during installation. In addition to the administrator password, some router vendors have created special so-called "back door" passwords for their systems, intended to be used by the vendor's tech support personnel so that if an administrator forgot the admin password, the vendor could help the administrator get back in. Of course, this system could also be exploited by hackers with knowledge of the secret "master" password.

Hackers can also obtain router passwords the same way they get the passwords for computers: using sniffer or spyware software, brute force attacks, or social engineering tactics. Whichever method the hacker uses to access the router, he or she can then create DoS attacks by changing routing table entries to send all messages to the same destination. In fact, if the router uses Routing Information Protocol (RIP) to dynamically update its routing tables, the attacker can send spoofed RIP messages to make the changes to the routing table without even needing to access the router directly.

Prevention and Response

Administrators can take a number of steps to help prevent exploits, including the following:

- You can protect Linux systems from SYN attacks by building the kernel with SYN cookies. Some versions of UNIX (such as Solaris 2.6 and later) have built-in protection against SYN attacks. In Windows servers, you can edit the Registry to protect against SYN attacks. For information and how-to instructions on hardening the TCP/IP stack against DoS attacks, see http://support.microsoft.com/kb/324270.

- You can configure routers to respond to directed broadcasts instead of passing them on to the subnet to guard against smurf attacks.

- You can configure DNS servers to respond with a "refused" response when they receive DNS queries from suspicious or unexpected sources to protect from DNS DoS attacks.

- You can configure the router to filter out incoming packets with a source IP address that appears to be from the local network.

- You can configure the system to ignore router redirects.

- You can disable SNMP, if it is not needed, to protect against exploits that rely on the protocol.

- You can change default passwords on routers and disable "back door" passwords.

Attacking with Trojans, Viruses, and Worms

Intruders who access networks and systems without authorization, or inside attackers with malicious motives, can plant various types of programs to cause damage to the network. These programs—often lumped together under the general term *viruses*, although there are other varieties—have cost companies and individuals billions of dollars in lost data, lost productivity, and the time and expense of recovery.

The cost of damage is impossible to determine accurately. Although you can calculate the hourly wage of a network administrator who must restore data from backups, or you can calculate the cost of AV software to purge the virus from systems, it is often difficult to calculate the monetary value of lost data. For example, if someone loses an unpublished novel on his or her computer, is it worthless because it isn't published, or has this person lost potential millions? Because of this, you hear wide ranges in how much a virus cost in damage. What is always certain is that there are new viruses every week, and more devastating ones always on the horizon.

Considering that Symantec provides a searchable database of viruses, Trojans, and worms on its site (www.symantec.com/security_response/index.jsp), it would be impossible to discuss all of them in this chapter. However, a number of viruses have had a great impact on networks, the Internet, and personal computers over the decades. By looking at these, we can get a better understanding of how they work:

- **CIH/Chernobyl** In the late 1990s, this virus caused a great deal of damage to business and home computer users. It infected executable files and was spread by running an infected file on a Windows 95/98 machine. There were several variants of CIH; these were "time bomb" viruses that activated on a predefined date (either April 26 —the anniversary of the Chernobyl disaster—or every month on the 26th). Until the trigger date, the virus remained dormant. Once the computer's internal clock indicated the activation date, the virus would overwrite the first 2,048 sectors of every hard disk in the computer, thus wiping out the file allocation table and causing the hard disk to appear to be erased. However, the data on the rest of the disk could be recovered using data recovery software; many users were unaware of this capability. The virus also attempted to write to the BIOS boot block, rendering the computer unbootable. (This did not work on computers that had been set to prevent writing to the BIOS.) This virus started to show up again in spring 2002, piggybacking on the Klez virus, described later in this list.

- **Melissa** This was the first virus to be widely disseminated via e-mail, starting in March 1999. It is a macro virus, written in Visual Basic for Applications (VBA) and embedded in a Microsoft Word 97/2000 document. When the infected document is opened, the macro runs (unless Word is set not to run macros), sending itself to the first 50 entries in every Microsoft Outlook Messaging Application Program Interface (MAPI) address book. These include mailing list addresses, which could result in very rapid propagation of the virus.

The virus also made changes to the Normal.dot template, which caused newly created Word documents to be infected. Because of the huge volume of mail it produced, the virus caused a denial of service on some e-mail servers. The confessed author of the virus, David Smith, was sentenced to 20 months in federal prison and was fined $5,000.

- **Code Red** In summer 2001, this self-propagating worm began to infect Web servers running Internet Information Server (IIS). On various trigger dates, the infected machine would try to connect to TCP port 80 (used for Web services) on computers with randomly selected IP addresses. When successful, it attempted to infect the remote systems. Some variations also defaced Web pages stored on the server. On other dates, the infected machine would launch a DoS attack against a specific IP address embedded in the code. CERT reported that Code Red infected more than 250,000 systems over the course of nine hours on July 19, 2001.

- **Nimda** In late summer 2001, the Nimda worm infected numerous computers running Windows 95/98/Me, NT, and 2000. The worm made changes to Web documents and executable files on the infected systems and created multiple copies of itself. It spread via e-mail, via network shares, and through accessing infected Web sites. It also exploited vulnerabilities in IIS versions 4 and 5 and spread from client machines to Web servers through the back doors left by the Code Red II worm. Nimda allowed attackers to then execute arbitrary commands on IIS machines that had not been patched, and denials of service were caused by the worm's activities.

- **Klez** In late 2001 and early 2002, this e-mail worm spread throughout the Internet. It propagates through e-mail mass mailings and exploits vulnerabilities in the unpatched versions of Outlook and Outlook Express mail clients, attempting to run when the message containing it is previewed. When it runs, it copies itself to the System or System32 folder in the system root directory and modifies a Registry key to cause it to be executed when Windows is started. It also tries to disable any virus scanners and sends copies of itself to addresses in the Windows address book, in the form of a random filename with a double extension (for example, file.doc.exe). The payload executes on the 13th day of every other month, starting with January, resulting in files on local and mapped drives being set to 0 bytes.

- **MyDoom** In January 2004, this worm (which is also called the Norvarg worm) set a record as to how fast it was disseminated, and actually managed to slow global Internet performance by 10 percent. The worm was spread as an e-mail that appeared to be an error message containing the text "Mail Transaction Failed." When someone opened the e-mail, the worm would spread further by being sent to any e-mail addresses found in address books on the machine. It spread further through shared directories used by the file-sharing program Kazaa. It was estimated that during the first hours the worm was disseminated, one in 10 e-mails sent over the Internet contained MyDoom. It is no longer a threat, because MyDoom was programmed to stop after February 12, 2004.

These are only a few examples of the damage and inconvenience caused by various forms of malicious code. There are three broad categories of this type of code, identified as *Trojans* or *Trojan horse programs*, *viruses*, and *worms*. We take a brief look at each of these attack types in the following sections.

Trojans

The name *Trojan* is short for *Trojan horse* and refers to a software program that appears to perform a useful function but in fact performs actions that the program's user does not intend or is not aware of. Trojan horses are often written by hackers to circumvent a system's security. Once the Trojan is installed, the hacker can exploit the security holes it creates to gain unauthorized access, or the Trojan program may perform some action such as:

- Deleting or modifying files
- Transmitting files across the network to the intruder
- Installing other programs or viruses

Basically, the Trojan can perform any action that the user has privileges and permissions to do on the system. This means that a Trojan is especially dangerous if the unsuspecting user who installs it is an administrator and has access to the system files.

Trojans can be very cleverly disguised as innocuous programs, utilities, or screensavers. A Trojan can also be installed by an executable script (JavaScript, a Java applet, ActiveX control, or the like) on a Web site. Accessing the site can initiate the program's installation if the Web browser is configured to allow scripts to run automatically. Trojans can use the default behavior of Windows to disguise their true nature. Because the file extension (the characters that appear after the last dot in a filename) are hidden by default, a hacker can name a file something such as vacation.jpg.exe and it will be shown in Windows Explorer as vacation.jpg, seeming to be an innocent graphics file when it is really an executable program. Of course, double-clicking it to open the "picture" will run the program. Trojans that are designed to allow a hacker unauthorized access across the network (such as Back Orifice) are sometimes called *remote access Trojans*, or *RATs*.

WARNING

Although Microsoft Office documents are not executable files themselves, they can contain *macros*, which are small programs that are embedded into the documents and can be used to spread malicious code. Thus, Office documents should be treated as though they are executables unless running macros is disabled in the Office program.

Viruses

Viruses are programs that are usually installed without the user's awareness and perform undesired actions that are often harmful, although sometimes merely annoying. Viruses can also replicate themselves, infecting other systems by writing themselves to any diskette that is used in the computer or sending themselves across the network. Viruses are often distributed as attachments to e-mail or as macros in word processing documents. Some activate immediately on installation, and others lie dormant until a specific date or time or a particular system event triggers them. For more information, see the article "How Computer Viruses Work" at www.howstuffworks.com/virus.htm.

Viruses come in thousands of varieties. They can do anything from popping up a message that says "Hi!" to erasing the entire contents of a computer's hard disk. The proliferation of computer viruses has also led to the phenomenon of the *virus hoax*, which is a warning—generally circulated via e-mail or Web sites—about a virus that does not exist or that does not do what the warning claims it will do.

Real viruses, however, present a real threat to your network. Companies such as Symantec and other AV software vendors design their products to detect and remove virus programs. Because new viruses are created daily, it is important to download new *virus definition files*, which contain information required to detect each virus type, on a regular basis to ensure that your virus protection stays up-to-date.

The types of viruses include:

- **Boot sector viruses** These are often transmitted via a diskette. The virus is written to the Master Boot Record (MBR) on the hard disk, from which it is loaded into the computer's memory every time the system is booted.

- **Application or program viruses** These are executable programs that, when run, infect your system. Viruses can also be attached to other, harmless programs and can be installed at the same time the desirable program is installed.

- **Macro viruses** These are embedded in documents (such as Microsoft Word documents) that can use macros, small applications or "applets" that automate the performance of some task or sequence.

Viruses that are programmed to "go off" (activate and destroy data or files) on a certain date are called *time bombs* or *logic bombs*. One of the first of this type to gain worldwide attention was the Michelangelo virus in the early 1990s, which attempted to erase the hard disks of infected PCs on March 6, the birthday of the famous painter. A few years later, a disgruntled ex-employee of Omega Engineering planted a time-bomb virus on the company's network that resulted in approximately $10 million in loss and damage. He was convicted of the crime and sentenced to 41 months in prison.

On the Scene

Understanding the Virus Threat

The most dangerous aspect of computer viruses (as is true of their biological counterparts) is their ability to "mutate" into something else. Of course, this mutation doesn't happen spontaneously, but virus writers build on the code of others to make relatively benign viruses more destructive—and to avoid detection by AV software.

Worms

A *worm* is a program that can travel across a network from one computer to another. Sometimes different parts of a worm run on different computers. Worms make multiple copies of themselves and spread throughout a network. The distinction between viruses and worms has become blurred. Originally the term *worm* was used to describe code that attacked multiuser systems (networks), whereas *virus* described programs that replicated on individual computers.

The primary purpose of the worm is to replicate. These programs were initially used for legitimate purposes in performing network management duties, but their ability to multiply quickly has been exploited by hackers who create malicious worms that replicate wildly and can also exploit operating system weaknesses and perform other harmful actions.

Prevention and Response

Protecting systems and networks from the damage caused by Trojans, viruses, and worms is mostly a matter of common sense. Practices that can help prevent infection include the following:

- Don't run executable (.exe) files from unknown sources, including those attached to e-mail or downloaded from Web sites.

- Turn off the Preview and/or HTML mail options in your e-mail client program.

- Don't open Microsoft Office documents from unknown sources without first disabling macros.

- Be careful about using diskettes that have been used in other computers.

- Install and use firewall software.

- Install AV software, configuring it to run scans automatically at predefined times and updating the definition files regularly.

- Use intrusion prevention tools called *behavior blockers* that deny programs the ability to execute operations that have not been explicitly permitted.

- Use *behavior detection* solutions such as Finjan's Real-Time Content Inspection (www.finjan. com) that can use heuristic techniques to analyze executable files and assess whether they are likely to be hostile.

- Use *integrity checker* software such as Tripwire (http://sourceforge.net/projects/tripwire) to scan the system for changes.

Recognizing the presence of malicious code is the first-response step if the system does get infected. Administrators and users need to be on the alert for common indications that a virus might be present, such as missing files or programs; unexplained changes to the system's configuration; unexpected and unexplained displays, messages, or sounds; new files or programs that suddenly appear with no explanation; memory "leaks" (less available system memory than normal) or unexplained use of disk space; and any other odd behavior of programs or the operating system. If a virus is suspected, a good AV program should be installed and run to scan the system for viruses and attempt to remove or quarantine any that are found. Finally, all mission-critical or irreplaceable data should be backed up on a regular basis in case all these measures fail.

Some virus writers create "proof of concept" viruses that do not cause damage and are designed merely to demonstrate that a particular type of virus can be written. For example, it was once thought that viruses could not be spread by simply reading e-mail; users were told that as long as they didn't open attachments, they were safe. The first viruses exploiting Hypertext Markup Language (HTML) e-mail to run and infect systems when a user opened the e-mail message (not an attachment) proved that the concept of a virus that could spread via e-mail alone. In June 2002, researchers at McAfee received a proof-of-concept virus called Perrun that is embedded in a JPEG image file. Although limited, this was the first known case of a virus embedded in a picture file that runs automatically when the graphic is viewed. That same month, Symantec reported the first cross-platform virus; it could infect both Linux and Windows systems.

The moral of the story is that virus writers are a creative and persistent bunch and will continue to come up with new ways to do the "impossible," so computer users should never assume that any particular file type or operating system is immune to malicious code. The only sure way to protect against viruses is to power down the computer and to leave it turned off.

Hacking for Nontechies

As we've mentioned, highly developed technical skills are no longer necessary for people who want to break into computer systems and networks. Some say that hacking was originally an art that required great talent, that later required only a bit of skill, and that today can be done by anyone who has enough hand-eye coordination to click a mouse. To put it more eloquently, "Hacking has devolved from a labor of love to unskilled labor." This process of deterioration began with the phenomenon of the *script kiddie*.

The Script Kiddie Phenomenon

You'll find a dozen definitions of *script kiddie*, depending on the source you consult. Webopedia (www.webopedia.com) defines the term as someone who "randomly seeks out a specific weakness over the Internet in order to gain root access to a system without really understanding what it is s/he is exploiting because the weakness was discovered by someone else." The Jargon Lexicon at www. faqs.org/docs/jargon/index.html is a bit more judgmental: "The lowest form of cracker ... People who cannot program but who create tacky HTML pages by copying JavaScript routines from other tacky HTML pages."

Regardless of the precise definition, most agree on one thing: Script kiddies don't have much technical expertise themselves, but they use code written by others to wreak havoc. In the hacker culture, they are generally regarded with contempt or at least with a lack of respect. Nonetheless, hackers who *do* understand the technology continue to distribute scripts and programs that the script kiddies use to do their dirty work.

The number of people who write their own code to hack systems is relatively low in comparison to those who have marginal skills and use the scripts and tools of others. Script kiddies and their cousins, *packet monkeys* (people who launch DoS attacks against Web sites for "no apparent reason"), have been around for many years, and have caused considerable damage to systems throughout the world. An example is the large-scale DDoS attack that brought down Yahoo!, eBay, ZDNet, and CNN. The Yahoo! attack was launched by a Canadian teenager called "Mafiaboy" who used a utility called Stacheldraht that was written by a German hacker.

The "real" hackers spend years playing with computer systems and learning the intricacies of complex operating systems, often preferring to work with UNIX. They take pride in their knowledge and in the "elegance" of their attacks. They regard script kiddies, who rely on scripts written by others and even stoop to using hacking tools with graphical interfaces, in much the way a master jewel thief regards a street thug. Because script kiddies are unskilled (and thus are less able to cover their tracks) and because they tend to crave attention (whereas most skilled hackers take pride in being able to stealthily invade a system and get out without anyone knowing), script kiddies make up a large proportion of the network intruders and attackers who are caught and prosecuted.

Despite their disrespectful nickname and the low level of regard they're given in the hacker community, script kiddies can do a lot of damage, and the randomness of their attacks makes them especially dangerous. As with drive-by shootings that target random victims, script kiddies' actions are impossible to predict and they place everyone at risk.

The "Point and Click" Hacker

As unsophisticated as script kiddies are, another variety of "wannabe" hacker is even less technically savvy. At least the average script kiddie knows enough to type a few commands to launch the script he or she got from somebody else. The newest incarnation of "do it the easy way" attackers is too unknowledgeable—or too lazy—to do even that. Instead, this new breed uses "point and click" utilities with pretty graphical interfaces or "fill in the blank" Web sites that serve as front ends to launch the chosen attack(s) against specified targets without the so-called hacker even needing to know how to download a file.

David Rhoades of Maven Security came up with the term *click kiddies* to describe these "rebels without a clue." Rhoades travels to computer security conferences around the world with his presentation, called "Hacking for the Masses." In his talk, he outlines just how easy it is for literally anyone to commit online breaking and entering—and much worse—with readily available tools that, to paraphrase Rhoades, are so user-friendly even your grandmother can bring down several servers before dinner.

> **NOTE**
>
> Rhoades' discussion of this type of hacker is available to view in his presentations, called "Hacking for the Masses" and "De-Evolution of the Hacker," which are available at www.mavensecurity.com/presentations.

Use of the Web-based attack tools favored by click kiddies also makes it more difficult to trace the origin of the attack, because the attack is coming from an intermediary (the Web site that provides the tool) instead of directly from the attacker.

Prevention and Response

The same preventive measures that we've already discussed apply to protecting a network from nontechie hackers. In addition, script kiddies can sometimes be lured in and caught by setting up a *honeypot*, which is a system designed specifically for the purpose of trapping attackers. The honeypot is a system or network that acts as an "open invitation" to hackers. It is connected to the Internet with minimal protection, running unpatched operating systems and application software that can be easily exploited. The systems are constantly monitored so that the attacker can be identified and traced before he or she has a chance to destroy evidence. We discuss honeypots in more detail in Chapter 14.

Understanding Wireless Attacks

In many corporate networks across the country, wireless devices are extending the network perimeter beyond the confines of the office walls and into neighboring buildings and public streets. No longer does an attacker need to gain network access by breaking into an office or attempting to bypass strict firewall policies. Now attackers can take advantage of an unsuspecting company that doesn't realize its wireless infrastructure security is so loose it can be hacked in less than 15 minutes.

You often read stories about hackers sitting in vehicles with a laptop and a high-powered wireless antenna, scanning for insecure wireless networks to compromise. These hackers may be looking for internal corporate intellectual property to sell to a competitor or data that may be used for blackmail or extortion. BJ's Wholesale Club, Lowe's Companies Inc., DSW, Wake Forest University School of Medicine, and TJX have all been victims of compromised wireless networks. The cost of these data breaches could be well into the millions of dollars, but their true cost remains difficult to calculate because we must take into consideration the money spent by the company to investigate the problem, provide damages to the victims, and fix the vulnerabilities, and factor in loss of revenue due to low consumer confidence.

As the cost to implement wireless networks continues to decrease, more and more companies and home users are using wireless technology. Since 2006, London has seen 160 percent more wireless access points, with New York increasing a substantial 49 percent. However, you don't need to look at statistics to realize that wireless networks are becoming more popular. Open your wireless configuration user interface and you will usually see three or four networks in the surrounding area. If you live in the city, that number can be as high as 15 to 20.

This section discusses the basics of wireless networks and the methods hackers use to attack them. Hackers have an advantage when it comes to wireless attacks due to anonymity and the difficulty of tracking down attacks. The attack surface is huge and the results are appealing because once a hacker gets in, he or she is on the internal network, bypassing many of the traditional network security barriers.

Basics of Wireless

A wireless access point connects the traditional wired network to wireless clients by transmitting network data through the air. The wireless access point acts as a relay between the wired network and wireless clients. Many companies implement many wireless access points that can hand off the wireless signal to ensure that the client does not get disconnected. These access points range from home or home office devices that cost less than $100 to enterprise access points that implement complex security features and allow for specialized configuration and management.

The wireless access points themselves simply provide a means for the data to travel from the wired network to the client. The network infrastructure services must still be provided to the client. Although most access points today have these features built into the device, you can also use your traditional servers to provide services such as Dynamic Host Configuration Protocol (DHCP) and routing.

For a client to connect wirelessly to a LAN, it must have a wireless network card compatible with the wireless standard used by the target network. With the majority of laptops today including built-in network devices, wireless networks are becoming a standard with most home and corporate networks. Although wireless LANs have traditionally been used for mobile devices, the ease and cost-effectiveness of extending the network has some companies implementing wireless cards on their desktop machines.

Even with all the advancements in recent years, installing a wireless network on your LAN is not something you should do without careful planning. Before adding wireless connectivity to your network, you should understand the major advantages and disadvantages of introducing wireless connectivity.

On the Scene

Different Types of Wireless Networks

Different types of wireless networks are available, the most common being 802.11 b/g. 802.11b was the first wireless standard developed for commercial use. It operates at 2.4 GHz and transfers data at a rate of 11 megabits per second (Mbps). Improving data transfer to 54 Mbps, 802.11 g was a welcome upgrade for consumers wanting faster throughput from their wireless infrastructure. Although the 2.4 GHz band would often lead to interference problems, backward compatibility and early adoption helped this combination become the standard for wireless devices.

For those companies that required less interference or that could not adopt the 2.4 GHz band as an acceptable solution, 802.11a was released that worked on the 5 GHz band. 802.11a improved on wireless stability, reducing dropped connections, while staying at the 54 Mbps transfer rate. The main downside is the expense of upgrading both the wireless access points and the client's wireless cards to devices that support this standard.

Wireless devices can also connect two remote locations by using line-of-sight antennas to send data from one location to another where the installation of cabling would not be feasible. A company that has a second building located less than a mile from the main building may choose to implement a line-of-sight wireless solution for Internet connectivity instead of spending the reoccurring cost of a traditional T1 line.

Advantages of a Wireless Network

Wireless networks offer users the following advantages:

- **Ease of accessing the network** No longer are employees bound to areas where they can plug into a wall jack to connect to the network. Being able to connect your laptop to the network from anywhere in the building allows for more freedom.

- **Reduced cost of running cable** The labor cost alone of wiring an office or office building can be quite high compared to the cost of purchasing and installing a wireless device and cards. With wireless cards available for desktop computers, an office can be network-available in a matter of minutes.

- **Productivity** Employees can now take their laptops with them to meetings or any other place required, and yet continue working.

Disadvantages of a Wireless Network

Wireless networks also have some disadvantages as well:

- **Security** The main disadvantage of wireless is its lack of security. If proper planning and configuration are not taken into consideration, any wireless network can be easily compromised.

- **Complexity and reliability** Although adding wireless access points increases accessibility to the wired network, it can also increase the complexity of the network design. System administrators must be aware of the impact that the wireless devices have on the network and troubleshoot problems such as weak signals and dropped wireless connections.

- **Network performance** Although the advertised speed of a wireless connection is 54 Mbps, the actual data throughput is often much lower, especially if many computers are using the same wireless connection. A wired network drop will almost always outperform a wireless connection.

Association of Wireless AP and a Device

To transmit and receive data through a wireless connection, the client must be associated with the access point. This association connects the two devices and allows the client to obtain an IP address and communication on the network. Signal power and security settings can interfere with the association process.

On Windows XP and Windows Server operating systems, Microsoft provides the Windows Wireless Zero Configuration (WZC) utility to assist the user with connecting to wireless networks. Although it does make the association process easier, it also introduces some security concerns you should be aware of.

If a preferred network is not available, WZC will probe for networks that are already connected. This information can be viewed by anyone using a wireless analyzer and can be used to set up fake access points to lure clients to connect. WZC will also attempt to connect to the wireless network with the strongest signal. Knowing this, an attacker can create fake wireless networks with high-power antennas and cause computers to associate with their access point rather than the legitimate one. When possible, it is recommended that you use the vendor-provided wireless management tool.

If you are using a wireless card from Linksys, Dell, or Netgear, you will likely have installed management software from the vendor that can control the association of the wireless device. This software has been designed by the manufacturer to work with the corresponding hardware and is typically more secure.

All wireless management software will require you to select the wireless network to which you would like to connect. You will select the service set identifier (SSID). The SSID is the public name of the wireless network. If the network has security enabled, you will be prompted to enter the passphrase or encryption key. If you do not know the key, you will not be allowed access to the network. If the network is open or you enter the correct security key, your computer will attempt to establish the connection.

NOTE

In Chapter 13, we'll discuss a number of security issues and methods used to protect wireless networks.

Wireless Penetration Testing

Wireless penetration testing involves using the same techniques that hackers use to attack wireless networks. A negative stigma is often associated with the use of hacker tools and methodologies. Network administrators and management frequently consider the use of these tools as the legitimization of hacker-based tactics and strategies. This attitude can lead to an insecure wireless network that has not been tested to determine the ability to prevent a true attack from succeeding.

Conducting penetration tests to determine the security of your wireless infrastructure is essential. Through the practice of learning, understanding, and implementing the same methods of attack the intruder will use, one can better assess vulnerabilities, overcome weaknesses, and fortify defenses. During a wireless penetration test, it is important to gather as much information about the network as possible. Most networks are discovered during *wardriving* (the process of scanning for insecure networks), so the attack may be targeted more toward a wireless vulnerability than a specific corporate network.

When conducting a penetration test you should conduct both are an internal and an external attack. The internal approach allows you to use information you already know about the network, such as encryption keys, network design, and signal ranges. This type of test validates the security of the network from an internal employee's point of view. External testing is done without using any knowledge of the network infrastructure. The tester uses tools an intruder would use and simulates an actual attack. It is important that a skilled security professional perform this test to ensure that these tools do not negatively impact network and server systems.

The key thing to remember during a wireless penetration test is that the goal is to assess the security of the wireless network. Management approval in writing of what tests are expected and the potential impact to the network is a good way to ensure no surprises for either side. Those performing the test should also do the following:

- Never do anything that will compromise or affect a neighboring wireless network.

- Never try any type of DoS attack on the network without approval.

- As various portions of the network are cracked (or are attempted to be penetrated), make sure to keep the results of the scan and penetration test confidential, and ensure that the results are stored safely.

- Report all findings to management with detailed explanations and security recommendations.

CyberLaw Review

Search Warrants

Before you can investigate a device owned by someone else, you will need permission from an authorized party (the owner of that device) or you may be required to obtain a search warrant. You must verify that the search warrant includes the proper authorization to perform on-site examinations of computer equipment such as wireless access devices. Do not perform any forensic analysis on equipment you are not authorized to analyze.

Direct Connections to Wireless Access Points

Users that are persistent in their desire to connect to an unauthorized access point will keep an eye out for security professionals completing wireless audits and simply unplug the access point until the scan is complete. The amount of effort required for physical wireless scans can often result in less frequent scans. Detecting wireless access points from your wired network has many advantages. You can set automated scripts that search your network on a continuous basis, saving you time and money. By using tools such as Nmap and Nessus, you can scan sections of your network not easily accessible to wireless scanning.

To perform wired network scans for access points, you must be connected to the internal network and have the ability to connect to all the subnets you want to scan.

Rogue Access Points

For enterprise-class access point detection, organizations may want to consider investing in a wireless IDS/IPS system. A wireless IDS/IPS is an intrusion detection/intrusion prevention system that provides 24/7 monitoring on the network and can dynamically respond to wireless threats.

In addition to detecting rogue devices, a wireless IDS/IPS can terminate them using air or port suppression on the switch, provide forensic analysis of packets sent and received, and provide location tracking of the device by triangulating the signal between multiple sensors.

Rogue access points represent a growing threat to network administrators because users can plug in a wireless access point with a minimal configuration and extend the network wirelessly. This creates a lack of control regarding where data is being sent, and worse, who is listening.

Wireless Connection to a Wireless Access Point

Before initiating an attack, a hacker will want to know as much about the target network as possible, using various wireless tools to perform information gathering. Once the hacker feels comfortable with the information gathered, he or she may use injection techniques to force information across the wireless network that can be used to crack encryption schemes. Once this data has been captured, it is matter of time before the encryption key is discovered and the hacker is connected to the internal network via the wireless access point.

The tools used to perform these attacks are freely available on the Internet and are included in live security distributions. Some of these tools include:

- **Aircrack-ng suite** (www.aircrack-ng.org) A suite of tools for auditing wireless networks. It includes Airodump-ng (which logs the coordinates of access points and captures raw 802.11 packets), Aireplay-ng (which can be used to inject frames into wireless networks), Aircrack-ng (which can recover keys once enough packets have been captured), and Airdecap-ng (which decrypts encrypted capture files).

- **Kismet** (www.kismetwireless.net) A Layer 2 wireless packet analyzer that works with wireless cards that support raw monitoring mode. Kismet can quickly identify wireless networks by capturing wireless packets and retrieving information such as whether they have security-enabled SSID cloaking, network channels, and an SSID of the network.

On the Scene

BackTrack

Getting all the tools necessary to perform penetration-testing tasks can be quite daunting. Compatibility issues with kernels and dependent drivers can have a security analyst spending most of the time getting the tools to work instead of testing the security of his or her applications or devices. Live CDs are bootable CDs that contain preconfigured operating systems and tools that are distributed by groups over the Internet. One of the premier Security distributions is BackTrack (www.remote-exploit. org/backtrack.html).

The BackTrack live CD distribution comes with many security tools already installed and ready to use so that the tester can spend more time performing the penetration testing and finding security vulnerabilities in the systems. BackTrack not only contains the majority of the tools that we will discuss in this chapter, but it also contains tools for information gathering, network mapping, vulnerability identification, penetration testing, privilege escalations, Voice over IP (VoIP) and wireless analysis, and digital forensics. All you need to get started is to download the International Organization for Standardization (ISO) image and burn it to a CD.

Logging

Most wireless access points have the ability to log traffic and connections. It is important to consider logging requirements before an incident occurs. Being able to go back to a specific time when an event is thought to have occurred gives the investigator the ability to analyze and determine whether there was indeed a wireless attack on the network.

The logging on most access points does not provide the kind of granularity required for effective logging. You can set up a wireless IDS/IPS to monitor and log any suspicious wireless activity using wireless sensors. These sensors detect malformed wireless packets and log the data for forensic analysis later.

Investigating wireless attacks is difficult due to the nature of the technology. This is exactly the reason attackers like to use this method to gain access to corporate networks. The best solution is to configure your wireless network securely to ensure that hackers will not be able to gain access easily. If a wireless incident does occur, an investigator can use the same tools the attacker used to determine how the attack was done and decide how much information may have been exposed. Proactively reviewing event logs on servers and network devices is always a good step toward identifying attacks early and handling them appropriately.

Summary

The sheer number of ways that a hacker can intrude or attack a network can be overwhelming. As soon as one security "hole" is plugged, dozens more are discovered or created. Some of these methods are so subtle that no one might ever realize that the network's security has been compromised. Others are so blatant that *everyone* will know instantly.

Attackers range from charmers with lots of "people skills" who can persuade legitimate users to provide the credentials they need to break into the system, to technical "whiz kids" who can exploit the characteristics of network protocols, applications, and operating systems, and technically unsophisticated hacker "wannabes" who use scripts, GUI tools, and Web sites created by others to carry out their attacks. The attacks themselves can range from denials of service that disrupt communications on the entire network, to "benign" viruses that do no more than pop up an annoying message window. In many cases, the goal of an attack is to plant a "back door" in the system that will allow the hacker to reenter later at will.

The state of hacking has reached the point at which anyone and everyone who wants to launch an attack can do so, and the incidence of "drive-by hacking" has increased with the advent of easy-to-use hacking tools. To protect systems, network administrators and management should use the same methods used by hackers to identify weaknesses in their networks. This can include using tools installed on individual computers, and using various tools designed to hack cabled and wireless networks.

Frequently Asked Questions

Q: Why aren't the tools described in this chapter—port-scanning utilities, packet sniffers, keystroke logging devices, and so on—illegal to create or download?

A: Many of these tools have legitimate uses. It is especially important for network administrators and security consultants to be able to use scanning tools to determine where the vulnerabilities are in their own or their clients' networks to take the appropriate steps to "harden" the systems. After all, if scanning tools were outlawed, only outlaws would have scanning tools. These utilities—like many other things—can be used either offensively or defensively. Keystroke logging devices and other "spyware" can be useful in situations in which monitoring users' activities is legal and appropriate—for example, for employers to keep tabs on what employees are doing on the network (especially when the employer could be held liable for those activities) and for parents to exercise control over children's online activities.

Q: If a company has a good firewall installed, won't that protect the company from all these attacks?

A: No. Firewall products are very useful for controlling what comes into or goes out of a network. But a firewall is like a computer (in many cases, a firewall *is* a specialized computer); it does only what the person who configures it tells it to do. Some types of attacks are recognized and can be stopped by firewalls, but others exploit the characteristics of the protocols commonly used for legitimate network communications, and packets might appear to be nothing more than a benign bit of data destined for a computer on the internal network. Trojans, viruses, and worms piggyback into the network as e-mail attachments or through remote file sharing. Firewalls won't catch them, but a good AV program, frequently updated and set to scan all incoming e-mail, might be able to do so. Many companies seem to operate under the assumption that installing a firewall is akin to invoking a magic spell that casts a force field of protection around their networks, rendering them completely immune to attack. Even the best firewall won't protect against social engineering attacks, nor will it do any good against internal attackers who have physical access to the network. Studies have shown that a large number of network-related crimes are actually "inside jobs." In Chapter 12, you'll learn in detail how firewalls work, which will make it easier to understand why they are not the "cure-all" solution to network security that they're sometimes made out to be.

Q: I think I understand the differences between a virus, a Trojan, and a worm. But what are all these other types of viruses I hear about: stealth viruses, polymorphic viruses, armored viruses, and cavity viruses?

A: *Stealth viruses* are able to conceal the changes they make to files, boot records, and the like from AV programs. They do so by forging the results of a program's attempt to read the infected files. A *polymorphic virus* makes copies of itself to spread, like other viruses, but the copies are not exactly like the original. The virus "morphs" into something slightly different in an effort to avoid detection by AV software that might not have definitions for all the variations. Viruses can use a "mutation engine" to create these variations of themselves. An *armored virus* uses a technique that makes it difficult to understand the virus code. A *cavity virus* is able to overwrite part of the infected (host) file while not increasing the length of the file, which would be a tip-off that a virus had infected the file.

Q: To hack into a wireless network would take a highly experienced hacker and I don't think anyone in my neighborhood would be able to do it.

A: The Internet has made it possible for anyone who is curious to become a viable threat when it comes to hacking, no matter where he or she lives or how much computer knowledge he or she has. Long gone are the days when a hacker would have to code an application from scratch to exploit vulnerabilities. Now, it is as simple as downloading the application and following instructions. BackTrack is a security operating system distribution that provides many of the tools discussed in this book, and is available free of charge. These days, the tools that security professionals use to test systems for vulnerabilities are often the same ones hackers use for malicious intent.

Q: How do I detect whether a hacker has associated to my wireless access point?

A: The first step is to look at the management interface and determine whether any machines look unfamiliar. Most management consoles will provide the client MAC address and computer name. Because this information can be spoofed, it should not be considered 100 percent reliable. Instability in the network may be another indication that an attacker is attempting to capture corporate data. The best solution is to implement an IDS/IPS. This system would monitor the network and search for suspicious network traffic, providing alerts to security and system administrators when an alarm is raised.

Q: Are wireless networks safe?

A: No network solution is 100 percent safe, but by taking proper precautions and using strong encryption techniques, you will be able to deter the majority of attacks. If wireless security is a top priority, investing in an IDS/IPS that is designed for wireless networks will provide the highest level of security. A wireless IPS can actually intercept and suppress wireless attacks in the air, preventing many of the most common attacks from reaching your access points. It can also detect rogue access points and provide wireless packet forensic analysis.

Chapter 11

Passwords, Vulnerabilities, and Exploits

Topics we'll investigate in this chapter:

- **Authentication**

- **Passwords**

- **Understanding Password Cracking**

- **Authentication Devices**

- **Social Engineering and Phishing**

- **Vulnerabilities and Exploits**

☑ **Summary**

☑ **Frequently Asked Questions**

Introduction

Operating systems, networks, and other systems that have integrated security (or the illusion of it) need to be able to identify who is attempting to use the system. In most systems, this is done through a combination of a username and password, although other methods of identifying the user may also be used. Once the system has established who you are, it can then give you the authorized level of access associated with your account. For example, on a network, the logon information would be used to determine whether you have access to certain folders on a server, or whether you are allowed to use specific printers. Conversely, failing to give the appropriate logon information will prevent you from being able to enter the system. Because passwords are so widely used and are so important in terms of controlling access, acquiring passwords (especially those of administrators) is a common objective of hackers.

In this chapter, we'll look at what makes a good password, and how to crack bad ones. We'll discuss various types of attacks used to acquire passwords, how passwords stored on a system can be discovered and exploited, and how hackers use social engineering to con authorized users into disclosing their passwords. Because passwords aren't the only way of proving the identity of a person, we'll also look at a number of authentication devices, such as smart card readers, fingerprint scanners, retinal and iris scanners, and voice analysis devices.

In addition to weaknesses in passwords, we'll also discuss other vulnerabilities that attackers commonly exploit to gain access to systems. Even if you have done everything correctly to prevent unauthorized people from guessing or acquiring your password, that doesn't mean that everything was done correctly when the operating system, application, or Web site was created and deployed. Hackers and malicious software can still exploit software bugs, system configuration mistakes, and other vulnerabilities, leaving your system open to attack.

Authentication

Authentication is the process of verifying the identity of a user, computer, or process. In other words, it is proving that someone or something is who or what it claims to be. You can use many different methods to authenticate a user's (or in some cases, a computer's) identity. In general, the user is asked to provide something that is associated with his or her user account that someone else could not easily provide. In information security, this falls into one of three categories, which are referred to as *authentication factors*:

- **Something you know** One way to determine that a person is really who he or she claims to be is to ask a question that only the "real McCoy" is likely to be able to answer. If you are engaging in online messaging with someone who purports to be your brother, before discussing personal or sensitive subjects, you might ask him what your mother's oldest sister's name is, or ask him to name the song that the two of you played in a piano duet as children. In information security, the "something you know" is usually a password or personal identification number (PIN).

- **Something you have** Passwords can be compromised. For example, as we'll discuss later in this chapter, someone can discover passwords through a brute force attack or by watching over a user's shoulder as he or she types the password. In many of these cases, the user doesn't know that someone else now knows the password. A better authentication method is to require that the user provide a physical object, such as a "smart card" (a credit-card-size device with an embedded chip that contains authentication information). If the card is lost or stolen, the user is likely to know about it. Smart cards are used to log on to computer networks and to access bank accounts and make purchases.

- **Something you are** Although a card or other physical object that must be in the user's possession is a step up from password authentication, cards can be lost or stolen or perhaps even duplicated. An even more secure method of proving identity is via what you are, that is, biological data such as a fingerprint, voice print, or retinal or iris scan. Biometric methods are much more difficult to defeat than other identification methods.

When Is Authentication Necessary?

Authentication is necessary in a number of different circumstances, and different authentication methods are used in different circumstances. For example:

- **Logon authentication** When a user initially accesses the computer or network (when he or she logs on), a secure operating system will require that the user authenticate to a security accounts database. When logging on to the local computer, the user must enter an account name and password that are stored in a local security database on that machine's hard disk. When logging on to a server-based network (such as a Windows domain or a NetWare network), the user must enter an account name and password that are in the authentication server's database. Additionally, Windows domains require that computers have a computer account to join the domain. (The computer's credentials are sent to the domain controller automatically, without any user intervention.)

- **Remote access authentication** When a user accesses the network over a remote connection (dial up or virtual private network [VPN]), security is especially important because the computer from which the user is logging on isn't physically wired to the local network. Different, additional protocols are used for remote access authentication. When a remote logon is initiated, the remote client and the remote access server generally negotiate an authentication method and protocols that both are configured to support. There are a number of different methods for authenticating remote users, some of which we discuss in the following section, "Authentication Protocols."

NOTE

In a network that uses an authentication server, users are authenticated when they log on to the network, and then access to individual network resources is controlled based on the permissions granted to the account with which the user logged on. In workgroup (peer-to-peer, or P2P) networks, there is no authentication server, but access to resources can be protected using *file-level security*. Passwords are assigned to individual resources, and those passwords are shared with users who are authorized to access them. Every time a user wants to open a particular file or use a particular printer, he or she must enter the correct password. This is not really authentication, because the user's identity isn't verified (the password is not associated with a user account), although entering the password does verify that the user is authorized to access the resource.

Authentication Protocols

The protocols used for authenticating identity depend on the authentication type. Some common protocols used for authentication include the following:

- **Kerberos** The default logon authentication protocol used by Windows 2000, XP, and Vista, as well as by Windows Server 2003 and Windows Server 2008. It is also used by Mac OS X. This protocol is based on secret key (symmetric) cryptography, which we'll discuss in Chapter 12. This system uses tickets that a central server issues to determine whether a user can access the network and its resources. Rather than being used to log on to each server, the tickets are used by all of the servers to determine what a user is permitted to access.

- **Challenge Handshake Authentication Protocol (CHAP)** Uses a sequence in which one party sends a challenge and the other responds with an answer. The most common form of this sequence is the server requesting a password, which the client provides to gain access to a system. Microsoft developed its own version of the protocol, called MS-CHAP.

- **NT LAN Manager (NTLM)** Another Microsoft logon authentication method that is supported by newer versions of Windows. NTLMv2 provides more security than NTLMv1, and uses a challenge-response sequence to authenticate the user. Unlike Kerberos, with NTLM, when a client wants to access a server's resources, that server must contact the domain controller to have the client's identity verified. The client doesn't have credentials already issued (the session ticket in Kerberos) that the file or application server knows it can trust.

- **Password Authentication Protocol (PAP)** A remote access authentication protocol used for Point-to-Point (PPP) or dial-up connections. Its distinguishing characteristic (and the reason it should not be used on secure networks) is the fact that it sends passwords in plain text. This means an unauthorized person can intercept and use the passwords during transmission. The only good reason to use PAP is if you face a situation in which the remote server doesn't support other, more secure authentication methods. Shiva PAP (S-PAP) addresses this problem by using a two-way reversible authentication method that encrypts passwords so that they will not be subject to interception and misuse.

- **The Remote Authentication Dial-in User Service (RADIUS)** Another means of authenticating remote connections that takes the authentication responsibility off each individual remote access server by providing a centralized server to authenticate clients securely.

- **Secure Shell (SSH)** Allows users to log on to UNIX systems remotely. Both ends of the connection (client and server) are authenticated, and data—as well as passwords—can be encrypted.

NOTE

In Chapter 12, we'll discuss a number of these protocols and how many of them use various types of encryption to ensure that data passed between a client and a server is secure.

On the Scene

Identity Confirmed; Now What?

Once a user's identity has been established, the next step in the security process is authorization, which is concerned with what that user is permitted to do. Authentication and authorization work together to provide a security system that takes into account the need for different users to have different capabilities on the network.

Administrators can control which files and other objects a user can access and the level of access (read only, change, and so on) by setting *permissions*. Most network operating systems provide a mechanism for associating specific permissions on an object with certain user accounts or groups. For example, Windows computers that have hard disks formatted as New Technology File System (NTFS) provide for two levels of permissions: *share permissions* that apply only to users accessing the resource across the network, and *file-level permissions* (also called NTFS permissions) that apply both across the network and to users accessing the resource from the local machine.

Administrators can also control which system wide actions a particular user (or group of users) can perform by setting *user rights*. User rights differ from permissions in that permissions apply to access of individual files, folders, printers, and other objects.

Passwords

The most common method used for authentication, and for determining whether someone should be allowed access, is the use of passwords. *Passwords* are a series of characters that are used to access computers, programs, and other secure systems that require security. They are used to prevent unauthorized access to computers, networks, and other technologies by forcing anyone who wants access to provide specific information. The password may consist of numbers, letters, symbols, or a combination of these.

Even though the password works like a key that gives you access, many people essentially leave the key under the mat by the front door. It's common that users don't consider the importance of their passwords, and use ones that are easy to remember, and thereby easy to guess. For example, a person may use the password "money" for his or her online banking, and administrators too often use the word "password" as a password for accessing servers or applications. Many systems also allow the use of spaces in the password so that multiple words can be used as a *pass phrase*. The problem with this is that users will often use easy-to-guess words, such as the name of their favorite sports team, or even their first and last names. Some of the other common errors people make when using passwords include:

- Using a sequence of numbers or letters, such as "1234" or "abcd".

- Using characters that are adjacent on the keyboard, such as "qwerty".

- Using common sources for passwords, such as your username, birthday, name of a loved one, and so on.

- Using words that appear in the dictionary (which can easily be cracked, as we'll see later in this chapter).

- Using numbers or symbols that look like letters, such as "P@ssw0rd". This practice is so common that hackers will try such combinations when cracking a password. After all, many of them have been spelling words like this in chat rooms since the early days of the Internet, or even earlier on bulletin board systems (BBSes).

To make passwords more secure, strong passwords should be used. A *strong password* is a password that is complex and secure. You can create strong passwords by using a combination of two or more of the following keyboard characters:

- Lowercase letters (a–z)

- Uppercase letters (A–Z)

- Numbers (0–9)

- Special characters (({}[],.<>;:'"?/|\`~!@#$%^&*()_-+=)

As you might expect, the more characters you use in a password, the more secure it will be. For this reason, many Web sites and networks require a minimum password length of eight or more characters. Unfortunately, by creating a long mix of characters, its not uncommon for people to forget their passwords.

A simple way to create a long password is to think of a sentence, and convert it to a strong password. For example, if we used the phrase "My daughter Sara is 5 years old," we could take the first letter of each word to create the password *MdSi5yo*.

CyberCrimeStopper

One Password, Many Places

Even if strong passwords are used, the same ones shouldn't be used again and again. A common practice is for people to have one or a few small passwords, and then reuse them on multiple sites. If you used a single password over and over, a person who acquired your password could then access multiple systems.

Password Policies

In the networking world, passwords (in combination with user account names) are normally the "keys to the kingdom" that provide access to network resources and data. To ensure the security of systems, policies should be in place dictating how a network user's password is created and changed. An effective password policy is a basic component of a security plan, but it is often more difficult to implement than it might appear at first glance. To be effective, a password policy must require users to select passwords that are difficult to "crack" yet easy for them to remember so that they don't commit the common security breach of writing the password on a "sticky note" that will end up stuck to the monitor or sitting prominently in the top desk drawer.

A good password policy is the first line of defense in protecting the network from intruders. Careless password practices (choosing common passwords such as *god* or *love* or the user's spouse's name; choosing short, all-alpha, one-case passwords; writing passwords down or sending them across the network in plain text) are like leaving your car doors unlocked with the keys in the ignition. Although some intruders might target a specific system, many others are just "browsing" for a network that's easy to break into. Lack of a good password policy is an open invitation to them.

Policy developers must remember that expensive, sophisticated firewalls and other strict security measures (short of biometric scanning devices that recognize fingerprints or retinal images, as we'll discuss later in this chapter) will not protect the network if an intruder has knowledge of a valid username and password. It is particularly important to use strong passwords for administrative accounts.

Best practices for password creation require that you address the following, each of which is discussed in the sections that follow:

- Password length and complexity.

- Who creates the password?

- Forced changing of passwords.

Password Length and Complexity

It's easy to define a "bad" password—it's one that someone other than the authorized user can easily guess. As we'll see later in this chapter, one way in which "crackers" do their work is via the *brute force attack*. In this kind of attack, the cracker manually or, more often, using a script or specially written software program, simply tries every possible combination of characters until he or she finally hits upon the right one. It goes without saying that using this method, it will be easier to guess a short password than a longer one because there are fewer possible combinations. For this reason, most security experts recommend that passwords have a minimum required length (for example, eight characters). Modern network operating systems such as Windows Server 200*x* allow domain administrators to impose such rules so that if a user attempts to set a password that doesn't meet the minimum length requirement, the password change will be rejected.

Who Creates the Password?

Network administrators might be tempted to institute a policy whereby they create all passwords and issue them to the users. This policy has the advantage of ensuring that all passwords meet the administrator's criteria in regard to length and complexity. However, it has a few big disadvantages as well:

- It places a heavy burden on administrators, who must handle all password changes and be responsible for letting users know what their passwords are. Of course, an administrator would not want to notify a user of his or her password via e-mail or other insecure channels. In fact, the best way to do so is to personally deliver the password information. In a large organization, this becomes particularly taxing if there is a policy requiring that passwords be changed on a regular basis.

- Users will have more difficulty remembering passwords that they didn't choose themselves. This means they are more likely to write the passwords down, resulting in security compromises. Otherwise, they might have to contact the administrator frequently to be reminded of their passwords.

- If the administrator creates all passwords, this means the administrator *knows* everyone's password. This might or might not be acceptable under the overall security policy. Some users (including management) could be uncomfortable with the idea that the administrator knows their passwords. Even though an administrator can generally access a user's account and/or files without knowing the password, it is less obvious to the users and thus less of a concern.

Allowing users to create their own passwords within set parameters (length and complexity requirements) is usually the best option. The user is less likely to forget the password because he or she can create a complex password that is meaningless to anyone else but has meaning to him or her. For example, it would be difficult for others to guess the password Mft2doSmis. It has 10 characters, combines alpha and numeric characters, and combines upper- and lowercase letters in a seemingly random manner. To a user, it might be easy to remember because it stands for "My favorite thing to do on Sunday morning is sleep."

Password Change Policy

Best practices dictate that users change their passwords at regular intervals and after any suspected security breach. Modern network operating systems such as Novell NetWare and Windows Server 200*x* allow the administrator to set a maximum password age, forcing users to change their passwords at the end of the specified period (in days). Password expiration periods can be set from one to 999 days. Individual user accounts that need to keep the same passwords can be configured so that their passwords never expire. This overrides the general password expiration setting.

Because it is the nature of most users to make their passwords as easy to remember as possible, policies should strive to prevent the following practices, all of which can present security risks:

- Changing the password to a variation of the same password (for example, changing from Tag2mB to Tag3mB)

- Changing the password back and forth between two favored passwords each time a change is required (that is, changing from Tag2mB to VERoh9 and back again continuously)

- "Changing" the password to the same password (entering the same password for the new password as was already being used)

Administrators can use operating system features to prevent these practices. For example, in Windows XP and Vista, you can configure the operating system to remember the user's password history so that up to a maximum of the last 24 passwords will be recorded and the user will not be able to change the password to one that has been used during that time. As shown in Figure 11.1, you can configure these settings in the Microsoft Management Console (MMC) by loading the Local Users and Groups snap-in, and modifying the settings found in Local Computer Policy | Computer Configuration | Windows Settings | Account Policies | Password Policy.

Figure 11.1 Password Policy Settings in Local Computer Policy on Windows XP

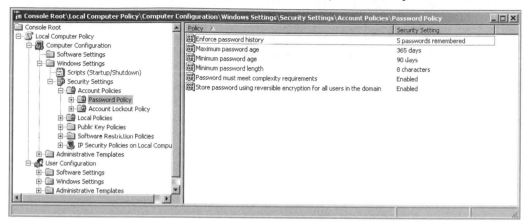

Summary of Best Password Practices

Here is a short overview of the best password practices:

- Passwords should have a minimum of eight characters.

- Passwords should not be "dictionary" words.

- Passwords should consist of a mixture of alpha, numeric, and symbol characters.

- Passwords should be created by their users.

- Passwords should be easy for users to remember.

- Passwords should never be written down.

- Passwords should be changed on a regular basis.

- Passwords should be changed anytime compromise is suspected.

- Password change policies should prevent users from making only slight changes.

On the Scene

How High Security Can Turn into High Risk

Paradoxically, overly restrictive security policies can even result in *lowered* security (while creating a false sense of high security) because frustrated employees will look for ways to circumvent security measures, intentionally or unintentionally. Gung-ho security enthusiasts who march in and "tighten up" a network without taking user needs into account can do more harm than good in the long run, despite the best of intentions.

Continued

The simplest example is the imposition of a policy that requires employees to use randomly generated 20-character passwords that change every week. Because they are unable to remember such passwords, employees are much more likely to resort to writing them down (even if that is a violation of policy) than if the employees themselves chose their own passwords so that the passwords would have meaning to the people who must remember them. Writing down the passwords (especially because people tend to keep that little note close to the computer, for convenience) poses a much greater security risk than the possibility that user-selected passwords might be a little easier to crack. A compromise solution here is to allow users to select their own passwords, but also to set policies (which can be enforced using appropriate software) requiring that user passwords meet a minimum length and complexity—for example, stipulating that both alpha and numeric characters must be included, and that the password must be at least eight characters long.

Locking Computers with Passwords

You also can configure computers to prevent unauthorized access by locking them with passwords. Computers can provide screensavers with password protection so that anyone without the password is unable to access the system. For example, Novell NetWare servers provide a password-protected screensaver that you can activate by entering the command *SCRSAVER ACTIVATE* from the server prompt. To deactivate the password, the user needs to enter a username and password with sufficient privileges. Windows computers also provide password protection on screensavers, which prevents access to the machines while the owner or designated user is away.

One of the problems with password-protected screensavers is that an intruder can bypass the protection by rebooting the machine. When the OS is loaded, the screensaver is off, so the intruder can access the data and applications on the machine. To ensure that this does not happen, you should use additional methods of protecting a machine with passwords. As we mentioned, you can set up local user accounts so that usernames and passwords must be entered to gain access once the OS has loaded. These types of accounts are different from network accounts, as they are used to control access on the machine itself. You can set up user accounts on a variety of OSes, including Windows XP and Vista, and provide protection from unauthorized access.

To set up local user accounts on Windows XP machines, you use the User Accounts applet in the Control Panel. As shown in Figure 11.2, the User Accounts applet provides an easy-to-use interface that allows you to create and maintain accounts on your computer. This is different from previous versions of Windows, in which all users could log on to the machine using the same account. In XP and Vista, each user is required to have his or her own account, allowing administrators to control what permissions and resources users have access to on the local machine. When you click on the **Create a new account** link, a wizard appears that takes you step by step through the process of setting up a new account. Once you've set up the new account, you can then click **Change an account** to modify a particular account's password, and other elements of the account.

Figure 11.2 The User Accounts Applet, Which You Use to Create Usernames and Passwords for the Local Computer

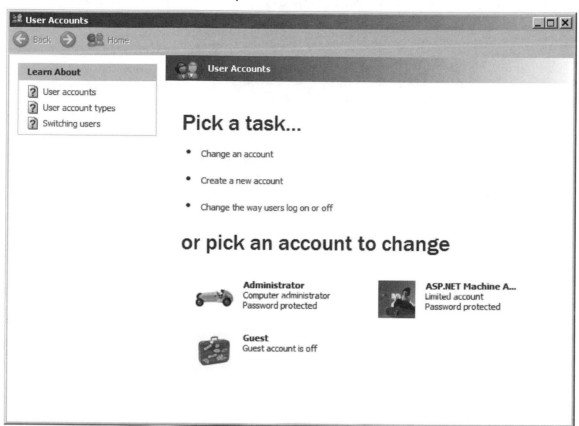

The alternative method of accessing a version of this tool is through the **Run** command on the Start menu. When you type **control userpasswords2** in **Start | Run** and then click **OK**, a dialog box similar to the one in Figure 11.3 will appear. As you can see from this dialog box, not only can you create and manage local users, but by checking the **Users must enter a user name and password to use this computer** checkbox, users are forced to have individual accounts that they must use to enter a username and password to log on to the computer.

Figure 11.3 The User Accounts Dialog Box, Which You Use to Force Users to Enter a Username and Password

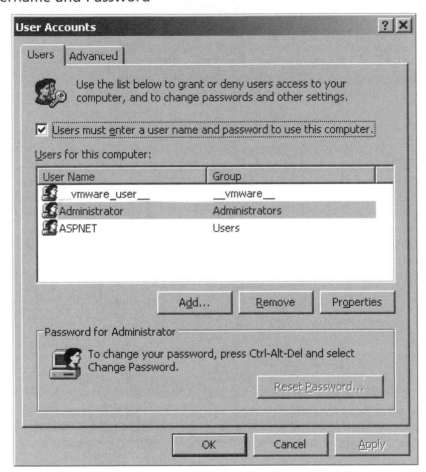

Although this prevents people without valid user accounts from using the machine, it does not prevent someone from accessing a system that a valid user has already logged on to. People often need to walk away from their computers, leaving themselves logged on with files open. Because it is not practical to shut down your computer every time you leave your desk, the Lock Workstation feature is available. The Windows Security dialog box appears when you press **Ctrl+Alt +Del** on machines running Windows OSes. When you click on the **Lock Computer** option, another dialog box requesting a username and password appears. Only the person logged on to the computer or an account that is a member of the Administrators group will be able to unlock the machine. A similar Lock Workstation feature is also available for machines running Novell NetWare.

You can force users to press **Ctrl+Alt+Del** to log on using either of two methods in Windows XP. When you open the User Accounts dialog box using the *control userpasswords2* command, the Advanced tab has a checkbox titled "Require users to press CTRL+ALT+DEL" which, when checked, forces users to log on in this manner. You can also configure this setting using the Local Security Settings applet that you can access through Administrative Tools in the Control Panel.

In Local Security Settings you would expand **Local Policies** and then click on **Security Options**. In the right pane, a listing of policies will appear. By double-clicking on **Interactive logon: Do not require CTRL+ALT+DEL**, you can enable or disable the policy.

Another method of protecting a machine is by setting passwords that prevent unauthorized users from starting up the machine and/or changing the settings. On many machines, you can access a setup program that allows you to configure the system by pressing the **F10** or **Del** key when the computer is first turned on. When the setup software appears, generally you'll see options that allow you to set passwords. You can set a Power-On Password, requiring anyone who starts the computer to enter a password before the OS loads. This prohibits hackers from using password-cracking tools to gain entry through the OS. You also can set another password in the Basic Input Output System (BIOS) to prevent unauthorized people from accessing the setup software and making changes to the computer. Setting this password also prevents malicious users from configuring Power-On and BIOS passwords, which would restrict valid users from starting the computer or making system changes.

Understanding Password Cracking

The best way to get into a system is to "trick" the system into thinking you're an authorized user. In many cases, you can do this simply by using a valid account name and password. This method is called *password cracking*. In this section, we look at the tools and resources hackers use to crack passwords. Investigators need to be aware of all the techniques and tools that can be used to impersonate a legitimate user and how they work. Understanding how a crack was accomplished provides valuable clues to the cracker's skill level and how determined he or she is to get into a particular network, as well as other characteristics that can help track down the culprit.

Password cracking involves acquiring valid passwords. You can do this in several ways, including:

- Via various types of attacks
- Recovery and exploitation of passwords stored on the system
- Use of password decryption software
- Social engineering

In the following sections, we look at each of these methods and ways to protect against them.

Types of Password Cracking

Ever since the first passwords were used, methods have been available for trying to crack the actual text-based version of the password. We can crack passwords for two reasons. One, users can select a weak password if the administrator has not enforced a strict password policy; two, some vendors have done a poor job scrambling the password. We will discuss several methods of attacking passwords. The methods are guessing, dictionary, brute force, syllable attack, rule-based, and hybrid.

Guessing Attack

In the guessing attack, perpetrators are successful when they are able to guess a person's password. This can occur if a user has selected a blank password. It can also occur if the user has chosen a simple password such as "password." Some users think they are smart, and will try a word in reverse, such as "drowssap." Another problem is when users select a password based on their kids, spouse, relative, or other personal information that is easy to identify.

Dictionary Attack

With a dictionary attack you load a file of dictionary words into the password cracking tool, and if the password is one of the words within the dictionary file it is cracked. It is important to note that dictionary files are available for many languages; therefore, it is a simple process of loading your dictionary for the country in which you are conducting the testing. Consultants have successfully cracked many passwords of foreign languages using this technique—a dictionary even exists for the Klingon language.

Brute Force Attack

In the brute force method of password attacking, the concept is to try every possible combination of characters until a password is found. It is the slowest method of attack, but given enough time and resources it will discover any password.

Syllable Attack

The syllable attack is a combination of brute force attack and dictionary attack. The technique usually is used when the password is known to be a nonexistent word.

Rule-Based Attack

The rule-based attack is used when the perpetrator is able to get some information about the password, usually following some form of enumeration that has identified the password policy in place for an organization. For example, if the policy indicates that the length of the password is not fewer than eight characters and must contain at least numbers and a special character, the perpetrator will adjust and customize the cracking tool for this.

Hybrid Attack

A hybrid attack is used to find a password that is a dictionary word with combinations of characters prepended or postpended to it. This attack is surprisingly successful, because in most cases users will select a password that is a dictionary word surrounded by additional characters.

Rainbow Attack

The rainbow attack technique works by calculating all the possible hashes for a character set, and storing them in a table. The password hash is presented to the tool that uses the rainbow algorithm, and a table search is made until the password is found. This is a much quicker method than the other types of attack; however, the limitation of the rainbow technique is the size requirements for a table, so you need to think in terms of terabytes for complex passwords.

Password Recovery Tools

A large number of password recovery programs are available on the Internet, and they are often marketed as security tools. You might not immediately think that password-cracking programs also have a legitimate use. An employee might leave a company or die suddenly without revealing passwords that were used to protect important files, which other employees now need to access. Even if they're still around, sometimes employees forget their passwords. Some companies do password recovery as a service. One such company is Password Crackers Inc. (www.pwcrack.com). Programs marketed for legitimate purposes are usually called *password recovery* programs, but of course crackers can use the same software for less-than-legitimate purposes.

> **NOTE**
>
> Some recovery programs are focused on operating system passwords and others on application passwords. The Passware software at www.lostpassword.com is a modular system that lets you select modules according to your needs, to recover passwords in Windows 2000, XP, Vista, and other operating systems, as well as Excel, Access, Outlook, Word, WinZip, WordPerfect, QuickBooks, ACT, and more. The Passware Kit includes all the modules, and you can download a free demo version from the site.

Some password protection schemes are more difficult to crack than others. The passwords on documents created with older versions of Microsoft Office and zipped files are notoriously easy to crack with readily available software. With any password scheme, the better (the longer and more complex) the passwords, the longer it takes to crack them. For difficult cracking jobs, some tools even allow you to divide the task into parts and use multiple machines simultaneously to work on it in a method called *distributed cracking*. In the sections that follow, we'll discuss a number of the most popular tools used by network administrators, computer forensic investigators, and crackers alike.

Decryption Collection Enterprise

Paraben's Decryption Collection Enterprise is an advanced password recovery suite with support for Windows Vista and Server 2003, EFS, SQL, and Lotus Notes along with support for everything included in the Standard Edition of the suite. One of its most advanced features is its ability to distribute its processing on a network of up to 16 computers. This allows brute force or dictionary attacks using several computers. This tool is available from www.paraben-forensics.com, and its features include:

- MD5 hash verification
- An easy-to-use interface that lets you just drag and drop the file to be recovered
- A listing of the most recent files recovered
- Hypertext Markup Language (HTML) reporting of recovery results
- A password cache for quick recovery of repeat passwords
- English password recovery accuracy of 90 percent and higher

Reactive Software

Reactive Software (www.reactive-software.com) has created a number of utilities that can decrypt the logon passwords used by instant messaging (IM) tools such as AOL Instant Messenger, Google Talk,

Miranda, MSN Messenger, Paltalk, Trillian, and Windows Live Messenger. The company also has tools for acquiring passwords used in other tools and services, such as File Transfer Protocol (FTP) tools (CuteFTP, WS FTP, and so on), online mail services (Hotmail, Gmail), Voice over IP (VoIP) tools such as Skype, and other utilities.

Cain and Abel

A Windows-based password recovery tool, Cain and Abel uses multiple methods to capture password hashes. It can get the hash from the network, or it can dump it from the local machine. Cain and Abel uses dictionary attacks, brute force, and other cryptanalysis techniques to crack passwords. In addition, it can sniff the network for data, can record VoIP conversations, and has other features that go beyond simple password cracking. Figure 11.4 shows the password cracking capabilities of this tool.

Figure 11.4 Password Cracking with Cain and Abel

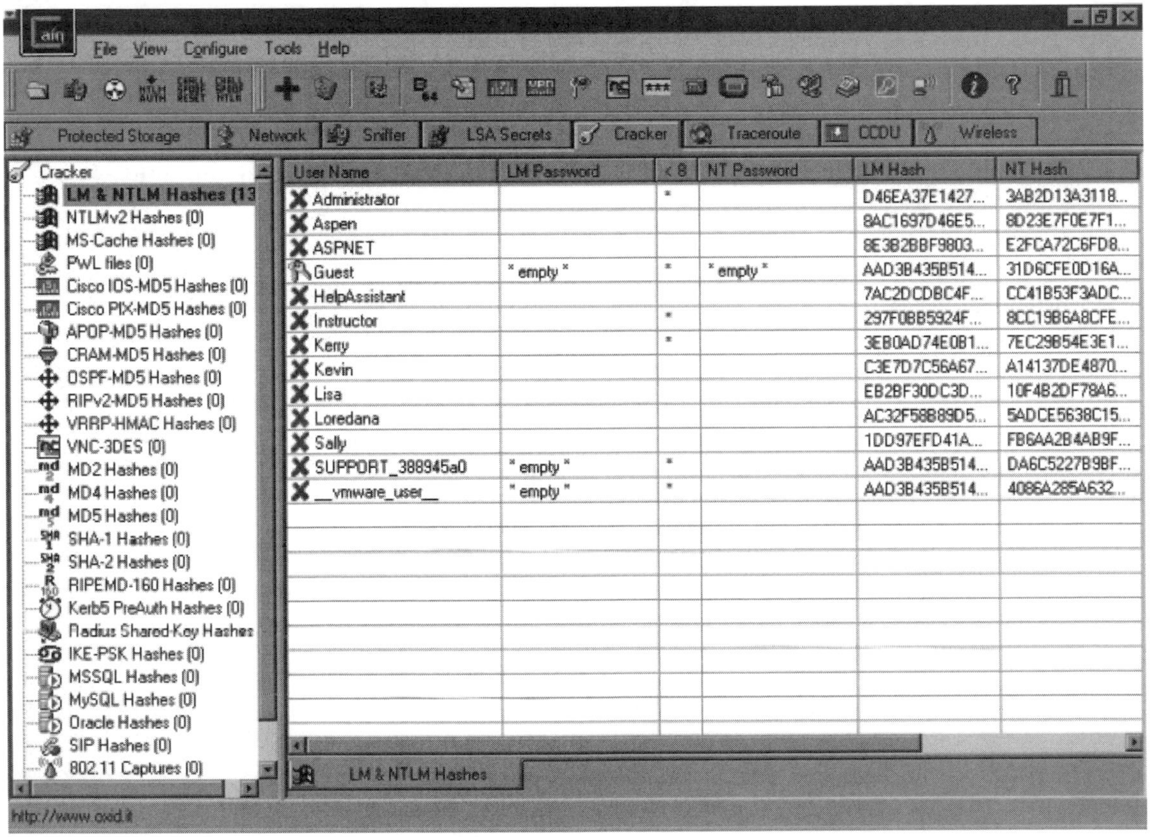

LCP

The LCP tool was developed as a free alternative to the very popular L0phtcrack tool that was the pioneer in cracking passwords on a Windows platform. L0phtcrack is no longer offered, and LCP is an excellent way to get the features that used to be available with L0phtcrack. The tool offers the ability to import from a variety of formats, and it uses dictionary, hybrid, and brute force attack methodologies to discover passwords. Figure 11.5 shows the LCP tool with a dump of the SAM database.

Figure 11.5 LCP with a Dump of the SAM Database

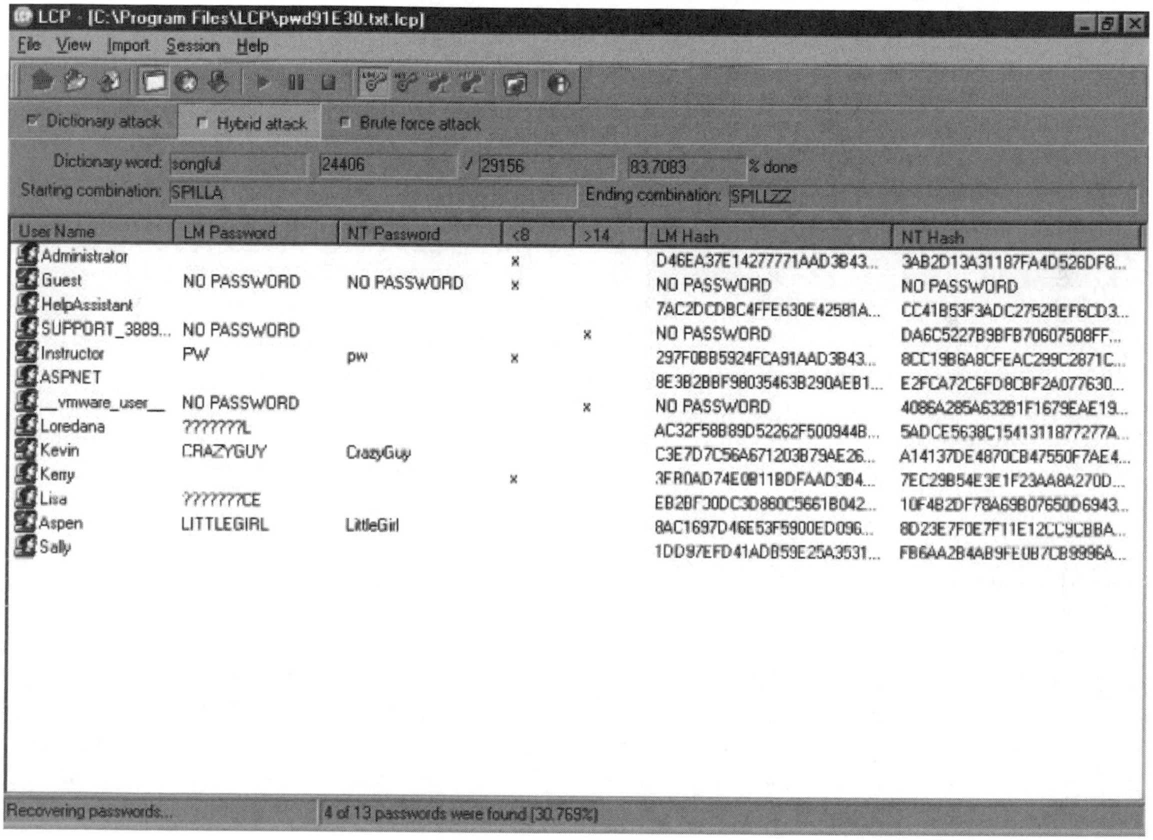

Ophcrack

Ophcrack is a Windows-based password cracker that uses the concept of rainbow cracking methodology by conducting the crack from existing rainbow tables. The algorithm deployed is based on the time-memory trade-off technique of precomputing all possible hashes and then applying the hash to the table.

John the Ripper

John the Ripper (JTR) is a fast password cracking tool that will not only crack Windows-based passwords, but also passwords on UNIX and Linux systems. The tool runs within UNIX and Linux environments.

Brutus

Brutus is a very fast and flexible password cracking tool that can perform cracks remotely. It commonly is used to crack Web site passwords. It is a Windows-based tool that can support up to 60 simultaneous target connections.

Exploitation of Stored Passwords

Trying to guess passwords, even with software to expedite the process, is a tedious business. It would be much easier if a cracker could just find a list of passwords lying around somewhere. Well, in some cases, that's exactly what happens—the list is right there for the taking on the computer's hard disk. Passwords have to be stored somewhere; after all, how else will the system know whether a user has entered the correct password? Additionally, most people have several different passwords in addition to their logon passwords; these are used for e-mail access, entry to restricted Web sites, and the like. Rather than memorizing all these secondary passwords, many users elect to have the system "remember" the password for them. Because computers have short memories (you'll recall that all the data in RAM is lost when the computer is rebooted), these "remembered" passwords must be stored in a file somewhere. All a cracker has to do is get his or her eager little hands on that file.

Thank goodness it's a little more complicated than that. In most cases, passwords are not stored in a plain-text file that the cracker can simply open and read, except in cases in which a forgetful user creates such a file, diligently recording passwords for various services and applications. Usually, stored passwords are *encrypted* or *hashed*.

For example, UNIX systems store passwords in a file located in one of several places—the /etc /passwd file, /etc/shadow (or /etc/master.passwd on BSD systems)—along with other user information. The passwords are encrypted with a hash function. The computer doesn't compare the actual password you type in to a list to determine whether to log you on; instead, the password you enter is hashed and the resultant hash value is compared to that of the stored (hashed) password.

This system sounds foolproof, but it's not. The cracking software just needs to be a little more sophisticated. If the cracker can get the password file, the program uses whatever hash function the system uses and encrypts possible passwords (generating them via brute force and dictionary methods), then compares the results with the encrypted passwords in the password file. This technique is called *comparative analysis*.

NOTE

UNIX and Linux systems can use *shadow passwords* to circumvent comparative analysis techniques. If *shadow passwords* are enabled, the encrypted password in the passwd file is replaced by an *x*. The real passwords are stored in another file, called /etc/shadow. What good does it do to store the information in a different file, especially when everyone familiar with UNIX knows the name and location of that file? The secret is that the /etc/shadow file can be accessed only by the root account. Although group accounts usually aren't assigned passwords, they can be. Group passwords can be shadowed like user passwords. In that case, the encrypted passwords are stored in a file called /etc/gshadow.

Why does all of this matter to the investigator? In some cases, an investigator can use his or her knowledge of how various operating systems store passwords to track criminals' actions. If security auditing is properly configured, investigators will be able to tell whether and when various files have been accessed. Logs that record access to password files could indicate that passwords have been or will be compromised.

Interception of Passwords

Crackers don't always have to access password files or resort to guessing (brute force) to learn usable passwords. When passwords are sent across the network via local or remote access connections in plain-text form, they can be intercepted, as can other data traveling across the network, using sniffer software. Telnet sessions to UNIX computers can be intercepted and the plain-text password extrapolated if security measures haven't been taken. Use of nonsecure authentication protocols such as PAP for remote access results in sending plain-text passwords across the link and should be avoided when possible.

NOTE

We discuss authentication protocols in more detail in Chapter 12.

Another means of intercepting passwords is to use a *keystroke logger*. This is a hardware device or software program that captures and records every character that is typed—including passwords. In many cases, when the program or tool is installed on a computer, there is no indication that the program is running. Users on the machine have no idea that everything they type is being recorded to a file, or in some cases e-mailed at regular intervals to the person who installed the program.

It is often possible to detect an unauthorized packet sniffer on the wire using a device called a time domain reflectometer (TDR), which sends a pulse down the cable and creates a graph of the reflections that are returned. Users who know how to read the graph can tell whether and where unauthorized devices are attached to the cable.

Other ways of detecting unauthorized connections include monitoring hub or switch lights, using Simple Network Management Protocol (SNMP) managers that log connections and disconnections, or using one of the many tools designed for the specific purpose of detecting sniffers on the network.

Password Decryption Software

Most password-cracking programs don't actually decrypt anything. However, if the encryption algorithm is weak or implemented incorrectly, it is sometimes possible to use a technique called *one-byte patching*, which is able to decrypt the password by changing one byte in the program. Another technique used with weak algorithms requires that the cracker already have obtained one or more files in decrypted form; then they can be used to decrypt others that use the same algorithm. This is called the *known plain-text method*. This technique is popular as an attack against password-protected .zip, .rar, and .arj files. All of these are extensions used for compressed archive files.

When strong cryptography is used and complex passwords are chosen, it is much more difficult to use direct decryption; in these cases, a dictionary or brute force attack is more often successful. PDF "decryptors" such as Guaranteed PDF Decryptor/Restrictions Remover (GuaPDF) use a type of brute force that involves testing all possible keys.

On the Scene

The Weak Encryption Debate

Many security experts feel that weak, easily broken encryption is worse than no encryption at all because it gives users a false sense of security, leading them to be careless with sensitive data because they believe it is protected. Others argue that weak encryption is better than no encryption because it at least keeps out the casual, merely curious, or technically unsophisticated "snoop." The truth, as usual, lies between the extremes; weak encryption might be beneficial in some situations—for example, for a noncritical document such as a personal journal that a user wants to protect from other, nontechnical users who share the computer. On the other hand, weak security can be disastrous in the case of vitally important information such as trade secrets or military data that is likely to be targeted by technically sophisticated crackers. In this situation, the weak encryption actually *can* be worse than none at all because the fact that the file is encrypted draws the attention of the cracker, who might otherwise have ignored it.

Authentication Devices

From the previous sections, it becomes apparent that despite the widespread use of passwords, they are not the safest way to authenticate a user … at least, not by themselves. Many organizations where security is a priority use multifactor authentication, in which a combination of authentication factors are used to identify who or what is attempting to access the system. To enhance security, usernames and passwords may be used with hardware-based solutions, such as:

- Smart card readers
- Fingerprint scanners
- Retinal and iris scanners
- Voice analysis devices

These devices can be used in environments that require a high level of security for secure and reliable network authentication. Microsoft has incorporated support for authentication devices such as smart card authentication for years, and continues to add new features that support hardware-based authentication.

Smart Card Authentication

The term *smart card* has several different meanings. In a broad sense, it refers to any plastic credit-card-size card that has a computer chip (a memory chip and/or a tiny microprocessor) embedded in it to hold information that can be changed (as opposed to less "smart" cards that use a magnetic strip that holds static information). A smart card *reader*—a hardware device—is needed to write to and read the information on the card. Smart cards can be used for different purposes, but one of the most popular is for authentication. Satellite television services use smart cards in the SATV receiver to identify the subscriber and that subscriber's service level. Banks use smart cards for conducting transactions.

Smart cards can also be used for network logon authentication. This provides an extra level of security, the "something you have" factor described earlier in this chapter. The cards are generally resistant to tampering and are relatively difficult for a hacker to compromise, because they are self-contained. They're also inexpensive in comparison to biometric authentication devices.

Smart cards used for logon authentication generally store a *digital certificate* that contains user identification information, the user's public key, and the signature of the trusted third party that issued the certificate, as well as a time for which the certificate is valid. As we'll discuss in greater detail in Chapter 12, digital certificates are used to prove the identity of users. The certificates are stored on the cards by an authorized administrator. To log on with a smart card, a user must insert the card in the reader or swipe it through and enter a PIN that is associated with the card. This PIN is a numeric sequence that serves the same purpose as a password. If the PIN is compromised, an administrator can change it or issue a new card. To use smart cards for network logon, the computer must run an operating system that supports smart card authentication, such as Windows 200x, XP, or Vista, or use add-on software such as Sphinx (www.securetech-corp.com/sphinx.html).

A number of companies manufacture smart cards and readers. Some vendors make keyboards that have built-in smart card readers, and there are combination fingerprint scanner/smart card readers for providing both card-based and biometric security.

Although smart cards provide for extra security, they (like all authentication methods) are not foolproof. Many cryptographers have been able to "break" smart card encryption. In general, there are two methods for defeating smart cards: logical and physical. An example of the logical attack is erasing parts of the data on the embedded microchip by raising or dropping the voltage; in some cases, this activity "unlocks" the security without deleting the data. A physical attack might involve actually cutting the chip out of the card and using a laser-cutter microscope to examine it. Although a determined attacker might be able to crack the smart card in this way, these methods are not easy and they don't always work.

Biometric Authentication

Biometric authentication devices rely on physical characteristics such as a fingerprint, facial patterns, or iris or retinal patterns to verify user identity. Biometric authentication is becoming popular for many purposes, including network logon. A biometric template or identifier (a sample known to be from the authorized user) must be stored in a database for the device to compare to a new sample given during the logon process. Biometrics is often used in conjunction with smart cards in high-security environments. The most popular types of biometric devices are the following:

- **Fingerprint scanners** These are widely available for both desktop and portable computers from a variety of vendors, connecting via a Universal Serial Bus (USB) or PCMCIA (PC Card) interface.

- **Facial pattern recognition devices** These devices use facial geometry analysis to verify identity.

- **Hand geometry recognition devices** These are similar to facial pattern devices but analyze hand geometry.

- **Iris scan identification devices** Iris scanners analyze the trabecular meshwork tissue in the iris, which is permanently formed during the eighth month of human gestation.

- **Retinal scan identification devices** Retina scanners analyze the patterns of blood vessels on the retina.

A large number of physiological characteristics can be used as identifiers, and devices have been developed that verify identity based on knee scans, ear geometry, vein pattern recognition, and even body odor recognition. In addition, some devices analyze and compare behavioral traits using methods such as voice pattern recognition, signature verification, keystroke pattern recognition, breathing pattern recognition, gait pattern recognition, and even brainwave pattern recognition, although many of these are only in experimental stages. Biometrics is considered to be among the most reliable authentication methods possible.

On the Scene

Defeating "Foolproof" Authentication Mechanisms

In 2000, a French engineer/hacker named Serge Humpich (and known as "the Count of Monte Crypto") was able to defeat the 640-bit encryption key used by smart cards issued by banks in France, which millions of French consumers used for purchasing items. The equipment he used to break the encryption key cost only $250.

Even supposedly "foolproof" biometric methods aren't foolproof. This is because the biometric data must be analyzed by a software program, and everyone who has worked with computers knows that there is no such thing as a software program that works perfectly. Thus, the vendors of biometric solutions establish fault-tolerance limits that are based on a certain level of false rejection and false acceptance rates (called FRRs and FARs, respectively). *False rejection* occurs when an authorized user is rejected by the system, and *false acceptance* occurs when an unauthorized user is "passed" by the software and is allowed access. In fact, fingerprint scanners have been defeated by such simple methods as blowing on the sensor surface to reactivate a fingerprint previously left there or by dusting a latent fingerprint on the sensor with graphite and then applying adhesive film to the surface and pressing on it gently. These techniques are examples of *latent image reactivation*. In a well-publicized case in May 2002, a cryptographer in Japan was able to create a phony fingerprint using gelatin, which he claimed fooled fingerprint scanners approximately 80 out of 100 times.

Social Engineering and Phishing

Hacking may be done through expert computer skills, programs that acquire information, or an understanding of human behavior. This last method is called *social engineering*. When social engineering is used, hackers misrepresent themselves or trick a person into revealing information. Using this method, a hacker may ask a user for his or her password, or force the user to reveal other sensitive information.

Hackers using social engineering to acquire information will often misrepresent themselves as authority figures or as someone in a position to help their victim. For example, a hacker may phone a network user and say that there is a problem with the person's account. To remedy the problem, all the caller needs is the person's password. Without this information, the person may experience problems with his or her account, or will be unable to access certain information. Because the person will benefit from revealing the information, the victim often tells the hacker the password. By simply asking, the hacker now has the password and the ability to break through security and access data.

Social engineering often involves subtler methods of acquiring information than simply asking for a password. In many cases, the hacker will get into a conversation with the user and slowly get the person to reveal tidbits of information. For example, the hacker could start a conversation about the Web site, ask what the victim likes about it, and determine what the person can access on the site. The hacker might then initiate a conversation about families and pets, and ask the names of the victim's family members and pets. To follow up, the hacker might ask about the person's hobbies. Because many users make the mistake of using names of loved ones or hobbies as a password, the hacker may now have access. Although the questions seem innocuous, when all of the pieces of information are put together, it can give the hacker a great deal of insight into getting into the system.

In other cases, the hacker may not even need to get into the system, because the victim reveals all the desired information. People enjoy when others take an interest in them, and will often answer questions for this reason or out of politeness. Social engineering is not confined to computer hacking. A person may start a conversation with a high-ranking person in a company and get insider information about the stock market, or manipulate a customer service representative at a video store into revealing credit card numbers. If a person has access to the information the hacker needs, hacking the system is not necessary.

The best way to protect an organization from social engineering is through education. People reveal information to social engineers because they are unaware that they are doing anything wrong. Often, they do not realize they have been victimized, even after the hacker uses the information for illicit purposes. Teaching users how social engineering works, and stressing the importance of keeping information confidential, will make them less likely to fall victim to social engineering.

Phishing

A variation of social engineering is *phishing*, or *phising*, in which a hacker uses e-mail to acquire information from the recipient. Because the hacker is fishing for information using the e-mail as bait, and hackers replaced "f" with "ph," the term phishing was born. A hacker will send e-mail to groups of people, posing as some authoritative source, and request that the recipient provide specific information. This may be a single department, the entire company, or (most often) sent as spam across the Internet. For example, common e-mails on the Internet pose as banks or companies such as eBay, and request that people fill out an HTML form or visit a Web site to confirm their account information.

The form asks for personal and credit card information, which can then be used to steal the person's identity. The same technique can be used to pose as network administrators, human resources, or other departments of a company, and request the recipient to confirm information stored in various systems. For example, it could ask them to provide their employment information (for example, name, position, department, Social Security number, and so forth), business information (business accounts, credit card numbers, and so forth), or network information such as usernames and passwords. Although many people are educated in this technique, it succeeds because out of the sheer number of people that are contacted, someone will eventually fall for the trick.

Phishing is particularly effective in business environments, because unlike banks or companies that don't use e-mail to collect information over the Internet, businesses may actually contact departments through internal e-mail to acquire information. For example, finance departments have requested that other departments provide information about their purchase accounts, credit cards, and other information, whereas human resources departments have requested updated information on employees. Because it takes knowledge to read the Multipurpose Internet Mail Extensions (MIME) information and identify whether e-mail was sent internally or externally, a member of a department may be easily duped by phishing. To prevent such problems, it is important to educate users and implement policies to specify how such information is to be collected. This may include stages, such as sending out internal e-mails stating that on a specific date, a request for such information will be sent out. It is equally important that measures be taken to inform users what sort of information is never requested, such as passwords.

Tailgating

Even with the most stringent physical security in place, there are ways of bypassing these methods and gaining access. One of the simplest methods is *tailgating*, or *piggybacking*, in which an unauthorized person follows an authorized person into a secure area. Regardless of whether a person has to use a key, PIN, card key, biometrics, or other methods to open a door and enter, all a second person needs to do is follow him or her through the door. Even if the first person notices the security breach, he or she may feel uncomfortable challenging the person who is tailgating, and not bother asking the person to provide identification, get out, or go back and use his or her own key or access to enter.

Intruders piggybacking on another person's access can be a real security challenge, because any existing security measures are rendered useless even though they're functioning properly. It is especially common if the authorized person knows the tailgater, such as when management, a coworker, or others who are visually recognized are piggybacking. It's common to see one person using a key card to enter a building and several others following their way in. However, even in these cases, you cannot be 100 percent sure whether one of them has been dismissed from the company, is under a disciplinary action (such as suspension), or is a contractor whose contract has ended. Even if the person legitimately works for the company, allowing him or her to piggyback into a server room could result in equipment being knocked over, sensitive documents (such as administrator passwords) being seen, or other problems.

Human nature can cause significant problems for any security measures you put in place, and there is no easy way to deal with it. Policies can be implemented that prohibit allowing anyone to enter an area unless he or she has used his or her own security access method (key, access card, PIN, and so forth), with procedures on what to do if someone does sneak in behind a person (such as challenging the person to produce ID, notifying security personnel, and so forth). However, most employees are neither trained nor willing to confront or physically remove a person from the premises, so often the policy may be ignored for personal safety reasons or because it is emotionally uncomfortable. After all, no one wants to ask his or her boss to get out of the building or room because the boss snuck in the door.

This makes education one of the best methods of combating the problem. Employees should be educated that tailgating is a security issue; that policies exist that make a person responsible for those permitted access; and that allowing an unauthorized person access could result in disciplinary actions (including termination of employment). Although this won't completely eliminate tailgating, it will limit the number of people who attempt or allow security breaches.

Dumpster Diving

Another threat that can be overlooked in companies is *dumpster diving*. As with tailgating, it is about as low-tech a method of threatening security as anyone could think of. It literally involves getting into a dumpster and going through the trash, searching through garbage bags, looking in wastebaskets, and rummaging through other places where people may have disposed sensitive information.

This method of breaching security remains popular because it is so effective. In addition to the rotting refuse of people's lunches, one can find discarded printouts of data, papers with usernames and passwords, test printouts that have Internet Protocol (IP) address information, and even old hard drives, CDs, DVDs, and other media containing the information you'd normally have to hack the network to obtain. Even the most innocuous waste may provide a wealth of information. For example, printouts of e-mail will contain a person's name, e-mail address, contact information, and other data that could be used for social engineering purposes (discussed in the next section).

There are many solutions to resolving dumpster diving as a security issue. Dumpsters can be locked with a padlock to limit access, or they can be kept in locked garages or sheds until they're ready for pickup. Companies can also implement a shredding policy so that any sensitive information is shredded and rendered unusable by anyone who finds it. This is especially important if the company has a recycling program, in which paper products are kept separate. If documents aren't shredded, the recycling containers make it even easier to find information, as all of the printouts, memos, and other documentation are isolated in a single container. Because discarded data isn't always in paper form, companies also need to implement a strict hardware and storage media disposal policy so that hard disks are completely wiped and old CDs and DVDs containing information are destroyed. By obliterating the data before the media is disposed, and protecting the waste containers used afterward, dumpster diving becomes difficult or impossible to perform.

Prevention and Response

Because passwords are the first—and in some networks, the only—line of defense in protecting a network from intruders, it is extremely important that steps be taken to ensure the integrity of all users' passwords. The following sections provide some general guidelines on protecting passwords and dealing with so-called social engineers.

General Password Protection Measures

Network administrators and users can take a number of measures to protect passwords, including the following:

- Follow guidelines for creating strong passwords.

- Configure settings so that user accounts are disabled or locked out after a reasonable number of incorrect password attempts.

- Use the Encrypting File System (EFS) on Windows 200x and XP computers, or BitLocker drive encryption on systems running Windows Vista and Windows Server 2008.

- Store critical data on network servers rather than local machines.

- Don't rely on the password protection built into most applications.

- Enable password shadowing on UNIX/Linux systems.

- Ensure that passwords are never sent across the network in plain-text form.

- Use antisniffer software and sniffer detection techniques to guard against crackers who try to intercept passwords traveling across the network.

Protecting the Network against Social Engineers

Administrators find it especially challenging to protect against social engineering attacks. Adopting strongly worded policies that prohibit divulging passwords and other network information to anyone over the telephone and educating users about the phenomenon are obvious steps that administrators can take to reduce the likelihood of this type of security breach. Human nature being what it is, however, some users on every network will always be vulnerable to the social engineer's con game. A talented social engineer is masterful at making users doubt their own doubts about his legitimacy.

The "wannabe" intruder could regale the user with woeful stories of the extra cost the company will incur if he or she spends extra time verifying his identity. The intruder could pose as a member of the company's top management and take a stern approach, threatening the employee with disciplinary action or even termination if he doesn't get the user's cooperation. Or the social engineer could try to make the employee feel guilty by pretending to be a low-level employee who is just trying to do his job and who will be fired if he doesn't get access to the network and take care of the problem right away. A really good social engineer is patient and thorough. He will do his homework and will know enough about the company he targets or the organization he claims to represent to be convincing.

Because social engineering is a human problem, not a technical problem, prevention must come primarily through education rather than technological solutions.

Vulnerabilities and Exploits

There is an expression among programmers: "If at first you don't succeed, call if version 1." The reason for this expression is because programs often have flaws or issues (called *bugs*) that may not be apparent until after they're used by others. When a program is written, it is hopefully tested before being released for others to use. We say *hopefully* because even though testing is a common procedure, many times in-house programs are written and released before proper testing is done (primarily due to pressure by management). Even when software is tested, some things can be missed. A program may appear to function properly, even though it has programming that is weak and can be exploited by hackers and malicious programs that can crash the software or access its data.

Known vulnerabilities are another issue that often arises when new systems are released on the market. New versions of operating systems and applications are often released with known vulnerabilities. For example, when Windows Vista was released, word quickly spread that it had literally thousands of known vulnerabilities. Despite such knowledge, Microsoft released the software with the thought that a service pack, patches, and other updates would be released afterward to fix these issues. Unfortunately, if the end-user doesn't visit the vendor's Web site to download and apply these patches, the vulnerabilities will continue to exist until he or she upgrades the software to the next version. As we'll discuss in the sections that follow, many kinds of vulnerabilities may be present in operating systems and applications.

Application Exploits

Application software exploits are those that take advantage of weaknesses of particular application programs; these weaknesses are often called *bugs*. Like protocol exploits, intruders use application exploits to gain unauthorized access to computers or networks or to crash or clog up the systems to deny service to others.

Bug Exploits

Common "bugs" can be categorized as follows:

- **Buffer overflows** Many common security holes are based on buffer overflow problems. Buffer overflows occur when the number of bytes or characters input exceeds the maximum number the program allows.

- **Unexpected input** Programmers might not take steps to define what happens if invalid input (input that doesn't match program specifications) is entered. This could cause the program to crash or open a way into the system.

- **Configuration bugs** These are not really "bugs," per se; rather, they are ways of configuring the software that leaves it vulnerable to penetration.

Popular software such as Microsoft Internet Information Server (IIS), Internet Explorer, and Outlook Express (MSOE) are the favorite targets of hackers looking for software security holes to exploit. ActiveX controls, JavaScript, and VBScript can be used to add animations or applets to Web sites or e-mail messages, but hackers can exploit these features to write controls or scripts that allow them to remotely plant viruses, access data, or change or delete files on the hard disks of unaware users who visit the page or open the mail and run the script.

Major software vendors regularly release security patches to fix exploitable bugs. It is very important for network administrators to stay up-to-date in applying these fixes to ensure that their systems are as secure as possible. The following sections take a closer look at some popular attacks that exploit application software.

Mail Bombs

A *mail bomb* is a means of overwhelming a mail server, causing it to stop functioning and thus denying service to users. A mail bomb is a relatively simple form of attack, accomplished by sending a massive quantity of e-mail to a specific user or system. Programs available on hacking sites on the

Internet allow a user to easily launch a mail bomb attack, automatically sending floods of e-mail to a specified address while protecting the attacker's identity. A number of types of mail-bombing techniques can be used against the popular Sendmail program, including:

- *Chain bombs,* in which massive numbers of e-mails are sent to an e-mail server on a script. When this e-mail server is overwhelmed, the remaining e-mails are then sent to the next server in the chain. This continues until all of the mail servers listed in the script are brought down.

- *Error message bombs,* in which massive amounts of undeliverable e-mail are sent to a mail server. Because the e-mail messages are sent to an undeliverable address, the mail server returns an error message. However, in sending the e-mail, the bomber uses the e-mail address of an intended victim. Massive amounts of error messages flood the victim's e-mail account, and may also overwhelm the mail server used by the victim.

- *Covert distribution channels,* in which e-mail and files are sent using an intermediate mail server. The e-mail may consist of hate propaganda, pornography, or other illicit files and messages. The victim is fooled into believing that the e-mail actually originated from the intermediate server.

- *Abuse-of-mail exploders,* in which the bomber sends massive amounts of e-mail using automated mailing lists. These lists distribute the e-mail to everyone on the list.

One variation on the mail bomb automatically subscribes a targeted user to hundreds or thousands of high-volume Internet mailing lists, which fill the user's mailbox and/or mail server. Bombers call this attack *list linking.* Examples of these mail bomb programs include Unabomber, Extreme Mail, Avalanche, Voodoo, and Kaboom.

The solution to repeated mail bomb attacks is to block traffic from the originating network using packet filters. Unfortunately, this solution does not work with list linking because the originator's address is obscured; the deluge of traffic comes from the mailing lists to which the victim has unknowingly been subscribed.

Browser Exploits

Web browsers are client software programs such as Internet Explorer, Netscape, and Opera that connect to servers running Web server software such as IIS or Apache and request Web pages via a Uniform Resource Locator (URL), which is a "friendly" address that represents an IP address and particular files on the server at that address. The browser receives files that are encoded (usually in HTML) and must interpret the code or "markup" that determines how the page will be displayed on the user's monitor. Browsers are open to a number of types of attack.

Exploitable Browser Characteristics

Early browser programs were fairly simple, but today's browsers are complex; they are capable of not only displaying text and graphics, but also playing sound files and movies and running executable code. The browser software also usually stores information about the computer on which it is installed and even about the user (data stored as cookies on the local hard disk), which can be uploaded to Web servers—either deliberately by the user or in response to code on a Web site.

All of these characteristics serve useful purposes. Support for running code (as "active content" such as Java, JavaScript, and ActiveX) allows Web designers to create pages that interact with users in sophisticated ways. Cookies allow users to set preferences on sites that will be retained the next time they visit the site. However, hackers can exploit these characteristics in many ways. For example, a hacker can program a Web site to run code that transfers a virus to the client computer through the browser, erases key system files, or plants a "back door" program that then allows the hacker to take control of the user's system.

Web Spoofing

Web spoofing is a means by which an attacker is able to see and even make changes to Web pages that are transmitted to or from another computer (the target machine). These pages include confidential information such as credit card numbers entered into online commerce forms and passwords that are used to access restricted Web sites. JavaScript can be used to route Web pages and information through the attacker's computer, which impersonates the destination Web server. The attacker can send e-mail to the victim that contains a link to the forged page or put a link into a popular search engine. Secure Sockets Layer (SSL) doesn't necessarily prevent this sort of "man in the middle" attack; the connection appears to the victim user to be secure because it *is* secure. The problem is that the secure connection is to a different site than the one the victim thinks he or she is connecting to. *Hyperlink spoofing* exploits the fact that SSL doesn't verify hyperlinks that the user follows, so if a user gets to a site by following a link, the user can be sent to a spoofed site that appears to be a legitimate site.

Web spoofing is a high-tech form of con artistry. The point of the scam is to fool the user into giving confidential information such as credit card numbers, bank account numbers, or Social Security numbers to an entity that the user thinks is legitimate and then using that information for criminal purposes such as identity theft or credit card fraud. The only difference between this and the "real-world" con artist who knocks on a victim's door and pretends to be from the bank, requiring account information, is in the technology used to pull it off.

There could be clues that will tip off an observant victim that a Web site is not what it appears to be, such as the URL or status line of the browser. However, the attacker can use JavaScript to cover his or her tracks by modifying these elements. An attacker can even go so far as to use JavaScript to replace the browser's menu bar with one that looks the same but replaces functions that provide clues to the invalidity of the page, such as the display of the page's source code.

Web spoofing was a particular problem in older versions of browser software, but features in today's browsers make Web spoofing more difficult.

Web Server Exploits

Web servers host Web pages that are made available to others across the Internet or an intranet. Public Web servers (those accessible from the Internet) always pose an inherent security risk because they must be available to the Internet to do what they're supposed to do. Clients (Web browser software) must be able to send transmissions to the Web server for the purpose of requesting Web pages. However, allowing transmissions to come into the network to the Web server makes the system—and the entire network, unless measures are undertaken to isolate the Web server from the rest of the internal network—vulnerable to attackers.

Web server applications, like other software, can contain bugs that can be exploited. For example, in 2001 a flaw was discovered in Microsoft's IIS software that exploited the code used for the indexing feature.

The component was installed by default. When it was running, hackers could create buffer overflows to take control of the Web server and change Web pages or attack the system to bring it down. Microsoft quickly released security patches to address the problem, but many companies don't upgrade their software or don't update it with available fixes, and new, different security holes are being found all the time in all major Web server programs.

Buffer Overflows

A *buffer* is a sort of holding area for data. To speed processing, many software programs use a memory buffer to store changes to data, and then the information in the buffer is copied to the disk. When more information is put into the buffer than it is able to handle, a *buffer overflow* occurs. Overflows can be caused deliberately by hackers and then exploited to run malicious code.

There are two types of overflows: *stack overflows* and *heap overflows*. The *stack* and the *heap* are two areas of the memory structure that are allocated when a program is run. Function calls are stored in the stack, and dynamically allocated variables are stored in the heap. A particular amount of memory is allocated to the buffer. Attackers can use buffer overflows in the heap to overwrite a password, a filename, or other data. If the filename is overwritten, a different file will be opened. If this is an executable file, code will be run that was not intended to be run. On UNIX systems, the substituted program code is usually the command interpreter, which allows the attacker to execute commands with Superuser privileges. On Windows systems, the overflow code can be used to send a Hypertext Transfer Protocol (HTTP) request to download malicious code of the attacker's choice.

Buffer overflows are based on the way the C programming language works. Many function calls don't check to ensure that the buffer will be big enough to hold the data copied to it. Programmers can use calls that do this check to prevent overflows, but many do not.

Creating a buffer overflow attack requires that the hacker understand assembly language as well as technical details about the operating system to be able to write the replacement code to the stack. However, the code for these attacks is often published so that others, who have less technical knowledge, can use it. Some types of firewalls, called *stateful inspection* firewalls, allow buffer overflow attacks through, whereas *application gateways* (if properly configured) can filter out most overflow attacks. We discuss firewalls in detail in Chapter 12.

Operating System Exploits

Some exploits are unique to a particular operating system or family of operating systems. These hacks exploit specific characteristics of the operating system code to carry out the attack. All operating systems have their own vulnerabilities.

A number of different sources can exploit these vulnerabilities. In addition to hackers using their own expertise to hack systems, prewritten scripts and tools are available on the Internet that novices (script kiddies) can use to hack systems. Tools such as Metasploit can be used to analyze systems for vulnerabilities, and then run previously developed exploits for penetration testing on your own systems or to hack those belonging to other people. Version 2 of this tool comes with more than 100 exploits that can be used. In addition to this, Trojan horses and other malicious programs take advantage of the vulnerabilities to access data or damage systems.

Most exploits are written to take advantage of vulnerabilities in the most popular operating systems, which as you would expect are versions of Windows. According to the Market Share

Web site (http://marketshare.hitslink.com/report.aspx?qprid=8), the market share of different operating systems was as follows:

- Windows, 91.57 percent

- Mac, 7.48 percent

- Linux, 0.61 percent

Although these are rough statistics, they do show that Microsoft dominates the market, which is why most of the tools and scripts available are designed to exploit the weaknesses of various versions.

Windows Registry Attacks

The *Registry* is a database in which critical system and application configuration and initialization information is stored, and it is used in all Windows operating systems after Windows 3.*x*. Having this information in one centralized location instead of scattered in multiple initialization and configuration files offers many benefits, but it also makes the Registry vulnerable to hackers and attackers.

The Regedit tool in Windows allows the user to connect to the Registry on a remote system across the network and make changes to Registry settings. As shown in Figure 11.6, you can connect to another computer's Registry by selecting the **Connect Network Registry** menu item on the **File** menu, and then specifying the computer to which you want to connect. A hacker can exploit this ability and alter important information that could bring down the system. Administrative privileges are needed to edit remote registries.

Figure 11.6 The Regedit Utility, Which You Can Use to Connect to and Edit a Remote System's Registry

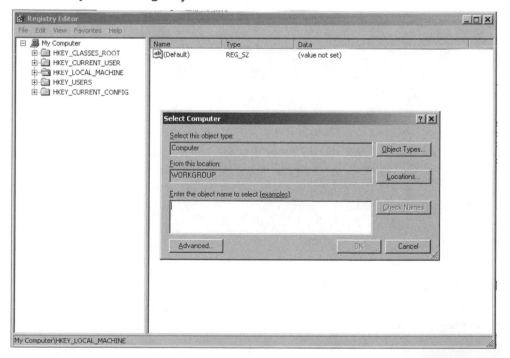

It can be difficult to detect Registry attacks, because the system accesses the Registry often, complicating the monitoring process. However, you can use utilities such as RegMon to track Registry access data, which you can compare with common attack models.

Other Windows Exploits

Many vulnerabilities have been discovered in the Windows operating systems. Microsoft is generally quick to patch these vulnerabilities once they become known, but as we mentioned, this doesn't help if these patches aren't applied to the computer after the operating system is initially installed. Some of the vulnerabilities that have appeared in various versions of Windows include:

- The Messenger service in Windows XP being vulnerable to a buffer overrun that allows a hacker to execute code with local system privileges.

- The Task Scheduler in Windows XP allowing arbitrary code to be executed remotely.

- A heap overflow problem in Windows Server 2003 that allowed arbitrary code to be executed, and also provided hackers with the ability to capture segments of the host memory space.

- The domain name system (DNS) server in Windows Server 2003 being vulnerable to Cache Snooping attacks, in which a hacker can see which hosts have been recently resolved.

- An issue where Windows Vista failed to properly disable AutoRun and AutoPlay features, because of a problem handling the *NoDriveTypeAutoRun* value in the Registry. This allowed AutoPlay to be enabled, even if Group Policy and Registry values had been set to disable it. As such, a hacker could get a user to inadvertently execute code on removable devices, such as USB flash drives.

CyberCrimeStopper

Keeping Up with Vulnerabilities

Windows users, administrators, and law enforcement officers can keep up with the latest Windows vulnerabilities by reviewing the Security Bulletins and Advisories section on the Microsoft TechNet Web site at www.microsoft.com/technet/security/bulletinsandadvisories/default.mspx. These bulletins are released on a monthly basis, provide information on vulnerabilities that have been discovered in Microsoft products, and advise on how to secure systems against them.

UNIX/Linux Exploits

Many UNIX/Linux exploits aim at gaining root access. In UNIX, the root account is the equivalent of the Administrator account on a Windows system. A user logged on with the root account has full control of the system and is able to clear the logs to cover his or her tracks. "Getting root" often involves finding a file that has Superuser ID (SUID) permissions and running a script (downloadable from hacker sites on the Web) or exploiting bugs in Sendmail or some other service.

Rootkit Attacks

Despite its name, a *rootkit attack* is not a method of obtaining root account privileges—at least, not directly. It is a group of programs which install a Trojan logon replacement with a back door, along with a packet sniffer, on UNIX boxes. The sniffer can then be used to capture network traffic, including user credentials, thus giving the user access to the root account by logging on with legitimate credentials. Software such as Rkdet is available to detect rootkit installation or packet sniffers running on a UNIX system.

Other UNIX Exploits

As with other operating systems, a number of different vulnerabilities can appear in different distros of Linux and systems running UNIX. Like their Windows cousins, vulnerabilities have appeared over the years inclusive to a variety of buffer overflow exploits, insecure default configurations, and programming flaws that hackers can use to compromise systems and networks. Some of the vulnerabilities with different distros have included the following:

- The DNS server in Slackware Linux 11.0, SUSE Enterprise 10, and Ubuntu 6.10 was vulnerable to Cache Snooping attacks, which allow hackers to view what hosts have recently been resolved.

- The Very Secure FTP server in Slackware Linux 11.0 permitted anonymous connections by default.

- The Web server in SUSE Enterprise 10 and Ubuntu 6.10 had a default configuration with TRACK method support, which allowed a cross-site scripting attack.

Mac OS Exploits

Some Apple commercials have promoted Mac computers as being more secure and less vulnerable than other operating systems (notably Windows). Although fewer viruses and malicious software are written to attack Macs (primarily due to their having a lower market share), they are not without vulnerabilities. This isn't to say that Macs aren't an exceptional system. They have a significant number of security features, and they are configured with security in mind (such as not having built-in servers enabled, which prevents them from exploited). However, some security features are not enabled when the system is installed. For example, Mac OS X includes a firewall called Internet Protocol FireWall (IPFW), but it isn't initially enabled. In addition to this, a number of vulnerabilities have appeared over the years:

- A vulnerability on the Mac OS X 10.4 server allowed Directory Services to be remotely shut down by making excessive connections to the server.

- The DNS Server in Mac OS X 10.4 server was found to be vulnerable to Cache Snoop attacks.

- Mac OS X was found to have a vulnerability that allowed malicious Web sites to compromise the system. The *help* URI handler allowed arbitrary local scripts to be executed using *help:runscript.* Script files and other arbitrary files could also be run by placing them in a known location, and then run on the computer using the *disk* URI handler.

CyberCrimeStopper

Keeping Up with Vulnerabilities

Apple provides a great deal of information regarding security features in its products, security guides, and updates to fix security issues. To ensure that your Mac is up-to-date with the latest patches, you should visit Apple's product security page at www.apple.com/support/security/.

Prevention and Response

Administrators can take a number of steps to help prevent exploits, including the following:

- Ensure that all systems have the latest security patches. This assurance protects against many denial-of-service (DoS) attacks, which rely on operating system or protocol "bugs."

- Disabling Java, JavaScript, ActiveX, and other active content in the Web browser thwarts many common browser exploits. We discussed browser security in greater detail in Chapter 9.

- Use application gateway firewalls to protect against buffer overflow attacks.

- Keep up-to-date by reviewing security bulletins regarding vulnerabilities that have been found in different systems. A good site to visit for this is the United States Computer Emergency Readiness Team (US-CERT) technical alerts site at www.us-cert.gov/cas/techalerts/.

Summary

Passwords, pass phrases, and PINs are common methods of authenticating a user to confirm his or her identity, before the user is given access to systems. A secure client operating system such as Windows XP or Windows Vista requires an interactive logon with a valid account name and password to access the operating system. These systems allow users to "lock" the workstation when they are going to be away from it, so someone else can't just step up and start using the computer. Other systems, such as Web servers, applications, and other software, also use passwords to control access to systems.

To enhance security, passwords can be used with other authentication factors. Even if a password was compromised, authentication devices such as smart card readers, fingerprint scanners, retinal and iris scanners, and voice analysis devices will prevent unauthorized access. These require the user to prove his or her identity in other ways, such as through possession of a card or through characteristics and features unique to that person.

Even in the most secure settings, weak links in a chain will exist. This can be the people who work there, and are vulnerable to social engineering techniques, or vulnerabilities in the software that's used and can be exploited by hackers and malicious programs. Despite these common weak points, there are ways to strengthen security. People can be educated in what to do, and what not to do (such as revealing passwords to others). The other good news is that you can take many steps to prevent technical exploits on your systems. In fact, applying all the current patches, fixes, service packs, and other upgrades and running good antivirus (AV) software with updated virus file definitions will go a long way toward keeping intruders out and attackers at bay. The bad news is that administrators must be constantly vigilant to guard against new threats that appear on a daily basis.

Frequently Asked Questions

Q: Why should people care about password security?

A: When someone can guess or acquires a password, it's analogous to him or her having the keys to your house. He or she can get in, and can have the same access that you have. By using strong a password and taking steps to protect it and change it regularly, it is less likely that someone will be able to crack your password and use it to access sensitive information.

Q: Someone is taking over my job temporarily. Can't I just given him my password, so he can do my job properly?

A: No. Although this is a common problem in organizations, when someone uses your password, he or she appears in network logs as though he or she were you. This means that if this person committed a violation of policy or a crime using your account, it would appear as though you did it. The best way to deal with such situations is to notify a network administrator, so he or she can set up a new account with the same level of access.

Q: What passwords are most easily cracked?

A: Easy-to-guess passwords are the easiest to crack. Even without the benefit of password recovery tools, a person will be able to type in words that relate to you. Anyone who knows you or has access to information about you would be able to guess the name of a significant other, child's name, pet's name, birth date, favorite sports team, or other facts about you that you probably used for a password.

Q: Exactly how does social engineering work? Why would anyone reveal his or her password to a stranger? Does this really happen?

A: Yes, it really happens—and more often than you might think. Skilled social engineers are good con artists; they are masters at making other people trust them. In large companies, employees often aren't personally familiar with all the other employees, so it's relatively easy for the social engineer to come strolling in or even call on the phone and persuade a user that he or she is a member of the information technology (IT) department and needs the user's password. The social engineer might have a convincing story, saying, for instance, that a hacker has gotten into the system and discovered all the password files, and now the IT department needs to know everyone's old password so that they can reset them and issue new ones to protect against the hacker. Like all con artists, the social engineer usually plays on common human emotions. For example, the engineer will play up the danger that the hacker can access and destroy all of the user's data if the "IT worker" doesn't get the password immediately and make the change. In other cases, the engineer might exploit other emotions, such as people's natural desire to help, claiming that the "IT worker" will get in trouble with the "big boss," maybe even get fired, if he or she is unable to get the password information that is needed. Social engineers are not above appealing to the user's ego or pretending sexual/romantic interest in the user to get the password, either. Although some might not categorize it as social engineering, another technique involves simply spying on the user to obtain the password ("shoulder surfing" or looking over the user's shoulder as he or she types the password) or going through the user's papers to find a written record of the password. Infamous hacker Kevin Mitnik is quoted as saying, "You can have the best technology, firewalls, intrusion detection systems, [and] biometric devices. All it takes is a call to an unsuspecting employee, and that's all she wrote, baby. They got everything." Visit http://searchsecurity.techtarget.com/originalContent/0,289142,sid14_gci771517,00.html for more on this topic.

Chapter 12

Understanding Cybercrime Prevention

Topics we'll investigate in this chapter:

- **Understanding Security Concepts**

- **Understanding Basic Cryptography Concepts**

- **Making the Most of Hardware and Software Security**

- **Understanding Firewalls**

- **Forming an Incident Response Team**

- **Designing and Implementing Security Policies**

☑ **Summary**

☑ **Frequently Asked Questions**

Introduction

Understanding what cybercrime is and how cybercrimes can be committed gives an investigator only half the picture. Just as every police officer needs a good grasp of physical defensive tactics, the cybercrime investigator must be aware of the tactics that are commonly used to defend a network from criminal intrusion or attack. In this chapter, we discuss the basic concepts involved in computer and network security. This includes the importance of multilayered security and the components that make up a multilayered security plan. We also emphasize the need for investigators to "talk the talk" by learning computer security terminology.

We delve into the fascinating and complex world of *cryptography*, the study of "hidden writing." We look at encryption technologies and algorithms and the many ways in which encryption can be used to protect data stored on computers or traveling across the network. You'll learn about the purposes of encryption in the context of network security and how it can provide for authentication, data confidentiality, and data integrity. We provide a brief history of cryptography and discuss common encryption protocols in use today. We also explain the differences between *encryption* and *steganography* and how these two techniques are used together for stronger security—by both the good guys and the cybercriminals. Finally, we discuss cryptanalysis and decryption techniques and how cryptographic software is being used today as a terrorist tool.

Moving from theory to implementation, we next discuss how organizations can make the most of both hardware- and software-based security products to protect their networks. First, we look at hardware devices, including firewall appliances. Then we discuss software-based security solutions, including cryptographic software, digital certificates, and the public key infrastructure.

The next section takes us into how firewalls—both hardware- and software-based—work "under the hood." You'll learn about layered filtering and how the best firewalls provide protection at the packet, circuit, and application levels. Then we discuss integrated intrusion detection and the way that many firewall products can be configured to perform predefined attacks when an attack occurs.

After covering the specifics of available security products, we turn to another aspect of creating an overall security plan—the issue of how to form an incident response team to deal quickly and effectively with attacks when they occur. But having a team in place will not provide the protection that an organization needs unless the team—and the users and information technology (IT) professionals who make up the "human side" of the network—are governed by specific, detailed security policies that bring the organization's security plan into focus and incorporate it into the everyday use of the systems and network. Thus, the last section of this chapter deals with why and how solid security policies can be developed and put in place, creating a foundation for the implementation of all the security measures that we've addressed as well as laying the cornerstone of the organization's cybercrime prevention plan.

Understanding Security Concepts

In Chapter 10, you learned about "technical" intrusions and attacks on networks and how hackers (and hacker wannabes) can exploit protocols, operating systems, and applications to commit the criminal acts of unauthorized access, interrupting network communications, and destroying or damaging computer data. It is important for investigators to have at least a basic understanding of how these attacks are carried out. It is also important for investigators to be aware of how networks can be defended from further attacks, for several reasons:

■ In the course of investigating an intrusion or attack, knowing what security measures were in place at the time of the incident might help narrow down the exact nature of the attack and even who could have perpetrated it.

■ Understanding how various security measures work can lead investigators to log files and other sources of information useful in the investigation.

■ Knowledge of security measures and concepts allows investigators to suggest to victims how they might prevent further incidents.

■ Some of the measures used by the "good guys" to protect their networks and data (such as encryption) can also be used by the "bad guys" to cover their criminal activities.

Knowledge is power. That's a famous hacker motto (along with such other gems as "Information wants to be free"). However, it is a truism that applies not only to people attempting to gain access to data they aren't supposed to see, but also to those who are trying to protect themselves from the intruders. The first step in winning any battle—and network security *is* a battle over the ownership and control of your computer files—is the same as it's always been: "Know thine enemy."

To protect a network's resources from theft, damage, or unwanted exposure, administrators must understand who initiates these things, why, and how they do it. Knowledge will make *you*, the investigator, powerful, too—and better able to track down and prosecute unauthorized intruders and attackers.

Applying Security Planning Basics

Securing a company's electronic assets from cybercriminals must involve much more than the IT department; it must involve the entire organization   just as a community policing effort, to be effective, must involve the police department as a whole and not just an isolated "community service division." For cyberinvestigators to understand the security planning and implementation process, they need to start at the beginning, with the very basics of computer security. The following sections illustrate how some of the most basic tenets of traditional security can be applied to the context of computer networking.

Defining Security

A generic dictionary definition of *security* (taken from the *American Heritage Dictionary*) is "freedom from risk or danger; safety." This definition is perhaps a little misleading when it comes to computer and networking security, because it implies a degree of protection that is inherently impossible in the modern connectivity-oriented computing environment.

This is why the same dictionary provides another definition, specific to computer science: "The *level to which* a program or device is safe from unauthorized use" [emphasis added]. Implicit in this definition is the caveat that the objectives of *security* and *accessibility*—the two top priorities on the minds of many network administrators—are, by their very nature, diametrically opposed. The more accessible the data, the less secure it is. Likewise, the more tightly you secure the data, the more you impede accessibility. Any security plan is an attempt to strike the proper balance between the two objectives.

The first step is to determine *what* needs to be protected, and to what degree. Because not every asset is equally valuable, some assets need stronger protection than others. This determination leads to the concept of instituting multiple layers of security.

The Importance of Multilayered Security

An effective security plan does not rely on one technology or solution, but instead takes a multilayered approach. Compare this approach to a business's physical security measures; most companies don't depend on just the locks on the buildings' doors to keep intruders and thieves out. Instead, they might also have perimeter security (a fence), perhaps additional external security such as a guard or guard dog, external and internal alarm systems, and to protect special valuables, further internal safeguards such as a vault. IT security should be similarly layered. For example:

- Firewalls at network entry points (and possibly a demilitarized zone [DMZ] or screened subnet between the local area network [LAN] and the network interface connected to the Internet) that function as perimeter protection

- Password protection at local computers, requiring user authentication to log on, to keep unauthorized persons out

- Access permissions set on individual network resources to restrict access of those who are "in" (logged on to the network)

- Encryption of data sent across the network or stored on disk to protect what is especially valuable, sensitive, or confidential

- Servers, routers, and hubs located in locked rooms to prevent people with physical access from hijacking data without authorization

The Intrusion Triangle

Crime prevention specialists use a model called the Crime Triangle to explain that certain criteria must exist before a crime can occur. We can adapt this same familiar law enforcement concept to network security: The same three criteria in the Crime Triangle must exist before a network security breach can take place. Figure 12.1 shows the three "legs," or points of the triangle.

Figure 12.1 The Three Legs of the Crime Triangle That Must Exist for a Network Intrusion to Occur

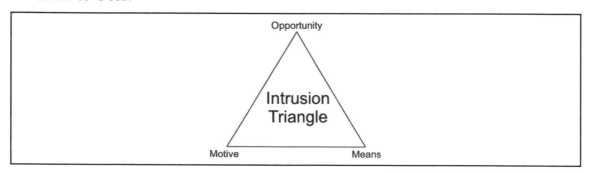

Let's look at each point on the triangle individually:

- **Motive** An intruder must have a reason to want to breach the security of the network (even if the reason is "just for fun"); otherwise, he or she won't bother.

- **Means** An intruder must have the ability (either the programming knowledge or, in the case of script kiddies, the intrusion software written by others) or he or she won't be able to breach your security.

- **Opportunity** An intruder must have the chance to enter the network because of flaws in the security plan, holes in a software program that open an avenue of access, or physical proximity to network components. If there is no opportunity to intrude, the would-be hacker will go elsewhere.

If you think about the three-point intrusion criteria for a moment, you'll see that the network administrator or security specialist has control over only one leg of the triangle. It is unlikely that anyone can do much to remove the intruder's *motive*. The motive is likely to be built into the type of data that's on the network or even the personality of the intruder him- or herself. It is also not often possible to prevent the intruder from having or obtaining the *means* to breach your security. Programming knowledge is freely available, and many experienced hackers are more than happy to help less sophisticated ones. The one thing that people who strive to prevent cybercrime *can* affect is the *opportunity* afforded the hacker.

Removing Intrusion Opportunities

Crime prevention officers tell members of the community that they probably can't keep a potential burglar from wanting to steal, and they certainly can't keep the potential burglar from obtaining burglary tools or learning the "tricks of the trade." What they *can* do is to take away, as much as possible, the opportunity for the burglar to target their own homes.

This means putting deadbolt locks on house doors (and using them); getting a big, loud dog that is unfriendly to strangers; and installing an alarm system. In other words, the homeowner's goal is not to prevent the burglar from burglarizing, but to make his or her own home a less desirable target. For network "owners," the objective is to "harden" the network so that all those hackers out there who already have the motive and the means will look for an easier victim.

The best and most expensive locks in the world won't keep intruders out of your house if you don't use them. And if those locks are difficult to use and they cause you inconvenience in your everyday comings and goings, you probably *won't* use them—at least, not all the time. A poorly implemented network security system that is difficult to administer or that unduly inconveniences network users might end up similarly; eventually the person burdened with maintaining it will throw his or her hands up in frustration and just turn the darn thing off. And that will leave the network wide open to intruders.

Talking the Talk: Security Terminology

Every industry has its own "language," the jargon that describes ideas, items, concepts, and procedures that are unique to the field. Lawyers speak "legalese," rife with *wherefores* and *hereuntos*; doctors and nurses use terms such as *crash cart* and *defib*, and police reports are sprinkled with references to *perps* and *vics* and *MVAs*. Computer networking is infamous for its "technotalk" and the proliferation of acronyms which often mystify outsiders. Specialty areas within an industry often have their own brands of jargon as well, and the computer security subfield is no exception.

It might not be absolutely necessary for the cybercrime investigator to understand all the technical aspects of how security measures work, but knowledge of the technical language used to describe security concepts and devices will serve a couple of important purposes:

- It will make you aware of what a hacker can and can't accomplish in a particular network environment.

- If you are able to "talk the talk"—to converse intelligently about security issues and measures—you will be better able to win the trust of and communicate with the IT professionals who provide much of the information necessary to your investigation.

It is not possible to provide a complete glossary of security-related terms within the scope of this chapter, but in this section, we define some of the more common words and phrases that you might encounter as you begin to explore the fascinating world of computer security:

- **Authentication** Verification of identity of a user, computer, or process.

- **Authorization** The actions that a user, computer, or process, once identified, is permitted to do.

- **Audit** To track security-related events, such as logging on to the system or network, accessing objects, or exercising user/group rights or privileges.

- **Breach** Successfully defeating security measures to gain access to data or resources without authorization, to make data or resources available to unauthorized persons, or to delete or alter computer files.

- **Cipher** A method used to encrypt data.

- **Cipher text** Data in encrypted form.

- **Confidentiality of data** Ensuring that the contents of messages will be kept secret. See also *integrity of data*.

- **Cryptography (crypto)** The science of hiding information.

- **Encryption** The process of converting data (plain text) into a format (cipher text) that cannot be read or understood by anyone except those authorized to receive it.

- **Encryption algorithm** A formula or calculation that is applied to data to encrypt, or scramble, it.

- **Integrity of data** Ensuring that data has not been modified or altered, that the data received is identical to the data that was sent.

- **Key** A variable that is used in conjunction with an algorithm to encrypt or decrypt data.

- **Penetration testing** Evaluating a system by attempting to circumvent the computer's or network's security measures.

- **Reliability** The probability of a computer system or network continuing to perform in a satisfactory manner for a specific time period under normal operating conditions.

- **Risk** The probability that a specific security threat will be able to exploit a system vulnerability, resulting in damage, loss of data, or other undesired results.

- **Risk management** The process of identifying, controlling, and either minimizing or completely eliminating events that pose a threat to system reliability, data integrity, and data confidentiality.

- **TCSEC** Trusted Computer System Evaluation Criteria, a method for evaluating a system's level of security.

- **Technical vulnerability** A flaw or bug in the hardware or software components of a system that leaves it vulnerable to security breach.

- **Vulnerability** A weakness in the hardware, software, or security plan that leaves a system or network open to the threat of unauthorized access or damage to or destruction of data.

NOTE

You can find extensive lists of definitions for security-related terms on the Internet by visiting such sites as www.whatis.com and www.mobrien.com/terminology.shtml.

Understanding Basic Cryptography Concepts

Cryptography is a word derived from the Greek *kryptos* ("hidden"), and the use of cryptography predates the computer age by hundreds of years. Keeping secrets has long been a concern of human beings, and the purpose of cryptography is to hide information or change it so that it is incomprehensible to people for whom it is not intended. Cryptographic techniques include:

- *Encryption*, which involves applying a procedure called an *algorithm* to plain text to turn it into something that will appear to be gibberish to anyone who doesn't have the *key* to decrypt it.

- *Steganography*, which is a means of hiding the existence of the data, not just its contents. This is usually done by concealing it within other, innocuous data.

NOTE

The words *cryptography* and *encryption* are often used interchangeably, but cryptography is a much broader term than encryption; encryption is a form of cryptography. In other words, all encryption is cryptography, but not all cryptography is encryption.

Understanding the Purposes of Cryptographic Security

Cryptographic techniques are an important part of a multilayered security plan. Some security measures, such as implementation of a firewall and use of access permissions, attempt to keep intruders out of the network or computer altogether, much like fences and door locks attempt to keep burglars off the grounds or out of the house. Cryptography provides an inner line of defense. Like a wall safe that is there in case the burglars *do* make it inside your house—and to protect valuables from people who are authorized to come into your house—cryptography protects data from intruders who are able to penetrate the outer network defenses and from those who are authorized to access the network but not *this* particular data.

Cryptographic techniques concern themselves with three basic purposes:

- **Authentication** Verifying the identity of a user or computer
- **Confidentiality** Keeping the contents of the data secret
- **Integrity** Ensuring that data doesn't change between the time it leaves the source and the time it reaches its destination

One or more of these goals may be a priority, depending on the situation. For example, if an investigator receives a message from his or her chief to fly to the West Coast to interview a witness in a case, the overriding concern might be to know that it was, indeed, the chief of police who sent the message and not a fellow officer playing a practical joke. In this case, *authentication* of the message sender's identity is of utmost importance. If the case relates to an internal affairs investigation and it is important that no one else in the department know where the investigator is going, *confidentiality* of the data might be important as well. And if the message states that the investigator is authorized to spend $3,000 on the trip, it might be important to ensure that the message has not been changed (after all, chiefs are not usually this generous) in transit—in other words, that the message's *integrity* has not been compromised.

All three mechanisms can be used together, or they can be used separately when only one or two of these considerations are important. In the following sections, we look more closely at how each one works in relation to network security.

On the Scene

A Historical Perspective on Cryptography

Cryptography has probably been around for almost as long as written language. According to *A Short History of Cryptography*, by Fred Cohen (www.all.net/books/ip/Chap2-1.html), the study of cryptography has been around for 4,000 years or more.

Continued

Whenever communications are recorded, the issue of protecting those recorded communications arises.

In both business and personal communications, it is often not desirable to share the contents with everyone—in fact, in many cases doing so could have disastrous results. Thus, early civilizations looked for ways to conceal the contents of messages from prying eyes. In ancient Egypt, deviations on the hieroglyphic language in use were developed for that purpose. The Greeks used a "transposition code" in which each letter of the alphabet was represented by another that indicated where, in a grid, the original letter was located. In early India, spies employed by the government used phonetic-based "substitution codes" (the same concept children use for pig Latin). In biblical times, a substitution cipher called *atbash*, which worked by replacing the last letter of the Hebrew alphabet with the first and so on, was used to encrypt writings. Encryption methods were used by such diverse historical figures as Julius Caesar (after whom the "Caesar cipher" was named), Thomas Jefferson (who invented the cipher wheel), and Sir Francis Bacon. Governments have long used encryption to protect sensitive military messages.

Authenticating Identity

As we discussed in Chapter 11, you can determine the identity of a user or computer in numerous ways, but it generally requires that the user provide something that is associated with his or her user account that someone else could not easily provide. The requested credential is generally one (or more) of the following:

- *Something you know*, such as a password or personal identification number (PIN)
- *Something you have*, such as a smart card or certificate
- *Something you are*, in which biometric devices are used to identify you on the basis of your physical characteristics

Because none of these authentication methods (or any other) is absolutely foolproof, it makes sense in a high-security environment to use a multifactor authentication system (sometimes called *two-way* or *three-way authentication*, depending on the number of authentication methods used) by combining two or more of them. That is, a user is required to provide both something he or she has *and* something he or she knows (in fact, most smart card implementations require that the user not only insert the card in a reader, but also enter a PIN), or the user must both undergo a biometric scan and provide a password before being granted access.

Another method of implementation is *layered authentication*, in which one form of authentication is accepted to provide a lower level of access, and additional authentication is required for a higher level of access.

NOTE

Some security literature mentions a fourth means of proving identity: *something you do*. An example would be a sample of your handwriting. Voice prints might also be considered to be in this category.

As we saw in Chapter 11, a wide number of protocols are used for authenticating users on a network, many of which use various types of encryption to ensure that the data being passed by the user to the authentication server can't be intercepted and viewed by others. Some of these protocols include:

- **Kerberos** A logon authentication protocol that is based on secret key (symmetric) cryptography. It usually uses the Data Encryption Standard (DES) or Triple-DES (3DES) algorithm, although with the latest version, Kerberos Version 5, algorithms other than DES can be used. Kerberos uses a system of "tickets" to provide verification of identity to multiple servers throughout the network. This system works a little like the payment system at some amusement parks and fairs where, instead of paying to ride each ride, customers must buy tickets at a central location and then use those tickets to access the rides. Similarly, with Kerberos, a client who wants to access resources on network servers is not authenticated by each server; instead, all the servers rely on "tickets" issued by a central server, called the Key Distribution Center (KDC). The client sends a request for a ticket (encrypted with the client's key) to the KDC. The KDC issues a ticket called a Ticket-Granting Ticket (TGT), which is encrypted and submitted to the Ticket-Granting Service (TGS). The TGS can be running on the same physical machine that is running the KDC. The TGS issues a session ticket to the client for accessing the particular network resource that was requested (which is usually on a different server). The session ticket is presented to the server that hosts the resource, and access is granted. The session key is valid only for that particular session and is set to expire after a specific amount of time. Kerberos allows mutual authentication; that is, the identities of both the client and the server can be verified.

- **NT LAN Manager (NTLM)** Another Microsoft logon authentication method. Unlike Kerberos, with NTLM, when a client wants to access a server's resources, that server must contact the domain controller to have the client's identity verified. It uses MD4/MD5 hashing algorithms and DES encryption.

- **Shiva Password Authentication Protocol (S-PAP)** A remote access authentication protocol used for Point-to-Point Protocol (PPP) or dial-up connections. Shiva PAP (S-PAP) uses a two-way reversible authentication method that encrypts passwords so that they will not be subject to interception and misuse.

- **Challenge Handshake Authentication Protocol (CHAP)** Uses a hashing algorithm and a shared secret (more about that later in this chapter, in the section on encryption) to protect the password. CHAP provides more security than PAP. Microsoft developed its own version of the protocol, called MS-CHAP, which uses the DES encryption algorithm and LM/NTHASH.

- **The Remote Authentication Dial-In User Service (RADIUS)** Also used for authenticating remote connections. Exchanges are encrypted using a shared key, and multiple RAD-IUS servers can communicate with each other and exchange authentication information.

- **Secure Shell (SSH)** Allows users to log on to UNIX systems remotely. When using SSH, both ends of the connection (client and server) are authenticated, and data (including passwords) can be encrypted. 3DES, Blowfish, and Twofish are encryption algorithms that are supported by SSHv2, which also allows the use of smart cards.

A concept that is closely related to authentication is *nonrepudiation*. This is a means of ensuring that whoever sends a message cannot later claim that he or she didn't send it. Nonrepudiation is sometimes considered to be a fourth, separate purpose of cryptography, but we include it here in the discussion of authentication because the two concepts go together; nonrepudiation just goes a step further than authentication.

Providing Confidentiality of Data

Confidentiality refers to any method that keeps the contents of the data secret. Usually this means encrypting it to prevent unauthorized persons from understanding what the data says even if they intercept it. In a high-security environment, where network communications necessarily involve information that should not be shared with the world, it is important to use strong encryption to protect the confidentiality of sensitive data. We discuss exactly how that is done in the upcoming "Basic Cryptography Concepts" section.

Ensuring Data Integrity

Data integrity, in the context of cryptography, means that there is a way to verify that the data was not changed after it left the sender, that the data that was sent is exactly the same as the data that is received at the final destination. It is essential to be able to count on data integrity in network transactions such as e-commerce.

NOTE

The term *data integrity* has a broader meaning in terms of general computing and networking than it does in the context of cryptography. In this sense, it refers to protection of data from damage or destruction; the integrity of data can be threatened by a power surge, a magnetic field, fire, flood, or the like as well as by persons who would deliberately modify it. You can install utilities such as Tripwire (www.tripwire.org) to monitor changes to system data on the hard disk.

Basic Cryptography Concepts

Cryptographic techniques such as encryption are the basis of *digital certificates*, *digital signatures*, and the *public key infrastructure*, or *PKI*. All of these technologies are important components of an enterprise-level security plan, and we discuss the use of each later in this chapter. Now that you understand the purposes of cryptography, we can look at the mechanics of how these technologies are implemented.

Scrambling Text with Codes and Ciphers

There are many different ways to "scramble" text or hide its meaning in such a way that only authorized persons (at least in theory) are able to read it. This scrambled (encrypted) text is called *cipher text*. A method for encrypting text is called a *cipher* or a *code*. Technically, a code uses substitution at the word or phrase level, whereas a cipher works at the level of individual letters or digits. The two words are often used interchangeably, but computerized cryptographic techniques generally rely on ciphers that operate on the binary form of the data by applying an *algorithm* (a mathematical calculation). Some common cipher/code types are:

- Substitution

- Transposition

- Obscure languages

Substitution Ciphers

Simple substitution is a method often used by children in their first experiments with secret code. A substitution cipher merely substitutes different letters, numbers, or other characters for each character in the original text. The most straightforward example is a simplistic substitution in which each letter of the alphabet is represented by a numerical digit, starting with 1 for A. The message *goodbye* then becomes 7-15-15-4-2-25-5. This code is obviously extremely easy to break.

The Caesar Cipher used a simple shifting method, in which each letter of the message is represented by the letter two places to the right in the alphabet (A becomes C, B becomes D, and so on). Other substitution methods can be much more difficult to crack. For example, if two parties exchanging communications have an identical copy of a particular book, they might create a message by referencing page, line, and word numbers (for example, 73-12-6 tells you that the word in the message is the same as the sixth word in the twelfth line on page 72 of the code book). In this case, anyone who doesn't have a copy of the book (and to cite the correct pages, it must be the exact same edition and print run) will not be able to decipher the message.

Some types of substitution ciphers are:

- **Monoalphabetic substitution** Each letter is represented by another letter or character in a one-to-one relationship.

- **Polyalphabetic substitution** Different cipher-text characters can represent the same plain-text letter, making it more difficult to decrypt messages using the frequency analysis technique. Renaissance architect and art theorist Leon Battista Alberti is credited with developing this technique, earning him recognition as the "father of Western cryptography."

- **Polygraphic (block) cipher** Several letters (or digits when we're dealing with binary data) are encrypted at the same time, using a system that can handle all the possible combinations of a set number of characters.

- **Fractionation** Multiple symbols are substituted for each plain-text letter, and then the letters or digits are transposed.

Transposition Ciphers

Transposition ciphers use tables in which the plain text is entered one way, and then read another way to create the encrypted text. For example, each character of text is entered into the table cells going across from left to right, and then the cipher text is produced by reading the characters in columns. A variation uses a square grid with holes that is placed on top of a sheet of paper, and then the message is written, rotating the grid at intervals.

Obscure Languages As Code

Obscure languages have been used as code by governments for military communications. Ancient ("dead") languages have been used in this way. The U.S. military even used Navajo "code talkers" (speakers of the complex and little known Navajo language) in World War II to send secret communications. This language was chosen because it was hard to learn, and only a few people in the world knew it. The Navajo language had never been written, which made it even more obscure. Members of the Navajo tribe were recruited to develop a code based on the language.

Mechanical and Electrical Cipher Devices

Cipher devices such as cipher wheels and cylinders can be used to encrypt and decrypt text. An early example of this technique was the *skytale cipher* or *staff cipher* used by the Spartans. They wrapped a sheet of papyrus around a staff and wrote their message down the length of the staff. When the sheet was unwrapped, the message couldn't be easily read unless it was wrapped around a staff of the same diameter as the original one.

Leon Battista Alberti used a set of disks that had the alphabet etched on them to employ his polyalphabetic ciphering system. He lined up the two disks to determine what cipher-text character would represent each plain-text letter. By rotating the disks at set intervals, he caused different cipher-text letters to represent the same plain-text letters at different places in the message.

Many different cipher machines have been developed by government and military entities. Most use multiple rotating disks to create letter substitutions, and they can be operated either mechanically or electrically. Thomas Jefferson invented a cipher wheel of this type. During World War II, the Japanese used cipher machines called RED and PURPLE, and the German Enigma machine (a wired rotor machine that has equally spaced electrical contacts on each side of a disk, which are connected to one another in scrambled order) is perhaps the most famous—or infamous—of the cipher devices.

Computerizing the Ciphering Process

The availability of computer technology made it much easier to encrypt messages using very complex methods that would be difficult or impossible to use by hand or with mechanical and electrical devices. As we discussed in Chapter 4, when you get down to the heart of the system, computers really do only one thing: perform calculations on numbers. However, they can do an incredible number of such calculations incredibly quickly. This is exactly what is needed for complex encryption algorithms. Of course, computers also make it much easier to *decrypt* encrypted data. Ciphers that would take hundreds or thousands of years to break with a team of top cryptanalysts working on them manually can be cracked in hours, days, or weeks using high-powered computers.

One of the first well-known computer ciphering systems was LUCIFER, an IBM project that formed the foundation of the popular DES cipher that is still widely used (along with its more secure version, 3DES). LUCIFER was a block cipher, as is DES. It used a 128-bit key to encrypt blocks of binary data that were 128 bits in length. The cipher was applied to each block several times. Even though LUCIFER uses a larger block and key than DES, it is less secure. That's because its key schedule is regular and thus more predictable. In the upcoming "Encryption Algorithms" section, we discuss DES and other modern ciphers used by computerized encryption schemes.

What Is Encryption?

Encryption is a form of cryptography that "scrambles" plain text into unintelligible cipher text. Encryption is the foundation of such security measures as digital signatures, digital certificates, and the PKI that uses these technologies to make computer transactions more secure. Computer-based encryption techniques use keys to encrypt and decrypt data. A *key* is a variable (sometimes represented as a password) that is a large binary number—the larger, the better. Key length is measured in bits, and the more bits in a key, the more difficult the key will be to "crack."

The key is only one component in the encryption process. It must be used in conjunction with an encryption *algorithm* (a process or calculation) to produce the cipher text. Encryption methods are usually categorized as either symmetric or asymmetric, depending on the number of keys that are used. We discuss these two basic types of encryption technology in the following sections.

Symmetric Encryption

Symmetric encryption is also called *secret key encryption*, and it uses just one key, called a *shared secret*, for both encrypting and decrypting. This is a simple, easy-to-use method of encryption, but there is one problem with it: The key must be shared between the sender and the recipient of the data, so a secure method of *key exchange* must be devised. Otherwise, if a third party intercepts the key during the exchange, an unauthorized person can easily decrypt the data.

Asymmetric Encryption

To address the problem of key exchange, another type of encryption was developed. *Asymmetric encryption* is also called *public key encryption*, but it actually relies on a *key pair*. Two mathematically related keys, one called the *public key* and another called the *private key*, are generated to be used together. The private key is never shared; it is kept secret and is used only by its owner. The public key is made available to anyone who wants it. Because of the time and amount of computer processing power required, it is considered "mathematically unfeasible" for anyone to be able to use the public key to re-create the private key, so this form of encryption is considered very secure.

The primary advantage of asymmetric encryption is that there is no need to securely transmit a secret key. Instead, the public key is published openly, made available to the entire world. There is no need to keep it secret, because it can't be used alone. The encryption process works like this:

1. The sender of a message uses the intended recipient's public key, which is freely available, to encrypt a message.

2. The recipient decrypts the message using his or her private key. Only the private key associated with the public key that encrypted it can be used to decrypt the message.

This key pair can also be used to provide for authentication of a message sender's identity using the keys a little differently: This time the sender uses his or her own *private* key to encrypt the message. This system provides no confidentiality, because anyone can decrypt the message using the owner's public key. However, it does verify the sender's identity, because if the associated public key will decrypt the message, it could only have been encrypted with that person's private key.

Obviously, the most important issue in public key cryptography is the protection of the private keys. This concept is especially important because compromise of a private key not only allows the unauthorized person to read private messages sent to the owner, but also allows the key thief to "sign" transactions emulating the owner, thus stealing the owner's identity. When the key pair is used for secure credit card or banking transactions, this loophole can be disastrous.

Securing Data with Cryptographic Algorithms

Literally thousands of different cryptographic algorithms have been developed over the years. Cryptographic algorithms can be classified as follows:

- *Encryption algorithms* that are used to encrypt data and provide confidentiality
- *Signature algorithms* that are used to digitally "sign" data to provide authentication
- *Hashing algorithms* that are used to provide data integrity

Algorithms (ciphers) are also categorized by the way they work at the technical level (stream ciphers and block ciphers). This categorization refers to whether the algorithm is applied to a stream of data, operating on individual bits, or to an entire block of data. *Stream ciphers* are faster because they work on smaller units of data. The key is generated as a *keystream*, and this is combined with the plain text to be encrypted. RC4 is the most commonly used stream cipher. Another is ISAAC.

Block ciphers take a block of plain text and turn it into a block of cipher text. (Usually the block is 64 or 128 bits in size.) Common block ciphers include DES, CAST, Blowfish, IDEA, RC5/RC6, and SAFER. Most Advanced Encryption Standard (AES) candidates are block ciphers.

NOTE

AES is a standard for cryptography used by the U.S. federal government to protect sensitive but unclassified information. A number of different algorithms were considered candidates for this standard. The National Institute of Standards and Technology (NIST) selected the Rijndael algorithm for the AES. You can find additional information on AES and its specifications at http://csrc.nist.gov/publications/fips/fips197/fips-197.pdf.

Encryption Algorithms

Some popular encryption algorithms (many of which were AES candidates) are:

- Rijndael (AES standard)
- DES and 3DES

- SAFER

- IDEA

- DEAL

- CAST-256

- MARS

- Blowfish and Twofish

Other encryption algorithms include SERPENT, RC4/RC5/RC6, LOKI-97, FROG, and Hasty Pudding.

Signature Algorithms

Signature algorithms are used to create digital signatures. A *digital signature* is merely a means of "signing" data (as described earlier in the section "Asymmetric Encryption") to authenticate that the message sender is really the person he or she claims to be. Digital signatures can also provide for data integrity along with authentication and nonrepudiation. Digital signatures have become important in a world where many business transactions, including contractual agreements, are conducted over the Internet. Digital signatures generally use both signature algorithms and hash algorithms.

When a message is encrypted with a user's private key, the hash value that is created becomes the signature for that message. Signing a different message will produce a different signature. Each signature is unique, and any attempt to move the signature from one message to another would result in a hash value that would not match the original; thus, the signature would be invalidated.

Hashing Algorithms

Hashing is a technique in which an algorithm (also called a *hash function*) is applied to a portion of data to create a unique digital "fingerprint" that is a fixed-size variable. If anyone changes the data by so much as one binary digit, the hash function will produce a different output (called the *hash value*) and the recipient will know that the data has been changed. Hashing can ensure integrity and provide authentication as well.

The hash function cannot be "reverse-engineered"; that is, you can't use the hash value to discover the original data that was hashed. Thus, hashing algorithms are referred to as *one-way hashes*. A good hash function will not return the same result from two different inputs (called a *collision*); each result should be unique.

There are several different types of hashing, including division-remainder, digit rearrangement, folding, and radix transformation. These classifications refer to the mathematical process used to obtain the hash value. Standard hashing algorithms include:

- **MD2, MD4, and MD5** These methods use a *message digest* (the hash value) that is 128 bits in length. They were created by Ron Rivest and are popularly used for digital signatures.

- **Secure Hash Algorithm (SHA)** There are several variations on this algorithm, including SHA1, SHA256, SHA384, and SHA512. The differences between them lie in the length of the hash value. SHA was created by a cooperative effort of two U.S. government agencies, NIST and the National Security Association (NSA).

How Encryption Is Used in Information Security

Encryption is used for a number of different purposes in organizations that deal with sensitive data of any type. In the "Designing and Implementing Security Policies" section later in this chapter, we discuss the types of information that should be protected. In this section, we look at the different ways encryption technologies can be used to protect that information.

Encrypting Data Stored on Disk

Disk encryption refers to encrypting the entire contents of a hard disk or other removable media. *File encryption* refers to encrypting data stored on disk on a file-by-file basis. In either case, the goal is to prevent unauthorized persons from opening and reading files that are stored on the disk.

Support for disk/file encryption can be built into an operating system or file system. The Encrypting File System (EFS) was introduced with New Technology File System (NTFS) Version 5, the native file system for Windows 2000 and later, and can be used to protect data on a hard disk or large removable disk. (EFS can't be used to protect data on diskettes because they cannot be formatted in NTFS format.) EFS allows encryption of individual files and/or folders. Windows Vista and Windows Server 2008 also uses BitLocker Drive Encryption, which uses the AES-CBC + Elephant diffuser encryption algorithm (which is the AES algorithm in CBC mode that's combined with a new component called Elephant) to encrypt entire volumes of data.

Third-party programs—such as DriveCrypt (www.securstar.com/disk_encryption.php) and SafeDisk (www.guardcomplete.com) for Windows operating systems and the Crypto File System and Transparent Cryptographic File System (TCFS) for UNIX/Linux—can be installed to provide encryption on file systems that don't natively support encryption or to provide partition-level or virtual drive encryption.

An excellent virtual drive encryption tool is Security Guardian from Frontier Information Enterprise, which is available from www.securityguardian.us.com. After installing it on a computer, inserting the Universal Serial Bus (USB) key into a USB port allows you to see a virtual drive on the machine. This virtual disk appears (and from the user's perspective functions) identical to a real hard disk, but data is actually stored on an area of your computer's hard disk. With the exception of the operating system, any files or programs can be installed in the virtual drive and encrypted using AES 256-bit encryption. As shown in Figure 12.2, by default, this drive is 32MB but can be resized up to 128GB using a utility that's accessed through an icon on the Windows taskbar. Because Security Guardian uses a combination of hardware and software to encrypt the data, anyone accessing the data must have the USB key to view the virtual drive and decrypt the data. Once the USB key is removed, the virtual drive is hidden. Anyone using the computer afterward will be completely unaware that a virtual disk even exists on the machine.

Figure 12.2 Security Guardian

In looking at tools such as Security Guardian, it is easy to see their importance in protecting sensitive data. By encrypting the data, you ensure that information stored on a hard disk remains secure, even if the hard disk is removed or the computer is stolen. If a thief stole the computer, the data would remain inaccessible without the USB key to decrypt the data. In day-to-day use (especially on computers used by multiple users), the tool can be used to hide encrypted data on a machine, preventing others from viewing any sensitive data stored in the virtual drive. However, the ability to hide data is why law enforcement officers need to be aware that tools such as Security Guardian exist. If a person were crossing the border or going through Customs with a laptop, a Customs official might never realize that a virtual drive with encrypted data resided on the computer. The ability to smuggle data becomes easier if it's concealed.

With partition-level and virtual drive encryption, a user does not have to explicitly set encryption properties on individual files and folders (as is true with file-level encryption). Instead, an entire partition is marked as encrypted or an encrypted virtual drive is created, and all data that is stored there will be automatically encrypted. Many users choose these methods because performance is better than with file-level encryption. Some file/disk encryption methods use a password to protect encrypted data; when someone wants to access an encrypted file, he or she must enter a password. Other methods rely on the user account that is logged on to determine whether access will be granted. EFS, for example, uses digital certificates that are associated with the user account. These latter methods require less user interaction, but they have their drawbacks. It might not be possible to share encrypted files with others without decrypting them in cases where only one particular account is allowed access. In addition, there is a security risk if the user leaves the computer while logged on; then anyone who sits down at the machine can access the encrypted data.

NOTE

According to the document "AES-CBC + Elephant diffuser: A Disk Encryption Algorithm for Windows Vista," by Niels Ferguson (available from www.microsoft.com/downloads), Microsoft's research shows that laptop computers are lost at a rate of around 1 percent to 2 percent per year. By encrypting the data on a laptop computer, it is less likely that a thief will be able to access the information on the computer if it is stolen.

Encrypting Data That Travels across the Network

In Chapter 11, we discussed how data can be intercepted and captured as it travels across a network and its contents revealed with a "sniffer," or protocol analyzer. When sensitive data is transmitted across the network, users can protect against its decoding by ensuring that it is encrypted so that if unauthorized persons *do* intercept it, they won't be able to read it. The industry-standard method for doing this on a Transmission Control Protocol/Internet Protocol (TCP/IP) network is to use the Internet Protocol Security (IPSec) encryption mechanism.

Specifications for IPSec are laid out in Request for Comments (RFC) 2401. (A number of additional RFCs pertain to different protocols used by IPSec.) IPSec can be used with different operating systems and platforms. Windows 2000/XP/.NET include built-in support for IPSec. IPSec can provide machine-level authentication (verification of the identity of the computer from which a network transmission originated). It can be configured to work in one of two modes:

- **Transport mode** This mode provides end-to-end security, from the source computer to the destination computer. It is also called *host-to-host mode.*

- **Tunnel mode** This mode provides for encryption between two secure gateways (the computers that act as gateways between an internal network and the Internet or other internetwork).

Because it is capable of tunneling, IPSec can be used to create virtual private networks on its own, and it is also used in conjunction with Layer 2 Tunneling Protocol (L2TP) to provide encryption in an L2TP virtual private network (VPN) tunnel.

Although often referred to as a protocol, IPSec is actually a security scheme that incorporates several different protocols. These include the following:

- **Authentication Header (AH) protocol** This protocol is used for authentication and to ensure data integrity by signing each data packet. AH signs the entire packet (including the Internet Protocol [IP] headers) but does not provide data confidentiality.

- **Encapsulating Security Payload (ESP) protocol** This protocol is used to encrypt data for confidentiality. It also signs the data portion of the packet for authentication and integrity, but it doesn't sign the entire packet.

These two protocols can be used separately or together (in the latter case, when both data confidentiality and signing of the entire packet are desired). Other protocols used by IPSec include:

■ **The Internet Security Association and Key Management Protocol (ISAKMP)**
This protocol creates security associations between two computers that communicate using IPSec, to define the process of exchanging information.

■ **The Oakley Key Generation Protocol** This protocol creates the keys used during the transaction. These are temporary keys that are discarded after the communication session is terminated.

Because IPSec uses shared keys (symmetric encryption), it is important that there be a way to exchange keys securely across the network. The *Diffie-Hellman Key Exchange algorithm* provides a way for the computers on both sides of the transaction to generate identical keys without ever actually sending the key itself across the network and exposing it to possible interception. The encryption algorithms used by IPSec are standard ciphers such as DES/3DES, IDEA, Blowfish, RC-5, and CAST-128.

Another important feature of IPSec is its ability to provide *antireplay*—protection against hackers who might try to capture transmissions and replay them to create a communication session, emulating one of the parties to the original transaction. IPSec is an important mechanism for protecting data during the vulnerable period when it is being sent across a network. The current version of IP, IPv4, allows the use of IPSec as an option; the next generation, IPv6, will require it.

Encrypting E-mail Communications

E-mail has become one of the most common forms of communication, including for messages that contain sensitive personal or business information. Several software programs encrypt e-mail; the most popular is Pretty Good Privacy (PGP), which was created by Phil Zimmermann in the early 1990s. Since then, PGP has become widely distributed, and versions are available for most common operating systems, including Windows XP and Mac OS X.

PGP first compresses and then encrypts the plain-text data using a one-time secret key (or *session key*), which is itself then encrypted with the public key of the intended recipient. The encrypted session key is sent to the recipient along with the encrypted data, and the recipient uses his or her private key to decrypt the session key so that it can be used to decrypt the message itself. Because both symmetric and asymmetric encryption is used in this process, PGP is called a *hybrid cryptosystem*. Different versions of PGP use different encryption algorithms. Version 2.6.x (sometimes called "classic PGP" and considered by some to be more secure than newer versions) uses a combination of the RSA asymmetric cipher and the IDEA symmetric cipher. The MD5 hash algorithm is also used to create a fixed-length replacement for very long text strings in digital signatures.

Public keys and private keys are stored in separate files called *keyrings* on the hard disk of the computer where PGP is installed. Both the sender and recipient must have PGP installed to use the program for secure communications.

PGP's biggest vulnerability is related to the fact that users have to use a passphrase to perform actions such as signing documents and decrypting messages (anything for which the private key is used). Protecting this passphrase is a big security issue; good security practices require that the passphrase not be revealed to anyone else or stored on the system for "automatic" entry. Anyone who knows the passphrase can read the encrypted messages or send messages that purport to be from the legitimate user. If the passphrase does become compromised, a key revocation certificate can be generated and issued to render the associated public key null and void. PGP also includes a wipe option (−*w*) that can be used to overwrite the contents of an encrypted file when you delete it so that it can't be easily recovered using data recovery utilities.

NOTE

For more information about PGP, see the International PGP home page at www.pgpi.org.

A number of tools and services use PGP or the Open PGP standard for encrypting e-mail. Many of these solutions are also available on the Web, including Hushmail (which we discussed in Chapter 9), but these are primarily for private use. Larger organizations commonly use services such as e-mail encryption software from Entrust (www.entrust.com/email-encryption/). Entrust uses Secure/ Multipurpose Internet Mail Extensions (S/MIME), PGP, and Entrust encryption formats to encrypt messages, and Entrust server software is available to encrypt messages on a network so that they can't be viewed after being to other networks such as the Internet. Entrust is used not only for e-mail programs such as Outlook, but also by mobile devices such as BlackBerry handheld devices.

What Is Steganography?

Steganography (from the Greek word for *covered writing*) refers to a method of hiding data—not just concealing its contents as encryption does, but concealing its very existence. Steganography is usually used in conjunction with encryption for added protection of sensitive data. This method ameliorates one of the biggest problems of encrypting data—the fact that it is encrypted draws the attention of people who are looking for confidential or sensitive information.

The concept of steganography has been around for a long time. The ancient Greeks are said to have sent secret messages by shaving the head of the messenger and writing the message on his scalp, then letting the hair grow back over it before sending him on his way to deliver the message. Early methods of steganography involved using "invisible ink" or concealing a message inside another message using a code whereby only every fifth word, for example, "counts" as part of the real, hidden message. One of the earliest books on the subject, *Steganographica*, by Gaspari Schotti, was published in the 1600s.

Steganography in the computer world also hides data inside other data, but the way it does so is a little more complex. Because of the way data is stored in files, there are often unused (empty) bits in a file such as a document or graphic. A message can be broken up and stored in these unused bits, and when the file is sent it will appear to be only the original file (called the *container file*). The hidden information inside is usually encrypted, and the recipient will need special software to retrieve it (and then decrypt it, if necessary). Messages can be concealed inside all sorts of other files, including executables and graphics and audio files. Another form of steganography is the hidden watermark that is sometimes used to embed a trademark or other symbol in a document or file.

A number of different software programs can be used for this purpose, including JP Hide and Seek, which conceals data inside .jpg files, and MP3Stego, which conceals data in .mp3 files. Steganos Security Suite is a package of software programs that provide steganography, encryption, and other services.

Other programs, such as StegDetect, are designed to look for hidden content in files. The process of detecting steganographic data is called *steganalysis*.

NOTE

For more information and links to lots of good steganography Web sites, see "Information Hiding" at http://www.jjtc.com/steganography.

Modern Decryption Methods

The use of cryptography naturally led to the science of *cryptanalysis*, the process of decrypting encrypted messages. One of the early methods for "cracking" polyalphabetic substitution ciphers was *frequency analysis*, which involved examining the encrypted text for repeated character strings and using the distance between the repeated strings to calculate the key length. (Repetitions of identical plain-text characters that are ciphered in the same way will occur at intervals that are a multiple of the key length.) Then statistical methods can be used to painstakingly determine which plain-text character each cipher-text character represents.

Cryptanalysts throughout history have used a number of different methods to break encryption algorithms, including the following:

- **Known plain-text analysis** If the analyst has a sample of decrypted text that was encrypted using a particular cipher, he or she can sometimes deduce the key by studying the cipher text.

- **Differential cryptanalysis** If the analyst can obtain cipher text from plain text but is unable to analyze the key, it can be deduced by comparing the cipher text and the plain text.

- **Ciphertext-only analysis** This is used when only the cipher text is available and the analyst has no sample of plain text.

- **Timing/differential power analysis** This is a means of measuring the differences in power consumption over a period during which a computer chip is encrypting information to analyze key computations.

- **Key interception (man in the middle)** The analyst tricks two parties to an encrypted exchange into sending their keys by making them think they're exchanging keys with each other.

CyberCrimeStopper

A Perfect Cipher?

A *perfect cipher* is one in which every possible cipher text is equally likely for every method, thus rendering the encryption unbreakable without the key.

In his paper "A Communications Theory of Secrecy Systems," published in 1948, Claude Shannon, a Bell Labs mathematician sometimes called the "father of information theory," postulated that given enough time and a large enough sample of the cipher text, every cipher can be broken. He held that a number he called the *unicity distance*, which represented the amount of cipher text that is needed to be able to decrypt a message, could be used as a measurement of how strong a cipher is. If the unicity distance is infinite (the sequence of numbers in the key is genuinely random and is at least as long as the message, and the key is used only for that one message), the cipher is called a *one-time pad* and the message is undecipherable.

Another example of an undecipherable message is one in which the length of the entire message is shorter than the amount of cipher text needed to break the key. If an alphabetical substitution cipher has a key length that is greater than the message length, the message can't be decrypted by analyzing the cipher text.

Mathematician Claude Shannon (see the sidebar in this section) put forth the theory of *workload*. This term refers to the fact that increasing the amount of work (and the time required to do it) that is necessary to crack an encryption system increases the strength of the encryption and is an alternative to increasing the unicity distance (the amount of cipher text needed to crack the encryption).

Computer encryption ciphers are difficult to crack, but it can be done. With enough time and patience, a brute force attack that tries every possible key will be successful. The goal of cryptographers is to create ciphers for which this process will take such a long time—even using supercomputers or distributed processing methods—that the effort will not be worthwhile. Today's popular encryption algorithms rely on this deterrent effect.

Cybercriminals' Use of Encryption and Steganography

We have been discussing the legitimate use of cryptographic techniques as part of an organization's security plan. There are many reasons to take steps to provide extra protection for data such as trade secrets, customer and client personal information, and so forth. However, these same technologies can be—and often are—also used by cybercriminals to conceal the self-incriminating information in messages they send to one another. Terrorists are believed to use steganography and encryption (as well as less technical code words inserted in seemingly innocuous e-mails or Web pages) to communicate with one another and coordinate their financial activities and attacks.

In cases of serious crimes, investigators might need to employ the services of a cryptanalyst to help decipher encrypted data that could contain information essential to identifying criminals or preventing future criminal activities.

On the Scene

Cryptography As a Terrorist Tool

According to an article in *USA Today* and later reported on the Wired Web site at www.wired.com/politics/law/news/2001/02/41658, government officials believe Al Qaeda terrorists use steganography to hide their secret communications "in plain sight" in messages and files posted on bulletin board Web sites and exchanged in Internet chat rooms, and encryption technologies to conceal the true content of e-mail messages. Encrypted files containing terrorist plans have been found on the computers of various terrorist suspects, including Pakistani terrorist Khalil Deek and the terrorist convicted of plotting the first World Trade Center bombing in 1993, Ramzi Yousef. In both cases, mathematicians working for the FBI were able to use supercomputers to decrypt the files, although in the case of some files, it took more than a year to do so.

For more information, see www.usatoday.com/life/cyber/tech/2001-02-05-bin-laden.htm.

Making the Most of Hardware and Software Security

A multilayer security plan will incorporate multiple security solutions. Security is not a "one size fits all" issue, so the options that work best for one organization are not necessarily the best choice for another. Security solutions can be generally broken down into two categories: hardware solutions and software solutions.

Implementing Hardware-Based Security

Hardware security solutions can come in the form of network devices: Firewalls, routers, and even switches can function to provide a certain level of security. In general, these devices are dedicated computers themselves, running proprietary software.

Hardware-Based Firewalls

Many firewall vendors provide hardware-based solutions. Some of the most popular hardware firewalls include the Cisco PIX firewall, SonicWALL, Sun's iForce VPN/Firewall, Sidewinder G2, and home-based firewalls from D-Link and Linksys. Hardware solutions are available for networks of all sizes. For example, the D-Link and Linksys products focus on small office/home office (SOHO) users, whereas the Cisco PIX comes in configurations that support up to 500,000 connections.

Hardware-based firewalls are often referred to as *firewall appliances*. A disadvantage of hardware-based firewalls is the proprietary nature of the software they run. Another disadvantage of many of these products, such as Cisco's highly respected PIX, is the high cost. Of course, the range in price is based on how many connections are supported, and features that aren't found in firewalls designed for home and small-business use. Hardware-based firewalls perform basically the same functions as software-based firewalls. Later in this chapter, in the section "Understanding Firewalls," we discuss how both of these work.

Authentication Devices

As we discussed in Chapter 11, you can use a number of hardware-based components to authenticate users, and you can implement them as part of your network security plan to provide extra security. These devices may use biometrics, which analyzes characteristics of the person, or smart cards that contain computer chips to help authenticate the user. The costs of these devices can vary, but they have dropped dramatically in recent years as security has become a priority for homes and businesses alike.

Implementing Software-Based Security

Software security solutions cover a much broader range than do hardware-based solutions. These solutions include the security features built into the network operating system as well as additional security software made by the operating system vendors or third-party vendors. Software security has its advantages: It is often less expensive than hardware-based solutions and it integrates more easily into the system and network. However, software security often suffers from decreased performance, compared to hardware-based security implementations, and security applications that run on popular operating systems can be easier to hack than the proprietary programs that run on dedicated hardware devices. Nonetheless, software security is popular and provides a full range of methods for protecting data and providing authentication, confidentiality, and integrity.

Cryptographic Software

Thousands of cryptographic products are available for different purposes: disk/file encryption, e-mail encryption, steganography, and more. We have mentioned some of these in the sections addressing how the technologies work. In addition to the commercial products, many encryption and authentication software programs are available as freeware.

Digital Certificates

As mentioned earlier, public key encryption is more secure than secret key encryption because there is no need to transmit a key across unsecured channels, but public key cryptography is also more complex, and it's more difficult to implement on a large scale. There must be a system that ensures that public keys that are posted to the Internet are not forgeries posted by someone who purports to be another user. If this happens, the data that is encrypted with that public key (and intended to be sent to the user whose name was associated with it) could be intercepted by the unauthorized user who posted the key. That unauthorized person would then be able to decrypt the data and read the message.

We need a mechanism that will provide a way for a trusted third party to confirm that the user who publishes the public key is in fact who he or she claims to be. A digital certificate provides this assurance. To understand how a digital certificate works, think of the way a driver's license or government-issued ID card is used for identity verification. If a store or bank requires that you prove your identity by producing a license or ID card, that entity is relying on the word of a trusted third party (in this case, the Department of Motor Vehicles [DMV]) that you are who you say you are. The store or bank presumes that the DMV has checked you out and would not have issued the official identification document unless your identity was confirmed.

Just as the store or bank accepts your driver's license as proof of your identity, another computer with which you want to exchange data or make transactions will accept the digital certificate issued by a trusted third party. In the case of digital certificates, the trusted third party is a *certificate authority (CA)*. The CA verifies that a particular identity is bound to the public key that is included in the certificate.

Some public CAs, such as VeriSign, issue certificates to persons on the Internet. Some private (internal) CAs are set up by organizations to issue certificates to users within the local network. The CA is a server that runs special software that allows it to issue, manage, and revoke digital certificates. The CA's role is to guarantee to other users, computers, and applications that a particular public key really belongs to the entity with whose name it is associated.

The Public Key Infrastructure

A *public key infrastructure*, or *PKI*, is a security framework based on digital certificates. The PKI provides a system for users to request certificates and for CAs to issue, manage, and revoke certificates and disseminate certificate revocation lists (CRLs) so that other entities will know when a particular entity's certificate is no longer valid. The PKI is based on the X.509 standards established by the International Organization for Standardization (ISO).

An important component of the PKI is the set of security policies that governs it. These policies should define the rules for issuance and use of digital certificates and the keys that are associated with them. Public certification authorities such as VeriSign are required to provide a certificate practice statement (CPS). This is a document that outlines in detail the procedures for implementing the PKI.

When multiple CAs are in the same PKI, as is the case in most large organizations, they are arranged in a hierarchical manner. The *root CA* is the most trusted CA in the PKI. Its certificate is self-signed, and it is responsible for issuing certificates to all the other CAs in the PKI, which are called *subordinate CAs*. The subordinate CAs issue certificates to users and computers, whereas the root CA generally issues certificates only to subordinate CAs. Public CAs are published in the Global Trust Register, which acts like a root CA for public CAs (albeit in printed form).

Certificates can be issued by a CA for many different purposes, including file encryption, smart card authentication, e-mail, IP security, and network logon. Users can export or import certificates, moving them from one computer to another. The export function is also used to create a backup of a certificate, which can then be restored to the *certificate store*, the location on the hard disk where certificates are kept, if the original certificate is destroyed. Certificates are issued automatically in some cases; in other cases, they must be explicitly requested by the user. There are different ways to request a certificate, depending on the CA software and the PKI policies. Requesting a certificate from a public CA usually involves filling out an application form on the CA's Web site.

It is very important that a PKI contain a mechanism for publishing certificate revocations so that other entities won't mistakenly rely on a certificate that is no longer valid. Certificates are revoked when the public key is compromised or when users leave the company or for some reason are no longer trusted. A CRL lists certificates that have been revoked and is updated regularly and distributed throughout the organization by the CA.

Software-Based Firewalls

In addition to the PKI software that provides for verification of identity, a vitally important type of software-based security is the *software firewall*. In reality, all firewalls are software-based. The hardware devices sold as firewalls run proprietary software that performs basically the same functions as a software program that can be installed on a regular PC. We use the term *software-based firewall* to describe firewall products such as Microsoft ISA Server, as opposed to hardware/software (or firmware) combination appliances such as those produced by Cisco Systems. Some vendors, such as Check Point, market both types of products. In the next section, we discuss in detail how firewalls work.

On the Scene

The Difference between a Firewall and a Proxy

Proxy servers have been around for quite a while. The original meaning of the term *proxy* was "one who is authorized to act for another." Perhaps the most famous—or infamous—use of the word came about in relation to the practice of marriage by proxy, in which a substitute would stand in for one of the parties, allowing a wedding ceremony to be performed even though the groom (or less commonly, the bride) was not physically present. Proxy weddings at one time were a popular way for a couple to get "hitched" while the groom was serving in the military.

Proxy servers are so named because, like the hapless stand-in who says "I do" when it's really someone else who does, they act as go-betweens to allow something to take place (in this case, network communications) between systems that must remain separate.

Proxy servers "stand in" between the computers on a LAN and those on the public network outside. Another good analogy is a gatekeeper who is stationed at the entrance to an estate to check all incoming visitors to ensure that they are on the list of invited guests. The proxy can actually hide the computers on the LAN from outsiders. Only the IP address of the proxy server is "visible" to others on the Internet; internal computers use private IP addresses (nonroutable over the Internet) that cannot be seen from the other side of the proxy.

In fact, a proxy can go further and function more like a prison guard, who not only makes certain that only authorized persons get in, but also sees that only those who have permission to go out are allowed to leave. Just as the guard checks his list before letting anyone in or out, the proxy *filters* outgoing and incoming data according to predefined criteria. At this point, the proxy is behaving like a *firewall*.

Understanding Firewalls

A firewall goes a bit further than just "standing in" for the local computers and hiding them from view on the global network, as a proxy server does. Firewalls are specifically designed to control inbound and outbound access, preventing unauthorized data from entering the network and restricting how and what type of data can be sent out.

The firewall gets its name from the building industry. In commercial structures, it is common to build a barrier wall made of fireproof material between two areas of a building. This wall is designed to prevent fire from spreading from one part of the building to the other. Another example is the heat barrier between the engine of an automobile and the passenger compartment, also called a firewall. Likewise, a network firewall acts as a barrier to prevent "bad data"—whether that is virus code or simply messages to or from unauthorized systems—from spreading from the outside network (usually the Internet) to the internal network. It also prevents packets of a particular type or to or from a particular user or computer from spreading from the LAN to the outside network.

In choosing among different firewall solutions, organizations encounter two basic firewall design options:

■ A firewall can be designed to *permit* all packets to pass through unless they are expressly denied.

■ A firewall can be designed to *deny* all packets unless they are expressly permitted.

Obviously, the second method is more secure, but it can result in the denial of access that administrators actually want to allow. The first method is easier to implement but is also more easily penetrated or circumvented.

How Firewalls Use Layered Filtering

Firewall products support the filtering of messages to either allow data to pass through or prevent it from doing so, according to specified criteria. The best firewalls support *layered filtering*. This means they can perform filtering at the packet layer, the circuit layer, or the application layer; some firewalls support only one of these filtering types, but most advanced firewall products, such as Microsoft ISA Server and Check Point's Firewall-1 product, support all three types. Firewalls that combine packet filtering, circuit filtering, and application layer filtering provide the highest level of security. These types of firewalls also tend to be the most expensive. In the following sections, we look briefly at how each filtering method works.

Packet Filtering

Packet filtering does most of its work at the network layer of the Open Systems Interconnection (OSI) networking model (equivalent to the internetwork layer of the Department of Defense [DoD] model), dealing with IP packets. Packet filters examine the information contained in the IP packet header of a message and then either permit the data to cross the firewall or reject the packet based on that information. When IP packet filtering is enabled, the firewall will intercept and evaluate packets before passing them on to a higher level in the firewall or to an application filter.

The information that the packet filter uses to make its decision includes the IP address of the source and/or destination computer(s) and the Transmission Control Protocol (TCP) or User Datagram

Protocol (UDP) port number. (Yes, the port numbers are in the transport layer header, so technically, although packet filtering generally operates at the network layer, it also processes some higher-layer information.) Packet filtering allows the data to proceed to the transport layer only if the packet-filtering rules allow for it to do so.

Packet filtering lets administrators block packets that come from a particular Internet host or those that are destined for a particular service on the network (for example, the Web server or Simple Mail Transfer Protocol [SMTP] server). *Dynamic packet filtering* provides higher security because it opens the necessary port(s) only when required for communication to take place, and then closes the port(s) immediately after the communication ends. *Static packet filters* are configured to allow inbound and outbound access to a predefined IP address (or group of IP addresses) and port number (or groups of ports).

It is important to note that packet filters cannot perform filtering that is based on anything contained in the data field of the packet, nor can they use the state of the communication channel to aid in making their decision to accept or reject the packet. If filtering decisions need to be made on the basis of either of these criteria, the firewall must be configured to use filtering that operates at a different layer (circuit or application filtering).

Circuit Filtering

Circuit filters operate at a higher layer of the OSI model, the transport layer (the host-to-host layer in the DoD model). Circuit filters restrict access on the basis of host machines (not users) by processing the information found in the TCP and UDP packet headers. This allows administrators to create filters that would, for example, prohibit anyone using Computer A from using File Transfer Protocol (FTP) to access Computer B.

When circuit filters are used, access control is based on TCP data streams or UDP datagrams. Circuit filters can act based on TCP and UDP status flags and sequencing information, in addition to source and destination addresses and port numbers. Circuit-level filtering allows administrators to inspect sessions rather than packets. A session is sometimes thought of as a connection, but actually a session can be made up of more than one connection. Sessions are established only in response to a user request, which adds to security.

Circuit filters don't restrict access based on user information; they also cannot interpret the meanings of the packets. That is, they cannot distinguish between a *GET* command and a *PUT* command sent by an application program. To do this, application filtering must be used.

Application Filtering

At times, the best tactic is to filter packets based on the information contained in the data itself. Packet filters and circuit filters don't use the contents of the data stream in making filtering decisions, but this *can* be done with *application filtering*. An application filter operates at the top layer of the networking model, the appropriately named application layer. Application filters can use the packet header information but are also able to allow or reject packets on the basis of the data contents and the user information.

Administrators can use application filtering to control access based on a user's identity and/or based on the particular task the user is attempting to perform. With application filters, criteria can be set based on commands issued by the application. This means that, for example, the administrator could restrict a particular user from downloading files to a specified computer using FTP. At the same time, the administrator could allow that user to upload files via FTP to that same computer. This is possible because different commands are issued depending on whether the user is retrieving files from the server or depositing them there.

Many firewall experts consider application gateways to be the most secure of the filtering technologies. This is because the criteria they use for filtering cover a broader span than the other methods. Sometimes hackers write malicious programs that use the port address of an authorized application, such as port 53, which is the domain name system (DNS) address. A packet or circuit filter would not be able to recognize that the packet is not a valid DNS request or response and would allow it to pass through. An application filter, however, is able to examine the contents of the packet and determine that it should *not* be allowed.

There are drawbacks to this filtering type. The biggest problem is that there must be a separate application gateway for every Internet service that the firewall needs to support. This makes for more configuration work; however, this weakness is also a strength that adds to the security of the firewall. Because a gateway for each service must be explicitly enabled, an administrator won't accidentally allow services that pose a threat to the network. Application filtering is the most sophisticated level of filtering performed by the firewall service and is especially useful in protecting the network against specific types of attacks, such as malicious SMTP commands or attempts to penetrate the local DNS servers.

Integrated Intrusion Detection

Many firewalls also incorporate an *intrusion detection system (IDS)* that can actually recognize that an attack of a specific type is being attempted and can perform a predefined action when such an intrusion is identified, such as one of the following:

- Send an e-mail message to the administrator

- Page the administrator

- Write an event entry to the event log

- Run a previously specified program or script

- Stop the firewall service

IDSes can recognize many different common forms of network intrusion, such as port scans, LAND attacks, the Ping of Death, UDP bombs, out-of-band attacks, and others. Special detection filters may also be built in, such as a Post Office Protocol (POP) intrusion detection filter that analyzes POP mail traffic to guard against POP buffer overflows, or a DNS intrusion detection filter that can be configured to look for DNS hostname overflow or length overflow attacks.

Forming an Incident Response Team

An intrusion or attack can be scary, frustrating, and maddening—as with a physical attack on one's person, the emotional reactions can make it difficult to exercise good judgment and make the correct decisions about how to respond. This situation is made easier if you have properly prepared for it. Many companies, taking the proactive approach, form incident response teams—called *computer incident response teams*, or *CIRTs*—made up of individuals who train together (much like a military unit or police SWAT team) in how to handle anticipated incidents. The goal is to be able to swing into action when an actual incident occurs, with each team member covering a preassigned area of responsibility and thus decreasing the amount of damage and increasing the likelihood of apprehending the perpetrator of the incident.

In their book *Incident Response: Investigating Computer Crime*, Chris Prosise and Kevin Mandia define an incident as "an event that interrupts normal operating procedure and precipitates some level of crisis." The CERT guidelines define specific incidents, including violation of security policy, attempts to gain unauthorized access, unwanted denial of service/resources, unauthorized use, and changes made to a system or data without the owner's knowledge, instruction, or consent. An incident can be anything from an attack that crashes all the servers and cuts off all network communications to an intrusion that causes no actual damage but demonstrates the vulnerability of the organization's systems. The various types of attacks described in Chapter 10 (for example, the many varieties of denial-of-service/distributed denial-of-service [DoS/DDoS] attacks) certainly qualify as incidents.

The response team should have its own hardware and software to use in conducting the investigation. It is important that the victim systems be preserved in the state they were in when the incident was discovered. Any changes made to these systems can compromise the integrity of the evidence and affect its admissibility in court.

Response team members may be called to testify in court if criminal charges or civil lawsuits are brought in relation to the incident. This is another reason to create extensive documentation that can be reviewed prior to giving testimony. Often, a case doesn't come to trial until months or even years after the incident, and the human memory often isn't reliable after so long a time without a little help. The team member who creates the documentation should be the one to testify to its authenticity if it is to be entered into evidence.

NOTE

It is important for team members to understand that their reports regarding the incident may end up being entered into evidence at trial. For this reason, such documentation should be kept in a special notebook with numbered pages, and the notebook should not contain any personal information, because the entire notebook may become part of the official record.

The steps involved in incident response include:

- **Training** Once versed in the theory of incident response, the team should train together in realistic scenario-based drills until response actions become automatic. Training should also address the law relating to privacy considerations and other issues that could affect or restrict team members' activities during the response.

- **Incident recognition** Monitoring should be conducted to ensure that team members are alerted to the possibility that an incident is occurring in its earliest stages.

- **Incident verification** This step involves examining logs, observing system/network behavior, interviewing witnesses, and so on to verify that an incident has in fact occurred.

- **Incident classification** An assessment should be conducted to determine the nature of the incident and the threat level.

- **Incident containment** Immediate steps should be taken to stop the incident and prevent any more damage.

- **Evidence preservation** Immediate steps should be taken to preserve all evidence of the incident for the purposes of tracking the offender and possible prosecution or civil litigation.

- **Incident analysis** A thorough investigation should be conducted to determine exactly what happened and how.

- **Restoration** Systems should be brought back to a working state as soon as possible, to minimize loss of productivity.

- **Follow-up activities** New security measures should be established to ensure that the same type of incident doesn't occur again.

- **Documentation** Each step of the response process should be documented and preserved for later review and use.

NOTE

Documentation may include "crime scene photographs"; photos or screenshots to preserve the information on the monitor might be desirable in some cases. A digital camera should be part of the investigative team's response kit.

It is not necessary for every member of the team to participate in every step of the response process. All team members should know their own roles and allow other team members to perform as assigned. Team member roles should be assigned according to each individual's area of expertise. Teams often include persons from the IT department, corporate security, management, legal department, and even the financial, human resources, and public relations departments. Response team members should be on call and able to respond to incidents at all hours and on any day of the week.

Incident response is the culmination of everything we've discussed in this book and the first step in the investigative process. In this chapter, we've moved from security theory and concepts to the "hands-on" aspects of a security plan: implementation of security measures and finally, should those fail, planning to respond to an attack. However, the document that brings all these topics together is the organization's *security policy*, which governs everything from the way security technologies are to be used to the procedures prescribed for the incident response team. The next section provides an overview of security policies: what they are (and aren't) and how they're developed. We include examples of some specific policy issues that every organization should address.

Designing and Implementing Security Policies

Security issues are at the forefront of organizational priorities today. Companies lose millions of dollars and untold hours of worker productivity due to lax security. Companies realize that protection of their assets—digital as well as physical—is no longer a luxury; in the twenty-first century, it has become a necessity.

An enormous amount of a company's most crucial information, including financial data, personnel records, customer information, and trade secrets, is concentrated in one virtual "place": the organization's network. This location renders this information vulnerable to unauthorized access and accidental or intentional destruction, both from within and (assuming the local network is connected to the Internet, as most today are) from outside intruders. Implementation of security measures, to be effective, must be based on an organized plan that takes into account all aspects of the organization's security needs. There must be rules and guidelines governing how the plan is put into action. These are disseminated throughout the organization as *policies*.

Understanding Policy-Based Security

Those of us in the security field often stress the need for detailed policies that are customized to fit the needs of each particular organization—sometimes to the point of sounding like a broken record. However, there's a good reason for this: The security policy is the foundation of an organization's security plan. It is the governing document, much like a police department's general orders, a city's charter, or a corporate board's mission statement. The following sections discuss the purpose and function of an IT *security policy* and the process of evaluating and defining security needs, developing the policy, and implementing it throughout the organization.

What Is a Security Policy?

A *security policy*, as the term is used here, refers to a written document that defines an organization's approach to security or a specific security area (in this case, computer and network security) and lays down a set of rules to be followed in implementing the organization's security philosophy.

NOTE

Guidelines usually function as recommended procedures rather than hard-and-fast rules. Guidelines can supplement policies, but they do not replace them.

Organizations may establish both written and unwritten rules pertaining to security matters and may issue a number of different types of documents dealing with these issues. How does the security policy differ from security-related memoranda and directives, standards, specifications, guidelines, and procedural documents?

Security Memoranda

Generally, a *security memorandum* or freestanding *security directive* is issued in response to a particular incident and may be used as a way to establish a rule that is not covered in the policy. If the rule applies only to a specific one-time situation or will be in effect for only a limited time, a memorandum might be all that's needed. If the rule will be permanent or long-term and is applicable to a broader spectrum of situations, it should be incorporated into the organization's formal policy as soon as possible. A memorandum can also be informational only, its purpose to make users aware of security considerations without laying out specific rules or guidelines.

Security Standards and Specifications

Standards and *specifications* are generally requirements that are to be met in implementing system-specific security procedures and may be used to measure or rate the overall reliability, compatibility, or other characteristics of the system. The *Common Criteria for Information Technology Security Evaluation* (which is commonly called the *Common Criteria*) is an international standard for computer security, which is outlined under ISO/IEC 15408. It is a framework that outlines the evaluation criteria for IT security. It evolved from the government standards used by several countries, and it provides a framework that is used by users, vendors, and testing laboratories to specify, implement, and test IT security.

Security Procedures

Procedural documents supplement the policy and may be incorporated into it as part of a policies and procedures manual. The procedural document gives step-by-step technical instructions for tasks that are required to implement the policies. For example, if the policy states that users must change their passwords every 30 days, you might have two associated procedural documents: one directed to network administrators that details how to set password requirements on the Windows domain controller to force users to change passwords at 30-day intervals, and another directed to users detailing how to change their passwords. When contained in separate documents, the policy section and associated procedural document(s) should reference one another.

Why This Information Matters to the Investigator

Investigators responding to cybercrimes that involve a corporate network need to have a thorough understanding of how security is implemented within the organization, just as an investigator responding to a home invasion needs to know the layout of the house, how and where commercial security devices are in place, what the family's security philosophy is, and so forth. Unlike most residential situations, corporations will often have formal, written documentation that lays out all the guidelines followed in implementing the security plan.

However, these documents aren't always easy to understand—unless you also understand the process by which they're created, adopted, and implemented. In the following sections, we provide an overview of that process: how organizations assess their security needs based on known risk factors, threat levels, and other factors that determine how much and what types of security will be implemented; how policy areas are defined; and how the document itself is developed (usually by a policy development team).

This background will make it easier for investigators to come into an organization and analyze its role as the victim or source of cybercrimes based on information contained in the policy document. For example, if an examination of the policies shows that the organization has an extremely strong password policy, and further investigative techniques such as interviewing employees reveal that the policies are universally enforced, this could indicate that intruders used techniques other than password cracking to gain access, or it could indicate that there is a "leak" inside the organization. In other words, understanding the policies can help to narrow the focus of the investigation. This is often one of the most difficult and most vital steps in the investigative process.

Evaluating Security Needs

If we accept the stated definition of security policy, it becomes obvious that there is not and cannot be a one-size-fits-all IT security policy that will work equally well for all organizations. Security needs differ, based on:

- Risk factors
- The perceived and actual threat levels
- Organizational vulnerabilities
- The organization's philosophy (open versus closed system)
- Legal factors
- Available funds

It is important to analyze all of these factors carefully when developing a policy that offers both adequate protection and a desirable level of access.

Components of an Organizational Security Plan

Security features are now built into operating system software; Windows XP, Vista, Server 2003, and Server 2008 include numerous security features. UNIX and Linux distributions as well as Mac OS X also come with built-in security features. IT security products, both hardware and software, abound. Security training and numerous security certifications are available, and IT professionals are seeking them out. These are all important components of an organization's overall security plan, but they are not enough. Effective coordination and interaction of all these parts require one more thing: a comprehensive security policy.

Defining Areas of Responsibility

To assess security needs accurately, someone should review the company's infrastructure, processes, and procedures and involve personnel at all levels of the organization and from as many different departments as possible. Ideally, the following tasks will be performed by a carefully selected team that includes, at a minimum, members of management, IT personnel, and a company legal representative. Each team member should be assigned specific areas of responsibility, and deadlines for completion should be provided.

Responsibility for Developing the Security Plan and Policies

The initial creation of a good security plan requires a great deal of thought and effort. The policy will impact those at all levels of the organization, and it is desirable to solicit input from as many representatives of different departments and job descriptions as is practical. An effective approach is to form a committee consisting of people from several areas of the organization to be involved in creating and reviewing the security plan and policies. A security planning committee of this type might include some or all of the following:

- The network administrator and one or more assistant administrators

- The site's security administrator

- Department heads of various company departments or their representatives

- Representatives of user groups that will be impacted by the security policies (for example, the secretarial staff, the data processing center)

- A member of the legal department who specializes in computer and technology law

- A member of the finance or budget department

- A member of upper management

Responsibility for Implementing and Enforcing the Security Plan and Policies

Security policies will generally be implemented and enforced by network administrators and members of the IT staff. Job descriptions and policies should designate exactly who is responsible for the implementation of which parts of the plan. There should be a clear-cut chain of command that specifies whose decision prevails in case of conflict. In some cases—such as physical penetration of the network—the company security staff will become involved. Written, clearly formulated policies should be in place, which stipulate which department has responsibility for which tasks in such situations.

The security plan should also address the procedures for reporting security breaches, both internally and if the police or other outside agencies are to be brought in. In addition, it should be specified who is responsible for or has the authority to call in outside agents.

As we mentioned in Chapter 5, when we discussed the investigation of policy violations, one of the most important factors in a good security policy is that it must be enforceable. If the policy can be enforced through security tools, this method is preferred. If the policies must be enforced through reprimand or other actions against employees who violate them, there should be clearly worded, universally distributed written documentation of what constitutes a violation and what sanctions will result, as well as who is responsible for imposing such sanctions.

Analyzing Risk Factors

Before the policy development team can set policies, they need to determine both the nature and the level of the security risks to the organization. Traditionally, risk analysis involves:

- Determining to what types of security breaches the organization is vulnerable

- For each type, determining the probability of such a breach occurring

- For each type, determining the extent of the loss that would be suffered if the breach did occur

This process is known as *quantitative risk analysis*. Another type of risk analysis, *qualitative risk analysis*, disregards the probability element and instead focuses on potential threats and the characteristics of the system or network that make it vulnerable to these threats. Then methods are developed for preventing or reducing the likelihood of breaches, detecting when breaches do occur, and decreasing and repairing the damage done if a breach does occur. To help identify threats and vulnerabilities, rate the threat level, estimate the impact on the organization, and recommend solutions, risk assessment tools may be used.

Why is a risk analysis necessary? There are several reasons, including the following:

- From the IT professional's point of view, a detailed risk analysis is the first and perhaps most important step in justifying to management the cost to implement needed security measures.

- From the business manager's point of view, the risk analysis document provides a solid, objective basis for making budgetary and personnel-impacting decisions.

- Data collected during the risk analysis process forces both IT and management to face and acknowledge threats and vulnerabilities of which they might not have been aware or which they previously might have been able to ignore.

- Risk analysis allows the organization to focus resources on the existing threats and vulnerabilities and avoid wasting time and funds on unnecessary measures.

Because the risk analysis process involves personnel throughout the organization, it can raise security awareness and help make appropriate security practices the responsibility of everyone who uses the computers and network. This is a basic tenet of crime prevention.

Assessing Threats and Threat Levels

The dictionary defines a *threat* as "somebody or something likely to cause harm." The threat assessment portion of the risk analysis should include:

- Sources of potential threats

- The nature of potential threats

- The likelihood of occurrence of each potential threat type

- The estimated impact of each potential threat type

Sources of potential threats can be divided into internal and external categories. Although many security policies focus on the threat of a security breach from outside the network or organization (across the Internet), in actuality many organizations find that their biggest potential losses come from inside—the deliberate or unintentional actions of employees, contractors, and others who have legitimate access to the network. It is important to address both categories when performing a threat assessment.

Defining threat sources further requires that the assessment team determine both *who* and *what* could pose a threat to the network. For example, people who could pose a threat include most of the cybercriminal types discussed in Chapter 3. The nature of possible threats is the *what* in this equation. Any of these people could initiate threats of one or more of the following natures:

- Unauthorized access to data

- Unauthorized disclosure of information

- Destruction of data

- Modification or corruption of data

- Introduction of viruses, worms, or Trojans

- Denial or interruption of service or network congestion/slowdown

NOTE

A thorough threat assessment program will not overlook the threats posed by events such as fire, flood, and power loss as well as those caused by human agents.

The next step in threat analysis consists of assigning a likelihood or probability to each type of threat event. A high probability indicates that the threat event is more likely than not to occur, as when there is a history of its occurrence in the past. A medium probability indicates that the threat event might or might not occur. A low probability indicates that the threat event is not likely to occur, although it is possible. Finally, the assessment team must evaluate the probable impact on the organization for each potential threat event. For example:

- If the company's customer database were destroyed, how would this affect such activities as sales, billing, and so on?

- If the company network were down for one day, what is the potential cost to the company in lost sales, lost employee productivity, and the like?

- If the company's client records were made public, what is the potential loss in terms of lawsuits, withdrawal of client business, or similar actions?

Once all of these questions have been asked and answered, it is a relatively simple matter to construct a threat assessment matrix that will put this information into perspective and help the policy development team focus the company's security policies on the threat areas of highest likelihood and most significant impact.

Analyzing Organizational and Network Vulnerabilities

In previous chapters, we discussed how to analyze a network's *technical vulnerabilities*. These vulnerabilities are those characteristics or configurations that an attacker can exploit to gain unauthorized access or misuse your network and its resources. Network vulnerabilities are often referred to as *security holes*. Security holes should be identified as part of the policy development process. These vulnerabilities can be caused by a programming characteristic or (mis)configuration of the operating system, a protocol or service, or an application. Examples might include:

- Operating system code that allows hackers to crash a computer by accessing a file whose path contains certain reserved words

- Unnecessarily open TCP/UDP ports that hackers can use to get into or obtain information about the system

- A Web browser's handling of scripts which allow malicious code to execute unwanted commands

The network's connections to the Internet and other networks obviously affect vulnerability. Data on a network that is connected 24/7 via a high-speed link is more vulnerable than data on a network that is only intermittently connected to the outside. A network that allows multiple outside connections (such as modems and phone lines on a number of different computers) increases vulnerability to outside attack. Dial-up modem connections merit special consideration. Although a dial-up connection is less open to intrusion than a full-time dedicated connection—both because it is connected to the outside for a shorter time period, reducing the window of opportunity for intrusion, and because it usually has a dynamic IP address, making it harder for an intruder to locate it on multiple occasions—allowing workstations on the network to have modems and phone lines can create a huge security risk.

If improperly configured, a computer with a dial-up connection to the Internet that is also cabled to the internal network can act as a router, allowing outside intruders to access not just the workstation connected to the modem, but also other computers on the LAN. One reason for allowing modems at individual workstations is to allow users to dial up connections to other private networks. A more secure way to do this is to remove (or in the case of laptops, disable) the modems and have the users establish a VPN connection with the other private network through the LAN's Internet connection. The best security policy is to have as few connections from the internal network to the outside as possible and to control access at those entry points (the *network perimeter*).

NOTE

Third-party software tools known as *vulnerability scanners* are designed to discover the vulnerabilities on a network, using a database of known commonly exploited weaknesses and probing for those weaknesses on your network.

Organizational vulnerabilities are those areas and data that are open to danger or harm if exposed to an attack. To determine these vulnerabilities, the policy team should first identify the assets that could be exposed to the types of threats previously identified. These could include financial records, trade secrets, personal information (including customer/client information), intellectual property, and marketing and strategy documents.

You should consider a number of factors when you are assessing vulnerabilities, including the nature of the data that goes through the organization's network. The vulnerability of data that is highly confidential (such as trade secrets) or irreplaceable (such as original artwork or writing) should be of highest priority. Vulnerability is also affected by the size of the organization and network. A larger number of people who have access to the network indicates a greater chance of exposure to someone who will want to do harm.

Analyzing Organizational Factors

The next step in evaluating security needs is to determine the philosophy of the organization's management regarding security versus accessibility. It is important to remember that the two are conflicting characteristics; the more of one that a system has, the less of the other it will have. The organizational philosophy determines where on the security-access continuum a particular network falls (and thus determines its policies).

Some companies institute a highly structured, formal management style. Employees are expected to respect a strict chain of command, and information is generally disseminated on a "need to know" basis. Government agencies, especially those related to law enforcement such as police departments and investigative agencies often follow this philosophy, sometimes referred to as the *paramilitary model*.

Other companies, particularly those in "creative" industries and other fields that are subject to little state regulation, are built on the opposite premise: that all employees should have as much information and input as possible, that managers should function as "team leaders" rather than authoritarian supervisors, and that restrictions on employee actions should be imposed only when necessary for the efficiency and productivity of the organization. This is sometimes called the *"one big happy family" model*. Creativity is valued more than "going by the book," and job satisfaction is considered to be an important aspect of enhancing employee performance and productivity.

In business management circles, these two diametrically opposed models are called *Theory X* (traditional paramilitary style) and *Theory Y* (modern, team-oriented approach). Although numerous other management models have been popularized in recent years, such as management by objective (MBO) and total quality management (TQM), each company's management style falls somewhere on the continuum between Theory X and Theory Y. The management model is based on the personal philosophies of the company's top decision makers regarding the relationship between management and employees.

The management model can have a profound influence on what is or isn't acceptable in planning security for the network. A "deny all access"-based security policy that is viewed as appropriate in a Theory X organization could meet with so much resentment and employee dissatisfaction in a Theory Y company that it disrupts business operations. Policy makers must always consider the company "atmosphere" as part of security planning. If there are good reasons to implement strict security in a Theory Y atmosphere, the restrictions will probably have to be justified to management and "sold" to employees, whereas those same restrictions might be accepted without question in a more traditional organization.

Considering Legal Factors

Security needs not only depend on the wishes of company managers, but they may also be dictated or at least guided by the criminal and civil laws in a particular jurisdiction. If the company's industry is subject to government regulations, the information on its network falls under privacy protection acts, or company contracts prohibit disclosure of information on the company network, these are legal factors that must be considered in establishing security policies.

It is important to protect the company from liability that might be incurred if employees or others using the network violate laws. For this reason, it is essential that the security policy development team include one or more attorneys who are well versed in applicable laws, and who are familiar with the terms of the company's contracts with partners, vendors, clients, and others.

Analyzing Cost Factors

Finally, but rarely of least concern, the needs evaluation must take into account the monetary cost of implementing heightened security. Determining the funds available for security upgrades will affect security policies by forcing the development team to differentiate the organization's security *needs* from security *wants*.

Cost factors can also force the team to prioritize security needs so that those threats that are most likely or most imminent can be addressed, those assets that are most important can be protected, and those vulnerabilities that are most egregious can be closed first.

Assessing Security Solutions

Once the company has identified and documented its security needs and established a working budget for addressing those needs, it is possible to assess solutions and determine which one(s) meet those needs within that budget. Network security solutions can generally be divided into three broad categories: hardware, software, and policy-only solutions.

Hardware Solutions

Hardware-based security solutions involve adding some physical device such as a dedicated firewall to protect the network or a smart card reader for logon authentication. Removal of diskette and CD/DVD drives from desktop computers to prevent unauthorized copying of files to removable media or introduction of viruses is also a hardware-based solution. Other security hardware devices include:

- Keystroke capture devices for monitoring computer use
- Hardware tokens for storing security keys
- Cryptographic hardware devices for offloading the processing of crypto operations
- Biometric authentication devices such as fingerprint or retina scanners

Hardware solutions can be more costly than software-only solutions, but they offer several advantages. Hardware security is usually more secure because there is less exposure of security information such as private keys, and it is more difficult to tamper with hardware than software. Hardware solutions also often offer faster performance.

Software Solutions

Software solutions include IDSes, packet/circuit/application filtering software, and security auditing software, as well as software firewall packages such as Microsoft's Internet Security and Acceleration

(ISA) Server, which combine these functions. Other software security solutions are antivirus (AV) programs such as those made by Symantec, "spyware" used to monitor how computers are being used (including packet sniffer software that can capture and analyze network traffic), and network management packages that incorporate security features. Operating system and application "fixes" that patch security holes can also be placed in this category.

Policy Solutions

Most hardware and software security measures have accompanying policies that prescribe when and how they are to be deployed and used, but many security measures consist of policies only. For example:

- Policies that prohibit users from disclosing their passwords to anyone else

- Policies that require users to lock their workstations when they leave their desks

- Policies that require users to get permission before installing any software on their machines

- Policies that prohibit users from allowing anyone else to use the computer after they've logged on

Of course, in many cases policies will be enforced via software or hardware. For example, a policy that prohibits users from copying network files to their local disks can be enforced by permissions that allow read-only access. A policy that requires users to change their passwords every 30 days can be enforced by setting passwords to expire after that time period.

Complying with Security Standards

The security policy document should lay out standards regarding such issues as confidentiality and integrity of data, authorization and authentication, access, appropriate use of network resources, and employee privacy issues. If compliance with federal standards (such as a C2 rating) or industry-specific standards (such as HIPAA for healthcare organizations) is required, the specifications should be included and mandated in the policy document.

Policies should be reviewed for compliance with international standards such as ISO 17799. You might want to reference related sections of ISO 17799 in individual policies similarly to the reference to related policies.

Government Security Ratings

Security ratings might be of interest in the development of a company's security policy, although they are not likely to be important unless the organization works under government contract requiring a specified level of security. An international standard for computer security is ISO/IEC 15408, which was based on TCSEC (United States, CTCPEC (Canada), and ITSEC (Western Europe). As we discussed earlier, this standard is called the *Common Criteria for Information Technology Security Evaluation* (or *Common Criteria* for short). Your security policy might specify adherence to this particular set of standards or specifications.

A copy of ISO/IEC 15408 is available from the ISO Web site at http://standards.iso.org/ittf/PubliclyAvailableStandards/index.html.

Utilizing Model Policies

Model security policies can be used to guide the policy development team in preparing a comprehensive policy document. Policy templates can be purchased from various sources (for example, RUSecure Information Security Policies), and sample policies are available for download from such organizations as the SANS Institute.

An advantage is that purchased model policies may be guaranteed to be compliant with ISO standards, HIPAA, or the like. However, policy makers should beware of simply copying a sample policy without an extensive review to ensure that the policies fit the organization's philosophy, budget, and business model. Sample policies are usually "sanitized"—that is, organization-specific issues have been removed to provide a generic policy that is designed to serve as a starting point in creating customized policies.

Common Policy Areas

In creating policies for an organization, a number of policy areas often need to be addressed. These include the following:

- *Password Policies* define the length and complexity of passwords, how often they must be changed, and other important qualities that we discussed in Chapter 11.

- *Server and workstation security policies* define rules governing physical security of network-connected computers, mandating logoff or password-protected screensavers when leaving a station unattended, system shutdown policies, sharing of workstations, and so forth.

- *Encryption policies* define when encryption should or shouldn't be used and the encryption technologies or algorithms that are acceptable. For example, a policy might mandate that specific proven algorithms such as 3DES, RSA, or IDEA be used and prohibit use of proprietary or nonstandard algorithms.

- *E-mail policies* govern such matters as opening e-mail attachments, using e-mail clients configured to display Hypertext Markup Language (HTML) mail, forwarding internal e-mail to people outside the organization, and so forth.

- *Remote access policies* define rules for connecting to the company network from outside using dial-in or VPN connections, specify what remote authentication methods can be used, prohibit "dual homing" (being connected to another network while simultaneously being connected to the company network), and so forth.

- *Wireless access policies* set forth standards for connecting to the corporate network using wireless equipment, requiring use of Wireless Equivalent Privacy (WEP) or other encryption technologies, prohibiting connection of unauthorized wireless access points to the network, and so forth.

- *Acceptable use policies* define what users are allowed to do or are prohibited from doing on the network, governing personal use (such as Web surfing, sending personal e-mail), downloading files, posting to newsgroups, prohibiting installation of unauthorized software applications, and so forth. We discussed this type of policy in Chapter 5.

Many other policy areas could be applicable to specific organizations; defining policy areas to be addressed is an important task for the policy development team. You can view examples of policy documents that cover the areas mentioned (and others) on the SANS Institute's Security Policy Project resource page at www.sans.org/resources/policies/.

Developing the Policy Document

The policy development team should ideally be chosen prior to and be involved in the needs evaluation process. The team should comprise management and IT personnel, along with someone from each department within the organization. The team should include a legal advisor. As they begin to solidify and codify your policies, the team members must work closely together to:

- Establish security priorities based on the threat assessment matrix.

- Consider and incorporate security standards as needed.

- Determine the practices and procedures that are necessary to achieve the desired level of security at both the administrative and user levels.

- Clearly define both required and prohibited behaviors.

- Determine and define consequences for violations.

- Determine what policies are enforceable and methods for enforcement.

- Policies should represent a consensus as to what is and is not appropriate computer-related behavior.

Establishing Scope and Priorities

The policy development team should determine the scope of the policy document. For example, will policies regarding telephone, mobile phone, and fax use be included in the IT security policy or be part of a separate policy document? Will procedures for purchasing hardware and software be covered, or will this area be addressed in an overall organizational purchasing policy document? The easiest way to create a policy nightmare is to have two policy documents with conflicting directives.

Funds might not be available to address all security needs. Even if enough funds are allocated, most organizations will not be able to implement all security measures simultaneously. Thus, the team must establish priorities to determine which policies will be implemented first. Prioritization will be based on such factors as:

- Immediacy of the threat

- Potential loss

- Ease of implementation

- Available funding

We discussed immediacy of the threat and potential loss in the threat assessment section. Ease of implementation can also be a factor in prioritizing. Policies that can easily and quickly be implemented can be put in place first, while work begins on those that require more time and effort. Policies generally mandate one or more of the following: physical safeguards, technical security mechanisms, and/or administrative procedures. It can often be faster and easier to change administrative procedures than to implement physical safeguards (which could require purchase and setup of equipment or modifications to the facilities) or technical mechanisms (which could require purchase of software as well as a learning curve for IT personnel and users).

Policy Development Guidelines

Policies can be divided into different policy types: *regulatory policies*, which must be implemented to comply with the law or regulatory agency requirements; *advisory policies*, which are strongly recommended though not mandated; and *information policies*, which provide information but do not prescribe or proscribe any action.

Security policies can serve a number of secondary purposes in addition to the primary purpose of preventing unauthorized use of the network. For example, the policies can be the basis for personnel action (discipline or termination), can be used in the company's defense (or against it) in a civil lawsuit, and can even be instrumental in building a criminal case for prosecution. Thus, it is imperative that the policies that are finally published be well thought out, reasonable, and clearly articulated.

Policy writers should avoid technical jargon insofar as is possible; the security policies must be understandable to and usable by company managers, human resources personnel, and the users to whom they apply, as well as IT personnel. It's a good idea to include a glossary to define the technical terminology that is unavoidable. It is also important to create accountability; the person(s) responsible for each area of network/computer security and that person's scope of responsibility should be identified in the policy document.

Policies should state what actions are required, recommended, or prohibited. In addition to defining the action, they should give an example of behavior that would constitute that action, or a violation. For example, if the policy states, "Each user is required to protect the secrecy of his or her network logon password," it should give concrete examples such as, "Users are required to memorize their passwords. Users are prohibited from possessing any written record of their passwords anywhere on company property and are prohibited from divulging their passwords to any other person. If any person asks a user to divulge his or her password, the user is required to report the request to the network administrator immediately."

Policies should clearly state the consequences for violation. Consequences should be based on the severity of the violation, damage/loss caused, intent or lack thereof, and history of past violations. It's always important to ensure that the policies are consistent—not just with one another within the IT security policy document, but also with other company and departmental policies. Finally, it's imperative to make sure that policies don't conflict with any local, state, or federal laws.

Policy Document Organization

The policy document should not be a hodgepodge collection of security directives. It should be logically organized so that related policies are brought together under broadly defined areas. For example, sections might include:

- Physical security (placement of servers, installation of hardware, securing cabling, securing printers, location of backup tapes, and access to rooms/buildings where computer equipment is located)

- Local system security (users' responsibilities in regard to securing their own workstations, installation of software, and copying files)

- Password security (policies governing length of passwords, complexity of passwords, changing passwords, and protection of passwords)

- Network security (policies governing use of firewalls, downloading/uploading of files, Web access, and using instant messaging [IM] software)

- Server security (access to servers, protection of Web servers, file servers, DNS servers, and authentication servers)

- Remote access security (policies governing telecommuters, on-the-road executives, after-hours access from home, and designated VPN software and configurations)

- Data management and document-handling policies (policies that govern transferring and exchanging data, securing databases, modifying directory structures, creating/deleting files, naming files, and classifying data sensitivity)

- E-mail security (policies governing sending/receiving attachments, use of HTML mail, and e-mail client configuration settings)

- Software development policies (governing security and control over in-house software code)

- E-commerce security (governing online sales and purchases)

- Wireless communication security (policies governing standards for use of wireless devices on the network)

- Intranet and extranet policies (governing terms of access, acceptable use)

- Backup policies (scheduling, responsibility, retention, and storage)

- Disaster prevention and recovery policies (continuity of service, power backup)

- Policies governing security violations (responsibility to report, response handling)

- Policies governing employees who leave the company, both on friendly and on hostile terms (e.g., turning over equipment and access cards, deactivation of network accounts)

The policy document should contain a detailed table of contents. Each individual policy should have the following components:

- A title that describes clearly what the policy pertains to and a notation of any policy that it supercedes or replaces

- The effective date of the policy (and duration or expiration date if the policy is temporary)

- Reference to related policies

- A section stating the purpose or objective of the policy

- A section identifying the threat or vulnerability being addressed

- A brief summary of the policy

- A section that lays out in detail the policy itself—that is, defining the act or acts that are required or prohibited; this should include identification of people responsible for implementing the policy, to whom the policy applies, and any exceptions to the policy

- Signature of the authority issuing the policy

Educating Network Users on Security Issues

The best security policies in the world will be ineffective if the network users are not aware of them or if the policies are so restrictive and place so many inconveniences on users that users go out of their way to attempt to circumvent them. The security plan itself should contain a program for educating network users—not just as to what the policies are, but *why* they are important and how the users benefit from them. Users should also be instructed in the best ways to comply with the policies and what to do if they are unable to comply or if they observe other users deliberately violating the policies. If users are involved in the planning and policy-making stages, it will be much easier to educate them and gain their support for the policies at the implementation and enforcement stages.

Policy Enforcement

To be effective, policies must be enforceable, and they must be enforced consistently. Policies that are unenforceable (perhaps because you don't have the means to detect violations) or that you are not willing to enforce are worse than useless; their existence undermines the credibility of the rest of the policies. Enforcement must not be selective; if exceptions to the policies are necessary for certain people or in certain circumstances, those exceptions should be laid out in the policy itself.

Enforcement authority should be divided among a number of people to provide a system of checks and balances. Employees should be made aware of who is responsible for policy enforcement, and the enforcement team must be given the authority to carry out the job (for example, the authority to monitor e-mail and Web access). Employees should be informed within the policy document that they may be subject to such monitoring.

Policy Dissemination

Copies of the IT security policy should be distributed to all personnel to whom the policies apply. All employees should be required to sign a statement acknowledging that they have received, have read, and agree to abide by the terms of the policy. Amendments to the policy should be distributed, and the distribution should be documented in the same way. This is important in the event that disciplinary action is taken against an employee for violation of the policy.

Copies of the policy can also be made available to organizational personnel in electronic format. This should be in addition to, not instead of, the procedure recommended earlier. One of the easiest ways to do this is on the intranet in HTML format. This allows the policy maker to create hyperlinks to reference documents and cross-reference related policies, and it makes it easy for users to search the document(s) for keywords and phrases. Security awareness and training policies might also be included and should specify required training for different levels of personnel (permanent staff members, temporary staff members, contractors, management, technical personnel, users of new systems, and so on).

Ongoing Assessment and Policy Update

The security policy is not a static document. Company business practices and priorities change, and new types of threats emerge as hackers learn new ways of accessing or attacking networks. The policy document should be reviewed on a regular basis and revised when necessary to meet new challenges and adapt to changing circumstances. The document itself should include a policy outlining the schedule for review, the person responsible for conducting the review, and the procedure for amending the document, as well as the procedure for disseminating changes to all affected personnel throughout the organization.

Summary

An understanding of basic security concepts gives a cybercrime investigator a distinct advantage in communicating intelligently with IT personnel and a better idea of exactly how a cybercrime was committed, based on the security measures in place at the time. Additionally, investigators should be proactive in helping the victims of cybercrime protect themselves against subsequent attacks. Although the investigator probably cannot and will not be expected to provide in-depth advice about the technical implementation of security systems, he or she should be able to discuss options in a general way and point crime victims in the right direction with some general suggestions.

A good investigator, like a good network security specialist or a good crime prevention officer, realizes that any security plan must be multilayered for it to be effective. It is important that all major security areas be addressed. These include physical security, perimeter security (through placement of firewalls at the network's entry points), security of data stored on disks (through file/disk encryption), security of data traveling across the network (through IP security), and a means of verifying the identities of users, computers, and other entities that have access to network resources (through the building of a PKI).

Many security technologies are based on or use cryptographic techniques. An investigator might encounter encrypted data or even suspect that the existence of additional data is being concealed using steganography. An understanding of how cryptography developed and how it works in the computerized environment can be invaluable in investigating many types of cybercrime. Knowing a little about different encryption types and the algorithms they use allows the investigator to assess just how secure a particular system is—whether it belongs to a cybercrime victim or to a cybercrime suspect.

Finally, it's useful for the investigator to understand the process involved in creating and deploying organizational security policies and to see samples of such policies to understand the "big picture" of where the policies came from (revealing the organization's overall security philosophy) and exactly how security is deployed within the organization to help narrow the focus of the investigation. A good cybercrime investigator has at least a surface knowledge of all aspects of IT security. He or she need not be a hands-on IT professional but should be able to "talk the talk" and understand what's being said when the real IT pros offer information about their organization's network.

Frequently Asked Questions

Q: Is it a good idea for an organization to buy encryption software that uses "secret" algorithms?

A: No. Most security experts advise that only well-known, trusted, and tested algorithms be used. Although a vendor may claim that its product is more secure because the algorithms it uses are proprietary or secret, in reality proprietary algorithms are considered to be generally unsafe. Most of the best algorithms are public ones; knowing the algorithm doesn't help a hacker crack the encryption if the cipher is a strong one. If a vendor doesn't want to make its algorithm public, that might mean the vendor isn't confident that the algorithm can stand up to public scrutiny.

Q: Is a firewall a foolproof, all-encompassing security method?

A: There is *no* foolproof, all-encompassing security method; the only effective security plan is one that uses multiple layers of security. A firewall is an important part of such a plan. It provides protection at the perimeter of the network, but firewalls don't protect against many types of security breaches, such as internal breaches, physical breaches, or intrusions caused by compromise of user passwords. The Firewall FAQ site (www.faqs.org/faqs/firewalls-faq) notes that many organizations place a firewall on the network and think they're protected when there are numerous other vulnerabilities (such as dial-up modems on individual computers), similar to a person who has a 6-foot-thick steel door installed in a wooden house with unlocked windows. Firewalls also don't usually do a very good job of protecting against viruses and Trojans. On the other hand, the better firewalls *do* allow for very granular filtering of both incoming and outgoing data at different levels, based on the organization's needs. Every business network (and home computers that are connected to the Internet) should have some sort of firewall. Firewall products range from proprietary hardware appliances that cost thousands of dollars or high-end software firewalls that cost hundreds of dollars to simple freeware and shareware products that are suitable for home use. Windows XP and Vista even come with a built-in firewall; although it is a simple one that shouldn't be relied on to protect mission-critical systems.

Chapter 13

Implementing System Security

Topics we'll investigate in this chapter:

- **Implementing Broadband Security Measures**

- **Implementing Web Server Security**

- **Understanding Operating System Security**

- **Understanding Mainframe Security**

- **Understanding Wireless Security**

- **Understanding Physical Security**

☑ **Summary**

☑ **Frequently Asked Questions**

Introduction

Cybercrime is possible because computers and networks are not properly secured. Law enforcement officers know that most criminals look for "easy" prey—that is, pickpockets look for victims who fail to secure their wallets or purses, and burglars hit the residences and businesses that take fewer steps to secure their property. It should come as no surprise that cybercriminals do the same. Most attacks against computer systems and networks exploit well-known vulnerabilities—vulnerabilities that, in many cases, can be fixed with a simple patch or configuration change. Often, applying these simple security measures costs nothing. Yet computer users and network administrators are as lax in protecting their valuable data as many citizens are in protecting their personal property. The fact that these known exploits still work most of the time shows that most individuals and companies are not performing due diligence in protecting their information technology (IT) assets before connecting them to the Internet.

There are many reasons for this behavior, including:

- The average computer user's lack of knowledge of security issues

- Busy network professionals' lack of time (the "I really meant to get around to it" syndrome)

- Psychological denial that leads people who are aware of the risk to think that even though such things happen, "it can't happen to me"

Of course, none of these reasons is good enough to justify potential loss due to cybercrime, and that fact hits home with a vengeance *after* the network and its data have been compromised. It's important to realize that it's not just naïve individuals or small businesses on tight budgets that neglect their security needs. Unfortunately, many companies are like the police agencies that "can't afford" to buy body armor for their officers—until one of their own is killed in a shooting. Human nature is such that it often takes a tragedy to motivate people in charge to take action.

How Can Systems Be Secured?

System security is not a *thing*; it's a *process*—the process of building a barrier between the network and those who would do it harm. The key is to make your barrier more difficult to cross than someone else's. In other words, IT security involves creating a deterrent to convince a would-be intruder or attacker that your system is more difficult to breach than some other system. However, if an attacker specifically wants to breach your security perimeter, given enough time, he or she will be able to do so.

Crime prevention officers tell residents at neighborhood watch meetings that there is no way to make a home completely impervious to burglars—and if you could, it would be a windowless fortress that would be unpleasant to live in. No lock will keep out someone who's determined to break in, but what good locks *will* do is slow an intruder. If you make it difficult enough to get in, a typical burglar will go elsewhere, looking for quicker and easier pickings. Likewise, no computer or network can ever be 100 percent secure unless it is disconnected from every communication interface and completely powered off—and of course, such a fully secured system is also completely useless to the user. What system security methods *can* do is raise the break-in difficulty level to the point where most would-be intruders will take their attacks somewhere else—especially because they'll find no shortage of networks that they can break into with little effort.

NOTE

Understanding that IT security cannot be 100 percent effective should focus your efforts on establishing the best security you can afford, rather than wasting your time and money searching for the "perfect" security solution.

The Security Mentality

Security is not something you can install right off the shelf, nor is it something you can ever achieve or complete. Security is an ongoing course of action that involves continually improving, tuning, and adjusting your systems to protect against new vulnerabilities and attacks. You cannot view security as a characteristic limited to computers, either; security must be an end-to-end solution. For your enterprise to be secure, you must address everything: computers, networking devices, connectivity media, boundary devices, communication devices, operating systems, applications, services, protocols, people, physical access, and the relationships among all of these components of your business.

A good network security specialist has at least one thing in common with a good law enforcement officer: Both are naturally suspicious—sometimes almost to the point of paranoia. Both subscribe to the philosophy that it's better to be safe than sorry. A security-conscious network professional sees a potential attack in every security hole. This can be annoying to other network users, just as a police officer's insistence on sitting with a clear view of the door can be annoying to civilian friends and family members. However, considering every possible threat is part of the job—both jobs. After all, just because you're paranoid doesn't mean they *aren't* out to get you—or your data!

On the Scene

Developing a Defensive Mindset

Early in their training, most law enforcement officers become familiar with the color codes that identify differing mental states of alertness. This color system is usually attributed to Colonel Jeff Cooper, a legendary firearms and personal defense expert, and is used to represent mental "conditions" as follows:

- **Condition White** Describes the mindset of most people as they go about their daily business, oblivious to possible danger and wrapped up in their own thoughts and activities

Continued

- **Condition Yellow** Describes the optimum mindset for self-protection under ordinary circumstances—relaxed but alert and looking for signs of potential danger

- **Condition Orange** Describes the mindset a person should be in when known dangers exist (for example, when walking down a street at night in a high-crime area), constantly scanning for possible threats and ready to escalate to a higher state if necessary

- **Condition Red** Describes the mindset of a person who has encountered a threat (or, as police officers put it, when the proverbial waste byproducts have already hit the oscillating instrument); in this condition, the body experiences an adrenaline rush and the person reacts—usually—in one of two ways: fight or flight

We can borrow these "mindset" codes to describe the state of our network's security. Unfortunately, too many networks operate in Condition White, with administrators and users oblivious to the many threats that exist. For our purposes, Condition Yellow is probably not enough to adequately protect computer systems and networks; any network that is connected to the Internet must be considered to be in a known high-crime area. Thus, network security professionals should remain in Condition Orange, a heightened state of alertness, constantly on the lookout for threats and ready to respond when (not if) intrusions or attacks occur.

Elements of System Security

System security is about much more than just keeping out malicious users and preventing attacks. It is also about maintaining and providing access to resources for authorized users, and it is about maintaining the integrity of the data and the infrastructure. These related but separate elements of system security are described using four terms: *authentication*, *confidentiality*, *integrity*, and *availability*. If network administrators fail to properly manage any one of these elements, they will fail in the task of providing security for the IT infrastructure.

Successfully designing, deploying, and maintaining security requires mastery of an ever-expanding body of knowledge. This book couldn't possibly provide you with all the details of locking down even a *single* operating system, much less the entire IT infrastructure of a small company or enterprise corporation. However, we can highlight some of the big issues you face in your security efforts.

Implementing Broadband Security Measures

Broadband is one of the buzzwords in Internet connectivity today. Broadband technologies have made it possible for both home users and small office networks to obtain reasonably high data-throughput rates at relatively low cost. According to a May 2006 report by the Pew Internet & American Life Project (www.pewinternet.org/pdfs/PIP_Broadband_trends2006.pdf), the widespread availability and implementation of broadband connectivity have made high-speed connections more prevalent. At least 42 percent of adults in the United States (84 million people) had a high-speed connection, and of these people, 50 percent use DSL and 41 percent use cable modems. As more end-users (customers) gained access to greater bandwidth, Web sites began to offer more resources, more multimedia content, and more volume than was feasible for slower modem connections.

However, a great deal of confusion, even among IT professionals, has arisen about what broadband really is. The term is sometimes used to refer to any high-speed connection, but it has a specific technical meaning. *Broadband* refers to a connection technology that uses multiple frequencies over a common networking medium (such as the coaxial cable used for cable television, or CATV) to exploit all available bandwidth. This allows data to be *multiplexed* so that it can travel on different frequencies (or channels) simultaneously and more data can be transmitted in a specified period of time than with *baseband* (one-channel) technologies such as Ethernet. Broadband is also sometimes called *wideband*.

NOTE

In addition to *broadband* and *baseband*, you'll sometimes hear the term *narrowband*. This term is often used to refer to technologies that carry only voice communications. In radio communications, narrowband refers to the 50cps to 64Kbps frequency range allocated by the Federal Communications Commission (FCC) for paging and mobile radio services.

Some factors that affect the data transmission capacity of a communications medium include its frequency range and the *quality* (or signal-to-noise ratio) of the connection. A single channel has a fixed capacity within those parameters, but capacity can be increased by increasing the number of communications channels. This is how broadband works.

Cable modems deliver a common form of broadband Internet connectivity. And in fact, cable has many advantages as an Internet technology. Cable companies have extensive network infrastructures in place for transmission of television programming. Because it is a broadband technology, computer data signals can be sent over the cable on their own frequency, just as each TV channel's signal travels over its own frequency. Cable Internet typically offers speeds ranging from 500Kbps to 1.5Mbps (roughly equivalent to T1, at prices at least 10 times lower), and the technology is capable of much higher speeds—up to 10Mbps or more.

Despite its advantages, cable has some significant disadvantages, including the following:

- Some cable companies' lines are capable of only one-way transmission (which, after all, is all that's needed for transmitting TV programs). In this case, users must send upstream messages via a regular analog phone line; only the downstream data comes over the cable. Fortunately, most cable companies have upgraded their infrastructures to support two-way transmission.

- Even with two-way cable, many cable companies throttle upstream bandwidth to 128Kbps. This is to prevent users from running Internet servers (which is also often prohibited by the subscribers' terms-of-service agreements).

- Another disadvantage, in some areas, is lack of reliability. The cable network might be "down" a lot, leaving users without an Internet connection for periods of time. Unlike expensive business solutions such as leased lines, no guaranteed uptime (or guaranteed bandwidth) is included in a typical cable contract for Internet access.

- Perhaps the most serious disadvantage comes from the fact that cable is a "shared bandwidth" technology. This means that all subscribers in any immediate area share the same connection medium. In other words, everyone in a neighborhood is connected to the same subnet and therefore has the potential to become a security threat to any other system in that neighborhood. This is the primary weakness of cable Internet technology. Keep in mind that to launch an attack against a computer you must be able to communicate with that computer. Being connected to the same network medium facilitates—some might even argue that it enables—malicious communications among those computers.

Digital Subscriber Line (DSL) technology provides broadband Internet connectivity over telephone lines. Asymmetric DSL (ADSL), the most widely available form of DSL, uses a signal coding technique called *discrete multitone* that divides a pair of copper wires in an ordinary telephone line into 256 subchannels. Via this technique, data can be transmitted at more than 8Mbps—but only for a relatively short distance, due to attenuation. The frequencies used are above the voice band; this means that both voice and data signals travel over the same phone line at the same time.

NOTE

For more information about how DSL works, see www.howstuffworks.com/dsl.htm.

Broadband Integrated Services Digital Network (B-ISDN) is another broadband technology that uses telephone lines. In this case, however, these are fiber optic phone lines rather than copper wiring. B-ISDN provides data transmission speeds of up to 1.5Mbps. The original ISDN technology was once intended to replace analog voice lines with digital lines, which are more reliable and less vulnerable to "noise" (interference). There are two types of ISDN services: Basic Rate Interface (BRI) and Primary Rate Interface (PRI). BRI is more often used by consumers and small businesses. It provides two channels (called *B channels* or *bearer channels*) on which data or voice can be transmitted at 64Kbps. These two channels can be used separately so that you can connect to the Internet at 64Kbps and use the other line for voice calls at the same time, or they can be aggregated to give you a 128KB data transmission rate. Another channel, called the *D channel* or *data channel*, is 16Kbps and manages signaling. PRI is much more expensive than BRI but provides more bandwidth: twenty-three 64Kbps B channels plus one 64Kbps D channel, for a total capacity of 1.5Mbps (this applies to the United States; in Europe, PRI provides 1.98Mbps).

DSL and ISDN connections are not shared connections. Instead, the connection medium is used only by the two endpoints of the connection. Because there are only two parties in these connections, they offer a more secure means of communication than cable modem. Those to whom security is important—and that should include everyone who uses the Internet—should opt for an unshared connectivity option if it is available and affordable. Satellite Internet technologies can also provide always-on Internet access at speeds of up to about 500Kbps in areas where cable and DSL aren't available. Satellite is available almost anywhere, as long as you have an unobstructed view of the sky where the satellite is located. (This is required because satellite is a line-of-sight technology.)

Broadband Security Issues

The benefits of high-speed broadband connectivity are complicated by problems and vulnerabilities unique to broadband. These issues arose directly out of the broadband implementation and were not palpable threats to the dial-up modem community. One threat is the always-connected aspect of broadband. No longer do users have to manually initiate a connection when they want to surf the Web or access e-mail, because broadband connections are always on. In the past, modem users typically disconnected from the Internet once they completed their online sessions. This removed their computers from the Internet and prevented crackers from accessing their systems or mounting attacks against them. With broadband connections that remain up 24/7 and automatically reconnect when interrupted, a computer is now available to be attacked on an ongoing basis.

A second aspect of this always-connected issue is the Internet Protocol (IP) address assigned to a system. With dial-up modem connectivity, a PC is usually configured to use Dynamic Host Configuration Protocol (DHCP) to obtain its address and is assigned a different IP address each time the connection is established. Thus, a modem-connected PC that has one address today will usually have a different address tomorrow, and the address it used yesterday will be assigned to a different system today. This makes tracking individual systems difficult. However, with broadband connectivity, systems using DHCP are connected for days or weeks at a time and are able to continually renew their assigned IP addresses so that their online identifiers remain consistent over a long period of time. They may also be assigned a static IP address, meaning that the IP address never changes. This makes tracking a specific system extremely easy.

Law enforcement officers can easily understand the impact on detection and apprehension; many traditional criminals—especially scam artists—are always on the move, living in motel rooms or with friends and changing addresses every few weeks or months. These offenders are much more difficult to track down than those who have established a permanent residence and a fixed address. The same is true of cybercriminals. The ones who use static (consistent) IP addresses are easier to find than those with ever-changing addresses. Although there are ways for technically savvy criminals to disguise their IP addresses, the advent of broadband, with a greater likelihood of static addressing, makes the investigator's job easier when dealing with cybercriminals who are less knowledgeable about the technology.

On the other hand, the longer a system remains online, especially when it retains the same IP address, the more vulnerable that system is to repeat brute force and port-scanning attacks. Given enough time, every system can be breached, even if security-conscious administrators have taken standard precautions such as deploying a firewall, installing patches, and assigning strong passwords. Remember, security is a deterrent—it is not an impenetrable barrier. Given enough time and determination, any security measure can be breached.

Simply powering down the computer when it's not in use isn't enough to protect against these threats. Through the power of automation, crackers can continuously scan an IP address to determine when the computer is on or off. Yes, it is possible to prevent the attack from progressing while the PC is powered down, but the attack can resume right where it left off once the system boots back up. Instead of relying on "security through obscurity" (attempting to hide the existence of a system or data from an attacker), you can take numerous proactive steps to reduce your vulnerability to broadband-specific attacks. We discuss these steps in the next section.

It might sound strange, but another flaw in broadband security is the speed at which it allows data to flow. First, this speed allows a faster attack against your system. A malicious user can send a significantly greater amount of data to your system over a broadband connection than is possible over a dial-up modem connection. Second, once your system is compromised, it takes an attacker less time to download or upload files.

Obviously, broadband connectivity has its drawbacks. But for many Internet users, it still offers an irresistible promise of lightning-fast connectivity at very low cost. It's important to first recognize that there is a problem and then take specific risk reduction measures, so in this section, we not only point out the flaws but also offer guidance on reducing the risks associated with using broadband connectivity.

When implementing risk-reducing strategies such as improving security, you must take into account the specific hardware and software configuration of each computer. This includes the operating system in use, the applications installed, and the services used on the connected computer. Implementing security precautions on just one aspect of your system does not provide adequate security. You must deploy a multilayered security solution so that there will be numerous barriers to unauthorized access.

> **NOTE**
>
> We discussed the concept of multilayered security in Chapter 12.

When a large company contracts with an Internet service provider (ISP) for a high-speed bandwidth connection, security is probably the most important item in the service contract. However, individual customers (and many small businesses) who obtain low-cost broadband connections often overlook security. This oversight primarily stems from the fact that few individuals or small-company employees are trained security professionals, and they simply don't know any better. Even when they have a vague idea that there are security risks they should be addressing, they might be overwhelmed by the complexity of the topic and the sheer number of competing security "solutions" available, as well as the high cost of implementing many such recommended solutions. The promise of fast Internet downloads for little cost blinds many users to other important issues, such as security and privacy, which should be carefully considered before broadband deployment.

In the following sections, we discuss specific risk-reducing strategies you can employ to improve the security of your computer or network using broadband connectivity. Readers who are implementing broadband must also consider the issues that we raise later in this chapter, when we discuss how to secure specific operating systems.

Deploying Antivirus Software

Security has many facets, two of which are the need to prevent *unauthorized* access and the need to support *authorized* access. All too often, the prevention of attacks comes at the expense of ensuring access to data by valid users. It is important to keep a balanced perspective when deploying any security measure. Think of security in terms of the popular policing motto, "To protect and to serve." If your security implementation fails to adequately support either of these elements, protecting your data and serving your authorized users, you have failed to implement a truly effective security plan.

This is a challenge because security and availability will always be at opposite ends of the continuum. The more you have of one, the less you have of the other. However, you *must* strike a balance, because a security policy that is too restrictive could have the same result as one that is too lax—that is, a negative (perhaps even catastrophic) impact on the company's bottom line.

Maintaining the *integrity* of your data so that it can be served to authorized users is just as important as preventing unwanted outsiders from stealing it. Many things—including human error, disgruntled employees, and even hardware failure—can threaten your data's integrity. But the most serious, prevalent, and imminent threat is corruption, destruction, or alteration of data by virus infection. A broadband connection is just as likely as a local area network (LAN) link or a dial-up connection to be a pathway for virus infection. No matter how your computer is connected to the Internet or other systems, you must protect it from viruses.

CyberCrimeStopper

One Hundred Percent Virus-Free E-mail

E-mail is the number-one virus delivery mechanism today, so it is essential to keep as much malicious e-mail out of your network as possible. With the increasing reliance on e-mail for commercial and private communications, balancing security against availability can be especially difficult in regard to electronic mail.

Some companies provide solutions to this problem. For example, MessageLabs offers a service that guarantees 100 percent virus-free e-mail delivered to your e-mail servers. This guarantee is based on MessageLabs' ability to adequately screen inbound e-mail for any possible virus infection or carrier agent. This task is accomplished by routing your inbound e-mail to one of the company's control tower systems. There each message is inspected by at least three antivirus (AV) solutions from reliable vendors as well as an artificial intelligence search tool that relies on heuristics, pattern matching, signature matching, and traffic flow analysis to detect unknown viral threats. After a delay of about 1.5 seconds, your e-mail is then delivered to your internal e-mail servers for distribution on your network. MessageLabs maintains an excellent track record for making good on promises. For more information, visit the company's Web site at www.messagelabs.com.

When striving to protect your data's integrity, you can obtain no greater bang for your buck than that gained by deploying reliable AV software. When selecting such a product, look for the following:

- The product should originate from a well-known, reputable company.
- The product should automatically update its virus definitions.

- The product should scan stored files, memory (RAM), removable media, e-mail, and Web-transmitted data.

- The product should clean or quarantine any infected files it detects.

Whenever possible, deploy two or more virus solutions together on the network, to work as a layered system. However, do not install two AV tools on the same computer, because doing so can often cause the system to crash or behave erratically. Many organizations opt to place an AV product on each border system (firewall, gateway, proxy, and so on), on each server, and on each client. This multilayered approach provides more thorough protection and eliminates the problems that can come with reliance on a single vendor's solution.

NOTE

We discuss viruses, Trojans, and other malicious code and provide additional information on how to protect systems from these threats in Chapter 10.

Defining Strong User Passwords

Only two elements are necessary to gain access to most computer systems: a user identity (username) and its associated password. Most usernames are obvious or very easy to guess—a person's first name, first initial and last name, or the like—and are therefore not confidential. Thus, access authorization is likely to be based solely on the password. Passwords must be very strong and kept secured to maintain control over access. This is true whether your system is linked to a broadband connection, a LAN cable, or a dial-up link. Because broadband connections are always on, however, they offer a potential intruder much more time than a dial-up connection to carry out a brute force attack (which is essentially a trial-and-error method that attempts various character combinations until the attacker stumbles onto one that works).

In Chapter 11, we discussed in detail how to create strong passwords that are difficult to crack and how to set and enforce password policies to ensure that none of the passwords in use in your organization creates an "easy in" for intruders.

Setting Access Permissions

Controlling access is an important element in maintaining system security. The most secure environments follow the "least privileged" principle. This principle states that users are granted the least amount of access possible that still enables them to complete their required work tasks. Expansions to that access are carefully considered before being implemented. Law enforcement officers are familiar with this principle in regard to noncomputerized information; this concept is usually termed *need to know*. Generally, following this principle means that the network administrators hear more complaints from users about being unable to access resources. However, hearing complaints from authorized users is better than hearing about access violations that damage an organization's profitability or its capability to conduct business. We discussed establishing and enforcing access policies in more detail in Chapter 12, and we will discuss access control for wireless networks later in this chapter.

Disabling File and Print Sharing

The ability to share files and printers with other members of your network can make many tasks simpler and, in fact, was the original purpose for networking computers in the first place. However, this ability also has a dark side—especially when users are unaware that they're sharing resources. If a trusted user can gain access, the possibility exists that a malicious user can obtain access as well. On systems linked by broadband connections, crackers have all the time they need to connect to your shared resources and exploit them.

File and Print Sharing allows others to access files and printers on your Windows operating system across the network. When enabled, the service provides access to files and printers attached to the machine. In Windows NT Server, Windows Server 200x, XP, and Vista, this is controlled by the Server service, and in nonserver Windows operating systems prior to XP, the File and Print Sharing service controls this ability.

Shared resources are advertised but may not offer security to restrict who is able to see and access those shares. Setting permissions on the shares controls such security. On older Windows operating systems, when a share is created, by default the permissions are set to give full control over the resource to the Everyone group—which includes literally everyone who accesses that system. Sharing a folder in Windows XP is somewhat different. Not only does it use the Server service, but it only provides Read permissions to the Everyone group, meaning that anyone can view and copy files from the shared directory, but not add, modify, or delete files in that folder. Windows Vista has gone a step further, providing a folder named Public that can be used to store files that are used by everyone in the organization. With Public folder sharing enabled, any files and folders in the Public folder are available to others on the network. However, unlike Windows XP, Vista does not allow simple file sharing. Any shared folders including the Public folder require a username and password.

Windows Vista provides a Network and Sharing Center tool that allows you to turn the following on and off:

- File sharing
- Public folder sharing
- Printer sharing
- Password-protected sharing
- Media sharing

If the user doesn't need to share resources with anyone on the internal (local) network, these options should be set to off. Similarly, File and Print Sharing should be disabled on computers running older operating systems. On networks where security is important, sharing of resources should be disabled on all clients. This action forces all shared resources to be stored on network servers, which typically have better security and access controls than end-user client systems.

Using NAT

Network address translation (NAT) is a feature of many firewalls, proxies, and routing-capable systems. NAT has several benefits, one of which is its ability to hide the IP address and network design of the internal network. The ability to hide your internal network from the Internet reduces the risk of intruders gleaning information about your network and exploiting that information to gain access. If an intruder doesn't know the structure of a network, the network layout, the names and IP addresses of systems, and so on, it is very difficult to gain access to that network.

NAT enables internal clients to use nonroutable IP addresses, such as the private IP addresses defined in Request for Comments (RFC) 1918, but still enables them to access Internet resources. NAT restricts traffic flow so that only traffic requested or initiated by an internal client can cross the NAT system from external networks.

If only a single system is linked to the Internet with a broadband connection, NAT is of little use. However, for local networks that share a broadband connection, NAT's benefits can be utilized for security purposes. When using NAT, the internal addresses are reassigned to private IP addresses and the internal network is identified on the NAT host system. Once NAT is configured, external malicious users are only able to access the IP address of the NAT host that is directly connected to the Internet, but they are not able to "see" any of the internal computers that go through the NAT host to access the Internet.

On the Scene

Deploying a NAT Solution

NAT is relatively easy to implement, and there are several ways to do so. Many broadband hardware devices (cable and DSL modems) are called cable/DSL "routers" because they allow you to connect multiple computers. However, they are actually combination modem/NAT devices rather than routers because they require only one external (public) IP address. You can also buy NAT devices that attach your basic cable or DSL modem to the internal network. Alternatively, the computer that is directly connected to a broadband modem can use NAT software to act as the NAT device itself. This can be an add-on software program such as the Smart Firewall included in Symantec's Norton Internet Security, or the NAT software that is built into some operating systems.

When NAT is used to hide internal IP addresses, it is sometimes called a *NAT firewall*; however, don't let the word *firewall* give you a false sense of security. NAT by itself solves only one piece of the security perimeter puzzle. A true firewall does much more than link private IP addresses to public ones, and vice versa.

Deploying a Firewall

As we discussed in Chapter 12, a firewall is a device or a software product whose primary purpose is to filter traffic crossing the boundaries of a network. That boundary can be a broadband connection, a dial-up link, or some type of LAN or wide area network (WAN) connection. The network can be an enterprise LAN, a single system, or anything in between.

The most typical use for firewalls is to restrict what types of traffic can traverse the boundary connections of your network. Several types of firewalls or filtering mechanisms are available to handle this job: packet filters, stateful inspection systems, proxy systems, and circuit-level filtering.

You will recall that *packet filters*, also known as *screening routers*, decide what traffic is allowed or blocked based on information found in Transmission Control Protocol (TCP) headers. The information used from the TCP header is typically the source or destination IP address and the corresponding TCP or User Datagram Protocol (UDP) port. Packet filters are static, always open, and therefore unable to properly manage dynamic port applications. Furthermore, packet filters are unable to monitor sessions or traffic content.

Stateful inspection systems inspect the ongoing activities within active communication sessions to ensure that the type of traffic detected is valid. Stateful inspection was designed to address deficiencies in packet filters, specifically to ensure that traffic over dynamic ports is valid and authorized.

Proxy systems, also known as *application gateways* or *application firewalls*, are able to filter traffic based on high-level protocols (such as Hypertext Transfer Protocol, or HTTP; File Transfer Protocol, or FTP; Simple Mail Transfer Protocol, or SMTP; and Telnet), applications, or even specific control commands. Proxy systems work well with dynamic port applications, although unfortunately, some services and applications don't lend themselves well to being proxied. Proxy systems also lower the network performance due to the amount of processing involved with fully inspecting each packet.

Circuit-level filtering makes traffic decisions based on the content of the session rather than individual packets. Circuit-level filters open ports only when internal clients make requests, thus supporting dynamic port applications such as FTP. This type of filter supports a wider range of protocols than a proxy system, but it does not provide the detailed controls that a proxy system does.

When selecting a firewall to protect broadband connections, the user should seek a product with all these filtering capabilities as well as extensive logging and auditing features and alarms and alerts. Another good idea is to seek out products with NAT and intrusion detection capabilities.

For individual, stand-alone, or home systems, several fairly inexpensive personal firewall products provide adequate security for nonprofessional computer use, such as ZoneAlarm from Zone Labs. Operating systems such as Windows XP and Vista also include a built-in personal firewall feature. However, to protect a business network, administrators cannot rely on "personal" firewalls. Companies should invest in a heavy-duty firewall that provides a higher level of security and greater configurability. Deployment might be simplified if you contract with a security outsourcing company to install, configure, maintain, and administer your firewall.

Disabling Unneeded Services

One of the primary tenets for maintaining physical security in a residence or business property is to reduce the number of pathways an intruder can take to gain access to it. This reduction typically involves locking doors and windows, sealing off access tunnels, and securing ventilation shafts. Administrators should apply the same perspective in regard to the electronic pathways into the network. Any means by which valid data can reach the network or computer is also a potential path for a malicious intruder or attack.

Systems linked to the Internet by broadband connections should have any unneeded protocols, applications, and services either disabled or completely removed or uninstalled. With the proliferation of poor programming practices that often lead to security vulnerabilities, it is essential to limit exposure to potential threats simply by not having removed unessential software from the network's computer systems. For example, many versions of Windows automatically install a Web server during default OS installation. If a system is not specifically intended for use as a Web server, that component of the OS must be disabled.

Configuring System Auditing

When a system is compromised, one of two things occurs:

- Bad things happen and you are clearly aware of them (system crash, deleted files, or the like).

- Bad things happen and you are unaware of them (a hacker toolkit is downloaded to your system, a user account is compromised, or a similar security breach).

Waiting for clear indications of system violations to appear is a poor security practice, especially because unseen compromises usually result in more severe consequences. Law enforcement officers can relate this concept to the difference between *reactive policing*, in which a law enforcement agency waits until a crime is reported to go into action, and *proactive policing*, which involves activities designed to prevent crimes from occurring in the first place. We all know that the proactive method is more effective in fighting crime, but it has one drawback: It's a lot more work. Unfortunately, system administrators, police officers, and other human beings are often tempted to take the path that requires the least amount of effort, and that's why preventable crimes—including network security breaches—proliferate.

The only way to know when your system has been breached or when an unsuccessful attempt to penetrate your security has occurred is to monitor or audit for unusual or abnormal activity—just as patrol officers drive through the neighborhoods on their beats, looking for anything out of the ordinary. Most OSes include native auditing capabilities. For example, Windows servers and client operating systems provide for security auditing that is tracked through a security log available to administrators through the Event Viewer administrative tool. At a minimum, administrators should audit logons and logoffs, changes to user accounts and privileges, and use of administrative-level functions. These are activities that are often involved in a security breach and can serve as indicators when the computer or network has been compromised.

If the amount of data the auditing system gathers is too much to manage manually, as might be the case on enterprise networks, it could be beneficial to invest in an intrusion detection system (IDS). An IDS automates the tedious task of looking for abnormal or suspicious system activity. An IDS uses pattern recognition and heuristic learning to detect suspect activities by authorized user accounts as well as external malicious users.

Implementing Web Server Security

Most companies and organizations today have a Web presence on the Internet. An Internet presence offers numerous business advantages, such as the ability to reach a large audience with advertising, to interact with customers and partners, and to provide updated information to interested parties.

Web pages are stored on servers running Web services software such as Microsoft's Internet Information Server (IIS) or Apache (on Linux/UNIX servers). Web servers must be accessible via the Internet if the public is to be able to access their Web pages. However, this accessibility provides a point of entry to Internet "bad guys" who want to get into the network, so it is vitally important that Web servers be secured. Protecting a Web server is no small task. Systems attached to the Internet before they are fully "hardened" are usually detected and compromised within minutes. Malicious crackers are always actively searching for systems to infiltrate, making it essential that you properly lock down a Web server before bringing it online.

First and foremost, administrators should lock down the underlying operating system. This process includes applying updates and patches, removing unneeded protocols and services, and properly configuring all native security controls. We discuss some of the important issues related to specific OS lockdown procedures later in this chapter.

Second, it is wise to place the Web server behind a protective barrier, such as a firewall or a reverse proxy. Anything that will limit, restrict, filter, or control traffic into and out of the Web server reduces the means by which malicious users can attack the system.

Third, administrators must lock down the Web server itself. This process actually has numerous facets, each of which is important to maintaining a secure Web server. We discuss these topics in the following sections.

DMZ versus Stronghold

There are two general lines of thought when it comes to Web server security. One is to assume that the Web server will be compromised and to plan accordingly. The other is to try to prevent any and all possible attacks at all costs. The first philosophy utilizes a deployment design called a *demilitarized zone (DMZ)*; the second relies on a design referred to as a *stronghold*.

A DMZ is a networking area where your Web server (and other servers that are accessible via the public Internet) is secured from most known common exploits, but it is known to be insecure at some level. Because the DMZ is a separate network, the internal network remains more secure. A DMZ assumes that the time and money required to protect against every possible attack are too great an expense to offset the value of the data hosted on the Web server.

NOTE

Microsoft uses the term *screened subnet* to refer to the DMZ in some of its documentation. You'll also hear the same concept called a *perimeter network*.

To compensate for the lack of front-line security, organizations that deploy a DMZ configuration typically have a duplicate Web server positioned on their internal LAN that maintains a mirror image of the publicly accessible Web server. In the event that the primary Web server is compromised, the mirror backup can be repositioned to act as the public Web server until the primary system is repaired. Other companies employ an even less expensive solution by maintaining only tape backups of the primary Web server. Such a company might assume that the time and money lost while its Web server is offline will not significantly impact the organization. It also might assume that the value of its Web presence does not justify a more fault-tolerant solution, such as the expense of creating and maintaining a backup system.

A *stronghold* is a networking area where the Web server is protected from all known exploits and significant effort is expended to protect against unknown new exploits. A stronghold assumes that the data hosted on the Web server is valuable enough to spare no expense in protecting it. This type of configuration is often deployed by organizations whose Web server integrity and availability are essential to doing business, such as e-commerce sites.

Each organization must choose the protection policy that is appropriate to its situation and that fits its needs best. A DMZ deployment is cheaper but more prone to attack than a stronghold. A stronghold deployment is more expensive than a DMZ but will repel most attacks.

Isolating the Web Server

For security purposes, the Web server should be separated and isolated from the internal LAN. Otherwise, if the Web server is compromised, the attacker could get a free ticket into the entire network. Separating the Web server from the internal production network prevents Web attacks from becoming organization killers.

Separating the Web server from the LAN can take many forms, such as:

- Deploying a separate domain just for the Web server and its supporting services

- Using a Web-in-a-box solution that has no capabilities other than Web page service

- Co-locating Web servers at an ISP

- Outsourcing Web services to an ISP or other third party

No matter what method an organization chooses, it is also wise to consider creating a sideband communication channel for all management, administration, and file transfer activities. A sideband communication channel can be as simple as using a unique protocol between your LAN and the Web server and preventing (blocking via unbinding) Transmission Control Protocol/Internet Protocol (TCP/IP) from crossing that link. A sideband channel could be a dial-up link, a dedicated ISDN line, or even a direct-connect serial port link. Using a sideband channel restricts the traffic that can flow between the Web server and the internal network. This system could dampen the speed or the capabilities of remote administration; however, it greatly reduces the possibility that a malicious user can cross over from a compromised Web server to the LAN.

If security is of utmost importance, organizations can deploy a firewall on the sideband channel or eliminate direct communication completely. If the administrator must be physically present at the Web server and must transfer data to and from it using removable media. This completely eliminates the possibility of a malicious user employing the Web server as a bridge into the LAN.

Web Server Lockdown

Locking down the Web server itself follows a path that begins in a way that should already be familiar to you: applying the latest patches and updates from the vendor. Once this task is accomplished, the network administrator should follow the vendor's recommendations for securely configuring Web sites. The following sections discuss typical recommendations made by Web server vendors and security professionals.

Managing Access Control

Many Web servers, such as IIS on Windows servers, use a named user account to authenticate anonymous Web visitors. When a Web visitor accesses a Web site using this methodology, the Web server automatically logs that user on as the IIS user account. The visiting user remains anonymous, but the host server platform uses the IIS user account to control access. This account grants system administrators granular access control on a Web server.

These specialized Web user accounts should have their access restricted so that they cannot log on locally or access anything outside the Web root. Additionally, administrators should be very careful about granting these accounts the ability to write to files or execute programs; this should be done only when absolutely necessary. If other named user accounts are allowed to log on over the Web, it is essential that these accounts not be the same user accounts employed to log on to the internal network. In other words, if employees will log on via the Web using their own credentials instead of the anonymous Web user account, administrators should create special accounts for those employees to use just for Web logon. Authorizations over the Internet should be considered insecure unless strong encryption mechanisms are in place to protect them. Secure Sockets Layer (SSL) can be used to protect Web traffic; however, the protection it offers is not significant enough to protect internal accounts on the Internet.

Handling Directory and Data Structures

Planning the hierarchy or structure of the Web root is an important part of securing a Web server. The root is the highest-level web in the hierarchy that consists of webs nested within webs. Whenever possible, Web server administrators should place all Web content within the Web root. All the Web information (the Web pages written in Hypertext Markup Language (HTML), graphics files, sound files, and so on) is normally stored in folders and directories on the Web server. Administrators can create *virtual directories*, which are folders that are not contained within the Web server hierarchy (they can be on a completely different computer) but appear to the user to be part of that hierarchy. Another way of providing access to data that is on another computer is *mapping* drives or folders. These methods allow administrators to store files where they are most easily updated or take advantage of extra drive space on other computers. However, mapping drives, mapping folders, or creating virtual directories can result in easier access for intruders if the Web server's security is compromised. It is especially important not to map drives from other systems on the internal network.

If users accessing these webs must have access to materials on another system, such as a database, it is best to deploy a duplicate server within the Web server's DMZ or domain. That duplicate server should contain only a backup, not the primary working copy of the database. The duplicate server should also be configured so that no Web user or Web process can alter or write its data store. Database updates should come only from the protected server within the internal network. If data from Web sessions must be recorded into the database, it is best to configure a sideband connection from the Web zone back to the primary server system for data transfers. Administrators should also spend considerable effort verifying the validity of input data before adding it to the database server.

Scripting Vulnerabilities

Maintaining a secure Web server means ensuring that all scripts and Web applications deployed on the Web server are free from Trojans, backdoors, or other malicious code. Many scripts are available on the Internet for the use of Web developers. However, scripts downloaded from external sources are more susceptible to coding problems than those developed in-house. If it is necessary to use external programming code sources, developers and administrators should employ quality assurance tests to search for out-of-place system calls, extra code, and unnecessary functions. These hidden segments of malevolent code are called *logic bombs*.

One logic bomb to watch out for occurs within Internet Server Application Programming Interface (ISAPI) scripts. The command *RevertToSelf()* allows the script to execute any following commands at a system-level security context. In a properly designed script, this command should never be used. If this command is present, the code has been altered, or was designed by a malicious or inexperienced coder. The presence of such a command enables attacks on a Web server through the submission of certain Uniform Resource Locator (URL) syntax constructions to launch a logic bomb.

Logging Activity

Logging, auditing, or monitoring the activity on your Web server becomes more important as the value of the data stored on the server increases. The monitoring process should focus on attempts to perform actions that are atypical for a Web user. These actions include, among others:

- Attempting to execute scripts
- Trying to write files
- Attempting to access files outside the Web root

The more traffic your Web server supports, the more difficult it becomes to review the audit trails. An automated solution is needed when the time required to review log files exceeds the time administrators have available for that task. IDSes are automated monitoring tools that look for abnormal or malicious activity on a system. An IDS can simply scan for problems and notify administrators or actively repel attacks once they are detected.

Backups

Unfortunately, every administrator should assume that the Web server will be compromised at some point and that the data hosted on it will be destroyed, copied, or corrupted. This assumption will not become a reality in all cases, but planning for the worst is always the best security practice. A reliable backup mechanism must be in place to protect the Web server from failure. This mechanism can be a real-time mirror server to back up the primary Web server or just a daily backup to tape. Either way, a backup is the only insurance available that allows a return to normal operations within a reasonable amount of time. If security is as much maintaining availability as it is maintaining confidentiality, backups should be part of any organization's security policy.

Maintaining Integrity

Locking down the Web server is only one step in the security process. It is also necessary to maintain that security over time. Sustaining a secure environment requires monitoring the system for anomalies, applying new patches when they are available, and adjusting security configurations to match the ever-changing needs of the internal and external Web communities. If a security breach occurs, the organization should reevaluate previous security decisions and implementations. Administrators could have overlooked a security because of ignorance, or they might have simply misconfigured some security control.

Rogue Web Servers

There is one thing worse for a network administrator than having a Web server and knowing that it is not 100 percent secure, even after locking it down, and that is having a Web server on the network that you're not aware exists. These are sometimes called *rogue Web servers*, and they can come about in two ways. It is possible that a technically savvy user on the network has configured Web services on his or her machine. More often, however, rogue Web servers are deployed unintentionally. Many operating systems include Web server software and install it as part of the default OS installation, or they can be accidentally installed if the Web server is selected as an option. If administrators aren't careful, when they install Windows (especially a member of the Server family) on a network computer, they can create a new Web server without even realizing it's there. When a Web server is present on a network without the knowledge of network administrators, no one will take all the precautions necessary to secure that system. This makes the system (and through it, the entire network) vulnerable to every out-of-the-box exploit and attack for that Web server.

CyberCrimeStopper

Hunting Down Rogue Web Servers

To check a system to see whether a local Web server is running without your knowledge, you can use a Web browser to access http://localhost/. If no Web server is running, you should see an error stating that you are unable to access the Web server. If you see any other message or a Web page (including a message advising that the page is under construction or coming soon), you are running a Web server locally. Once you discover the existence of such a server, you must either secure it or remove or disable it. Otherwise, the system will remain insecure.

Understanding Operating System Security

Regardless of the operating system being used, you should take certain steps to ensure that the system is up-to-date and secure. These include:

- Installing patches and service packs
- Verifying user account security

- Removing any applications and network services that aren't required (and installing and configuring only the applications and network services that are required)

- Configuring logging to record significant events

- Backing up important data

Installing Patches and Service Packs

Even if you've just installed the latest version of an operating system, it's possible that the system is already out-of-date. This is especially true if the operating system is an older one, or one that was released a number of months or years previous. Operating systems are often released with bugs and vulnerabilities that were either known or overlooked when the operating systems were made available on the market. The reasoning for this is that patches and service packs can be released to fix the problem.

With many applications and operating systems, there is a need to visit the vendor's Web site to determine what patches and updates are available. Microsoft provides an easy solution to downloading and installing patches through the Windows Update site. In Internet Explorer, you can click on the **Tools** menu and then click the **Windows Update** menu item. In Windows Vista, you can also click on **Start | All Programs | Windows Update**. Doing so will take you to www.update.microsoft. com. Here, using a combination of scripts and ActiveX components, the site can analyze your system to determine what updates are needed for Windows and Internet Explorer, allowing you to then download and install them. By installing the *Microsoft Update* tool, it can also identify whether updates are required for Microsoft Office, SQL Server, and other Microsoft applications installed on your computer.

Systems running Windows XP and Vista can also use the Automatic Updates feature. Turning on this feature will allow the computer to automatically connect to Microsoft's Web site and download any necessary updates. The feature can be turned on from the computer, or by clicking a link on the Windows Update site.

Network administrators may not wish to allow users to update their own machines, and often download the necessary updates. These updates can then be applied remotely, or by making configurations that allow the updates to be installed automatically when the user logs on, or uses a particular tool (as in the case of Novell NetWare where software can be automatically installed when the user accesses the ZENworks application launcher). An alternative is to use tools such as Offline Update, a freeware tool that downloads updates for the operating systems you specify, including Windows 2000, XP, Vista, and Server 2003, as well as updates for Microsoft Office 2003 and 2007. Once downloaded, Offline Update can write an International Organization for Standardization (ISO) file that can be burned to a CD or DVD, allowing you to install updates from the CD or DVD without connecting to the Internet.

Verifying User Account Security

A number of different accounts are common to operating systems, and some applications that require usernames and passwords, which should be modified immediately after installation. A Guest account is often used for temporary users, and this should be disabled to prevent unauthorized users from gaining entry. If a temporary user account is needed, you should change the name from "Guest" (which is well known and easy for hackers to guess) to something less obvious. Another common account name is "Administrator" or "Admin," which is used for administration of the computer and has the highest level of access. Because hackers can guess the name of this well-known account name, it too should be changed to a less obvious username. A strong password should also be set for the account for both of these accounts, if they are used and enabled.

Just as the Administrator account provides full access to the system, an Administrator group may also be used on the computer's operating system or the network operating system. The Administrator group provides the highest level of access to any users who are part of this group, but administrative privileges should be limited to only those who need them. Many computer users log on to the operating system using an account with this level of access, or the actual Administrator account. This means that the user could install programs that he or she doesn't need and that could contain viruses or Trojan horses. Also, because any malware installed on the machine would have the same privileges as the user who's logged on to the machine, this means the malware would be able to access anything on the system.

It is important that users have only the level of access they need to perform their work, or in the case of home users, perform the actions they'd do on a regular basis. Each user should have his or her own account, and should have a password set. This will prevent anyone with physical access to the machine from using the computer, and in the case of network accounts from accessing network resources.

Removing Applications That Aren't Required

As we mentioned earlier, operating systems often have services that automatically run, and any services that aren't required should be disabled. In addition to the services, applications that are installed on your computer can be used as a means for hackers to gain access to systems. Vulnerabilities in the program may be exploited, or may conflict with other aspects of the system. In addition to this, programmers may have developed the program with malicious code programmed to activate on a given date, or use other services on the computer to provide a back door to systems. By installing only the applications a user needs to perform his or her work, there is less chance that the program will cause conflicts with the system. By setting Group Policies that prevent the user from installing additional software, you will remove the possibility that unnecessary programs will cause unnecessary problems.

Logging

Auditing significant events on a computer can go a long way toward identifying problems, including intrusions to the system. Many operating systems and applications that are security-minded provide methods of logging certain actions that a user takes, such as logging on or accessing specific data. A review of these logs can provide vital information during an investigation, and can be a primary source of identifying whether someone has attempted to hack a system or access data he or she is not authorized to use.

Auditing Events on Windows

Windows operating systems such as Windows 200x, XP, and Vista provide the ability to generate logs that track events. Auditing is disabled on some systems such as Windows 2000 and XP, but should be enabled to track the success or failure of certain events through the following steps:

1. From the **Start** menu, select **Settings**, and then click on **Control Panel**.
2. Double-click on the **Administrative Tools** icon.

3.   Double-click on **Local Security Policy**.

4.   When the Local Security Settings applet appears, expand **Local Policies** in the left pane, and then click on **Audit Policy**. By double-clicking on different policies in the right pane, you can then set the different events you want to log.

When logging is enabled, any events you've set to be logged are tracked. As shown in Figure 13.1, these events can include logging the success and/or failure of account logons, account management, logon events, policy changes, and system events. At a minimum, these events should be logged, as they can help determine whether someone has attempted to guess a user's password and try and log on as that person, or performed other actions that would indicate an attempt to access the system using another person's account.

Figure 13.1 Local Security Settings

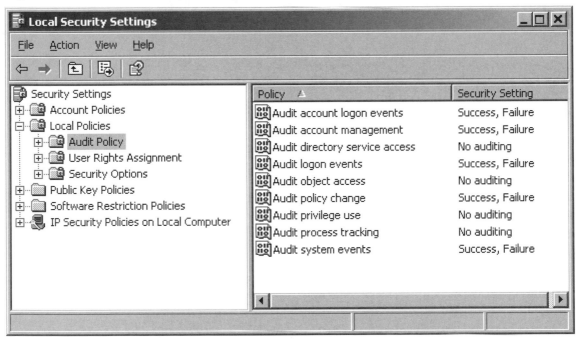

Once logging is enabled, you can view the log using the Event Viewer. In Windows 200x, XP, and Vista, you also can access this tool in the Administrative Tools folder in the Control Panel. By double-clicking on the Event Viewer icon in this folder, the tool shown in Figure 13.2 will appear. As you can see in this figure, by selecting different categories of events in the left pane, you can then view information on events related to those categories in the right pane. Double-clicking on a particular event in the right pane will provide more detailed information.

Figure 13.2 The Event Viewer

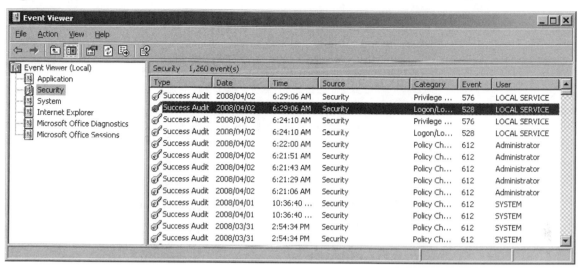

Monitoring user activity is an important part of the forensic process. Unusual user activity may be just an indicator of system problems, or it may be a real security issue. By analyzing the user activity reported in your system logs, you can determine authentication problems and hacking activity.

An important aspect in determining relevant events in your system logs is determining which behavior is benign and which behavior indicates trouble. For example, if a user fails to authenticate one time in a one-week span, you can be pretty certain that the user simply mistyped his or her password and is not trying to hack into your system. Alternatively, if a user has two failed authentication attempts hourly for an extended period you should look more deeply into the problem. We will be covering these types of events and going over how to make the critical determination as to whether a behavior is benign or a warning sign. Security is, and always should be, a top priority for anyone working on key infrastructure systems.

Access to files can also be audited on a machine. As shown earlier in Figure 13.1, double-clicking on **Audit object access** in Local Security Settings allows you to set whether the success and/or failure of accessing objects such as files and folders is audited. By using Windows Explorer, you can right-click on the file or folder you want to audit, and then click **Properties** on the menu that appears. When the Properties dialog box appears, you would then click on the **Security** tab, and perform the following steps:

1. Click the **Advanced** button.

2. When the Advanced Security Settings screen appears, click the **Auditing** tab.

3. To add a new user or group to audit, click the **Add** button, type the name of the user or group to audit, and then click **OK**.

4. As shown in Figure 13.3, you can then set what will be audited. Checking a **Successful** checkbox will audit events that were successful, whereas checking a **Failed** checkbox will audit unsuccessful events.

Figure 13.3 The Auditing Entry for a Folder

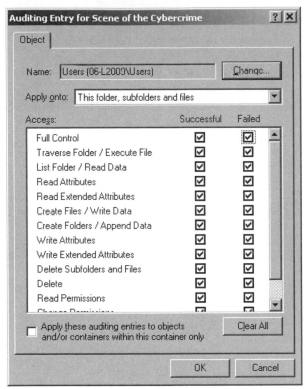

Log Parser

Log Parser is a tool from Microsoft that can read text-based files, XML files, and comma-separated value (CSV) files, as well as data sources on Windows operating systems such as the Registry and Event log. It is available as a free download from Microsoft's Web site at www.microsoft.com/technet/scriptcenter/tools/logparser/default.mspx.

Tools such as Log Parser can help you identify events that could indicate a potential hack attempt or even just a user attempting to look at something he or she shouldn't be looking at. By enabling file access auditing and using Log Parser to examine the results, you can even track down potential security issues at the file level. Digging through these same log files to track down this data manually is both tedious and unnecessary with the advanced capabilities of Microsoft's Log Parser utility.

Backing Up Data

As we've stressed throughout this book, important data should always be backed up. Some organizations use policies to enforce users saving data to locations on a server so that only the server's data needs to be backed up and not each individual computer. If data is saved to the local hard disk of each computer in an organization, the folders where data is stored should be routinely backed up. This not only includes documents that the users have saved, but also data that may be stored in databases on the local machine.

Microsoft Operating Systems

Microsoft is one of the leading vendors of server and desktop operating systems, and each new version of Windows has included new features to improve (or attempt to improve) security. However, even with Microsoft's widespread use, the company's track record for security has been less than spotless (of course, the same is true for every other operating system). To make your Windows operating system more secure, you should perform certain steps.

Disabling Services

Services are programs that perform specific tasks or functions, and run in the background while the computer is running. Although certain core services need to be running for Windows to operate, your system may not require many others. Unfortunately, with the exception of Windows 2003 that requires the network administrator to enable the services that he or she deems necessary, the services are installed and enabled by default regardless of whether you want them. These unneeded services use up memory and take up processing time from the CPU, and can make the computer run slower. Even worse, if there are any programming flaws in the services, these may be exploited by hackers and viruses. Although patches are released to fix these vulnerabilities, it may take months or years after the operating system has been released before the problem is identified, and a patch is made available. Even when patches are available, it doesn't mean that users will download and install them immediately.

Because of the security risks and other issues that unneeded services can cause, it is wise to disable any unnecessary services on the computer. You can disable services through the Services applet (found in the Administrative Tools folder of the Control Panel), which you can alternatively open by clicking **Start | Run**, typing **services.msc** in the **Open** field, and clicking **OK**. As shown in Figure 13.4, the right pane of this tool provides a listing of all services installed on the computer. When you select a service, a description of the service appears to the left.

Figure 13.4 Services

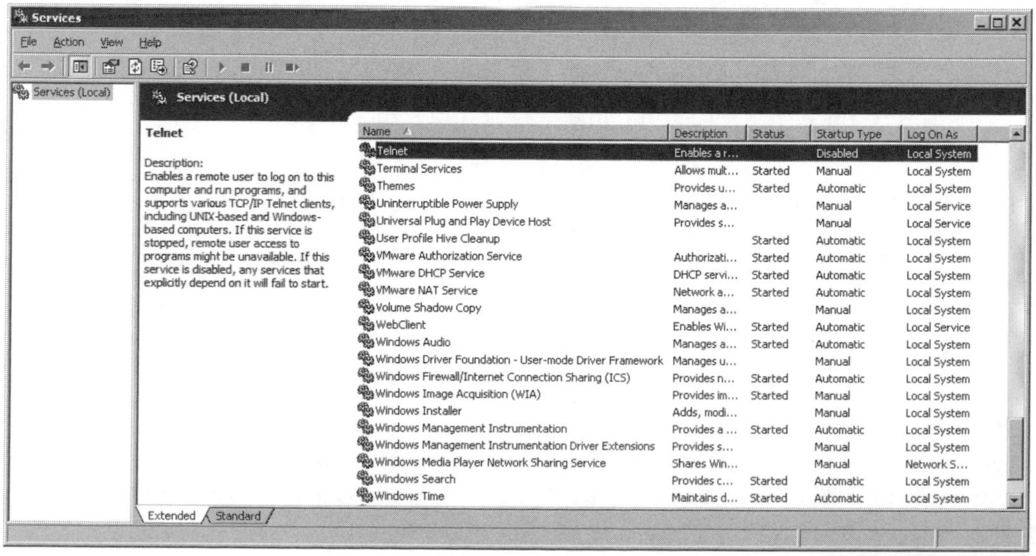

Double-clicking on a service will display the Properties dialog box for it. By clicking on the **General** tab, you will see a drop-down list titled **Startup Type**. This list allows you to set what happens with the service when the computer starts. The different startup types in the list are:

- Automatic, which causes the service to automatically start when Windows starts
- Manual, in which the service starts only when the user or another service needs it
- Disabled, in which the service will not start under any circumstances

When you select the services you don't need and set the startup type to Disabled, the service cannot be started. When services are stopped, programs that use the service will be unable to use its functions. If services are disabled, any services that depend on it will fail to start. Therefore, you will need to ensure that the services aren't needed by applications or services that you do require. The various services that aren't required by Windows XP to run include:

- Alerter, which notifies specific users and computers of administrative alerts. This should be disabled if the computer is not on a corporate network.
- ClipBook, which allows the ClipBook Viewer to store information and share it with other computers on the network. This tool isn't commonly used anymore, and is generally safe to disable.
- Messenger, which (despite its name) isn't related to Windows Messenger. The service is used to transmit net send and alerter messages between clients and servers. It is often used to send spam, and is already disabled in some installations.
- SSDP Discovery Service, which is used for discovering Universal Plug and Play (UPnP) devices on a home network.
- Telnet, which is used by remote users to log on to the computer and run programs.
- NetMeeting Remote Desktop Sharing, which allows authorized users to access the computer remotely using NetMeeting. It may be used on corporate intranets, but should be disabled if NetMeeting isn't used.
- Remote Registry, which allows remote users to modify Registry settings on the computer. This isn't a needed service on home networks or stand-alone machines, and should be disabled if it isn't used on corporate networks.
- Smart Card, which manages access to smart cards read by the computer. If smart cards aren't used, it should be disabled.
- Routing and Remote Access, which is used for routing services to businesses in LANs and WANs. Again, this isn't needed on stand-alone machines and home networks, and should be disabled if not used on a corporate network.

NIC Bindings

Microsoft Windows operating systems use a mechanism known as *binding* to associate specific services and protocols with particular network interfaces. A network interface can be any port into or out of the computer, including a network interface card (NIC), a modem, or even a serial port. By default,

Windows enables every possible binding when the OS is first installed and when a new interface or new service or protocol is installed. This is done to ensure that everything "just works"—it's easier and more convenient for less knowledgeable users than having to troubleshoot communication problems and enable the correct bindings. However, it also opens up security holes, so each time a significant change is made to a system, you should inspect the bindings to make sure no unwanted bindings are enabled.

One of the most common problems arising from this situation occurs when a system is connected to a broadband communication device for the first time. Windows automatically binds TCP/IP to the new interface as well as the Microsoft Networking service and File and Print Services. This effectively transforms a "stand-alone" system into a member of a network comprising other systems on the local broadband segment. This situation poses a significant security risk. To return the system to a more secure configuration, you must disable the bindings for every service and protocol other than TCP/IP on the new Internet interface.

Understanding Security and UNIX/Linux Operating Systems

UNIX and Linux systems seem to have a reputation for being more secure than Windows operating systems. To some extent, this reputation might be justified, but UNIX and Linux have a significant number of unique security vulnerabilities as well as sharing some common vulnerabilities with Windows OSes. Remember: No operating system is without security problems. Because UNIX has been around for decades, it has already been through numerous attack and repair cycles. For that reason, its current manifestations are generally more secure than many Windows OSes. Linux is based on UNIX architecture, and has been around since 1991. It is generally more secure than Windows for two reasons: It lacks several of the biggest pitfalls of Windows (such as support for NetBIOS) and it is less a target for attackers who prefer to concentrate on developing attacks for the most widely deployed operating systems, which means Windows. Nonetheless, both UNIX and Linux still have security problems.

For example, the passwd program used by some versions of UNIX *appears* to require somewhat secure passwords: That is, it requires passwords that contain at least five letters (or four characters if numerals or symbols are included). But this requirement is an illusion, because the program will accept a shorter password if the user enters it three times—thus overriding the "requirement."

Many UNIX machines use accounts with names such as *lpq* or *date* that are used to execute simple commands without requiring users to log on. Often such accounts have blank passwords and a user ID of 0, which means they execute with superuser permissions. This is a big security hole because anyone can use these accounts, including hackers who might replace the command that is supposed to be run by the account with one of his or her own commands.

When securing a deployment of UNIX or Linux, you must take the following measures. This list is not exhaustive and does not apply to every version of UNIX or Linux.

- Use strong passwords.
- Implement password aging.
- Implement a shadow password file.

- Eliminate *shared accounts*. This is a type of "group account" that differs from the security groups used on Windows, NetWare, and UNIX systems. The latter contains user accounts; the UNIX shared group account is a single account that many different people use—often members of a team working together on a particular project. Instead of using group accounts, you should place the user accounts in groups by editing the /etc/group file.

- Be careful about implementing the "trusted hosts" concepts. They allow users to designate host computers that are to be considered trusted, so the users will not have to enter a password every time they use the network. This system can be exploited, so the best security practice is to disallow trusted hosts. If trusted hosts are allowed, only local hosts should be trusted; remote hosts should never be trusted. (Trusted hosts are listed in the /etc/hosts.equiv file.)

- Remove the "secure" designation from all terminals so that the root account can't log on from unsecured terminals, even with the password. Authorized users will still be able to use the *su* command to become a superuser.

- Ensure that network file system (NFS) security is enabled. Some UNIX implementations have no NFS security features enabled by default, which means that any Internet host (including untrusted hosts) can access files via NFS.

- Disallow anonymous FTP unless it is necessary.

- Disallow shell scripts that have the *setuid* or *setgid* permission bits set on them.

- Set the sticky bit on directories to prevent users from deleting or renaming other users' files. The sticky bit isn't supported on all versions, as it has been dropped by Linux, FreeBSD, and Solaris.

- Set default file permissions so that group/world read/write access is not granted.

- Write-protect the root account startup files and home directory.

- Use only secured applications and service daemons. Secure NFS, Network Information Service (NIS), X Windows, and so on. Disable the *r* commands if they are not used.

- Remove unnecessary services and protocols. You can remove unneeded services by editing the /etc/inetd.conf and /etc/rc.conf files.

- Log all connections to network services, and use a TCP wrapper to track connections.

- Prevent domain name system (DNS) hostname spoofing.

- Set appropriate permissions on all files.

- Employ packet filtering.

- For remote logons, use a secured shell instead of Telnet, FTP, RLOGIN, RSH, and so on.

- For file encryption, use add-on programs that use strong algorithms (such as 3DES) rather than the standard UNIX *crypt* command, which is easily broken.

- Ensure that device files such as /dev/kmem, /dev/mem, and /dev/drum cannot be read by the world. Most device files should be owned by user "root."

- Use the *who* command to determine who is currently logged on to the system. This command displays the contents of the /etc/utmp file, which lists the logon name, terminal, logon time, and remote host of each logged-on user. Use the *last* command to display a log of each logon session (including FTP sessions) as well as the time of each shutdown and reboot. The /etc/ security scripts that run daily can be used to monitor security-related events.

- Run the syslog daemon (syslogd) in secure mode to prevent receiving forged UDP datagrams from other systems.

- If you are not using programs that require Remote Procedure Call (RPC), disable the port daemon.

- Sendmail is enabled by default on some UNIX systems. Turn it off if you don't need it. If you are using Sendmail, be sure it has the latest patches and ensure that spammers can't use your system to relay spam.

For a detailed step-by-step description of locking down a UNIX or Linux system, see the excellent UNIX security checklist on the CERT Web site at www.cert.org/tech_tips/unix_security_checklist2.0.html.

Understanding Security and Macintosh Operating Systems

In 2001, Apple released the new Macintosh operating system, OS X. More than just the latest version of the Macintosh operating system in a string of upgrades, OS X is a completely rewritten OS based on the UNIX OS FreeBSD. Apple calls its implementation of BSD *Darwin* and has made it an open source project. OS X is more like UNIX than it is like OS 8 or 9. This is a positive move in terms of stability and security, but it also means Mac users will encounter new security issues. In addition, many utilities, programs, and services previously available only on UNIX systems are now or will soon be available for OS X. Thus, maintaining vigilance is essential to the long-term security of an OS X system.

OS X has some security advantages compared with many other UNIX implementations. Many of its network services (Telnet, HTTPD, Sendmail, and the like) are turned off by default, and the root account has to be specifically enabled before it can be used. However, you should take some security measures specific to OS X, including the following:

- Deselect the **Automatically log in** option in the System Preferences | Login panel (on the Login Window tab) and ensure that the Login window is set to display as "name and password entry fields," rather than displaying a list of the user accounts on the computer.

- Set the screensaver to ask for authentication information (through the Screen Savers panel of System Preferences).

- Remove the SetUID and SetGID permission bits from the RCP, RDUMP, RRESTORE, RLOGIN, and RSH utilities, or remove these utilities if they aren't used.

- Review the files in legacy directories (those that were already on a Mac OS 9 machine prior to upgrading to OS X) and change the permissions; by default, files and folders used by the Classic environment have read and write permissions assigned to the world.

- Configure the IPFW firewall included in OS X; for easier configuration, install Flying Buttress (formerly called Brickhouse), a graphical interface for creating rule sets.

- Use a file integrity checker that supports OS X (such as Osiris) to track system changes.

To stay abreast of the security concerns for Macintosh systems, visit the Apple Web site at www.apple.com/support/osfamily/ and the Macintosh Security Site at www.securemac.com.

Understanding Mainframe Security

Mainframes remain a significant presence in many educational and research environments. Mainframes offer significant computing power, rigid access controls, and the ability to employ thin clients in a host-terminal configuration. Traditionally, mainframes have been less vulnerable than personal computers to security breaches, but that was when access to the mainframe was only through in-house terminals. Now Internet connectivity and the addition of more features (such as Web server and e-commerce capabilities) have opened up mainframe systems to many of the same problems that plague administrators of PC-based networks. To maintain the security of a mainframe environment, you must take the following measures:

- Use strong passwords.

- Eliminate unused accounts, and set expiration dates on temporary accounts.

- Remove unnecessary services and protocols.

- Log all connections to network services.

- Set access permissions on files and folders.

- Configure auditing.

- Perform regular backups and secure the backup media.

- Install and update AV software.

- Use nonadministrative accounts for nonadministrative activities.

- Use a firewall to filter traffic.

- Secure the links between the mainframe and remote clients.

Mainframe security products include CA Top Secret and IBM's Resource Access Control Facility (RACF). For more information about Top Secret, see http://ca.com/products/product.aspx?ID = 141. For information about RACF, see www-03.ibm.com/servers/eserver/zseries/zos/racf/overview.html.

Understanding Wireless Security

The ability to stay connected to your network while roaming around the office, not tied down by a cable, has gained widespread popularity very quickly. The capabilities and throughput of wireless networking technologies have approached those of traditional wirebound networking solutions. This surge in efficacy has convinced many network administrators to deploy this simple and reasonably priced technology. Wireless NICs and access ports have dropped in price, and have become affordable for home and business networking. This means anyone can plug a port into an Ethernet jack on a hub, install a wireless NIC, and have fully functional wireless networking with little or no additional configuration.

The goals of wireless security are the same as within a wired network: authentication of users and computers, providing confidentiality of data, and ensuring data integrity. However, wireless presents special challenges because the signals pass through the airwaves, using radio frequencies. This makes eavesdropping easier in a wireless LAN (WLAN) than in a cabled network.

Most wireless networking technologies are based on the 802.11b standard. Although this standard does define several security mechanisms to protect wireless traffic, there are numerous exploits to circumvent or crack the restrictions. Unfortunately, the wireless access ports are usually connected to an internal network behind the firewall. This effectively grants external users with the right equipment nearly the same type of access as they would enjoy if they were able to plug into an open port in the company's wiring closet.

One form of eavesdropping, called *wardriving*, is the act of driving around with an antenna to locate insecure wireless networks. This activity has become a popular hacker pastime. The really alarming part of wardriving is that anyone can build an antenna with parts that cost less than $5, and often homemade antennas are more sensitive and directional than commercial devices. Organizations using wireless networking solutions might assume that the signals are contained within the walls of the office, but this assumption is not based on fact. Signals strong enough to support connectivity can be detected blocks away, even around corners and on the other side of line-of-sight blocking structures.

Once a malicious user has discovered a wireless connection, it is only a matter of time before he or she gains access to any and every part of the network. Hackers can use packet sniffing, brute force attacks, and other information discovery attacks to find weaknesses to exploit them. Fortunately, the goal of most wardriver efforts is to tap into high-speed corporate Internet access for free rather than to infiltrate the internal network. However, unauthorized use of company equipment and services costs money, time, and productivity, so their actions can't be regarded as benign.

One common way to improve the security of wireless connectivity is to use a virtual private network (VPN) link over the wireless network. Such a link is typically deployed by attaching the wireless portal directly to a VPN server that serves as a gateway for authorized clients and a firewall for unauthorized clients. This setup forces the client systems to properly authenticate before being granted access to the network and encrypts all data passing over the wireless link. Additionally, it removes the wireless port from the internal network so that its traffic cannot be intercepted by a sniffer and internal systems cannot be directly accessed without successful VPN authentication.

Other options to improve the security of wireless technologies include taking the following actions:

- Isolate all wireless access points from the internal network. Require additional authentication or connection mechanisms before access to the internal network or Internet gateway is granted.

- Disable wireless network broadcasting of service set identifiers (SSIDs). This action disables many of the automatic configuration features for clients, but manual configuration greatly reduces the ability of unauthorized clients to connect.

- Require specific Media Access Control (MAC) addresses from authorized wireless cards to establish connectivity.

- Be on the lookout for "rogue WLANs," unauthorized wireless access points set up by employees within the company for their own convenience. For example, a member of the firm who wants to be able to take his or her laptop to meetings and maintain network connectivity might buy an inexpensive access point and plug it into the Ethernet jack in the office, unaware of the security risks involved.

- Enable Wired Equivalent Privacy (WEP) on the wireless system. Although it has some security flaws, WEP does provide some measure of security. By default, most wireless systems have WEP disabled, which leaves the network completely vulnerable.

Access Control

To secure the wireless network as much as possible, security controls can be implemented to minimize the ability of an attacker to gain access. These access controls can be used independently or they can be combined to provide additional protection. The access controls available to you will depend on the type of wireless access point you are configuring. Most access points will allow the configuration of encryption and MAC filtering.

Encryption

Wireless data is being transmitted in the air that is susceptible to unauthorized users capturing this data and reading the contents. To eliminate data being sent over the air in clear text, wireless networks adopted encryption as part of the network standard. Unfortunately, early implementations of encryption for wireless soon became trivial to crack. As wireless networking matures, the encryption is becoming more complex and difficult to crack. Different technology is also being implemented, such as certificate-based encryption, as an alternative to preshared keys.

WEP

WEP is an optional security feature that was specified by the 802.11 protocol to provide authentication and confidentiality in a wireless access point. It was one of the original methods of sending secure information using a wireless network. When the IEEE committee recommended WEP be used as a mechanism, it also said WEP should not be considered an adequate security and strongly recommended it not be used without an authentication process for key management. WEP employs a symmetric key to authenticate wireless devices and guarantee the integrity of the data by encrypting the transmissions. Each wireless access point and client must share the same key for authentication to take place. Once WEP has been enabled, it then begins a challenge and response authentication process. WEP encrypts data before it is sent from the system, and then decrypts it at the access point. It has been shown to be severely inadequate in its security methods, and as such was replaced as the wireless encryption method of choice in 2003. It uses the stream cipher RC4 (Rivest Cipher). Its method of authentication is essentially that of Shared Key Authentication because both the access point and the wireless device possess the same key. WEP keys are always either 40-bit or 104-bit. The advertised 64-bit and 128-bit encryption results from the fact that the Initialization Vector (IV) is 24 bits. With the encryption method used by WEP, an attacker with enough IVs can crack the key used and gain full access to the network. In studies, WEP networks have been broken into extremely quickly. Recently, at an information security conference, the FBI demonstrated how to crack WEP—and they did it in three minutes.

Overall, the use of WEP can create in the casual user a false sense of security. In the worst-case scenario, an attacker can gain full access to the network extremely quickly—as such, this should not be used to secure a sensitive network. In today's access points, WEP is not considered a secured method of securing a wireless access point.

WPA

Wi-Fi Protected Access (WPA) resolves the issue of weak WEP headers as explained earlier, or the IVs, and provides a way of ensuring the integrity of the messages that passed the integrity check using Temporal Key Integrity Protocol (TKIP) to enhance data encryption. WPA-PSK is a special mode of WPA for home users without an enterprise authentication server and provides the same strong encryption protection. In simple terms, WPA-PSK is extra-strong encryption where encryption keys are automatically changed (called *rekeying*) and authenticated between devices after a specified period of time, or after a specified number of packets has been transmitted. This is called the *rekey interval*. WPA-PSK is far superior to WEP and provides stronger protection for the home/small office/home office (SOHO) user for two reasons. The process used to generate the encryption key is very rigorous, and the rekeying (or key changing) is done very quickly.

WPA is an improvement over WEP because it uses a per-session encryption key. Every time a station associates, a new encryption key is generated based on randomization and the MAC addresses of the wireless access point.

Unfortunately, though, the easiest way to use WPA actually makes it easier to crack than WEP. When 802.1x authentication is not used in WPA, a simpler system called Pre-Shared Key (PSK) is utilized instead. A preshared key is a password that all clients need to be configured with to access the access point. Most consumer routers have the capability of using the WPA with the PSK preshared key.

With WPA-PSK, and almost all passwords, if you make a short character password, you are susceptible to an offline dictionary attack where an attacker grabs a few packets at the time a legitimate station joins the wireless network, and then can take those packets and recover the PSK used. An attacker can get what he or she needs to guess the PSK and get out without anyone noticing. This can occur because the attacker doesn't have to be near the WLAN for more than a few seconds, and the LAN doesn't have to be very busy. This attack depends on the choice of a password, although cracking techniques get better and better. Thus, WPA has been defeated. Most wireless access points have a mechanism built into WPA, which converts an 8- to 63-character string you type in to the 64-digit or 128-digit key (as used with WEP). However, most wireless access points won't be able to use the whole 64-bit key with passphrase mode.

The innate problem is that a passphrase is easy to guess. The IEEE committee that wrote 802.11i pointed out that an eight- to 10-character passphrase actually has less than the 40 bits of security that the most basic version of WEP offers, and said that a passphrase of less than 20 characters is unlikely to deter attacks. As with WEP, wireless cracking tools exist that are specifically designed to recover the PSK from a WPA-protected network (such as Kismet) which are easily available to download.

WPA with 802.1x authentication (sometimes called WPA-Enterprise) makes for a much more secure network. 802.1x offers strong positive authentication for both the station and the WLAN infrastructure, while deriving a secure, per-session encryption key that is not vulnerable to any casual attack. This is typically used with a Remote Authentication Dial-in User Service (RADIUS) server for authentication. The best wireless security mechanism out there with the most access points is 802.1x authentication, combined with WPA's improved encryption.

But instead of pointing out all of the inherent flaws in passing data over unlicensed radio frequencies, WPA, which comes with most new consumer routers, is an excellent way to keep your Internet surfing and home network as safe as it can be Add VPN connections and MAC filtering and you basically have the same security as you do with an alarm system on your home. It deters people from getting access without considerable resolve.

MAC Filtering

With few exceptions, network devices contain a physically unique burned-in MAC address. The purpose of this is to give a unique identifier to that piece of equipment. It is preassigned to the devices by its manufacturer, and in theory it is completely unique. In most cases, the MAC address is 48 bits long. A standard format exists for writing MAC addresses, which consist of three groups of four hexadecimal digits separated by dots. The more common method of writing is to use six groups of two hexadecimal digits, which are in turn separated by colons or hyphens—for example, 00-07-E9-E3-84-F9.

Because each MAC address is unique, it can be used to limit network access. The steps to do so will vary by access point, but will always involve the following:

- Finding the MAC address for the devices that will be allowed to access the network (you can find this either by looking on the actual device itself, or by using the *ipconfig /all* command in the Windows command console, and *ifconfig – a* for Linux and OS X consoles)

- Entering the MAC address into the configuration for the access point (this will vary by device)

In theory, once the MAC addresses are entered into the access point, they will be the only devices allowed to access the network. In practice, a number of issues can come up, including, but not limited to, the fact that anytime a new system is used in conjunction with the access point (such as a visiting client who needs to connect to the network), its MAC address must be entered individually into the access point. This can pull the network administrator away from other tasks of monitoring the network. The administrator must also periodically remove the information for devices that are no longer being used.

Another problem that exists is that of MAC address spoofing. Although the address is typically encoded to the physical medium of the network device, software exists that can make a device access point have a different MAC address than it actually does. Though this does have legitimate and useful purposes, including privacy and interoperability, it can also be changed to access a system illegally. Because of this large security hole, MAC address filtering should not be used by itself, and should instead be included in a wider security policy involving encryption and other authentication methods.

Cloaking the SSID

The SSID is essentially the name of the access point or wireless network seen by the user. A client can find out its SSID in only two ways: The access point can actively tell the client, or you can passively put it in the client's configuration. When it is given out automatically, it is called Open

Network mode, but it is known as Closed Network mode when "cloaking," meaning the SSID is not broadcast over the radio frequency. Automatic delivery of the SSID typically occurs every 100 milliseconds and is called a *beacon*, within which is contained synchronization information such as channel, speeds, timestamps, encryption status, and other information.

In Closed Network mode, the SSID is not broadcast out to the user or administrator programs. Thus, the client must probe the access point, and if the SSID matches, it will synchronize and go through the authentication process. Authentication can occur using an open system or via a shared key. An open system does not need any credentials supplied. The SSID is used in wireless networks to identify the wireless access point and its associated network. It can be up to 32 alphanumeric characters long and is attached to all packets sent over the wireless connection. Additional access points in the area can broadcast the same SSID, so its use as a security or authentication method is negligible. However, the SSID may be changed and cloaked (meaning it is not set to be broadcast by the AP) in an attempt to minimize the visibility of the network. By default, most APs broadcast their SSID to the surrounding area. This beacon method occurs roughly every 0.1 seconds. Most APs ship with a default SSID which is widely known and can be found on a number of Internet sites. Using a default SSID may draw malicious users who suspect that additional settings on the AP are set to default settings as well (such as the administrative password). From a security standpoint, changing the SSID may cause some possible attackers to choose a wireless network that uses default settings. Changing the SSID is reasonably simple for a nontechnical user, and though minor, it is a step toward securing the AP. It is important to note that disabling the broadcast of the SSID does not completely cloak the AP. It simply makes it less visible.

On the Scene

Wigle (Wireless Geographic Logging Engine)

Wigle (www.wigle.net) is the consolidation of thousands of wardriving efforts to create a database of wireless networks around the world. Wigle accepts WAP information by NetStumbler, DStumbler, Kismet, and Pocket Warrior exports. You can also use the Web site's online submission form to enter wireless networks.

In just more than five years, Wigle has collected information on 10,953,561 unique wireless networks with locations. Of these networks, 44.4 percent are encrypted with WEP (which we know can be cracked in minutes) and 18.5 percent still maintain the default SSID or network name, which leads us to believe that these networks may still maintain the vendor's default settings.

The danger of so much wireless access point data being available to hackers is that by searching for APs by SSID or network name, BSSID or MAC address, longitude and latitude, or street address, anyone can find an insecure wireless network.

Understanding Physical Security

When people consider computer and network security, the focus revolves around accounts, passwords, file permissions, and software that limits and monitors access. However, even though a user's account has been denied access to files on a server, what is to stop that user from opening files directly at the server instead? Worse yet, what is to prevent someone from stealing the server's hard disk? Issues such as these are why physical security is so important to the protection of data and equipment.

Physical security involves protecting systems from bodily contact. It requires controlling access to hardware and software so that people are unable to damage devices and the data they contain. If people are unable to have physical access to systems, they will not be able to steal or damage equipment. This type of security also limits or prevents their ability to access data directly from a machine, or create additional security threats by changing account or configuration settings.

Not all equipment is at risk from the same threats. For example, a workstation at a receptionist's desk is vulnerable to members of the public who may be able to view what is on the monitor or access data when the receptionist steps away. Equipment is also vulnerable to accidental or malicious damage, such as when a user or visitor accidentally knocks a computer off a desk or spills something on a keyboard. A server locked in the server room would not be subject to the same types of threats as the receptionist's workstation, because access to the room is limited to members of the IT staff. Because the level of risk varies between assets and locations, risks must be evaluated for each individual device.

When creating measures to protect systems, it is important to note that threats are not limited to people outside the company. One of the greatest challenges to physical security is protecting systems from people within an organization. Corporate theft is a major problem for businesses, because employees have easy access to equipment, data, and other assets. Because an employee's job may require working with computers and other devices, there is also the possibility that equipment may be damaged accidentally or intentionally. Physical security must not only protect equipment and data from outside parties, but also those within a company.

A good way to protect servers and critical systems is to place them in a centralized location. Rather than keeping servers in closets throughout a building, it is common for organizations to keep servers, network connectivity devices, and critical systems in a single room. Equipment that cannot be stored in a centralized location should still be kept in secure locations. Servers, secondary routers, switches, and other equipment should be stored in cabinets, closets, or rooms that are locked, have limited access, are air-conditioned, and have other protective measures in place to safeguard equipment.

Access Control

Physical security is a way of controlling access so that only authorized people can gain entry to an area. Without access control, anyone can enter restricted locations that contain vital equipment, data, or personnel. If an unimpeded person has malicious intentions or causes accidental damage, the impact on people, data, and systems could be severe. Physical security is needed to manage who can and cannot enter sensitive areas.

Identification is a common method of determining who has access to certain areas. Badges, cards, or other IDs can be used to show that a person has gone through the proper security channels, and has an established reason for being in a particular location. For example, the identification may distinguish the person as an employee, visitor, or another designation. To obtain such an identification card, the person would need to go through established procedures, such as being issued a card upon being hired, or signing a logbook at the front desk.

Access logs require anyone entering a secure area to sign in before entering. When visitors require entry, such as when consultants or the vendor support staff needs to perform work in a secure room, an employee of the firm must sign the person in. In doing so, the employee vouches for the credibility of the visitor, and takes responsibility for this person's actions. The access log also serves as a record of who entered certain areas of a building. Entries in the log can show the name of a visitor, the time this person entered and left a location, who signed him or her in, and the stated purpose of the visit.

Even after a visitor has been given access to an area, a member of the organization should accompany the visitor whenever possible. Doing so ensures that the visitor stays in the areas where he or she is permitted. It also provides a measure of control to ensure that the visitor does not tamper with systems or data while he or she is there.

Chaperoning someone who has been given clearance to an area is not always possible or desirable. For example, if you have hired an outside party to install equipment that is needed for Internet access, you may not want to stand beside the installer for an extended period of time. However, workers can be monitored in high-security locations using video cameras to provide electronic surveillance. This provides a constant eye, and allows for review of their actions if an incident occurs.

Alarms are another method of notifying people of unauthorized access. Alarms can be put on doorways, windows, and other entrances, and can be set to go off if someone enters an area and fails to follow proper procedures. If someone enters an incorrect personal identification number (PIN) to unlock a door, or opens a door without deactivating the alarm properly, a noise will sound or a signal will be sent to a person or company that monitors alarms. Additionally, any number of added defenses can be used to sense entry into a secured location. Motion detectors can be used to sense any movement in a room, heat sensors can be used to detect body heat, and weight sensors can be used to detect the added weight of a person on the floor. Although such elaborate methods may not be needed everywhere within a building, they are viable solutions to detecting unauthorized entries.

Although the methods discussed here provide varying degrees of security, each provides an additional barrier to unauthorized access to a machine. Mixing different methods of access control makes it increasingly difficult for intruders to gain access to data, applications, system settings, and other important aspects of a computer.

Environment

Even with educated users and all critical systems locked behind closed doors, equipment and data are still at risk if the environment beyond those locked doors is insecure. *Environment* refers to the surroundings in which the computers and other equipment reside. If an environment is insecure, data and equipment can be damaged. To prevent the environment from affecting a system's safety and ability to function, the following elements should be considered:

- Temperature
- Humidity
- Airflow

- Electrical interference
- Electrostatic discharge (ESD)

If a computer overheats, components inside it can be permanently damaged. Although the temperature of the server room may feel comfortable to you, the inside of a computer can be as much as 40 degrees warmer than the air outside the case. The hardware inside the case generates heat, raising the interior temperature. Computers are equipped with fans to cool the power supply, processor, and other hardware so that temperatures do not rise above 110 degrees. If these fans fail, the heat can rise to a level that destroys the hardware.

Computers are also designed to allow air to flow through the machine, keeping the temperature low. If the airflow is disrupted, temperatures can rise. For example, say you removed an old adapter card that a computer no longer needed. Because you did not have a spare cover, there is now an opening where the card used to be. Because air can now pass through this hole, you might expect that this would help to cool the hardware inside, but airflow is actually lost through this opening. Openings in the computer case prevent the air from circulating inside the machine as it was designed to, causing temperatures to rise.

A common problem with computers is when fans fail, causing increases in temperature within the case. These fans may be used to cool the processor, power supply, or other components. As with other causes of temperature increases, the machine may not fail immediately. The computer may experience reboots, "blue screens of death," memory dumps, and other problems that occur randomly. To determine whether increases in temperature are the cause of these problems, you can install hardware or software that will monitor the temperature and inform you of increases. When the temperature increases past a normal level, you should examine the fans to determine whether this is the cause. Variations in temperature can also cause problems. If a machine experiences sudden changes in temperature, it can cause hardware problems inside the machine. Heat makes objects expand, and cold makes these same objects contract. When this expansion and contraction occurs in motherboards and other circuit boards, *chip creep* (also known as *socket creep*) can occur. As the circuit boards expand and contract, it causes the computer chips on these boards to move until they begin to lose contact with the sockets in which they are inserted. When the chips lose contact, they are unable to send and receive signals, resulting in hardware failure.

To prevent problems with heat and cold, it is important to store servers and other equipment in a temperature-controlled environment. Keeping machines in a room that has air conditioning and heat can keep the temperature at a cool level that does not fluctuate. To assist in monitoring temperature, alarms can be set up in the room to alert you when the temperature exceeds 80°F. Other alarms can be used that attach to the servers, automatically shutting them down if they get too hot.

ESD is another threat to equipment, as static electricity can damage hardware components so that they cease to function. If you are unfamiliar with ESD, think of the times when you have walked over a dry carpet and received a shock when you touched someone. The static electricity builds up, and electrons are discharged between the two objects until both have an equal charge. When you receive a shock from touching someone, the discharge is around 3,000 volts. To damage a computer chip, you need a discharge of only 20 or 30 volts. Humidity levels can increase ESD. If the humidity in a room is below 50 percent, the dry conditions create an atmosphere that allows static electricity to build up. This creates the same situation as mentioned in the preceding paragraph. A humidity level that is too high can also cause ESD, as water particles that conduct electricity can condense and stick to hardware components. Not only can this create ESD problems, but if the humidity is very high, the metal components may rust over time. To avoid humidity problems, keep the levels between 70 percent and 90 percent. Humidifiers and dehumidifiers that respectively raise and lower the level of humidity can be used to keep it at an acceptable point.

Poor air quality is another issue that can cause problems related to ESD and temperature. As mentioned earlier, fans in a machine circulate air to cool the components inside. If the air is of poor quality, dust, smoke, and other particles in the air will also be swept inside the machine. Because dust and dirt particles have the ability to hold a charge, static electricity can build up, be released, and build up again. The components to which the dust and dirt stick are shocked over and over again, damaging them over time. If the room is particularly unclean, dust and dirt can also build up on the air intakes. Because very little air can enter the case through the intake, temperatures rise, causing the components inside the machine to overheat. Vacuuming air intakes and installing an air filtration system in rooms with critical equipment can improve the quality of air and avoid these problems.

Shielding

Shielding can be used to prevent data signals from escaping outside an office. Not only can communication signals leak *out* of a prescribed area, but unwanted signals can also leak *in* and interfere with communications. Thus, shielding is also necessary to prevent data from being damaged in transmission from radio frequency interference (RFI) and electromagnetic interference (EMI). RFI is caused by radio frequencies emanating from microwaves, furnaces, appliances, radio transmissions, and radio-frequency-operated touch lamps and dimmers. Network cabling can pick up these frequencies much as an antenna would, corrupting data traveling along the cabling. EMI is cause by electromagnetism generated by heavy machinery such as elevators, industrial equipment, and lights. The signals from these sources can overlap those traveling along network cabling, corrupting the data signals so that they need to be retransmitted by servers and other network devices. When EMI and RFI cause interference it is called "noise."

To prevent data corruption from EMI and RFI, computers and other equipment should be kept away from electrical equipment, magnets, and other sources. This will minimize the effects of EMI and RFI, because the interference will dissipate as it travels over distances.

When cabling travels past sources of EMI and RFI, a higher grade of cabling should be used, which have better shielding and can protect the wiring inside from interference. Shielded twisted-pair (STP) is a type of cabling that uses a series of individually wrapped copper wires encased in a plastic sheath. Twisted-pair can be unshielded or shielded. When the cabling is STP, the wires are protected with foil wrap for extra shielding.

Coaxial cable is commonly used in cable TV installations, but can also be found on networks. This type of cabling has a solid or stranded copper wire surrounded by insulation. A wire mesh tube and a plastic sheath surround the wire and insulation to protect it. Because the wire is so shielded from interference, it is more resistant to EMI and RFI than twisted-pair cabling.

Another alternative is to use fiber-optic cabling, in which data is transmitted by light. Fiber-optic cable has a core made of light-conducting glass or plastic, surrounded by a reflective material called *cladding*. A plastic sheath surrounds all of this for added protection. Because the signal is transmitted via light, data that travels along fiber-optic cable is not affected by interference from electromagnetism or radio frequencies. This makes it an excellent choice for use in areas where there are sources of EMI or RFI.

One way or another, fiber-optic cabling has become a common element in many networks. If it is a small company, most of the internal network will probably be made up of cabling that uses some form of copper wiring (UTP, STP, or coaxial). However, even in this situation, Internet access is probably provided to users on the network, meaning they will connect out to a backbone that utilizes fiber optics. In larger companies, it has been increasingly common to connect different locations together using fiber-optic cabling. If buildings are connected together with fiber optics, it doesn't mean that copper cabling isn't present on the network. UTP (or some other cabling) will generally be used within buildings to connect computers to the network or connect networks on different floors. Because of this, EMI and RFI will still be an issue.

When installing cabling, it is important that the cable is not easily accessible to unauthorized people. If an intruder or malicious user accesses the cable used on a network, he or she can tap the wire to access data traveling along it, or the cabling can be physically damaged or destroyed. Cable should not be run along the outside of walls or open areas where people may come into contact with it. If this cannot be avoided, the cable should be contained within tubing or some other protective covering that will prevent accidental or malicious actions from occurring.

Summary

Why does all this matter to the cybercrime investigator? Only by understanding how computer security works—and how it sometimes doesn't—can you predict where and how network attacks and intrusions will occur, track the actions of cybercriminals who break into systems, build evidence based on those break-ins, and help the victims of cybercrime protect themselves from future attacks.

The first step in preventing cybercrime is to secure computer systems and networks against attacks. No system can be completely secure, but the goal of security is to present a barrier significant enough to repel most—if not all—attackers. Generally, the elements or issues that must be addressed to create a secure environment are the same for any type of system. But the specifics of how to implement a security policy and how to make individual security changes vary from one operating system to the next, and different technologies such as broadband, mainframe systems, and wireless networks present their own unique challenges.

With the widespread use of inexpensive high-speed broadband connections, more home and professional systems than ever before are vulnerable to sustained Internet attacks. Proper security precautions must be taken to protect these 24/7 connections against attacks from the Internet. These include deploying AV software, using strong passwords, disabling file and print sharing, and using a firewall.

When planning security, you must take into consideration not only the method by which Internet access is brought to a system, but also the software programs used to interact with Internet-based resources. Web browsers are notoriously vulnerable to numerous attacks. However, with a bit of effort to keep the software up-to-date and configure settings for the best security, most common attacks can be avoided.

Organizations that host Web sites for public consumption provide useful content for visitors, but they must also take steps to protect the Web server from malevolent intruders. Protecting a Web server involves securing the host OS as well as the Web server software itself. When securing a Web server, administrators must choose between a modest effort and an all-out effort to protect against security incidents, based on the importance of the data that stands to be compromised. In any case, isolating the Web servers from the organization's internal LAN is an essential part of keeping the network secure.

Physical security is the process of safeguarding facilities, data, and equipment from bodily contact and environmental conditions. This security is provided through access control methods such as physical barriers that restrict access through locks, guards, and other methods. Unfortunately, even with these methods, nothing can prevent security from being breached through social engineering, in which the user is tricked into revealing passwords and other information.

When locking down individual systems, the operating system deployed on that system determines the specific steps that must be taken. Each OS has unique vulnerabilities and security solutions. Understanding these idiosyncrasies and staying informed about new patches and vulnerabilities are essential to the prevention of many types of cybercrime.

Frequently Asked Questions

Q: Our company is very small. Why would an attacker want to gain access to our network?

A: Most hackers are going to go after easy-to-hack networks and try to gain as much information as possible. The motivation for many black hat hackers is financial gain. If your company uses the Internet to read corporate e-mail, access password-protected Web sites, or conduct online transactions, a hacker may attempt to disrupt the operation.

Q: I've heard that understanding the mindset of a hacker or cracker can help thwart their attempts to infiltrate your network. How can I accomplish this without putting my systems or myself at additional risk?

A: Just as there are numerous reputable security companies on the Internet that offer tools and utilities to test and improve the security of your systems, there are groups of crackers or hackers with a Web presence. These "underground" community resources are often invaluable collections of documentation and tools that you can't find anywhere else, especially from commercial sites. However, you should take the precaution of visiting these sites only from a secured system that is not connected to your production environment. If you download any materials from such sites, take extra precautions to test for viruses and Trojans before moving the material to a production system.

Q: How can I verify that the security barriers I've erected and the patches I've applied have successfully eliminated specific security vulnerabilities?

A: The best way to do this is to attack your own system. Using a corruption of the Golden Rule, Ed Tittel, author of numerous IT books and articles and technical editor of this book, often states, "Do unto yourself, before others do unto you." Basically, you should employ common attack methods used by crackers and hackers to see whether their exploits are successful against your hardened system. In addition to deploying manual attacks against your own systems, you can refer to several Web sites, service groups, and products that can perform automated security auditing and stress-testing against your network. Several of these sites are included in the resource list that follows.

Chapter 14

Implementing Cybercrime Detection Techniques

Topics we'll investigate in this chapter:

- Security Auditing and Log Files
- Firewall Logs, Reports, Alarms, and Alerts
- Commercial Intrusion Detection Systems
- IP Spoofing and Other Antidetection Tactics
- Honeypots, Honeynets, and Other "Cyberstings"

☑ Summary

☑ Frequently Asked Questions

Introduction

In the preceding chapter, we turned our focus from an analysis and explanation of cybercrime, who's involved in perpetrating such crimes, and underlying computer and networking security basics to an investigation of what's involved in countering potential threats—namely, we covered various aspects and areas in which it's essential to implement system, network, and communication security. Unfortunately, our security measures won't always work. Another important part of preparing for potential threats and related risks of criminal mischief, intrusion, or attack is being prepared to deal with the aftermath of a cybercrime and to start gathering the information that will be necessary to build a case for prosecution.

Once an attack has occurred or a system or network has been compromised, it's essential to be able to sift through the evidence of what's happened. From a technical information technology (IT) perspective, this means knowing how to find, recognize, and locate the visible evidence of a cybercrime. From a law enforcement perspective, this means knowing how to handle such evidence to make sure it will be admissible in court if necessary. However, these roles overlap somewhat. A good investigator also needs to know the technicalities of where and how evidence can be located, to properly put together the offense report and help the prosecutor formulate questions for witnesses. Likewise, the IT professional needs an understanding of how evidence must be treated to preserve its integrity in the eyes of the law.

In this chapter, we focus primarily on the former activity; we introduce various sources and potential types of evidence that investigators can gather to provide evidence of attempts to perpetrate cybercrimes. In some cases, this evidence may be collected whether the attempted crime succeeds or fails; in other cases, such evidence may be available only as a byproduct of a successful attack.

To some extent, computers and other network devices are capable of recording information about activity that occurs within them or passes through them. When evidence of cybercrime is needed, this kind of data can be an essential element in making a successful case or in making a decision to prosecute the people responsible. But as with so many other aspects of system and network security, it's necessary to understand the underlying technologies and software that must be put to work to make it possible to produce such evidence. It's also necessary to understand what this evidence looks like, how it may be interpreted, and what kinds of telltale signs or data to look for that could not only help document that a cybercrime was committed, but also help identify the responsible party or parties involved and prove to the satisfaction of a jury that they did it.

As we've noted elsewhere in this book, a lack of due diligence in protecting IT assets and information is very often involved in exposing companies and organizations to loss or harm. This loss or harm may occur as a result of either an insider attack (from an employee, consultant, or other person "in the know") or of an attack mounted from outside the network boundary. We've also mentioned that there is no such thing as perfect security, so it's also necessary to concede that even a remote chance of successful attack, penetration, or compromise means that it's necessary to be able to monitor, detect, and react to security incidents if and when they occur.

Thus, an important part of the due diligence necessary in dealing with security matters is to be ready to perform subsequent analysis and investigations to determine causes and to identify perpetrators whenever possible. Whether or not an organization decides to prosecute a security incident is almost beside the point. To the organization and its IT professionals, the real value of understanding how to gather and interpret evidence of cybercrimes comes from the ability it confers to improve or harden security after the fact, to prevent any recurrence of the attacks or circumstances that permitted such crimes to occur in the first place.

Even if the company or organization never actually decides to pursue legal remedies for attempted or successful attacks, the ability to gather, interpret, and respond to the information inherent in the tracks and traces of such events is an essential part of a proper security regime. Finally, it's important to realize that maintaining proper system and network security requires active checks on how security policy is implemented and how well it's working to determine whether potential or actual vulnerabilities exist.

Think of this as a "how are we doing?" kind of check, security-wise, that acts not only to make sure that whatever security controls have been implemented match what a security policy requires, but also to repeatedly assess vulnerabilities to new security exploits and attack techniques as they occur. This is not unlike the continuous training and preparation for a violent confrontation that most police officers undergo on a regular basis. Even if there is no reason to expect violence, officers are always prepared for a situation to turn bad, and during and after any contact related to a call, officers are constantly monitoring the situation. Likewise, a savvy security professional knows that he or she must check the status of the network on a regular basis, if only to be sure nothing untoward or unexpected is in progress or has already happened. This empirical form of assessing security posture is a key ingredient in maintaining strong security at all times and is the first step in incident response.

Security Auditing and Log Files

An important concept in system and network security is what's often called the AAA, or "triple-A" model of security. In this case, the acronym is subject to several interpretations, including:

- Administration, authorization, and authentication
- Authentication, authorization, and accounting

Although both expansions of the acronym are pretty widespread, the second is the one that we use in this chapter.

The idea behind AAA is that strong security rests on a three-legged foundation in which:

- *Authentication*, as discussed in detail in Chapter 11, ensures that users, processes, and services that seek to consume system resources or access their contents provide sufficient proof of identity to enter systems and networks before any such requests may be issued.

- *Authorization* (sometimes also called *access control*) ensures that requests for resources will not be granted unless requesters have the permissions necessary not only to read or otherwise inspect the contents of the resources they want to access, but also that they have explicit permissions to perform the kind of operation they seek to perform on the resource. Some individuals may be granted read-only access to information to which they have no permissions to make changes (or to delete such information altogether), whereas other individuals may be granted the ability to modify or delete such information at will.

- *Accounting* relates to monitoring and tracking system activity. Some companies or organizations put a monetary value on computer resources, usage, and access. In this situation, accounting tracks such activity to assess so-called "chargebacks" for use of computer or network services based on actual consumption. But from a security standpoint, the other form of monitoring or tracking involved under the general heading of accounting is called *auditing*. As in its formal meaning in financial accounting, auditing means tracking access and use of resources—in this case, communication links, systems, networks, and related resources, so that activity may be logged. This auditing deposits tangible data into various kinds of computerized records so that they may be analyzed for all kinds of purposes after the fact. Such logs provide a key source of evidence in detecting and analyzing cybercrimes, whether only attempted or successfully completed.

Note that both authentication and authorization put various kinds of barriers or checks between users (or consumers) and the resources they seek to utilize. Only accounting tracks what actually happens on the networks and systems it monitors. Thus, accounting—or, more properly, auditing—is the essential activity that closes the loop between what is supposed to happen from a security standpoint and what actually occurs on the systems and networks to which authentication and authorization controls apply.

Auditing is a capability that's built into most computer operating systems and network devices. But because creating audit trails means generating files in which activity records may be stored, auditing is generally viewed as a discretionary form of tracking and monitoring, rather than something to be applied to all user activity and resource access across the board. A good general principle to apply when deciding whether to audit certain kinds of activity or access to specific resources is based on a careful assessment of the risks involved. In other words, it's wise to audit for potentially harmful or dangerous activities and for access to sensitive files and other resources. But it's also important to recognize that auditing everything is just as impractical as auditing nothing. These general exhortations will make more sense if we look at how certain operating systems handle auditing and what kinds of activities and accesses they can track and monitor. Following that discussion, we can generalize further about auditing and the trails that auditing leaves behind (usually called *logs* or *log files*) with a little more specificity and precision.

Auditing for Windows Platforms

Starting with the earliest versions of Windows NT, all installations of the Windows operating systems (with the exception of Windows 9x/Me) maintain three audit logs to track user and system activity. You can view these logs through the built-in Event Viewer utility:

- **Application log** Shows messages, status information, and events reported from applications and nonessential services on the Windows computer. (Note that some system services write to this log rather than to the System log.)

- **System log** Records errors, warnings, and information events generated by the Windows operating system itself and related core system services.

- **Security log** Displays success and failure records from audited activities. When you enable auditing and set specific auditing policies or settings in Windows, this is the log in which such items appear.

The last log is, of course, the one that is most obviously important for our purposes, although investigators should not ignore the other two. Relevant information, such as the starting or stopping of a service or abnormal behavior of an application, can be obtained from the Application and System logs as well.

NOTE

Other logs may appear in the Event Viewer in addition to the standard Application, System, and Security logs, if certain services are running (such as Active Directory and domain name system [DNS] server services).

Launching the Event Viewer varies by platform, but you can usually fins it under the Administrative Tools menu, as in Windows NT and 2000, or through the Microsoft Management Console (MMC) in Windows 2000, XP, and Vista, Windows Server 2003, and Windows Server 2008. The Event Viewer is a good starting point when investigating abnormal or unusual system activity and for monitoring system activity in general.

In Windows, *Group Policy Objects*, or *GPOs*, control the level of auditing performed by the operating system. Only someone logged on with an account with administrative-level permissions can enable auditing or establish audit policies. To enable auditing, you simply create a GPO and configure it to monitor success and failure for one or more of various classes of defined events. As shown in Figure 14.1, by using the Local Security Settings, you can edit the Audit Policy of the computer. In looking at this figure, you'll notice that by default, the audit policies are disabled, meaning that if you initially viewed the Security Log in the Event Viewer, it would be empty. To enable the policy, you would double-click on the event(s) you wanted to audit, and then choose whether to audit the success and/or failure of that event.

Figure 14.1 Audit Policy on a Windows XP Computer

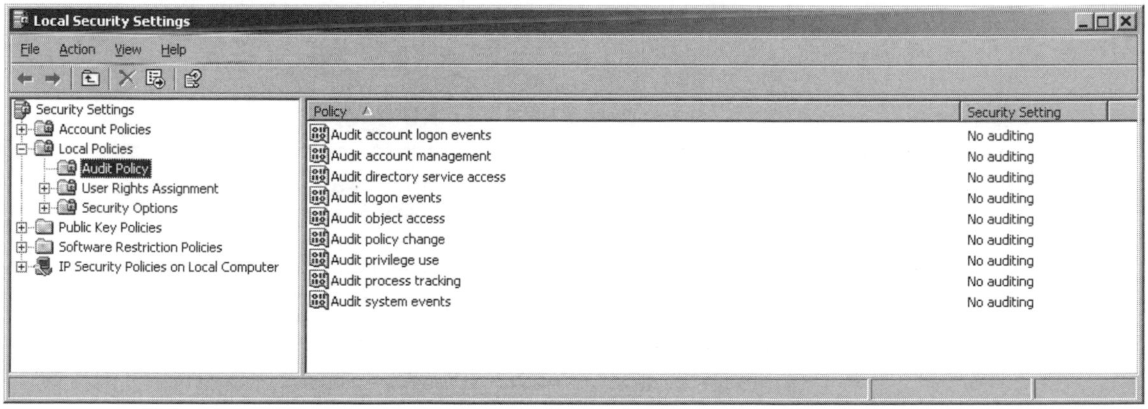

Previous to Windows Vista and Windows Server 2008, nine classes of events or activities could be audited:

- **Account logon events** Use this to monitor user account logon activity.

- **Account management** Use this to monitor administrative account management activities (creating, deleting, disabling, or changing account settings).

- **Directory service access** Use this to monitor use of Active Directory services and objects.

- **Logon events** Use this to monitor all logon events for system accounts, service accounts, and user accounts (a superset of account logon events, in other words).

- **Object access** Use this to enable auditing of individual files, folders, printers, or other computer resources (which must also be configured for auditing individually and separately).

- **Policy change** Use this to monitor GPO creation, deletion, or modification. This tracks important administrative activities on Windows systems.

- **Privilege use** Use this to monitor use of user and administrative privileges on a Windows system. This also tracks important administrative activities on Windows systems, as well as object owner/creator and user use of privileges.

- **Process tracking** Use this to monitor process creation, threads, and deletion. This is seldom used for security purposes (but may sometimes be helpful).

- **System events** Use this to monitor operating system activities. This is also seldom used for security purposes.

In Windows Vista and Windows Server 2008, the number of audit policies increased from nine to 50. Each of the original nine has subcategories that allow you to audit events on a more granular level. Table 14.1 lists the policies and their subcategories.

Table 14.1 Audit Policies in Windows Vista and Windows Server 2008

Audit Policy Name	Top-Level Category	Subcategory
Audit System Events	System	Security State Change Security System Extension System Integrity IPsec Driver Other System Events
Audit Logon Events	Logon/Logoff	Logon Logoff Account Lockout IPsec Main Mode IPsec Quick Mode IPsec Extended Mode Special Logon Other Logon/Logoff Events Network Policy Server

Continued

Table 14.1 Continued. Audit Policies in Windows Vista and Windows Server 2008

Audit Policy Name	Top-Level Category	Subcategory
Audit Object Access	Object Access	File System Registry Kernel Object SAM Certification Services Application Generated Handle Manipulation File Share Filtering Platform Packet Drop Filtering Platform Connection Other Object Access Events
Audit Privilege Use	Privilege Use	Sensitive Privilege Use Non Sensitive Privilege Use Other Privilege Use Events
Audit Process Tracking	Detailed Tracking	Process Creation Process Termination DPAPI Activity RPC Events
Audit Policy Change	Policy Change	Audit Policy Change Authentication Policy Change Authorization Policy Change MPSSVC Rule-Level Policy Change Filtering Platform Policy Change Other Policy Change Events
Audit Account Management	Account Management	User Account Management Computer Account Management Security Group Management Distribution Group Management Application Group Management Other Account Management Event
Audit Directory Service Access	DS Access	Directory Service Access Directory Service Changes Directory Service Replication Detailed Directory Service Replication
Audit Account Logon Events	Account Logon	Kerberos Service Ticket Operations Credential Validation Kerberos Authentication Service Other Account Logon Events

Once audit policies have been enabled, the information captured from the audit is stored in the security log for viewing with the Event Viewer. Figure 14.2 shows a security log open in the Event Viewer. Note that successful and failed logon events are audited.

www.syngress.com

Figure 14.2 The Security Log Showing Event Types for Which Auditing Is Enabled

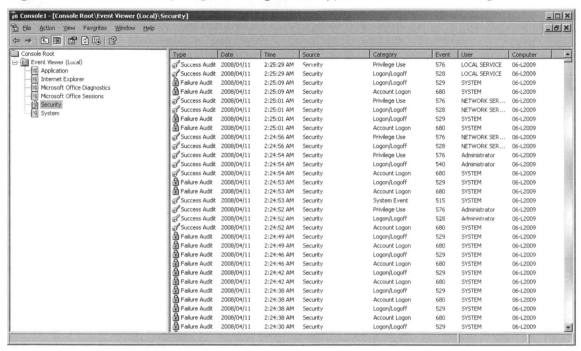

The profound trade-offs between auditing and system performance are manifested in at least two ways:

- The more objects and activities that are audited, the more impact that the collection and recording of such data will have on system performance and consumption of disk space (because all of those logged activities are written to files on disk).

- The more objects and activities that are audited, the more data administrators and investigators will have to dig through to find items of interest among the routine or benign events or activities that will also be recorded.

If a large amount of data is collected, however, all is not lost. You can configure the Event Viewer to filter logged events so that only certain event types (for example, only failures) or only events that originate with specific sources, users, or computers are displayed in the log. Other options include displaying only events that occurred on a specified date and/or time or within a specified period, or events in a certain category or that are marked with a specific event ID. Figure 14.3 shows the dialog box that is used to configure display filtering.

Figure 14.3 Configuring Display Filtering to Display Only Specified Logged Events

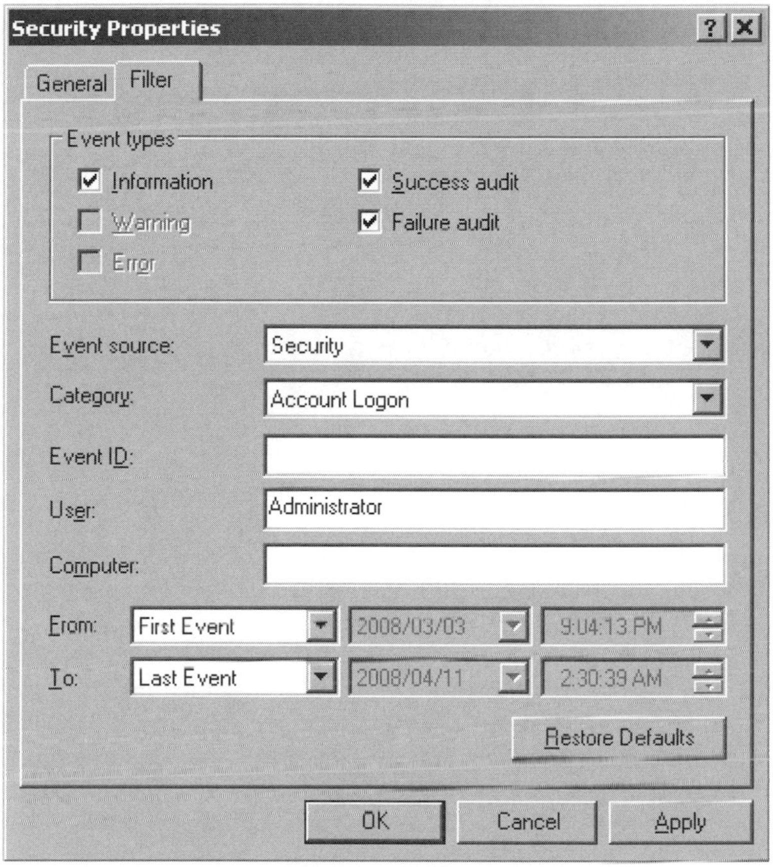

On the Scene

Designing Effective Audit Strategies

Ultimately, what the IT administrator chooses to audit depends on the kinds of activity that occur on the server or device in question, the kinds of attacks or intrusions that are anticipated, and the kinds of information or other assets the organization seeks to monitor (and protect). Thus, it might make sense to audit specific intrusion signatures at the periphery of the network (on firewalls, screening routers, application gateways, and so forth). But on those servers where sensitive files reside, it probably makes sense to audit access to such files, including attempted and successful accesses. In general,

Continued

it's also a good idea to monitor administrative activities on all such devices (and to advertise that policy) so that IT professionals know they will be held accountable for all official (and unsanctioned) administrative activities they perform.

In some situations—perhaps when an account may be compromised—it may make sense to disable that account (and set up a new account for the old account's user), and then audit subsequent attempts to use the old account. This practice permits administrators to determine whether such activity originates inside or outside the local network boundary and can help to establish an intruder's identity.

The general principle at work here is to audit for suspicious activities, to track administrative activity, and to monitor information or assets of known value or interest. By combining these activities into the auditing strategy, it's easier to strike the right balance between audit data volume and the amount of useful information that can be discerned from that data.

Auditing for UNIX and Linux Platforms

Every different distribution and version of UNIX and Linux logs critical audit information in its own unique way and stores the resultant log files in particular locations using specific platform-dependent formats. Nevertheless, most UNIX and Linux operating systems support extensive logging capabilities and share numerous common features.

The Syslog daemon (syslogd) is a clearinghouse for all kinds of log information on UNIX and Linux systems. The daemon is a process that diverts different system messages to different log files, depending on the type of message and how urgent or severe it is. For example, on a FreeBSD system, successful and failed File Transfer Protocol (FTP) logons are shown in the ftp.log file, information about access to Apache Web sites is stored in access_log, and information about failed logons resides in secure.log.

Most networks that incorporate UNIX or Linux systems also set up special network drives to record logging data, so it can all reside in a single centralized location. In addition, the Syslog daemon receives event data from various operating system and user applications (listed in Table 14.2); it also stores all log data using a single standardized format for easy interpretation and analysis. (The same consistency, alas, is not found for all logs on Windows systems, where the Event Viewer uses one format for its logs, but other applications and services use other formats.)

In fact, Syslog even prioritizes event or error messages according to a predefined scheme (listed in Table 14.3). Higher-priority messages appear at the top of this table, and lower-priority messages appear at the bottom of this table.

As mentioned previously, various specific UNIX or Linux log files store particular types of events or information. Thus, the *loginlog* records failed logon attempts, and the *sulog* records *su* (superuser) command activity on a specific system and identifies the user account where the activity originated. The *utmp* log identifies all users who are currently logged on to a system, and the *wtmp* log stores snapshots of *utmp* information at regular intervals. These are only some of the many log files you'll find on most Linux and UNIX systems; please consult your system documentation and man pages to obtain a complete listing of logging facilities, formats used, and (default) storage locations.

Table 14.2 Common Syslog Facilities

Facility	Description
Auth	Authorization systems (for example, *login* and *su*)
Cron	The *cron* daemon drives scheduled scripts and commands and executes them as scheduled.
Daemon	Miscellaneous daemons not covered by other facilities
Kern	Abbreviation for *system kernel*—the operating system's memory-resident core code
local0-local7	Reserved for local use (numbered 0 through 7)
Lpr	Print spooling (line printer remote) system
Mark	A timestamp service that emits a timestamp for logging every 20 minutes (1,200 seconds)
Mail	E-mail system
Syslog	Internal *syslog* data

Table 14.3 Syslog Priorities

Priority	Description
Emerg	Panic conditions broadcast to all users
Alert	Conditions requiring immediate intervention
Crit	Critical errors, such as a device failure
Err	Standard priority errors
Warning	Warning messages
Notice	Notifications that may require some action or response
Info	Informational messages
Debug	Shows messages written to Syslog when programs run in debug mode

Firewall Logs, Reports, Alarms, and Alerts

In Chapter 12, we discussed the function of firewalls and the part they play in a network security plan. Because firewalls sit on the boundary between internal and external networks, they're ideally positioned to observe incoming (and outgoing) traffic. Thus, it should come as no surprise that firewalls not only represent a first and important line of defense to foil or deflect attack, but also that you can configure them to monitor and track activity that can point to incipient attacks as they commence. Unless attackers are savvy enough to erase log files (and alas, many are indeed smart enough to do this), firewall logs can also help you document successful or attempted attacks after the fact. Most boundary devices, which include not only firewalls but also screening routers, application gateways, proxy servers, and so forth, can—and indeed should—log various kinds of activity routinely. Given that such logs can be very important sources of evidence in cases where strong evidence is needed, most such devices log a wide range of traffic and various types of activity.

Because so many such devices run in UNIX-based or UNIX-like environments, the good news here is that the same information covered in the preceding section about the Syslog facility and general Linux or UNIX logging techniques often applies to firewalls, routers, and other devices. For example, even though Cisco devices run a Cisco proprietary operating system, known as the *Internet Operating System* or *IOS*, this software environment uses a reasonably standard Syslog implementation to support its logging capabilities. With the proviso in mind that low-level details vary from system to system and implementation to implementation, our general coverage of logging facilities and operation remains applicable to many (if not most) boundary devices in wide use.

> **NOTE**
>
> Add-on software products that can monitor and analyze firewall logs are available. For example, *firelogd* is a daemon that monitors Linux firewall logs. *Fwanalog* is a shell script that parses and summarizes firewall log files on UNIX and Linux systems. *Stonylake Firewall Reporter* is a server application that runs on Windows and Linux, and provides more than 150 reports to help in data analysis. *ZoneLog Analyzer* imports the logs from the ZoneAlarm firewalls into an easily queried database. Web Trends makes a Firewall Suite that processes log files from Check Point, Cisco, Microsoft ISA Server firewalls, and others.

Logging is only one of the ways in which firewalls and other boundary devices can provide information about the activity and traffic they handle. Firewalls (and other boundary devices) do indeed create log files, where all kinds of data may be written and stored for the long term. But these devices also support various types of other outputs, some of which can be quite important:

- **Alarms** These systems can be instructed to issue high-priority messages in various formats should particularly suspicious activities or events occur. Many such systems can send e-mail messages to specific respondents and even page designated telephone numbers, in addition to logging information when specified events occur. This functionality permits these systems to provoke immediate responses from responsible individuals. Because routers, firewalls, and other boundary devices may be subjected to ping floods or other denial-of-service (DoS) attacks, and because they may witness repeated failed logon attempts that can likewise signal that attacks have commenced, immediate action is sometimes essential in responding to such events.

- **Alerts** Some types of traffic activity are less obviously symptomatic of attack but should be looked into nonetheless. This explains why many boundary systems can also issue alerts when particular conditions occur. Although these alerts may also result in e-mail or pager calls, they are usually less urgent than outright alarms.

- **Reports** Although reportable events fall into the more mundane category of cataloging and categorizing traffic, activity, errors, and failed logon or other access attempts, most boundary devices can also report aggregate behavior and statistics over some specific period of time (daily, weekly, monthly, and so forth). Such reports are important indicators of overall system health and security and should be consulted regularly as part of the security monitoring and maintenance process.

In fact, most operating systems have some kind of alarm or alert facility as well. For example, Windows NT, 2000, XP, Vista, Server 2003, and Server 2008 support system alerts to alert administrators of system performance- or error-related events. Although the Event Viewer provides no way to configure alerts when security events occur, some third-party software packages such as IPSentry (www.ipsentry.com) monitor the Windows event logs and send alerts when triggering events occur.

When it comes to working with firewall logs (or responding to related alarms or alerts), some of the most common types of information you'll encounter relate directly to attacks and exploits documented elsewhere in this book. Thus, it should come as no surprise that the following types of activities or traffic might be noteworthy from both an attack detection and a post-attack perspective:

- **Internet Control Message Protocol (ICMP) traffic** Excessive pinging, ping scans, echo requests to broadcast address, ICMP time exceeded packets, distributed ICMP echo reply hits

- **Regular, systematic scanning behavior** Internet Protocol (IP) address range scanning, Transmission Control Protocol/User Datagram Protocol (TCP/UDP) port scans, NetBIOS name scans

- **Attempts to access specific well-known port addresses** Addresses associated with remote access software (pcAnywhere, Back Orifice [BO2K], and so forth), instant messaging (IM), or specific Trojan horse applications

In fact, any type of traffic or activity pattern—otherwise known as an *attack signature*, or more simply as a *signature*—that can be directly associated with a specific type or method of attack represents events that should be logged if at all possible. Sometimes recognizing a signature can involve more intelligence than a typical boundary device such as a firewall or screening router might possess, however. For that reason, we return to this subject later in this chapter when we discuss a class of systems known as *intrusion detection systems*, or *IDSes*, that are expressly built with this very kind of capability.

As to what kind of information occurs in a firewall log, it usually consists of fairly simple text records that document various aspects of network traffic underway. Though here again the details will vary to some extent, no log record is complete without including at least the following information (and usually more than appears in this deliberately brief list of common log entry fields):

- **Timestamp** Date and time at which the event, activity, or communication occurred
- **Source address** Reported IP address for traffic source
- **Source domain name (if available)** Reported domain name for traffic source
- **Destination address** Target delivery address for traffic
- **Protocol** Name of IP protocol or service in use

- **Message type or class (where applicable)** Type of message being sent
- **Port address (where applicable)** TCP or UDP port to which the message is directed
- **Socket address (where applicable)** Socket address to which the message is directed

In some cases, log entries also include what's called a *reverse DNS lookup* or a *backtrace.* You can configure some boundary devices to double-check the official IP address associated with domain names reported for inbound traffic against the actual IP address included in incoming traffic. When these two values differ, it can be a definite indicator of spoofing, which in turn may mean that suspicious activity (if not an outright attack) has ensued. This type of detection usually triggers an alert or alarm for that reason.

Commercial Intrusion Detection Systems

Earlier, we mentioned that firewalls and other simple boundary devices lack some degree of intelligence when it comes to observing, recognizing, and identifying attack signatures that may be present in the traffic they monitor and the log files they collect. Without sounding critical of such systems' capabilities, this deficiency explains why intrusion detection systems (often abbreviated as *IDSes*) are becoming increasingly important in helping to maintain proper network security. Whereas other boundary devices may collect all the information necessary to detect (and often, to foil) attacks that may be getting started or may already be underway, they haven't been programmed to inspect for and detect the kinds of traffic or network behavior patterns that match known attack signatures or that suggest that potential unrecognized attacks may be incipient or in progress.

In a nutshell, the simplest way to define an IDS might be to describe it as a specialized tool that knows how to read and interpret the contents of log files from routers, firewalls, servers, and other network devices. Furthermore, an IDS often stores a database of known attack signatures and can compare patterns of activity, traffic, or behavior it sees in the logs it's monitoring against those signatures to recognize when a close match between a signature and current or recent behavior occurs. At that point, the IDS can issue alarms or alerts, take various kinds of automatic action ranging from shutting down Internet links or specific servers to launching backtraces, and make other active attempts to identify attackers and actively collect evidence of their nefarious activities.

By analogy, an IDS does for a network what an antivirus (AV) software package does for files that enter a system: It inspects the contents of network traffic to look for and deflect possible attacks, just as an AV software package inspects the contents of incoming files, e-mail attachments, active Web content, and so forth to look for virus signatures (patterns that match known malware) or for possible malicious actions (patterns of behavior that are at least suspicious, if not downright unacceptable).

To be more specific, intrusion detection means detecting unauthorized use of or attacks on a system or network. An IDS is designed and used to detect and then to deflect or deter (if possible) such attacks or unauthorized use of systems, networks, and related resources. Like firewalls, IDSes may be software-based or may combine hardware and software (in the form of preinstalled and preconfigured stand-alone IDS devices). Often, IDS software runs on the same devices or servers where firewalls, proxies, or other boundary services operate; an IDS *not* running on the same device or server where the firewall or other services are installed will monitor those devices closely and carefully. Although such devices tend to operate at network peripheries, IDS systems can detect and deal with insider attacks as well as external attacks.

Characterizing Intrusion Detection Systems

IDSes vary according to a number of criteria. By explaining those criteria, we can explain what kinds of IDSes you're likely to encounter and how they do their jobs. First and foremost, it's possible to distinguish IDSes on the basis of the kinds of activities, traffic, transactions, or systems they monitor. In this case, IDSes may be divided into network-based, host-based, and application-based IDS types. IDSes that monitor network backbones and look for attack signatures are called *network-based IDSes*, whereas those that operate on hosts to defend and monitor the operating and file systems for signs of intrusion are called *host-based IDSes*. Some IDSes monitor only specific applications and are called *application-based IDSes*. (This type of treatment is usually reserved for important applications such as database management systems, content management systems, accounting systems, and so forth.) Read on to learn more about these various types of IDS monitoring approaches:

- **Network-based IDS characteristics**

  Pros: Network-based IDSes can monitor an entire, large network with only a few well-situated nodes or devices and impose little overhead on a network. Network-based IDSes are mostly passive devices that monitor ongoing network activity without adding significant overhead or interfering with network operation. They are easy to secure against attack and may even be undetectable to attackers; they also require little effort to install and use on existing networks.

  Cons: Network-based IDSes may not be able to monitor and analyze all traffic on large, busy networks and may therefore overlook attacks launched during peak traffic periods. Network based IDSes may not be able to monitor switch-based (high-speed) networks effectively, either. Typically, network-based IDSes cannot analyze encrypted data, nor do they report whether attempted attacks succeed or fail. Thus, network-based IDSes require a certain amount of active, manual involvement from network administrators to gauge the effects of reported attacks.

- **Host-based IDS characteristics**

  Pros: A host-based IDS can analyze activities on the host it monitors at a high level of detail; it can often determine which processes and/or users are involved in malicious activities. Though they may each focus on a single host, many host-based IDSes use an agent-console model where agents run on (and monitor) individual hosts but report to a single centralized console (so that a single console can configure, manage, and consolidate data from numerous hosts). Host-based IDSes can detect attacks undetectable to the network-based IDS and can gauge attack effects quite accurately. Host-based IDSes can use host-based encryption services to examine encrypted traffic, data, storage, and activity. Host-based IDSes have no difficulties operating on switch-based networks, either.

  Cons: Data collection occurs on a per-host basis; writing to logs or reporting activity requires network traffic and can decrease network performance. Clever attackers who compromise a host can also attack and disable host-based IDSes. Host-based IDSes can be foiled by DoS attacks (because they may prevent any traffic from reaching the host where they're running or prevent reporting on such attacks to a console elsewhere on a network). Most significantly, a host-based IDS does consume processing time, storage, memory, and other resources on the hosts where such systems operate.

- **Application-based IDS characteristics**

    Pros: An application-based IDS concentrates on events occurring within some specific application. They often detect attacks through analysis of application log files and can usually identify many types of attacks or suspicious activity. Sometimes application-based IDSes can even track unauthorized activity from individual users. They can also work with encrypted data, using application-based encryption/decryption services.

    Cons: Application-based IDSes are sometimes more vulnerable to attack than host-based IDSes. They can also consume significant application (and host) resources.

In practice, most commercial environments use some combination of network- and host- and/or application-based IDSes to observe what's happening on the network while also monitoring key hosts and applications more closely.

IDSes may also be distinguished by their differing approaches to event analysis. Some IDSes primarily use a technique called *signature detection*. This resembles the way many AV programs use virus signatures to recognize and block infected files, programs, or active Web content from entering a computer system, except that it uses a database of traffic or activity patterns related to known attacks, called *attack signatures*. Indeed, signature detection is the most widely used approach in commercial IDS technology today. Another approach is called *anomaly detection*. It uses rules or predefined concepts about "normal" and "abnormal" system activity (called *heuristics*) to distinguish anomalies from normal system behavior, and to monitor, report on, or block anomalies as they occur. Some IDSes support limited types of anomaly detection; most experts believe this kind of capability will become part of how more IDSes operate in the future. Read on for more information about these two kinds of event analysis techniques:

- **Signature-based IDS characteristics**

    Pros: A signature-based IDS examines ongoing traffic, activity, transactions, or behavior for matches with known patterns of events specific to known attacks. As with AV software, a signature-based IDS requires access to a current database of attack signatures and some way to actively compare and match current behavior against a large collection of signatures. Except when entirely new, uncataloged attacks occur, this technique works extremely well.

    Cons: Signature databases must be constantly updated, and IDSes must be able to compare and match activities against large collections of attack signatures. If signature definitions are too specific, a signature-based IDS may miss variations on known attacks. (A common technique for creating new attacks is to change existing, known attacks rather than to create entirely new ones from scratch.) Signature-based IDSes can also impose noticeable performance drags on systems when current behavior matches multiple (or numerous) attack signatures, either in whole or in part.

- **Anomaly-based IDS characteristics**

    Pros: An anomaly-based IDS examines ongoing traffic, activity, transactions, or behavior for anomalies on networks or systems that may indicate attack. The underlying principle is the notion that "attack behavior" differs enough from "normal user behavior" that it can be detected by cataloging and identifying the differences involved. By creating baselines of normal behavior, anomaly-based IDSes can observe when current behavior deviates statistically from the norm. This capability theoretically gives anomaly-based IDSes capabilities to detect new attacks that are neither known nor for which signatures have been created.

Cons: Because normal behavior can change easily and readily, anomaly-based IDSes are prone to false positives where attacks may be reported based on changes to the norm that are "normal," rather than representing real attacks. Their intensely analytical behavior can also impose sometimes-heavy processing overheads on systems where they're running. Furthermore, anomaly-based systems take awhile to create statistically significant baselines (to separate normal behavior from anomalies); they're relatively open to attack during this period.

Today, many AV packages include both signature-based and anomaly-based detection characteristics, but not all IDSes incorporate both approaches.

Finally, some IDSes are capable of responding to attacks when they occur. This behavior is desirable from two points of view. For one thing, a computer system can track behavior and activity in near-real time and respond much more quickly and decisively during early stages of an attack. Because automation helps hackers mount attacks, it stands to reason that it should also help security professionals fend them off as they occur. For another thing, IDSes run 24/7, but network administrators may not be able to respond as quickly during off hours as they can during peak hours (even if the IDS can page them with an alarm that an attack has begun). By automating a response to block incoming traffic from one or more addresses from which an attack originates, the IDS can halt an attack in process and block future attacks from the same address.

By implementing the following techniques, IDSes can fend off expert and novice hackers alike. Although experts are more difficult to block entirely, these techniques can slow them down considerably:

- Breaking TCP connections by injecting reset packets into attacker connections causes attacks to fall apart.

- Deploying automated packet filters to block routers or firewalls from forwarding attack packets to servers or hosts under attack stops most attacks cold—even DoS or distributed denial-of-service (DDoS) attacks. This works for attacker addresses and for protocols or services under attack (by blocking traffic at different layers of the Advanced Research Projects Agency [ARPA] networking model, so to speak).

- Deploying automated disconnects for routers, firewalls, or servers can halt all activity when other measures fail to stop attackers (as in extreme DDoS attack situations, where filtering would work effectively on only the Internet service provider [ISP] side of an Internet link, if not higher up the ISP chain, as close to Internet backbones as possible).

- Actively pursuing reverse DNS lookups or other ways of attempting to establish hacker identity is a technique used by some IDSes, generating reports of malicious activity to all ISPs in the routes used between the attacker and the attackee. Because such responses may themselves raise legal issues, experts recommend obtaining legal advice before repaying hackers in kind.

NOTE

For access to a great set of articles and resources on IDS technology, visit http://searchsecurity.techtarget.com and use the site's search engine to produce results on *intrusion detection* as a search string.

Commercial IDS Players

Literally hundreds of vendors offer various forms of commercial IDS implementations. Most effective solutions combine network- and host-based IDS implementations. Likewise, most such implementations are primarily signature-based, with only limited anomaly-based detection capabilities present in certain specific products or solutions. Finally, most modern IDSes include some limited automatic response capabilities, but these usually concentrate on automated traffic filtering, blocking, or disconnects as a last resort. Although some systems claim to be able to launch counterstrikes against attacks, best practices indicate that automated identification and backtrace facilities are the most useful aspects that such facilities provide and are therefore those most likely to be used.

A huge number of potential vendors can provide IDS products to companies and organizations. Without specifically endorsing any particular vendor, the following offer some of the most widely used and best-known solutions in this product space:

- Cisco Systems is perhaps best known for its switches and routers, but Cisco offers significant firewall and intrusion detection products as well (www.cisco.com).

- GFI LANguard is a family of monitoring, scanning, and file-integrity-check products that offer broad intrusion detection and response capabilities (www.gfi.com/languard).

- Network-1 Security Solutions offers various families of desktop and server (host-based) intrusion detection products, along with centralized security management facilities and firewalls (www.network-1.com).

- Tripwire is perhaps the best known of all vendors of file integrity and signature-checking utilities (which are also known as Tripwire). But Tripwire also offers integrity check products for routers, switches, and servers, along with a centralized management console for its various products (www.tripwire.com).

On the Scene

Weighing IDS Options

In addition to the various IDS vendors mentioned in the preceding list, judicious use of a good Internet search engine can help network administrators identify more potential IDS suppliers than they would ever have the time or inclination to investigate in detail. That's why we also urge administrators to consider an additional alternative: deferring some or all of the organization's network security technology decisions to a special type of outsourcing company. Known as managed security service providers, or MSSPs, these organizations can help their customers select, install, and maintain state-of-the-art security policies and technical infrastructures to match. Law enforcement professionals may find these organizations to be particularly knowledgeable sources for information, help, and support when tackling technology questions or teasing apart IT security puzzles.

IP Spoofing and Other Antidetection Tactics

Despite your best efforts to backtrace unwanted e-mail or attack traffic, sometimes you will still be unable to determine its real source or conclusively identify the person or persons behind that activity. The primary reason for the phenomenon is that hackers typically generate network traffic or messages that contain fabricated data for the source address, port numbers, protocol IDs, and other information that normally permits such information to be conclusively associated with an originating IP address, if not also an originating process identifier (and by extension, the user or service responsible for creating that process). This is a deliberate and calculated technique to prevent identification of attackers and to deflect interest from the real source of such traffic to unwitting or uninvolved third parties.

The most common form of spoofing occurs when attackers try to insert fabricated traffic or messages that purport to originate inside a local network through an outside interface. That explains why the most common antispoofing rule enforced at most screening routers and firewalls is to drop any packets that arrive on an external interface that report an originating address that should appear only on an internal interface. Other forms of spoofing may be detected by using a backtrace or reverse DNS lookup to compare domain names and associated IP addresses (when that data is available) and dropping all packets where these two information items show no correlation (as when the reported IP address originates outside the range of addresses assigned to the organization from within which it claims to originate).

The real problem with spoofed traffic occurs when IDS or human administrators try to follow the traffic back to its source and hit various types of dead ends. Recall, for example, that various types of DoS or DDoS attacks rely on compromised intermediate computers, sometimes called zombies or agents, and you'll quickly understand why tracing attacks back to their source can't always identify attackers. When you determine where certain attacks originate, you may only be able to identify other victims rather than finding a "smoking gun" which points to an attacker. The savvier and more sophisticated the hacker who perpetrates an attack, the less likely it is that he or she will provide direct clues that lead directly to his or her primary presence on the Internet. Rather, you'll find your identification efforts will lead you down a trail of intermediaries, cut-outs, and anonymizer services, each of which you must then investigate to look for clues to the identity of the mastermind behind the cybercrimes you are pursuing.

This also explains why contacting service providers who may be forwarding attacks—and working with them not only to trace back the origination of attack traffic, but also to block it from going through unwitting intermediaries—is an important part of the process of handling security incidents and fending off future attacks. In addition, numerous Web sites and Internet services maintain lists of known IP addresses, domain names, and e-mail addresses from which attacks have originated in the past. By subscribing to such services and using them to configure packet and e-mail filters, administrators can fend off many potential sources of attack preemptively—as many ISPs themselves do—and avoid interacting with known sources of trouble.

Numerous sources for information about spammers and attackers are available online; we mention only a couple of examples here. To find more, use a good Internet search engine to search on strings such as *spam database*, *attacker database*, *spam prevention*, and so forth:

- List of all known DNS-based spam databases: www.declude.com/junkmail/support/ip4r.htm
- Lists of spammers, harassers, mail bombers, and other e-mail abusers: www.ram.org/ramblings/philosophy/spam/spammers.html and www.spamhaus.org

Honeypots, Honeynets, and Other "Cyberstings"

Although the strategy involved in luring hackers to spend time investigating attractive network devices or servers can cause its own problems, finding ways to lure intruders into a system or network improves the odds that you might be able to identify those intruders and pursue them more effectively. A *honeypot* is a computer system that is deliberately exposed to public access—usually on the Internet—for the express purpose of attracting and distracting attackers. Likewise, a *honeynet* is a network set up for the same purpose, where attackers will find not only vulnerable services or servers, but also vulnerable routers, firewalls, and other network boundary devices, security applications, and so forth. In other words, these are the technical equivalent of the familiar police "sting" operation.

CyberLaw Review

Walking the Line between Opportunity and Entrapment

Most law enforcement officers are aware of the fine line that they must walk when setting up a "sting"—an operation in which police officers pretend to be victims or participants in crime with the goal of getting criminal suspects to commit an illegal act in their presence. Most states have laws that prohibit entrapment; that is, law enforcement officers are not allowed to *cause* a person to commit a crime and then arrest him or her for doing it. Entrapment is a defense to prosecution; if the accused person can show at trial that he or she was entrapped, the result must be an acquittal.

Courts have traditionally held, however, that providing a *mere opportunity* for a criminal to commit a crime does not constitute entrapment. To entrap involves using persuasion, duress, or other undue pressure to force someone to commit a crime that the person would not otherwise have committed. Under this holding, setting up a honeypot or honeynet would be like the (perfectly legitimate) police tactic of placing an abandoned automobile by the side of the road and watching it to see whether anyone attempts to burglarize, vandalize, or steal it. It should also be noted that entrapment applies only to the actions of law enforcement or government personnel. A civilian cannot entrap, regardless of how much pressure is exerted on the target to commit the crime. (However, a civilian could be subject to other charges, such as criminal solicitation or criminal conspiracy, for causing someone else to commit a crime.)

The following characteristics are typical of honeypots or honeynets:

- Systems or devices used as lures are set up with only "out of the box" default installations so that they are deliberately made subject to all known vulnerabilities, exploits, and attacks.

- The systems or devices used as lures include no real sensitive information—such as passwords, data, applications, or services on which an organization must really depend or which it must absolutely protect—so these lures can be compromised, or even destroyed, without causing real damage, loss, or harm to the organization that presents them to be attacked.

- Systems or devices used as lures often also contain deliberately tantalizing objects or resources, such as files named *password.db*, folders named *Top Secret*, and so forth—often consisting only of encrypted garbage data or log files of no real significance or value—to attract and hold an attacker's interest long enough to give a backtrace a chance of identifying the attack's point of origin.

- Systems or devices used as lures also include or are monitored by passive applications that can detect and report on attacks or intrusions as soon as they start, so the process of backtracing and identification can begin as soon as possible.

Although this technique can certainly help identify the unwary or unsophisticated attacker, it also runs the risk of attracting additional attention or ire from savvier attackers. Honeypots or honeynets, once identified, are often publicized on hacker message boards or mailing lists and thus become *more* subject to attacks and hacker activity than they otherwise might. Likewise, if the organization that sets up a honeypot or honeynet is itself identified, its production systems and networks may also be subjected to more attacks than might otherwise be the case.

The honeypot technique is best reserved for use when a company or organization employs full-time IT security professionals who can monitor and deal with these lures on a regular basis, or when law enforcement operations seek to target specific suspects in a "virtual sting" operation. In such situations, the risks are sure to be well understood, and proper security precautions, processes, and procedures are far more likely to already be in place (and properly practiced). Nevertheless, for organizations that seek to identify and pursue attackers more proactively, honeypots and honeynets can provide valuable tools to aid in such activities.

Numerous quality resources on honeypots and honeynets are available on the Internet by searching on either term at http://searchsecurity.techtarget.com or www.techrepublic.com. The Honeynet Project at www.honeynet.org is probably the best overall resource on the topic online; it not only provides copious information on the project's work to define and document standard honeypots and honeynets, but it also does a great job of exploring hacker mindsets, motivations, tools, and attack techniques.

Summary

Why is cybercrime detection important to investigators? Only by detecting that cybercrimes have occurred (or are occurring) will investigators be able to get a step ahead of the criminals and start the investigation while the trail is still "hot." Furthermore, only when suspicious activity is detected or observed do investigators know that they must take the steps necessary to obtain, secure, and prepare the evidence that will be necessary if any kind of legal charges are to stick. By following attack traffic from its targets back to its sources—even if those sources point only to other victims and not to the real attacker, as may often be the case—investigators can work with intermediate service providers to inform them about attacks and to help administrators and security personnel prevent such attacks from recurring. Even when prosecution isn't possible, or when those who have been attacked decide not to pursue legal remedies, the information obtained and shared during the investigation can still have an overall positive impact on the security posture and awareness of the various parties investigators contact in the process.

One key element in obtaining evidence of cybercrimes may be found by enabling auditing of suspicious events in the boundary devices and operating systems that are likely to be subject to attack. IT professionals should understand how to instruct these systems and devices to log such data and should also be aware of what kinds and classes of events are most worth logging. These events include logon attempts, access to sensitive resources, use of administrative privileges, and monitoring of key system and data files. Likewise, law enforcement professionals should be aware not only that these logs exist, but also that they often provide the most salient evidence of attempted or successful cybercrimes, and they must be aware of how to make appropriate efforts to secure and protect these logs before and during the investigation. Firewalls, routers, proxy servers, network servers, and IDSes can all contribute logs (plus related reports, alarms, and alerts) to substantiate allegations that unauthorized access, alteration, destruction, or denial of service occurred for information assets or services and, in some cases, to help track down the origin of the activity.

In the security model known as triple-A (authentication, authorization, and accounting), accounting is what makes auditing and logging of suspicious or illicit activity possible. IT and law enforcement professionals alike must understand this concept. Administrators must practice proper auditing and logging techniques to make sure they can detect cybercrimes (preferably before they succeed at compromising or damaging an organization's IT assets or infrastructure), obtain evidence that can help document illicit or unwanted activity, and assist in identifying the parties involved. Note also that boundary devices, Windows, and UNIX/Linux systems all have their own methods for enabling and recording such data, but that evidence is readily obtainable to those who know what to ask for and where to find what they seek.

On the proactive, preventive side of system and network security, boundary systems and servers should be configured to prevent or deflect common known attacks while also auditing and logging any evidence that related activities may be occurring. Log data usually includes timestamps, putative source addresses and domain names, and other information that can be used to trace attacks to their systems of origin. E-mail messages include similar information so that unwanted e-mail can be tracked back through the systems that forwarded it from its sender to its ultimate receiver. All too often, however, such trails lead only to additional victims or to unwitting participants in cybercrimes rather than to the actual perpetrators.

When tracing the origin of cybercrimes and the paths their network activity takes from the point of origin to the point of attack, investigators will find numerous tools and utilities useful in obtaining information. Firewalls, screening routers, and IDSes can often seek out and obtain such information automatically, and numerous Windows and Linux or UNIX tools and commands also exist to reacquire or confirm such information manually. Both IT and law enforcement professionals should understand how to use such commands and utilities, particularly those that help map IP addresses to domain names, and vice versa, to help identify points along the path of attack as well as its ultimate origin.

IDSes not only help detect and actively foil cybercrimes, but they also often help gather evidence about their patterns of attack, specific details about related activities, and so forth. Many IDSes operate on so-called attack signatures, which provide specific patterns of activity, network traffic, or behavior against which ongoing network activity may be compared to identify (and sometimes even foil) attacks as they occur. Like AV software and its signature databases, the IDS must also be constantly updated to keep its attack signatures up-to-date. Some IDSes also seek to identify anomalous behavior on systems or networks as a way to detect potential attacks for which signatures may not yet have been defined. In addition, IDSes can focus on individual hosts, applications, or networks to look for evidence of attacks or suspicious activity.

Despite investigators' real abilities to trace attacks and identify their points of origin, spoofing techniques can often foil their efforts to identify the real perpetrators of cybercrimes. Often, initial suspects in cybercrimes turn out to be themselves victims of cybercrimes that make them only intermediaries for real perpetrators, or they may only be unwitting participants in activities that originate elsewhere. That's why antispoofing techniques are important components when configuring firewalls, screening routers, and so forth to avoid potential attack and why investigators must be prepared to follow trails of attack further, rather than rely on what the initial available evidence reveals.

Some companies and organizations may choose to expose deliberate lures to attackers—sometimes known as honeypots (for individual systems that act as lures) or honeynets (for entire networks that act as lures)—as a way of attracting their attention, then distract them long enough to increase the odds of identifying the perpetrators involved. Although this strategy does incur some additional risks (much like those associated with what insurance professionals call an "attractive nuisance" or what law enforcement professionals can readily identify as "sting operations"), when properly implemented and practiced, it can produce definite, usable results.

In the final analysis, the proper practice of security includes planning for potential intrusion or compromise, with attendant tools and settings in place to gather evidence of the existence and operation of illicit or unwanted activities. Because such evidence is essential to detecting cybercrimes, preventing recurrence, and enabling successful prosecution, it's a key element of any proper security policy. This also explains why tracking and monitoring represents an essential "reality check" to make sure security is working properly and to be able to deal with unforeseen or unexpected attacks or vulnerabilities if and when they occur.

Frequently Asked Questions

Q: What steps should IT or law enforcement professionals take to inventory logs, audit trails, and other potential sources of evidence or supporting data when investigating cybercrimes?

A: The short answer to this question is inventory, inspect, filter, document, and preserve. Let's expand on that a bit:

- **Inventory** Take stock of all firewalls, screening routers, IDSes, systems, and servers in use through which attack traffic may have passed or at which attack traffic or activity may have focused. Examine each element to identify related log files or audit trails, and take note of their names and locations.

- **Inspect** Examine the various log files or audit trails to determine whether they contain records or entries that contain any traces of or evidence related to the incident under investigation. If so, add the name and location of each such audit trail to your list of evidence files.

- **Filter** Mathematics professionals call this step *data reduction* because it consists of ignoring entries that have no bearing on the incident you're investigating and collecting only those that are relevant to the matter at hand. Most log or event viewers include powerful data filtering tools; those that do not can usually be imported into a spreadsheet or database where those applications' built-in search tools can help you separate what's important from what's not. Make sure your notes include the name and location of the original source file and that you (or an expert witness) can attest that (a) data filtering is a common practice in log and event trace analysis and (b) you can demonstrate a direct relationship between the original file and the filtered file.

- **Document** Explain how the captured log entries, event listings, and so forth provide evidence of a cybercrime. In addition, document extensively the original sources for such data, including their locations; original filenames; current locations of original, unaltered files or drives; and how the data was handled since initial detection of the incident occurred.

- **Preserve** Take all steps necessary to preserve the original source of the log files or event data. This may require removing a hard drive from a system or even taking a system out of service so as to preserve the evidence in its most pristine possible state.

Q: Given the need to interpret and explain the contents of some specific log file or event trace, how can an investigator obtain the information necessary to perform this task?

A: We've noted repeatedly that although the kinds of information recorded in logs and event traces are similar across multiple operating systems and boundary devices, the details vary according to each system and implementation. To document the layout and interpret the significance of log files and event traces, you will need to contact the vendor of the operating system, application, or device in question and ask the company to provide you with its documentation for those log files or event traces. In many cases, you'll be able to find this information for yourself if you use the vendor's search engine on its Web site or consult its technical support database or other information resources the vendor makes available online. If this doesn't produce the desired results, you may need to call the vendor's technical support operation and ask for assistance in identifying and obtaining the right information. In most cases, this should be an entirely routine matter and relatively easy to handle.

Q: How can an organization be sure that its IDS and other boundary devices are completely up-to-date and that they include the latest attack signatures, patches, fixes, and so forth?

A: In most cases, the system or software vendor that provides the IDS or other boundary device will also offer a notification service, online update information, and perhaps even tools you can use to assess the status of databases, patches, and fixes for such systems or services. Usually, a search on the vendor's Web site for the product in question will provide direct pointers to such information because the vendor understands the importance and urgency of that information as much as its customers do. When in doubt, contact the vendor's technical support operation. Here again, obtaining this information (or pointers to it) should be an entirely routine matter and easy to complete.

Q: If an organization becomes subject to an attack that appears to be unknown or for which no signatures appear to be available, how and to whom should this kind of information be reported?

A: The odds against falling prey to the first (or an early instance of an) attack are pretty low, but one unlucky organization must inevitably be the first victim of new vulnerabilities or be subjected to as-yet-undocumented attacks, as they occur. When this happens, it's important to notify all parties that might be concerned, including the following:

- Notify your upstream ISP and any other upstream ISPs that might sit between your network and the Internet.

- Contact any vendors whose products handle traffic related to such an attack, including firewall, proxy server, screening router, IDS, application, AV (where applicable), and operating system vendors. Most companies have formal reporting mechanisms they provide to customers who want to report security incidents. It will help if you can identify these companies in advance so that your response during an incident isn't slowed by researching this information.

- All the big general-incident clearinghouses should also be notified, including www.cert.org, and other more-focused security organizations that focus on your particular industry or market niche.

- In the United States, if your state has criminal laws that cover network attacks (such as unauthorized access or denial/disruption of network services) contact your local police or sheriff's office.

- In the United States, the FBI and Secret Service have developed guidelines intended to encourage companies to report cyberattacks. See *CIO Cyberthreat Response & Reporting Guidelines* (in PDF format) at www.cio.com/research/security/incident_response.pdf for detailed information.

- Outside the United States, contact the national or regional agency responsible for making and enforcing cybercrime laws.

Chapter 15

Collecting and Preserving Digital Evidence

Topics we'll investigate in this chapter:

- **Understanding the Role of Evidence in a Criminal Case**
- **Collecting Digital Evidence**
- **Preserving Digital Evidence**
- **Recovering Digital Evidence**
- **Documenting Evidence**
- **Computer Forensic Resources**
- **Understanding Legal Issues**

☑ **Summary**

☑ **Frequently Asked Questions**

Introduction

In previous chapters, we discussed methods of detecting that cybercrimes have occurred and tracking down the person(s) responsible. The next and perhaps most important step in prosecuting the offender is to collect the evidence that will be used to build the case to be presented at trial.

The field of computer forensics involves identifying, extracting, documenting, and preserving information that is stored or transmitted in electronic or magnetic form (that is, digital evidence). Like fingerprints, digital evidence can be visible (such as files stored on disk that can be accessed via the normal directory structure using standard file management tools such as Windows Explorer) or it can be latent (not readily visible or accessible, requiring some sort of processing—via special software or techniques—to locate and identify it). An important aspect of computer forensics involves finding and evaluating this "hidden data" for its evidentiary value.

Standards have been developed that apply to the collection and preservation of digital evidence, which differs in nature from most other types of evidence and thus requires different methods of handling. Following procedures that are proper, accepted, and, in some cases, prescribed by law in dealing with evidence is vital to the successful prosecution of a cybercrime case. The proper handling of these procedures comes into play at two different points in a trial:

If evidence is not collected and handled according to the proper standards, the judge may deem the evidence inadmissible when it is presented (usually based on the opposing attorney's *motion to suppress*) and the jury members will never get a chance to evaluate it or consider it in making their decision.

If the evidence is admitted, the opposing attorney will attack its credibility during questioning of the witnesses who testify regarding it. Such an attack can create doubt in jury members' minds that will cause them to disregard the evidence in making their decision—and perhaps even taint the credibility of the entire case.

The entire investigation will be of little value if the evidence that shows the defendant's guilt is not allowed into the trial or if the jury gives it no weight. Thus, proper handling of evidence is one of the most important issues facing all criminal investigators and, because of the intangible nature of digital evidence, cybercrime investigators in particular.

Because this is such an important topic—not only for investigators, but also for prosecutors, judges, and justice system professionals involved in cybercrime cases—many organizations and publications are devoted solely to issues concerning digital evidence. The International Organization on Computer Evidence (IOCE; www.ioce.org) was established in 1995 to provide a forum for law enforcement agencies around the world to exchange information about issues regarding computer forensics; its U.S. component is the Scientific Working Group on Digital Evidence (SWGDE; www.swgde.org). The International Association of Computer Investigative Specialists (IACIS; www.cops.org) is a nonprofit organization that is dedicated to educating law enforcement professionals in the area of computer forensics. The *International Journal of Digital Evidence* (www.ijde.org/) is an online publication devoted to discussions of the theory and practice of handling digital evidence. Many other similar resources that focus on computer forensics are available, and more broad-based organizations such as the American Academy of Forensic Sciences (www.aafs.org) address computer crimes and digital evidence along with other topics in that area.

A glance at any of these resources will reveal that digital evidence handling is a huge topic that could easily fill several books (and already has). It is far beyond the scope of this chapter to cover every aspect of collecting and preserving digital evidence. This chapter provides additional material to what we've already covered regarding the role evidence plays in a criminal case (particularly in a cybercrime case) and discusses standard procedures for dealing with digital evidence, as well as specific evidence location and examination techniques. We also outline procedures for documenting digital evidence and discuss some of the legal issues involved in evidence collection and handling. Finally, we provide many excellent online resources that furnish detailed instructions for performing the tasks described in this chapter and provide information about commercial services and equipment that can aid in the evidence recovery process.

Understanding the Role of Evidence in a Criminal Case

The process of collecting, examining, preserving, and presenting evidence is a legal process and is governed by the laws of the jurisdiction of the court in which the evidence will be introduced. Thus, it is extremely important for investigators to become familiar with the applicable laws. These rules are adopted by statute and are usually codified into a document titled "Rules of Evidence."

The rules of state courts may differ from those of federal courts, and the rules for evidence in criminal trials may differ from those for civil trials. Generally, evidence must be *authenticated*, which in this context usually means that some witness must testify to its authenticity. In the case of digital evidence, this could be a witness who has personal knowledge of the evidence (for example, a person who shared the computer with the accused and observed the document or file in question on the computer). It could also be the first responder who saw the evidence on-screen when responding to the incident or an expert who examined the computer and evidence after it was seized. One of the most important aspects of preparing to introduce evidence in court is determining which witnesses will testify as to its existence and validity, describe the circumstances of its discovery, and verify that it has not been tampered with.

CyberLaw Review

When Authentication Is Not Required

Certain types of evidence are sometimes held by the rules of evidence to be self-authenticating. This means testimony as to authenticity isn't required and usually refers to such things as public documents under seal, certified copies of public records, official publications, and the like. It is also possible for both sides at trial to agree to *stipulate* as to the authenticity of a piece of evidence, in which case it does not have to be authenticated through testimony. When both sides agree to the stipulation of a fact (such as the fact that the evidence is authentic), the judge will advise the jury that they are to presume the fact is true and that it is not a matter that has to be proved or disproved at trial.

Defining Evidence

Evidence can generally be defined as the means by which an alleged fact, the truth of which is subjected to scrutiny, is established or disproved. The legal significance of any given piece of evidence lies in its influence on the judge or jury at trial. There are three categories of evidence:

- **Physical evidence (sometimes called real evidence)** Consists of tangible objects that can be seen and touched

- **Direct testamentary evidence** The testimony of a witness who can give an account of facts based on personal experience through the use of the five senses

- **Circumstantial evidence** Not based on personal observation of the offense but on observation or knowledge of facts that tend to support a conclusion indirectly but do not prove it definitively

CyberLaw Review

It's "Only" Circumstantial

The news media and (via movies and novels) the entertainment industry—not to mention defense attorneys—often refer to evidence as "merely circumstantial," with the implication that circumstantial evidence does not really constitute evidence or that it is inherently inferior to direct evidence. In fact, circumstantial evidence is equally admissible in court, and most criminals are convicted based on circumstantial evidence. This is because in many cases criminals do not commit their offenses in front of witnesses, so there is no one to testify to having seen or heard the offense occur. It is the *totality of the evidence* in the minds of the jury members that matters—whether all that evidence, taken together, persuades them beyond a reasonable doubt that the defendant committed the crime.

Here is an example of direct evidence as compared to circumstantial evidence:

- **Direct evidence** John Smith **testifies** under oath that he was in the room with his friend, Joe Hacker, when Joe broke into the ABC Corporation's computer network and that John saw the break-in take place on Joe's computer screen.

- **Circumstantial evidence** The network administrator of ABC Corporation testifies that an intruder using the Internet Protocol (IP) address *xxx.xxx.xxx.xxx* penetrated the network at 2:20 a.m. on December 12, 2001. Internet service provider (ISP) records show that the IP address in question was assigned via Dynamic Host Configuration Protocol (DHCP) to Joe Hacker's computer at that time on that date. Joe's girlfriend testifies that

Continued

Joe was in the study "doing something on the computer" between the hours of midnight and 4:00 a.m. on that date. No one actually saw Joe perform the intrusion, and none of the evidence definitively proves that he did, but taken together, the evidence supports the conclusion that Joe Hacker broke into the ABC Corporation network.

In a computer crime case, evidence tends to be one of the following types, as classified by the SWGDE/IOCE standards:

- **Digital evidence** Information of value to a criminal case that is stored or transmitted in digital form

- **Data objects** Information of value to a criminal case that is associated with physical items

- **Physical items** The physical media on which digital information is stored or through which it is transmitted or transferred

Digital evidence can be classified as *original digital evidence* (that is, the physical items and data objects associated with those items at the time the evidence was seized) and *duplicate digital evidence* (referring to an accurate digital reproduction of all the data objects contained on an original physical item).

"Written" evidence is also sometimes classified as either demonstrative evidence or documentary evidence. *Demonstrative evidence* is that which reconstructs the scene or incident in question and allows jurors to view it, using visual aids such as graphs, charts, drawings, and models. *Documentary evidence* usually refers to written documents that constitute evidence. For example, a letter or photograph is generally considered documentary evidence. As we'll discuss in Chapter 17, when documents are introduced as evidence, the entire document must generally be admitted even though only part of it might be read to the court. In some cases of digital evidence, there is debate among legal scholars as to whether it should be classified as documentary or demonstrative. Computer evidence is not quite like other documentary evidence (which is usually paper) for several reasons: A copy of a digital file is generally identical to the original, and a document can be copied without physically removing it from its location or leaving behind any indication that it has been copied. Many legal experts consider digital evidence to be more demonstrative than documentary, because the field of computer forensics basically concerns itself with reconstructing the crime scene. However, this view could vary depending on the type of digital evidence associated with a particular crime.

Under the *best-evidence rule*, the original document must be presented as evidence unless it has been destroyed or falls under other exceptions. However, the Federal Rules of Evidence recognize that computer evidence is different from other written evidence. Rule 1001-3 addresses this issue, saying, "If data are stored by computer or similar device, any printout or other output readable by sight, shown to reflect the data accurately, is an original." The burden is on the party introducing the evidence to show that it does indeed reflect the data accurately. It must be proven that the evidence is what it is claimed to be and that it hasn't been changed since it was taken into custody. Otherwise, the evidence will be deemed inadmissible.

Admissibility of Evidence

There are a number of requirements for evidence to be admissible in court. The evidence must be *competent* (that is, reliable and credible), it must be *relevant* (it tends to prove a fact of the case), and it must be *material* (it substantiates an issue that is in question in the case).

In addition, to be admissible in U.S. courts, evidence must be obtained legally. That is, it must be obtained in accordance with the laws governing search and seizure, including laws expressed in the U.S. and state constitutions. If evidence is obtained through an illegal search, even though it proves the guilt of the defendant, the evidence is considered to be "tainted." This is known as the "fruits of the poisonous tree" doctrine, or the *exclusionary rule*.

Case law in some jurisdictions sets special rules for the admissibility of scientific evidence. Under the Federal Rules of Evidence, Rule 402, all relevant evidence is admissible except as otherwise provided under the U.S. Constitution, by Act of Congress, or under the Federal Rules of Evidence themselves (for example, evidence obtained in violation of a suspect's constitutional rights). Rule 401 defines relevant evidence as "any evidence having a tendency to make the existence of any fact that is of consequence to the determination of the action more probable or less probable than it would be without the evidence." This is known as the *relevancy test*. Another standard sometimes applied to scientific evidence is the *general acceptance test*, also known as the *Frye standard*, which holds that a scientific technique must be generally accepted in the field before the results of the technique can be admitted as evidence.

Forensic Examination Standards

Although the rules of evidence regarding digital data are not clear-cut, it is always safest to exceed the minimum requirements for admissibility. When investigators take extra precautions to ensure the integrity of evidence, above and beyond what the court might find acceptable, not only will the possibility of having the evidence excluded by the judge be avoided, but the impression on the jury will be more favorable as well.

As we mentioned earlier in this chapter, a number of organizations provide standards governing forensic examination procedures for their members. Showing in court that you adhered to such high standards in conducting the investigation will enhance your case.

Most organizations and experts involved in computer forensics agree on some basic standards regarding the handling of digital evidence, which can be summarized as follows:

- The original evidence should be preserved in a state as close as possible to the state it was in when found.

- If at all possible, an exact copy (image) of the original should be made to be used for examination so as not to damage the integrity of the original.

- Copies of data made for examination should be made on media that is *forensically sterile*—that is, there must be no preexisting data on the disk or other media; it should be completely "clean" and checked for freedom from viruses and defects.

- All evidence should be properly tagged and documented and the chain of custody preserved, and each step of the forensic examination should be documented in detail.

Collecting Digital Evidence

A network administrator or another member of the IT staff will often be the first person to become aware of a cybercrime in a corporate setting, and the IT incident response team (if the company has one) will take the initial steps to stop the crime in progress and "freeze" the crime scene before law enforcement personnel take over. Even after the police are called in, the process of collecting digital evidence usually involves several people, who we previously discussed in detail in Chapter 5:

- *First responders*, who are officers or official security personnel who arrive first at the crime scene. These people are responsible for identifying the crime scene, protecting it, and preserving evidence.

- *Investigators*, or an investigative team, who is responsible for establishing a chain of command, conducting a search of the crime scene, and maintaining the integrity of the evidence.

- *Crime scene technicians and specialists*, who are called out to process the evidence, and who are responsible for preserving volatile evidence (which we'll discuss later in this chapter), duplicating disks, and preparing evidence for transport (including shutting down systems, and packaging, tagging, and logging evidence).

It is important that one person be designated in charge of the scene and be given the authority to make final decisions as to how the scene will be secured, how the search will be conducted, and how the evidence will be handled. This is usually the role of the senior investigator. It is equally important that each member of this team understand his or her role and adhere to it. The ability of the team to work together is essential to the successful collection of evidence.

Evidence Collection

Collection is a practice consisting of the identification, processing, and documentation of evidence. When collecting evidence, a crime scene technician will start by identifying what evidence is present and where it is located. For example, if someone broke into the server room and changed permissions on the server, the room and server would be where you would find evidence. When establishing this, the crime scene technician will then ensure that the crime scene has been secured, and that others have been prevented from entering the area and accessing the evidence. If the area wasn't secured, suspects could enter the area and alter or contaminate evidence. For example, if fingerprints were being taken to determine who broke into the server room, merely touching the door and other items would distort any findings. Maybe the perpetrator left the fingerprints while in the process of breaking in, or maybe someone else left them when the crime scene was not secure.

Once the evidence that is present has been identified, the next step is to identify how the evidence can be recovered. Evidence on computers may be obtained in a variety of ways, from viewing log files to recovering the data with special forensic software. If data recovery is needed, the computer's operating system should be identified, along with the media used to store the evidence. Once you've determined this, it is then possible to decide on the techniques and tools needed to recover the data.

In addition to photographing the screen of a computer to record any volatile data that's displayed, you should also photograph how the equipment is set up. When you've transported the equipment and are ready to begin examining it, you will need to set it up exactly as it was at the crime scene. After the case is completed, setup may also be required if the equipment is returned to the owner. To ensure that the equipment is set up properly, you should photograph the front and back of the machine upon seizing it. Photographs or diagrams should be made showing how cables and wires were attached.

Backup media should also be collected, as analyzing any backup tapes may show that an incident began earlier than expected. In some cases, you may find that data that was backed up days or even weeks before shows that an intruder entered a system, or a virus infected data on hard disks. If this were undetected, it is possible that you could unknowingly restore a virus to the system as part of the recovery process, and create a repeat of the initial incident.

Preserving Digital Evidence

Digital evidence is, by its nature, fragile. Some data is *volatile*—that is, it is transient in nature and, unlike data stored on disk, will be lost when the computer is shut down. Data on a computer disk can be easily damaged, destroyed, or changed either deliberately or accidentally. The first step in handling such digital evidence is to protect it from any sort of manipulation or accident. As we discussed in Chapter 6, the best way to do this is to immediately make a complete bitstream image of the media on which the evidence is stored.

> **NOTE**
>
> As we've mentioned in previous chapters, a *bitstream image* is a copy that records every data bit that was recorded to the original storage device, including all hidden files, temp files, corrupted files, file fragments, and erased files that have not yet been overwritten. In other words, every binary digit is duplicated exactly onto the copy media. Bitstream copies (sometimes called *bitstream backups*) use cyclic redundancy check (CRC) computations to validate that the copy is the same as the original source data.

The "mirror image" should be an exact duplicate of the original, and the original should then be stored in a safe place where its integrity can be maintained. (See the "Environmental Factors" section later in the chapter.) The copy is made via a process called *disk imaging*. In some cases, evidence could be limited to a few data files that can be copied individually rather than creating a copy of the entire disk. In the following sections, we review a number of factors in preserving evidence and ensuring the integrity of disks used for imaging or copying. We consider environmental factors that can affect the integrity of evidence, as well as preservation concerns related to specific types of storage media.

Preserving Volatile Data

The data that is held in temporary storage in the system's memory (including random access memory [RAM], cache memory, and the onboard memory of system peripherals such as the video card or network interface card [NIC]) is called *volatile data* because the memory depends on electric power to hold its contents. When the system is powered off or if power is disrupted, the data disappears. According to the IEEE Internet draft titled "Guidelines for Evidence Collection and Archiving," the most volatile evidence should be collected first. This makes sense because the most volatile evidence is the most likely to disappear before it can be documented or collected. The draft lists the "order of volatility" as follows:

1. Registers and cache

2. Routing tables, Address Resolution Protocol (ARP) cache, process tables, and kernel statistics

3. Contents of system memory

4. Temporary file systems

5. Data on disk

Collecting volatile data presents a problem because doing so changes the state of the system (and the contents of the memory itself). Some experts recommend that investigators or crime scene technicians capture such data as running processes, the network status and connections, and a "dump" of the data in RAM, documenting each task or command they run to do so. You can do some of this work by running such commands as *netstat* (on both Windows and UNIX systems) and *nbtstat* (on Windows only) to view current network connections. The *arp* command will tell you what addresses are in the ARP cache (and thus have recently connected to the system). You can use the *dd* command to create a snapshot of the contents of memory on UNIX machines, and the *ps* command to view the currently running processes. On Windows machines, you can use the downloadable *pslist* utility to list running processes, or you can view them in the Task Manager. You can use other commands such as *ipconfig* (Windows) and *ifconfig* (UNIX) to gather information about the state of the network. You should run these programs from a special CD that you bring with you (instead of running the same commands from the hard disk of the suspect computer), and they should not require any programs or libraries from the computer's hard disk to run.

Special Considerations

Because certain kinds of digital evidence can be incredibly volatile, and all digital evidence can be damaged or compromised by improper copying, storage, or handling, it's essential to exercise extreme care and diligence when gathering and handling such evidence. Therefore, numerous special considerations can come into play, including environmental factors, retention of timestamps and date stamps, and ways to preserve specific types of data. We discuss these concerns in the following sections.

Environmental Factors

Magnetically encoded data can be destroyed or damaged (scrambled) by exposure to a magnet or an electromagnetic field generated by many types of electronic equipment. Radio frequency (RF) transmissions can also damage digital data, as can exposure to static electricity or extreme heat.

It is very important for investigators and crime scene technicians to be aware of environmental factors that can affect the integrity of data. They must be sure that digital evidence is packaged in such a way as to protect it from damage and that it is stored in an electromagnetically "clean" environment that is properly cooled.

When you're packaging magnetic or optical media (tapes, CDs, DVDs, hard disks, diskettes, ZIP/Jaz disks, and so on), first place the media inside an antistatic bag, and then place it in a box that has enough extra room so that you can "pad" it with bubble wrap, Styrofoam "peanuts," or other protective material. Try to anchor the media against the bottom or side of the box so that it won't move around in transit. Be sure to list the contents on the outside of the box and identify it as evidence (with the case number). Labels warning carriers to handle the package carefully might also be appropriate. If you are shipping or mailing the package, use a method that allows tracking (registered mail when using the U.S. Postal Service).

Retaining Timestamps and Date Stamps

The time and date of creation or modification of a file can be an important issue in a criminal case. Remember that the timestamp and date stamp on the files will be in accordance with the time and date set on the system clock. Some systems default to a particular time zone (usually Greenwich Mean Time, or GMT). If the user set up the system without configuring the proper time zone or if the user deliberately changed the date and time settings, the timestamp and date stamp on the files might not correlate to "real-world" occurrences regarding when the files were created.

This can be a problem if, for example, the system records show that a file was created on a particular date and the suspect is able to prove that he or she was nowhere near the computer on that date. For this reason, you should note the system time and date settings before shutting down the computer and document them with a photograph, if possible; otherwise, with written notes.

Opening a file changes the file's time and date records. Thus, it might be prudent to photograph the screen showing the file access or modification times prior to opening the file. You should be prepared to testify as to your actions and provide expert testimony that the actions you took changed the timestamp and date stamp but did not modify the contents of the file in any way. When you do all your work on an image rather than the original, the original times and dates will be on the original disk. You can create a second copy of the original to illustrate this fact.

Write Protection

Write protection prevents any data from being written to storage media so that in the case of a forensic investigation, the data on the original hard disk isn't modified or deleted. Write protection is important in forensics, because even the slightest modification to a file could destroy information that might be important in an investigation, and bring the validity of the data into question in court.

Probably one of the easiest examples of showing how write protection works is a floppy disk. As shown in Figure 15.1, on the upper-left corner of the back of a 3.5-inch floppy disk is a tab that you can switch to an open or closed position. When you slide the tab to a bottom position so that the hole is closed, you can write to the disk. If you were to open a file that was saved on the disk, the *LastAccessed Date* property of the file would be modified, showing that it was last accessed at the current date and time. To avoid modifying the disk, you could slide the tab to the top position, creating a hole in the disk and write-protecting the disk. In doing so, if the file were opened, the file and its properties could not be modified, so the date that the file was last accessed would still show a previous date.

Figure 15.1 Write Protection on a Floppy Disk

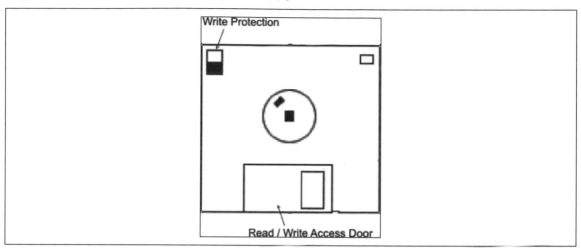

Other media may not even require that you worry about modifying the data. For example, when a CD-R or DVD-R is being examined, it cannot be modified because once the data has been stored on the disk, it cannot be written to again. This may not be the case, however, if you were accessing rewritable optical disks, such as a DVD-RW or CD-RW, which can be written to and modified multiple times.

When dealing with hard disks and other storage devices that can be written to over and over again, simple measures such as flipping a tab aren't available, so you must use other methods. To ensure write protection, you can use hardware- or software-based solutions. Some forensic software provides write protection so that any data suspect's computer isn't modified as an image is being created on another storage device. An even better solution is hardware-based write blockers. The hard disk is connected to the hardware, while a Universal Serial Bus (USB), FireWire, serial, or parallel cable is used to connect the write blocker to the examiner's computer. The forensic software connects to the hard disk through this device, which passes data from the hard disk to the examiner's computer, where an image of the disk is created. In doing so, no data is modified on the original drive.

Recovering Digital Evidence

In some computer crime cases, the evidence you need will be neatly stored on the hard disk (or on easily accessible removable media), with the files conveniently labeled to indicate their contents. In other cases, the investigator is not quite so lucky. Cybercriminals might get wind of the fact that they're about to be "busted" and delete incriminating data or even format and/or repartition the disk. Some particularly tech-savvy cybercriminals use sophisticated techniques to hide data in unlikely or nontraditional areas. Other times, the data that would be useful to the investigator is never stored on disk at all—at least, not to the computer user's knowledge. However, a great deal of *ambient data* is stored in locations such as cache files, swap/page files, and temporary (temp) files, as well as "leftover" data that occupies the "unallocated" space on the disk, the "slack" space in clusters that are larger than the files they hold, and the "gaps" between partitions or sectors. In the following sections, we review and expand on some of the ways that investigators can recover data that is not immediately apparent when browsing the file structure but that can prove critical to building a criminal case.

> **NOTE**
>
> Recovery of digital data, especially data that is partially destroyed or supposedly erased, is sometimes referred to as *electronic dumpster diving*.

Deleted Files

Many computer users—including cybercriminals—think that when they delete a file, it is erased from the hard disk. Even so-called computer experts have been heard to say on television and radio that once the Windows "trash" has been emptied, the files there are gone from the disk. As we saw in Chapter 7, this simply isn't true. Deleting a file does not remove the contents of the file; it merely removes the pointer to that file from the File Allocation Table (FAT), Master File Table (MFT), or other scheme that the operating system uses to pinpoint the location of a particular file on the disk. Data is stored on the disk in *clusters*, which are units consisting of a set number of bits. Because parts of a file are not always stored in contiguous clusters on the physical disk, but instead parts of it could be spread across the disk in separate locations, removing the pointer makes it difficult for the file to be reconstructed—but *difficult* does not equal *impossible*.

When the file is deleted, the disk location in which it is stored is marked as *unallocated space*, which means that it is available when new data needs to be written. However, on a large disk it might be a long time before that particular part of the disk is used to write new data. In the meantime, the old data is still there and can be recovered if the investigator has the proper tools.

A brand-new disk is thought of as being "clean," or completely empty, but in reality it is full of *format characters*, which are repeated characters that are made by the test machine at the factory. When files and directories are created and saved to disk, they overwrite the format characters. When the files or directories are deleted, the clusters in which they are stored are not reallocated until new data is written there. Formatting the disk does not remove this data. Even if the disk is repartitioned, the data is still there until those clusters are overwritten.

Supposedly erased data can be located in many places on a computer. For example, when a disk is repartitioned, it is possible for data from the previously configured partitions to end up in the space between partitions, called the *partition gap*. Disk search tools can locate this hidden data, which can then become a potential source of evidence for investigators.

Data Recovery Software and Documentation

In Chapters 6 and 7, we discussed a number of different tools that you can use to acquire evidence using disk imaging, or perform other tasks related to a forensic investigation. To make it easier to analyze data acquired with these tools, many of these tools include features that allow you to review the data stored in the image files. Tools such as X-Ways Forensics, EnCase, and other include the following features:

- A gallery view so that you can view thumbnails of images recovered from a suspect computer or other media

- A file preview capability to view the data contained in different types of files (for example, Microsoft Word documents, Excel spreadsheets, PDF files, and so on)

- A calendar view to view when data was stored on specific areas of the computer

Many of these tools provide documentation features so that the actions taken while acquiring the data are recorded and can be printed in a report. EnCase will document when the acquisition of data from a suspect machine began and ended, can generate a report with thumbnails and other information about pictures found on the computer, lists files and their locations, and generates other reports that reduce the amount of information you manually have to keep track of.

Decrypting Encrypted Data

As you learned in Chapter 12, encryption is a method of scrambling data so that it can't be read by anyone who doesn't have the password or key to decrypt it. Cybercriminals often use encryption to conceal the criminal nature of their data. They could encrypt e-mail messages that include incriminating statements, or they could encrypt documents that could be used as evidence or pornographic pictures of children that constitute contraband.

Cryptanalysts specialize in "cracking" encryption algorithms. Strong encryption is difficult to break, but in many cases cybercriminals use relatively weak methods such as the password protection for Office documents that comes built into the applications. As we discussed in Chapter 11, a number of "password recovery" programs exist ostensibly for use by legitimate users who protect documents and then forget their passwords. These programs can also be used to crack the passwords on Word or Excel documents. They are basically brute force/dictionary attacks. Some programs are designed to crack the passwords used by the Outlook Express e-mail client, Internet Explorer passwords for protected Web sites, files created by Quicken and QuickBooks financial management programs, password-protected PDF files, password-protected .zip files and other archives, and many more. For information about many of these password-cracking programs, see www.crackpassword.com.

Finding encrypted documents stored on a suspect machine can be relatively easy. Tools such as X-Ways Forensics provide a feature that automatically detects encrypted Microsoft Office and PDF files. Paraben (www.paraben-forensics.com) also markets a "decryption collection" software suite as part of its line of forensic programs. The suite is designed to crack passwords for a large number of popular software programs and file types, including the Windows operating systems, Exchange, VBA Visual Basic modules, and many more.

Documenting Evidence

Throughout this book, we've stressed the importance of documenting how evidence is collected and acquired through the use of forensic hardware and software. According to Digital Evidence Standards and Principles, developed by the SWGDE and IOCE in 1999 and published in the April 2000 issue of *Forensic Science and Communications* (a publication of the FBI), "[C]ase notes and observations must be in ink, not pencil, although pencil (including color) may be appropriate for diagrams or making tracings. Any corrections to notes must be made by an initialed, single strikeout; nothing in the handwritten information should be obliterated or erased. Notes and records should be authenticated by handwritten signatures, initials, digital signatures or other marking systems."

As we'll discuss in Chapter 17, documentation may also be useful as a personal reference, should the need arise to testify in court. Because of the technical nature involved, you may need to review details of the evidence before testifying at trial. Without it, your memory may fail you at a later time, especially if a case doesn't go to court until months or years later. You can also refer to these notes on the stand, but doing so will have them entered into evidence as part of the court record. As the entire document is entered into evidence, you should remember not to have notes dealing with other cases or sensitive information about the company in the same document, as this will also become public record.

In the following sections, we discuss the evidence documentation procedures in a cybercrime investigation. We look first at how evidentiary items should be tagged or marked and the practice of keeping an evidence log. Then we discuss how the analysis of evidence should be documented by the person(s) performing the forensic examination. Finally, we discuss the chain of custody and the importance of documentation to preserving the integrity of the chain.

NOTE

Documentation plays a vital role in any investigation. You should remember that documentation must be maintained throughout an investigation, and that it may be used in court. Documentation may be referred to, it may be used to challenge what you did, or you may use it when providing testimony as a personal reference.

Evidence Tagging and Marking

Evidence management begins at the crime scene, where it is bagged and/or tagged. When the crime scene is being processed, each piece of evidence should be sealed inside an evidence bag. An evidence bag is a sturdy bag that has two-sided tape that allows it to be sealed shut. Once the bag is sealed, the only way to open it is to damage the bag, such as by ripping or cutting it open. The bag should then be marked or a tag should be affixed to it, identifying the person who initially took it into custody. The tag would provide such information as a number to identify the evidence, a case number (which shows the case with which the evidence is associated), the date and time, and the name or badge number of the person taking it into custody. A tag may also be affixed to the object, providing the same or similar information to what's detailed on the bag. However, this should be done only if it will not compromise the evidence in any manner.

Information on the tag is also written in an evidence log or chain of evidence form, which is a document that inventories all evidence collected in a case. In addition to the data available on the tag, the chain of evidence form will include a description of each piece of evidence, serial numbers, identifying marks or numbers, and other information that's required by policy or local law.

Evidence is tagged and/or marked by the person who originally takes it into custody. That person places his or her initials or name on the item, along with the date and time and the case number. Physically marking the evidence is preferable when possible, because tags can become separated from items, thus damaging the chain of custody. Items that can't be physically inscribed can be placed in a bag or contained and sealed, and then the container can be marked. The mark should be made using a permanent ink or marker.

NOTE

In some cases involving digital evidence, you can use a cryptographic (digital) signature if you can do so without modifying the evidence.

Evidence Logs

The *evidence log* is a document that lists all evidence collected in a criminal case, with a description of each piece of evidence, who discovered and collected it, the date and time of collection, and the disposition of the evidence. The description should be detailed enough to differentiate the item from others like it and should include serial numbers and other identifying numbers when possible. The log should show all transfers of custody of the evidence from one person to another. This process of logging the transfer of evidence is tangible proof of the preservation of the chain of custody.

Documenting the Chain of Custody

The term *chain of custody* refers to continuity of the evidence. That is, you must be able to trace the route that the evidence has taken from the moment it was collected until the time it is presented in court, every person whose hands it has passed through, and when and where it was transferred from one person to another. Documentation of the chain of custody is one of the most important purposes of the evidence log.

Any break in the chain of custody opens the prosecution to allegations that the evidence has been tampered with or that other evidence has been substituted for it. Proof of chain of custody is provided by testimony of the person who collected the evidence, establishing that the item presented in court is in fact the same evidence that was collected (or is an exact representation of that evidence), that the evidence was not tampered with while in his or her custody, and when and where custody of the evidence was transferred to the next person in the chain. This same process can be followed with each person who had custody of the evidence.

Obviously, the fewer people who handle the evidence, the easier it will be to preserve the integrity of the chain. It is a best practice to designate one person as the custodian of the evidence. Sometimes computer evidence must be delivered to a lab or service that handles data recovery/computer forensics, however. If the designated custodian is unable to stay with the evidence (keeping it within his or her sight) while it is processed, the lab or technician should provide a receipt when the evidence is delivered, and the evidence should be examined by the custodian when it is retrieved, to ensure that it is the same evidence. The lab technicians will also need to testify as to what happened to the evidence while it was in their custody and how it was stored and protected at the lab.

The Chain of Custody Form

A *chain of custody* is also sometimes referred to as a *chain of evidence*, as it shows how evidence made it from the crime scene to the courtroom. To prove where a piece of evidence was at any given time, and who was responsible for it, a chain of custody form is often used to document who had possession of it and to establish that the integrity of evidence wasn't compromised.

The chain of custody form provides a log that details who had custody of the evidence. This document will be used to describe who had possession of the evidence after it was initially tagged, transported, and locked in storage. To obtain possession of the evidence, a person will need to sign in and sign out evidence. Information is added to a chain of evidence form to show who had possession of the evidence, when, and for how long. The form will specify the person's name, department, date, time, and other pertinent information.

In many cases, the investigator will follow the evidence from crime scene to court, documenting who else had possession along the way. Each time possession is transferred to another person, it is written on the form. For example, the form would show the investigator had initial custody, and the next line might show that a computer forensic examiner took possession on a particular date and time. Once the examination is complete, the next line would show that the investigator again took custody. Even though custody is transferred back to the investigator, this is indicated in the log so that there is no confusion over who was responsible on any date or at any time.

Documenting Evidence Analysis

When the bitstream image of the suspect computer's disk(s) is analyzed, a log should be kept documenting the evidence analysis. This log should show each step of the analysis process, including who was present, what was done (for example, running a software utility to remove binary data from a swap file), the result of the procedure, and the time and date. As the data on the disk is assessed for its evidentiary value, you should document all potential evidence that is found. For example, if you open a .jpg file that appears to be a pornographic photo of a child, document the filename, where on the disk it was located, the date stamp and timestamp, and other file properties. In addition to the volatile data and obscure areas on the disk where data hides that we discussed earlier (slack space, unallocated space, partition gaps, and so forth), some of the data that should be examined for evidence, depending on the type of cybercrime offense, includes:

- A list of Uniform Resource Locators (URLs) recently visited (obtained from the temporary Internet files or Web cache and History folders)

- E-mail messages and a list of e-mail addresses stored in the suspect's address book; the filename depends on the e-mail program in use—for example, the .pst file for Outlook (in some cases, this information will be stored on an e-mail server, such as an Exchange server)

- Word processing documents; the file extensions depend on the programs used to create them—common extensions are .doc, .wpd, .wps, .rtf, and txt

- Spreadsheet documents; the file extensions depend on the programs used to create them— examples include .xls, .wg1, and .wk1

- Graphics, in the case of child pornography cases; the file extensions include .jpg, .gif, .bmp, .tif, and others

- Chat logs; the filename depends on the chat program

- The Windows Registry (where applicable)

- Event viewer logs

- Application logs

- Print spool files

The Final Report

Once evidence has been examined, the documentation that has been compiled is used to create a final report that outlines what actions have been taken, and what has been found on the suspect's machine. The final report will include a statement regarding what occurred during the investigation process, information you acquired and generated during the analysis of a suspect machine, and printouts of pertinent data. For example, in an Internet luring case (where an online predator seduces a child into having sex), the chat logs from their conversations would be included in the final report. Excerpts from the chat may be included to indicate important parts of the document that the investigator should be aware of, as well as the complete log. In situations where pornography was found on a machine, printouts of thumbnails would also be included in the report, with information on the filename, full path to its location on the suspect's hard drive, file size, and time and date information. As you can see from this, the specific information included in the final report can depend on what the case involved, and on what was found on the machine.

Computer Forensic Resources

Computer forensics is a relatively young field, with standards that were quickly established and are still evolving. A large number of resources are available to aspiring computer forensic experts. Cybercrime investigators who want to expand their knowledge, corporate IT personnel who are interested in specializing in this area, and crime scene technicians who want to learn to deal with digital evidence will all find a plethora of training programs, equipment, and software available. Investigators who prefer to "farm out" the technical aspects of digital evidence examination will find many commercial services that do imaging, data recovery, and related tasks. Many of these services employ people qualified to testify as expert witnesses in court. Several associations and organizations provide white papers, articles, and other information sources to keep computer forensic personnel updated on the latest developments in the field. The following sections provide an overview of some of these resources.

Computer Forensic Training and Certification

Training programs are available through private companies that make forensic software and equipment, such as NTI (www.forensics-intl.com/training.html) and DIBS (www.dibsusa.com/training/training.html), through community colleges and universities, through some law enforcement in-service academies, and through computer crime/forensic associations and organizations.

There are at least a couple of recognized certification programs in computer forensics:

- IACIS provides a Certified Forensic Computer Examiner (CFCE) certification for individuals, both in law enforcement and outside law enforcement, who submit an application demonstrating extensive knowledge, training, and/or experience in the field of computer forensics, along with an understanding of forensic procedures, standards, ethics, and legal and privacy issues. Candidates must have technical knowledge and skills and have the equipment necessary to conduct forensic examinations. To earn the certification, candidates undergo a rigorous testing process in which they must complete a number of hands-on problem-solving exercises, prepare reports and present the evidence obtained, and then pass a written examination. For more information about the CFCE certification, visit the IACIS Web site at www.cops.org.

- The High Tech Crime Network (HTCN) offers basic and advanced Certified Computer Forensic Technician and Certified Computer Crime Investigator certifications. To obtain the certifications, applicants must demonstrate a minimal level of combined education and experience (in either law enforcement or corporate environment) and submit documentation derived from at least 10 cases. For more information, see www.htcn.org/cert.htm.

A good computer forensic training course should cover theory, process, and methodology and include hands-on practice in techniques and tools.

Computer Forensic Equipment and Software

A number of companies including Guidance Software (www.guidancesoftware.com) and DIBS (www.dibsusa.com) market special equipment to aid in forensic examinations. The following types of equipment can be useful to investigators and forensic technicians:

- **Imaging equipment** These devices allow you to rapidly make bitstream copies of hard disks onto another hard disk, an optical cartridge, or a tape. Portable units that fit into a suitcase are available and can be easily transported to the crime scene to make disk copies on-site before the computer is shut down. The target media include write-protection features to ensure that data cannot be tampered with after the copies are made.

- **Forensic workstations** These are complete computer workstations set up for easy reconstruction and analysis of copied drives, usually with removable drive racks that allow booting of the "working copies" of suspect disks. Analysis software is installed to assist in searching for particular types of data using artificial intelligence techniques or fuzzy logic to conduct searches when the investigator isn't sure of the text strings or file types he or she is looking for. Data recovery software is installed to locate data from "deleted" or "erased" files. Mobile workstations set up on portable computers are also available. Examples include the DIBS forensic workstations and F.R.E.D., the Forensic Recovery of Evidence Device, which is made by Digital Intelligence (www.digitalintel.com/fred.htm).

- **Forensic software** Packages provided by companies such as Guidance Software, NTI, and DIBS include imaging software, "undelete" programs, comprehensive file and text string search programs, programs that can verify the accuracy of bitstream copies, programs that can remove binary characters from data to ease analysis of the data, programs that quickly document lists of files and directories, programs that can capture the data in unallocated space or file slack space, programs that can rebuild cache, uncompression tools, system-checking utilities, steganography detection software, password recovery programs, and much more. For a list of some of the best computer forensic software programs, see the Timberline Technologies Web site at www.timberlinetechnologies.com/products/forensics.html. Also, NTI provides several free forensic tools at www.forensics-intl.com/download.html.

On the Scene

Building a Forensic Workstation

You can build your own forensic workstation using either a portable or a desktop computer instead of buying the prepackaged hardware/software combination. The system should be powerful enough to run forensic application software, and to avoid having to upgrade the equipment too soon, it should have the most powerful processor and most amount of RAM available (or at least that you can afford). To store evidence files that are created, you will also need a significant amount of hard disk space. It is not uncommon for computer forensic labs to have terabytes of hard disk space to store the evidence files, which will also need to be backed up on a regular basis in case of a hard disk failure or other problems.

The workstation should run an operating system compatible with your forensic application software. You might find it useful to set up a dual-boot configuration so that you can boot into either Windows or Linux, or you can run VMware (www.vmware.com) virtual machines to allow you to view an New Technology File System (NTFS) formatted disk, for example, from within the Linux operating system using a Windows virtual machine.

Computer Forensic Services

A huge number of companies offer data recovery and other computer forensic services. Many of these services work on a consultant basis and provide expert witnesses for court testimony. Services might bill by the hour or by the job, and some services offer discounts or even free services to law enforcement agencies. Full-service companies might also rent forensic equipment to investigators who want to do their own forensic work, and they might provide training in computer forensics.

Most medium-size to large U.S. cities have one or more local firms specializing in computer forensics or offering these services as part of their businesses. From one-person operations to large, well-known companies such as Ernst & Young, this hot field is expected to expand even more as computer crime awareness continues to grow. This is particularly true in the wake of terrorist attacks and subsequent information that terrorist networks use the Internet and might plan future attacks on critical IT infrastructures.

We recommend that when you consider employing a computer forensic service or expert, you inquire about his or her training and certification, professional association memberships, and past experience and ask for references from past clients. Law enforcement agencies should also keep in mind that in many cases, other law enforcement agencies will provide forensic services, either as a courtesy or for a fee, to smaller agencies that don't have the equipment or personnel to do their own computer forensic work. Check with larger municipal and county agencies in your area, the state police or department of public safety, and, in cases of high-profile or important cases, the FBI and other federal agencies for assistance.

Computer Forensic Information

Computer forensics is a field that is not only growing fast but changing fast as well. New techniques and technologies are being developed and proven all the time, and it's important that investigators keep up with the latest news in the field. There are several ways to stay current, including:

- Reading computer security information available through government and computer security sites on the Internet.

- Attending seminars and conferences that focus on computer crime and cybercrime, which may be hosted by law enforcement organizations or private companies. An example of one such conference is the Techno-Security Conference, of which information is available at www.techsec.com.

- Joining associations of computer forensic and cybercrime investigation professionals, such as IACIS (www.cops.org), the International High Technology Crime Investigation Association (http://htcia.org/), the High Tech Crime Consortium (www.hightechcrimecops.org), and others.

Understanding Legal Issues

Computer forensics is concerned as much with complying with the law and following prescribed procedures for evidence collection as it is with the technical aspects of collecting digital evidence. Evidence that is inadmissible in court is worse than useless; not only can illegal search and seizure damage or destroy the prosecution's case and result in a cybercriminal going free, but it can also result in administrative or even criminal actions against officers who violate the rules.

Thus, it is imperative that law enforcement officers and others who will be involved in the collection and preservation of evidence understand the legal issues under which they operate. The laws vary from one jurisdiction to another and change on a regular basis, so all cybercrime investigators should make it a practice to stay up-to-date on passage of statutes and court decisions that apply to their jurisdictions.

This chapter does not purport to give legal advice. The following sections are intended only to provide an overview of some of the laws and court cases that pertain to search and seizure of computers and digital evidence.

Searching and Seizing Digital Evidence

A *search* was legally defined by the courts in *State v. Woodall* as "an examination of a man's house or other buildings or premises, or of his person, or of his vehicle, aircraft, etc., with a view to the discovery of contraband or illicit or stolen property, or some evidence of guilt to be used in the prosecution of a criminal action for some crime or offense with which he is charged" (according to *Black's Law Dictionary*). A *seizure* was defined in *Molina v. State* as "the act of taking possession of property, e.g., for a violation of law or by virtue of an execution" [of a warrant].

Traditional ideas of search and seizure did not take into account the ways in which computers are used today as a repository of information (and potential evidence). The courts have had to develop interpretations of the law to apply to the unique aspects of these digital "places" and the types of evidence that can be found there. For example, the laws generally restrict entering a person's private premises to conduct a search without a warrant, except under certain restricted circumstances. Courts have generally held that a person has a reasonable expectation of privacy when information is stored in a computer, similarly to the contents of a closed container. On the other hand, when evidence is in plain view in a public place, the law allows officers to seize it.

Some general principles govern search and seizure in the United States based on the federal laws and the U.S. Constitution. Be aware, however, that states can impose further restrictions on police powers within their boundaries, so understanding federal guidelines is only the starting point. In the following sections, we discuss these general principles with these caveats in mind.

U.S. Constitutional Issues

The Bill of Rights of the U.S. Constitution consists of 10 amendments designed to protect the citizenry from government oppression and guarantee certain basic human rights to the people of the United States. One of the most important amendments in terms of its impact on law enforcement is the fourth, violation of which is common grounds for suppression of evidence in criminal trials.

Understanding the Fourth Amendment

The Fourth Amendment to the U.S. Constitution prohibits "unreasonable" searches and seizures. Specifically, it states: "The right of the people to be secure in their persons, houses, papers, and effects, against unreasonable searches and seizures, shall not be violated, and no warrants shall issue, but upon probable cause, supported by oath or affirmation, and particularly describing the place to be searched, and the persons or things to be seized."

Perhaps one of the most important things to understand about the Fourth Amendment is that its restrictions apply only to agents of the government such as the police and other public employees or public officials. A private party cannot violate a suspect's Fourth Amendment rights unless acting at the direction of the police or another government agency. In other words, if a landlord searches a tenant's home or an employer searches an employee's office, it is not a Fourth Amendment violation. However, such a search could be a violation of privacy and a basis for a civil suit in some cases and not in others; for example, courts have held that an employee generally does not have an expectation of privacy in an office owned by the employer.

How does this interpretation apply to search and seizure of computers? Again, only an agent of the government is prohibited by the Fourth Amendment from searching a computer's hard disk. In *United States v. Hall*, a case involving a computer repair person who found child pornography on a client's computer, the court held that "the Fourth Amendment does not apply to searches conducted by private parties who are not acting as agents of the government," and in *United States v. Jacobsen*, the court held that "the Fourth Amendment is wholly inapplicable to a search or seizure, even an unreasonable one, effected by a private individual not acting as an agent of the Government or with the participation or knowledge of any governmental official."

Thus, if a private party searches a computer and finds evidence of a crime, and then contacts law enforcement authorities who obtain a search warrant based on the private party's information, this does not constitute a violation of the computer owner's constitutional rights.

In fact, the Supreme Court has held (*United States v. Jacobsen*) that law enforcement agents can reenact the original private search without a warrant and that this does not constitute a violation of reasonable expectation of privacy. However, if officers exceed the scope of the original search, evidence can be suppressed, as it was in *United States v. Barth*, when a computer repair technician found child pornography on a customer's computer and agents looked at additional files that the technician had not viewed in his original search. The evidence originally viewed by the technician should have been used to obtain a search warrant to seize and view the additional files.

NOTE

Whether or not a search or seizure is permissible under the Fourth Amendment is only one aspect of its legality. Privacy acts and other statutes could apply in particular cases.

Case Law Governing Search and Seizure

We can look to many court cases for guidance in regard to search and seizure in general and search and seizure regarding computer equipment and electronic evidence in particular. *Katz v. United States* held that a search is considered to be constitutional if it doesn't violate a person's reasonable or legitimate expectation of privacy. Circumstances under which a person does or does not have a reasonable expectation of privacy are open to debate and generally must be decided by the courts in a particular case, although there is case law that establishes certain premises:

- In *Payton v. New York*, the Supreme Court held that there is a reasonable expectation of privacy when a person is inside his or her own home.

- In *United States v. Ross*, the Supreme Court held that there is a reasonable expectation of privacy regarding the contents of closed opaque containers.

Some court cases have established that a person has a reasonable expectation of privacy in the data stored on the hard disk of a computer (*United States v. Barth* and *United States v. Blas*). On the other hand, courts have ruled that when a person makes computer information publicly available, the reasonable expectation of privacy is lost. *Katz v. United States* held that "what a person knowingly exposes to the public, even in his own home and office, is not a subject of Fourth Amendment protection." Posting information on a Web site open to the public would obviously eliminate the expectation. Generally, information in transit (such as a message sent across the Internet) has been held not to constitute public exposure or sacrifice the expectation of privacy. However, the expectation might be lost when the message reaches the recipient. It has also been generally held that a person relinquishes the expectation of privacy if he or she turns information over to someone else whose use of it he or she cannot reasonably expect to control. Other cases have found that "mere information" revealed to third parties does not fall under reasonable expectation of control or privacy.

When there is no reasonable expectation of privacy, such as when property is abandoned or when evidence of a crime is displayed in plain view in a public place, officers generally can search and seize without a warrant. When circumstances create a reasonable expectation of privacy, a search warrant is required.

Search Warrant Requirements

A *search warrant* is a document signed by a magistrate giving law enforcement officers the authority to search a specified place for specific items that are particularly described in the warrant. A warrant must be based on another document called an *affidavit*, which is signed under oath by some person (a police officer or any other person) expressing the belief that certain items will be found at the location to be searched and giving facts that support the belief. Those facts must constitute *probable cause* that the objects of the search will be found at the described location. Only those items specifically named in the warrant can be searched for. A warrant can authorize the search and seizure of computer hardware, digital information, or both. Overly broad language (such as authorization to seize "all records" or "all computers") can result in the warrant being invalidated; the warrant must specify the crime(s) to which the evidence pertains.

On the Scene

Affidavit Checklist

The affidavit for a search warrant should articulate probable cause that:

- An offense has been committed (specify by name and penal code number).
- Digital evidence is located at the named location.
- The digital evidence is associated with the crime (tell how).
- The digital evidence is associated with a particular person/suspect (name or describe).

The affidavit should be specific enough to satisfy the legal requirements but remain as general as possible so as not to exclude any evidence that might be found.

Search warrants can be obtained to search for specific types of property or for a person. State laws usually define exactly for what things a search can be issued. For example, under the Texas Code of Criminal Procedures, section 18.02, search warrants can be issued to search for any of the following:

- Property that was acquired illegally (through theft, fraud, and so on)
- Property that was made, designed, or adapted for use to commit an offense and implements or instruments that were used in committing a crime (the tools of the crime, such as a computer used to launch a network attack)
- Contraband (property that is illegal to own; this would include child pornography intended for the suspect's own use)
- Illegal drugs, prohibited weapons, and illegal gambling equipment
- Obscene material for commercial distribution (this would include child pornography intended for commercial distribution as well as other materials deemed "obscene" that are intended for commercial distribution)

- Evidence of a crime

- A person

Search warrants and the supporting affidavits must follow strict guidelines as to form and content, and the reliability of the affiant (the person signing the affidavit) must be established to the satisfaction of the magistrate who issues the warrant. From the officer's point of view, it is always preferable to have a search warrant rather than searching without a warrant, because a warrant relieves the officer of the responsibility of showing that probable cause and/or applicable exceptions to the search warrant requirements existed.

> **NOTE**
>
> Generally, a copy of the search warrant must be served on the person in control of the premises being searched or left or posted in a prominent place if there is no one there to accept service. In some cases, courts have authorized so-called "sneak and peek" warrants that do not require officers to provide notification that a search has been conducted.
>
> A related matter is the "no-knock" warrant. Generally, officers are required to announce their presence when they serve a search warrant and identify themselves as law enforcement officers. However, courts have held that the announcement is not required if it would result in danger to the life of some person or destruction of evidence. Because computer evidence can be so easily and quickly destroyed, officers with search warrants for digital evidence are often held to be justified in foregoing the announcement.

Special problems can arise in constructing search warrants for electronic evidence, because of the intangible nature of the evidence. For example, a suspect can move or destroy computer data quickly and easily without leaving the premises. A person with technical expertise should advise the officers and magistrate regarding the technical aspects of searching for and collecting digital evidence based on the facts of a particular case. It is just as important, if not more important, to gather all the information possible about the object of the warrant in a computer-related case as in one involving the search of a physical location. This includes the hardware platforms, operating system environment, and software applications in use, as well as the network connections and configuration. This specificity will help pinpoint the types of files to look for in the search and possible locations where they might be stored.

Searches without Warrants

In some circumstances, Fourth Amendment protections don't apply because the action is deemed *not* to be a search. If police take a vehicle into custody (for example, because they have arrested the person who was driving it), they are allowed to *inventory* the contents of the vehicle as a standard procedure. This does not constitute a search because it is not done for the purpose of looking for evidence of a crime but for the purpose of protecting the owner's property (and protecting the agency against claims of theft). However, this exception does not allow police to open locked containers, such as a briefcase, as part of the inventory process. To do so, they would generally need a warrant (unless some other exception, such as exigent circumstances, applies). A laptop or other computer that is in the vehicle when it is seized would generally be treated like a closed container in that in most cases law enforcement agents should obtain a warrant to open it and view the data on it.

There are a number of other exceptions to the requirement for a search warrant, as established by statutes and court cases. These include:

- Consent searches
- Abandoned property
- Exigent circumstances
- Plain view
- Search incident to arrest

Consent Searches

If the party who has control over the premises or thing to be searched gives voluntary consent to the search, officers don't need a warrant. This is called a *consent search*. Officers don't even need to show probable cause of a crime; they can legally search with consent even if there is no reason whatsoever to believe that a criminal offense has occurred. The key element here is that the consent must be voluntary. If consent is obtained under duress, threat, or intimidation, it is not voluntary and thus is not valid.

Furthermore, the person giving consent must have the authority to do so. For example, courts have held that a landlord cannot give consent for officers to search a tenant's home. On the other hand, courts have also held that employers can give consent to search employees' offices and school administrators can give consent to search students' lockers. In determining the legality of a search, courts consider the authority of the person giving consent and the scope of the consent. That is, if a person gives consent to search his house, does that include searching the contents of his computer's hard disk?

On the Scene

The Joint Ownership Dilemma

Generally, if two or more people have joint ownership of a computer (for example, two roommates), consent has to be obtained from only one of the owners to conduct a legal search. The computer is then considered to be a "common area," much like the shared areas of a home. However, one party does not have the authority to give consent to search the other's "private areas" such as a bedroom used exclusively by one roommate. Likewise, the roommate could not legally give consent to search a computer solely owned by the other roommate. Even on a commonly owned computer, the use of password protection or file encryption by one roommate can establish that

Continued

those files are part of a "private area" on the computer, and if the other roommate has not been given the password or key, he or she does not have authority to consent to a search of those files.

Generally, a spouse can give valid consent to search the property of the other spouse, and parents can give consent to search the property of their children who are under 18 years old. In the case of adult children who live with their parents and pay rent, the situation becomes more like that of roommates, in that parents can consent to searches of common areas but not private areas where the children have demonstrated expectation of privacy (for example, by putting locks on the doors or encrypting files).

In most cases, system administrators have been held to have the authority to give consent to search files stored on a network, if network users have no reasonable expectation of privacy in files stored on the network (as in the case in which the files are created in the course of an employee's job and are stored on the employer's network). If the administrator does not have clear authority to give consent, it must be determined who does (such as senior management).

NOTE

Although a verbal consent to search can be legal, it is always best practice for law enforcement officials to get a signed consent form. Officers should carry a supply of preprinted Consent to Search forms for this purpose.

Abandoned Property

Law enforcement officers are generally allowed to search property that has clearly been abandoned without obtaining a warrant. For example, if a suspect is carrying a CD or USB flash drive and, upon observing that police are in the area, throws the disc in a public trashcan, officers can lawfully retrieve it.

Exigent Circumstances

Another situation in which searches can be conducted without a warrant is the case of *exigent circumstances*—that is, an emergency in which there is no time to get a warrant and the search is required immediately to save a life or prevent physical injury to some person, to keep the suspect from escaping, or to prevent evidence from being destroyed. This last situation is most applicable to digital evidence because of its fragile nature. It is very easy to destroy evidence that consists of computer data. In *United States v. David* and *United States v. Romero-Garcia*, the courts held that seizure of electronic evidence without a warrant was legal because the evidence was about to be destroyed.

An important tenet regarding the exigent circumstances exception is that law enforcement officers cannot create the exigency. In *United States v. Reyes*, the court ruled against the government when the argument was made that incoming messages or battery failure could destroy the evidence in a pager, because the officers created the exigency by turning the pager on.

Plain-View Searches

The concept of *plain view* (sometimes also referred to as the *open fields doctrine*) rests on the premise that the law enforcement officer is legally in a particular place where he or she can see obvious evidence of a crime in plain view. Because the contents of a file stored on a computer are usually not in plain view (unless the officer lawfully entered the room where the suspect had the file open on the screen), this doctrine is not often applied to electronic evidence.

This issue has come into play when officers had a warrant to search for evidence of one crime (for example, child pornography) and during that legal search came across evidence of a different crime (for example, a photo indicating that the suspect had committed a murder). Courts have generally held that the plain-view doctrine applies, but upon finding the evidence of the second offense, officers should return with that evidence to the magistrate to establish probable cause for issuance of a search warrant to search for further evidence of the second crime.

Searches Incident to Arrest

Officers may search a person and his or her immediate surroundings when making an arrest, without obtaining a search warrant. The courts have interpreted this to mean that officers can go through a person's wallet or purse, address books, and the like. The courts have held that information stored in a pager may be accessed when arresting the person wearing the pager. A number of cases support this ruling, including *United States v. Reyes*, *United States v. Thomas*, and *United States v. Lynch*. Whether this ruling would also apply to personal digital assistants (PDAs) and handheld or laptop computers is not clear.

NOTE

Yet another exception to the requirement for a search warrant is the border inspection. Routine searches of persons entering or leaving the United States are allowed without probable cause or any indication of criminal activity. This was held to apply in a case where a computer disk was seized and accessed as part of a "routine export search" of a man who was leaving the country (*United States v. Roberts*).

Seizure of Digital Evidence

There are several different ways digital evidence can be seized when it is located. Early computer crime investigators often printed incriminating files or made digital copies (on floppy disks or other removable media) of the files in question. Another option is to seize all the computer equipment and go through the data stored on it at another location. As we mentioned previously, the best accepted practice today is to first make a complete exact bitstream copy of the hard disk(s) before shutting down the computer. These copies can be used to reconstruct the suspect disk and analyze it at another location later. After making the copies, investigators should seize the equipment and original disk, mark it as evidence, and store it in a secure location.

The search and seizure process should be well planned in advance. Determine the best day and time of day for the process, and estimate the number of officers and technicians and levels of expertise that will be needed on-site when the search and seizure are conducted.

Forfeiture Laws

Computer equipment used as a tool or instrumentality of certain crimes (for example, illegal drug trafficking) can be subject to state and federal asset forfeiture laws. This means that the ownership of the equipment is transferred to the state or the law enforcement agency making the seizure and can be converted to their own use or sold.

Privacy Laws

The U.S. Privacy Protection Act (PPA) covers search and seizure of items that fall under the First Amendment (freedom of speech and freedom of the press) protections. The Privacy Act was intended to protect journalists, publishers, and other such people who might have evidence of criminal activity but are not suspected of having committed any criminal act. This law applies to materials that are created for the purpose of disseminating information to the public (which could apply to writings intended to be posted to Web sites, because this is a form of publishing to a public forum).

If there is reason to suspect that the person who has the materials is committing the crime that the materials pertain to, or if there is a danger to some person of physical injury or death that could be prevented by seizing the evidence, the search and seizure are not a violation of the Privacy Act. Violation of the act is a civil rather than a criminal matter. Violators of the act are subject to civil lawsuit, but a violation does not mean that the evidence will be thrown out of court, as is the case with a violation of constitutional rights.

The Electronic Communications Privacy Act (ECPA) was passed to protect the privacy rights of customers of ISPs when their personal information is disclosed. Penalties for violation include civil damages and, in some cases, criminal charges. The ECPA provisions are laid out in Title 18 of the U.S. Code. However, the passage of the U.S. Patriot Act made changes to some of the provisions of the ECPA, which we discuss in the next section.

NOTE

Some states have their own privacy statutes that can be applicable in specific cases in addition to the federal Privacy Protection Act. Furthermore, special rules under both federal and state laws govern information held to be confidential or privileged by statute, such as that arising from the physician/patient, attorney/client, or clergy/parishioner relationship. These are called *legally privileged documents.*

Summary

Evidence is the foundation of every criminal case, including those involving cybercrimes. The collection and preservation of digital evidence differs in many ways from the methods law enforcement officers are used to using for traditional types of evidence. Digital evidence is intangible, a magnetic or electronic representation of information. Its physical form does not readily reveal its nature. In addition, digital evidence is fragile. It is very easy for a criminal to deliberately delete crucial evidence in an instant or for an officer or technician to unintentionally damage or destroy it.

Fortunately, in many cases, evidence that appears to be gone is still on the disk or other media and can be recovered. A number of data recovery software packages are on the market, several of which are designed specifically for computer forensic work and are marketed with law enforcement use in mind. Also, many commercial data recovery services will perform the recovery operation for a fee, using sophisticated equipment that might be beyond the budget of many law enforcement agencies.

Computer forensics is still a relatively new field, but standards have been established and continue to evolve. To ensure that digital evidence is admissible in court, it is best to adhere to accepted current standards and practices and to use software that has been tried and tested. The primary objective in conducting an examination of a suspect computer's data is to leave the original in the same condition in which it was found. This means that, whenever possible, disk-imaging technology should be used to create an exact duplicate of the suspect hard disk, and this duplicate alone should be used for examination. To recover data that might be hidden in obscure areas of the disk or left behind after deletion or erasure, the copy must be a bitstream image, in which every bit is copied, sector by sector, from the original disk to the duplicate. This duplicate ideally should be made on-site when the computer is seized, before the computer is shut down. At the same time, steps should be taken to record or preserve volatile data that will be lost when the computer's power is turned off.

Once one or more duplicates have been made, the original can be locked up securely in an evidence locker or evidence room until needed. Chain of custody must be maintained throughout the entire process. The duplicate disk can be examined for evidence of criminal activity. This examination not only should address those files that are visible in the file system, but also should include a search for ambient data that is not obvious and that the user of the computer might not know still exists on the disk. For this task, you will need special forensic software, which can be installed on a forensic workstation set up for this purpose.

Collection of evidence involves not just technical know-how; it also requires knowledge of the laws pertaining to evidence. Violation of those laws can result in the evidence being thrown out of court, regardless of its technical quality and regardless of how definitively it proves the guilt of the defendant. In the United States, admissibility of evidence often hinges on the Fourth Amendment to the Constitution, which protects citizens against unreasonable search and seizure. If the search and seizure of computer equipment and/or digital data violate the suspect's constitutional rights, the judge will suppress the evidence and the jury will never see it. Other federal laws and state laws govern the admissibility of evidence in criminal trials as well. These laws are generally collected in codifications called *rules of evidence*, which we'll discuss in greater detail in Chapter 17, and every investigator should be intimately familiar with the laws in his or her jurisdiction.

Frequently Asked Questions

Q: Why is documentation so important? Doesn't the evidence speak for itself?

A: In many computer-related criminal cases, the evidence speaks a language that most of the members of the jury (and often the judge, prosecutor, and law enforcement officers) don't understand. At one time, juries were likely to accept the testimony of expert witnesses without question, but as the public has become more technically sophisticated and expert testimony has been called into question in high-profile cases such as the O.J. Simpson case, juries have become more skeptical of experts' infallibility and are more likely to accept the opposing attorney's challenges that raise doubts about evidence-processing methods and forensic techniques. This is why it is so important to document the actions of law enforcement officers and technicians every step of the way. Documentation is also important to refresh the memories of people who must testify in the case. Often, trials are delayed for months or even years, and by the time an officer or technician is required to take the stand, he or she has handled many other cases.

Q: Why is it important that all the software used by law enforcement officers be licensed and registered? Law enforcement budgets are often tight; why not use freeware as much as possible?

A: Some freeware and shareware tools that are available on the Internet are good tools, and the price is certainly right. However, there are some dangers in using these programs for forensic purposes. First, you never know exactly what you're getting when you download a free program (and you certainly can't ask for your money back if it doesn't work properly). Downloads can be infected with viruses or Trojans that can damage the systems on which you use them. Using unlicensed software (illegal copies) is even worse. The opposing attorney(s) will have a field day if they discover that the police used pirated or "borrowed" software in the investigation. This behavior can destroy the credibility of the people who conducted the forensic examination and can even result in losing the case. In addition, with properly purchased and registered software, you will be able to get technical support from the vendor if necessary. Makers of computer forensic software often offer discounts to law enforcement agencies, making it easier to afford the proper tools for the job. After all, officers and agencies probably wouldn't suggest saving money by buying their duty weapons from a pawnshop; that's because these are essential tools of the trade and they must be as reliable as possible. For the cybercrime investigator or technician, the same is true of the forensic software that is used to collect and preserve evidence that can make or break a criminal case.

Chapter 16

Building the Cybercrime Case

Topics we'll investigate in this chapter:

- Major Factors Complicating Prosecution

- Overcoming Obstacles to
  Effective Prosecution

- The Investigative Process

☑ Summary

☑ Frequently Asked Questions

Introduction

Experienced investigators know that, contrary to the philosophy of the modern murder mystery, discovering "who dun it" is not the end of an investigation—it's only the beginning. In the previous chapter, we discussed how to collect and preserve evidence. Although in a cybercrime case this can be one of the most difficult aspects of the investigation, it's still not the final step. To result in prosecution of the offender, a criminal investigation must culminate in the building of a solid *case file* containing documentation of all the evidence that can be used to obtain a conviction in court.

Constructing a criminal case is a long, often complex process. The more technical the facts of the case, the more difficult it is to build a good case that presents the evidence in a way that can be thoroughly understood by the following key players:

- The prosecuting attorney or a grand jury (one of which, depending on the level of the offense and the governing code of criminal procedure, will make the decision as to whether to bring the case to trial)

- The trial jury (which ultimately decides guilt or innocence in a felony case and sometimes sets the penalty)

- The judge (who may decide guilt or innocence in a misdemeanor case and who often is responsible for setting the penalty even in cases where guilt or innocence is decided by a jury)

The investigator is not the only person involved in constructing the case, but he or she usually plays the most important role and often coordinates the tasks of others who are involved. These others can include first-response law enforcement officers, crime scene technicians, crime lab personnel, and members of assisting agencies (for example, when local law enforcement agencies send digital evidence to the state police or FBI for enhancement or interpretation). Because of the technical nature of some cybercrimes, it is also common to call on private sector specialists or experts to provide assistance during the investigation. The criminal investigator in charge of the case will need to work closely with such outside experts to help them understand their roles and provide the type of documentation necessary for the case file.

Investigative techniques, tools, and processes are basically the same in a cybercrime case as in any other criminal case, but special considerations apply and several factors complicate the prosecution of these types of crimes. In this chapter, we discuss such complicating factors as the difficulty of defining the crime, jurisdictional issues, and special problems related to the nature of some of the evidence. We also take a brief look at how the authoritarian attitudes of many law enforcement officers, the elitist and anti-authority attitudes of many information technology (IT) people, and the natural adversarial relationship that often exists between the two can complicate an investigation. Then we provide an overview of the investigative process as it applies to the typical cybercrime case, including discussion of investigative tools, the steps involved in an investigation, and the importance of defining areas of responsibility and preserving the chain of custody. Finally, we look at the trial process and offer tips on testifying in a cybercrime case, either as an evidentiary witness providing direct evidence or as an expert witness offering conclusions and opinions.

Major Factors Complicating Prosecution

Few criminal prosecutions are as simple as they seem at first glance. Even a lowly, seemingly straightforward speeding ticket can turn into a complex matter if it goes to trial. Officers can be required to prove that they have been adequately trained in the use of radar equipment, and the veracity of that equipment can be brought into question based on myriad theoretical technical possibilities. Prosecuting more serious offenses requires even more preparation on the parts of all who will testify, as well as people who won't be called to the stand but who are involved in handling evidence or putting together the documentation for the case file.

Cybercrimes are inherently complex by their very nature. Computers—which are complicated machines and which many people find confusing—always play a key role in every cybercrime case. Cybercrimes are often poorly defined in the statutes that govern them. This is partly because the legislators who make those laws don't understand the technology. It is also in part because the theories on which the criminal justice system is based were formulated long before computers existed and did not anticipate the changes they would bring to criminality. Jurisdictional ambiguities create nightmares for investigators and prosecutors alike. As though that weren't enough, much of the evidence in a cybercrime case might be both intangible and circumstantial. In the following sections, we address each of these obstacles to prosecution and then discuss some ways to overcome them.

Difficulty of Defining the Crime

The first step in investigating a reported crime is to determine that a crime has in fact been committed. Many people who don't work in the legal field—including tech people—have only a vague understanding of the law and of what constitutes a crime. We've all heard (and most of us have said) the phrase "There ought to be a law," but unless there *is* a law—one that specifically describes the act that was committed—we can't prosecute no matter how "wrong" that act seems to be.

Not everything that's immoral or unethical is against the law, and we should be thankful for that. The justice system is already overcrowded, and the more laws there are on the books, the more potential there is for two conflicting but equally undesirable developments:

- There is more potential for abuse of the laws, resulting in innocent people being punished.

- There is more potential for the laws to be ignored, resulting in guilty people going unpunished.

A society that tries to regulate everything and protect its citizens from every possible unpleasantness (even from themselves) soon finds that it has also stifled the spirit and creativity of those people and created a police state in which the oppression is not worth the illusion of security. On the other hand, a society that seeks to make no rules and accepts the premise that "it's all good" and that everyone should be free to do his or her own thing soon descends into anarchy and chaos. The challenge of finding a sensible balance between these two extremes is a job for the legislative branch of government, and it is a challenge that is currently facing those legislators in regard to the formerly largely unregulated regions of cyberspace. Crime in the context of cyberspace is being defined and redefined regularly as government bodies seek to provide adequate—but not overly oppressive—legislation that balances our desire for control and order with the rights to free speech and the benefits of a free flow of ideas.

In the following sections, we look at how criminality is defined in terms of bodies of law and basic criminal justice theory, and we discuss the concepts of elements of the offense and burden and level of proof on which the criminal justice system rests.

Bodies of Law

Computers, networks, and the data that passes through them are, like other aspects of our lives, subject to a confusing number of laws that have been enacted by legislative bodies at different levels of government (local, state, national, and international), created by courts in the form of case law, or set down through administrative orders or regulatory bodies. Because the law is such a maze of complicated and ever-changing rules, many nonlawyers don't even try to understand how the legal system works, the differences between different bodies and types of law, and how all of these different laws interact with one another.

NOTE

In the United States, individual laws are passed by a legislative body, and then groups of related laws are gathered into collections called *codifications* or *codes*. For example, a penal code contains criminal laws; a motor vehicle code contains laws pertaining to driving, traffic offenses, and the operation and maintenance of vehicles; a family code contains laws related to child custody, adoption, marriage and divorce, and other family matters.

Generally, laws can be divided into three different "bodies." Each body of law has its own rules of procedure, different penalties for violation, and different enforcement agencies and courts that have jurisdiction. The burden of proof and the level of proof required to win a case are different, depending on the applicable body of law. The three bodies of law are:

- Criminal law
- Civil law
- Administrative/regulatory law

In the following sections, we discuss each of these bodies of law and the differences among them

NOTE

The information in this chapter pertains directly to the U.S. legal system. Other countries have similar divisions of law, but these might differ. For more information about international issues, see the resources listed later in this chapter where we discuss international laws.

Criminal Law

When we hear or use the term *illegal*, we generally think of a violation of criminal law. We consider something that is "against the law" to be an act for which a person can be jailed or at least fined by the state. However, many acts that violate the law are not *crimes*, but rather civil infractions or breaches of civil contract. For example, in the tech industry you often hear it said that "it's illegal" to give away a copy of software that you purchased. Although software *piracy* (which involves making and distributing copies of copyrighted software without the authorization of the copyright holder) is a criminal offense in some circumstances and jurisdictions, giving away a copy you purchased legally is not. However, doing so might be a breach of contract—the end-user license agreement (EULA) that a person "signs" when he or she installs the software. This means the software vendor could file a lawsuit against you in civil court asking for monetary damages, but you could not be put in jail for it.

A *criminal offense* must be specifically defined as such by a locality's, state's, or country's written statutes. (We discuss statutory law a little later in this chapter.) Criminal laws are designed to protect society, as well as individual persons, from harmful acts. They are also designed to punish offenders as a deterrence both to the offender and to others, and in some cases they are intended to ensure that the offenders are unable to pose a further risk to society by placing them in jail or prison or even, in extreme cases, by taking their lives.

Criminal complaints can be filed by the individual(s) who are harmed or by law enforcement officers or citizens who observe the offense. However, the charges are prosecuted not on behalf of the victim, but on behalf of the government entity having jurisdiction. That is, a crime defined in the state penal code is prosecuted by the state, and a federal crime is prosecuted by the federal government. The *style of the case* is the term used to describe the language at the top of all court documents identifying a case. If the case is brought under criminal law, the style will read something like this: *The State of Texas v. John Smith* or *The United States of America v. Jane Doe*. In a criminal case, the person or entity that files the charges is referred to as the *complainant*, and the person (or company) against whom the charges are brought is called the *defendant*.

Penalties for violating a criminal law can include monetary payment or loss of liberty and range from light to severe, including:

- A warning citation (usually in the case of traffic laws or other lowest-level misdemeanors)

- A citation that imposes a fine (monetary payment that goes to the state)

- Compensation or restitution (monetary payment that goes to the victim)

- Community service (mandatory "volunteer" work for some charitable organization or government body)

- Probation (supervision or oversight by the government for a specified period of time in lieu of confinement, which can include court-order restrictions on behavior such as no use of computers or required attendance at counseling sessions)

- Confinement in jail (usually for a limited time, such as a few days to a year)

- Confinement in prison (usually for a more extended time, ranging from a few months to life)

- The death penalty (in some jurisdictions; usually limited to people convicted of murder)

> **NOTE**
>
> Different jurisdictions handle offenses differently. For example, in some U.S. states, traffic offenses such as speeding and running a red light are considered criminal misdemeanors, and in other states they are considered civil violations.

Criminal offenses are generally classified according to the seriousness of the crime and the severity of the penalty. These classifications can include the following, depending on the jurisdiction: *violations*, the least serious offenses, the penalty for which is only a fine; *misdemeanors*, more serious than violations with a penalty of fine or jail term; and *felonies*, the most serious offenses, which carry a penalty of imprisonment (and in some jurisdictions, the death penalty for the most serious cases). Cybercrimes span the range of classifications and penalty grades. In many jurisdictions, offenses such as theft, property damage, and others that cause monetary loss are classified according to the dollar amount of the loss or damage. That is, a network intrusion that causes little loss is a misdemeanor, whereas an attack that results in large monetary losses to the victim is a felony.

CyberLaw Review

Defining the Law

Generally, in the United States each state adopts a code of criminal procedure and a penal code that define, respectively, how criminal laws are enforced and the criminal offenses themselves. The penal code generally sets forth the way in which offenses are classified (violations, misdemeanors, and felonies), *penalty grades* within each classification (such as Class A, B, and C misdemeanors and first-, second-, and third-degree felonies), and the penalty range for each grade of offense.

In the United States, the Constitution gives persons accused of serious crimes (felonies) the right to trial by jury. The accused can waive the right if desired and have the case decided by a judge.

Civil Law

The objective of civil law is to settle disagreements between persons or entities (*parties* to the suit or action). Thus, the style of the case will usually name two private parties (such as *John Smith v. Joe Jones* or *Jane Doe v. BrandX Corporation*), although government entities can be parties to civil suits as well. Civil wrongs are not crimes; they are called *torts*, and civil litigation is the legal process of petitioning a court for compensation or correction of these wrongs. In a civil suit, the party who initiates the lawsuit is called the *plaintiff*, and the person against whom the suit is brought is called the *respondent*. (Although you might hear the respondent referred to as the *defendant*, that term is not technically correct in these cases.)

The losing party in a civil suit does not generally go to jail or prison unless also convicted of a criminal offense such as contempt of court. Instead, he or she is subject to one of two types of court orders:

- An order requiring that the respondent pay monetary damages. These damages can include *compensatory damages* for the actual and anticipated losses suffered by the plaintiff—both tangible and intangible—and *punitive damages* beyond the actual losses, designed to punish the party who committed the wrong.

- An injunction requiring that the respondent do some specified act or *not* do some specified act. For example, an injunction could order that the party stop sending e-mail to the plaintiff. An injunction is a legally binding order, and ignoring it can result in criminal charges.

NOTE

An important distinction between criminal and civil law is that people sued in civil court do not have the same rights, protections, and presumption of innocence as do criminal defendants.

An act can be both a crime and a civil wrong. Thus, cybercrime investigators may find that the evidence in their cases is also evidence in a civil lawsuit. When a company's network is invaded, in addition to filing criminal charges against the hacker, the company can also file a civil suit that seeks to directly collect monetary compensation for damages such as loss of worker productivity and lost sales due to the hacker's actions.

Another important concept in civil law is that of *vicarious liability*. This is the legal responsibility that one person or entity has for someone else's actions. Vicarious liability is usually created by some sort of "oversight" relationship. That is, a person or entity that has oversight or control over another person can be held civilly liable for wrongs committed by that person. This means a parent can be held liable for a child's acts, and an employer can be held responsible for an employee's acts. Thus, if a hacker uses company equipment and time to illegally break into other networks, to send child pornography, or to commit other cybercrimes, the employing company could be sued for allowing it to happen.

NOTE

It is important to understand that vicarious liability generally applies only to civil law. There are limited circumstances in criminal law (such as criminal conspiracy) in which a person can be charged for an offense actually committed by someone else, but in general, criminal responsibility requires *culpability* (overt involvement in commission of the prohibited act) before a charge can be brought.

Administrative/Regulatory Law

A third body of law, often overlooked in discussions of criminal and civil law, is *administrative law*, also called *regulatory law*. This body of law consists of rules and regulations that are enacted by a government agency under authority given to it by the legislative body and that apply to a particular occupational field or govern a particular area of life. Examples include Environmental Protection Agency regulations as well as rules that govern the practice of medicine, law, engineering, and the like.

Administrative laws are neither criminal nor civil but have the authority of law within their areas of jurisdiction. For example, an administrative action can be brought against a doctor or lawyer who violates the state regulatory agency's rules. If found guilty, the accused person might be censured, be fined, or have his or her license revoked. (If the latter occurs, and the person continues to practice, criminal charges of practicing without a license could be brought.) Administrative actions are usually conducted according to procedures set out by law that are similar to those of a court, but the councils or other bodies that hear the cases are not officers of the court. Thus, the proceedings are called *quasijudicial*.

NOTE

In some cases, one act can be subject to more than one body of law. For example, killing a person could result in both a murder charge (under criminal law) and a wrongful death lawsuit (under civil law). Likewise, a cybercriminal working in the finance industry who discovers and misuses insider information in a stock trade might be subject to both criminal charges and administrative sanctions.

Types of Law

Laws of all three types—criminal, civil, and administrative/regulatory—come into being in one of three ways: They're passed by a legislative body, they're created through court decisions, or they arise out of tradition and practice. The origin of a law determines whether it is considered to be statutory law, case law, or common law.

Statutory Law

Statutory law carries the most weight of the three types of law and is what we usually think of when we think of "the law." Statutory laws are created through a formal process known as *legislation*. They are introduced as proposed laws, or *bills*, debated, sometimes amended, voted upon, and passed by one or more legislative bodies and signed into law by an executive officer of the jurisdiction. In most cases, both the members of the legislative body and the executive officer are elected by popular vote of the citizens. Statutory laws are written and published as statutes, then *codified* (collected into codes) and enforced by police and other law enforcement agencies.

Case Law

Case law is based on judicial interpretation of laws that have been enacted by legislative bodies (statutory law) and governing documents (for example, the U.S. or state constitution or the city charter). Case law doesn't carry the same weight as statutory law because different courts can issue drastically different interpretations, and court decisions are subject to the appeals process.

Nonetheless, even though case law is not binding as is statutory law, the judicial opinions that form the basis of case law do establish *precedent*, which means case law is given weight by other judges making decisions in subsequent cases. In both criminal and civil court, an attorney cites previous case decisions to back up his or her case, and this forms an important part of the basis for a judge's decision.

Often, the principles set down by judges in case law find their way later into statutory law. For example, in the famous case *Miranda v. Arizona*, the U.S. Supreme Court held that law enforcement officers must inform suspects in criminal cases of their constitutional rights before questioning them in relation to a crime. This decision was not based on any statute but on the justices' interpretation of the due process guarantees in the U.S. Bill of Rights. However, after this landmark case, legislative bodies in many states passed statutory laws requiring that officers *Mirandize* (read the rights to) criminal suspects.

NOTE

Case law is important in cybercrime enforcement because many of these offenses haven't been on the books for a long period of time and thus their interpretations haven't been clearly defined in court. In ambiguous areas such as jurisdiction, in particular, it is important for investigators and prosecutors to stay up-to-date on applicable case law, because it can determine whether a case is prosecutable.

Common Law

Common law has grown less prominent over the years as more and more formal laws have been passed governing matters that once were ruled by tradition and custom. In the early days of the United States, common law (based on the English common law system) was an important way of governing society in a time when far fewer laws were formally enacted. Common law is based on practice, or "the way we've always done it."

A good example of common law still in existence is common law marriage, which is legal in many U.S. states. Two persons can become legally married without obtaining a marriage license from the state by meeting the common law requirements, which usually include a public declaration that they are married and living together, co-mingling funds, and otherwise acting as a married couple. Because common law is open to ambiguity (for example, in the case of common law marriage, if one party denies that the marital relationship exists, it can be difficult for the other to prove that it does), in the United States and other countries more and more matters that were once subject to common law are being formally legislated.

One might say that in the early days of the Internet, a form of common law governed. Although there were no governmentally imposed laws that directly pertained to online activity, "netizens" set their own rules based on consensus. For example, "flamers" (people who launched verbal and personal attacks on others) and spammers (those who deluged lists and individuals with unsolicited advertising) were often shunned and even kept out of Internet Relay Chat (IRC) channels and mailing lists. There was even a sort of "profiling" that took place, as people with certain e-mail addresses (for example, those ending with @aol.com) were immediately suspected. As in earlier societies, traditions were quickly established defining what was and wasn't acceptable behavior. These traditions still persist in many areas of the Net today and they influence online behavior. As with common law in earlier societies, these rules are now finding their way into formal legislation as governing bodies introduce bills aimed at criminalizing spam and other such activities.

Levels of Law

Statutory laws are enacted at different levels of government. Often, these laws overlap so that one act might be both a state and a federal crime, for example. Generally, the *scope* of law falls into one of four categories:

- Local laws
- State laws
- Federal laws
- International laws

The processes of enacting these laws are very similar; the differences are the legislative body that enacts them, the executive officer who signs them, and the geographic jurisdiction within which they can be enforced.

Local Laws

In the United States, *local law* generally refers to laws enacted by a city or town council or by a county commission, signed into law by the mayor or a county judge. Some cities and counties give the executive officer the power to veto laws; in others, the signing is a mere formality. Local laws are usually called *ordinances*. Cities and counties can enact ordinances making certain acts criminal offenses, but generally only at the lowest levels. For example, in Texas a criminal offense under city law is a Class C misdemeanor, the lowest level of criminal offense. Local laws can be enforced only within the boundaries of the city or county that enacts them.

People accused of violations of ordinances are tried in municipal or county courts. These courts often are not *courts of record*—that is, no court reporter records the proceedings. A guilty verdict in these lower courts can be appealed to a higher court of record. Cities and counties could pass laws regarding computer and network usage, but this generally isn't done at the local level.

> **NOTE**
>
> Local law is subject to state and federal law. A locality cannot pass a law that would violate the U.S. or state constitution or specific laws that grant sole control over certain behaviors to the state. For example, some states have laws that prohibit cities and counties from passing gun control laws, reserving that right for the state. On the other hand, in many states you'll find that some cities have laws imposing curfews on juveniles or requiring helmets for bicyclists, whereas other cities in the same state do not.

State Laws

Most penal laws (criminal offenses) enforced by police—including municipal police and county sheriff's offices—are *state laws*, passed by a state legislature and signed into law by the state's governor. Many states have a bicameral legislature patterned after the U.S. Congress, so the laws must be passed by both houses. In some states, the governor has veto power.

States can pass criminal laws at all offense grades (misdemeanors and felonies), with penalties ranging from fines to the death penalty (in states that allow it). States have wide latitude in the types of behaviors that can be outlawed. In general, unless the U.S. Constitution or federal law prohibits a state from regulating a particular behavior, the state is free to do so. Many U.S. states now have some laws regarding computer crime, but these laws vary widely from state to state.

Federal Laws

The U.S. Constitution grants all federal legislative powers to Congress, which consists of two branches: the Senate and the House of Representatives. Federal laws are introduced as bills in either the House or the Senate (designated by *HR* or *S* before the bill number to identify its origin) and are generally debated and amended in committee, where public hearings may be held to obtain citizen input, before being brought to the full body for a vote. After passage by one branch, the bill must go to the other. If changes are made there, it comes back to the originating body for approval, and it goes back and forth until agreement is reached. Alternatively, a conference committee with members from both the House and Senate may be appointed to resolve the differences. Once a law has been passed by both bodies, it goes to the president, who can sign it, veto it, or let it pass into law without signature. A presidential veto can be overridden by a vote of two-thirds majority of both the House and Senate.

Federal criminal laws are enforced by the FBI and other enforcement agencies that specialize in particular areas of law, such as the Drug Enforcement Administration (DEA); the Bureau of Alcohol, Tobacco, and Firearms; and the Criminal Investigation Division of the Internal Revenue Service. The FBI investigates federal cybercrime offenses, and the Computer Crime and Intellectual Property Section (CCIPS) of the Criminal Division of the U.S. Department of Justice (DOJ) provides legal expertise to federal prosecutors. The Federal Rules of Criminal Procedure govern the proceedings in these cases. Most federal criminal laws are contained in Title 18 of the U.S. Code (the federal equivalent of a state's penal code).

The federal government doesn't have general police powers within the states. That is, the FBI cannot arrest people for violations of state laws. The federal government does have general criminal jurisdiction over U.S. locations that are not within state boundaries, such as federal land, U.S. territories, and the District of Columbia.

International Laws

Laws can also originate through treaties, which are agreements entered into between countries. For example, Congress enacted the infamous Digital Millennium Copyright Act (DMCA) in 1998 to implement the World Intellectual Property Organization (WIPO) copyright treaty concluded at Geneva, Switzerland, in 1996. WIPO is an agency of the United Nations that has 179 member states. These treaties allow crimes to be effectively investigated and prosecuted even though the victim, offender, and investigators may reside in different countries.

Because cybercrimes are committed around the world, many people in the United States assume that legislation similar to that found in North America exists around the world. This couldn't be further from the truth. Many countries rely on existing laws to deal with cybercrime and might update those laws only after it becomes apparent that they fail to apply to cybercrimes (just as U.S. state laws often were not updated—and in some cases still haven't been—until the need became obvious). Ineffective law is as bad as no law whatsoever, and when the legal elements of an offense don't quite fit the actual crime, the law is ineffective—at least, for the purposes of prosecuting that particular crime.

In some countries, no laws whatsoever apply to crimes commonly associated with computers and the Internet, making it legal "by default" to perform actions that would subject a person to arrest in North America. However, the international attitude toward cybercrime has changed in many ways, and new laws are appearing around the world. Keeping up with all of these changes presents a challenge to people who must work with the laws of different jurisdictions.

In comparing the laws of nations around the world, the overwhelming conclusion is that many countries are failing to address the problem of cybercrime because they don't have legislation that deals with it specifically, whereas others have been more aggressive than the United States in addressing these issues. As we've seen throughout this book, many computer-related crimes are variations on old themes. For example, a country can have child pornography laws on the books and make no distinction as to whether the illegal materials are distributed in a paper or digital format. The fact that the crime is now being committed over the Internet is merely a new way to do something that's already illegal. In these cases, existing statutes might apply to someone committing the crime, regardless of whether a computer is involved.

On the other hand, they might *not*. If the legislation is too vague, it can be interpreted in a way that disqualifies any cyber-based variation. An example of this situation is the Love Bug virus that attacked systems around the world and resulted in estimated billions of dollars in damages. Investigation found that the author of the virus was located in the Philippines, and a suspect named Onel de Guzman was arrested under the Philippine Access Devices Act of 1994, which is also known as Republic Act 8484. This act, traditionally applied to cases involving credit card theft, dealt with the illegal use of account numbers and passwords. Unfortunately, after determining that the law wasn't applicable to this case and didn't address virus dissemination or the havoc it created, the charges were dropped. Even if the act could have been used to prosecute this crime, it imposes a penalty of only six months to six years in prison. The same crime, if committed in the United States, could be prosecuted under laws that carry a penalty of up to 20 years' imprisonment.

Because the existing laws of the time were inadequate to prosecute the Love Bug author (and other cybercriminals), the Philippine government found itself in the position of having to create new laws that dealt with cybercrime effectively. The creation of legislation that addresses computer and Internet-related crime is often a similar reactive approach to inadequate legislation.

To address the issues of all these computer and Internet-related crimes, numerous countries have joined together and signed the Council of Europe (COE) Convention on Cybercrime that requires members to criminalize activities related to cyberterrorism and other forms of cybercrime. Nonmember states such as the United States, Canada, Japan, and South Africa have also signed. Through this cooperative effort, activities such as hacking, interference with computer systems, fraud, forgery, and other related offenses are made illegal in each country that signs the convention. The convention also supports cooperation between countries to detect, investigate, and prosecute such crimes and to collect evidence through electronic methods of offenses related to terrorism, organized crime, and other crimes that are carried out on a global scale using computers and networks. You can view the convention itself on the COE's Web site at http://conventions.coe.int.

Basic Criminal Justice Theory

Investigating and prosecuting crimes of any type requires a basic understanding of criminal justice theory. Even experienced criminal justice theorists are challenged by the need to fit a type of criminality that didn't exist when these theories were established into a system designed to deal with less complex crimes that involve tangible property and evidence. In this section, we discuss some of the concepts on which the U.S. criminal justice system is based and the ways in which cybercrimes fit into these concepts.

Mala Prohibita and Mala in Se

Crimes can be divided into two groups based on whether they are considered to be acts that are inherently evil or acts that are "wrong" only because a legislative body made them illegal:

- Historically, acts that are considered to be *true crimes* under the laws of nature or God are described as *mala in se*, meaning "bad in itself." Acts such as murder, stealing, rape, robbery, and so forth are examples of this type of crime.

- Offenses that are not universally considered to be criminal but are made so by act of legislature are described as *mala prohibita* crimes. Examples include driving 80mph in a 50mph zone, possessing a gun without a permit in a state where that's required, or drinking alcohol when under a certain age.

The classification of some cybercrimes is a matter of debate. Is copying data from someone else's network without permission more akin to picking flowers on state property (*mala prohibita*) or stealing tangible goods that belong to another (*mala in se*)? The distinction between *mala in se* and *mala prohibita* offenses is not very important from a legal standpoint—the two types of law are enforced identically—but is interesting from a philosophical point of view.

Corpus Delicti: The Body of the Crime

The concept of *corpus delicti*, which literally means *the body of the crime*, is another important criminal law concept. This term describes the essence of the crime, or material evidence showing that a crime has been committed. It derives from the historical rule in a murder case that a dead body is necessary to prove that a murder has been committed. This rule has evolved over time to allow the *corpus delicti* to be established through *presumptive evidence*—that is, conclusive evidence that would lead a reasonable person to presume that a person has been murdered, even though the body is never found. For example, large amounts of blood established by DNA testing to be that of the presumed victim, along with the disappearance of the victim, would constitute presumptive evidence.

One factor that makes prosecution of cybercrimes difficult is the absence of a concrete *corpus delicti*. That is, there might be no tangible evidence of a crime at all.

Actus Reus and Mens Rea

Before a criminal offense can be charged, two essential elements must exist:

- ***Actus reus* (Latin for *guilty act*)** This is the act or omission that is prohibited by the criminal law. For example, the act of taking an item from a store shelf and removing it from the store without paying for it is the prohibited act for the offense of shoplifting (theft). The act of accessing a file on a network that you don't have permission to enter is a prohibited act under the offense of unauthorized access. In addition to overt acts or omissions, criminal laws might also prohibit mere possession, as with drug laws and some weapons offenses.

- **Mens rea (Latin for *guilty mind*)** This term refers to the state of mind that the prosecution must prove to convict the defendant in a criminal case. This is also sometimes referred to as the *culpable mental state*. The particular mental state required to constitute an offense is defined in the statute for that crime and differs depending on the crime.

The U.S. criminal justice system is based on the principle of *actus reus non facit reum nisi mens sit rea*. This is Latin for "An act does not make a person guilty of a crime unless his mind be also guilty." In other words, to convict, the prosecution must prove not only that the accused committed the prohibited act, but also that the accused possessed the culpable mental state at the time of the offense.

Most penal codes define the culpable mental states as follows:

CyberLaw Review

Understanding Criminal Culpability

Generally, criminal culpability includes one of four mental states: intentional, knowing, reckless, or negligent. Often, a single act can be interpreted as different offenses depending on the perpetrator's mental state. Here's an extreme example—the act of killing a person by running over him with a motor vehicle:

- If a person sees a pedestrian crossing the street in front of him, notices that it is his archrival whom he has long wished dead, and deliberately aims the car at the pedestrian and accelerates, killing him, the mental state is *intentional* and the crime is murder.

- Even if he doesn't have the intent to kill, if the driver sees the pedestrian, simply doesn't feel like slowing down, and runs him over, the mental state is *knowing*. The crime is still murder in most jurisdictions because the murder statutes generally specify "intentionally or knowingly" as the required level of culpability for that offense.

- If a person is driving much too fast for conditions, breezing through stop signs and paying no attention to the road as he "bops to the tunes" on his car stereo and in so doing he runs over a pedestrian at a crossing and kills him, the mental state is *reckless* and the crime is manslaughter.

- If a person knows that his brakes are bad, has had them go out several times but continues to keep driving the car without having them fixed, sees the pedestrian crossing the street in front of him and tries to stop but

Continued

> is unable to do so and kills the pedestrian, the mental state is *negligent* and the crime is criminally negligent homicide.
>
> ■ On the other hand, if a person is driving down the street, obeying the speed limit and traffic signs and otherwise taking care, and a pedestrian suddenly darts into the road from between two parked cars right into the path of the car and is hit and killed, there is no culpable mental state and there is no crime; the incident is an accident.

- **Intent** It is the deliberate desire of the person to obtain the outcome of the act (such as the death of a person).

- **Knowledge** The person is aware that the act will result in the outcome.

- **Recklessness** The person knows there is a substantial risk that if he or she engages in the act, it will result in the outcome.

- **Negligence** The person *ought to have known* that there was a substantial risk that if he or she engaged in the act, it would result in the outcome.

How do these definitions apply to cybercrimes? It is important for cybercrime investigators to realize that as with other criminal offenses, there must be evidence to prove *mens rea* as well as *actus reus*. That is, a person who "stumbles into" a network without intent to do so (for example, by running some program or script a hacker left on the computer, without knowing what that program or script will do) or who accidentally deletes critical files on a system does not have the intent or knowledge that is necessary under some statutes to obtain a criminal conviction

Elements of the Offense

The prohibited act and the culpable mental state are the two most important of the *elements of the offense*. The elements are those things that the prosecution must prove to obtain a conviction. Most penal codes define additional elements, such as:

- **Required result** Some offenses require a specific result of the act before that offense can be charged. For example, murder cannot be charged unless a death occurs as a result of the accused person's act. (Most jurisdictions also provide for an offense called *criminal attempt* that can be charged when an offense is attempted but is unsuccessful.)

- **Negation of exceptions** Some offenses provide in the statute for *exceptions* to prosecution. An exception differs from a defense to prosecution in that if the exception applies, the offense can't be charged. A person can still be charged with the crime even if there is an applicable statutory defense; it's up to the defendant to prove the defense (at trial), but it's up to the prosecution to prove the negation of exceptions.

All elements of an offense that are laid out in the statute must be present before a suspect can be arrested. Cybercrime investigators must be familiar with the statutes under which they plan to bring charges and ensure that each and every required element is present before making the arrest.

On the Scene

Analyzing the Elements of an Offense

Texas Penal Code Section 33.02 defines the offense of Breach of Computer Security as follows:

(a) A person commits an offense if the person knowingly accesses a computer, computer network, or computer system without the effective consent of the owner.

(b) [defines penalty grades]

Section 33.03 defines defenses as follows:

"It is an affirmative defense to prosecution under Section 33.02 that the actor was an officer, employee, or agent of a communications common carrier or electric utility and committed the proscribed act or acts in the course of employment while engaged in an activity that is a necessary incident to the rendition of service or to the protection of the rights or property of the communications common carrier or electric utility."

If we analyze the statute, we find that the prohibited act is "accessing a computer, computer network, or computer system without the effective consent of the owner." The culpable mental state (*mens rea*) is "knowingly." The defense to prosecution can be argued in court, if applicable. If the defendant can prove that the defense applies, he or she will be acquitted. If this were an exception instead of a defense, the law enforcement officers would have to ensure that it didn't apply before they could make a lawful arrest. This particular offense does not have a required result other than "access." It is not necessary that damage or loss occur to bring charges.

Level and Burden of Proof

Two important differences between criminal and civil law are the *level of proof* required to find a person legally accountable for an act and the side on which the *burden of proof* lies—that is, which side must prove its case to win at trial.

As we'll discuss in the next chapter, in a criminal case, the burden is on the prosecution to prove its case; if it does not, the defendant will be acquitted without having to provide any case at all. This is based on the presumption of innocence until proven guilty that is the basis of U.S. criminal law. The level of proof required in criminal cases is very high: Guilt must be proven *beyond a reasonable doubt*, and in a jury trial, all jurors must agree on the verdict.

Some countries' criminal justice systems operate on the opposite presumption; under the Napoleonic Code, which forms the basis of the criminal laws of France and other European countries, a person accused of a crime is presumed guilty and the burden is on the accused to prove his or her innocence.

In a civil case, the burden is generally on the respondent who is accused of a civil wrong to prove that he or she isn't liable. The level of proof required is much lower than in a criminal trial; the party that proves its case by a *preponderance of the evidence* (that is, there is slightly more evidence supporting that side than the other) wins the case. In many civil cases, only a majority of the jurors must be convinced; the decision doesn't have to be unanimous.

Cybercrime investigators must always be cognizant of the fact that criminal cases work toward two different levels of proof at different points in the investigation. *Probable cause* (facts and circumstances that would cause a reasonable and prudent person to believe that the accused person committed the crime) is the first level and is required to make a lawful arrest. Conviction requires much more evidence—enough to constitute proof beyond a reasonable doubt in the minds of an entire jury. This is the reason that follow-up investigations are so important, even after enough evidence has been gathered to arrest the suspect.

Jurisdictional Issues

Cybercrime cases, more than most others, often involve complex jurisdictional issues that can present both legal and practical obstacles to prosecution. To understand why jurisdiction presents such a problem in enforcing cybercrime laws, we have to look at how jurisdiction is defined, including the different types of jurisdictional authority, levels of jurisdiction, and statutory and case law pertaining to jurisdiction. In the following sections, we discuss these issues and explore the complications that arise when multijurisdictional cases take on an international flavor. We also examine the practical considerations that make it difficult to prosecute cases that span jurisdictional lines.

Defining Jurisdiction

Legal jurisdiction refers to the scope of authority given to a law enforcement agency to enforce laws or to a court to pronounce legal judgments. All governmental powers are jurisdictional in nature. That is, they are applicable only in regard to specific places or subject matter. A law passed in France does not apply to Americans unless they travel to France. At least, that's the way it used to be. Cyberspace complicates matters because a person can now—via computer—commit an act in France (or any other country accessible through the Internet) without physically being there. Does this mean that the American who has never set foot in France can be charged with a crime under French law? Later in this chapter we look at an actual case that addresses that very question. First, however, we need to discuss the different types and levels of jurisdictional authority.

Types of Jurisdictional Authority

The jurisdiction of an enforcement agency or of a court can be based on several things. These include:

- **The legal system under which the law falls** Police agencies have jurisdiction over criminal cases but no jurisdiction over civil matters. Citizens often ask police officers to intervene in civil disputes, but police are legally unable to do so. This must be done by agencies of the civil system. In some states, for example, county constables' deputies have the authority to enforce civil orders such as evictions and seizure of property to satisfy civil judgments. Regulatory agencies may have enforcement arms that have jurisdiction over their specific scope of responsibility. Courts likewise have jurisdiction over either civil or criminal cases; some courts have jurisdiction over both.

- **The case type** Municipal and state police have jurisdiction over all state criminal offenses, but some enforcement agencies have jurisdiction over only certain types of cases. For example, the state alcoholic beverage commission has jurisdiction over crimes pertaining to the sale, use, and transport of alcoholic beverages; the state racing commission has jurisdiction over criminal acts related to horse racing; and the state pharmacy board can enforce criminal laws related to controlled substances. Courts sometimes are limited to jurisdiction over specific types of cases (for example, family courts that hear only child custody and juvenile cases).

- **Offense grade** Courts often hear cases related to particular grades of offense. Thus, in Texas, municipal courts hear cases related to Class C misdemeanor offenses, county courts hear cases related to Class A and B misdemeanors, and district courts hear cases related to felony offenses.

- **Monetary damages** Some civil courts hear cases based on limits on the amount of monetary damages claimed. The most common example is small claims court, in which damages are limited to no more than a few thousand dollars. This court is often presided over by a justice of the peace, an elected judicial officer who, unlike judges of higher courts, often is not required to be a licensed attorney.

- **Government level** Both enforcement agencies and courts are assigned jurisdiction based on level of government. Courts, too, operate at the municipal, county, state, and federal levels.

- **Geographic area** *Geographic jurisdiction* refers to the physical area over which an agency or court has jurisdiction. Municipal police officers have jurisdiction within their city limits, state police have statewide jurisdiction, and so on. In many states, however, police officers have legal jurisdiction throughout an entire state, although their agency policies often restrict them to making arrests only within the limits of the city or county for which they work. Courts likewise have jurisdiction within specified geographic areas. For example, a municipal court in the city of Houston has jurisdiction over Class C misdemeanors—but only those that occur within the city limits.

Geographic jurisdiction is what most of us think of when we hear the term *jurisdiction*. However, it's important to realize that the scope of jurisdictional authority can be based on many things other than geographic area.

Level of Jurisdiction

Levels of jurisdiction correspond to the levels of law. Jurisdiction of enforcement agencies and courts can be local (city or county), statewide, federal, or international. Jurisdictional levels can overlap. Most U.S. citizens are familiar with the concept of *double jeopardy*. Based on the Sixth Amendment to the U.S. Constitution, this principle states that no one can be subject to being tried twice for the same offense. What many people don't understand is that a person can indeed be charged and tried twice for the same act if those charges are brought at different jurisdictional levels. This is what occurred when Sgt. Stacey Koon and other Los Angeles Police Department officers were tried and acquitted at the state level for police brutality in the Rodney King case in the 1990s, and were then tried again and convicted at the federal level. This is *not* considered to be double jeopardy.

Likewise, a cybercriminal could be charged with unauthorized network access under a state's computer crimes laws and also be charged at the federal level for the same act if the offense involved matters that come under federal jurisdiction (for example, if the computer belongs to a financial institution).

On the Scene

Multijurisdictional Task Forces

One way that enforcement agencies at different jurisdictional levels can cooperate to address special crime problems such as cybercrime is through a *multijurisdictional task force*. The U.S. Secret Service has assisted agencies by forming these types of task forces composed of members from local, state, and federal law enforcement agencies. The model for this type of task force was the New York Electronic Crimes Task Force (NYECTF) that was located in the World Trade Center in New York City prior to the September 11, 2001 terrorist attack that destroyed the Trade Center buildings.

The Problem with Cyberspace

Jurisdiction presents a special problem in cybercrime cases because the offenses are by definition committed in cyberspace, which is not a physical "place." The criminal and the victim are often miles apart, and the criminal might never set foot in the state or country where the harm occurs.

Another complicating factor is the cyberspace culture. Many believe that the Internet should remain a "free zone" where no government regulation or laws apply. Others believe that existing laws are sufficient and can be effectively applied to the cyberspace environment. Still others think we should have special "cybercops" whose jurisdiction *is* the Internet. The latter solution, although intriguing, brings up more questions: For whom would these cybercops be employed—an international entity such as the U.N.? If so, would they have jurisdiction only in member nations? Would an international body have authority to pass laws regulating behavior on the Internet? What would happen if or when those laws conflicted with laws in the states or nations that belong to the international body?

Statutory Law Pertaining to Jurisdiction

Most U.S. states have laws that address the jurisdiction of the states' laws and courts. For example, the Texas Penal Code, section 1.04, titled Territorial Jurisdiction, says:

"(a) This state has jurisdiction over an offense that a person commits by his own conduct or the conduct of another for which he is criminally responsible if:

1. either the conduct or a result that is an element of the offense occurs inside this state;

2. the conduct outside this state constitutes an attempt to commit an offense inside this state;

3. the conduct outside this state constitutes a conspiracy to commit an offense inside this state, and an act in furtherance of the conspiracy occurs inside this state; or

4. the conduct inside this state constitutes an attempt, solicitation, or conspiracy to commit, or establishes criminal responsibility for the commission of, an offense in another jurisdiction that is also an offense under the laws of this state."

This code gives the state broad authority to bring charges in a wide range of cases and would cover most cybercrimes that originated within the state or when a "result" (such as loss of intangible property) occurs within the state even though the perpetrator might be in another state or even another country. Legally, then, Texas could bring charges against citizens of other states or countries who had never been inside Texas. Practically, this would require extradition, which might or might not be granted by the state or country where the accused is physically located. Later in this chapter, we look more closely at how practical considerations can complicate prosecution.

Case Law Pertaining to Jurisdiction

We mentioned the case of *Tennessee v. Robert and Carleen Thomas* earlier in this book. In the Thomas case, the long arm of the law reached approximately 2,000 miles from a Tennessee court to California, where the Thomases lived and worked. The grand jury in Tennessee handed down an indictment against the Thomases for violating the Tennessee obscenity statutes, even though their adult bulletin board system (BBS) had already been declared legal in Santa Clara County, California, where they were located, and the Thomases were tried and convicted in Tennessee and sent to prison. This was a landmark case in the matter of jurisdiction as it applies to acts committed in cyberspace.

Another case that proved to be important in terms of international jurisdiction took years to resolve. In May 2000, a court in France ordered Yahoo!, the U.S.-based Web service, to remove all Nazi paraphernalia that was offered for sale on its site (which is hosted in the United States). The reason for this order is because the sale of Nazi-related material is illegal in France, and Yahoo! made no efforts to block the sale of these items from French customers. Yahoo! refused to abide by the order, and in November 2000 the French court threatened to fine Yahoo! $13,000 per day if the company didn't comply. The next month, Yahoo! filed in U.S. court for a declaration that the French order couldn't be enforced by the U.S. government, and in November 2001, the U.S. District Court issued a decision that enforcement of the French order would violate Yahoo!'s constitutional right to freedom of speech. In February 2002, the French court countered that it would take Yahoo! to trial in France for condoning war crimes. The decisions that were reached in this case were controversial, and varied. Although Judge Jeremy Fogel initially found in favor of Yahoo!, the 9th U.S. Circuit Court of Appeals later reversed this decision. Although Yahoo! was fighting that it had the First Amendment right to violate French law and facilitate French citizens to violate the same law, there was no certain extraterritorial right under the amendment. Ultimately, Yahoo! and other auction sites such as eBay banned the sale of hate-related items. As with the Thomas case, the act committed is not a crime in the jurisdiction where the accused is located, but it is considered a crime in another location where the "criminal" items can be accessed over the Net.

The potential for many similar jurisdictional sparring matches exists now that it's so easy for a criminal to use the Internet to "reach out and touch someone" in a state or country other than the one in which the criminal is located.

International Complications

In international law, the concept of *territoriality* is based on the principle that nations should not exercise their jurisdiction outside their own territory (*Dictionary of Law*, Oxford University Press). However, nations are allowed to exercise jurisdiction inside their territory over acts committed by their own citizens when outside their territory. Furthermore, they generally are permitted to exercise jurisdiction over a criminal act in which part of the act occurred within their territory (that is, the offense either originated in their territory and was completed outside or originated outside their territory and was completed inside).

Treaties such as the Council of Europe Convention on Cybercrime provide a common ground in defining cybercrime (although, as we stated earlier in this book, these definitions are broad in nature). Through the use of such treaties, it makes it easier for law enforcement to investigate and prosecute cybercriminals who operate or victimize others in different countries. This isn't the case if no treaty exists between the country investigating the crime and the one in which the cybercriminal resides. If no laws exist in the other country and extradition isn't possible, the suspect cannot be punished. As we said, if there is no law to make an act illegal, no crime has been committed.

Practical Considerations

Legalities aside, for a number of practical reasons law enforcement agencies and prosecutors choose not to pursue cybercrime cases that take them outside their normal jurisdictions. These reasons include the following:

- The cost of travel to investigate leads in distant cities, states, or countries
- The difficulty of bringing in witnesses and records from far away for the trial
- The difficulty of extraditing a suspect who is located in another jurisdiction
- The political reality that citizens generally want their police agencies to address local crime first
- The lack of technical understanding and expertise within the enforcement agency and prosecutor's office
- The paperwork and "red tape" that are often involved in obtaining the cooperation of agencies in other jurisdictions, especially in other countries
- The language barriers that often make it difficult to communicate with agencies and witnesses in other countries

The fact that an agency has the legal authority to bring criminal charges in a particular case doesn't mean that it will necessarily do so, especially if it is deemed more cost-effective or more politically expedient not to do so. In this, cybercrimes are no different from other types of offenses. However, there might be more reasons *not* to prosecute in a cybercrime case than in the typical criminal case.

Investigating an International Cybercrime

The ability to perform investigations that go outside jurisdictional boundaries almost always relies on cooperation with law enforcement entities in those areas. Police in one country generally have no official jurisdiction in other countries. However, when police in different countries work together, the impact on crime can be significant. This impact is seen in a number of collaborative efforts between police and other law enforcement agencies in various countries.

Extraditing and Prosecuting

The ability to investigate and prosecute cybercrimes can become complicated when a single crime crosses one or more international borders. Although a suspect might be physically sitting at a machine in one country, the information he or she taps into could go across many jurisdictions as it flows from another computer in a foreign land. In some cases, the cybercriminal might use anonymous e-mail addresses or technologies that make him appear to be working in a different country than the one he is actually in. By attacking a system in this way, the crime becomes more difficult to detect and even more difficult to prosecute. Other difficulties inherent in prosecuting international cybercrimes include:

- **The language barrier** Difficulty of communicating with law enforcement and others in countries where you don't speak the language.

- **Time factors** Any cybercrime investigation can stretch out over months or even years. Keeping the investigation alive is difficult enough when all the parties involved are in the same geographic area, but it becomes even more difficult across national boundaries.

- **Cost** Traveling to a foreign country or countries could be necessary to pursue an international case. Few police agencies have budgets that cover such expenses, except in the most heinous and high-profile crimes.

- **Political factors** Even when law enforcement agencies in different jurisdictions want to cooperate, they might be restricted by political factions above them.

In many cases, the source of a crime might originate in one country where legislation differs from that of your own country or where the act is not a crime at all. For example, although child pornography might be defined as pornographic images of persons younger than 18 years of age in North America, the legal age to pose for such images in other countries might be considerably younger. This difference can cause a dilemma for law enforcement officers, because it is legal for a Web site in one country to distribute the images but illegal for people in other countries to download them. Investigators can arrest people in possession of the pornographic files, but they might be powerless to shut down the Web site distributing the pornography.

Another area where jurisdictional issues can arise is in cases of Internet luring. Although NBC's *Dateline* has run numerous episodes of online predators being arrested for engaging in sex chats and meeting to have sex with girls who are (or more accurately, are presented as being) underage, the legal age of consent varies in many states. To make things more difficult, the age of consent is equally inconsistent in different countries. For example, even though it may be illegal to have sex with a person under the age of 18 in your area, the legal age of consent in Canada is 14 years of age (unless that person is in a position of authority, such as a teacher or priest). As such, even if there are laws that protect children against Internet luring in your state or country, what constitutes as being a child or someone mature enough to engage in sex will vary from place to place.

When there is a need to extradite the offender, it isn't always possible. Extradition requires the cooperation of the country in which the offender resides. In the case of the person who authored the

Love Bug virus, U.S. law enforcement officers tried to have the culprit extradited to the United States from the Philippines. As has been the case with numerous crimes committed on one nation's soil when the offender is located in another nation, the request for extradition was denied by the Philippine government. Many countries have laws and punishments that differ from those in the United States, and they might refuse extradition if they feel the punishment that the offender would be subject to in the United States for a particular crime is unjust under their law. In other cases, they could feel it is bad precedent to turn their citizens over into the hands of a foreign nation anytime they're asked to do so. Although the person who allegedly wrote the Love Bug virus was charged in the Philippines, as we noted, it was found that he couldn't be prosecuted there because no laws existed that explicitly dealt with the dissemination of viruses.

> **NOTE**
>
> Under international law, there is no obligation for a country to extradite unless a treaty between the countries creates such an obligation. This situation gives nations a lot of leeway in granting or refusing extradition. The extradition treaties that the United States has signed generally require that evidence be provided showing the accused person has violated both U.S. law and the law of the country requesting extradition. Often, extradition treaties specify the particular offenses for which a person can be extradited. Unlike the United States, some European nations try their own citizens for crimes committed in other countries.

Once a suspect is extradited to your jurisdiction, additional international cooperation is usually needed. Witnesses might need to be flown in from the other countries. If they choose not to come voluntarily, a subpoena can be issued. Ignoring the subpoena can be declared contempt of court by the judge, who can then have a warrant issued for the witness's arrest. However, because the witness is in another country and might never set foot in yours, the warrant can't be served and is effectively useless. The criminal suspect might have been extradited, but it is doubtful that an extradition request will be granted for a witness who failed to show at trial. If the witness does comply, he or she will need to be transported to the location of the court and provided with proper accommodations and food during the trial. It might be necessary to hire interpreters if the witness speaks a foreign language. All these factors increase the cost of prosecuting the offender, which may lead the prosecutor to drop charges or never file them to begin with.

The Nature of the Evidence

In addition to the difficulty of defining the offense and the jurisdictional issues that complicate prosecution, another obstacle that stands in the way of building and winning a case against a cybercriminal is the nature of much of the evidence. The law generally recognizes three types of evidence:

- **Physical evidence** Tangible items that provide proof of the commission of an offense and/or the identity of the offender (for example, the "smoking gun" that was used to commit a murder)

■ **Direct evidence** The testimony of witnesses who saw the offense occur, observed the accused taking preparatory steps toward committing the offense, or otherwise have direct knowledge of the crime

■ **Circumstantial evidence** Facts and circumstances that tend to support the theory that the accused person committed the offense but that do not offer definitive proof

Much of the evidence in cybercrime cases is digital; this means that it is not tangible evidence, but rather is made up of electronic or magnetic pulses that are stored in the form of electromagnetic charges on a disk or tape. Not only is this evidence largely intangible, but it is also fragile, much like evidence consisting of a footprint in the snow. A record of the evidence's existence must be captured before it "melts away." As with the footprint, it might be impossible to preserve the original cybercrime evidence for presentation in court, and the inability to produce the original evidence tends to weaken the prosecution's case.

Hackers with technical expertise can destroy the evidence by going through multiple servers to get to their targets and then, once they've accomplished their objective, deleting the log files on each server to cover their tracks. According to fraud investigator Dan Clements, quoted at http://news.com.com/2009-1017-912708.html, this is the digital equivalent of "vacuuming up the crime scene."

Because digital evidence is intangible, fragile, and easily destroyed (either deliberately or accidentally), proper evidence handling is even more important in cybercrime cases than in other types of crimes. As we discussed in Chapter 15, investigators should immediately make copies of disks that might contain evidentiary material and work only on the copies, preserving the integrity of the original evidence. In addition, all such evidence should be documented carefully.

Human Factors

The obstacles to prosecution of cybercrime cases that we have discussed thus far pertain to legal or technical issues. However, other factors make it difficult to build a cybercrime case; these might be thought of as *human factors*. These factors pertain to the necessity that law enforcement officers and IT professionals work together to most effectively put together a prosecutable case and the difficulties that both sides often encounter in doing so.

Law Enforcement "Attitude"

Law enforcement officers have a saying: *Nobody understands a cop except another cop*. In many ways, it's true. Police officers are put on the streets and are given an incredibly difficult job to do, saddled with a tremendous responsibility and burdened with impossible expectations. Often with too little training, they are given positions of authority but are placed under close public scrutiny, restricted by law and departmental policies and tasked with making split-second decisions in life-threatening situations. Later their decisions will be critiqued at leisure by people with no street experience who hold the officers' careers in their hands.

Law enforcement agencies are, by and large, paramilitary organizations—with the emphasis on *para*. Military personnel generally have a clearly defined mission. Police agencies often operate at the whim of politicians and bureaucrats and are expected to be all things to all people—"tough on crime" yet unfailingly nice to citizens, heroes who save the day from the bad guys yet are sensitive enough to never offend anyone. Officers are often undertrained, underpaid, overworked, and overstressed. Salaries are low, hours are long, and divorce, alcoholism, and suicide rates are high.

It's no wonder that many police officers have "an attitude." Most eager young police recruits really do join the force because they want to help people and make the world a better, safer place to live. Because officers see the worst side of humanity day after day, they can slowly become cynical and suspicious, developing an "us versus them" mentality that excludes everyone who's not a cop (including, all too often, their own families).

This is the law enforcement culture. People on the other side of the "thin blue line" must understand it to work effectively with law enforcement officers. Investigators generally must have several years of experience on the streets before they're eligible for promotion to detective, so the "attitude" is often firmly engrained. IT professionals who want to be part of the investigative team need to learn to think like cops, just as the police investigator needs to learn to think like a hacker to penetrate the hacker culture and understand what they do and how they do it. Understanding law enforcement types isn't really difficult, if you keep in mind a few basic facts:

- **Most police officers are not as confident as they seem** "Command presence" is a job requirement, and officers get good at "bluffing," but those who come off as most authoritarian are often the least confident in themselves.

- **Most police officers don't understand technology** There are exceptions, of course. However, the majority of officers are not technically savvy. They often know a lot about radios, light bars, and other traditional police paraphernalia but think computers are for "nerds." This attitude is changing as computers become more ubiquitous within departments, but the changes come slowly. This point of course applies more to seasoned officers than new recruits, who grew up with the technologies discussed in this book.

- **Most police officers don't like not understanding** They are suspicious, and perhaps a bit envious, of people who do know about computers. IT professionals generally make a lot more money than cops do, without having to put their lives on the line. For that reason, a little resentment on the part of the police officer is understandable.

- **Many police officers feel pretty powerless** Despite the "police power" myth, many officers feel weighted down by the highly structured agency environment, where the slightest misstep results in disciplinary measures, and by the weight of the law, policies, political factors, and public relations requirements.

All of this leads to a touch of police paranoia about working with "outsiders"—those who aren't sworn police officers. That being said, officers who cling to this mentality are often a liability to investigations and other duties that require direct involvement and cooperation with civilians. As a civilian police employee who worked in computer forensics, I can say that the worst officers to deal with were the ones who held the cardinal belief that police officers were better than anyone else, and would treat "outsiders" with contempt. This attitude was summarized by one officer that told me "you're a civilian … you're the lowest of the low." Although such extreme attitudes of privilege and entitlement are often seen in officers who themselves are investigated, at the least this stance toward majority of the population makes it extremely difficult to assist an officer.

This attitude must be overcome if the police are to work effectively with IT professionals, corporate management, and the general citizenry to fight cybercrime. For officers and investigators, the first step in overcoming negative attitudes is to recognize the problem. For IT professionals, the first step is to recognize how the sharp contrast between the highly structured police environment and the more relaxed high-tech lifestyle widens the chasm.

The High-Tech Lifestyle

Now that the dot-com bubble has burst and many high-tech companies have disappeared off the map, the high-tech lifestyle has moved down a notch, from the ridiculous to the merely sublime. At least, it seems that way when the average police officer compares his or her earnings to the salaries and perks that come with many technology industry jobs. The lifestyle differences, however, are about much more than just money.

Police officers, who work in a highly structured environment, tend to live structured lives outside the job as well. The typical cop is straitlaced and punctual and believes in doing things "by the book," according to the rules. The typical techie takes a more relaxed approach to life, living on Jolt and pizza and often admiring those who are smart enough to bend or get around the rules. The majority of police officers are political conservatives, whereas high-tech workers tend to be politically liberal. Police officers tend to stay with one job, often retiring from the agency where they went to work at an early age. Officers tend to grow "roots," staying in the same community all or most of their lives. Tech workers tend to jump from job to job, often moving from one geographic location to another for bigger salaries and better opportunities. It's no wonder cops and techies don't understand one another.

Natural-Born Adversaries?

At first glance, police officers and IT professionals don't mix at all. In addition to their differences, it's not unusual to find an elitist mentality on both sides. Police officers feel superior by virtue of their governmental authority, whereas tech people feel superior based on their positions in the business world. There is a mutual mystique at work. Cops carry guns, something many techies have no experience with and of which they're more than a little fearful. Techies can make computers do their bidding, and (to varying degrees) many police officers are a little afraid of those mysterious machines.

The gap between police officers and IT professionals has narrowed immensely in recent years. Although many police officers don't understand or appreciate the difference between black-hat and white-hat hacking, nor do they recognize that the same skills used by cybercriminals can also be used for legitimate purposes, they do understand computers. Younger officers have grown up using technologies that may still baffle senior officers, and may have indulged in downloading an illegal music file or two. Like IT professionals, they too are computer enthusiasts. More seasoned officers have also had to become more familiar with computers, as they are a common piece of equipment in the police station and the cruisers they drive. They may have been issued BlackBerry devices, laptop computers, or other devices. As IT professionals have learned, officers often find that they couldn't imagine working without them.

As far apart as the two careers might seem, you don't have to look far to find common ground. Police officers and IT professionals actually have many things in common:

- Both work long, odd hours. Who can you often find hard at work at 3:00 on a Sunday morning when the rest of the world is sound asleep? Police officers and programmers.

- Both generally are dedicated to their jobs and would not want to do anything else.

- Both suffer from caffeine addiction, although they might argue the merits of Jolt Cola versus thick black police station coffee.

- Both want things (law, code) to "make sense" and they get frustrated when they don't.

- Both are problem solvers by nature.

In this last commonality lies the key to overcoming all the differences and working together as part of a team. Both jobs involve identifying problems or potential problems and taking action to solve them. Police officers and IT professionals who are able to see beyond the surface will find that they're really not so different after all, at least not in the ways that count when it comes to fighting cybercrime together.

Overcoming Obstacles to Effective Prosecution

Despite the many obstacles that stand in the way of effectively prosecuting cybercrime cases—including the difficulty of even defining the crime in the first place, the jurisdictional nightmares that arise when suspect and victim are in different geographic locations, and the attitudes and lifestyle differences that make it difficult for police and IT professionals to work together—it *is* possible to overcome all these challenges and put together a case that will stand up in court.

Law enforcement agencies can work with prosecutors to clarify definitions and ensure that they understand the elements that must be proven to arrest and convict in a cybercrime case. IT personnel who anticipate working with law enforcement on cybercrime cases must learn the basics of how the criminal justice system operates, and both must know the differences among civil, criminal, and regulatory laws and which specific acts fall under which bodies of law in their jurisdiction.

Speaking of jurisdiction, investigators must be prepared for legal complications when cybercrimes cross state or national boundaries—as they so often do. Investigators must also be realistic enough to understand that even when they legally have jurisdiction, many practical factors can prevent successful prosecution of multijurisdictional cybercrime cases.

Law enforcement officers and IT professionals can learn to work together on cybercrime cases, resulting in much more effective investigations than either could conduct alone. An important part of building the bridge is learning to "talk the talk." Police officers need to learn technical terminology, and IT personnel need to become comfortable with the language of law and police jargon so that the two can better understand one another. A successful prosecution is based on the work of many people and on many factors. An important element in building a solid case hinges on proper implementation of the investigative process.

The Investigative Process

Cybercrime investigators must be familiar with the process of gathering data, materials, and information that might be related to the commission of an offense; this is, in fact, the definition of *criminal investigation*. IT professionals who work with law enforcement officers to facilitate the process might be intimidated by the word *investigation* and its official implications, but it's easier to understand if you realize that we all conduct investigations, all the time. Whenever we meet a new person, make a major purchase such as a home or automobile, or make a major life decision such as changing jobs or getting married, we *investigate*—the gist of which is simply gathering information. Certainly a network administrator often has reason to investigate; he or she investigates when a server goes down, when a user is unable to access a network resource, when a software application doesn't work properly, and so forth.

The only differences between the sorts of investigations that are a normal part of everyday life and a police investigation are the formality and the ultimate goals of the investigation. In both cases, the primary objective is to gather information. In a criminal investigation, that information is ultimately used to prove the guilt of the accused person in court. Thus, the process must be formalized to provide a standard structure that ensures compliance with the laws that govern evidence collection.

However, it is important for investigators to remember that even evidence that's not admissible in court can still be useful during the course of the investigation because it can help the investigator reconstruct the circumstances of the illegal act or omission and can lead to other, admissible evidence. For presentation in court, evidence must be evaluated in light of the following questions:

- **Is it relevant?** In other words, does it relate to this case? If you are investigating a hacker suspected of launching a denial-of-service (DoS) attack on a computer network, the discovery that this hacker was once arrested for using a blue box to make illegal long distance calls has no bearing on the current case and probably won't be admissible as evidence (although such information *can* be introduced, in many jurisdictions, during the sentencing phase of the trial, after the defendant is found guilty).

- **Is material it?** In other words, does it prove one of the essential elements of the case? Does the evidence provide proof that the suspect committed the prohibited act, show the suspect's culpable mental state, support the fact that a required result occurred, or negate the existence of statutory exceptions?

- **Is it competent?** Is the evidence believable? If the evidence is witness testimony, is that witness credible? If the evidence is digital, is its meaning clear, and can you show that it hasn't been tampered with?

An investigation should be objective; after all, the purpose of an investigation is not to indict a particular person but to determine the truth. Investigators should put aside personal feelings and approach the investigation in the same way a good journalist approaches a story. In fact, it is useful for the investigator to use the rule of thumb journalists are taught to use in collecting information for publication: Find out *who*, *what*, *when*, *where*, *why*, and *how*, also known as the *5WH method*. These are the questions that must be asked and answered before you—as a writer or as an investigator—can rest, assured that you have the whole story. Table 16.1 shows a breakdown of the objectives of a criminal investigation and how the journalistic approach can be used to accomplish them.

Table 16.1 Investigative Objectives and the 5WH Approach

Objective	Questions to Answer
Determine whether a crime has been committed.	*What* happened? *Who* was involved?
Protect the crime scene.	*Where* did the illegal act occur? *When* did it happen?
Identify the suspect.	*Who* had motive, means, and opportunity?
Identify the M.O.	*How* was the act committed?
Prove that the suspect did it.	*Who* observed the crime or its results? *Where* was the suspect when the crime occurred? *What* records/documents/logs identify the suspect?

When these questions have been answered, the next step in the process is to effect a lawful arrest. This doesn't mean the investigation is over. At the time of arrest, you must have collected enough evidence to constitute probable cause, but that's not enough to convict—proof beyond a reasonable doubt is required—so the investigation continues as you prepare an effective case for prosecution.

> **NOTE**
>
> *Probable cause* is required in two situations: to obtain a search or arrest warrant or to make an arrest without a warrant. Evidence does not have to be admissible at trial to be used as a building block of probable cause.

In a cybercrime case, as in any other criminal case, the investigator might need to revisit witnesses, and new evidence may be discovered at any time up to the start of the trial. Under the U.S. system of justice, the existence of evidence must be made known to the defense attorneys under the rules of *pretrial discovery*.

Investigative Tools

An investigator builds a case using standard investigative tools. The "Three I's" that form the nexus of the investigator's toolkit are:

- Information
- Interview and interrogation
- Instrumentation

In the following sections, we look at each of these tools in detail and discuss their applicability to a typical cybercrime case.

Information

Information, the foundation of the case, can be obtained in many different ways. Here we refer to the information that an investigator can gather through observation, examination of documents or electronic data, and examination of physical evidence. One important means of obtaining this information is through the *crime scene search*. In the case of a cybercrime, much of the evidence might be on the computer—stored on its hard disk or even still in memory. However, it's important for investigators to resist tunnel vision that leads them to focus solely on the computer, because the crime scene can encompass the area around the computer as well.

If there is evidence on the system showing that a particular computer was used to commit a cybercrime, you still must establish a link between the computer and the suspect. Then traditional crime scene techniques are appropriate, such as dusting for fingerprints and conducting a thorough area search that can turn up such evidence as printouts of computer data, notes jotted by the suspect that pertain to the offense, backup tapes containing evidentiary information, and so forth. It is also important to remember that evidence can be stored off-site where it has been uploaded over the Internet or physically transported on removable media.

Interview and Interrogation

Interview and interrogation refer to the questioning of persons involved in the cybercrime in some way. The difference lies in the person's role in the crime and in the manner of questioning. An *interview* involves questioning witnesses, victims, and other people who might have information relevant to solving the crime. These people could include technical experts who can explain how the crime was committed and who may also testify as expert witnesses at trial or who may merely provide background information to help the investigator understand the technicalities of the offense. An interview is basically a conversation (recorded or documented by the interviewer) with the objective of obtaining facts that will help identify the perpetrator of a crime and build a case against that person.

> **NOTE**
>
> Although witness interviews should be recorded or documented, in most cases the witness in a criminal case will need to personally testify to the facts in court. The U.S. justice system in most cases gives the accused the right to face his or her accuser(s), and hearsay evidence (third-party evidence) is generally not admissible. There are exceptions, including child abuse cases (including child pornography and child rape cases that might be cybercrimes), dying declarations, and other cases in which the witness is emotionally or physically unable to personally testify.

An *interrogation* involves questioning persons suspected of committing or aiding in the commission of the offense. The interrogation is generally recorded, and it is important to document that the suspect has been advised of his or her rights before questioning, either by recording the advisement or by obtaining a written waiver of rights from the suspect, or both. The objective of an interrogation is to obtain incriminating statements and/or a confession.

> **NOTE**
>
> In certain circumstances, statements may be used against a suspect without that suspect first being advised of and waiving the Miranda rights, including *res gestae* statements (statements made suddenly and not in response to questioning—"blurted out").

An interrogation is often adversarial in nature, but it doesn't have to be. One of the best ways to get useful information from a suspect is to gain his or her confidence, make the suspect think that you're sympathetic to his or her cause. In cybercrimes involving hacking and technical exploits, it can be useful to have an officer who is technically savvy interrogate the suspect, because someone who "speaks the same language" might be able to draw the suspect into bragging about the technical prowess necessary to pull off the job. The old familiar "good cop, bad cop" routine might also work, especially if you set up a team that features a young, "techie" type good cop playing against an older, apparently technophobic bad cop. There are many different interrogation techniques, and the investigator should use those that work best for and come most naturally to him or her. Some tried and true techniques, in addition to the sympathetic approach, include:

- **The logical approach** Use reasoning to convince the suspect that it's in his or her best interest to confess.

- **Indifference** Pretend you don't need a confession because you already have enough evidence without it. This can work well with multiple suspects when you can imply to each that the other(s) has already "spilled the beans."

- **The facing-saving approach** Allow the suspect to provide excuses for the behavior and show understanding of why he or she committed the crime.

On the Scene

Confession Is Good for the Soul—and for the Prosecution's Case

To be admissible in court, a confession must be voluntary; that is, it must be given without duress, bribery, or other undue influence. Some jurisdictions hold that a confession cannot be admitted unless there is independent *corroboration* of some sort. For example, if a person admits to being the one who sent threatening e-mail to another party, this could be corroborated by his knowledge of the specific contents of the e-mail, which had not been made public and would not be known by anyone other than the recipient, law enforcement officers, and the sender of the e-mail.

Investigators must always be on guard for the possibility of *false confessions*. Why would someone confess to a crime he or she didn't commit? Most such confessors do it to get attention, and many high-profile crimes attract a number of people who line up to claim "credit." This can be a problem in the case of a "popular" crime, such as a Web site defacement that expresses a popular political idea or a network attack against a corporation that has a bad reputation with the public. This is one reason investigators don't publicize all the facts of a case or even sometimes "leak" false or misleading information about the case to the media. Confessions can then be measured against the true facts of the case, which would be known to only a few people, one of whom is the person who actually committed the offense.

For both interviews and interrogations, the same basic guidelines apply to cybercrime witnesses and suspects as in other types of cases:

- Separate the persons being interviewed or interrogated. Even in the case of witnesses who are not innocent of any crime, witnesses can be influenced by one another's statements. Suspects can reveal their guilt by telling conflicting stories.

- Use *kinesic interview techniques*; note body language, voice tone, facial expression, and other nonlinguistic communication that provide clues to whether a person is telling the truth. Use *mirroring*, in which the investigator subtly emulates the other person's body language to create a sense of rapport with the person.

- Have a tactical plan for the interview or interrogation; be aware of all the available facts about the case and know exactly what information you're seeking going in.

- Ensure that standard procedures are followed for recording and/or obtaining written statements.

Once you've obtained information in the course of an interview or interrogation, that information should be analyzed to determine its value and admissibility. This analysis can be based on the answers to the following questions:

- Does the information substantiate one or more elements of the offense (is it material)?

- Could the information negate a suspect's defense or alibi?

- Does the information corroborate a suspect's confession?

Investigators often use a "two-pronged test" to evaluate the credibility of witness information. This test consists of separately evaluating both the witness giving the information and the information itself, as shown in Table 16.2.

Table 16.2 The Two-Pronged Test for Evaluating the Credibility of Witness Information

Evaluating Witness Credibility	Evaluating Information Credibility
Has the witness given information in the past that proved to be true?	Does the information fit with the facts observed or obtained from other sources?
Is the witness an "upstanding" member of the community, considered honest, and so on?	Does the information make sense?
Is the witness objective (in other words, does he or she have a personal stake in the investigation or a personal relationship with the victim or suspect)?	Is the information something that the witness would be in a position to know?

Instrumentation

Instrumentation refers to the use of technology to obtain evidence. In cybercrime cases, use of data recovery techniques to recover "deleted" and "erased" information on disks is a type of instrumentation. Other, more traditional examples include forensic techniques for collecting and analyzing trace evidence, DNA analysis, and the like.

On the Scene

Bad Luck, Good Investigations, or Both?

Sometimes the bad guys have a run of bad luck, making investigators' lives easier. The following report summarizes some of the cyber-related elements of a recent arrest, made after the suspect attempted to extort funds by means of the Internet. The alleged perpetrator, "James Palmer," has been arrested and has pled guilty to federal charges. Palmer also has been charged with several state offenses.

The case came to the attention of local and federal authorities when an individual, "Timothy Vaughan," reported to Major Eastern University police the receipt of e-mail messages that threatened injury to Vaughan's family if money was not paid to the sender of the e-mail message. Over a two-week period, the messages built in severity of threatened actions and in specificity of details about the recipient's personal life. It later turned out that an acquaintance of Palmer was a coworker of Vaughan's wife. A key feature in this extortion attempt was Palmer's perceived ability to maintain his anonymity throughout the series of communications. That perception on his part turned out to be incorrect.

Palmer sent Vaughan a large number of messages, generally during the late afternoon. After Vaughan filed a complaint, the university police department queried the public e-mail service Palmer used. The service allows users to establish e-mail addresses anonymously, and thus the service was unable to provide direct information about the sender's identity. However, the service was able to provide the Internet Protocol (IP) addresses used. The IP addresses of the PCs Palmer used were traced to various PCs at another, nearby college. Unlike the computers on many networks, the computers Palmer used had fixed IP addresses. This was Palmer's first bit of bad luck. As a result, the college IT personnel were able to provide the investigators with a complete listing and location diagram of each Internet-enabled PC on campus. Palmer's second piece of bad luck was to choose a college with IT staff members who were eager to put some energy into the investigation, and they identified Palmer rather quickly.

On the day that Palmer had established as the deadline for meeting his payment demand, the investigators had real-time telephone contact with Vaughan and the e-mail service provider. The investigators were also on-site at the sending college. They were

Continued

quickly able to establish the location of the sending PC, in a temporarily unused computer laboratory. Palmer was sitting at a PC with his back to a glass panel that separated him from the hallway. The investigators watched him for about an hour as he continued to send a long series of e-mails to Vaughan. These e-mails were confirmed as emanating from the observed PC at that location.

Palmer was arrested in mid-message, and the PC he used was seized as evidence. Unfortunately for Palmer, even more bad luck was coming his way. The third piece of bad luck involved Palmer's meticulousness in using the e-mail service's spellcheck function. The e-mail service Palmer chose saves, in temporary Internet files, screenshots of spelling checks. A final piece of bad luck: When Palmer was arrested, he was in possession of printouts of many of the e-mails he had sent.

Contributed by Dr. Bernard H. Levin, professor, Blue Ridge (VA) Community College, and commander, Waynesboro Police Department; and Robert S. Baldygo, vice president, Blue Ridge Community College. The names of the victim and cybercriminal as well as the college involved have been changed.

Steps in an Investigation

Investigators should follow the same step-by-step process each time they conduct investigations. This will help avoid the possibility of skipping steps or neglecting important tasks. These steps should be documented in a procedure manual that can be part of the agency's policies and procedures. A suggested set of steps follows:

1. Analyze the complaint.
2. Collect physical evidence.
3. Seek expert advice, if necessary.
4. Interview witnesses and interrogate suspects.
5. Construct the case file.
6. Analyze the case.
7. Conduct follow-up investigations.
8. Decide whether to prosecute.

Analyzing the Complaint

Upon receiving a complaint or notification that a cybercrime has occurred, the investigator first must analyze the complaint to determine:

- Whether a crime was committed
- If so, what crime was committed

The analysis includes evaluating the plausibility of allegations that a violation of the law has occurred, considering the nature and seriousness of the crime, and considering other factors that might complicate the crime's prosecution. In an ideal world, all complaints would be thoroughly investigated and all criminal actions would be prosecuted. In our less-than-ideal world, manpower limitations and other considerations can prevent the pursuit of less serious cases. If the analysis of the complaint determines that a crime was committed and warrants a preliminary investigation, the next step is to start collecting evidence.

Collecting Physical Evidence

Physical evidence in this context refers to tangible items that can be gathered, marked or tagged, and stored in a secure location until trial. Although the evidence itself may be digital in a cybercrime case, the disk on which it is stored is a tangible item. There might be other physical evidence in addition to digital information, including fingerprints, documents, and so forth. These should be preserved in accordance with standard crime scene practices.

Traditional crime scene techniques such as making crime scene sketches, photographs, and videotapes can be useful. This is especially true if, when investigators seize the computer, there is information on the screen that is not saved on disk. There might be information in memory and status information (network connections that are open, applications and processes that are running, and the like) that is useful as evidence but will be lost when the computer is powered down. Saving the contents of memory or other information or dumping the contents of memory to a file changes the system so that you've altered it and can no longer testify that it is exactly as you found it. One way to avoid this problem is to use photography to record the displayed information. Another is to transfer the data to another computer. Remember that every time you perform a task on a computer, even something as simple as saving a file, you change it in some way. See Chapter 15 for more information on how to handle digital evidence so that no changes are made and what to do if changes have already been made (for example, if IT personnel took preliminary investigative steps before law enforcement investigators became involved in the case).

> **NOTE**
>
> Crime scene sketches, photographs, and videotapes all serve separate purposes in documenting the crime scene; none of these takes the place of another. The sketch shows perspective, whereas the videotape provides an overview of the scene. Still photographs are used to document specific items or information. None of these is admissible as evidence unless accompanied by a witness (usually the sketch artist, photographer, or videographer) who can testify under oath to the circumstances in which they were made and that they represent the scene as he or she remembers seeing it.

Seeking Expert Advice

When a crime involves technical details that are beyond the knowledge of the investigator and/or prosecutor, it is often necessary as part of the investigation to seek advice and help from an expert in the field, much as you would seek the services of an interpreter if all the witnesses at a crime scene spoke a language with which you weren't familiar. The ideal situation is to have technically savvy law enforcement officers on board or available on loan from other agencies. Because this is often not the case, investigators might have to seek outside help.

When investigating a cybercrime in which a corporate network is the victim, why not just use the IT personnel there as your experts? Although this might save the agency some time and effort, it might not be the best idea. The expert you consult for technical advice should be objective, and it is often difficult to obtain objective opinions from people whose own networks have been victimized. Even if the company IT professionals *are* completely objective, there could be a perception that they are otherwise, and this perception could be exploited if defense attorneys discover that they provided you with technical guidance. Agencies might be able to find IT experts within the community who are willing to volunteer their expertise for a good cause. One good place to look is the academic world; computer science and computer security instructors at local colleges are often happy to help with technical questions in cybercrime cases. Associations of computer professionals might also be able to point you in the right direction.

Interviewing and Interrogating

Interviewing witnesses and interrogating suspects can be an ongoing process throughout the investigation. As more information is gathered, new witnesses might be discovered and new suspects might come to light. Follow-up interviews with witnesses who have already been interviewed might be necessary as the case develops.

Investigators should be sure to get contact information from all witnesses, even those who might not need to be interviewed at the time. This information includes work addresses and phone numbers *and* home addresses and phone numbers. It is not unusual for witnesses to leave a company or to move during the course of an investigation, making them difficult to locate if you have only one set of contact information. It is also a good idea, in today's mobile, connected world, to get witnesses' e-mail addresses. Many people retain the same e-mail address when they move and/or leave a job, so this could be the only contact information that remains constant.

Constructing the Case

After physical evidence has been gathered and documented and interviews and interrogations have been conducted, the next step is to start putting together the physical case file. This is an important element in *case preparation. Black's Law Dictionary* defines a *case* as "an aggregate collection of facts which furnishes occasion for the exercise of the jurisdiction of a court." *Preparation*, according to *Webster's New Collegiate Dictionary*, is "the action or process of making something ready." From these definitions, we can extrapolate that a simple definition of *case preparation* is "a compilation of information made ready for court presentation."

The case file will contain all documentation of the case, including (but not limited to):

- An initial incident report from the officers or investigator who responded to the complaint
- Follow-up reports
- Documentation of evidence collection by crime scene technicians
- Lab reports by forensic lab personnel
- Written statements of witnesses, suspects, and experts
- Crime scene sketches, photographs, and videotapes
- Printouts of digital evidence, where applicable

The case file is used to organize information and evidence in one place and will be used by the prosecutor in making a decision as to whether to prosecute the case and at trial. The case file *must* contain documentation of proof of the elements of the offense, the legality of the entry/search/seizure/arrest, and the preservation of the chain of custody.

Analyzing the Case

When the case file has been constructed and all documentation is included, the next step is to analyze the legal significance of the information and the evidence it contains. This step should usually be done in conjunction with the prosecutor, who might be able to provide the investigator with guidance as to the weaknesses of the case and what additional information or evidence needs to be obtained to strengthen it. This could be the first of several *pretrial conferences* between members of the prosecution team and the investigator(s).

Following Up

After the case analysis, you might need to obtain additional evidence or clarify facts and information. Interviewing witnesses again at this point can serve several purposes. In addition to obtaining specific additional information, the second interview will help to refresh witnesses' memories about the case, refresh the investigator's memory about the case, and prepare the witnesses for the courtroom process if and when the case goes to trial.

Deciding to Prosecute

After all the additional information has been collected and the case file is considered complete, the prosecutor will decide whether to prosecute (or he or she will refer the case to a grand jury, depending on the jurisdiction and its procedures). At this time, charge selection will also take place. In some cases, several different offenses could be charged. The prosecutor will select based on the provability of the elements and the difficulty of obtaining a conviction as well as the severity of the punishment. For example, a suspect's actions might contain the elements of two different offenses—for example, unauthorized access and theft of trade secrets. If the latter charge is a felony and the former is a misdemeanor, the prosecutor may choose to charge only the more serious offense. In other cases, both charges would be brought. Generally, if one offense is a *lesser included offense* of another, the jury can find the defendant guilty of the lesser charge even though only the higher charge was filed.

Defining Areas of Responsibility

Rarely will a complex investigation be conducted by one person. The investigative team might consist of one or more detectives, crime scene technicians, crime scene photographers and videographers, evidence recorders and custodians, and specialists such as computer forensics team members.

It is important that only one person be in charge of the investigation. This is the team leader and is often a senior investigator. The team leader should assign each team member a specific *area of responsibility*. Team members should be accountable for their designated areas of responsibility (for example, collecting, tagging, documenting, and securing the physical evidence) and should not overstep their bounds and perform tasks that fall under other members' areas of responsibility, unless approved by the team leader.

Summary

Building a cybercrime case is a complicated process, more so than is true for some other types of criminal cases. This is because special factors that present obstacles to prosecution must be considered and dealt with if the investigator is to successfully put together a winning case. Because many of the offenses under which cybercrimes are prosecuted are relatively new, the elements are not always clearly defined, and often there has not yet been time to clarify and interpret the statutes through the process of case law. It is important for cybercrime investigators to keep up-to-date on relevant court cases that might affect the applicability of the local, state, and federal laws that pertain to cybercrime.

Understanding the complex system of laws which govern our lives and how they interact with one another is essential to building a criminal case. Investigators and those who work with them should be aware of the function of various bodies of law, understand the differences between different types of law, be aware of the existence of different levels of law, and learn the legal terminology necessary to communicate intelligently within the system.

Jurisdictional issues are one of the biggest challenges to the cybercrime investigator and to prosecutors who attempt to bring cybercriminals to justice. It is important to acquaint yourself with just what jurisdictional authority means and the issues affecting multijurisdictional cases. The intangible nature of much of the evidence in a cybercrime case creates yet another obstacle.

Law enforcement officers and IT personnel must work together as a team to prosecute cybercrimes effectively, because each plays an essential role in building the case. IT professionals understand the hacker mindset, know where to look for digital evidence, and understand what can and can't be done with the technology. Law enforcement personnel know the law and investigative procedures that must be followed to preserve the integrity of evidence. Together, the two can fight cybercrime effectively, but they must overcome the natural distrust and adversarial relationship that often hamper the cooperative process.

The investigative process is basically the same in a cybercrime case as in any other criminal case, but investigators must be cognizant of the importance of defining the roles of everyone on the investigative team and ensuring that each team member has an assigned area of responsibility. A good case file is the result of hard work on the parts of many different people, but the ultimate goal is to bring the case to trial—and win. Toward that end, both law enforcement investigators and IT personnel with direct knowledge of the crime may be called to testify in court as evidentiary witnesses. IT pros may also be qualified to testify as expert witnesses, who are allowed to analyze evidence, give opinions and draw conclusions, and/or explain the technical aspects of the case to the court and jury.

Frequently Asked Questions

Q: Should cyberspace be treated as a distinct "place" for purposes of jurisdictional issues?

A: Some legal experts think that's the most logical approach. David R. Johnson and David G. Post, writing in the *Stanford Law Review* in 1996, posited that geographic boundaries are irrelevant when considering legal issues in the online world and that treating the Internet as merely a "transmission medium" confuses the issue and has ultimately unsatisfying results. They propose that when engaged in online activity, a person should be considered to be in a distinct "place" or jurisdiction that has its own laws, just as a geographic jurisdiction does. They argue that cyberspace has distinct boundaries in that you are either online or not at a given time, and thus there is no ambiguity about whether and when your actions would fall under that jurisdiction. Furthermore, they argue that treating the process of going online as crossing a border would greatly simplify the ability to set and enforce laws regulating behavior in the online "space." For a complete discussion of their ideas, see the paper "Law and Borders: The Rise of Law in Cyberspace" at the Cyberspace Law Institute's Web site at http://www.cli.org/X0025_LBFIN. html#II.%20%20A%20New%20Boundary%20for%20Cyberspace.

Q: There appear to be thousands of computer forensic expert witnesses advertising on the Internet. How can an investigator determine which one to use?

A: Many companies and individuals do provide this service. Some are highly qualified, and others have little experience or expertise. In the United States, there is no regulation of fields such as computer forensics. "Experts" don't have to meet any particular educational or experience standards, and there are no standard certifications or training programs. Basically, anyone can hang out a shingle and call him- or herself a computer forensic expert. In selecting from among the many self-proclaimed experts, then, you'll need to put your investigative skills to work. Find out what the expert's background is: Does he or she have a degree(s) in computer science and/or forensic studies? How about actual job experience in addition to academic experience? At how many trials has the expert testified, and what was the outcome of those trials? In other words, ask all the same questions that the court will want answered in qualifying this person to testify as an expert witness. Ask for references (from previous clients) and check them out. Ensure that you get someone who is experienced in testifying in *criminal* matters, because the rules of procedure and other aspects of testifying in civil trials are different. These are issues we'll further address in Chapter 17.

Chapter 17

Becoming an Expert Witness

Topics we'll investigate in this chapter:

- **Understanding the Expert Witness**
- **Testifying As an Expert Witness**

☑ **Summary**

☑ **Frequently Asked Questions**

Introduction

A cybercrime investigation and building of the case file is aimed toward one end result: obtaining a conviction of the cybercriminal in a court of law. No matter how good the evidence you obtain—log files showing unauthorized access to the network, hard disks seized from the suspect's computer containing clear-cut indications of the criminal activity, network records tracking the intruder back through Internet servers to his or her computer—none of this evidence can stand alone. Under most judicial systems, physical and intangible evidence must be supported by testimony. Someone must testify as to when, where, and how the evidence was obtained and verify that it is the same when it is presented in court as it was when it was collected.

Even though you should treat every case as though you were expecting it to go to court, actually testifying in court can be a stressful experience. If you've never been in a courtroom before, it can feel similar to your first day at a new school. You're unfamiliar with the environment, don't know the procedures, and may even make mistakes that will cause you to cringe later. Even when you know what to expect, it can still feel like you're walking into the principal's office (or at times like you're walking onto the playground to be beat up). Testifying generally isn't a pleasant experience, although it can be made easier through knowledge and experience. With enough preparation, the occasion can even be something you'll remember with pride.

Understanding the Expert Witness

Testimony in court is provided by witnesses, which are people who have firsthand knowledge of a crime or incident, or whom offer evidence during a trial, tribunal, or hearing. When evidence is technical in nature and difficult for laypersons to understand, experts may be required to testify to explain the nature of the evidence and what it means to the case. In a cybercrime case, police investigators and information technology (IT) personnel may both be required to take the witness stand. Two types of witnesses can be called to testify in criminal actions:

- Evidentiary witnesses
- Expert witnesses

An *evidentiary witness* is someone who has direct knowledge of the case. For example, a network administrator might be called to testify as to what he or she observed during an attack on the network, or an investigator might be called to testify as to the evidence that he or she observed on a computer that was seized pursuant to a search warrant. An evidentiary witness can only testify as to facts (what he or she saw, heard, or did) and cannot give authoritative opinions or draw conclusions.

An *expert witness* is different from an evidentiary witness in that he or she can give opinions and draw conclusions about facts in the case. The expert witness may have no direct involvement in the case but has special technical knowledge or expertise that qualifies him or her to give professional opinions on technical matters. Expert witnesses sometimes prepare reports that outline their opinions and give reasons for each opinion.

Even though the expert witness can present conclusions, he or she is limited in the opinions that can be expressed. For example, an expert in computer technology may testify that a threatening e-mail was traced to an account that was owned by the defendant, and how analysis of the defendant's computer showed that it was in fact sent from that machine. The witness cannot present a conclusion that the defendant is thereby guilty as sin. After all, a person is considered innocent until proven guilty, and the neutrality of the expert witness should follow that philosophy. The expert in computers also cannot speak about the mindset of the defendant as the e-mail was being sent, as psychology isn't the witness's expertise. A witness is limited to testifying about what he or she saw, heard, or did, and expert witnesses can speak only to this and/or about information that is within the scope of their knowledge and experience.

The prosecution and defense attorneys are both permitted to have expert witnesses testify in a case, although they aren't always deemed necessary by one or either side. As such, experts aren't used in most trials. In many cases, the weight of evidence is evaluated and a plea bargain is reached. A *plea bargain* is an agreement whereby the defendant pleads guilty to a lesser crime to have more severe charges dropped. Even when a case does go to trial, often the evidentiary testimony is all that a prosecutor or defense attorney needs to argue the guilt or innocence of a defendant. For each case going to trial, an attorney must determine whether the facts would benefit from an expert opinion, or whether the evidentiary testimony and evidence can stand on its own.

The expert witness should also not be confused with experts that serve as consultants, which both sides may use to understand different types of evidence. For example, in a trial involving a car accident, the defense lawyer may contact an expert in safety standards to understand issues related to the air bags used in a particular make and model of car. Although the expert can provide clarity in understanding aspects of the case, he or she isn't an expert witness because:

- The person hasn't been subpoenaed or sworn in as a witness.

- No testimony has been given in court.

- The court hasn't recognized the person as an expert.

As we'll see in the next section, whether someone is designated as an expert witness is primarily at the discretion of the judge. The expert witness provides information about his or her qualifications, and both the prosecution and the defense review the person's education, experience, and other credentials. Either side may challenge the person's qualifications in court, or they will both agree that the person is an expert in a particular field. Ultimately, however, it is up to the judge to recognize the person as an expert.

Qualifying As an Expert Witness

The standards for qualifying as an expert witness vary around the world. In some countries, expert witnesses must be registered as experts in a particular field. In the United States and Canada, experts must generally prove their expertise by presenting their credentials in court.

Determining whether a person qualifies as an expert witness, and whether the person's testimony is admissible, involves a process of examination, cross-examination, and being recognized by the court. The attorney calling the potential expert witness will generally read his or her qualifications into the record, and/or may ask a series of questions. These questions are designed to show the person's credentials as an expert. Such questions might include:

- What degrees, diplomas, or certificates do you have?

- What positions have you held in this field?

- What lectures or courses have you taught in this field?

- What additional training or courses related to this field have you taken?

- What memberships in organizations related to this field do you have?

- What books or papers have you written pertaining to this field?

- What is your past experience as an expert witness in this field?

The quality of your answers to these questions will help determine whether you'll be recognized as an expert in a particular area. However, in looking at these questions, don't feel that you have to have a positive answer to every one. For example, if you have education and experience but don't have any teaching experience, you might still be declared an expert. The key factor is the overall expertise, not whether you have an impressive answer to each and every one of these questions. After all, the first time anyone testifies in court, the answer to whether he or she has testified before is a resounding "no."

Once the witness has been called to the stand and examined, the court will be asked to accept him or her as an expert. The opposing side will then have the opportunity to accept the witness as an expert or challenge its admissibility. If a challenge is made, the opposing side can cross-examine the witness on his or her qualifications.

The opposing side may challenge the expert witness's credentials in an attempt to have that person's testimony deemed inadmissible, or prevent him or her from stating opinions and conclusions about the evidence. The attorney making this challenge has a heavy burden in attempting to exclude evidence or testimony at any stage of litigation. Not only must he or she attack the credibility of such witnesses, their testimony, and any evidence they've provided, but he or she must do so with limited knowledge. The attorney may be an expert in law, but he or she may have minimal or no expertise in the field of the witness.

As we'll see in later sections of this chapter, an attorney can use a number of tactics and resources when cross-examining a witness and challenging him or her as an expert. Such tactics can include ways of asking questions, and tricks that are often successful in tripping up a witness's testimony. To understand technical aspects of the case and ask more effective questions, the attorney may hire his or her own expert, who can be consulted before the trial and/or during the proceedings. Because the challenging side's expert is never sworn in as a witness, the identity of the expert may never be known to the opposing side, and will never be cross-examined. Although this can greatly help a lawyer's case, costs involved with hiring an expert can be prohibitive, so they aren't used in most cases.

Once the opposing side has cross-examined the witness, the court will hear arguments from both sides on the issue of whether the person should be recognized as an expert. In addition to challenging that the expertise of a witness hasn't been established, and that the person is thereby unqualified to give opinions on subject matter, arguments may be made that the person's expertise is limited. Challenging the limited expertise of a witness can be done during cross-examination. If the person's expertise is deemed limited, the person may still be able to give opinions, but his or her testimony will be given little weight.

Regardless of whether the witness's qualifications are challenged, the final decision rests with the judge. If the judge is satisfied that the witness has sufficient education and experience to testify and form opinions on subject matter related to the case, the court will recognize that the person is an expert. The area of expertise that's recognized may be broad (such as being an expert in computer technology) or limited to a narrow field of knowledge (such as being an expert on a particular piece of software).

Just because a person is an expert in one trial doesn't necessarily mean that he or she will be recognized in another trial. Being declared an expert applies only to that particular case, and doesn't carry forward to any other cases in which you might testify in the future. For each trial, the process of being recognized as an expert must begin again.

Curriculum Vitae

Curriculum vitae is a Latin term meaning "course of life," used to refer to a document that outlines a person's education, experience, and other credentials. A curriculum vitae (CV) is commonly referred to as a resume, although there are a number of differences between them. CVs are used in court cases to state the qualifications of a prospective expert witness, and you should submit one to the attorney you'll be working with before going to court to qualify as an expert. Once the attorney receives this information, he or she can then forward a copy to the opposing counsel. By allowing both the prosecution and the defense attorneys to review your CV before attending court, you can minimize the number of questions they will need to ask about your qualifications.

A CV can easily be compared to a resume, but in doing so you will see a great deal of disparities. A resume provides an overview of your abilities and achievements and serves as your introduction to a prospective employer. It may include information on why you left a previous employer, your salary history, and a list of personal references. A CV contains none of these elements. It is a detailed synopsis of the qualifications that make you an expert in a particular field. A CV is also generally longer than a resume. Although the recommended length of a resume is no more than one or two pages, a CV can be two or more pages in length. Because it is used to showcase your credentials, it is important that it contains all of the education and experiences you've had that correspond to a particular area of expertise.

NOTE

Just as many people searching for employment have different resumes that correspond to different types of jobs, many people who serve as experts also have several CVs prepared. For example, you might have one that focuses on computer forensics and another that stresses your education and experience with networks. When a case requires a particular expertise, you can then use the CV that is best suited for that particular case.

Writing a Curriculum Vitae

You can use a number of different formats to write a CV, but most of them contain the same elements and perform the same purpose: They describe who you are as a professional. The CV should identify who you are and how to contact you, and should describe what qualifications you can bring to a case to bring a better understanding of evidence.

Writing a CV begins by providing your name at the top of the document. The attorney who will call you to the stand will need the correct spelling of your name so that you can be added to the witness list. As such, the CV should have your full legal name, as it would be read into the official record when qualifying as a witness.

A CV can also include a line at the top of the document that specifies in what field you are an expert. In doing so, the type of testimony you can provide is easily identifiable to those reading it. For example, a line might be included stating "Specialist in Computer Forensics, Computer Technology, and Information Systems" or "Computer Expert Witness with Emphasis in the Areas of…." This is not required, but the latter example commonly appears on CVs belonging to expert witnesses that are hired to testify.

Below this, you would type your contact information. This includes not only a phone number, Post Office Box (POB) number, and/or other addresses, but also any electronic methods of contacting you, such as an e-mail address and Web site. Contact information is important, as the attorney you're working with will want to be able to reach you as needed. In addition to this, a current address is needed so that the court can notify you of a court date by having you subpoenaed (as we'll explain later in this chapter).

In writing your contact information, you should refrain from using a home address. Doing so can impact your personal safety. After all, if the case involved a violent offender or someone who possessed child pornography on his or her computer, you wouldn't want this person knowing where you lived. If you are creating a CV because of a case you were involved with at work, whether your involvement was as part of an incident response team or as an agent of law enforcement, you could use your employer's address, phone number, and the extension at which you can be reached. Alternatively, if you've been hired as an expert, you should buy a POB and then use the POB number in your contact information.

Below the contact information, you should also include a brief biography, which serves as a summary of your qualifications. Essentially, this captures the highlights of the CV within a few short paragraphs. It should provide a brief overview of education and key points relating to your experience within the field.

The bulk of the CV appears under this information, as this is where your education and experience are listed. The CV should be organized into categories, with qualifications related to each category listed and/or described underneath. Some of the categories under which you could organize your background information might include:

- Formal education, including degrees, diplomas, and certifications. You should also include any additional courses, conferences, or workshops you've attended, and list the number of hours of training involved in taking these courses.

- Related employment.

- Teaching and research experience.

- Grants and fellowships.

- Licenses and memberships in professional associations.

- Publications you've written or to which you have contributed. For each item under this category, you should identify the publisher, name of the publication, and publication dates.

- Awards and honors.

- Previous testimony experience, with specific reference to any cases in which you were previously recognized as an expert witness.

Any information appearing under these categories should be related to the field of knowledge to which you'll be testifying. In other words, limit your information to what's pertinent. Even though you probably graduated high school, you can generally omit that from the CV because it's irrelevant. What lawyers will be looking for is any post secondary education related to this field. Similarly, unlike a resume, you wouldn't include information about your interests, hobbies, or anything else that doesn't reflect the scope of your expertise in the area in which you'll be testifying.

CyberLaw Review

Falsifying Credentials

In writing the CV, you should be absolutely honest. Although some people will pad their resume with useless and fraudulent information, lying on a CV used to qualify you as an expert witness could lead to perjury charges against you. Remember that any information appearing on the CV may be verified when questioning you in court, so you'll be faced with either the embarrassing situation of coming clean under oath, or continuing the lie and possibly going to jail later.

An example of someone who used bogus credentials and put himself on the wrong side of the law is James Earl Edmiston, who admitted to committing perjury in two cases in which he falsified his qualifications as an expert witness. In declarations prepared between April 3, 2006 and July 19, 2006, he falsely claimed to have had a master's degree from California Institute of Technology, and degrees from University of California or University of Las Vegas. Not only did he lie about this, but he also neglected to mention a prior criminal record for forgery convictions that had included a prison term. In May 2007, Edmiston pled guilty to two counts of perjury, which carries a maximum penalty of 10 years in prison and a $500,000 fine.

Experts Who Are Not Witnesses

Lawyers are taught never to ask a question to which they don't know the answer. However, even though he or she has expertise in practicing law, the lawyer will have limited knowledge of technology or other specialized fields. To compensate for this lack of knowledge, lawyers can use experts as consultants.

Regardless of whether a professional consulting with the lawyer testifies in court, the prosecution or defense attorneys may use the consultant to provide greater insight into a case throughout the course of a trial. The attorney may consult with experts prior to a trial and/or during proceedings. In many cases, the expert will write reports that explain technical aspects of a case in layman's terms, and report any mistakes apparent in witness statements that contain technical information or in the processing of evidence. Because of the information provided by the expert, the attorney can better prepare for the potential testimony of witnesses, and cross-examine them on technical aspects of a case. Because the consultant is never formally used in court (that is, sworn in to provide testimony), one side might never know the name or existence of a consultant being used by the other side.

In some cases, experts may also be present in court. The expert will listen to testimony, provide information on technical anomalies or other facts in what a witness testifies to, and may even provide some follow-up questions that the attorney can use. When the opposing side attempts to qualify a witness as an expert, the consultant can assist in clarifying areas of the witness testimony, and suggest questions for cross-examination that may disqualify the witness as being an expert.

Experts in various fields are also used for the purpose of testing evidence that will be used in a case. For example, DNA evidence may play a key role in a murder trial, or in a trial involving sexual assault or paternity. A DNA expert might be hired to test blood or semen samples. Through such tests, the validity of this evidence can be determined and the expert can show that the sample matches a defendant or has been tainted in some way. Also through such tests, the guilt or innocence of a person may be established, and may determine whether a case is dismissed. Needless to say, if any of the results were used in court, the person would then be called as a witness the tests and any related findings, and probably go through the process of being qualified as an expert witness.

Although experts may be used in a case without ever appearing as witnesses, expert witnesses are also commonly used in the capacity of a consult. The attorney who called the witness may request that the person remain in the courtroom to provide insight into technical issues, or assist in other ways. Because the court has already recognized the person as an expert, there is an advantage of being able to call the witness to the stand again to provide further testimony on facts as they arise during the trial.

Types of Expert Witnesses

An expert witness testifies in relation to subject matter in which he or she has expertise, so it should come as no surprise that because there are so many different subjects, there are many different types of expert witnesses. Although experts exist in many fields, some of the more common ones used in trials include:

- Criminal litigation experts
- Civil litigation experts
- Computer forensic experts
- Medical and psychological experts

Criminal Litigation Experts

Criminal litigation experts are used to assist in the prosecution and defense of individuals involved in a crime. Criminal litigation involves actions against individuals who have committed illegal acts, and who are brought to court by the government to address charges of breaking specific laws. To assist in understanding the technical details of a case, evaluate and present evidence, and perform other functions that can best be addressed by an expert in a related field of knowledge, expert witnesses are used.

The specialties of criminal litigation experts used in court vary greatly. There are experts in almost any field you can think of who may be used to explain any type of evidence or aspect of a case. In criminal cases, the majority of experts used by the prosecution will be members of the police, or others involved in the investigation. As we've discussed, the person who performed a computer forensic examination will often be called as a witness, and may be qualified as an expert in a particular area of technology. Similarly, in a case involving a car accident, a police officer trained as an accident reconstructionist will collect evidence at the scene of the accident, and reconstruct the cause, effects, and other events that led to the accident from these clues. The defense may also use experts to support their position in the trial. These experts may be used to perform tests and review facts of the case, as well as provide alternative interpretations of the evidence. Providing this expertise to a case can clarify the facts of the case for the judge, jury, and other parties involved.

As we mentioned previously, experts are also used to provide technical consulting to legal counsel, and they serve as a resource for explaining technical details. This insight will prove useful not only during the trial, but also during discovery and depositions, which we'll discuss later in this chapter.

On the Scene

Hiring Experts

In looking at the kinds of professions in which expert witnesses have education and experience, you might wonder why they would be so willing to testify in court. In many cases, the expert witnesses used in a trial are paid for their time and expenses. Payment is usually on a *per diem* basis and may include travel expenses and accommodations during the trial. Many people hire themselves out as expert witnesses, specializing in many different technical or scientific fields, including computer forensics. Although it's more common to hear of people trying to get out of court duties, or of people who are anxious to testify only if they have a vested interest, many such expert witnesses advertise their services on the Internet. For example, The Expert Pages (www.expertpages.com/experts/computers.htm) is a database listing expert witnesses in many fields, available throughout the United States and Canada.

Civil Litigation Experts

In addition to criminal cases, experts are used in civil litigation, in which one party sues another to reclaim what they feel is owed them. In doing so, civil litigation courts provide a forum for resolving these disputes. Different types of civil litigation can include any number of lawsuits between individuals and/or businesses, including:

- Libel and slander
- Land disputes
- Probate of wills
- Wrongful dismissal
- Malpractice
- Personal injury

- Wrongful death

- Contract disputes

- Other disputes between individuals and/or businesses

In looking at the various legal actions that may occur in civil court, you can see that not all of them involve suing for monetary settlements. In many cases, civil litigation attempts to determine the rights of an individual, the scope of an agreement, or the intention of a contract. For example, if a person died without a will, the court may be required to determine the wishes of the deceased and how to best divide the estate among the person's spouse, children, and other interested parties. To determine the facts of a case and come to an equitable decision, expert witnesses may be used to evaluate and assist in understanding the details of the case. These experts are often the same types as those that may be used in a criminal trial, including forensic accountants, medical experts, and other professionals who specialize in any field that could provide insight to aspects of the case.

Even though civil court is different from criminal court, the two often overlap. In addition to using the same types of experts in both areas of law, a case that is held in criminal court may later appear in civil court. A popular example of this is the O.J. Simpson trial in which Simpson was acquitted of the murders of two people, but was later found responsible in civil court and was ordered to pay damages in a wrongful death suit. Just because an individual is tried in criminal court doesn't mean he or she can't be sued later in civil court.

Computer Forensic Experts

As you well know from reading this book, computer forensics is the collection, examination, preservation, and presentation of digital evidence. Computer forensic experts acquire and examine potential evidence during an investigation, including data that's been deleted, encrypted, or damaged. Any steps taken during this process are documented, and methodologies are used to prevent the evidence from being altered, corrupted, or destroyed. As we've stressed throughout this book, any case involving computer forensics should always be treated as though it were going to court, and that any documentation and evidence will eventually be turned over to a prosecuting attorney.

In criminal cases, the defense attorney may also hire his or her own expert to review the evidence and determine whether any errors were made during the examination of the computer. The expert will also document the actions he or she took, which will generally be incorporated into a final report that's submitted to the lawyer. This expert may also be required to testify in court, but this time on behalf of the defense attorney.

While serving as an expert for the defense, the computer forensic expert should remain impartial and perform many of the same functions as that of the prosecution. Any examinations he or she performs would involve examining, preserving, and presenting evidence, and could also require collecting additional evidence that was missed during the investigation. In doing so, the expert would attempt to find alternative reasons for the presence of data, such as identifying whether a Trojan horse, botnet, or other malicious software was present on the machine. Because he or she is working on behalf of the defense, it is important that any client-attorney information that is inadvertently acquired is kept private and is not divulged without the consent of the attorney or under order of the judge.

Computer forensic experts may also be used in civil litigations. Because information dealing with a case may be stored on computers or other devices, computer forensic experts may be used to search for data such as e-mail, text messages, chat logs, Web site history, calendar files, spreadsheets, documents, images, and other files on a machine. Examining this data may reveal facts that reveal an adulterous affair, fraud, malfeasance, downloading or visiting illegal or disturbing material (such as pornography), or other activities that could determine the outcome of a lawsuit.

Because the data acquired through computer forensics includes documents, spreadsheets, and other files that contain information outside the computer expert's scope of knowledge, additional experts will be used to explain what has been found. In such situations, the investigation and ensuing criminal or civil litigations will often use other experts that are suited to the evidence.

Medical and Psychological Experts

Like computer forensic experts, medical and psychological expert witnesses can be used in both civil and criminal litigation. Medical and psychological experts respectively provide insight and assistance in physical and mental issues that may be involved in a court case. They may be used by either side in a court case to perform tests, evaluate existing diagnoses, or testify about technical details related to evidence.

Medical experts are doctors or health professionals that are dedicated to specialized fields of medicine. They may be used to perform DNA or toxicology tests, testify to the extent of injuries suffered by a victim or plaintiff, or provide information on diseases, disabilities, practices, and/or procedures. Some of the other areas in which they provide specialized assistance include:

- Dentistry, which can include forensic dentistry and bite marks.

- Drugs, which may involve testifying about prescription medication or illegal drugs taken by an individual. This type of expert can testify about different types of drugs and their effects, or perform and evaluate drug tests on an accused person or individuals involved in a case.

- Malpractice, in which errors made by doctors or medical professionals are evaluated, reported, and presented in court.

Psychological experts are doctors and medical professionals who specialize in areas of mental health, psychology, and psychiatry. They may be used to evaluate and testify to the competency of an accused person or individual involved in the case, such as when it needs to be determined whether a person is fit to stand trial, or to establish the mental state of a person when a crime took place. In hearings involving children, they may also be used to establish whether a parent is unfit, or should be allowed to have unsupervised access to children. Some of the areas in which they provide specialized assistance include:

- Diagnosis and treatment of mental illnesses

- Medications and psychotropic drugs

- Standards of care

- Emotional distress and effects of a crime or event

Because medical and psychiatric experts may be used during an investigation, they may be required to testify in relation to information they provided earlier or evidence they acquired. For example, if a forensic or behavioral psychologist were used to develop a profile of a serial killer and victims associated with the case, the information previously provided to police would appear as evidence in a trial. The expert would then need to testify, to explain the techniques that were used, and to explain details that may not be clearly understood to the court.

Testimony and Evidence

Testimony and evidence fall hand in hand with one another in a court case. Evidence often needs some narrative to put it into the context of the case, and it relies on witness testimony to do that. When someone providing technical details of a case gives testimony, that testimony can fall into one of two categories:

- Technical testimony
- Expert testimony

Technical testimony is statements given under oath that present facts of a technical nature. In presenting the information, the witness must be technically accurate while translating complex and scientific issues to simple terms and concepts. In other words, in addition to testifying about the case, he or she must also teach the jury and/or judge so that they understand the relevance of these technical facts. Because it is vital that those in the court understand what is being discussed on the stand, there are a number of things you can do while testifying to make your testimony more understandable to laymen, including:

- Refraining from using jargon.

- Explaining the meaning and relevance of terms and acronyms. For example, "EnCase is forensic software that was used to acquire data from the computer. It's a proven product which has been used by the FBI for many years."

- Providing a glossary of technical terms and concepts to legal counsel. This may also be used by the court reporter when transcribing your testimony.

- Providing diagrams and pictures that will allow the jury and/or judge to better understand what's being discussed.

It is often useful when relating technical information to speak in a slow, gentle tone of voice. Although you should talk slow enough that the court reporter can effectively transcribe your statement and the judge and jury can follow the progression of your testimony, you shouldn't talk so slow that it appears you're patronizing those in the room. Practicing the pace and timbre of your voice on friends and family before testifying can help you identify the best way to speak clearly.

Because many people may not understand certain technologies being discussed and will find it difficult relating to your testimony, you should try to use analogies when explaining difficult concepts. For example, "Internet Protocol addresses are similar to street addresses. The same way your home address lets other people know where you live, IP addresses are also unique addresses that identify one computer to others on a network." When you use a familiar concept, people can more easily relate to what you're saying.

Unless you are qualified as an expert, you should refrain from offering any opinions about the case, as they will be deemed inadmissible. You should state the facts, and answer questions without providing any personal or professional conclusions.

Expert witnesses also commonly give technical testimony, but they are able to expand on their comments by expressing opinions and conclusions. *Expert testimony* is statements given under oath by a witness who's been recognized as an expert in a particular field. In providing facts that will help a jury and/or judge better understand the case, the witness may express an educated opinion related to his or her area of technical or specialized knowledge. The scope of this knowledge is established when qualifying the witness as an expert, and it determines what the witness is and isn't allowed to express during the trial. Any opinions that are outside the person's expertise are considered inadmissible.

Rules of Evidence

The guidelines that dictate whether a person can be recognized as an expert witness, and the admissibility of evidence, are governed by the laws of the jurisdiction of the court in which the evidence will be introduced. Thus, it is extremely important for investigators to become familiar with the applicable laws. These rules are adopted by statute and are usually codified into a document titled "Rules of Evidence."

In the United States, Congress adopted the Federal Rules of Evidence (FRE) as a set of standards that determine how evidence is presented and deemed admissible in court. Because state and federal laws are different, many states have also adopted their own sets of rules, some of which are identical to those in the Federal Rules. The FRE contains a considerable number of rules, but those dealing with opinions and expert testimony are explained under Article VII. The rules under this article consist of the following:

- Rule 701, Opinion Testimony by Lay Witnesses
- Rule 702, Testimony by Experts
- Rule 703, Basis of Opinion Testimony by Experts
- Rule 704, Opinion on Ultimate Issue
- Rule 705, Disclosure of Facts or Data Underlying Expert Opinion
- Rule 706, Court Appointed Experts

CyberLaw Review

Rules of Evidence

Laws can change over time, so it's important to review them from time to time and ensure that any changes will not impact your ability to testify as an expert witness. The latest version of the Federal Rules of Evidence (at the time of this writing) is available on the U.S. House of Representatives Committee on the Judiciary Web site at http://judiciary.house.gov/media/pdfs/printers/109th/31310.pdf.

Rule 701, Opinion Testimony by Lay Witnesses

Rule 701 addresses evidentiary witnesses who are not in court to provide expert testimony. Because of this, the scope of testimony is limited to events that transpired, and to what a person saw, heard, or did. Any opinions and inferences that the witness does make are limited to the following criteria:

- They must be rationally based on the witness's perception.

- They are helpful to achieving a clear understanding of the testimony or determination of a fact in issue.

- They are not based on scientific, technical, or specialized knowledge.

Although this rule does provide the ability for the witness to have an opinion on the events he or she witnessed, it limits this opinion to a narrow scope. For example, if a mugger held a gun to your head and said "Give me all your money, you don't want to die," a rational perception of this event would be that the mugger was going to kill you if you didn't give him your money. Such opinions are void of any specialized knowledge and deal only with clarifying the event, and what you believed was occurring.

Rule 702, Testimony by Experts

Rule 702 addresses testimony by expert witnesses who can have opinions based on scientific, technical, or specialized knowledge. As we discussed earlier, for this rule to apply, the witness must be qualified as an expert before he or she can testify in court. Rule 702 states the following:

> "If scientific, technical, or other specialized knowledge will assist the trier of fact to understand the evidence or to determine a fact in issue, a witness qualified as an expert by knowledge, skill, experience, training, or education, may testify thereto in the form of an opinion or otherwise, if (1) the testimony is based upon sufficient facts or data, (2) the testimony is the product of reliable principles and methods, and (3) the witness has applied the principles and methods reliably to the facts of the case."

In looking at this rule, you will see that the function of providing expert testimony is to assist in understanding, determining, and relating to the evidence and facts presented in a case. The information provided by the expert must be based on facts or data, and must use reliable principles and methods. In other words, any methods used can be reproduced.

Scientific methods that not accepted also cannot be used for expert testimony. For example, let's say that an expert based his conclusions that a defendant was guilty on physiognomy, which is a pseudoscience where criminal behavior is can be determined based on a person's facial appearance, head shape, and other physical features. Because this isn't a reliable or accepted science, the expert's opinions, conclusions, and possibly his or her entire testimony would be inadmissible.

Rule 703, Basis of Opinion Testimony by Experts

Rule 703 is another major rule for expert witnesses and the opinions they may express in testifying. This rule states:

"The facts or data in the particular case upon which an expert bases an opinion or inference may be those perceived by or made known to the expert at or before the hearing. If of a type reasonably relied upon by experts in the particular field in forming opinions or inferences upon the subject, the facts or data need not be admissible in evidence in order for the opinion or inference to be admitted. Facts or data that are otherwise inadmissible shall not be disclosed to the jury by the proponent of the opinion or inference unless the Court determines that their probative value in assisting the jury to evaluate the expert's opinion substantially outweighs their prejudicial effect."

The basis of this rule is that experts who have access to evidence or information prior to a trial. In such cases, the expert may form an opinion on these facts, even if they are not used or inadmissible in court. For example, a psychology expert might be aware that a defendant on trial for possession of child pornography had prior convictions for child molestation. Even if the jury isn't allowed to hear about these prior convictions, the psychologist could use this information to form an educated opinion that the defendant is a pedophile. The expert couldn't mention the prior convictions in court, but could state an opinion that was formed by this information.

Rule 703 is controversial to some, as evidence that can't be used in court is being used in an indirect manner. The evidence used by the expert doesn't completely provide a back door to submitting evidence, although there is some validity to this argument. If the jury has difficulty evaluating the expert's opinions, the judge could provide them with information and evidence that was used by the expert, even if it was otherwise inadmissible.

Even though the expert's opinions are considered vital to a trial, and can even outweigh the prejudicial effect of certain evidence, this isn't to say that opposing sides are powerless to the conclusions of an expert. The witness can still be cross-examined to challenge the validity of his or her opinions, and the opposing side can call their own expert witnesses to provide alternative conclusions and opinions on the facts of the case. However, a problem with this tactic is that when experts are called to challenge or provide conflicting opinions to a previous expert, the end result is that the jury can become confused and even disinterested. Because the opinions expressed can ultimately be discarded, it is known as *junk testimony*.

Rule 704, Opinion on Ultimate Issue

Rule 704 deals with the ability of legal counsel to object to opinions made by an expert, and what an expert can testify to in certain situations. In most cases, an attorney cannot object to an opinion made by an expert, because its validity should be decided by the facts of the case. In other words, cross-examination and evidence in the case should help evolve a decision as to whether the expert is correct. However, an objection can be made if the expert testifies about the mental state of a defendant in a criminal case, and whether the defendant had this mental condition while committing the crime or when using it as a defense. The expert isn't permitted to make such a conclusion, as the facts of the case should decide this issue, not the opinions of a witness.

Rule 705, Disclosure of Facts or Data Underlying Expert Opinion

Rule 705 addresses issues raised in Rule 703 regarding facts and data that were used to form an expert opinion being disclosed to the jury. In this rule, the expert may provide an opinion without releasing information or evidence that helped to form that opinion. He or she may be able to disclose these facts if the judge instructs him or her to do so, or may be required to disclose certain facts during cross-examination. This rule states:

> "The expert may testify in terms of opinion or inference and give reasons therefore without first testifying to the underlying facts or data, unless the Court requires otherwise. The expert may in any event be required to disclose the underlying facts or data on cross-examination."

Rule 706, Court Appointed Experts

Rule 706 provides guidelines on how experts should be appointed by the court. The rule provides information dealing with:

- How they are appointed

- The monetary compensation they receive

- Disclosure, which simply states that the court may inform the jury that the court appointed an expert witness

- That legal counsel (that is, the prosecution and defense) may also call their own expert witnesses

Testifying As an Expert Witness

Testifying as an expert witness can be an intimidating and stressful experience, especially if it's your first time. You may be unfamiliar with the courtroom, its layout, what's expected of you, and what will happen in court. Although you may receive some preparation from the attorney who will call you as a witness, often you receive little to no preparation and feel like you're simply thrown in the lion's den.

Although the courtroom can appear professional and reverent, the moments between cases and breaks in court can be absolutely chaotic. Paperwork needs to be processed, exhibits need to be prepared, witnesses need to be organized and updated, and those involved in a trial become embroiled in a flurry of activity behind the scenes. Although this chaos can filter into the trial, what most people see when entering a courtroom is an ordered and sober environment. Each person involved in a trial has his or her own place in the room and his or her own tasks to perform, including the following:

- **Judge** This is a court official who is either appointed or elected to preside over the court, and make judgments on issues in trials and hearings.

- **Court reporter** This is a court officer who transcribes the testimony and arguments made in the trial, which will become an official record of the proceedings.

- **Court clerk** This is a court officer who performs administrative duties, such as swearing in witnesses, handling exhibits, and performing other duties for the court.

- **Bailiff** This is a court officer who is responsible for maintaining order and decorum in the courtroom. In some jurisdictions and countries, the bailiff may instead be court security, and may be designated as a special constable of the police. The bailiff has custody of the jury and will escort them in and out of the courtroom. The bailiff may also perform other duties, such as calling in witnesses waiting outside the courtroom.

- **Prosecutor** This is the lawyer representing the state (or Crown in Canada and the United Kingdom) in criminal court cases. In doing so, the prosecutor represents the people and is responsible for taking legal action against the defendant and putting him, her, or them on trial.

- **Defense attorney** This is the lawyer representing the defendant in a criminal court case.

- **Plaintiff** This is the person suing a defendant in civil litigation. In civil litigation, both the plaintiff and the defendant may also have their own legal counsel.

- **Defendant** This is the person charged with a crime (in criminal court) or the person being sued (in civil court).

- **Jury** This is a group of citizens who have been selected to hear evidence and render a verdict.

- **Witnesses** These are individuals who are testifying to events that occurred or evidence that is presented as exhibits in the trial.

- **Spectators** These are members of the public and/or media watching the trial. They may consist of friends and family of the defendant, or interested parties who have come to watch the proceedings.

Of these roles, serving as a witness can be one of the most demanding to fulfill. Without the testimony and evidence a witness provides, it would be impossible to achieve a conviction. Although testifying can be uncomfortable even if you have years of experience as an evidentiary or expert witness, knowing about the process relieves much of the stress. In the sections that follow, we'll discuss aspects of the courtroom, trial proceedings, the tactics that may be used by prosecutors and defense attorneys, and what you can expect when testifying. The fewer surprises you have and the better prepared you are, the fewer problems you'll encounter on the stand.

Layout of a Court Room

Courtrooms are traditionally laid out in a specific manner, with chairs and other furniture arranged for special purposes. Dissimilarities may be apparent when comparing courtrooms that are used for different purposes or judicial systems, such as when comparing family court to a military court martial, or those of different countries. However, even when these differences are seen, similarities in functionality can usually be recognized.

As shown in Figure 17.1, the layout of a courtroom can consist of numerous individual components, including:

- **Judge's bench** A desk area where the judge is seated to preside over the trial.

- **Witness stand** An enclosed seating area where the witness gives testimony.

- **Court reporter's desk** Where the sworn proceedings of the trial are transcribed.

- **Court clerk's desk** Where records of the court are maintained.

- **Jury box** Seating for members of the jury.

- **Prosecution's table** Where the prosecutor is seated. In a civil litigation, this would be the plaintiff's table.

- **Defendant's table** Where the defendant and his or her legal council (defense attorney) are seated.

- **Podium** Where the prosecutor and defense attorneys will stand when formally addressing the court and examining/cross-examining witnesses.

- **Well of the courtroom** The main area of the courtroom where proceedings of the trial take place.

- **Bar** A railing separating the gallery from the well of the courtroom.

- **Gallery** An area where members of the public, media, and other spectators are seated.

Figure 17.1 Sample Layout of a Courtroom

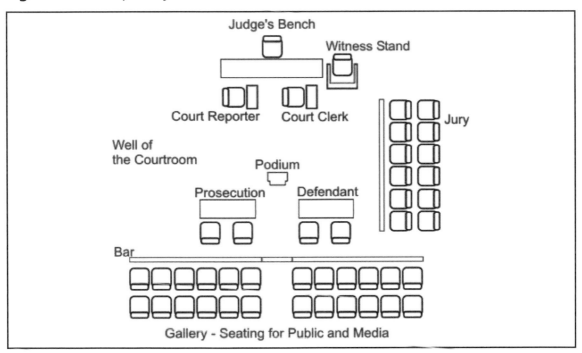

A courtroom serves as the staging area of a trial, and has a theatrical design. When looking at Figure 17.1, you can see that it is intended to accommodate an audience, as most trials are open to public spectators. Although public trials provide accountability to how they are conducted, the design of a courtroom is also influenced by the centuries-old practice of it being a form of public entertainment. The layout of a courtroom is designed to give maximum visibility to those watching the trial (whether they be judge, jury, or spectators), and focus their attention on the actions and actors involved in the courtroom process.

To help achieve this, the components of a courtroom are layered to varying heights. The judge's bench is positioned higher than other seating areas in the room. This allows him or her to rule over the court from a vantage point that overlooks everything, but it also conveys the judge as an authoritative and imposing figure that has control over the room. The witness stand may also be raised, but it is lower than the judge's bench, forcing anyone giving testimony to look up at the judge, but to remain at eye level with the lawyers who stand at a podium in the well of the courtroom when conducting their examination and cross-examination. Less visible are the court officers who sit at the foot of the judge's bench. Whereas the court reporter generally remains unnoticed during the trial while transcribing the proceedings, the court clerk is generally noticed only when swearing in witnesses or performing other court functions. To the side of the judge, a jury box provides the next best possible seats. In a jury trial, the jurors will be able to see and hear everything in the trial as it plays out in front of them, much like the spectators who sit in the gallery to the backs of the lawyers and the accused.

Technology in the Courtroom

Although tradition has dictated the design, technology has also influenced the courtroom. Newer courtrooms are often built with technology in mind, whereas older ones may be retrofitted to accommodate computers and display digital evidence more easily. Because there are no standards for the availability of technology, what you may see can vary greatly between courtrooms.

Even in older courthouses, a certain amount of technology will be present. Microphones are used in the witness box, judge's bench, and podium to allow voices to be heard throughout the courtroom, and lawyers will often use laptop computers to maintain their notes and other information brought to court. Although newer courtrooms are designed to have a sufficient number of electrical outlets, this generally isn't the case in older courthouses. As such, these and any other devices brought to court may require extension cords and/or power bars to be taped or draped across the floor. This can be a little surprising to see when walking to the witness stand, and having to step over a mat or duct tape covering electrical cords.

In newer or retrofitted courtrooms, technology and the justice system are better integrated. Some of the advanced technology you may find in these courtrooms includes that following:

- **Document camera** A device on which documents or small to medium-size objects can be placed so that their image can be captured by an overhead camera. The camera may project the image to a screen (much like an overhead projector would) or transmit it to monitors networked together in the room.

- **Display monitors** Used to display images, multimedia presentations, or other output from a computer or a document camera. These can be flat panel displays that are located on the judge's bench, witness box, court officer's table(s) (court clerk, court reporter), and legal counsel's tables, and between pairs of jurors in the jury box.

- **Annotation monitors** Monitors located at the podium and witness box that allow on-screen drawings to be made, such as diagrams or other information that enhances what is displayed on other monitors in the courtroom.

- **Real-time transcription** Allows transcribed testimony to be directed to the judge's bench and counsel tables.

- **Translation and listening devices** Allow any testimony in another language to be spoken into a microphone, translated by another person, and then broadcast via infrared or other technologies to listening devices (headsets and so on) that are worn by the judge, jurors, legal counsel, court officers, and others directly related to the trial.

■ **Videoconferencing** Involves cameras fixed in the courtroom that are focused on the judge, witness, and legal counsel at the podium. Other cameras may also be set up in other rooms of the courthouse, such as the judge's chamber or a room used for testimony by individuals who have been excused from testifying in the courtroom. The images captured by these cameras can then be used for pretrial conferences, remote witness testimony, or other proceedings. For example, a child who was sexually abused might be excused from facing his or her abuser in the courtroom, and be able to testify from a remote location.

■ **Computer-ready counsel tables** Tables used by the prosecution and defense attorneys. These may be discretely fitted with electrical outlets and ports that allow connections to display monitors or other features available through the courtroom.

■ **Printers** Allow information displayed on monitors to be printed, as well as data from any or specific computers in the courtroom.

Because the level of technology available in a courtroom may vary, you may need to confer with the prosecution regarding whether certain equipment will be accessible for your testimony. For example, if your testimony relies on showing the images or other files found on a hard disk, it would be beneficial to know whether they can be displayed on monitors already in the courtroom, if a computer projector and screen are available, or if you will need to bring your own equipment. By being prepared and understanding what's available to present your testimony, you can avoid situations that make testifying chaotic and stressful.

Order of Trial Proceedings

The trial process actually begins when a suspect is arrested or a warrant is issued for a suspect's arrest. After the arrest, the defendant is taken before a magistrate (a judge or, in some cases, the mayor of a city or town) within a specified time period—usually within 48 hours—and *arraigned*. This arraignment is an informal process whereby the magistrate tells the defendant what charges have been filed against him or her, Mirandizes the defendant, and sets or denies bail.

A preliminary hearing usually takes place within a few days. In this hearing, the prosecution must present enough evidence to convince the judge that the defendant should go to trial. In some cases, the defendant goes before a grand jury instead of a judge. This is a secret proceeding in which the grand jury decides whether to hand down an *indictment*. Next, a formal arraignment may be held, at which the defendant can enter a plea for the charges against him or her.

Before the actual trial, there is usually a pretrial conference or hearing at which motions can be filed (for example, asking for a change of venue). Finally, the case goes to trial. If the defendant pleads not guilty to the charges, a jury is selected through the *voir dire* process, during which each side gets to question potential jurors and *strike*, or exclude, a certain number of them. The judge instructs the jury on the applicable law, and then the attorneys each give an opening statement.

Because the burden of proof is on the prosecution, the prosecuting attorney gets to go first with an opening statement. After the defense attorney's opening statement, the prosecution calls witnesses. With each witness, the prosecution asks questions; this process is called *direct examination*. Then the defense attorney is allowed to question the witness about the matters that were brought up during direct examination. Afterward, the prosecution can *redirect*, after which the defense can *recross*. This process occurs with each witness until both attorneys are finished questioning that witness.

An investigator or IT professional testifying as to personal knowledge of the evidence in the case (an evidentiary witness) will be testifying as a prosecution witness and thus will be directly examined by the prosecutor and cross-examined by the defense attorney. Expert witnesses may testify for either side, but must be qualified as experts prior to testifying so that any opinions they have may be included in the testimony.

When the prosecution has presented all of its witnesses and evidence, the defense attorney usually makes a motion to dismiss the case due to lack of evidence. If this motion is granted, the trial is over and the defendant goes free. If not, the defense presents its case, calling witnesses to testify. These witnesses are cross-examined by the prosecutor, and so forth, in the same manner as the prosecution witnesses. After the defense has presented its case, the prosecution is allowed to call rebuttal witnesses, and the defense can rebut those witnesses.

Finally, when all the rebuttals are done, the attorneys make their closing statements (which side goes first depends on the court) and the judge gives more instructions to the jurors, who are then sent out to reach a verdict.

Subpoenas

A *subpoena* is a legal document that is issued by the court to notify you that you are required to attend court to give evidence as a witness. The court may subpoena you on behalf of the prosecution, the defense, or both. In looking at the subpoena shown in Figure 17.2, which is an actual subpoena with the pertinent data removed, you will see that it contains a considerable amount of information regarding a trial, including the following:

- The name and address of the person being summoned to court

- The date and time you are required to attend court

- The name of the defendant

- What the defendant is charged with

- The address of where the trial will take place

- The name and contact information of the officer in charge of the case

- The name of the attorney subpoenaing you

- Instructions to bring any books, documents, writing, or other exhibits related to this case with you

Figure 17.2 Example of a Subpoena

CANADA
PROVINCE OF ONTARIO
PROVINCE DE L'ONTARIO

CRIMINAL SUBPOENA
Assignation en matière criminelle
Form 16, section 699 C.C.C.
Formule 16, article 699 C.C.C.

File No. / N° Du Dossier

IN THE SUPERIOR COURT OF JUSTICE
COUR SUPÉRIEURE DE JUSTICE

Elizabeth the Second, by the Grace of God of the United Kingdom, Canada and Her other Realms and
Elizabeth Deux, par la Grâce de Dieu, Reine du Royaume-Uni, du Canada et de ses autres royaumes et

Territories QUEEN, Head of the Commonwealth, Defender of the Faith.
Territoires, Chef du Commonwealth, Défenseur de la Foi.

To: / A: Name of Witness
Address of Witness

Whereas/*Attendu que* Name of the Person Charged has been charged that/*a été accusé d'avoir*

HE/SHE DID COMMIT: **First Degree Murder**
Section **235(1)** of the Criminal Code of Canada

and it has been made to appear that you are likely to give material evidence for the PROSECUTION/*la poursuite et qu'on a donné à entendre que vous êtes probablement en état de rendre un témoignage essentiel pour*
Court House, Address of Courthouse

THIS IS THEREFORE TO COMMAND YOU to attend before/*À CES CAUSES, LES PRÉSENTES ONT POUR OBJET de vous enjoindre de comparaître devant* **The Superior Court of Justice**
On the/*le* **11**th **day of /jour de** **October, 2005**
At/à **10:00 o'clock**/*heures à/* in the forenoon at The Superior Court of Justice, **Address of Court City of Court**

To give evidence concerning the said charge and to bring with you and produce any books, documents, writings
Pour rendre témoignage au sujet de ladite accusation et d'apporter avec vous tous les livres, documents, écrits

or other exhibits in your possession or control that relate to the said charge, and more particularly the following:
ou autres preuves en votre possession ou sous votre contrôle qui se rattachent à ladite accusation et en particulier les suivants:

NOTE: You are required by the Criminal Code to attend from day to day until the end of the trial unless you are excused by the presiding Judge.

REMARQUE: *Le Code criminel exige que vous demeuriez présent chaque jour jusqu'à la fin du procès à moins que le juge président ne vous dispense de cette obligation.*

GIVEN UNDER MY HAND AND THE SEAL OF THE SAID COURT,
SIGNÉ DE MA MAIN ET REVÊTU DU SCEAU DE LADITE COUR,
this/*en ce* **29th** day of/*jour de* **August, 2005**
at/*à* St. Catharines, Ontario.

Deputy Registrar/*Greffier adjoint*

This subpoena requires you to attend at the Sittings of this Court and remain until this case is tried. However, to convenience you, it is suggested that you contact the officer in charge of this case, **Name of Officer, Address of Police Department**
Phone number of Police Department   , since it may not be necessary for you to attend on the exact date mentioned on this subpoena. In order to be compensated for your transportation costs to court (at $.29/km), please report to the Crown Attorney's Office upon your arrival EACH DAY.

Name of Attorney

The subpoena is hand–delivered to you by a summons officer or other court officer, who will use information on the subpoena and other contact information that you may have previously supplied to the investigator or attorney. Once you have been served with the summons to appear in court as a witness, you are required to attend. If you fail to attend, criminal charges may be pressed against you, and if convicted you could face imprisonment and/or a fine.

On the Scene

Not Appearing in Court

There may be situations when attending court is not possible. When there is a good reason not to attend court, you should notify the attorney who subpoenaed you and the officer in charge of the case as soon as possible. If a reason is good enough, you may be rescheduled or (in cases where your testimony is pivotal to the case) the trial itself may be rescheduled.

An example of not being able to attend court occurred the first time I was subpoenaed to appear as an expert witness in a trial. When I saw the date of the case, I realized it was the due date that my wife was to give birth. I informed the investigator and attorney, and mentioned that the chances of my wife actually giving birth on the due date were slim. As fate would have it, my son was right on time, born on the day I was scheduled to testify.

Although I had warned those involved of this possibility, I was on the phone in the delivery room explaining how I wouldn't be able to attend court. I should also mention that I had the good sense to call *after* my wife had delivered our son. The attorney prosecuting the case offered congratulations and I was rescheduled to testify the next day. The thought was, I would be the first to testify, and then could return to the hospital to bring my wife and son home after they were discharged.

Although I generally recommend a witness getting a good night's sleep, I managed to get three hours of rest before dropping off my daughter at a babysitter and showing up to court the next day. Upon arriving at court first thing in the morning, I found that my scheduled testimony had been delayed due to another witness needing to complete her testimony from the previous day. I waited for the other witness's testimony and cross-examination to be completed, and then found that another witness was being moved ahead of me to offer his testimony. By that afternoon, I was wondering if I was even going to be called to the stand, or if I would be rescheduled to the next day. I explained that my wife and newborn son had been discharged from the hospital, but were waiting for me to pick them up. Although my wife was patiently waiting for me to be finished, she had now been waiting all day in the maternity ward for a ride home. The attorney who called me as a witness told me to leave court, pick her up from the hospital, and bring my family home … and then rush back and testify.

Continued

> After unceremoniously dropping my wife and newborn son off at home, I returned to court, where other witnesses were still being examined and cross-examined. When I was finally called to the witness stand, I received congratulations from the judge and court officers, gave my testimony, and then proceeded to be grilled by the defense lawyer until the day concluded. Few witnesses ever remember one of the most stressful times testifying in court as also being one of the happiest days of their life.

Depositions

Depositions are a process of questioning witnesses prior to a trial, and are used in the pretrial stages of both civil and criminal cases. In a deposition, the witness is under oath and is required to tell the truth as though in the trial. Legal counsel can examine and cross-examine the witness, and may even use this as an opportunity to discover information that may be used in the later trial. Because the deposition doesn't require a public forum, it may not necessarily be held in the courtroom, but instead in a meeting room or another venue that's been agreed upon.

Throughout the deposition, a court reporter or a stenographer documents the questions and statements made so that they can be preserved for future reference. Although the deposition doesn't replace testifying during the trial, unless there are exceptional circumstances for why the witness is unable to attend (such as dying before the trial starts), the information gathered in the deposition can later be used in trial. Attorneys may use statements made in a deposition to show contradictions in later testimony, thereby discrediting the witness by showing inaccuracies between incongruous statements made under oath.

Testifying in a deposition is generally less formal than the trial itself, although the same etiquette of showing respect for the court and those involved in the process applies. Because of this, requests for a break can be made whenever needed. Although it can be less formal, you should never assume anything is off the record. Any remarks made during the deposition will be recorded, so you should refrain from saying anything you don't want preserved for posterity until you are away from the court reporter and the location where the deposition is held.

Once a deposition has been transcribed, a witness is given the opportunity to review its contents for any inaccuracies and make corrections. It is important that you read the transcription thoroughly; once it's read and signed, it becomes an official record. When reviewing the document, you should look for mistakes in dates, times, quantities, or technical details that may appear later during the trial as evidence. The more accurate the deposition is, the less chance a mistake will be used to contradict truthful statements made later in court.

TIP

When testifying in a deposition or trial, you are generally given a glass of water immediately upon taking the witness stand. This is because your mouth and throat can get parched from talking so much, from nervousness, and (especially in older courthouses) from the dry environment of the courtroom. Just as you should go to the washroom before going on the witness stand (no pun intended), you should be careful how much water you drink, or your testimony may take on an unintended urgency from needing a recess.

Swearing versus Affirming

When serving as a witness, you are obviously expected to tell the truth. To declare that you will do so, one of two brief formal procedures is performed in which you promise to be honest. They are:

- Swearing in
- Affirming

For various reasons, most witnesses in the Western World are sworn in. This involves either holding your right hand on the Bible or taking a Bible in your right hand and holding up your left hand. After doing so, you are then asked whether you swear to tell the truth "so help you God." Some courts no longer mention the word *God*, although most continue to do so. In swearing to tell the truth, you are now a witness and can continue to the task of providing testimony.

If you are an atheist or have religious beliefs that prohibit you from swearing to God, there is also the option of affirming. When you affirm, you may be asked to raise your hand while making an oath to promise to tell the truth. With affirmation, no Bible is used and God is not mentioned. Once this is done, you are affirmed and you have completed a declaration of honesty that carries the same weight as being sworn in.

Affirming or swearing to tell the truth occurs immediately after you've been called as a witness and taken the stand. Once you've entered the witness box, the judge or court clerk will ask whether you would like to be sworn in or affirmed. Which you choose is entirely up to you, and has no effect or bias on the events that follow, while you're testifying. Regardless of whether you've been sworn in or affirmed, if you lie you can be charged with perjury.

Being affirmed or sworn in can occur in either civil or criminal proceedings, as well as depositions and affidavits (which we'll discuss next). The reason they are used in so many areas of law is simple: It is crucial for the witness to tell the truth. If the truth isn't presented to the court, an accurate determination of events cannot be made, and a proper ruling cannot be made.

Affidavits

An affidavit is a formal statement of facts. When you are a witness in a criminal trial or civil dispute you may be required to provide an affidavit that outlines the facts as you know them. This provides a written version of your formal statement. This written document states what you saw, heard, or otherwise know to be the truth. In terms of an expert witness, this would be information that is within your area of expertise. It is signed by you to validate that everything you have written is true, and also by another person who has you take an oath. The oath is that you either swear or affirm that everything stated in the document is true. The oath is taken by someone authorized by the court, such as a notary public or a court officer, which formalizes the document as being true and legal.

Legal Etiquette and Ethics

As with any official gathering, you should follow certain codes of conduct when attending court. In accordance with legal etiquette and ethics, you are expected to conduct yourself with a specific level of professionalism when attending court. *Etiquette* is the rules of socially acceptable behavior and courtesy, and *ethics* are moral principles or values. Together, they define how a person behaves in the courtroom.

Courtrooms are intended to be solemn, reflecting the serious nature of the forum they provide. Conducting yourself in a manner that maintains this atmosphere shows respect not only to the court itself, but also to those who must attend and have their fates decided in trials. Just as you would behave in a serious and thoughtful manner at a memorial service, ceremony, or other formal event, you should show the same level of respect in the courtroom. Some of the ways to show this respect include:

- Dressing conservatively in business attire (such as a suit, dress, or other conservative clothing you might wear to a business meeting or solemn occasion).

- Arriving early and being available to testify when called.

- When speaking to the judge, referring to him or her as "your honor."

- Not whispering or talking in the courtroom unless it is absolutely necessary. If information must be exchanged, it is better to pass a note to the attorney or other person with whom you are conferring.

- Bringing only the notes you will use on the stand. Do not bring magazines or other reading material to pass the time.

The legal etiquette and ethical behavior you show in a courtroom apply not only to those attending as jurors and legal counsel, but also (and especially) to witnesses. The way you behave in the courtroom and on the witness stand will be observed by others in the courtroom and will affect the way they perceive your credibility as a witness under direct and cross-examination.

TIP

If you are testifying as an expert witness, you may not see the defendant until you are called as a witness. Because of this, avoid talking to others about the case, and limit your contact with other people who may be waiting outside the courtroom. You don't want to accidentally get into a discussion with someone against whom you'll later be giving testimony.

Direct Examination

Direct examination refers to the process of a witness being questioned by the attorney who called him or her to the stand. Because the attorney who called you to the stand wants you to give good testimony, any questions that are asked are for the purpose of eliciting facts about the case. In other words, the lawyer asks these questions to help you in providing evidence.

The first rule for giving direct testimony (or any sworn testimony) is to always tell the truth. Witnesses should not be afraid to say "I don't know" or "I don't remember" when that's the truth. Telling the truth is vital to providing facts to the case, and failing to tell the truth is a serious matter. Lying under oath is a criminal offense called *perjury*, and can result in imprisonment and fines being imposed on you.

In addition to this most important and basic element of being a witness, there are a number of best practices for testifying in court. Remember that the jury will evaluate the credibility of each witness and decide whether to believe the testimony based on that evaluation. Here are some ways to enhance your credibility as a witness:

- **Be on time or slightly early for court** Although we mentioned this and the following point in the previous section, attending court early allows you time to prepare and scope out the layout of the courtroom, the route you'll walk from your seat in the courtroom to the witness stand, and so on. Arriving late makes a bad impression on the jury and detracts from your credibility.

- **Dress professionally** Appearance does count, and your credibility will be enhanced by conservative business attire.

- **Don't appear to be nervous** Juries expect people to act nervous when they're lying. You might not be able to control how you *feel*, but with practice you can control any visible manifestations of nervousness, such as repetitive gestures.

- **Keep good posture** Juries will look at a person's body language when approaching, leaving, or sitting in the witness box. Standing and sitting up straight conveys confidence, whereas slouching can appear as though you're uncomfortable and trying to hide something. Although you want to be relaxed on the stand, don't forget what your mother told you about sitting up straight.

- **Remain calm and don't get angry** The opposing attorney might try to make you lose your temper; doing so will damage your credibility with the jury. Witnesses should never argue or be sarcastic in response to an attorney's questions. Similarly, you should refrain from showing hostility toward the defendant, as this can make it seem like you have a personal agenda against the person. Remaining calm and professional will strengthen the case.

- **When applicable, answer with "yes" or "no"** Although this goes hand in hand with our next point, when answering a question to the affirmative or negative, you should always use the word "yes" or "no." On the stand, people often make the mistake of nodding or shaking their head to answer, grunting answers, or using terms such as uh-huh, yep, nope, or similar phrases. Whenever this occurs, the attorney questioning you will correct you and tell you to answer with yes or no, which can get monotonous and irritate everyone very quickly.

- **Don't volunteer extra information** Answer the questions you are asked, but don't provide more information or veer off the topic. Don't provide hearsay evidence (what other people said to you), because it's generally inadmissible.

- **Avoid making absolutes in your statements** Making an absolute statement such as "I always …" or "I never …" can create an adversarial situation in later cross-examination, which may be used to prove you wrong. After all, very little is absolute. Even saying "the sun always shines in the sky" is incorrect when you consider eclipses and nighttime.

- **Don't discuss the case with anyone but the attorney** When attending court as a witness, you may spend little time in the actual courtroom. You'll generally be restricted from entering the courtroom until being called, and adjournments and recesses will allow you to leave court for a period of time. During these moments, you'll be exposed to others who may testify, victims and defendants in a case, and possibly even the media. Because you probably won't know who most of these people are, you should never discuss the case with anyone. Doing so can taint the testimony of others or provide sensitive information to the wrong people.

- **Consider the question carefully before you answer** Be sure you understand the question, and if you don't, ask the attorney to repeat it. Don't start to answer until you're sure that the attorney is finished asking the question.

- **Speak clearly and confidently** An effective witness doesn't shout, but speaks loudly enough to be heard by the judge, jury, and attorneys. Testimony as an evidentiary witness should be limited to "just the facts, ma'am, just the facts." Don't offer opinion or speculation; in an impartial, objective manner, simply tell what you did or observed.

- **If the judge or attorney begins to speak, stop talking** When testifying, attorneys or the judge may interject to obtain a better understanding of a particular point, or stop you from revealing information that is inadmissible. When either of them speaks, immediately stop your testimony and listen to what he or she is saying.

- **Avoid memorizing answers** Although it's important that you review the notes and fully understand specifics of your testimony beforehand, preparing answers to anticipated questions can make your testimony appear scripted and unreliable.

- **Remain impartial and speak to the facts** Remember that as a witness, you are presenting facts of the case. Never exaggerate, never guess, and never manipulate answers to an attorney's question to favor one side or the other. Simply tell the truth, regardless of whose side the answer may benefit.

Cross-Examination

Cross-examination is the process of providing the opposing side in a trial the opportunity to question a witness. In any trial, the prosecution has the right to question witnesses called by the defense, and the defense has the right to question witnesses called by the prosecution. It is the job of the cross-examining attorney to discredit the opposing side's witness. Attorneys may use psychological techniques to attempt to discredit witnesses. When testifying, be careful not to fall into their traps. Be prepared for and ready to avoid such cross-examination tactics as:

- Rapid-fire questions with no time to answer between questions

- Leading questions ("Isn't it true that what you saw was ... ?")

- Repeating your words with a twist that changes their meaning

- Pretending to be friendly, and then turning against you suddenly

- Feigning bewilderment, outrage, or shock at what you've said

- Being silent for a prolonged period of time to cause you discomfort in the hope that you'll say more

The most important thing for you to remember when subjected to these tactics is this: Don't take the attorney's tactics personally; he or she is just doing a job. Our advice to the witness is, just do *your* job; keep your cool and state the facts.

You can use a number of tricks to deal with the tactics an attorney may employ during cross-examination. Lawyers will often attempt to gain a pace to their questions, starting by asking questions with some time between them, and then progressing the time between questions until they're being fired off in quick succession. This limits the time you have to think of an answer and increases the possibility of being caught in a trap. Many times, a question will be asked one way, and then asked a different way later. If you change your answer, the lawyer will use this to discredit your testimony. A simple way to defuse these rapid-fire questions is to force a delay before answering. By quietly tapping your foot three times before giving an answer, you give yourself a moment to think, and you control the pace of the questions and answers being given. Because you are sitting in an enclosed witness box, no one can see you discretely tapping your foot and defusing the attorney's attempt at rapid-fire questioning.

It is important to always listen to the questions being asked, and to be ready to respond. A lawyer may ask a question, wait for an answer, and then repeat what you've said but twist the words. Doing so can change the meaning of your statement and twist what you've said to the lawyer's favor. If the lawyer restates it as a question (such as by beginning with "So, you're saying that …") and you're not paying attention, you could actually agree with something you never said. Never be afraid to say, "That's not what I said" in these situations, and reiterate your previous statement.

TIP

The way to answer questions when testifying is to stop, think, and then answer. Always consider what is being said and the way it is asked. If you don't understand the question, say so, and the attorney will attempt to rephrase it.

Another common method that lawyers use is to start questioning a witness with points of agreement. In doing so, the lawyer conducting the cross-examination appears friendly and brings your guard down. You will generally be more cooperative, and the lawyer can then either dismantle previous statements by asking follow-up questions, or ask leading questions that may cause you to make statements that will be positive to the opposing side's position. Often, once your guard is down, the lawyer will turn from being friendly to suddenly attacking what you've said or becoming confrontational. This can confuse you and leave you feeling a little betrayed the first time it happens, and it allows the attorney to take the upper hand in questioning you.

Other psychological ploys can involve saying very little or nothing at all. Once you've finished answering, the attorney may delay asking the next question, choosing instead to pause for a long period of time. Because the prolonged silence can be uncomfortable, you may feel that you should say more. If you add nothing, the lawyer will undermine your comments by saying "Oh, I'm sorry, are you done?"

Many of the methods used by attorneys are implemented throughout the trial process, including when a witness is being qualified as an expert. When challenging a witness, the attorney will ask a series of questions to probe details of his or her qualifications and evaluate his or her level of knowledge. In general, the challenging party is given a fairly loose reign in the questions asked about a person's credentials, and judges and attorneys calling a witness may allow a line of questioning to continue until it appears the witness is being unfairly attacked. How legal counsel undercuts the witness's authority will vary, as lawyers have different styles of cross-examining witnesses.

One method that is used to varying degrees is to review the witness's credentials, and then undermine them by repeating facts in a snide tone of voice. For example, if a computer technician graduated from community college, the lawyer might repeat the name of the school in a sarcastic tone, and then ask, "So, you never went to a university?" Similarly, if a witness had a CompTIA certification, the lawyer would repeat "CompTIA?" as though the witness was making it up. It is a simple tactic that requires little to no knowledge about a subject.

Because there is an element of theatre to court, lawyers will often act a part. They may pretend to be avid proponents of justice, or that they actually care and believe in their client's innocence. Although this may be true of some court officers, the fact is that lawyers will defend clients regardless of whether they are guilty or innocent. Despite this, they will use a tactic of pretending to be morally outraged, baffled, or shocked by a statement. Because lawyers are also generally bad actors, this can be more annoying than surprising when it occurs. The attempt is made to play into the hands of the jury, and make themselves look good by making you look bad.

NOTE

After a cross-examination, the attorney who initially examined the witness will have the opportunity to redirect the witness. After this, the attorney who conducted the cross-examination will have the opportunity to recross. This gives both sides the chance to clarify and ask any questions that may have arisen during the preceding testimony.

Refusing to Answer

While serving as an expert witness, the possibility of refusing to answer would be extremely rare, but there are situations in which you may not want to answer a question that's posed to you. A lawyer may ask a question that is personally embarrassing, or that you find irrelevant to the case. In such situations, you can ask the judge whether you're required to answer the question. If the judge agrees that it isn't relevant to the case or necessary to answer, he or she will instruct you not to answer if you don't wish to. If the judge instructs you to answer the question, however, you have no real choice but to comply, or risk being cited with contempt of court.

Another situation in which you may refuse to answer is when doing so would cause you to confess to a crime. Under the Fifth Amendment of the U.S. Constitution, and under the protection of the Charter of Rights and Freedoms in Canada, you do not need to testify if it will incriminate you, because by answering in a way that doesn't incriminate you, you are essentially forced to commit perjury.

Using Notes and Visual Aids

What if you're required to testify as a witness, but your memory isn't so great? What if you're afraid of forgetting important facts, especially difficult-to-remember information such as numbers? Is it legal for you as a witness to take notes along to use as a reference when testifying?

Police officers and other witnesses use notes as a memory aid during court testimony all the time. There are advantages and disadvantages in doing so. Some jurors might be impressed by the fact that you're reading from notes, because they might trust the written word more than someone who relies on memory alone. On the other hand, others might think you're being coached or prompted if you refer to notes; they believe that if what you're saying is the truth, you would remember it without notes.

A very important consideration in deciding whether to use notes is the fact that if a witness does so, the notes will be entered into evidence and taken into the custody of the court for the duration of the trial. If you do choose to use notes, therefore, it's important to be sure that the notebook or paper on which they're written doesn't have other notes that refer to matters not related to the case, because the opposing attorney can question you about anything in the notes.

Visual aids are another common element, especially in cases that involve evidence such as digital images, or that require maps of a location. When referring to visual aids, such as photographs or diagrams, it is important to be as descriptive as possible. Rather than raising your hand and saying, "Here we see," you should try to focus the attention on what you're talking about, such as by saying, "In the lower-right-hand corner." Not only does this make it easier for those watching your testimony to understand what you're talking about, but it also makes it easier to understand in the transcription of the testimony.

On the Scene

Notes As Evidence and Witness Resources

Anyone involved in an incident, including investigators and computer forensic examiners, may be called to testify in court if criminal charges or civil lawsuits are brought in relation to the incident. In addition to documentation being used as evidence, the ability to use notes as a resource is another reason to create extensive documentation that can be reviewed prior to giving testimony. Often, a case doesn't come to trial until months or years after the incident took place, and the human memory often isn't reliable after so long a time without a little help. In situations where an incident response team or group responded to an incident, the person who creates the documentation should be the one to testify to its authenticity if it is to be entered into evidence.

It is important for team members to understand that their reports regarding the incident may end up being entered into evidence at trial. For this reason, such documentation should be kept in a special notebook with numbered pages, and the notebook should not contain any personal information, because the entire notebook may become part of the official record.

Summary

When most people think of a witness, they often think of a person who actually saw the crime take place. However, many witnesses in cybercrime cases offer information about the effects of a crime, or facts about evidence that was obtained during an investigation. Testimony explaining this evidence is used to show when, where, and how a crime occurred, what was affected, and who was identified as being responsible.

Testimony may be given in civil court (where one person or organization sues another), or criminal court (where the government brings the person to court for breaking the law). The person giving testimony may be both an evidentiary witness, who can speak about evidence and events that occurred, or an expert witness, who can also provide opinions based on his or her knowledge and experience in a particular field. There are many different types of expert witnesses, including those specializing in computer forensics, medicine, psychology, and other fields. The Rules of Evidence, which is a set of rules set at the state or federal level that dictates what and how evidence can be presented in court, regulates any testimony and evidence that may be presented in court.

In being a witness, you will be called to the stand and given the option of swearing in or affirming to tell the truth. Upon doing so, you will then be given the chance to give direct testimony, where the attorney who called you will ask a series of questions. The opposing attorney can then cross-examine you, in which he or she will then ask his or her own questions. After this, the attorney who called you has the option of redirecting the witness (asking questions to clarify information given under cross-examination), and after this the opposing attorney can recross. Once this process has completed, you're excused and can leave the courtroom, but should remain in the courthouse in case you're recalled to the stand.

Frequently Asked Questions

Q: I'm a witness in a criminal case, and I have discovered that a friend of mine has been called as a juror to the same case. What should I do?

A: Tell your friend to inform the court that he or she knows one of the witnesses. During the jury selection process, jurors are asked if there's any reason(s) that should prevent them from being a juror. This could include knowing the defendant, being involved in the investigation, knowing witnesses, or other issues that would affect the outcome of the trial. By having a relationship to one of the witnesses, a person could be released from jury duty.

Q: I'm part of an incident response team, and I became involved in an incident that will probably go to court. Who can I talk to about this?

A: Although you could talk generically about the case to anyone, you should try to avoid any conversations about it with anyone who isn't connected to the case. In other words, although you can talk to the attorney in charge of the case, you shouldn't talk to friends, significant others, or coworkers about the specifics of the case. By telling someone who isn't involved, there is a chance this information could be passed on to others, including members of the media. In addition, you could inadvertently talk to someone who knows or is related to the defendant, or who may be a potential juror.

Q: How do I know when and where I'm supposed to testify in a case?

A: When you're summoned to be a witness, you'll be served with a subpoena by an officer of the court. The subpoena has information on the location of the trial, and when you're to attend court to testify. Unless the attorney who has called you indicates otherwise, you will need to attend the courthouse every day that the trial continues in case you're recalled to the stand.

Q: My religious beliefs prohibit me from the practice of placing my hand on the Bible and swearing to God that I'll tell the truth. When being called to testify, what should I do?

A: When you are called to the stand, you have the option of swearing or affirming. When sworn in, you will hold your hand on a Bible and swear to God that you'll tell the truth. Affirming doesn't require this. When being affirmed, you simply promise that any testimony you give will be truthful.

Q: On my statement, I wrote an incorrect date and didn't realize my mistake until after the statement was sent to the prosecutor. Now I've been subpoenaed to testify about the facts. What should I do?

A: Notify the investigator and prosecutor immediately about the mistake before any depositions or the trial begins. By being honest and pointing out the mistake early, you can avoid any unnecessary questions during the trial about inconsistencies in the information you've presented.

Index